A DESCRIPTION OF THE CHARACTER, MANNERS, AND CUSTOMS OF THE PEOPLE OF INDIA AND OF THEIR INSTITUTIONS RELIGIOUS AND CIVIL

A DESCRIPTION OF THE CHARACTER, MANNERS, AND CUSTOMS OF THE PEOPLE OF INDIA AND OF THEIR INSTITUTIONS RELIGIOUS AND CIVIL

ABEE J. A. DUBOIS

Translated From The French Manuscript
With Notes Corrections
and Additions

Rev. G. U. Pope

Third Edition

GYAN

Published by

Gyan Publishing House
5, Ansari Road
Daryaganj, New Delhi-110002
Phone: 011-47034999, 9811692060
E-mail: books@gyanbooks.com

Distribution Network
gyanbooks.com
India, USA, Canada, UK, Australia, France

ISBN : 978-81-212-3307-1 (PB)
First Published, 1879

2nd Impression 2020

Printed at: Gyan Press, Delhi.

A Description of the Character, Manners and Customs of the People of India
Author: Abee J. A. Dubois

A DESCRIPTION OF THE CHARACTER, MANNERS, AND CUSTOMS OF THE PEOPLE OF INDIA;

AND OF THEIR INSTITUTIONS, RELIGIOUS AND CIVIL,

BY THE ABBÉ J. A. DUBOIS,

Missionary in the Mysore.

With Notes, Corrections and Additions

BY

REV. G. U. POPE, D.D.,

PRINCIPAL OF BISHOP COTTON'S GRAMMAR SCHOOL AND COLLEGE, BANGALORE, ETC., ETC.

Third Edition.

Translated from the French Manuscript.

MADRAS:
HIGGINBOTHAM AND CO.,
LONDON—TRÜBNER AND CO., LUDGATE HILL.
CALCUTTA—THACKER SPINK AND CO.
BOMBAY—THACKER AND CO.

1879.

TO

The Right Honorable

THE GOVERNOR IN COUNCIL

OF FORT ST. GEORGE.

as a mark (however inadequate) of His Sincere gratitude for the constant protection he has met with during a period of nearly thirty years he has lived under their control,

as well as

for a great many and personal favors bestowed on him.

This Work

is respectfully presented by their most obedient and faithful Servant,

J. A. Dubois,
Missionary.

Seringapatam,
1st December 1820.

ADVERTISEMENT TO THE FIRST EDITION.

The French Manuscript, of which a Translation is here offered to the Public, was meditated and composed in the midst of the people whom it describes. The absolute retirement of the Author from European Society, for a series of Years, well qualified him for penetrating into the dark and unexplorable recesses of the Indian character; but it has also veiled himself, in an equal degree, from the curiosity of his readers.

The little that is known of him in this country may be collected from the following despatch of the Governor in Council at Fort St. George, of the 24th December, 1807, *to the Honorable Court of Directors of the East India Company, which they have been pleased to allow the Translator to publish:*

" We request your reference to the Minutes noted in the margin
" relative to a work which has been lately compiled by the Abbé
" Dubois, a gentleman of irreproachable character, who, having
" escaped from the massacres of the French Revolution, sought
" refuge in India, and has since been engaged in the zealous and
" pious duty of a Missionary, in the performance of which he has
" acquired a degree of respect among both the European and Native
" inhabitants that we believe to have been rarely equalled in persons
" of his sphere. It is amongst natives, however, that the time of
" this Missionary has been chiefly passed, and he has availed
" himself of the long intercourse, to compile a distinct account of
" the Hindû Customs and Manners. In order that you may be par-
" ticularly informed of the character of the work, we have inserted
" the following extract of a letter from Major Wilks, late Acting
" President at Mysore, in which country the Abbé Dubois has chiefly
" resided, addressed to the Military Secretary of our late President:

" 'The Manuscript of the Abbé Dubois on Indian Castes, was
" put into my hands by the author early in the year 1806, and so
" far as my previous information and subsequent inquiry have

" enabled me to judge, it contains the most correct, comprehen-" sive, and minute account extant in any European language of " the Customs and Manners of the Hindûs. Of the general " utility of a work of this nature, I conclude that no doubt can " be entertained. Every Englishman residing in India is inter-" ested in the knowledge of those peculiarities in the Indian " castes which may enable him to conduct with the natives the " ordinary intercourse of civility or business without offending " their prejudices. These prejudices are chiefly known to Euro-" peans as insulated facts, and a work which should enable us to " generalize our knowledge by unfolding the sources from which " those prejudices are derived, would, as a manual for the younger " servants of the Company, in particular, be productive of public " advantages, on which it seems to be quite superfluous to " enlarge.

" ' Being desirous of obtaining for the work the advantage of " a testimony to its merits of greater weight than any which I " could presume to offer, I submitted it to the perusal of a gen-" tleman of high literary eminence, who returned it to me with " an eulogium which more than justified the opinion I had pre-" viously formed, but without the permission (which had been the " chief object of my communication) to make a public use of " his name.'

" The Manuscript was communicated to Lord William Bentinck " previously to His Lordship's departure, and Mr. Petrie has explain-" ed in a separate Minute the reasons which prevented the subject " from being earlier noticed. The Abbé Dubois having no means " of editing the work at his own charge, and it being obviously of " public importance that so useful a compilation should not be " withheld, it became necessary to decide on the most proper " mode of effecting the publication of it.

" After full consideration, we decided to purchase it on account " of the Company for the sum of two thousand pagodas, which " though a moderate sum for a work which must have been attended " with considerable labour, it was ascertained would be acceptable to " the author. We beg at the same time to observe, that it is pro-" bable that this sum will be fully repaid by the sale of a publication " which may be expected to excite considerable interest."

The prior consultations of the Madras Government on this subject have been also communicated to the Translator, and shew the importance that was attached to the work and the active zeal with which it was patronized. Lord William Bentinck, after his retirement from the Government, in laying the Manuscript before the Governor in Council, thus speaks of it: "It is described by Sir James Mackintosh as "being the most comprehensive and minute account extant, in "any European language, of the Manners of the Hindoos."

It was generally understood that Sir James Mackintosh felt his own judgment, on this occasion, confirmed by its coincidence with that of Mr. W. Erskine of Bombay, a gentleman of distinguished talents, and conversant equally with the Mythology, Literature, Manners, and Institutions of India.

My Lord William Bentinck sums up his own opinion as follows: "The result of my own observation during my residence in India is, "that the Europeans generally know little or nothing of the customs "and manners of the Hindoos. We are all acquainted with some "prominent marks and facts, which all who run may read; but "their manner of thinking, their domestic habits and ceremonies, "in which circumstances a knowledge of the people consists, is I "fear in great part wanting to us. We understand very imperfectly "their language. They perhaps know more of ours; but their "knowledge is by no means sufficiently extensive to give a des- "cription of subjects not easily represented by the insulated words "in daily use. We do not, we cannot, associate with the natives. "We cannot see them in their houses, and with their families. "We are necessarily very much confined to our houses by the heat; "all our wants and business which would create a greater intercourse "with the natives is done for us, and we are in fact strangers in "the land. I have personally found the want of a work to which "reference could be made for a just description of the native opinions "and manners. I am of opinion that, in a political point of view, "the information which the work of the Abbé Dubois has to impart "might be of the greatest benefit in aiding the servants of the "government in conducting themselves more in unison with the "customs and prejudices of the natives."

In the continuation of Major Wilks's Letter, that gentleman, so advantageously known to the world by his own writings, suggests, in liberal criticism of the Manuscript, that, "though absolutely divested

" of all political matter, it contains for example a variety of opinions " on the utility of the subdivision of the castes, on the origin of the " Hindû system, &c. which like all speculative opinions, are liable " to be questioned, and may perhaps be left to find their own " supporters and opponents, the public having only to do with the " facts; and in the general arrangement of the matter, I believe few " faults or errors will be found. But if it should be deemed expedient " to divest the work of any of the opinions to which I have adverted, " the most convenient mode would probably be in the first instance " to purchase the manuscript."

The work was accordingly brought over, and remained for a considerable time in the Company's Library, accessible to the curious, until the beginning of the present year, when the translation was commenced under the sanction of the Honourable the Court of Directors, Charles Grant, Esq., M. P., being then Chairman, and Thomas Reid, Esq., Deputy Chairman of the Court. It is now submitted to the Public without any attempt to alter or improve the speculations of the Author. His candour, sincerity, piety, and high sentiment are so uniformly conspicuous and expressive, that no danger is likely to attend any of his doctrines or theories. And if his zeal may at any time betray him, in argument, to conclusions apparently a little at variance, it would have been found but an ungrateful service to interrupt the reader with notes for the purpose of exposing small incongruities or in attempting to reconcile them. The scientific portions, and whatever would require the aid of a library to compose, will not be harshly criticised in an author undoubtedly of an ingenuous and cultivated mind, in the midst of a reserved and bigotted people, drawing his whole materials from the recollections of his early studies, and having no other resort, as he tells us, but his Bible.

But in the great and important object of the work, the delineation of the people and whatever distinguishes them from other nations, books would have been comparatively of no great avail. Little, from that source, could have been added to the brief though correct outline of Herodotus and the few excellent inquirers and good writers of more modern times who, during the last century, have been but little known. Here our author, following the only path that has ever yet led to any invention or discovery in human concerns, has eagerly studied, collected, and arranged the phænomena which a persevering curiosity and rigid self-denial had brought within his observation.

In communicating his stores, he generally exhibits that fervour which perhaps is inseparable from a mind conscious of imparting something before unknown. From this cause redundancies may sometimes arise; which might be easily pruned, though not perhaps without injury to the flavour and raciness of the fruit.

A work on Manners and Customs is, in some measure, a book of Natural History; which, with the beauties of nature, must also describe what is unseemly and offensive. The grossness and indecency of the Indian character under many circumstances, it was impossible to overlook, and it would have been dishonest to conceal. But the indignant appeals of the author to true modesty, and the veil afforded by our own language, it is not doubted, will protect the most delicate sensibility from a wound.

The author rarely appears in his own person throughout the book, but a single anecdote which we have before us, from another authentic source, will suffice to leave a pleasant impression of him on the mind: "Of the history and character of the author," *Major Wilks subjoins in his Letter to the Madras Government,* "I only know that he "escaped from one of the fusillades of the French Revolution, "and has since lived amongst the Hindûs as one of themselves; "and of the respect which his irreproachable conduct inspires it "may be sufficient to state that when travelling, on his approach "to a village, the house of a Brâhman is uniformly cleared for his "reception, without interference, and generally without communica-"tion to the officers of government, as a spontaneous mark of "deference and respect."

LONDON, 2d *December,* 1816.

THE AUTHOR'S PREFACE.

THOUGH Europeans have been in possession of regular and permanent establishments amongst the people of India for more than three hundred years, it is wonderful to observe how little authentic information they have collected respecting the various nations which inhabit that vast region.

We possess many details concerning several of the savage tribes of Africa, and also concerning the hordes of beings in the shape of man that are scattered over the vast continent of the new world; a race apparently formed by nature, nurture, and manners, to humble and degrade the whole of the human species. Yet a certain nation exists, cultivated from the earliest ages, the only one perhaps in the universe which has never sunk into barbarism, and which, of all ancient nations, may most deserve to fix the attention of the philosopher; one which attracted the admiration of antiquity by its successful cultivation of the sciences and arts, and by the admirable system which it invented for the maintenance of subordination in the community as well as of good order in private life. This nation spread its renown over the whole extent of polished antiquity, compelled the most enlightened of all people to confess its pre-eminence by alluring into its bosom the wisest of the philosophers of Greece. These, in spite of their pride and high pretensions, felt not degraded by pursuing a long and dangerous journey into India to consult the wisdom of its Bráhmans, who had flourished there in long succession, and to acquire from them a knowledge of the philosophy and the sciences which they had cultivated until their fame extended even into Europe. How wonderful, then, that such a nation remains almost unknown to the Europeans, who dwell in the midst of it, and who bear rule over a large portion of its soil!

The greater part of the ill-informed and often contradictory narratives that have been left us by travellers and other modern authors respecting the nations of India, has deservedly fallen into discredit and contempt. This has, in a great measure, been brought about by the literary associations which have been established in the country itself, consisting of a great number of persons of real judgment and learning, who have made a particular study of the language, the religion, the manners, education, and domestic economy of these people. They have had access to the first sources of information, and have been able to avail themselves of numerous interesting documents, derived from sources, or drawn from records held in high and sacred estimation by the native sages of the country.

Still, though what we have yet learned with certainty, concerning the people of India is but little in comparison with what remains to be known on so interesting a subject, it is not to be concealed that all the writings and documents to be met with amongst the Hindûs are unfortunately blended with the most extravagant fables; so that there is little hope of our being able to draw from such authorities a true and connected history of the country and of the various nations that inhabit it.

Among the ancient historical works still to be found in the country, the most esteemed and the most generally known are the *Râmâyaṇa*, the *Bhâgavata*, and the *Mahâ-Bhârata*; but the history which these books give us of the epochs of the dynasties of kings, of the series of wars, of battles, and of heroes, in the various revolutions which the country has undergone, as well as what relates to the introduction of arts and sciences, are so enveloped in darkness and intermixed with innumerable fables, each more incredible than the preceding, that the most skilful author would in vain attempt to avail himself of such faithless guides.

We shall see in the course of this work, how incredibly far the Hindûs carry their love of the marvellous. Their early historians, and especially their poets, in their enthusiasm, took advantage of this disposition of the people in writing their narratives, because they well knew they could not interest their readers, or fix their attention without recounting abundance of wild and surprising adventures; and accordingly they sacrificed all regard for truth to the desire of raising a name by humouring the taste of the public. Succeeding writers outdid their predecessors by constantly adding to the ancient fables innumerable inventions still more absurd.

Now, however, the attention paid to the Eastern tongues by the many learned Europeans who reside in the country, the progress they have made in Indian literature, the successful researches they are continually making into the books and other ancient remains of the nation; together with the ample means which a liberal and enlightened government possesses for collecting together the documents furnished by many well informed individuals who labour under its direction, the encouragement and rewards which it holds out to persons of every class who have it in their power to discover authentic and interesting memorials: all these considerations would lead us to hope that we may at last behold the reality of Indian history through the thick clouds which still obscure it. We may at least be enabled to separate what is credible from the mass of absurdity and fable, with which the Indian authors abound; and an able compiler may surely find sufficient materials to construct a full and authentic history of a nation, whose undoubted antiquity, the success with which it cultivated the arts and sciences in the remotest times, the wise domestic controul which it established at its origin, through which it has to this hour maintained an admirable police, render it an object of the highest interest, independently of the peculiar nature of its idolatry and superstitious rites.

But while such a work is only hoped for, I may be allowed, though incompetent for so great a task, to offer the present details, which will be found to contain many interesting particulars that are but imperfectly known to most readers, and may even be useful to any author who shall undertake a more methodical and comprehensive history of the Indian nations.

It was chiefly with this view that I was led to collect the numerous details of which this work is composed; for I aim not at the rank of an author, which is neither suited to my talents nor the secluded state to which my profession confines me amongst the natives of the country.

It will be readily perceived by the reader that the arrangement of the various subjects on which I have treated, was formed before the commencement of those last revolutions by which the people of the peninsula have been delivered from the iron yoke of that long succession of tyrants who oppressed them for so many ages, and before they had passed under the rule of a nation distinguished throughout the world for its beneficence, its moderation, its generosity, and above all, for its impartial administration of justice to all classes of people who live under its sway.

The spirit of justice and of prudence with which that nation rules the people of India who have become its subjects, and particularly the inviolable respect which she has constantly shewn for the customs and prejudices, civil and religious, which are inherent in every district and caste, together with the impartial protection which she extends alike to the feeble and the strong, to the Brâhman and the Pariah, to the Christian, the Mahometan and the Pagan; have more exalted her name and established her power in the east than even her victories and her extensive conquests.

The wonderful revolution effected of late years for the advantage of the people of the south of the peninsula has not induced me to alter the original plan of my work, where I treated of them as living under the arbitrary government of their despotic Princes.

It is a number of years since I first formed my design, in consequence of notices in the public papers calling for authentic documents regarding these people, for the use of the historiographers of the Honourable Company engaged in writing a history of India.

From that period, I have employed my leisure in accumulating materials and authentic documents for my work. My information has been drawn from the diligent study of some of the works in greatest estimation among the Hindûs, and some detached memoirs that accidentally fell into my hands, the veracity of which I am well assured of by personal observation. But I am chiefly indebted to an exact and regular system of inquiry which I was enabled to maintain by a residence of between seventeen and eighteen years among the people whom I describe, and a close and familiar intercourse with persons of every caste and condition of life through the great number of districts which I have traversed.

During the long period that I remained amongst the natives, I made it my constant rule *to live as they did*, conforming exactly in all things to their manners, to their style of living and clothing, and even to most of their prejudices. In this way I became quite familiar with the various tribes that compose the Indian nation, and acquired the confidence of those whose aid was most necessary for the purposes of my work.

My great object was to gain authentic information; which I here communicate in a style simple and unadorned. If, in the great variety of subjects on which I treat, I have at any time ventured to hazard an opinion of my own, and to enter upon discussions which neither my abilities nor opportunities of investigation qualify me for, I entreat my readers not to impute such digressions to ostentatious vanity, or to any affectation of learning, in which I feel my deficiency, but merely to the desire which I entertain of affording to other authors, better qualified than myself, occasional hints on subjects fit to exercise the genius of the profoundest inquirer.

The work would have been more complete and more satisfactory to most readers, if I had had the means of referring to the ancient authors, or to their European commentators, with regard to the quotations I make, and the comparisons I draw between the Indians and other ancient nations as to their religious and civil customs. But here I found myself destitute of all help but what I received from my Bible, or some modern authors whom chance rather than preference put into my hands; or, finally, in the imperfect traces which my memory supplied of books I had consulted in my early years.

I hope my readers will be indulgent to me in this particular, and attribute the inaccuracies they will discover in my references, and the imperfect parallels I sometimes attempt to draw, to my exclusion during so many years from every resource but what my limited understanding could supply.

In my description of the Indian castes, I must be understood to have in view chiefly those that people the southern provinces of the peninsula, within the Krishna. It is not unlikely that the habits and customs on this side of that river may differ from those beyond it, or that the provinces of the north may have some peculiar to themselves.

The religious and civil regulations which I describe in this work form a general bond of social union among the Hindûs in the south of the peninsula; and nearly the whole of them are of indispensable observance.

But there are also many other rules peculiar to each several caste, people, and district. Indeed there is no tribe of Hindûs that has not, in addition to the general rules of the society, some domestic usages peculiar to itself. Some have customs that are merely local and followed only by a few. A perfect acquaintance with such customs is not to be attained, because they defer in every part, and are brought to no standard by the natives themselves.

A more interesting and a more useful study than that of the peculiar usages of the castes, would be to trace the various nations that people the vast empire of India; for, although these nations are all united together by the bands of the same religion, and also by those of the same education, as far as good behaviour and decent intercourse in society go, yet great differences appear amongst them, in language as well as in character, in manners, inclinations, and habits. A good observer will remark, under all general points of resemblance, as much difference between a Tamil and a Telugu; between a Kanarese and a Mahrata, as one would perceive in Europe between an Englishman and a Frenchman, an Italian and a German.

There are some countries in India peopled from time immemorial by different nations, who, though mixed together in the same province and even in the same district, still preserve their distinct language, character, and national spirit. On the Malabar coast, for example, within a space of forty or fifty leagues from north to south, from Telichery to Onore or to Nagara, there are no less than five different nations peopling that small territory; and all of them appear to have been settled there upwards of a thousand years. These five nations are the *Nairs*, or *Naimârs*, the *Kûrgs* or *Kudagu*, the *Tuluvu*,[a] the *Kaunguni*, and the *Kanarese*. These are not merely names of castes, as might be supposed, but they distinguish five different nations, each of which is divided, like all other Indian nations, into a variety of castes; and although these five races dwell in the same district, each has its peculiar language, by which it is as much discriminated as by its national customs, spirit, and character.

In every country of the peninsula great numbers of foreign families are to be found whose ancestors had been obliged to emigrate thither, in times of trouble or famine, from their native land, and to establish themselves amongst strangers. This species of emigration is very common in all the countries of India; but what is most remarkable is, that in a foreign land, these emigrants preserve from generation to generation their own language and

---

[a] The District of Viziapûr.

national peculiarities. Many instances might be pointed out of such foreign families settled four or five hundred years in the district they now inhabit, without approximating in the least to the manners, fashions, or even to the language of the nation where they have been for so many generations naturalized. They still preserve the remembrance of their origin, and keep up the ceremonies, the usages of the land where their ancestors were born, without ever receiving any tincture of the particular habits of the country where they live.

Under all the circumstances that have been mentioned, there is nothing to be seen but the most absolute toleration amongst the aboriginal inhabitants of every district; and so long as the stranger settled amongst them conforms to the accustomed rules of decorum, each may follow his own national customs, preserve his native language in his family, and in all things follow the usages of his ancestors, without any man attempting to find fault with the singularity of his manner of living.

The facility of intercourse which the Europeans now enjoy with the different nations which people the peninsula of India, will no doubt soon afford us interesting details on the various subjects which do not fall within the scope of this work, and which indeed would require the labour of more than one author.

In attempting a description of the Indian Castes, and of the customs and usages which unite them together, I have been most solicitous to pourtray that discriminating peculiarity, which though the most curious of all, is still the least understood. Those who have visited India will appreciate the difficulty of holding any communication with the Brâhmans. They know the vast distance at which this class holds itself from the rest of the community. They know their hatred and sovereign contempt for all strangers, but particularly for Europeans, their close reserve and their jealous caution to prevent the mysteries of their religion, or of their science, or even of their domestic discipline from being divulged to other men.

By various means I surmounted many of the obstacles which have effectually opposed other authors in this career. If my details on the Brahmans and the other castes of Hindûs, are not in general so full as many readers would desire, and as I myself would have expected, if I could have had all the aid I required, I have yet the vanity to think they will appear interesting, and even satisfactory to many readers who have learned nothing on the subject but from ill-informed authors.

I have subjoined to the whole an Appendix, containing a brief account of the sect of the Jains, of their doctrines, the principal points of their religion, and their peculiar customs. Other writers possessing more information than I do, will hereafter instruct us more fully concerning this interesting sect of Hindûs, and particularly respecting their religious worship, which probably, at one time, was that of all Asia, from Siberia to Cape Comorin, north to south; and from the Caspian to the Gulf of Kamtchatka, from west to east; and which was probably one of the earliest kinds of idolatry which appeared on the earth, at the time when men, forgetting the idea of their Creator, deified the stars, the elements, and other striking objects, and even mortals like themselves; fashioning images to preserve their memory by clothing them with a visible form.

NOTICE BY THE EDITOR TO THE SECOND EDITION.

To the present edition of the Abbé's most valuable work I had intended to prefix an account of his life; but was deterred from doing so by two circumstances. Authentic details of his history are not abundant, and a full use of those which are available would lead to a revival of controversies now happily at rest.

The Abbé after many years of labour among the Hindûs in the Mysore kingdom, on his return to Europe, wrote and published a letter in which he declared his conviction that the conversion of the Hindûs was impossible; though, when going on board ship, he cast his eyes back towards the shore and exclaimed with emotion that he hoped to return. This he did not do; but became the head of the French Institution "for the propagation of the Faith," from which several eminent Missionaries of the Roman Catholic Church have come out to India. There he laboured with zeal and energy for some years and died, universally respected, in 1853.

But although the simple and laborious career of the self-denying Missionary affords scanty material for his life, we know enough of him to inspire the fullest confidence in the accuracy of his statements. The late Professor Wilson has borne testimony to his accuracy whenever he relates what he saw or knew; and in regard to other matters, such as the Mythology, Philosophy and History of Southern India, in which it may be acknowledged that he was not deeply learned, many valuable works, readily to be obtained, render the Abbé's deficiencies in these respects of little importance. The more I have examined the more have I become, in most cases, persuaded of the accuracy of the Abbé's statements.

It must be borne in mind, however, that he professed only to write of Southern India, and, in fact, that the Kingdom of the Mysore and the modern Collectorate of Coimbatore were the districts of India with which alone he had a minute personal acquaintance.

Nor must it be forgotten by those who may, at first sight, from their own more superficial acquaintance with Hindû manners and customs, doubt the truth of some of the statements of the work, that it is very difficult indeed to obtain a real insight into the native character and habits. He who would obtain this must pay for it the price Dubois paid: he must conform to native manners, yield much to native prejudices, and win the confidence and respect of those whom he would thoroughly know. This, it may safely be said, very few can do. The Missionaries of Southern India, have doubtless been permitted to effect more among the natives of this land than any other Europeans since the days of Xavier, Beschi, and de Nobilibus; but their very success in gathering together congregations of professing christians has confined the greater number of them in great measure to a pastoral intercourse with their people, which has prevented them from gaining that knowledge, at once comprehensive and minute, of the peculiarities of the different tribes of Hindûs, which the Abbé certainly possessed.

The impression may be felt in many minds that a work written half a century ago must be of little practical use at present, being superseded by more recent publications, or rendered useless by the inevitable change of manners among the people. The fact is, however, that, with the single exception of the 4th Volume of Dr. Graul's Reise-nach Ostindien, and a few monographs of more or less value published by Missionaries, little has been written of late years calculated to give a European an insight into South Indian life and manners.

Nor have the main features of Hindû character materially changed within the last hundred years.

The same natural causes that kept the *pagani* pagans, when Christianity had leavened the masses in the large cities of the Roman empire, have operated in South India to preserve the ancestral traditions and customs of the rural population unchanged; and the villagers, unmindful of the rise and fall of dynasties, have performed the same ceremonies, maintained the same distinctions, and plodded in nearly the same beaten track of thought as their forefathers did five hundred years ago.

I am not indeed disposed to consider the Hindûs to be the apathetic, unchanging people they have often been represented to be. The career of Chaitanya in Bengal and of Nanak in the Punjab, and the traditions which are in every one's mouth regarding the progress and fate of different systems in India, shew that the Hindûs are not impressionless, nor by any means slow to take in new ideas and to attach themselves to new systems. *We* have found them apathetic, for we have not striven to interest and arouse them, and have not, in many cases, studied them or their books with sufficient care, to enable us to talk with them mind to mind. Between them and us there has been *a great gulf fixed.* How shall it be bridged over?

But during this century no such changes have occurred as to render the Abbé's work in any sense obsolete.

Some changes there are, which the Editor has noted during a residence of 22 years in India, in habits of somewhat close and intimate intercourse with the people.

1. There has been a slow but certain diminution of Brâhmanical, and in general, of caste influence. Where the higher castes retain their influence it is the result of their having thrown themselves heartily into the struggle for pre-eminence in the new studies and the new systems, which have come into existence around them. In many districts the indigenous Brâhmans live contentedly upon their farms and leave all positions of influence and authority to Veḷḷâḷar or to Mahratta Brâhmans and others.

The effect of education, the gradual increase of wealth among the lower castes, association with foreigners, the influence to a certain extent, of the Christian system, which has modified men's opinions, even where it has been violently opposed, have all combined to bring about this result. Hence much of what is said in the opening chapters regarding caste institutions must be taken with some modification. Railways too, and the other attendants on advancing civilization, are gradually but surely abating the tyranny of caste and custom.

2. With this decrease of caste feeling is connected a gradual reform in many matters relating to their religious usages. Certainly the obscene figures on the cars and the more offensive of their public exhibitions have disappeared more by the influence of police regulations than by amelioration of sentiment in the masses of the people; but there is a very marked change, and those who feel inclined to doubt the assertions of Dubois regarding the impurities of the popular

Hindû system may rest assured that his statements fall short in many cases of the truth. In relation to this subject I would make the remark that the people of India are strangely inclined to impute to Europeans the use of human sacrifices, shewing, I think, incontestably how agreeable to the genius of their own system such sacrifices are.

Constantly are reports circulated and believed, on the consecration of a church or the marriage of the daughter of any one in authority, that a child is to be sacrificed, and the Native mothers at such times keep their little ones carefully within their sight. This species of report arises continually in all parts of the land; and seems to me to show how deeply the people are imbued with the idea that human sacrifices are of a peculiar efficacy. Their own worship of Kâli requires human heads to be suspended in her temple, if we credit their own traditions.

3. There is also in every part of India, but more especially in the South, a very great tendency to substitute for the ordinary religious system, or to add to it, a kind of philosophic pietism which, under such names as *Gnânam,* (wisdom) *and the Vedânta,* has great influence among the people. The more thoughtful among them explain away much of what is offensive in Hindûism and take refuge in an esoteric system professing to be founded upon the popular religion, and to be the real essence of it. Thus the Śaiva worshippers have their Śiva—Gnânam, with numbers of works, in which Śiva is represented as an all-pervading essence, his various manifestations are dwelt upon, and affection for him and intense desire for communion with him are expressed. The most remarkable of these Śaiva works is the collection of poems by *Tâyumâna-swâmi* of Trichinopoly, a devotee who lived about a hundred years ago, and whose verses are recited with intense enthusiasm. Certainly the Roman Catholic Missionaries, who laboured with such singular zeal and ability, have been instrumental in diffusing a higher sentiment which has penetrated the masses, and has found its expression in composition such as these. Christian influences are unmistakeably to be traced in these *Gnâṇa* verses. So the Vaishṇavas have their *Gnâna-Vâsishtam* and other works in which the worship of Vishṇu is idealized and sublimated into a refined pietism. The *Tiru-vây-mori, Tiru-vâsagam,* and others works of this school are in great repute.

Paṭṭanattu Piḷḷai's writings are full of tender and beautiful sentiments.

The *Vêdânta* of the south is a kind of *Neo-vêdantism*, differing in many essential points from the system of the Sûtras of the Vêdânta-Śâra. Its foundation is the doctrine of Mâyâ or illusion. The great text book of this system in the South is the *Panja-daśa-prakaraṇam* or fifteen Lectures. This work was composed in Sanskrit by *Mâdhava Âchârya* at *Vijayanagaram* in the 14th Century, during the reign of Bukka Râjah. It is translated into Tamil, and widely circulated. The same subject is treated of, with a more directly practical aspect, in the *Kaivalya-navanîta*, a more modern work, full of evidences of Christian influences. Both have been translated into German by Dr. Graul. These books are the real Vêdas of the great majority of the really thoughtful natives of the south. The 15 lectures begin with "*the picture: the four states of the Supreme.*" "The picture-canvass, before anything is painted on it, is called a *white picture;* when sized it is called the *sized picture;* when its outlines are drawn in charcoal it is the *outline picture;* when painted, the *coloured picture:* what are the corresponding states of the *Supreme Spirit*—Bramha?

"He is himself the picture ground, the white picture, *illusion* (Maya) is the colour which paints on this ground the universe.

"Man in his ignorance thinks all this to be real, and asserts his own individuality. Wisdom—the Vêdanta system—will teach him to know the supreme; then the vivid colours will by degrees fade away till only the outline is seen; those outlines themselves will finally disappear, the very habits of mind that tended to this foolish self-assertion will be eradicated, and at last Bramha will be all in all."

This is essentially different from the proper Vêdanta system; and is developing, gathering to itself and assimilating, many elements from other systems, more especially from the Mohamedan Sufiism and from Christianity, and exercises a great and growing influence upon the people of the South. It should, of course, be studied by all who wish to know, or to influence, the Hindûs of this Presidency.

It only remains for me to indicate to those who are beginning an Indian career the sources of information that are open to them in regard to the History, language, antiquities and manners of the people of whom the Abbé treats.

1. The student of the languages of India cannot be too earnestly advised to obtain some knowledge of Sanskrit as the best means of aiding his labours and making real progress in any of the Vernaculars.

For this purpose he will require Professor Monier Williams' Grammar, Dr. Ballantyne's Sanskrit Primer, Bopp's Sanskrit Grammar, Johnson's Hitopadêśa, Bopp's Glossary, and Wilson's Dictionary, of which a new edition is being issued in parts. Bopp's edition of Naḷa, Stenzler's Raghuvamsa, Williams' Sakuntala, the Bhagavat Gîtâ, and Dr. Otto Frank's Vêdânta Sâra, will furnish him with good and useful reading.

2. In applying his knowledge to the study of the Hindû religion and antiquities, Muir's Sanskrit texts will be invaluable to any one possessed of a tolerable knowledge of the language. Wilson's Vishṇu purâṇa is a mine of information. If to these Professor Max Müller's work on the ancient Sanskrit literature be added, the student will possess enough to enable him to judge for himself as to other works to be studied. The series of text books in Hindû philosophy published by Dr. Ballantyne is invaluable.

By the aid of these books the learner may investigate for himself the nature of the Vêdic, purâṇic and philosophic systems. Wilson's Hindû sects will give him the best view of the popular religious systems.

3. In order to make himself acquainted with the History and Topography of Southern India, he may study the following works: Mill's India, Brigg's Mahomedan power in India, Wilk's Mysore, Orme's Hindûstân, Eastlake's handbook of the Madras Presidency and Dr. Graul's Reisenach Ostindien.

4. The Tamil student may be referred to my Hand-book (2d ed.) for information in regard to the literature of that language. To the books there spoken of I must add Rottler's Dictionary, or that edited by Dr. Winslow, which is the work of a long series of able men.

To those who have acquired the Tamil language, the following additional books are recommended:

(1.) Gnâna Vâsishṭam, ஞானவாசிஷ்டம் a vedantic poem, exemplifying in a great variety of histories the advantage of studying the Gnâna system.

(2.) Kaivalya navanîtam, கைவல்லிய நவநீதம்.

This is a complete exposition of the Neo-vêdantic system.

(3.) The poems of *Tâyumâna-swâmi.*

(4.) The works of *Paṭṭanattu-piḷḷai.*

(5.) The drama of "*Harichandra*": Harichrandra-vilâsam.

(6.) The 15 lectures: பஞ்சதசப்பிரகரணம்.

These works read with a good Munshi will give the student a thorough mastery of the systems which have most influence over the Tamil mind.

5. The Telugu student has the advantage of using a long series of works by one of the most indefatigable and successful of students, C. P. Brown, Esquire, late of the Madras Civil Service.

Brown's Telugu Grammar, Dictionaries and Reader (3 vols.), are especially recommended.

An edition of *Vêmana*, published by Mr. Brown with an English translation is a very valuable introduction to poetical Telugu. Campbell's Telugu Grammar, with a preface by Ellis, is nevertheless all but indispensable.

6. In Kanarese, a compendious Grammar by Rev. T. Hodson, of the Wesleyan Mission, Rev. D. Sanderson's enlarged edition of Reeve's Dictionary, Kanarese dialogues and 70 stories all published at the Wesleyan Press, Bangalore, are most useful. The more advanced student will find the volumes of the *Bibliotheca Karnaṭaca* of great utility, especially the *Basava Purâṇavu.*

7. In Malayâlam, Rev. Mr. Peet's Grammar and Rev. H. Bailey's Dictionary must be used. Dr. Gundert has published a Grammar in Malayâlam, which is of special interest as shewing the intimate connection between Tamil and that language. A. J. Arbuthnot, Esquire, has published a small volume of stories with apparatus for a beginner, which should be re-printed.

But there is need of another Grammar and Dictionary, better adapted to the present state of the language.

The Maḷayaḷam literature is very scanty, and consists almost wholly of translations from the Sanskrit.

8. It hardly falls within my plan to speak of Hindûstâni literature. I may observe however that a small Grammar by Col. Brown, and a work called Subuq-u-Sulîs, seem to be the very best and easiest introductions to this language.

9. Among works which the student will find most helpful to him in the Madras Presidency may be mentioned, (1) Wilson's Glossary; (2) Caldwell's Draviḍian Grammar, and (3) Brown's Zillah Dictionary.

I have given these details regarding the Vernacular literature, because it is certain that no one can really know the people who is unable to converse with them and to read their standard Works. The fact that all intelligent natives now learn English (and this should be encouraged by every means in our power) does not render it unnecessary for us to learn—to study thoroughly—to master, their languages. Only thus can we know the height and depth of Hindû character, its undoubted excellencies and its equally manifest defects.

If a language be a fair exponent of the capabilities of the people that uses it, the South Indian races most certainly may aspire to great things.

No language more readily lends itself to severe and exact reasoning, is more flexible and more forcible, than Tamil. Not even the Italian of Dante and Petrarch is softer, sweeter, more mellifluous than Telugu.

The Native writings abound in passages of great beauty, in happy similes and apt illustrations.

They shew at times much depth of feeling and more liveliness of fancy. They are full of subtle distinctions, of exhaustive (and to the beginner, very exhausting) enumerations, classifications, divisions and sub-divisions.

Add to this that Native writers use words and epithets with great exactness and discrimination.

On the other hand excessive ornament, wearisome minuteness, bad taste, puerile conceptions, useless and even absurd distinctions, want of genuine love of nature, the absence of all freshness of feeling, the straining after effect, and frequent sacrifices of sense to sound, render it difficult for us to read through any of their works with real pleasure.

To revive a decaying civilization is confessedly difficult; yet with all the resources of Western Science, all the means and appliances of British wealth, power, and influence and, above all, with a religion which breathes into all who receive it in sincerity, *"the spirit not of fear, but of love, and of power, and of a sound mind,"* we ought to—we certainly must—effect much among the races of whose manners and customs this work gives so true and lively a picture.

The whole work has been thoroughly revised and collated with the MS. which contains the author's final corrections, obligingly lent to the publisher by the Madras Government.

Every statement has been examined, and I have omitted whatever did not seem to be capable of verification.

For *all the notes* in this edition the Editor is alone responsible. He hopes that the utility of the work may be in some measure increased by his labours, however imperfect.

G. U. POPE.

Ootacamund Grammar School, July 1, 1862.

CONTENTS.

Portrait of Dubois, taken from an Oil Painting in the College Hall.

PART I.

GENERAL VIEW OF SOCIETY IN INDIA.

A
DESCRIPTION
OF
THE PEOPLE OF INDIA, &c.

PART I.
GENERAL VIEW OF SOCIETY IN INDIA.

CHAPTER I.

DIVISIONS AND SUBDIVISIONS OF CASTES.—DISTINCTION OF RIGHT HAND AND LEFT.

THE word *Caste* is a Portuguese term, which has been adopted by Europeans in general, to denote the different classes or tribes into which the people of India are divided. The most ordinary partition, and at the same time the most ancient, is that which arranges them in four principal tribes. The first and most distinguished of all is that of the *Brâhmans:* the second in rank is that of the *Kshatriya* or *Râjas:* the third the *Vaisya* or *merchants* and *cultivators,* and the last that of *Śûdras* or *cultivators subordinate to the others.*

Each of these four principal tribes is subdivided into several more, of which it is difficult to determine the number; for this subdivision varies in different districts, and several castes known in one province do not appear in another.

Among the Brâhmans, for example, there are in the South of the Peninsula three or four principal divisions: and each of these admits of at least twenty subdivisions, which prevent them from intimate association and especially from intermarriage.[a]

The tribe of Râjas and that of Merchants are likewise split into many divisions and subdivisions. They are seldom met with in the South of India; but the former tribe is numerous in the North; although the Brâhmans affirm that the true Kshatriyas are extinct; and that the present claimants of the name are a spurious race.[b]

The tribe of Śûdras is that in which divisions are multiplied most of all. I have never found any man in the provinces where I have lived, able to fix with precision the number and the species of them, although it is proverbially said, that there are eighteen chief subdivisions, and one hundred and eight others.

---

a From Port. *Casta,* race. The Sanskrit word for Caste is *Varṇa* — colour; thus showing that upon the difference in colour between the Âryan Brâhmans and the aboriginal inhabitants the distinction of caste was originally founded.

b See Appendix. Note A.

The most numerous of the four principal tribes, then, is that of the Śûdras or cultivators, and I reckon them, including the Pariahs, to amount at least to five-sixths of the population of India.

Most of the professions, and almost all the trades, with the arts and employments which are indispensable to society, belong to the tribe of the Śûdras: and as, by the prejudices of the country, no caste and no individual can be of two trades, a particular tribe being exclusively set apart for each occupation and each trade, it is not surprising that the divisions and subdivisions of castes should be so exceedingly numerous in this tribe, or that it should stand so high in point of number.

But there are several castes of cultivators not known except in particular countries. Of those elsewhere unknown, the Tamil country appears to me to have the most subdivisions. There are not nearly so many even in the Deccan, nor in the Mysore, nor on the Coast of Malabar. In none of those parts have I found any castes corresponding to those in the Tamil territory, known in their language, under the names of Muđali,[a] Agambaḍiya,[b] Nattamâu,[c] Uḍaiyân,[d] Toṭṭiyan,[e] Valeyan,[f] Upiliyen,[g] and several others.

It is to be observed however, that the tribes of the Śûdras, to which those employments belong, which are every where indispensable, must necessarily be found in all the countries, under different appellations. The most considerable of the castes that are universally spread are the following: the *Herdsmen*, who keep the cows; the *Shepherds*, who tend the sheep; the *Weavers;* the *Pânchâlas*, meaning the five castes of artizans, which comprehend the carpenters, goldsmiths, blacksmiths, stone-cutters, founders, and in general all workers in metals; the *Barbers;* and the *Oṭṭar*, whose chief employment is to excavate tanks, repair their banks, erect mud walls, and the like. There are also distillers and sellers of oil, fishermen, potters, washermen, and many others.

These last kinds of labour, with some others, being equally required in all places, the castes which exercise them, and upon whom they are exclusively imposed, are of course found in every country.

The castes which we have enumerated belong entirely to the tribe of the Śûdras: but the several castes of the cultivators take

---

[a] முதலி [= chief one]: a highly respectable class of traders chiefly.

[b] அகம்படியர் [= *those who belong to the steps of the dwelling*]: this is a name given to those who performed menial offices in the temples and palaces of Râjas.

[c] நத்தமான் [= one belonging to a village without a river]: a subdivision of the caste of cultivators.

[d] உடையான் [= a proprietor]: a land owner.

[e] தொட்டியன் [= digger]: a caste of labourers.

[f] வலையன் [= net man]: a caste of people who live by snaring birds.

[g] உப்பிலியர் [= salt man]: these live by boiling down sea water to obtain salt.

precedence of the rest, and look down with contempt on the tribes of tradesmen and labourers.

In some districts, castes are to be seen that cannot be met with elsewhere, and which are to be distinguished from all others by singular peculiarities.

I am not aware, for example, that the very remarkable caste of *Nâymârs* or *Nâyars*, in which the women enjoy a plurality of husbands, is to be found any where but in the forests of the coast of Malabar.

The caste of *Kaḷḷar* or Robbers, who exercise their profession without disguise, as their birthright, is found but rarely beyond the *Maravu*,[h] a territory bordering on the fishing coast. The princes of this little state belong to the tribe and profession of *Robbers*, and conceive their calling no way discreditable to themselves or their tribe, as having legitimately descended to them by right of inheritance. So far from shrinking at the appellation, if one of them be asked who he is, he will coolly answer that he is a robber. Indeed the tribe is accounted one of the most distinguished among the Śûdras, in the province of Madura, where it flourishes.

There is another caste in the same province, called the *Tôṭṭyar*, in which brothers, uncles, nephews, and other kindred, hold their wives in common.

In the east of the Mysore there is a tribe known by the name of *Marasa okkiliyar*, in which when a mother gives her eldest daughter in marriage, she herself is forced to submit to the amputation of the two middle fingers of the right hand, as high as the second joint; and, if the mother of the bride be dead, the bridegroom's mother must submit to the cruel ceremony.[i]

In many other districts there are castes famous for practices no less irrational than those we have mentioned.

In general it may be remarked that, in addition to those customs and ceremonies, civil and religious, which are constant and invariable, and unite the whole race in things essential, there is no tribe that does not exhibit some particular and local varieties of its own by which it is discriminated from the rest. Some distinguish themselves by the cut and colour of their clothes, some by the manner in which they put them on. Others are remarkable for some particular shape of their trinkets, and others for the arrangement of them on different parts of the body, in particular modes. In some you will observe certain peculiar forms in celebrating the ceremonies of marriage or of mourning; and in others the decorations and the flags of various colours which the custom of the country gives them the right to use on similar occasions.

---

[h] Consisting of the Zemindaries of *Sivagangai* and *Râmnâd*, in the Madura Zillah. Hence in Tinnevelly, these people are called *Marravar*. (மறவர்.)

[i] I am informed that the bride herself submits to this operation and not her mother. A similar custom prevails among some tribes in New Holland. See Appendix. Note B.

Extravagant, however, as many of their modes and customs are, they never draw down from castes of the most opposite habits and fashions the least appearance of contempt or dislike. Upon this point there is, through the whole of India, the most perfect toleration, as long as the general laws of good behaviour are not infringed. With this exception every tribe may freely and without molestation follow its own domestic course, and practice all its peculiar rites.

There are, however, certain customs to be noticed in some districts, which though they are universally practised amongst them, are so decidedly contrary to the laws of decency and propriety observed in other countries, that they cannot be alluded to without feelings of disgust and even of horror. The practice amongst several of the lower castes in the east of the Mysore, subjects the women to attend upon those of the family and even upon visitors, when they go forth upon the calls of nature. The woman waits, and, when it is time, she advances with her bason of water, and performs her task of ablution.

This practice, regarded as infamous in other parts, is among these castes considered to be one of the indispensable requirements of good breeding.

The use of intoxicating liquors, which is rigorously forbidden to all the good castes in other parts, is permitted to the inhabitants of the forests and mountains on the coast of Malabar. There, the highest castes of Śûdras drink, openly and without shame, arrack and toddy; not excepting even the wives and children. Each inhabitant in those parts has his toddy dealer, who regularly brings him the daily supply, and takes in return an equivalent in corn when the harvest comes round.

The Brâhmans and Lingamists, who inhabit these districts, are prohibited the use of toddy or arrack under the penalty of exclusion from their caste or sect. But they supply the defect by opium, the use of which is universally interdicted, but not held so much in detestation as that of the toddy and other inebriating liquors.

The inhabitants of these moist and unwholesome countries no doubt have perceived that the moderate use of spirits and opium is necessary for the preservation of their health, by correcting the noxious vapours they are constantly obliged to inhale. Nothing indeed but absolute necessity could have overcome the shame and the remorse of breaking down one of the most venerable barriers of Hindû civilization.[j]

[j] It may be doubted whether abstinence from intoxicating liquors was so rigidly enforced in the earlier periods of Hindû history. The Tamil student will find that the Poet Kamban represents the venerable King of Ayodhya, Daśarathan, with all his family and retinue, male and female, as indulging in the use of toddy, and in fact as all getting drunk together: "*paçu narrâ mândal, mêyinâr,*" "they desired the fresh, odorous beverage." Their drunken frolics are described without a shadow of reprobation in 67 elaborate quatrains. Râm. I. xvii.

The fierce denunciations of drunkenness in the Vêdas, in Manu, and in many more modern books, show that in India there has ever been the same difficulty in checking this vice as in other countries. The Hindûs of any caste cannot claim the merit of superior sobriety.

There are likewise certain usages purely religious, which are observed only by particular castes, or in particular territories. For example, it is but in the districts on the west of the Mysore that I have observed Monday in every week kept nearly in the same manner as Sunday is among Christians. On that day the inhabitants abstain from labour, and particularly from that which requires the use of oxen and kine, and from tillage. It is a day of rest for their cattle rather than for themselves. It is consecrated to *Basavâ* or the Bull,[k] and set apart for the special worship of that deity.

This practice however does not subsist universally excepting in the districts where the Lingamists, the followers of Śiva, rule. That sect paying more particular homage to the Bull than the other Hindûs, keep up in the districts where they predominate the strict observance of the day which they have consecrated to their divinity, and compel the other castes to respect it also, by making it a day of rest to their cattle.[l]

Independently of the divisions and subdivisions common to all the castes, and the migration from one tribe into another through all India, a farther distinction arises from one family making alliance with another. This distinction is still more to be attended to in the case of intermarriage. For the Hindûs of good castes, avoid as much as they can any new alliance, and the heads of families use their utmost endeavours to dispose of their children amongst families with whom they are already connected either by consanguinity or affinity. Marriages are more easily contracted in proportion as the parties are more nearly related. A widower re-marries with the sister of his former wife: the uncle espouses his niece, and the cousin his cousin. Persons so related possess an exclusive privilege to intermarry, upon the ground of such relationship: and, if they choose, they can prevent any other union, and enforce their own preferable right. But there is one singular exception from the rule; for the uncle will take to wife his sister's daughter, but by no means his brother's: the children of a brother will intermarry with those of the sister, but not the children of two brothers or of two sisters.

This distinction is invariably kept up through all the castes, from the Brâhman to the Pariah. And however remote the persons related are from the original stock, so long as the memory is preserved of their springing from the same root, although in the fiftieth generation, or in the twentieth degree of relationship, the male line retains its right in all cases to connect itself with the female; but never can the children of the male line intermarry with each other, nor those of the female line unite.

Agreeably to this distinction, a custom has arisen, which, as far as I know, is peculiar to the Brâhmans. They are all supposed to know the *Gôtram* or root from whence they spring; that is to say,

---

k Corrupted from the S. *paśu*.

l The best idea of this system may be gained from the *Basava Purânavu*, published in Kanarese, in the Bibliotheca Karnaṭaca.

they know who was the ancient *Muni* or devotee from whom they descend; and in order to avoid intermixture with a daughter or descendant of this original stock they find a reason for marrying into a different Gôtram.

The Hindûs who cannot form a suitable connection among their relations are still bound to marry in their own caste, and even in that branch of it, to which they belong. In no case will any pretext avail them for contracting a marriage with a stranger. Neither can the *Iḍaiyan* of the Tamil country form an alliance with the Gollavâḍu of the Telugu country, although these two castes are but one, which is that of the herdsmen differently denominated in the respective dialects.

The *Okkiliyaru* of the Karnâṭaka districts, will on no account intermarry with the Tamilian Vaḷḷâḷar, although these two castes differ only in name: and the case is the same with other tribes.

The most distinguished amongst the four great tribes into which the Hindûs were originally separated by their first legislators, is that of the Brâhmans, as we have already observed. The next are the Râjas. The superiority of rank is more contested between the Śûdras or Cultivators and the Vaisya, or Merchants. But the precedency seems to be universally denied to the latter excepting in the Hindû books, where they are uniformly placed before the Śûdras. This caste, however, in all the transactions of life hold themselves high above the Vaisya, and consider themselves entitled in most cases to show their superiority over them by demonstrations of contempt.

The Brâhmans however do not hold the highest rank in society undisputed. The *Pânchâlas* or five castes of artisans who have been already mentioned, obstinately refuse, in several districts, to acknowledge the superiority of the Brâhmans, although these five castes themselves are considered to be of very low rank among the Śûdras, and are held in great contempt. And the Brâhman ascendency is still more warmly disputed by the *Jains,* of whom we shall speak hereafter. (See appendix I.)

With regard to the particular subdivisions of the tribes, it would be difficult to determine which exceed the rest in dignity, because some castes which are decried in one part are frequently esteemed in another according as they conduct themselves with propriety, or exercise the more reputable employments. Or if it should happen that the prince of a district belongs to a particular caste, although otherwise of the least consideration, it rises to distinction, and all its members partake in the lustre of its chief.

After all, public opinion is the only sure ground of superiority among the castes; and a very slight acquaintance with the customs of a province, and with its inhabitants will suffice for fixing the station which each caste has acquired by common consent.

In general, it will be found that the tribes which are most attentive to propriety of demeanour, in the rigid sense in which it is understood by Hindûs; who are constant in their ablutions; who abstain from animal food; who are exact in the rules prescribed for family alliance; whose wives are the most recluse, and most vindictively punished when they err; those who most resolutely maintain the customs and privileges of their order: such are the castes that are reputed the most noble.

Of all the Hindûs, the Brâhmans strive the most to keep up the feeling of purity by frequent ablutions and most rigorous abstinences, not only from all kinds of food that has had the principle of life, but even from many of the simpler productions of nature which their superstitious prejudices lead them to consider as impure or capable of communicating defilement. It is chiefly this unfailing sentiment of propriety which raises that high caste into the respect and reverence which they enjoy in the Hindû world.

Amongst the different tribes of the Śûdras, on the other hand, those who allow to widows the privilege of marrying again, are considered as beneath the other tribes, and have almost sunk into contempt. Excepting the tribe of the *Pariahs*, I hardly could name one where such marriages could be openly celebrated or obtain the countenance of the caste.

The division into castes is the paramount distinction amongst the Hindûs; but there is still another division; that of *Sects*. The two best known, are those of *Śiva* and *Vishṇu*. These two great sects are subdivided into a vast number of subordinate ones, which shall be afterwards considered.

There are several castes, too, that may be distinguished by certain symbols or marks which they assume and exhibit in some way peculiar to each. It is in this way that the Brâhmans of the North of the peninsula, called *Uttarâśâ Brâhmaṇa*, are recognized in public, by a perpendicular line which they draw on the middle of the forehead with a paste made of sandal-wood. The Brâhmans of the farming provinces are known by a line or stripe horizontally drawn on the same part, while those in the south, being for the most part attached to the sect of Vishṇu, take for their mark the figure called Nâman, which will be described hereafter.

Of the four great tribes, the three first, namely, the *Brâhmans*, the *Râjas*, and the *Merchants*, distinguish themselves from the various castes of Śûdras by a narrow belt of thread, which they always wear suspended from the left shoulder to the opposite haunch like a sash. But being borne also by the Jains and even by the Pâñchâlas, or five castes of artisans, the mark is rather equivocal.

From what has been said it will appear after all that the name of a caste forms its best discrimination. The names of several of the Hindû tribes have a known meaning; but in general they are so ancient that it is now impossible to trace the meaning.

There is another division of the different tribes still more general than those that have been yet mentioned. It is that of *Right-hand* and of *Left-hand*. It appears to be but a recent invention, as it is not mentioned in any of the ancient books of the country; and I have been assured that it is almost unknown in the north, and is indeed confined to a part of the southern provinces.

But although there is reason to think that this distinction of *right-hand* and *left* never entered into the contemplation of the sages who gave laws to the Hindûs, yet they have afforded us no stronger proof of their sagacity than in conceiving the division of the people into several castes.

This particular distinction, however, which we have alluded to, by whomsoever invented, has turned out to be the most baneful that could have been imagined for the tranquillity of the state, and the most injurious to the peace of the citizens. It has proved the perpetual fountain of disturbance and insurrections amongst the people, and a continued principle of endless jealousy and animosity amongst all the members of the community.

The greater number of the Hindû castes belong either to the *left-hand* or to the *right*. The first division consists of the whole tribe of the *Vaisya*, of the *Pânchâla*, or five castes of artisans, and of some other mean tribes of the Śûdras. This hand also includes the most infamous of all castes, that of the *Cobblers* or *Chakili*, who are reckoned to be its principal support.

The *right-hand* has, among its partisans, the most distinguished castes of the Śûdras. That of the *Pariah* forms its strongest bulwark, as a proof of which they still glory in the title of *Valangay Mattâr*, or friends of the Right-hand.

The fiercest opposition arises out of this separation; and of all the contests to which the people are accustomed, the battles between the two *Hands* always produce the greatest alarm and the severest evil.

The Brâhmans, the Kshatriyas, and several tribes of the Śûdras are considered neutral, and enjoying all the privileges and honours attached to both *Hands*, they take no part with either. These neutral castes are frequently called upon to arbitrate in the fierce disputes between the two parties of the *Hands*.

The opposition between the *Right-hand* and the *Left-hand* arises from certain privileges to which they both lay claim; and when any encroachment is made by either it is instantly followed by tumults which frequently spread over whole provinces, accompanied with every excess, and generally with bloody contests. Gentlest of all creatures, timid under all other circumstances, here only the Hindû seems to change his nature. There is no danger that he fears to encounter in maintaining what he terms his right, and rather than yield it he is ready to make any sacrifice, and even to hazard his life.

I have repeatedly witnessed instances of these popular insurrections excited by the disputes between the two *Hands*, and pushed to such an extreme of fury that the presence of a military force under arms had no effect to quiet them, nor even to allay their clamours, or stop their outrageous course in what they conceive the rightful cause.

I have known instances of attempts made by the magistrates to sooth these uproars by remonstrances and other means of conciliation, and when these have produced no effect they have been obliged to resort to measures of compulsion. Some shots of musquetry would then be tried, but neither this nor the certainty of its being followed up with stronger measures, has the slightest effect in abating their insolence. Even when an overwhelming military force has fully put them down, it is only for the moment; and whenever an opportunity occurs they are instantly up again, without reflecting on the evils they formerly suffered, or showing the smallest tendency to moderate their impetuous violence.

Such are the excesses to which the timid, the peaceable Hindû, sometimes abandons himself; whilst his bloody contests spring out of motives which, to an European at least, would appear frivolous and trifling. Perhaps the sole cause of the contest is about his right to wear pantoufles; or whether he may parade in a palanquin or on horseback, on the day of his marriage. Sometimes it is the privilege of being escorted by armed men; sometimes that of having a trumpet sounding before him, or the distinction of being accompanied by the country music at public ceremonies. Perhaps it is the ambition of having flags of certain colours, or with the resemblances of certain deities displayed about his person on such great occasions. These are some of the important privileges, amongst many others not less so, in asserting which the Indians do not scruple occasionally to shed each other's blood.

As it not unfrequently happens that one of the *Hands* makes an attack on the privileges of the other: this occasions a quarrel which soon spreads and becomes general, unless it be appeased at its commencement by the prudence or the vigour of the magistrate.

I may perhaps be thought to have said quite enough of the effects of this direful distinction of right-hand and left. But I may be permitted to relate one instance at which I myself was present. The dispute was between the caste of Pariahs and the Cobblers, or Chakili, and produced such dreadful consequences through the whole district where it happened, that many of the peaceable inhabitants had begun to remove their effects and to leave their villages for a place of greater safety, with the same feelings as when the country sees an impending invasion of a Mahrata army, and with the same dread of savage treatment. Fortunately in this instance, matters did not come to an extremity, as the principal inhabitants of the district seasonably came forward to mediate between these vulgar castes, and were just in time, by good management, to disband the armed ranks on both sides that only waited the signal of battle.

One would not easily guess the cause of this dreadful commotion. It arose forsooth from a Chakili, at a public festival, sticking red flowers in his turban, which the Pariahs insisted that none of his caste had a right to wear.

CHAPTER II.

ADVANTAGES RESULTING FROM THE DIVISION OF CASTES.

There are many persons that have thought so little about the genius and character of the different nations that people the earth; of the influence of education, of religion, of climate, of food, upon their manners, desires, and customs; that they are astonished how beings radically of the same nature and of the same feelings, should so exceedingly differ from each other. Such men are trammelled by the prejudices of education. They can see nothing well ordered but in the civilization and culture of their own country. Every thing there being on a good system, they desire to put all nations of the earth on the same footing; and whatever does not fall within their limits, is denounced by them as barbarous or ridiculous. They will not consider that, though the nature of man is universally the same, it is nevertheless subject to be modified by the circumstances of the country, by the climate, the education and prejudices incident to each people; and that the rules laid down and followed in one nation would be subversive of another.

I have heard many individuals, otherwise of great judgment, so full of the prejudices they had brought with them from Europe, as to decide most erroneously (according to my opinion) on the subject of multiplied divisions of the Hindû castes. This distinction appeared to them, not only as not promoting the good of society, but also as ridiculous, and calculated merely to oppress and disunite the members of the state.

For my part, having been in a situation to observe the character of the Hindûs, and having lived amongst them for many years, as a friend, I have formed an opinion upon this subject altogether opposite. I consider the institution of castes amongst the Hindû nations as the happiest effort of their legislation; and I am well convinced that if the people of India never sunk into a state of barbarism, and if, when almost all Europe was plunged in that dreary gulf, India kept up her head, preserved and extended the sciences, the arts and civilization; it is wholly to the distinction of castes that she is indebted for that high celebrity.

We have it in our power to form some judgment of what the Hindûs would degenerate to, if the restraint of the division, the rules and the police of castes were abolished, by considering what the *Pariahs* of India are; who, being exempt from all restrictions of honour and shame, which so strongly influence the other castes, can freely and without reserve abandon themselves to their natural propensities.

Every man who carefully considers the character and conduct of such a class of men as this, being the most numerous of all, I think will agree with me, that a state consisting entirely of such members could not long endure, and could not fail to decline very quickly into the worst degree of barbarism. For my own part, who know the inclinations and sentiments of this species of men, I am persuaded that a nation of Pariahs, left to themselves, would speedily become worse than the hordes of cannibals that wander in the deserts of Africa, and would soon fall to the devouring of each other.[m]

I am no less convinced, that the Hindûs if they were not restrained within the bounds of decorum and of subordination by means of the castes, which assign to every man his employment, and by regulations of police suited to each individual; but were without any curb fit to check them, or any motive for applying one, would soon become what the Pariahs are, or worse; and the whole nation sinking of course into the most fearful anarchy, India, from the most polished of all countries, would become the most barbarous of any upon earth.[n]

The legislators of India set out from that grand principle which has been recognised by all the ancient legislators, that no man is to be permitted to be useless to the commonwealth. But they saw, at the same time, that the people for whom they acted were naturally so indolent, and that this propensity was so greatly aggravated by the climate, that unless every individual had a profession or employment rigidly imposed, the state could not exist, but must quickly tumble into the most deplorable anarchy, and end in savage barbarism.

Those legislators, being also well aware of the danger of all innovations in matters political or spiritual, and being desirous to establish durable and inviolable rules for the different castes into which they divided the Hindû people, could find no surer basis of an orderly government than the two grand foundations of religion and policy.

Accordingly we find hardly any of their civil observances that are not combined with some religious mixture, either as the motive or the object. Every thing, in short, is blended with superstition; whether it be the manner of salutation, the mode of dress, the shape and colour of the clothes, the placing of their trinkets and other ornaments, the manner of erecting their houses and other buildings; the side where the fire place is to stand, or where the household utensils; and even the rules of civility and politeness which they are called on to observe.

I have closely viewed their customs and observances for more than fifteen years, and I have scarcely remarked any one, however simple or indifferent, or, I may add, filthy and disgusting, that had not superstition either for its motive or end. Nothing is left unregulated among them and the foundation of all their regulations is religion.

---

m I do not imagine that Pariahs will, on the whole, be found to be more immoral in their habits than any other tribe of Hindûs.

n Some of the Abbé's statements, (and the general experience of Europeans confirms them) seem to shew that the Hindûs are far from being among the most polished nations of the earth.

It is thus that the Hindûs hold all their customs as sacred and indispensable, because being united with religion they partake of its sacred and inviolable quality.

The same distinction of castes existed amongst the Egyptians as amongst the Hindûs; and in both, the trade or employment was immutable from father to son, and no man, in either country, could exercise two professions.

There was this difference, however, between the Egyptians and the people of India, that amongst the former, all employments, to the very lowest, were held equally in esteem, and it would have been highly censurable in any man to treat contemptuously persons in any trade that contributed to the general good: whereas, amongst the Hindûs, there are certain employments to which prejudice or perhaps more powerful reasons have attached such ignominy, that those who practise them are universally despised and looked down upon by the castes that move in a higher sphere.

It must be remarked, however, that the four great employments without which a civilized state could not exist, namely, the soldier, the agriculturist, the merchant, and the weaver, are held in honour through India. All castes, from the Pariah up to the Brâhman, may exercise any one of the three first without disgrace; and even the last is not despised by the better castes amongst the Sûdras.

This same division of the people into tribes which we observed among the Hindûs, subsists to the present time among the Arabs, and probably may have been common to all nations in ancient times.

Several other ancient legislators seem to have employed the division of the people into tribes as the groundwork of the civilization which they wished to introduce. Cecrops divided the people of Athens into four tribes or classes, which were afterwards subdivided into ten more. The great legislator Solon respected this division, and confirmed it in many particulars.

Numa Pompilius saw no better method of quieting the jealousies and animosities which subsisted amongst the people whom he governed, composed chiefly of Romans and Sabines, than the division of the whole into classes or castes. This division had the desired effect; and those two communities when combined into one national mass forgot their discordant interests and thought no longer but of what concerned the caste or class.

Those who were admirers of this plan of dividing a people into tribes could not but perceive that in proportion as the distinction into classes is firmly established in any society, so much the more completely may order and good arrangement be introduced amongst them, together with the facility of directing them and the preservation of good morals.

And in truth it is the influence of this artificial order, and the separation into castes amongst the Hindûs, which make the whole tribe feel the faults of one member as reflecting disgrace on the rest as long as they remain unpunished. The caste is thus obliged to take justice into its own hands, for the purpose of avenging its honour and to restrain within the bounds of good order all the individuals that compose it. For every caste has its ancient customs, agreeably to which, like the patriarchs of old, it can inflict the severest punishment upon the guilty.

Thus, in several tribes, adultery is punished with death. Young women and widows who allow themselves to be seduced, and the seducers also, suffer the same punishment.

The magnificent temple of *Kânchi-puram (Conjeveram)*, in the Carnatic, an immense structure, is said to have been erected at the charge of a very wealthy Brâhman who was convicted of intercourse with a woman of the tribe of the Pariahs. His own caste condemned him to expiate his crime by this enormous sacrifice; although it was not inflicted so much to punish the crime as the meanness of condescending to so unworthy a partner.

There are many other faults of a scandalous nature on which the caste has a right to determine, and not only against the perpetrator but all those who may have been his abettors: so that it may be affirmed that it is the influence of custom in the caste that preserves morality among the Hindûs, represses their vices, and prevents the nation from sinking into barbarism.

The good police and the wise sentiments inculcated on the greater number of the tribes, form not only a powerful rampart to keep up the Hindû nation in a state of civilization, but serve to counterbalance in a certain degree the evil effects which a religion that encourages vice and the depravity of morals by all its ceremonies would certainly occasion, if it were not counteracted by the sentiment of the people.

In India, where the Princes live in extreme indolence, and take little pains to make their people happy by the reign of justice and good morals, there are no other means of attaining this end and of preserving good order but by the authority and customs of the castes. The worst of it is that in many cases this authority is not sufficiently extensive, while in many others it is employed in animadverting upon transgressions of frivolous rites rather than in extirpating real crimes, for which a culpable indulgence is too frequently shewn.[o]

This authority of the castes likewise forms a defence against the abuses which despotic princes are ready to commit. Sometimes one may see the traders through a whole canton shutting up their shops, the farmers abandoning their labours in the field, the different workmen and artisans quitting their booths, by an order from the caste, in consequence of some deep insult which it had suffered from a governor or some other person in office.[p]

---

[o] Just so: Caste is arbitrary, visiting petty deviations of its absurd rules heavily and overlooking moral offences, while it is notoriously partial in the use of its terrible authority.

[p] That is, caste institutions may work in India mischiefs analogous to those caused by the one-sided trades-unions in Europe.

The labours of society continue at a stand until the indignity is repaired or the injustice atoned for, or at least till the offended caste has come to an accommodation with the persons in power.

Another important advantage arising from the division into castes is the continuation of families, and of that species of nobility peculiar to the Hindûs, which consists in never contaminating its blood with any foreign mixture. Each individual must unite only with one of his own family, or at least of the caste from which he sprung. In India the reproach will not hold, which is so often made in Europe, of families becoming debased and degenerate by unsuitable and ignoble connections. A Hindû of a good caste, without pedigree or any other tables of genealogy but the fact of his being born of the caste, can point backward to his extraction for two thousand years, if he pleases, without fear of contradiction or the slightest suspicion of a blot in his pedigree. He may also, with no other recommendation than that of being a member of the caste, and in spite of poverty, aspire to advancement; and wherever he goes he will be better received and more courted for an alliance than others in easier circumstances, but of blood less pure.

There are some districts and tribes, undoubtedly, where the purity of alliances is not so narrowly scrutinized. But this laxity is considered as derogatory, and as an open violation of propriety; and it is so universally condemned that those who are guilty of it conceal it as far as they are able, that they may avoid the public shame it would bring upon them.

I might be justified in asserting further, that it is by the division of castes that the arts[q] are preserved in India; and there is no reason to doubt that they would arrive at perfection there, if the avarice of the rulers did not restrain the progress of the people.

It was with this view that the Egyptians were so strictly divided into tribes, because (as Bossuet observes) their wise legislators perceived that by such means all the arts and trades would arrive at perfection; and that a person would learn to do that well which he had always had before his eyes, and which he had been constantly practising from his infancy.

This high perfection in art and manufacture would undoubtedly be attained by a people so patient and industrious as the Hindûs, if it were not perpetually checked by that avarice of their great men which I have before alluded to. For as soon as it is known that an artist of great skill exists in any district, he is immediately carried off to the palace of the ruler, where he is shut up for life and compelled to toil without remission and with little recompense.

This practice, which is common through all the provinces of India that are subject to princes, cannot fail to extinguish all industry and to deaden emulation. It may therefore be considered as the prin-

---

q None but the most mechanical have been preserved, and these even have retrograded.

cipal and perhaps the only cause which has kept the Hindû people so far behind other nations whom they have for so many ages preceded in civilization : for their artists and workmen are endowed with dexterity and industry, perhaps in a superior degree to the Europeans.[r]

In the countries that are under the government of Europeans, where the workmen are paid according to their merits, I have seen many articles of furniture executed by the natives so exquisitely that they would have been ornamental in the most elegant mansion. Yet no other tools were employed in the manufacture but a hatchet, a saw, and a plane, of so rude construction, that a European artisan could not have used them.

In those parts, I have known travelling goldsmiths, who, with no implements but what they carried in their moveable booth, consisting of a small anvil, a crucible, two or three hammers, and files, would execute with so simple an apparatus, toys as neat and well finished as any that could be brought from distant countries at a great expense. To what perfection might not such men arrive, if they were instructed from their infancy under fit masters, instead of being guided by the simple dictates of nature ?

In order to form a proper idea of what the Hindûs are capable of, in arts and manufactures, if their natural industry were properly encouraged, it is only necessary to go into the work-shop of one of their weavers, or painters on cloth, and to attend minutely to the humble machinery with which they execute those beautiful muslins and matchless cloths which are every where admired, and constitute the finery of Europe. In performing those ingenious labours, the workman employs his feet as much as his hands.

On the other hand, the weaving loom, the whole apparatus for spinning the thread before it is woven, and all the utensils necessary for his trade, are so few and simple, that altogether they form no heavy load for a man to carry ; and it is no uncommon thing to see one of those artisans who manufacture the splendid works we have mentioned, moving from one village to another, bearing on his back every thing that is necessary for commencing his work the moment he arrives.

Their paintings on cloth, which are not less admired than their works of the loom, are performed with means as little complicated. Three or four bamboos to stretch the cloth, two or three pencils to apply the colours, a few bits of a broken dish to hold the paints, and a piece of stone to grind them, are the only implements of the cloth painter.

I will now venture one political reflection on the advantages produced by the division into castes. In India, paternal authority is but little respected ; and the parents, partaking of the indolence so prevalent over all the country, are at little pains to inspire into their chil-

---

r This exceptional practice of tyrannical Hindû Râjas cannot be the cause of the stagnation which the abbé acknowledges to exist : caste, the great petrifier, is the real cause.

dren that filial reverence which is the greatest blessing in a family, by preserving the subordination necessary for domestic peace and tranquillity. The affection and attachment between brothers and sisters, never very ardent, almost entirely disappears as soon as they are married. After that event, they scarcely ever meet, unless it be to quarrel.[1]

The ties of blood and relationship are thus too feeble to afford that strict union, and that feeling of mutual support which are required in a civilized state. It became necessary therefore to unite them into great corporations, where the members have a common interest in supporting and defending one another. And, to make this system effectual, it was requisite that the connection which bound them together, should be so intimate and strong as that nothing can possibly dissolve it.

This is precisely the object which the ancient legislators of India have attained by the establishment of the different castes. They have thus acquired a title to glory without example in the annals of the world; for their work has endured even to our days, for thousands of years, and has remained almost without change through the succession of ages and the revolutions of empires. Often have the Hindûs submitted to a foreign yoke, and have been subdued by people of different manners and customs. But the endeavours of their conquerors to impose upon them their own modes have uniformly failed, and have scarcely left the slightest trace behind them.[2]

The authority maintained by the castes has every where preserved their duration. This authority in some cases is very large, extending, as we have already observed, to the punishment of death. A few years ago, in a district through which I was passing, a man of the tribe of Râjaputras, put his own daughter to death, with the approbation of the people of his caste, and the chief men of the place where he resided. His son would have shared the same fate if he had not made his escape; but no person imputed any blame to the Râjaputra.

There are several offences, real or imaginary, which the castes have the power of punishing capitally.

A pariah who should disguise his real caste, and, mixing with the Brâhmans or even with the Śûdras, should dare to eat with them or touch their food, would be in danger of losing his life. He would be overwhelmed with blows on the spot, if he were discovered. But a capital punishment, inflicted under such circumstances, would not be considered as a judicial act, but rather as proceeding from an immediate feeling of indignation, as a burst of zeal or noble fanaticism; of which we have some examples in the history of the Jews.

But, though the punishment of death is authorised in certain cases by some of the castes, it is inflicted but seldom. Ignominious punish-

[1] All is merged in caste feeling.

[2] That is: caste has prevented the Hindûs from availing themselves of the opportunities afforded them of acquiring the sciences, arts and civilization of nations with whom they have come into contact.

ments are more common; such as shaving the heads of lewd women. Sometimes the criminals are forced to stand for several hours in presence of the chiefs of the caste assembled, with a basket on their heads filled with earth; sometimes they are set upon an ass with their face towards the tail. On some occasions their faces are smeared with cowdung; or the cord is stripped from those who have the right to wear it. At times they are expelled from the tribe; or some other mark of ignominy is inflicted.[u]

---

[u] More than twenty years of a somewhat intimate intercourse with Hindûs have led me to a very different conclusion from the Abbé in regard to the effects of caste on the well-being of the people of South India.

He attributes the preservation and extension of the arts, sciences and civilization among the Hindûs to caste; yet this work shews, what is notorious enough, that these have not flourished, but rather declined, during the last thousand years.

Nor will it be possible to shew that the arbitrary distinctions of caste are similar to the divisions into tribes among the Egyptians and other ancient nations.

The original division into castes by the Hindû legislators has become obsolete, for the Kshatriyas and Vaisyas are now hardly to be found. The multitudinous subdivisions of the Brâhmans, Sûdras and of the various communities who are excluded from the name of Hindû by the upper castes, have originated in local circumstances, and have their real foundation in the instinct of segregation so peculiar to the people of India. Nothing is too slight to become the occasion for a separation of the different parts of a tribe or family into communities, which refuse henceforth to intermarry or to associate on terms of intimacy.

Patriotism, enlarged and comprehensive feelings of benevolence, or expanded views of social and moral obligations, are rendered impossible by this pernicious system.

From this work even, it is abundantly manifest that Hindû caste sets up impassible barriers to social progress, upholds immutable distinctions by arbitrary and absurd laws, which are enforced by irresponsible authority, maintains a standard of right and wrong entirely independant of the essential principles of moral science, and disunites and weakens the whole people so as to render them any easy prey to every invader.

The Abbé himself bears witness to the fact that customs however disgusting and degrading are perpetuated by some castes, and viewed, if not with complacency, yet with perfect toleration, by their neighbours, simply because they are in accordance with the law of the caste.

Caste and its offspring *varakkam* or Mâmûl (custom) are among the greatest hindrances to all good in India.

CHAPTER III.

EXPULSION FROM THE CASTE.

Of all sorts of punishment, the most severe to a Hindû is that of being cut off and excluded from his caste. The right of inflicting it belongs to the *Gurus* of whom we shall afterwards speak; or, where there are none, it is assumed by the chiefs belonging to the body. These may generally be found in every district of moderate extent, and recourse is had to them in all cases relating to the police of the caste. They are assisted in their office by the elders or principal men of the place where they are consulted.

Expulsion from the caste, which is the penalty inflicted on those who are guilty of infringing the accustomed rules, or of any other offence which would bring disgrace on the tribe, if it remained unavenged, is in truth an insupportable punishment. It is a kind of civil excommunication, which debars the unhappy object of it from all intercourse whatever with his fellow creatures. He is a man, as it were, dead to the world. He is no longer in the society of men. By losing his caste, the Hindû is bereft of friends and relations, and often of wife and children, who will rather forsake him than share in his miserable lot. No one dares to eat with him, or even to pour him out a drop of water. If he has marriageable daughters they are shunned. No other girls can be approached by his sons. Wherever he appears, he is scorned and pointed at as an outcast. If he sinks under the grievous curse, his body is suffered to rot on the place where he dies.

Even if, in losing his caste, he could descend into an inferior one, the evil would be less. But he has no such resource. A Śûdra little scrupulous as he is about honour or delicacy, would scorn to give his daughter in marriage even to a Brâhman thus degraded. If he cannot re-establish himself in his own caste, he must sink into the infamous tribe of the Pariah, or mix with persons whose caste is equivocal. Of this sort there is no scarcity wherever the Europeans abound. But, unhappy is he who trusts to this resource. A Hindû of caste may be dishonest and a cheat; but a Hindû without caste has always the reputation of a rogue.

The exclusion from the caste is frequently put in force without much ceremony; sometimes even out of hatred or caprice. These cases happen when individuals, from whatever motive, refuse, in whole or for the greater part, to assist at the marriages or funerals of any one of their relations or friends, or to invite, on such occasions of their own, those that have a right to be present. Persons excluded in this way never fail to commence proceedings against those who have offered them the insult, demanding reparation for their wounded honour. Such instances are commonly terminated by arbitration and in that case the exclusion is not attended with the hateful and ruinous consequences before described.

It is not necessary that offences against the usages of the caste should be either intentional or of great magnitude. It happened to my knowledge not long ago that some Brâhmans who live in my neighbourhood, having been convicted of eating at a public entertainment with a Sûdra, disguised as a Brâhman, were all ejected from the caste, and did not regain admission into it without undergoing an infinite number of ceremonies both troublesome and expensive.

I witnessed an example of this kind more unpleasant than what I have alluded to. In the caste of the Ideiyar, the parents of two families had met and determined on the union of a young man and girl of their number. The usual presents were offered to the young woman, and other ceremonies performed which are equivalent to betrothing among us. After these proceedings, the young man died, before the time appointed for accomplishing the marriage. After his death, the parents of the girl, who was still very young, married her to another. This was against the rules of the caste, which condemn the betrothed girl to remain in a state of widowhood, although the husband for whom she was destined dies before marriage. Accordingly all who had assisted at the ceremony or who had been present at it, were cut off from the caste, and no one would afterwards form any connection with them. Long after this happened, I saw some of the individuals, advanced in age, who remained in a solitary state for this reason alone.

Another incident of this kind occurs to me, which was rather of a more serious complexion than the preceding. Eleven Brâhmans, in travelling, having passed through a country desolated by war, arrived at length, exhausted by hunger and fatigue, at a village, which contrary to their expectation, they found deserted. They had brought with them a small portion of rice, but they could find nothing to boil it in but the vessels that were in the house of the washer-man of the village. To Brâhmans, even to touch them would have been a defilement almost impossible to efface. But being pressed with hunger they bound one another to secrecy by an oath, and then boiled their rice in one of the pots, which they had previously washed a hundred times. One of them alone abstained from the repast and as soon as they reached their home, he accused the other ten before the chief Brâhmans of the town. The rumour quickly spread. An assembly is held. The delinquents are summoned, and compelled to appear. They had been already apprised of the difficulty in which they were likely to be involved; and when called upon to answer the charge, they unanimously protested, as they had previously concerted, that it was the accuser only that was guilty of the fault which he had laid to their charge. Which side was to be believed? Was the testimony of one man to be taken against that of ten? The result was, that the ten Brâhmans were declared innocent, and the accuser, being found guilty, was expelled with ignominy from the tribe by the chiefs, who though they could scarcely doubt of his innocence, yet could not help being offended with the disclosure he made.

From what has been said, it will no longer be surprising that the Hindûs should be as much attached to their castes as the gentry of Europe are to their rank. Prone to abusive altercation, they use the most unmeasured language to each other, and instantly forget it: but if one should say of another that he was a man out of caste, it would be an injury that could admit of no pardon.

From this attachment to caste arises that which they entertain for their customs, which may be said to constitute their whole police. It is an attachment which is often more powerful than the desire of life; and in certain cases death would appear the lighter evil; as, for example, in eating food dressed by the Pariahs. I have seen examples of this feeling; and if I have met with still more instances of the contrary, these were at least concealed.

Upon the same principle, we are to account for the hatred and contempt which the Hindûs bear to all other nations and particularly the Europeans. These from being but little acquainted with the usages of the natives, or out of carelessness, openly violate them upon all occasions. They never shew the smallest desire to conciliate the regard of the people among whom they live, by making any sacrifice to their prejudices. But what the Hindû conceives to be the greatest indignity is their taking Pariahs for their servants, or keeping women of that abominable caste. The proud Hindû, on observing this, immediately concludes, as his habits and education lead him to do, that master and servant, husband and wife are all of one tribe, and that all Europeans are of the vile caste of the Pariah; because, according to their notions, Pariahs alone would admit other Pariahs into their service. Their principles, however, do not hinder them, upon this point, to act with the lowest submission when their interest requires it.

CHAPTER IV.

RESTORATION TO THE CASTE.

After exclusion from the caste, the individual may be reinstated, in several cases. When the exclusion has proceeded from his relations, the culprit, after gaining the principal members, prostrates himself in a humble posture before his kindred assembled on the occasion. He then submits to the severe rebukes which they seldom fail to administer, or to the blows and other corporal chastisement to which he is sometimes exposed, or discharges the fine to which he may be condemned; and, after shedding tears of contrition, and making solemn promises to efface, by his future good conduct, the infamous stain of his expulsion from the caste, he makes the *Sâshtângam*, or prostration of the eight members, before the assembly. This being completed, he is declared fit to be reinstated in his tribe.

As we shall often have occasion to make mention of the *Sâshtângam* in the course of this work, it is now proper to give a definition of the word. It signifies literally *with the eight members of the body;* because when it is performed, the feet, the knees, the belly, the stomach, the head, and the arms must touch the ground. This is the greatest mark of reverence that can be given. It is used no where but in the presence of those to whom an absolute and unlimited deference is due. This reverence is made only before the highest personages, such as kings, gurus, and others of lofty rank. A child occasionally performs it before its father; and it is common to see it practised by various castes of Hindûs in presence of the Brâhmans.

This sign of reverence is not confined to the Hindûs, but is common to several other nations of Asia; which is confirmed by the most ancient of all books, the Bible, where this extraordinary mark of reverence is called by the name of *adoration*, even when it is applied to mere mortals. It is said in the book of Genesis that Abraham ran to meet them from the tent-door, "and bowed himself toward the ground."* Lot also, "rose up, and bowed himself with his face toward the ground."† In the interview with his brother Esau, Jacob "bowed himself to the ground seven times, until he came near to his brother."‡ In the history of Joseph the same obeisance is more than once described.§ There are many other passages in scripture where this salutation is alluded to, from which it appears that this extraordinary degree of respect was employed amongst the Chaldeans, Egyptians, and other ancient people commemorated in the sacred writings, under circumstances and for purposes exactly similar to those in which it is still employed to this day in India.

---

* Gen. chap. xviii. 2. † Gen. chap. xix. 1.

‡ Gen. chap. xxxiii. 3. § Gen. chap. xlii. 6. chap. xliii. 26. chap. l. 18.

When a man is expelled from his caste for reasons of great moment, they sometimes slightly burn his tongue with a piece of gold made hot. They likewise apply to different parts of the body iron stamps, heated to redness, which impress indelible marks upon the skin. In other parts they compel the culprit to walk on burning embers; and, last of all, to complete the purification, he must drink the *Panchagavyam*; a word which literally signifies the *five things*[v] proceeding from the cow; namely, milk, butter, curd, dung, and urine, all mixed together. This is a term not to be forgotten, as it will frequently occur in the course of this work. The last of the five things, namely, the urine of the cow, is held to be the most efficacious of any for purifying all imaginable uncleanness.[w] I have often seen the superstitious Hindû accompanying these animals when in the pasture, and watching the moment for receiving the urine as it fell, in vessels which he had brought for that purpose to carry it home in a fresh state; or catching it in the hollow of his hand to bedew his face and all his body. When so used it removes all external impurity; and when taken internally, which is very common, it cleanses all within.

The ceremony of the Panchagavyam being closed, the person who had been expelled must give a grand entertainment. If he be a Brâhman he gives it to the Brâhmans, who flock to it from all parts; or if he belong to another caste, those that belong to it are his guests. This finishes the whole ceremony, and he is then restored to all his privileges.

There are certain offences, however, so heinous in the eyes of Hindûs as to leave no hope of restoration to those who have been excluded from their caste for committing them. Such would be the crime of a Brâhman who had publicly married a woman of the detested tribe of the Pariah.[x] If the woman were of any tribe less base, it is possible that, after repudiating her, and disclaiming all his children by her, many acts of purification and a large expense might at length procure his restoration. But very different would be the case of one who should be so abandoned as to eat of the flesh of a cow, supposing the idea of such enormous wickedness to enter into the heart of a Brâhman or any other Hindû of respectable caste. If such a portentous crime were by any possibility committed, even by compulsion, the abhorred perpetrator would be beyond all hope of redemption.

When the last Musalman prince reigned in Mysore, and formed the ambitious desire of extending his religion over all the peninsula of India, he seized a great number of Brâhmans and had them circumcised. Afterwards he made them eat cows' flesh, in token of renouncing their caste and their customs.[y] After the war which liberated that people from the yoke of the tyrant, I know that not a few of those who had been forced to become Musalmans, made every effort, by

---

[v] Manu, chap. xi. 166.

[w] Manu, ch. xi. 171.

[x] Manu, ch. v. 124.

[y] Wilkes, Vol. III. ch. xxii. p. 15.

offering large sums of money, to be re-admitted into their caste which they had not abandoned but through force. Assemblies were held in different parts for examining into this business, and the heads of the caste out of which they were formed decided unanimously that, after many ceremonies and expensive purifications, those who petitioned for re-admission might be cleansed from the complicated pollution contracted in their communication with the Moors. But when it was ascertained that those who were circumcised had been also under the necessity of eating cows' flesh, it was decided with one voice, in all their assemblies, that a pollution of that nature and such a prominent crime could by no means admit of forgiveness; that it could not be obliterated by presents, nor by fine, nor by the Panchagavyam. This decision was not confined to the cast of the Brâhmans; for I know well that many Śûdras in the same situation had no better success, and were all obliged to continue Musalmans.

The Râjaputras, as well as the good castes among the Śûdras, are still more difficult than the Brâhmans in receiving back those who have been expelled. Amongst the former, indeed, this degrading punishment is not inflicted but upon grave offences; whereas among the latter it is the punishment of slight breaches of their customs.

But whatever the caste may be from which one has been expelled, much cost and many ceremonies are required to reinstate him. Even when he has regained his place, he never overcomes the scandal. The blot continually remains; and in any altercation he may fall into, his former misfortune is sure to be commemorated.

CHAPTER V.

ANTIQUITY AND ORIGIN OF THE CASTES.

NOTHING appears to be of greater antiquity than the castes of the Hindûs and the customs which pertain to them. The ancient Greek and Latin authors who had made mention of India, speak of those institutions as the groundwork of Hindû civilization established from time immemorial. The inviolable attachment of that people to their customs is a strong evidence of their antiquity. They are bred in the principal of invariably clinging to their customs, so that any new habit is a thing unheard of among them; any man attempting to introduce one would rouse the whole nation and would be proscribed as a dangerous innovator.[a] So difficult would it be, that I believe it has never yet entered into the imagination of any intelligent Hindû. Every thing relating to their customs proceeds evenly, and is transacted with inflexible uniformity, and the minutest particulars are treated as of utmost importance; because they have been taught that it is by the strict nicety with which small matters are attended to that the most momentous concerns are sustained. Accordingly there is no nation on the earth that can boast of having kept up for so long a time its domestic rules and customs without any perceptible change.

Some modern philosophical writers among them, such as Vêmana[b] who has written his performance in the Telugu language; and Tiruvaḷḷuvar who has written his in the Tamil, are distinguished highly, and have made the Hindû customs the subject of their satire, throwing the sharpest ridicule upon the religion and habits of the

---

a *Tasmin dêśê ya chârah pâramparya kramâgatah Varṅanâm sântarâlanâm sa sadâchâra uchyatê.*

"In that land whatever institution is derived from ancestral tradition of the castes which are pure, that is pronounced to be a good institution."

Manu ii. 18.

and

Swakarma paryutsrijya tu yad anyat kurutê narah.
Ajnânât at'havâ lôbhat sa hatah patitô bhavêt.

Grihya-sûtras.

Comp. Müller's Antient Sanskrit Literature, p. 50, 51.

b The writings of *Vêmana* are extremely popular among the Telugu people. An edition of them by that very accomplished Telugu scholar C. P. Brown, Esq., with a translation was published in 1829. Nothing can exceed the sweetness and rythm of the Versification. The following triplet is a specimen of his style:

Âru ruchulu vêru, sârambu okkaṭi;
Satyanishṭ'ha vêru, satyam okkaṭi;
Parama rishulu vêru, bhâvyuṇḍu okkaṭi.—
Diverse are the six flavours, the essence one:
Diverse the conclusions regarding truth, one the truth;
Diverse the excellent sages, their mental conception ONE.

country.[c] But while these authors are exercising all their skill and raillery in ridiculing the religious ceremonies established in the nation, they never fail to recommend the practice of them, and are strictly attentive to it themselves. The works of the two authors I have named are always read and quoted with delight by all intelligent Hindûs, although there be not a page in their wr ngs that does not contain satirical reflections aimed at their gods and the worship and rites of the country.

One of the most artful contrivances made use of by the early Hindûs for preserving their customs, has been that of clothing them with ceremonies, which make a strong impression on the senses, and communicate something holy to the practice. These ceremonies are rigorously observed. It is never permitted to any one to treat them as matters of form which may be practised or omitted at pleasure. The omission of any, even of the least important, would not be allowed to pass unpunished.

---

c This is not true as regards the truly great poet of the Tamilian people *Tiruvalḷuvar.* He was a Pariah, and seems to have been in religion an eclectic. He had evidently imbibed some of the ideas of the Jains. His works seems to me to show that he had some knowledge of the institutes of Manu, and traces of an acquaintance with the Christian system are perceptible here and there. His great friend was *Èléla-Singan*, a sea-captain, according to current tradition; and he lived in St. Thomé, where he must have had opportunities of knowing any foreigners who arrived, and of making himself acquainted with their habits and ideas. It seems certain that christian missionaries had visited St. Thomé before Tiruvalluvar's time, probably about the tenth century.

But no ridicule of any Hindû religious customs, or indeed more than one or two special references to them, are to be found in his whole work. The following verse is the most express reference to popular religious practices in the book: "shaving the head or wearing long locks are not needed, if you forsake what the common consent of mankind reprobates."

The shaving of the head is peculiar to the *Śiva dandis*, as wearing the hair long to sanyâsis of various kinds. These wear their hair and beard long, and are distinguished by the Jatâ (சடை) or long matted braid of hair, which they wear twisted round the top of the head.

This work written by a Pariah, treating of ethical matters, and abounding in simple, practical, striking precepts for guidance in the affairs of every day life, with a studious avoidance of all reference to the Hindû popular religious system and to caste, has had a vast influence for good on the people of South India.

I subjoin a few of his triplets.

1. Save to those who approach the foot of Him with Whom is Majesty and Mercy, (Andaṇan=am + taṇ + an.) the sea of goodness, it is hard to reach the further shore of this sea of life." Chap. i. 8.

2. "The flute is sweet" "the lute is sweet" say they, who never heard the prattle of children of their own." vii. 6.

3. Is there any restraining bar to love? The loved one's tear raises a tempest in the loving soul." viii. 1.

4. Like the earth that bears up those who are digging into its bosom, to bear with those who use us despitefully is the highest virtue. xvi. 1.

5. If he scrutinize his own faults as though they were those of an enemy, is there any evil to be apprehended by living man? xix. 10.

6. A woman separated from her husband says

"This grief of mine buds with every dawn, blossoms with every rising sun, and every evening expands into a full blown flower." cxxiii. 7.

Some of their most important tenets are not peculiar to them, but are common to many ancient nations. The rule of marrying within the family is of this sort. When settled in a strange country, it is their usual practice to send perhaps upwards of a hundred leagues to the place of their nativity for wives and husbands to their sons and daughters.

But the origin of the castes amongst the Hindûs goes back to a much higher æra than that of any other people, if credit be given to their ancient books, in which it is written that the whole was the work of the God Brâhma, when he replenished the earth with inhabitants. From his head sprung the Brâhmans; the Kshatriya or Râjas, from his shoulders; the Vaisya or merchants from his belly; and the Śûdras or farmers from his feet.[d]

It is easy to perceive that this tale is a pure allegory, alluding not only to the rank which the castes maintain in relation to each other, but also to the different functions of those who compose them. The Brâhmans, no doubt, being generally engaged in the spiritual concerns of life, must have burst from the head of the Creator. Power being the attribute of the Râjas who were ordained to the arduous duties of war; from whence could their origin be derived but from the shoulders and arms of Brâhma? The Merchants, solely occupied in providing food, clothing and other necessaries of life, were no less appropriately drawn from the belly of the god: and the plodding Śûdras, doomed to the humble drudgery of the field, were shaken out of his feet.[e]

Dropping this fabulous origin of the castes, which is familiar to every Hindû, their writers give countenance to another, which refers that establishment to the remote æra of the subsiding of the universal deluge: for this awful event, which made a new world, was almost as distinctly known to the Hindûs as to Moses.

We will revert to this subject hereafter; but in the meantime we may observe that a famous personage, distinguished by the Hindûs under the name of *Manu* was saved from the flood by the aid of a bird, together with the seven famous penitents who will be mentioned in the next chapter. After the flood, this new renovator of the human race, discriminated men, as Hindû authors say, into the different castes which still prevail in India.

The name Manu deserves notice. Whatever may be the etymology of the word, the similarity of sound seems to point out Manu to be the same as the Menes of the ancient Egyptians, and the great Noah of the Scripture, who stands the highest in consideration and the most venerable of mankind after Adam.

---

d Manu ii. 31. 87—91. Vishṇu Purâṇa. ch. vi.

e The references to distinctions of caste in the Vêdas are few and equivocal. It seems doubtful whether they existed, at least in any thing like the form they afterwards assumed. See Colebrooke, Asiatic Researches. Vol. VII. p. 251.

CHAPTER VI.

THE FABULOUS ORIGIN OF THE BRÂHMANS.—ON THEIR NAME AND ORIGINAL FOUNDERS.—CONJECTURES ON THEIR REAL ORIGIN.

THE true origin of the Brâhmans, as well as that of the other Hindû tribes, is not distinctly known; and we are therefore reduced to fables or mere conjecture.[f]

The fabulous tradition which is most current among them is that which derives them from the head of Brâhma; and they draw their name from his. The other castes, having sprung from the same stem, would seem entitled to bear the same appellation. But the Brâhmans being the first, and emanating from the noblest part of their common father, consider themselves exclusively entitled to that sacred name.

They also produce other claims to establish their sole right to this venerable title. The Brâhmans, they say, were the first to comprehend Brâhma in perfection; and having the clearest conception of this great being, it pertains to them only to explain his nature and attributes to the other tribes. They alone have the distinguished privilege of perusing the books that treat of this divinity; and, for these and many other reasons not less conclusive, they assume the name of Brâhmans.

But, however well founded their pretensions may be to this great distinction, certain it is, that they derive it from the word Brâhma. In the scientific languages of the country, they are called *Brâhmaṇa* from which the name Bracmanes used by the Latin authors is undoubtedly derived.

A *Brâhman* is in a very different situation from a *Râja*, a *Vaisya*, or a *Śûdra*. These are born in the condition in which they continue to live. But a Brâhman becomes such only by the ceremony of the Cord, which will be afterwards fully explained. He is till then only a Śûdra; and by birth he possesses nothing that raises him above the level of other men. It is after this rite that he is called *Dwija* (twice born). The first birth admits him to the common rank of mortals; the second, which he owes to the ceremony of the triple cord, exalts him to the lofty rank of the tribe to which he belongs.

The seven castes of the Brâhmans have for their special origin the seven famous *Rishis* or penitents. Two of these were not originally of that rank; but they practised so long and so severe a penance, that they obtained the remarkable favour of being raised to it by the ceremony of the cord. From penitent Râjas they

---

[f] The most valuable materials for the full and independent study of this important subject are to be found in Muir's Sanskrit Texts, on the origin and history of the people of India. Williams and Norgate.

became penitent Brâhmans; and their rise was from a still lower rank, if we believe what is sung upon the subject by the philosophical poet Vêmana.

These seven *Rishis* or penitents, of whom frequent mention will be hereafter made, are highly celebrated in the annals of the country. They are the holiest and most venerated personages that the Hindûs acknowledge. Their names are held sacred and are invoked by all the people. They are inculcated on their children; and are as follows: *Kaśyapa, Atri, Bharadwajâ, Gautama, Viswâmitra, Jamadagni, Vaśishṭa, Vaśishṭa* and *Viswâmitra* were considered worthy, from the rigour of their penance, to be admitted into the caste of the Brâhmans.[9]

It is certain that these seven Rishis were of great antiquity, since they must have existed prior to the Vêdas, which make mention of them in many passages. They were favoured by the gods, and particularly by Vishṇu, who preserved them at the time of the flood from the universal destruction, by making them and their wives embark in a ship in which he himself acted as the pilot.

Some of the gods have suffered not a little from incurring their displeasure; for even against them the wrath of the Rishis would pursue evil conduct and infamous debauchery.

The seven penitents, after giving an example on earth of all the virtues, were translated into heaven, where they still hold their place among the most brilliant of the stars. Those who have a desire to see them, have only to look up to the seven stars in the great bear: for these are no other than the seven famous Rishis themselves; not emblematically, but in strict reality. And it is believed that, without ceasing to sparkle in the firmament, they can descend, and actually do pay an occasional visit to the earth to know what is going on.

If the fabulous stories which are told of the origin of certain great families in Europe shed a lustre upon them by proving their antiquity; how much more reason has the Brâhman to vaunt his noble pedigree? and if the honour of being sprung from an illustrious family, sometimes leads its descendants to look down with contempt upon the lower ranks, we cannot surely wonder at the arrogance and haughtiness of the Brâhman, and the high disdain which he shews to every caste but his own.

The idea of preserving the memory of their great men and of making them immortal, by assigning them a place among the constellations which shine in the sky, appears to be common to all ancient tribes. The worship of the stars accordingly seems to have been universally and most religiously observed amongst all idolatrous nations ancient and modern. This species of idolatry being the least unreasonable of any, and of the longest duration, the lawgivers of antiquity and the founders of false religions, perceiving the powerful hold which it had already acquired over the human mind, made use of it as the most efficacious means of perpetuating the memory of their

[9] Vishṇu Purâṇ. B. III. Cap. I.

heroes and other great men: for, by thus transforming them into stars, they set them up as objects always to be seen, and always to strike the observer. It was in this way that the Greeks and Romans consecrated their chief divinities and most celebrated heroes; and it was for the same purpose that the Hindûs placed their seven famous Rishis in the brightest zone of the starry sphere; being sure that this was the infallible method of keeping up their memory amongst a people insensible to all objects but those that strike vividly on their senses.

But there is at least one thing which is not fanciful in this question; which is that in the countries situated to the north-east of Bengal, beyond the Ganges, there were neither castes nor Brâhmans till within these four or five hundred years. The people who inhabited those provinces, beginning then to see that it would be of advantage to them to adopt the customs of their neighbours, demanded to have Brâhmans. The order was soon created by selecting and setting apart a number of their youths, who were trained up in the manners of that caste; into which they were duly embodied by the ceremony of the cord. From that period, they have been considered as true Brâhmans, and hold equal rank with those who are of a far more ancient order.[h]

In the southern countries they do not like to be reminded of this anecdote, although they are obliged to admit its authenticity, as well as that of the two penitents who were at first only Râjas.

There is a puzzling objection frequently urged against the Brâhmans. If it be the ceremony of the cord, it is asked, that creates you Brâhmans, how come your wives, who do not undergo that ceremony, to be any thing but Śûdras? You are therefore married to wives not belonging to your caste; a principle held sacred and inviolable amongst all Hindûs.

Their solution of this difficulty is an answer that has been continually made to all their antagonists; namely, that they are guided in this particular by the usage of the caste from time immemorial.

After reporting what the fables of India afford respecting the origin of the Brâhmans, I wish to offer, with deference, what appears to me no improbable suggestion. What I am going to say may perhaps appear of little weight to most of my readers: but I give my opinion without arrogance, or the vain pretension of forming a connected system, where all the documents that can be had, are founded only on the most extravagant fables. My view of it may be tolerated by those who in the midst of the thick darkness in which the origin of nations is obscured, would rejoice in one spark that might serve to guide their steps, and assist them in discovering what at least approaches most nearly to truth.

---

h The same thing has occurred among the Badagar (or immigrant Kanarese) on the Nilagiri Hills. Certain families have been set apart to perform such offices as are usually rendered by Brâhmans, and among their own family receive the name and honours of Brâhmans.

It appears tolerably certain, that India has been peopled from the earliest times, and not long after the deluge, which converted the earth into a vast desert. It is close to the plains of Shinar, where the descendants of Noah remained fixed for a long time. Its happy climate and fertile soil would naturally retain the wanderers who settled there. I need say nothing of the subsequent conquests of Hercules, Bacchus, and Osiris.[i] The best authorities hold them to be entirely fabulous, though some are inclined to admit their history to be fundamentally true, and content themselves with rejecting its extravagant embellishments.

The history of Sesostris, though also abounding in fable, is evidently more connected and better founded. The few monuments of antiquity that have descended to us, represent this celebrated hero as the greatest, and indeed the only warrior that pacific Egypt can boast of during its long career as an independent nation, extending to more than sixteen hundred years. He is also described as the most extensive conqueror that ever existed on earth ; for the boundaries of his empire embraced the enormous sweep between the Danube and all the nations which then inhabited the provinces of India ; but his conquests there turned out to be neither more secure nor more permanent than those that were made, long after, by his competitor in glory, Alexander the Great.

The establishments which were made by the Arabians in India, as they are represented by some modern writers, appear more plausible to superficial minds. The restless disposition of that people, the wandering life which they have always led, together with their vicinity to India, would seem to give a colour of probability to this opinion. Nay, its supporters may even add that it is from the Arabs that the Hindûs derive their division into castes, and that it still subsists among the people of Arabia. But, in order to give weight to the supposition, it would be necessary to prove that the division into castes has not existed amongst all ancient nations, and equally to the Arab and the Hindû.

It is not therefore through the channel of Egypt or Arabia that I am inclined to introduce the Brâhmans into India. I do not conceive them to be the descendants of Shem, but of Japhet. I think it supposable that they penetrated into the country by the north or the north-west, and that we must seek for their origin in the long chain of mountains, known in Europe by the name of Mount Caucasus.

Their books make frequent mention of two celebrated mountains situated in the middle of *Jambudwîpa*, (which is their name also for the habitable world,) remotely situated beyond the most northern boundaries of India. One of these mountains is designated by the name of

---

[i] See Plutarch's Isis and Osiris. ch. 35.

Mahâ Mêru, or Great Meru, and the other by that of Mount Mandara.[j] Frequent allusions to these two mountains, or, as I conceive, to the same under different names, are made in the prayers of the Brâhmans, in their religious and civil ceremonies, and in the principal occurrences of life. According to them and their books, this mountain is situated in the remotest quarter of the north, and from its bosom they still agree that their ancestors took their origin. This country, they tell us, is so far distant, that its precise situation is unknown to the modern Brâhmans; and that is not very surprizing in a country whose inhabitants have so little knowledge of practical geography, that the utmost reach of it extends only to the countries between Kâśi and Cape Comorin.

It is in these retired regions of the north that they fix the residence of the seven famous penitents of whom we have spoken, whom they consider as the first of their ancestors; and from them proceeded those descendants who gradually penetrated into the southern provinces of India.

This notion of the first origin of the Brâhmans deduced from the Hindû books, and kept up to this day by the members of that caste, is confirmed by the manner in which they treat one another. Those of the north of India consider themselves to be more noble and of higher distinction than those of the south; on the ground of their being less distant from their original seat, and consequently their descent from the great fountain being less dubious.

The Seven Penitents, or Philosophers of the north, from whom they spring, may have been the seven sons of Japhet, who, with their father at their head, at the time of the dispersion of men, carried with them the third part of the human race towards the west. The whole of that family did not go over to Europe. Many of them having approached its boundaries, turned towards the north, under the direction of Magog, the second son of Japhet, and advancing through Tartary as far as Mount Caucasus, formed considerable colonies in that wide region.

The name of Magog may be traced among the Seven Penitents, from whom the Brâhmans say they are descended. It seems to arise from that of *Gauta Maha*. *Mâ* or *Mahâ* signifies *great*, and *Gauta* is the same as *Got* or *Gog*, the *a* before a vowel and the final *a* being both elided in Sanscrit words: so that Gauta Mahâ, signifies the great Got or Magog, Magoth.

---

j Vishṇu purâṇa Book II. Chap. II. Jambu-dwîpa is the centre of the seven great insular continents. In its centre is the golden mountain *Mêru*. Its shape is that of an inverted cone, like the flower of the Dhatura. Mount Mandara is one of the buttresses of Mount Mêru, to the East of it. "There can be doubt that these mountains and other mentioned as lying around them, refer to the Altai, Tian-Shân, Kuen-lûn, and Himâlaya ranges, which traverse Central Asia from East to West, and from which flow the great rivers that water Siberia, China, Tartary, and Hindustân."

Much of this seems extremely fanciful. Max Müller's Essay on Antient Mythology in the Oxford Essays for 1856, should be consulted.

The history of other ancient people would supply me with conjectures for supporting the opinion I have embraced on the origin and antiquity of the Brâhmans. The learned acknowledge several Prometheuses. The most famous was the Prometheus of Greece, whom they consider to be the son of Japhet. He formed men from the soil, in imitation of the gods, and animated them with the fire which he stole from heaven. This boldness irritated Jupiter, who bound him to Mount Caucasus, where a vulture constantly devoured his liver as it grew. This grievous punishment continued till Hercules slew the vulture, and so delivered the son of Japhet.

Was not Brâhma the same as Prometheus? The Indian god is also called *Brâhma*, and *Prumé* in some dialects. These names well accord with the Prometheus of the Greeks. That is to say the god Promé or Prumé is the same as Brâhma. The latter as well as the former, is regarded as the author of the creation of men, who sprung from various parts of his body. He was their lawgiver, by the Vêdas which he wrote with his own hand. He had more than once occasion for the aid of Vishṇu, as Prometheus had for that of Hercules, in order to be delivered from his enemies.

This claim of the Indian Prometheus to be recognized as the creator of men and as a god, has descended, at least in part, to the Brâhmans, his eldest born. They denominate themselves without ceremony, and take the title, without any offence to their modesty, of the *Gods Brâhmans*, the Gods of the Earth; and on certain occasions they receive the homage of being adored on bended knees, like deities.

But, granting that the original natal soil of the Brâhmans was Tartary, or the environs of Mount Caucasus, it will not be easy to determine the exact epoch of their establishment in India. It appears, however, that they were there, and in a flourishing condition, more than nine hundred years before the Christian æra; for it is recorded that, about that time, Lycurgus went to visit them. The high reputation they had already acquired for learning, and particularly their skill in the occult sciences, had spread even into Europe, and appears to have at that distance determined one of the wisest and most profound philosophers that antiquity boasts of, to undertake a voyage into India to profit by the lessons and the example of those wise Brâhmans, who had been settled there for ages. It is pretty clear that such a personage as Lycurgus was not likely to risk so painful and tedious a voyage if the reputation of the philosophers whom he went to consult had not been established long before.

The Brâhmans of those remote ages were indeed very different in their principles and conduct from those of modern days. The former are represented in the Hindû books chiefly (if not exclusively) in the light of penitents or philosophers, devoted wholly to the culture of sciences, or to a life of contemplation and the practice of the moral virtues. They did not at that time form a tribe wholly intolerant and exclusive, like the hermits of the present days. Neither could penitents of a different origin become Brâhmans, and be initiated into their caste, by the ceremony of the *Dakshina*, or the investment of the triple cord: of which various proofs may be shewn in the Hindû books.

The simple and innocent manners of those early Brâhmans, their contempt of honours and wealth, their moral virtues, and above all their temperance, raised them into respect amongst kings and people. For, even the monarch did not conceive himself degraded by paying such homage to them as he would not have exacted from his own subjects for himself.

Those philosophers, secluded as they were, had wives, and multiplied exceedingly. The Brâhmans of our days are their descendants. The present race, though altogether degenerate from the virtues of their ancestors, still preserve a great deal of their character and habits; inasmuch as they shew to the present day a predilection for retirement and seclusion from the bustle of the world, selecting for their residence villages quite retired, into which they permit no person of any other caste to enter. Those villages, inhabited by none but Brâhmans, are in great numbers in the present different divisions of the peninsula, and are generally described under the name of the *Agrahâra-grâma* or superior villages.[k]

The modern Brâhmans approach nearer to the manners of their ancestors, by their frequent feasts, their daily ablutions, and the manner, nature, and subject of their sacrifices; and above all their scrupulous abstinence not only from meat, and all food that has ever had the principle of life, but also from many other productions of nature to which their prejudices and superstition have attached some idea of impurity.

The religious system of the modern Brâhmans, and the irrational theology which they have introduced into India, appear to me to be the particulars in which they have chiefly departed from the rules and precepts of their primitive founders. I am far from believing that the wise legislators who prescribed laws for the Hindûs could ever have formed an idea of introducing among them a species of worship so abominable and so ridiculously absurd as that which we see in use amongst them at the present time.

Their mythology and the external objects of their worship were at first mere allegories, represented under visible shapes, for the purpose of engraving them more vividly on the memory of a people who appeared quite insensible to all objects that did not make an immediate impression on the senses. But men of a gross, indolent, careless, and superstitious disposition would naturally soon forget what the worship signified, and attach themselves exclusively to the material objects represented in corporeal shape; so that all perception of a latent meaning would gradually vanish.

---

k Agrahâra-grâma = Endowed village: most of these having endowments bestowed upon them by antient Râjas.

The primitive religion of the ancient Brâhmans appears to have been altered and almost wholly perverted by their successors. The first species of idolatry into which all nations fell as soon as they forgot the traditions of their first ancestors, concerning the unity of God, and the sole and exclusive worship which he requires from all his creatures, was the adoration of the stars and of the elements.[l] It appears that this was the worship that prevailed amongst the ermitical Brâhmans or Penitents, from whom those of the present day take their rise. It was not till long after their time, that their descendants, falling into the last stage of idolatry, fashioned images or statues, which at first were merely typical of the objects of their religion, but which an ignorant race began at last to worship. It was then that India split into various schemes of religion, which subsist to the present times, and that one set embraced the fables of the Trimûrtti, and another the doctrines of Buddha.[m]

These two sects have probably the same origin. The one may have been a corruption of the other: or both may have been drawn from the purer religion of the ancient Brâhmans. Some modern authors have imagined that the religion of *Buddh* or *Buddha* was anciently that of all India and probably of all Asia, from Siberia to Cape Comorin and the Streights of Malacca, and from the Caspian Sea to the Gulph of Kamtchatka. But, be this as it may, the worship of Buddh or Buddha appears fully as ancient as that of the Trimûrtti. It is well known that the former species of idolatry is still in vigour and prevails in Tartary, in the two Thibets, and in China. It

---

l For a sketch of the Vaidic religion, see the introduction to Wilson's Rig Vêda sanhitâ. There is a great difference between the theology of the Purânas and the Vêdas.

The names of Śiva, Mahâdêva, Durgâ, Kâli, Râma and of Kristṇa never occur in the Vêdas. Neither is there, the slightest hint of the Trimûrtti. This is a Triune combination of Brahmâ; Vishṇu and Śiva, as typified by the Mystic syllable OM (= A + U + M.)

Comp. Max Müller's antient sanskrit liter. p. 32.

After the primeval physiolatry, which was common to all the members of the Aryan family, had, in the hands of a wily priesthood, been changed into an empty idolatry, the Indian alone of all the Aryan nations, produced a new form of religion, which has now been called subjective, as opposed to the more objective worship of nature. That religion, the religion of Buddha, has spread, far beyond the limit of the Aryan world, and to our limited vision, it may seem to have retarded the advent of christianity among a large portion of the human race.

The religion of Buddha is of all others the most hostile to the old belief of the Brâhmans,—the Buddhists standing to the Brâhmans in about the same relation as the early Protestants to the Church of Rome. It was only in India, where people had been prepared by thought and meditation, as well as by the very corruption of the old Brâhminical system, to embrace and nurture the religious ideas of Buddha sâkyâ Muni (+500 B.C.) that those new doctrines took an historical shape and grew into a religion which, if truth depended on majorities, would be the truest of all forms of faith. No religion is more extensively prevalent than the religion of Buddha, and though it has been banished from India, and no living follower of that faith is now to be met with in that country, yet it has found a refuge and second home in Ceylon, (543. B.C.) Siam, Ava, Pegu, the Birman Empire, China, Thibet, Tartary, Mongolia and Siberia, and is, even in its present corruption, looked upon and practised as the only true faith by many millions of human beings.

m On this subject the reader is recommended to consult the late Professor H. H. Wilson's "sketch of the religious sects of the Hindûs," contained in the Asiatic Researches, Vols. XVI. XVII.

was introduced from Siam and not through Cape Comorin, as La Loubere has demonstrated in his account of the kingdom of Siam. It is practised almost exclusively in the kingdoms of Pegu, of Las, of Cambogia, of Japan, and probably in all the countries beyond the Ganges. It extends also to the island of Ceylon.

Besides the worship of the Trimûrtti and that of Buddha, the two predominant religions in India, there exists a third, which, till lately, had been but little known. It is that of the *Jainas,* which keeps aloof from the rest, and equally detests the Brâhmans and the Buddhists and their respective doctrines.

The Jainas maintain that the Trimûrtti and Buddhism, are both modern innovations, of evil tendency, and corruptions of the primitive religion of India, which they insist is exclusively maintained by themselves. They affirm that they are the only successors of the ancient Brâhman devotees, whose practice and doctrine they preserve; whilst the modern Brâhmans and the Buddhists are sadly tainted and disfigured by the introduction of monstrous innovations which have overrun the country.[n]

These innovations of the Brâhmans in matters of religion were not introduced without a long and violent opposition on the part of the Jainas. The latter assert, and the Brâhmans admit, that the Brâhmanical worship at present professed in the country was not received till after a long and bloody war, in which the Jainas were subdued and reduced to the cruel necessity of submitting without reservation to whatever conditions their enemies the Brâhmans chose to prescribe. The Brâhmanical system thus acquired the ascendant, and perverted the popular faith.

But whatever may be the pretensions of the Brâhmans, the Jainas and the Buddhists, concerning the antiquity of their religion and the various points of doctrine in which they disagree, it appears extremely probable that all three derive their origin from the same source. The fundamental dogma of the metempsychosis, which is common to all the three, and the worship which they equally pay to images, not dissimilar in form, and which appear to be nothing else than allegorical representations intended to pourtray to the external senses the object of their original devotion; exhibit a striking resemblance among them. Their religious institutions also consist alike of priests, monks, and religious devotees; they offer up in most cases the same species of sacrifice; and the language used by

---

n Vishnu purâṇa, p. 272—277.

Vyâsa is commonly called vêda-vyâsa.

Twenty-eight persons bearing this name are enumerated, and it is probable that Vyâsa was a name given to any distinguished sage, author of any part of the Vêdas. The Vyâsa who is looked upon as the actual arranger of the Vêdas was the Muni Krishṇa Dwaipâyana. He is also said to be the author of the Mahâbhârata.

Vyâsa means simply *arranger*.

Comp. Müller's ant. sansk. lit. p. 476.

the priests in the discharge of their functions is also similar. This language is called *Pâli*, and is unquestionably employed by the Bonzes or priests of Buddha in the kingdom of Siam, and derived from the Sanskrit, the only idiom used by the Brâhmans and Jainas of the peninsula in their ceremonies.[o] These and many other points of coincidence among the three religions seem to leave little doubt of their origin being the same.

The sect of the Jainas, though much spread over several provinces of the South of the peninsula, being but little understood by Europeans till of late, I propose, in an Appendix to this work, to give a short sketch of their doctrines and the principal points in which they differ from their enemies the Brâhmans. I should have been likewise desirous to add a similar account of the doctrine of the Buddhists; but not having succeeded in obtaining authentic documents concerning that sect, it is out of my power to satisfy the curiosity of my readers on that subject. Persons residing in the island of Ceylon, where the religion of Buddha prevails, might supply the defect which such an omission occasions in my work.[p]

---

[o] The Pâli is the sacred language of the Bûdhistic writings, and was substantially the popular dialect of the district of Magadha (Berar) in which that system first arose. It is derived from sanskrit, according to certain Euphonic rules, and stands in the same relation to the mother language as Italian does to Latin.

[p] This has been done by a variety of modern authors, Turner, Burnouf, Lassen and others.

CHAPTER VII.

OF THE DIFFERENT KINDS OF BRÂHMANS.

THE tribe of Brâhmans is divided into seven branches, each of which recognises as its chief one of the famous penitents of whom we have spoken in another chapter; and each Brâhman knows from which of the seven he is descended.

Another and a more general division separates them into four distinct classes, each of which appertains to one of the four *Vêdas.* These Vêdas are four books held by them in such reverence that no eye of any other caste has ever perused them. The Brâhmans are so jealous about this privilege, or rather they have so great an interest in preventing the other castes from learning what these books contain, that they have invented a story, which obtains universal belief all over the country, that if a Śûdra or any other of the profane should make an attempt to read even the title of these sacred books his head would instantly cleave asunder. They conceal them with the utmost care, and never read them but in a low voice, and never but where they are sure to be unseen. The least punishment that a Brâhman would undergo who should have the boldness or indiscretion to shew these sacred volumes to profane eyes, would be the expulsion from his tribe without hope of ever regaining it. We shall afterwards resume the subject of these books.

There are Brâhmans denominated *Yajur Vêda, Sâma Vêda, Rig Vêda* and *Atharva Vêda.* Of the last species there are very few, and many people suppose they no longer exist.[q] But the truth is, they do exist though they conceal themselves with more caution than the others, from the fear of being suspected to be initiated in the magic mysteries and other dreaded secrets which this work is believed to teach. Any one saying that he had it in his possession, would not fail on that ground alone, to be branded with the detested name of a magician.

At the great sacrifice of the *Yajna* to be afterwards described, Brâhmans of all the four Vêdas assist.[r]

The prayers which the members of this tribe are bound to repeat three times daily, are taken from those sacred books. They differ somewhat, according to the Vêda from which they are taken; each Brâhman extracting from the Vêda to which he is attached.

But in the intercourse of life, they appear to pay little attention to this distinction of Brâhmans by the Vêda, nor to give the preference to one Vêda over another. Perhaps they are right in this; for if there

---

q Müller's anc. sanskrit lit. p. 121.

r Yajna sacrifice or oblation; from *yaja* worship.
Comp. introduction to Stevenson's Sâma Vêda.

be any truth in what the author of the *Bhâgavata* says, (a poem famous over India,) there was formerly no distinction of one Vêda from another, and the whole composed but one work. It was the penitent Vyasa who divided them into four books. This same author of the Bhâgavata has supplied an introduction and commentary to render the text more intelligible. He ascribes also to Vyasa the eighteen *Purâṇas;* which, it is well known, are eighteen rhapsodies, each more ridiculous than another, giving a detail of the grossest fables of Hindu idolatry.

Another race of Brâhmans widely spread over the south of the peninsula, is formed of individuals of that tribe who profess a particular veneration for Vishṇu, and who bear imprinted on their foreheads the mark of his particular worship, which is formed of three perpendicular lines joined at their base, and thus representing the figure of a trident.[s] The middle line is red or yellow, and those on each side are painted with a piece of white earth, called Nâma: and it is from this that the whole figure goes by the name of *Nâma.* Several castes of the Śûdras professing to do particular honour to Vishṇu, also wear the Nâma inscribed on their foreheads in the same manner as the Brâhmans.[t]

Those of the latter caste who bear the mark, are very numerous in the southern provinces of the peninsula within the Krishṇa, where they are generally known by the name of *Vishṇavas,* which signifies "devotees of Vishṇu." They are desirous of assuming an air of superiority over the other castes of Brâhmans, with whom they refuse to eat or to form alliances; but it is in fact the other castes that reject them as being of a lower degree, on account of their associating themselves with a particular sect. This is displeasing to the Brâhmans in general, who being of a more liberal and tolerant disposition, give equal honour to the three great divinities of India without pre-

---

s The followers of Vishṇu in the south are mostly followers of *Râmânuja,* who appeared in the 12th century. He studied at Kânchi (Conjevaram,) resided chiefly at Śri Ranga, near Trichinopoly, from whence he made excursions to various parts of India, disputing with the śaivas, reforming abuses among the Vaishṇavas, establishing the worship of Vishṇu where it had been discontinued and rescuing several magnificent temples, especially that of Tirupaḍi (Tripety) in the extreme north of the Tamil country.

The Vaishṇavas are divided into *Ten-galai* and *vada-galai,* or the *Southern* and *Northern* sects. (*Ten* = South, *vada* = north. *Kalai* = science.)

See Buchanan's Mysore Vol. I, 143, and II, 80.
At Mail-koṭṭai in Mysûr is one of their greatest temples.

t From Sanskrit NÂMAN, *a name.*

The white earth used is called *Gopi-chandana.* [The sandal wood of the cowherds' wives] a kind of magnesian clay. It is supposed to be brought from *Dwâraka,* where the milkmaids drowned themselves on hearing of Krishṇa's death.

Their *mantra* or *upadêśa,* as Buchanan calls it is ÔM RÂMÂYA NAMAH, *ôm! salutation to Râma.*

Their system is that called the *Vaśishtadvaita,* that is the system which regards the Deity as one with the universe (*a,* not; *dvaitam,* duality;) but as having attributes (viśishṭa, *endowed with qualities,*) which the Vêdântis deny. As the soul of the universe he is the first cause of all things, and in the form of matter he is the efficient cause.

See Wilson's Hindû sects; Buchanan's Mysore in India under Râmânuja; and Dr. Graul's Reise nach Ostindien. Vol. IV, p. 133—140.

ferring one to the others. We shall speak farther respecting this species of Brâhmans in the following chapter.

The Brâhmans called *Śaiva* are the most despised of any belonging to this tribe. They appear to make a distinct band among themselves, and to admit the superiority of the others. They are employed in many places as servants in the temples, to wash the idols, and bring up the offerings of incense, of flowers and fruits, of boiled rice and other things which are presented by the devout, and form the materials for the sacrifice.[u]

In many pagodas the Śûdras are employed in the same manner, as sacrificers. This office is assigned to them exclusively in the temples where fowls, sheep, hogs, buffaloes, and other living creatures are immolated. It is probably by exercising this kind of service in the temples, that the Śaiva Brâhmans have fallen into such contempt. A servile office, which even a simple Śûdra has the right to perform, is degrading in their estimation. The employment of *Pûjâri* or sacrificer to a temple is not held very honourable amongst the Hindûs, and the occupations carried on by such individuals are considered as purely servile. But where there is no other resource, a man has no choice. "To serve his belly, a man will play any game." Such is the favourite proverb of the Brâhmans, which serves them for an excuse under all circumstances where their conduct is opposite to their principles, and particularly in the case before us.

I will say nothing of those who are called in derision *Flesh Brâhmans* and *Fish Brâhmans.* I have been assured that, in the north of India, and even on the Malabar coast, there are some of them who would eat of both, publicly and without scruple. And it is added, that this conduct brings no reproach upon them from the Brâhmans who abstain. But whether this be so or not, it is certain that if Brâhmans who eat meat and fish were to appear in the southern provinces, and were detected, the Brâhmans of the place would peremptorily refuse to eat with them, and would expel them out of their society. Whether those in the south have refined on the practice, or whether the others have degenerated from the rules of their early ancestors, I will not attempt to decide. The second supposition, however, would appear to be the more probable, because the usages of the Brâhmans, particularly as relating to abstinence from flesh meat, are less difficult in the observance in the warm countries of the south than they are in the cold or temperate regions of the north.

---

[u] Brâhmans who officiate in temples are undoubtedly looked down upon by the others; but not on account of their adherence to the Śaiva system. They are called *Nambis* among the Vaishṇavas and are supposed to be descended from a Ksatriya mother and a Brâhman mother.

CHAPTER VIII.

OF THE SECTS OF VISHṆU AND ŚIVA.—CAUSES OF THE OPPOSITION OF THE ORDINARY BRÂHMANS TO THE VISHṆU BRÂHMANS AND OTHER SECTARIES.

THE Brâhmans recognize six sects which they designate *Sashṭa mata,* the six sects, each of which has numerous partisans. Brâhmans only, strictly speaking, are members of these sects, and each has its own metaphisical system. Yet these differences in regard to scholastic matters do not separate them so far as to lead them to hate or persecute one another: they are rather the subjects of controversies similar to those which take place among learned men in other lands who differ in regard to speculative matters of a metaphisical and philosophical character. I shall now speak chiefly of the two great divisions which effect the Śûdras, as well as Brâhmans.

The great body of Hindûs profess to pay equal honours to all the gods of the country, particularly the three principal ones, *Brahma, Vishṇu,* and *Śiva,* without any preference of one to another. But great shoals of sectaries are likewise found among them, of whom some attach themselves exclusively to the worship of Vishṇu, and some to that of Śiva. The former are very generally known by the appellation of *Vishṇu Bhaktaru,*[v] which signifies *devotees* of *Vishṇu,* and the other by that of *Śiva Bhaktaru* or devotees of Śiva. These are also called *Lingadhari,* and the devotees of Vishṇu *Nâmadhari.* These last appellations are taken from the marks of distinction which each of the parties bears. That of the Vishṇuvites is the Nâma and is traced on the forehead, as has been described in the preceding chapter. On the other hand, that of the partisans of Śiva is called the Linga, which they wear sometimes stuck in the hair or attached to the arm in a small tube of gold or silver; but it is more frequently seen hanging by a riband from the neck, and deposited in a silver box which dangles on the breast.

In place of the *Nâma,* some devotees of Vishṇu content themselves with drawing in a particular way a single perpendicular line of red down the middle of the forehead; and instead of the *Linga,* some of the devotees of Śiva are satisfied with rubbing the forehead and some other parts of the body with the ashes of cow dung.

Vishṇu's worshippers are met with in great numbers in all the provinces of the peninsula of India, and are known by the several names of Râmâ-andis, Dâśaris, Râmanujas, Vairâgis, and some more.

---

v S. B'HAKTI=*pietas,* devotion. This idea is not found in the Vêdas, nor did the intense devotion to one deity and faith in him constitute any part of the Hindû systems, before the time of the Bengal reformer Chaitanya in the early part of the 16th Century. The Vêdas inculcate general submission to the Supreme, the performance of certain fixed duties and teach the method of deliverance from material bonds; but the Bhakti system proposes some one deity as the especial object of love, faith and devotion.

Besides the Nâma, the least ambiguous mark of this sect, the greater number of its members may be discovered by the fantastic dress which they wear. Their clothes are always of the deepest yellow, bordering upon red. Many of them wear across their shoulders for a cloak, a kind of particoloured garment formed of patched work of all colours. The turban with which they cover the head is likewise made up of cloth of three or four tints, braided with each other. Some, instead of the clothing we have mentioned, hang a tyger's skin over their shoulders, which reaches the ground. The most of them adorn their necks with several rows of necklaces of black beads of the size of a nut.

Besides their ridiculous dress, which frequently resembles that of Harlequin in a European pantomime, the disciples of Vishṇu, when they travel or go a begging, equip themselves with a round plate of brass, about a foot in diameter, and a large shell called *Śankha*, shaped like a sea conch; with either of which they can make a sufficient noise to announce their approach from afar. With one hand they beat upon the brass plate with a stick, which makes a sound like a bell, and at the same time they apply the śankha to their mouth with the other hand, and by blowing into it they raise a sound sharp and always monotonous. These two last mentioned articles, the śankha and the circular plate of brass, are always seen in the hands of that portion of the devotees of Vishṇu who make it their profession to solicit alms, and indeed are a sort of religious mendicants.[o]

These religionists of Vishṇu, also, for the most part, wear a plate of copper on the breast, on which is engraved the image of *Hanuman*, or some one of the *Avatârs*, or incarnations of their god. Besides this, many of them have numbers of little bells hung from their shoulders, and sometimes fastened on their legs, the tinkling of which announces their approach from a distance. Some of them add to all this apparatus an iron ring which they carry on their shoulders, at each side of which a chafing-dish of the same metal is suspended, for the purpose of carrying the fire which they use in burning the incense when they sacrifice.

The principal business of the devotee of Vishṇu is to seek alms. It is a privilege inherent in the sect; and in general, throughout India, every person of the religious calling exercises that profession as matter of right.

It is chiefly when they go on a pilgrimage to some holy place that these religious beggars make use of this right. Sometimes one meets them in troops of more than a thousand: and in the districts through which they pass, they spread themselves in the different villages, where each of the inhabitants gives lodging to several of them; by which means they save the expense of travelling. In other circumstances, also, they generally go in bands to solicit alms, but not in such numbers as in their travelling excursions.

---

o. This applies to the *Dâsaris* or begging devotees. See Buchanan's Mysore.

In all cases they demand alms with insolent audacity, and often with threats, as a matter which is their due. When they are not readily served they redouble the uproar, setting up shouts all at once, beating on the sonorous plate of brass, and exciting harsh and shrill sounds from their śankha. If all this fails of success, they sometimes enter into the houses, break the earthen dishes, and overturn every thing within their reach.

It is commonly in a dance that these religious beggars apply for alms, singing hymns in honour of their gods, and still more frequently indecent songs.

The devotees of Vishṇu, and particularly the religious beggars of that sect, are detested by the people in general, chiefly on account of their intemperance. One would imagine that they give themselves up to that vice from a spirit of contradiction to their opponents the Lingamites, whose extreme moderation in eating and drinking equals, if it does not surpass, that of the Brâhmans, in imitation of whom they abstain from all animal food. The sectaries of Vishṇu, on the contrary, eat publicly of all sorts of meat, excepting that of the cow, and drink toddy, arrack, and all other liquors that the country supplies, without shame or restraint.[w]

Among the objects of worship held in the highest veneration by the Vishṇu devotees, are the Ape, the Monkey, the bird called Garuda, and the serpent Capella. One would expose himself to serious consequences who should be imprudent enough to kill or even to maltreat in their presence any of those animals.[x] A man so offending would be forced to expiate his crime by the ceremony or sacrifice called the *Pâvâdam.*

The Pâvâdam is known to very few, as I believe, and is therefore entitled to a short description. It is a ceremony peculiar to the sect of Vishṇu, and they resort to it only in circumstances of the weightiest kind, such as the necessity of expiating the crime of causing the death of any of the animals which are the objects of their worship; or for obtaining reparation for some breach of honour occasioned by any deep injury which an individual of their tribe may have received from some other person, and which would be felt as redounding to the disgrace of the sect if it remained unpunished. The Pâvâdam is a ceremony of the most serious kind, since it demands no less than the sacrifice of a human victim, and its resuscitation afterwards.

As soon as it is publicly known that any one has given occasion for the Pâvâdam, by any of the crimes that have been mentioned, or by any deep insult cast upon the sect, the votaries crowd from all quarters to the place where the culprit resides, and having assembled to the number sometimes of more than two thousand, each bringing his sounding plate of brass, and his śankha or great shell, they pro-

---

w This account can only apply to a few fanatics among the Vairâgis. In fact I doubt the truth of this whole paragraph.

x To this may be added the Squirrel. These are under the especial care of the Vishṇu dâsharis. The poor farmer is obliged to rid himself of these plagues by stealth.

ceed to the ceremony. The first step is to arrest the person who is the cause of their assembling, and then they spread a tent at a small distance, which is immediately encompassed with several ranks of partisans assembled for the occasion.

The chiefs having selected from the multitude a fit person who consents to become the victim for sacrifice, exhibit him to the crowd of people collected from all parts to witness the sight. A small incision is then made on his belly, deep enough for the blood to flow; upon which the pretended victim shams a fainting fit, tumbles on the ground, and counterfeits death. He is then carried into the tent which is fitted to receive him, and is there laid out as a corpse.

Of the great concourse of people gathered together, part watches night and day round the tent, which nobody is suffered to approach; while another division surrounds the house of the individual who has given occasion for the ceremony. Both parties raise continual cries and frightful howlings, which being mixed with the clanking sound of the brazen plates and the shrill squeak of the śankha, produce a confusion and uproar, in the midst of which it is almost impossible to exist. This overwhelming disorder continues without interruption till the person who was the cause of it pays the fine imposed upon him, which generally exceeds his means.

In the meantime the inhabitants of the village and of the neighbourhood finding it impossible to live in the midst of the confusion and disorder occasioned by the fanatical crowd, come to terms with the chiefs and pay at least a part of what has been required of the culprit, in order to obtain a speedy termination to the *Pâvâdam*, and to induce the great multitude to go to their homes.

The chiefs, when satisfied, repair to the tent to conclude the ceremony, which is effected by restoring to life the pretended dead man, who lies stretched out before them. For this purpose they choose one of their number, and, making an incision in his thigh, they collect the blood which runs from it and sprinkle the body of the sham corpse, which being restored by the efficacy of this simple ceremony is delivered over alive to those who assist at it, and who have no doubt whatever of the reality of the resurrection.

After this ceremony, for effacing all traces of the crime or the affront which had been complained of, the fine is laid out in a grand entertainment to all the persons present; and when that is over, the whole of them quietly return to their homes.

It is not very long since the Pâvâdam was celebrated in a solemn manner in a village next to that where I lived. The cause from which it originated was, that an inhabitant of that village had cut down (without being aware of it, as it is said) a tree or shrub called *câcâ-mara,*[y] which produces yellow flowers, and to which the sectaries of Vishṇu offer up adoration and sacrifices.

The sect of Śiva is not less widely spread than that of Vishṇu. It

---

y *Cassia fistula.*

bears rule over several provinces of the peninsula. On the west, to the whole extent of that long chain of mountains which make the separation between the countries called by the Europeans by the generic name of Malabar and Coromandel, the Lingamites or devotees of Śiva compose at least half the population, over a space of two or three hundred miles from north to south.

This sect has several customs peculiar to itself. In common with the Brâhmans it will on no account partake of animal food or of any thing that has enjoyed the principle of life, such as eggs, or of many of the simple productions of nature. They agree with the greater part of the other tribes in burying their dead and not burning them. But they differ from the most of them in not admitting the principles so generally adopted among all the other castes respecting uncleanness, and particularly that which is incident to women by child-birth, and periodical occurrences, or by the death and funeral of any relation; as well as in some other domestic regulations particular to themselves, in which they seem to be at variance with the manner of living and the customs generally observed by the other Hindûs.

Their disregard of the rules regarding uncleanness and the decent propriety of conduct, so religiously observed among all the other tribes, has given rise to a proverb which circulates in the country, the meaning of which *that there is no river for a Lingamite;* alluding to the people of that sect hardly in any case acknowledging the merit and virtue of the ablutions practised by the other Hindûs.

The Lingamites, as well as the Vishṇuvites, have amongst them a great number of religious beggars under the names of *Paṇḍâram,*[z] *Oḍeyaru,*[a] *Jangama,*[b] and several others. The greater part of these devotees of Śiva have no other means of living but by alms, which they demand in bodies; with the exception of a few who live retired in *Matas,* which are a species of convents usually having some lands attached to them, the produce of which, together with the offerings brought by the devotees of their sect, serve them for sustenance.

The dress of the penitents of Śiva scarcely differs from that of the devotees of Vishṇu, both being clothed in a way equally fantastical and ridiculous. The colour of their garments is also the *Câvi;* that is a very deep yellow inclining to red. This colour is worn in general not only by the devotees of Śiva and Vishṇu, but also by all those who make religion a profession; by the Fakirs, Gurus, and all the Indian clergy, as uniformly as black is worn by the clergy of Europe.

The devotees of Śiva have, nevertheless, some particular marks of distinction, (independent of the Linga which they always wear) by which they are easily known. Of this kind are the strings of large beads called *Rudrâksha,*[c] of the size and nearly of the shape and colour

---

z The śaiva *paṇḍâram* answers to the Śiva *dâsari.* Wilson supposes it to be a corruption of *Pâṇḍurangah* = pale complexioned, from their smearing themselves with ashes.

a Kan. *oḍeyaru* = lords.

b S. JANGAMA = moveable: wandering devotees.

c S. Rudrâksham, *Śiva's eyes:* the berries of the Eleocarpus.

of a nutmeg, which they suspend at their necks, and the ashes of cow-dung with which they daub the forehead, the arms and several other parts of the body.

Among the objects of their worship, the two principal are the Linga and the Bull, of which we shall afterwards speak at greater length.

Although the children commonly embrace the sect of their fathers; yet they are not by right of birth alone, entitled to become Vishṇuvites or Lingamites; they are not admitted into the sect of their parents until a certain age, and they are then associated by the Guru of the sect, who administers to the candidates the ceremony of the *Dîkshâ*, which means *initiation*. This solemn ceremony of the Dîkshâ, is a species of baptism amongst the Hindûs; and, indeed, the Christians in India give baptism the name of *Jnâna Dîkshâ* or spiritual initiation. The ceremony we have been describing consists in pronouncing over the novice several *Mantras* or prayers, adapted to the occasion, and in whispering in his ear certain secret instructions. But the whole is done in a language generally not understood by the Guru himself who presides at the ceremony. After the Dîkshâ, the newly initiated acquire a perpetual right to all the privileges belonging to the sect into which they are admitted.

Persons of any caste may be admitted into the sect of Vishṇu, and then they may bear the *Nâma* on the forehead, which is its distinguishing mark. Even the Pariahs, or any of the vilest tribes belonging to them, will not be rejected.[d]

I conceive also that all persons without distinction, may be permitted to join with the sect of Śiva; but as those initiated there must renounce for ever all animal food and inebriating liquors, a condition too hard to be easily submitted to by the low castes who are accustomed to those indulgences, we do not often see in the sect Śiva any other than the best castes of the Śûdras. There are some Pariahs in certain places, but they are very few in number. It is a common thing to see apostates going over from one of these sects to the other, as their interest prompts them; and some from spite or caprice.

Either of these castes will admit freely and without any examination such of the extraneous Hindûs as shew a desire to be incorporated with them.

In some castes of the Śûdras a singular peculiarity in this respect may be observed, where the husband belongs to the sect of Vishṇu and bears the mark of the Nâma, while the wife adheres to the sect of Śiva and shews the Linga. The husband eats animal food; while the woman is absolutely debarred from it. But this difference of religion between the husband and wife, disturbs in no degree the peace of the family or their conjugal happiness. Both follow quietly their separate modes of religion, and adore in their own manner the god they have severally chosen, without any disposition to contend with each other on the subject.

---

d The influence of caste is weakened by the schisms among the Hindûs; The influence of the Brâhmans gives way before that of the heads of the sects.

In other cases we see the two sects striving to exalt the respective deities whom they worship and to revile those of their opponents. The followers of Vishṇu maintain that it is to the providence of their god that we owe the preservation of whatever exists in the universe. They say it is to him that Śiva owes his birth and being, and that Vishṇu has preserved him in many perils, which would otherwise have involved him in utter perdition. They vehemently insist that he is far superior to Śiva and is alone worthy of all honour.

The disciples of *Śiva*, on the contrary, no less obstinately affirm that Vishṇu is nothing, and has never done any act but tricks so base as to provoke shame and indignation. They confirm these assertions by some particulars in the life of that deity, which their adversaries cannot deny, and which certainly do not redound to his credit. They hold that *Śiva* is the only sovereign lord of all things that exist, and that he alone is entitled to our praises.[e]

According to the Vishṇuvites, one cannot fall into a deeper sin than by wearing the Linga or mark of Śiva: while, according to the votaries of this god, all who bear the Nâma shall be tormented in hell, when they die, with a three pronged fork in the shape of that emblem.

It is a very common thing to see disputes and altercations amongst these sectaries, of great vehemence, respecting the pre-eminence of their respective gods. These religious quarrels are generally fomented by the bands of vagabond fanatics, those religious mendicants who are to be found in crowds through the whole extent of the country.

In the throngs in which they frequently assemble to support the dignity of their respective gods, their fanaticism on some occasions rouses them to such a pitch that when they are tired out with pouring every species of abuse upon each other, and voiding the most abominable blasphemies against the deity they oppose, they sometimes come to blows, and the religious controversy ends in a fight, in which there is rarely much spilling of blood, but a good belabouring with fisticuffs on both sides, the scattering of many turbans, and the tearing of much apparel into rags. Thus the fray generally ends, without spirit on either side to carry it to extremities.

But it is in the naturally timid and indolent character of the Hindû that we are to seek for the true cause why these holy wars do not overspread the whole land, or produce the dreadful excesses of every kind which religious phrenzy has occasioned in Europe, and in other regions, for so many ages. Or perhaps there is a still more powerful reason to be found in the indifference of most of the people to all forms of worship, which allows them to give equal honour to Vishṇu and to Śiva, without any concern about either, and at the same time disposes them to interfere between the religious combatants, and to mitigate the disputes in their origin.

---

e Thus in the Padma Purâṇa: "*na Vishṇu nâmapi na vaktavyam kadâchana.*" *The name even of Vishṇu is not to be uttered!* But on the other side in the Bhâgavat: "*Bhava vrata d'harâh pâshaṇḍinastê B'havantu sat Śâstra paripant'hinaḥ:*" *adherents of Śiva worship are heretics and enemies of the good Śâstras!*

But, nevertheless, if we are to give any faith to a tradition, very general in many provinces, it is scarcely to be doubted that, even in recent times, there have been waged in many parts of the peninsula, general wars upon religion, excited by vast numbers of fanatics who overran the country, and fomented also, as it is believed, to the utmost of their power, by the Râjas and other princes, who supported sometimes the one sect and sometimes the other, as their interest required, and became Vishṇuvite or Śivite, and mounted the Linga or the Nâma, as best suited their temporal concerns.

Those who are acquainted with the nature of the *Vairagi* and of the *Gosain* in the north of the peninsula, of the *Daśari* and the *Jangama* of the south, will readily believe that it would still be an easy matter for two ambitious princes to arm, in the name of the gods and of religion, those bands of fanatics, from one end of the country to the other, impelling them to deluge the land with blood, unfurling the standard of *Hanuman* on one side, and that of *Baswa* on the other, and persuading them that they were cutting each other's throats for the interest of religion.

In the more limited contests about religion which actually take place, the Vishṇuvites appear the most violent and most bigotted. They are almost always the aggressors; and the Śivites in general appear more peaceable and tolerant.

The generality of the Hindûs, and above all the Brâhmans, take no part whatever in those religious dissensions. The system of the latter is to hold in equal reverence the principal divinities of the country; and although, upon the whole, they appear more inclined to the worship of Vishṇu, they never pass a day without offering up in their houses a sacrifice to the Linga, the idol of Śiva.

The Vishṇuvite Brâhmans, making profession of honouring Vishṇu, if not exclusively, at least with a visible partiality, and upon many occasions expressing their contempt for S'iva, it is not surprizing that the tolerant party should look down upon them with eyes of contempt as a set of men that, by a marked adherence to such a sect, appear to place themselves on a level with the offscourings of the Śûdras.

That which lessens them the most in the esteem of persons of their own tribe is the affectation of appearing in public with the figure of Nâma engraved on their foreheads, which we have already seen is the distinctive badge of the followers of Vishṇu. This symbol is uniformly adopted by all the members of this sect, whatever their caste or origin may be. But, to assume for an ornament a token which persons of the lowest extraction, without excepting even the Pariahs, may wear, seems to the true Brâhmans, a self-abasement and a voluntary degradation to the level of those who are otherwise so much beneath them.

The same distance which the tolerant Brâhmans observe towards the Vishṇuvite Brâhmans would be extended also to the Lingamite Brâhmans if there were many of that persuasion. For my own part, I have never met with any of them, and I do not believe that there are any to be found in the South of the peninsula, from the banks of the Krishna to Cape Comorin. Yet I have been informed (though not in a way to put the matter out of all doubt) that there are certain cantons in the North of the peninsula where *Sivite* Brahmans are to be found, bearing the mark of the Linga like all other individuals of the caste.

The *Vishṇuvite* Brâhmans are not met with but in the Southern provinces of India situated on this side of the Krishna. None are seen beyond that river.

The contempt which the tolerant Brâhmans manifest for the Vishṇuvite Brâhmans is not wholly confined to them : the same feeling of aversion being universal against this class of Brâhmans, whom I never heard mentioned but in terms of reproach and contempt. I do not conceive, however, the feeling of dislike for them on the part of the Śûdras can have arisen out of the special attachment of that class of Brâhmans to the sect of Vishṇu ; but that it is rather to be ascribed to their extreme haughtiness and their insolent behaviour to all other tribes. And though the vices imputed to them are common to the whole Brâhmans, yet it is universally observed that they belong to the Vishṇuvite caste of them in a higher degree than to the others.

But, however, that may be, it is certain that this sect of Brâhmans stands aloof from the rest. The tolerant Brâhmans do not admit them to their tables or to their ceremonies ; and they, in their turn, are excluded under the same circumstances, by the Vishṇuvites. The estrangement and distrust which they mutually entertain is visible in the whole intercourse of society. The tolerant Brâhmans, when in power, invest the Vishṇuvite Brâhmans with no employments of trust, and they again, when they have the superiority, associate exclusively with each other.

Besides the general division into the sect of Śiva and that of Vishṇu, each of these is farther divided into several others, which the Hindûs include under the general appellation of *Matam* or *Matâchâram.*

Each of these different sects has its peculiar system, its secrets, its Mantras, its sacrifices, and a difference in its practice as well as its faith.

Their heads never unite nor associate together. They have frequent disputes upon the points of doctrine which disunite them. They combine, however, forgetting all subordinate quarrels, when it becomes necessary to protect the general interests of the sect in the controversies which sometimes break out between the Vishṇuvites and the Sivites.

Besides the Vishṇuvite Brâhmans already mentioned, who are considered as separate from the rest, and are excluded as obstinate and incorrigible heretics, there are among the tolerant Brâhmans the sects of the *Smârtta* Brâhmans,[f] and the philosophical sects of the *Dwaitam; Adwaitam,* and several others. In the sequel of this work, an enquiry will be made into the principles of the sects, and occasion will then be taken to examine the particulars in which they differ.

---

[f] The Smârtta Brâhmans are followers of Śankarâchârya. They derive their name from SMRITI = *tradition.* They are those then who adhere to the antient tradition, in opposition to the modern sects. These latter are all more or less founded in opposition to the prescriptive Brâhmanical system.

CHAPTER IX.

OF THE GURUS OF INDIA.

THE word *Guru* properly means *master;* whence fathers and mothers are sometimes called *Mahâ-gurus*, or great masters of their families; kings the Gurus of the kingdom, and masters Gurus of their servants.

But the appellation is specially applied to certain persons of distinguished rank who attain a character of sanctity, which invests them with power both spiritual and temporal. The latter consists chiefly in a superintendance over the different castes, by inforcing the due observance of their general and particular customs, and punishing the refractory. They have also the power of expelling from the tribe, and of restoring those who had been expelled.

Besides this temporal authority, which is never called in question, they possess an equal extent of spiritual jurisdiction. The *sâshtangam*, or prostration of the eight members, is made before them, and when followed by their benediction, or *âśirvâdam*, is effectual for the remission of all sins. The look even of a Guru has the same efficacy. Their *prasâdam*,[g] or present, which they confer upon their disciples, consists in some matter otherwise of small value, such as a portion of cow-dung ashes, to beautify the forehead, flowers that were previously offered up to the idols, the crumbs from their meals, or the water in which they had washed their feet, which is preserved and sometimes drank by those who receive it. These and other things of the like nature, or indeed whatever comes from their holy hands, possess the virtue of purifying body and soul from all uncleanness.

But if the benediction of the Gurus and the other little tokens of their favour, which they bestow on their disciples, have so wonderful an influence in attracting the respect and reverence of the silly populace; their curse, which is not less powerful, fills them with terror and awe. The Hindû is persuaded that it never fails to take effect, whether justly or unjustly incurred. Their books are full of fables which seem invented for the express purpose of inspiring this belief; and, to add greater force to it, the attendants of the Guru, who are interested in the success of the impostor's game, do not fail to recount many marvellous stories respecting him, of which they pretend to have been eye-witnesses; and to avoid any possibility of detection, they lay the scene of the miracles in some distant country.

Sometimes they tell of a person struck dead on the spot by the

---

[g] This is properly rice which has been offered to an idol and then is distributed to the worshippers.

curse of the Guru : sometimes of one suddenly seized with a shivering through every joint, which goes on, and will never cease until the malediction is stayed. At other times it is a pregnant woman whom they describe as miscarrying by it ; or a labourer, perhaps, that was doomed to see all his cattle perish in a moment.

Nay, I have heard from these men stories still more ridiculous, and given with the utmost gravity ; of a man, for example, being changed into a stone, and of another converted into a hog by their Guru's malediction.

The silly Hindû gives implicit credit to such tales, and therefore it is not surprising that he should carry his dread and reverence for his Guru to the most extravagant pitch. He naturally avoids whatever may be displeasing to him ; and rather than incur the awful danger of his anathema, a Hindû has been known to sell his wife or one of his children, having nothing else to part with, to procure for his Guru the tribute or presents which he unmercifully exacts.

Each caste and sect has its particular Guru. But all of them are not invested with an equal degree of authority. There is a gradation among the Gurus themselves, according to the dignity of the castes they belong to, and a kind of hierarchy has grown up among them, which preserves the subordination of one to another. In short there is an inferior clergy, very numerous in every quarter, while each sect has its particular high priests, who are but few in number. The inferior Gurus pay them obedience, and derive their power from the superior authority of the priests, who can depose them at pleasure, and appoint others in their room.

The place of residence of the Hindû Pontiffs is commonly called *Simhâsana* which signifies a *throne.* There are several of these episcopal sees, as they may be called, in the different provinces of the peninsula. The different castes, and each sect, have their own *Simhâsana* and their particular pontiffs. Thus, for example the Brâhmans of the sect called *Smârtta* submit to one, and that of the Vishṇuvite Brâhmans to a third.

In the sect of Vishṇu and in that of Śiva the higher and lower clergy are innumerable. Each subdivision of the two sects has its pontiff and corresponding Gurus. Among the Vishṇuvites, the single sect of Kârnânujas has no less than four Singhâsanas or episcopal sees, and seventy-two *Pîṭhas* places of residence of the inferior Gurus ; without reckoning a great number of a lower rank, who spread over the country to extend their visits to every place within their bounds.[h]

The other subdivisions of the same sect have in like manner their Gurus in great abundance.

In the sect of Śiva, also, each subdivision has its Singhâsana or episcopal seat and its *Pîṭha* or places of residence of the inferior

[h] Buchanan says that Râmanuja founded 300 Mat'hans of which 4 only remain, of these the chief is Mêl Kôṭai.

clergy. The Gurus of this sect are known by the names of *Paṇḍâram, Jangamas,* and others, according to the different idioms of the places.

The pontiffs and all the clergy of the sect of Śiva are taken out of the tribe of Śûdra; but the greater part of the high Gurus of Vishṇu and Brâhmans of Vishṇu, who ordain the inferior clergy pertaining to the sect.

It is the Brâhmans also who are most frequently the pontiffs among the tolerant Hindûs, that is to say, such as are attached neither to the sect of Vishṇu nor that of Śiva.

The pontiff or Guru of a caste or sect has no authority out of it. In any other sect they would disregard his *Prasâdam,* his blessing and his curse. There are but few instances therefore of any attempts at such an intrusion.

Besides the Gurus that pertain to the different tribes and sects, great personages, such as kings and princes, have them of their own, attached to their households and accompanying them wherever they go. Every day they present themselves before their Guru, and receive his blessing and *Prasâdam.* When they are engaged in any dangerous enterprize, the Guru generally tarries behind. On such occasions he contents himself with loading the great man with blessings and offering him some little hallowed gifts, which are received and kept as a precious relic, having the power to avert all evils that might otherwise happen in the absence of the Guru.

The princes take a pride in entertaining these associates (whom they call their chaplains) with the greatest magnificence. They invest them with a splendour which sometimes eclipses their own. Besides the presents which they frequently bestow, for the support of their rank and dignity, they also assign them land estates of considerable revenue for their ordinary expenses.

The great Gurus never appear in public without the utmost degree of pomp; but it is when they proceed to a visitation of their district that they are seen surrounded with their whole splendour. They commonly make the procession on the back of an elephant, or seated in a rich palanquin. Some of them have a guard of horse, and are surrounded with numerous troops both cavalry and infantry, armed with pikes and other weapons. Several bands of musicians precede them, playing on all the instruments of the country. Flags in all the varieties of colour wave round them, adorned with the pictures of their gods. Some of their officers take the lead, singing odes in their praise, or admonishing the spectators to be prepared to pay the mighty Guru, as he comes up, the honour and reverence which are due to him. Incense and other perfumes are burnt in profusion; new cloths are spread before him on the road. Boughs of trees, forming triumphal arches, are expanded in many places on the way through which he passes. Bands of young women, or the dancing girls of the temples, relieve each other, and keep up with the procession, enlivening it with lewd songs and lascivious dances. This the custom of having Criers on such solemnities to make their proclamations of praise before all great personages when they appear in public is common through all India. They repeat with a loud voice, or sing, the renown of their masters, with a long display of their illustrious birth, exalted rank, unbounded power and high virtues, and counsel all who hear them to pay the honours due to such illustrious men.

This pompous shew attracts a crowd of people, who throng to prostrate themselves before the Guru. After paying their adoration, they join in the train and make the sky resound with their shouts of joy during the whole course of the ceremony.

I shall not be understood to mean that every Guru meets with a reception like this, as it is only the pontiffs or Gurus of the first order that are accompanied with this extraordinary state. Those of inferior degree proportion their pomp to their narrower means. The common Gurus of the sect of Vishṇu, are generally mounted on a sorry horse, and some are even reduced to the necessity of travelling on foot. The wealthiest of the Gurus of the sect of Śiva, called *Jangama* or *Paṇḍâhram,* sometimes go on horseback and sometimes in a palanquin. But the greater number are mounted on bullocks, the favourite animal of this sect.

The Gurus, in general, rank as the first and most distinguished order of society. Those who are elevated to this great dignity, receive in most cases, marks of reverence or rather of adoration which are not rendered even to the gods themselves. But this is not surprising when it is understood that the power of controuling the gods is generally attributed to them, by which it is supposed they have the means of obtaining whatsoever the deities can bestow.[i]

The Gurus generally make a tour from time to time among their disciples, perhaps in a circle of two hundred leagues round their place of residence. During this visitation, their principal, and I may say their only object, is to amass money. Besides the fines which they levy from persons guilty of offences or any breach of the ceremonies of the caste or sect, they often rigorously exact from their adherents a tribute to the utmost extent of their means. This method of collecting money they denominate *Pâđa-Kâṇikai,* which signifies an offering at the feet. Nor can any person, however distressed, evade the payment of the Pâđa-Kâṇikai to the Guru. There is no affront or indignity which the Gurus are not disposed to inflict on any disciple, who fails, either from inability or unwillingness, to produce the sum at which he is rated. Rather than relax in the smallest degree from their extortion, they compel them to approach in a humiliating attitude, load them with reproach and abuse before

---

i The proverbial saying is

SARVA DÊVA MAYÔ GURUḤ.

The Guru is the embodiment of every divinity.

the multitude, and order mud or cow-dung to be flung in their faces. If this ignominious treatment does not succeed, they insist on being supplied with a person to work for them during a certain period, or till the sum is paid. Gurus have been known, in cases where a man was unable to pay the amount of his tax, to force him to deliver up his wife, to be kept for their use or given to some of their dependants.[j]

In the last resort, they threaten to inflict the *curse;* and such is the credulity of the timid Hindû, and such his dread of the evils which would spring from the malediction of a Guru, that this extreme denunciation seldom fails to extract the payment.

In addition to these ordinary requisitions levied for the support of the Gurus, they have several other sources of revenue under the name of *Guru-Dakshiṇâ*, which are imposed on the occasions of a birth, of the Diksha or initiation into the sect, or of the marriage or death of their disciples.

The castes, however, being obliged to defray the expence of the visits of their Gurus, the pomp and splendour of which, particularly in the case of the grand Gurus or Pontiffs, would be ruinous if often repeated, it is sometimes a long while before they are renewed. Some do not traverse their district more than once in three years, and some in five years or even less frequently.

Some of the Gurus are married; but in general they live in celibacy. The latter, however, are not reputed to be very strict in the observance of the virtue of continence which they profess.

But the foolish vulgar, who believe that their Gurus are moulded of a better clay than other mortals, and that they are not subject to fall into evil, look upon this arrangement without scandal. People of understanding deplore it, and without attempting a change, endure it as a necessary evil, and say they must lay to the charge of human weakness what even Gurus themselves are not exempt from.

Although the Brâhmans style themselves the Gurus of every caste, and claim the exclusive right to that title and to the honours which attend it, there are nevertheless many Ŝûdras elevated to that dignity. The Brâhmans, indeed, will on no account recognize their right. But they disregard that, and take the full enjoyment of the

---

j A Guru never allows his fees to remain in arrears if he can help it.

The following Tamil verse is in common use.

Âv'îna, maṛai poṛiya, illam vîṛa,
Agattinaḷ nôyđanil varunđa, aḍimai çâga,
Mâ îram pôguđ' enru viḍai koṇḍ ôḍa,
Variyilê kaḍankârar marrittu koḷla,
Çâvôlai koṇḍ' oruvan eđirê çella,
Taḷḷâđa virunđu vara, sarppam tîṇḍa,
Kôvênđar tamađ' urimai-paguđi kêḍpa,
Gurukkaḷ vanḍu dakshaṇaikku kurrukk'iṭṭârê!

"My cow calved, it poured with rain, my house fell, my wife fell sick, my servant died, the fields were saturated with moisture and I ran to sow the seed, in the way I was arrested for debt, a messenger met me with a warrant for my execution, a guest who could not be put off stood at my door, a snake bit me, they came to demand the king's taxes: *the Guru came and put in his claim for his fees.*"

honours and profits belonging to the title among the caste or sect which is willing to acknowledge them.

Excepting during their visitations, the Gurus live in retirement. They commonly reside in a kind of monasteries or insulated hermitages, generally called *Matam*, and shew themselves but seldom in public.

Some of them reside in the neighbourhood of the great Pagodas; but the chief Gurus or Pontiffs, who require greater convenience for their supply and that of their household, generally live in the towns.

In their different retirements these Gurus give audience to great numbers of their disciples, many of whom come from a great distance to pay them their adorations, to receive their blessing and gift, to offer them a present, to consult with them, to carry to them complaints of the infraction of customs of the caste, and many other similar purposes.

The Hindûs, in presenting themselves before the Gurus, make the Sâshṭângam, or prostration of the eight members. The sect of Śiva, after rendering this first mark of reverence to the *Jangamas*, as their Gurus are called, immediately proceed to a ceremony which deserves to be noticed. It consists in washing the feet of the Jangama, and receiving the water as it falls down into a vessel of copper. They pour a part of this water over their heads, and drink the remainder. This practice is general among the sectaries of Śiva, and is not uncommon with many of the Vishṇuvites, in regard to their Guru. Neither is it the most disgusting of the practices that prevail in that sect of fanatics, as they are under the reproach of eating as a hallowed morsel the very ordure that proceeds from their Gurus, and swallowing the water with which they have rinsed their mouths or washed their faces, with many other practices equally revolting to nature.

From their *Matam*, the Gurus annually send out one of their agents delegated with their authority to collect the *Pâḍa-Kâṇikai*, and the *Guru-Dakshiṇâ*, or tribute which they impose, and the fines inflicted on those who have committed any offence, as well as the gifts which it is the custom to present them with.

After discharging all the duties which their profession requires of them towards their disciples, and performing their daily sacrifices and ablutions, the Gurus are bound by the rules of their order to employ what remains of their time in meditation, and the study of the sacred writings.

The dignity of Guru descends, when married, from father to son: but upon the death of one who has lived single, a successor is appointed by some one of the grand Gurus, who, in the exercise of this power, generally nominates one of his own dependents. The Pontiffs, on the other hand, commonly assume coadjutors in their lifetime, who succeed to them at their death.

In the sects of Śiva and Vishṇu they admit a kind of priestesses, or women specially ordained to the service of their deities. They are different from the dancing-women of the temples; but they follow the same infamous course of life with them. For the priestesses of Śiva and of Vishṇu, after being consecrated, become common to their sect, under the name of spouses to these divinities: they are for the most part women who have been seduced by the priests of Vishṇu and of Śiva, who, to save their own credit and the honour of their families, whom they have thus disgraced, lay the crime to the charge of their respective gods, to whom they impute the deed. They devote these women to the divine service by the use of certain ceremonies, after which they are declared the wives of the god of the sect to which they belong; and the priests of that sect may then, without scandal, make use of them, in the name and stead of the god whose ministers they are.

Those who are consecrated in this manner in the sect of Vishṇu have the name of *Garuḍa-Bassivi,* or women of *Garuḍa,* and bear upon their breast, as a mark of their dignity, an impression of the form of Garuḍa, which is the bird consecrated to Vishṇu.

The priestesses of Śiva are known in public by the appellation of *Liṇga-Bassivi* or women of the Linga, and have the seal of the Liṇga imprinted on the thigh, as the distinctive badge of their profession.

These women are held in honour in public by their own caste; although in reality they are nothing better than the prostitutes of the priests and other chiefs of the sect.

CHAPTER X.

OF THE PURÔHITAS OR MASTERS OF THE CEREMONIES.

To prognosticate what are good and what are evil days for beginning any affair, or for putting it off; to avert, by the Mantras or prayers, the pernicious effects of maledictions or of the influence of malign constellations; to assign the name to new born children and calculate their nativity; to bless new houses, wells, or tanks; to purify temples and consecrate them, to give life to the statues and other inanimate objects of an idolatrous worship, and to imbue them with the divine essence: all these ceremonies, and many others of smaller importance, are the province of the Brâhmans called *Purôhitas*, whose office it is to preside over and conduct them.

The most important of their ceremonies are those of Marriage and Burial. They are so complex that an ordinary Brâhman would be found incapable of performing them. A regular study is necessary for the exactness and precision which they require; and the forms of Mantras or prayers are also requisite, with regard to which the greater part are ignorant. The Purôhitas alone are accomplished in the management of these rites, the detail of which they have in writing, in certain formularies, which they permit nobody to see, not even the other Brâhmans. Indeed the principal Mantras that are used are not reduced into writing, from the fear that some other Brâhmans might acquire them and so become their rivals, to the diminution of their exclusive profits. The father teaches them to his son, and thus they pass from generation to generation in one family. This shows that it is self-interest rather than superstition which occasions this reserve. By hindering the other Brâhmans from learning these ceremonies and the corresponding Mantras, the Purôhitas render themselves more necessary to the people and to the Brâhmans themselves, who cannot dispense with their services on many occasions.

The Purôhita Brâhmans not being numerous, those who are of that rank are often brought from a great distance. They attend the summons with alacrity, particularly when they are certain that the person who calls them is capable of recompensing their labours in a liberal way. And when they cannot undertake the journey themselves they send some one of their family whom they have trained up to the duty by teaching them the Mantras which are necessary for the due solemnization. At times their place is supplied by ordinary Brâhmans, especially among the Śûdras, who are much more brief in regard to ceremonies than the Brâhmans: and although the substitute be not acquainted with the true Mantras which pertain to each ceremony, he does not desist on that account, but pronounces an unmeaning string of Sanscrit words, which appear more than sufficient to the stupid Sûdras, who understand nothing of the matter. But abuses of this kind never fail to excite fierce disputes between the real Purôhitas and those intruders, whom they treat as sacrilegious usurpers of their functions and of the rewards which would attend them.

One of the highest privileges attached to the profession of the Purôhita is the exclusive right of publishing the Hindû Almanack. The greater number of them being unable to compose it, they are under the necessity of purchasing a copy every year from the Brâhmans, who make the calculations. There are but few who are found capable of this; perhaps one or two only in a district. It is not upon a knowledge of the motions of the stars that the Hindû Almanack is compiled, but upon the approximation and agreement of tables and formulæ of great antiquity, and extremely numerous; and therefore the calculation is very complicated, and requires much time, attention, and labour to arrive at exact conclusions.

This book is absolutely necessary to the Purôhita, to instruct him not only respecting good and evil days, but also the favourable moments in each day; for it is in such moments only that the ceremonies which they preside over can be commenced. They are often consulted respecting the happy or unfortunate issue of matters in the most ordinary occurrences of life. Neither is it the populace only that are addicted to this species of superstition; for the princes are more intangled with it than the people themselves. They have always at least one Purôhita retained in their service at their palaces, who comes every morning to wait upon them, and to announce what the almanack contains for the day. But the most ridiculous part is, that he afterwards proceeds to perform the same service to the Prince's elephant and the idols. The Purôhita is consulted many times every day upon the most ordinary occurrences of life. The Prince will not go a hunting nor take a walk without his decision whether it will be for his health or otherwise. Neither will he receive visits from strangers without the same precaution: and if there be the least ambiguity in the augury, he will wait for a more favorable moment, or put off his excursion to another day.

The Hindû Calendar is called *Panchângam*, which signifies the *five members*, because in truth it contains five principal heads, namely, the days of the month, the sign in which the moon is each day to be found, the day of the week, the eclipses, and the place of the planets. It likewise marks the good days and the evil; those on which one may journey towards any of the four cardinal points; for each point of the compass has its lucky and unlucky days; and a person who might to-day travel very successfully towards the north, would expose himself to some grievous danger if he took a southward course. It farther contains a vast number of predictions of all sorts which would be too tedious for this place.

On the first day of the year the Purôhita assembles the principal inhabitants of the place where he lives. In their presence he announces, by sound of trumpet, who is to be king of the gods for that year, and who is to be supreme over the stars; who are to be the ministers and generals of the people; who is to be god of the crops; what sort of grain will thrive the best. He determines also the quantity of rain and of drought, and whether the locusts and other destructive insects will devour the plants, or if the repose of men is to be greatly disturbed by bugs and fleas. He foretells, in short, whether it is to be a year of health or of disease; whether the deaths or the births shall predominate; whether a war is impending, from what side it will break out, and who shall gain the advantage: together with many other contingencies of equal importance.

There are many who care little about these predictions and appear to hold them in derision. But even among these some will be found consulting the almanack, and even the very man who invents and publishes it, especially when a war, famine, or other great calamity really seems to approach: so irresistible is the power of superstition over the minds of those even who affect to be liberal thinkers and elevated above the vulgar.

Finally, we may remark, that nothing appears to be more ancient in India than the establishment of the Purôhitas.[k] They are noticed in all the Hindû books, and if we can give credit to their authors, the highest honours were paid to them in ancient times. They strive above all others to maintain the usages and customs of the castes, and raise their voice the loudest against those who infringe or neglect them. Their interest may prompt them to this: but it is to them that we owe the chief part of the books of science that exist among the Hindûs. They have preserved them in the midst of the revolutions which have so often subverted the nations.

This class of persons is carefully to be distinguished from the Gurus described in the last chapter, although it belongs to both to watch over the observance of the customs of their castes. In other points they greatly differ, as in the profession of celibacy. All the Purôhitas are married. Indeed I believe it is held absolutely necessary that they should be so, to qualify them for the performance of the ceremonies; and a widower, who did not remarry would not be endured, as his presence would be thought to bode misfortune.

---

k "The most ancient name for a priest by profession was Purôhita, which only means *præpositus* or præses. The Purôhita, however, was more than a priest. He was the friend and counseller of a chief, the minister of a king, and his companion in peace and war. The office was often hereditary and partook of a political character. The original occupation of the Purôhita may have been to perform the usual sacrifices; but, with the ambitious policy of the Brâhmans, it soon became a stepping stone to political power." Max Müller, p. 485.

CHAPTER XI.

OF THE MANTRAS, OR FORMS OF PRAYER.

THE *Mantras,* so celebrated in all the Hindû books, are nothing more than certain forms of prayer, or words of efficacy, which (to borrow a Hindû expression on the subject,) have such virtue as to be able to *enchain* the gods themselves. They are of various sorts, invocatory, evocatory, deprecatory, conservatory. They are beneficent or hurtful, salutary or pernicious. By means of them, all effects may be produced. Some are for casting out the evil spirit and driving him away; some for inspiring love or hatred, for curing diseases or bringing them on, for causing death or averting it. Some are of a contrary nature to others and counteract their effect; the stronger overcoming the influence of the weaker. Some are potent enough to occasion the destruction of a whole army. There are some even whose awful summons the gods themselves are constrained to obey. But I should never finish if I attempted to enumerate in detail the whole of the pretended virtues of the Mantra.[1]

The Purôhitas, of all the Hindûs, understand them best. They are indispensably necessary to them for accompanying the ceremonies which it is their office to conduct. But, in general, the whole of the Brâhmans are conversant with these formulæ, agreeably to this Sanscrit strophe, which is often in their mouths:

> Dêvâd'hînâm jagatsarvam,
> Mantrâd'hînam taddêvatâ,
> Tanmantram Brâhmaṇâd'hînam,
> Brâhmaṇa mama Dêvatâ.

Which may be translated: "all the universe is under the power of the gods; the gods are subject to the power of the Mantras: the Mantras are under the power of the Brâhmans; the Brâhmans are therefore our gods." The argument is regular in form, and the conclusion technical; and accordingly in many books, as I have elsewhere mentioned, they are called *the terrestrial gods.* They assume these names to themselves, and listen with pleasure when they are applied to them by the other castes.

To place the efficacious virtue of the Mantras in a clear point of view, I will only refer to the following quotation from the *Brâhmôttarakhâṇḍa,* a well known Hindû poem written in honour of *Śiva:* "Daśara, King of Mathura, having espoused Kalâvati, daughter of the King of Kaśi or Benâres, this princess, on the very day of the marriage, apprized him that it would be absolutely necessary for him to abstain from making use of the right which his title of husband gave him,

[1] Mantras are properly Hymns of invocation.

because the Mantram of the five letters which she had learned, had penetrated her with purifying fire which would permit no man to come near her, with the risk of perishing, unless, before familiar intercourse, he should have been purified from his sins by the same means which she herself had practised: that, being his wife, she could not point out to him this purifying Mantram, because in doing so she would become his Guru, and consequently his superior.

"The following day, they went together in quest of the great Rishi, or penitent, *Garga*[m]; who having learned the purpose of their visit, ordered them to fast a whole day, to wash themselves in the river Ganges on the day following, and then to visit him again. This being complied with, and the prince having returned, the penitent made him sit down upon the ground with his face turned towards the east. Garga sat down beside him with his face towards the west, and secretly whispered these two words in his ear, *namaḥ Śivâya.* That is the Mantram of five letters, or five syllables, and signifies, 'health to Śiva.' As soon as Daśara had learned these two wonderful words, he perceived that he was excited by their purifying fire, and at the same moment, there sprung out from all parts of his body a multitude of crows, which flew up into the sky and disappeared. These were the sins committed by the prince in preceding generations.

"This history," says the author, "is certain. I had it from my Guru, *Vêdavyâsa,* who had learned it of *Para-Brahma.* The king and his spouse, thus purified, lived together for many years, and retired at last to re-unite with Para-Brahma in the abode of bliss, without being obliged to be re-born any more upon earth."

When the Brâhmans are rallied upon the present state of their Mantras, wholly divested of their boasted efficacy and power, they answer, that this loss of their influence is to be attributed to the *Kaliyugam,* which means that age of the world in which we now live, the true iron age, the time of evil and misfortune, in which every thing has degenerated. Nevertheless, they subjoin, it is still not uncommon to see the Mantras operate effects as miraculous as formerly; which they confirm by stories not less authentic than such as we have already reported.

Of all the Mantras, the most celebrated, and at the same time the most effectual for blotting out all sins, and of such potency as to make the gods themselves to tremble, as the Hindû books affirm, is that to which they give the name of *Gâyatrî,* which signifies the Mantram of the twenty-four letters or syllables. It is so ancient and so powerful as to have given rise to the *Vêdas.* The Brâhman when about to recite it, makes a previous preparation by prayers and the deepest meditation. Before pronouncing a word, he closes all the apertures of his body, and keeps in his breath as long as it is possible to retain it; and then he recites it in a low voice, taking good care that

---

m One of the ten Munis.

it shall not be intelligible by the Śûdras and the rest of the profane. Even his wife, especially at certain periods, is not allowed to hear it.

This famous Mantram consists of the following words :

"Tat Savitur vareṇyam b'hargôdêvasya
"D'hîmahi d'hiyô yô naḫ prachôdayât."

This then is the celebrated Mantram of four and twenty letters or syllables. The meaning is very dark, and unintelligible to the Brâhmans themselves.[n] I have never met with any one who could give me a tolerable explication of it. Such as it is, it would be a horrible sacrilege and an unpardonable crime in any Brâhman to communicate it to any profane or foreign ears. We may add that there are other Mantras which bear the name of *Gâyatrî*, but they are of much lower repute than this.

Although the Brâhmans alone are held to be the true depositaries of the Mantras, yet there are many persons of other castes who scruple not to pronounce them. There are professions also in which it is indispensable. The Physicians themselves, who are not Brâhmans, would be considered as ignorant beings and unworthy of the public confidence, however much entitled to it in other respects, if they were unacquainted with the Mantras suited to each disease as regularly as with the medicines which are applied in the cure. The cure is considered as arising from the Mantras as much as from the medical applications. One of the principal reasons for which the European physicians are held in such discredit in India, as far as regards their profession, is, that they administer their medicines without any accompaniment of Mantram.

The Midwives are called in some parts *Mantra Śâri*, or women who understand the Mantras; and never can those holy prayers be more necessary than at that crisis when, according to the notions of the Hindûs, a tender infant and a newly delivered mother are particularly liable to the fascination of evil eyes, to the malign conjunctions of the planets, the influence of unlucky days, and many other dangers, each more perilous than another. A skilful midwife, stored with good and serviceable Mantras, pronounced at the proper moment, provides against all such fears and dangers.

But those who are considered to be the most skilful in this kind of knowledge, and at the same time the most dangerous, are the persons who deal in the Occult Sciences; such as Magicians, Sorcerers, and Soothsayers. It is this sort of practitioners who pretend to be possessed of the true Mantras which can strike with sudden death, cure and inflict diseases, call up or lay the fiends, discover thefts, concealed treasures, distant objects, or future events. Such persons will always abound in a country where ignorance, superstition, and quackery so universally prevail.

The *mischievous magicians* being very much dreaded and hated,

---

[n] See Vishṇu Purâṇ, p. 222. The meaning is : "*We meditate on that excellent light of the divine Sun: May he illuminate our minds!*"

Compare Manu, Chap II. 77

never fail to be punished when they are believed guilty of having brought down evil upon any one by their spells. The ordinary way of punishing them on such occasions is by drawing the two front teeth of the upper jaw, which prevents them from speaking plainly, and is supposed to mar their utterance of the evil Mantras. Now, the slightest imperfection or defect in pronouncing the Mantram is so offensive to their god or demon, for both are invoked in their magical rites, that if it occurred he would infallibly turn upon themselves the whole evils which they imprecated upon others.

Among the numbers who thus lose their teeth in the cause of magic, I knew one individual, who came to me the very day on which the cruel operation was performed, and threw himself at my feet, mumbling his innocence, and imploring my counsel and assistance to procure reparation for the injustice they had done him in knocking out his front teeth, and in imputing to him the hateful practises of a magician. The poor man seemed to me to have very little of the appearance of a conjurer; but having neither the power nor the inclination to interfere in the affair, I got rid of him as I best could.

All the magical Mantras are hard to pronounce; and it is this difficulty which gives them all their importance, because if a sorcerer pronounces a single syllable amiss the whole evil he was invoking would fall upon himself.

The Mantram on which this art chiefly depends cannot easily be expressed in European characters: *Ôm, śrî, hsan, hgita, Ramâya namah.* The four first are barbarous words and without meaning. The two last signify "Salutation to Rama."

I believe no nation on earth is so infatuated as the Hindûs are with these notions of magic. The greater part of the cross accidents that befal them in life are attributed to the jealousy of some enemy who has had recourse to this wicked art for the purpose of injuring them. If they lose a wife or children by premature death; if a contagion breaks out among the cattle; or if a married woman continue unfruitful: none of these occurrences is believed to have had a natural cause, but they are all ascribed to preternatural arts employed by some secret enemy of their prosperity. Diseases, particularly such as are of long endurance, are attributed to the same cause, and if they should happen to take place while any quarrel or law-suit subsisted between the parties, the whole is laid to the charge of the opponent, who is accused of having devised it by magical contrivance. So serious a charge, to be sure, is not in general very patiently borne by the party accused; and thus a new cause of dissension is engendered.

It is to counteract the effects of this Wicked magic that a vast number of vagabonds roam over the country, calling themselves *Beneficent Magicians,* who are supposed to possess the Mantras that have power to heal the disorders and other evils occasioned by the *Sapanam*° or malignant magic, to render barren women fruitful, to cast out devils

° Literally: *Cursing.*

from those who are possessed with them, to check the murrain among cattle, to destroy the insects which ravage the fields, and to produce other beneficial effects. After reciting all their Mantras and carefully performing their whole ceremonies, they give amulets to their patients, on which are inscribed some unmeaning words. These sacred symbols they direct to be worn about their persons, as having virtue to complete the cure which the Mantram had begun. They then take their fee and go in quest of fresh dupes.

But as this delusion will be discussed more largely hereafter, we now return to the subject of the *Mantras*. There is one species of them differing from any we have yet mentioned, and capable of much more wonderful effects. It is called *Bîjâksharam*, or *Radical Letters;* such as *shrûm, craûm, hrîm, hrûm, hrû, hû,* and others of the like sound. Those who understand their true pronunciation, combination, and application, may perform prodigies as fast as he pleases. Let us take the following example.

Śiva chose to communicate the knowledge of them to a bastard boy, the son of a widow of the Brâhman caste, who, on account of the ignominy of his birth, had the mortification to be excluded from a wedding feast. He took his revenge by merely pronouncing two of the radical syllables at the door of the apartment where the guests were assembled, and by the power of the two syllables the viands on the table were instantly turned into toads. Such an accident would naturally occasion much confusion in the party. None of them doubted but that it was the little bastard who had played them such a trick, and that, if they still kept him out, he might go on with his pranks. Accordingly they opened the door for him, and upon entering the room, he pronounced the same syllables, only reversing their order, when immediately the toads changed again into what they were at first, and the different dishes took their original form.

I must leave it to men skilled in antiquity to point out any thing in their researches equal in extravagance to this of the Hindûs, or which could possibly have served them in it for a model.[p]

[p] It may possibly appear to the European reader that some of the popular superstitions among Western Nations are not less absurd and extravagant than those of which the Abbé speaks.

CHAPTER XII.

OF THE CEREMONIES PRACTISED ON THE BRÂHMAN WOMEN WHEN BROUGHT TO BED, AND ON INFANTS OF TENDER AGE.

WITHOUT stopping at present to enumerate the many ceremonies practised with regard to the wives of the Brâhmans when in a state of pregnancy, from the time when it is first ascertained, to that of parturition, some of which shall be noticed elsewhere, I will content myself with describing a few which are never omitted to be used towards the mother, and to the child after it is born.

A *Brâhmaṇi* or *Brâhmaṇâri,* the wife of a Brâhman, is pronounced to be unclean for ten days after her lying-in, and the stain is in some measure communicated to every person in the house where she is brought to bed. On the eleventh day they send all the linen she has used to be washed, and the house is thoroughly cleaned in the Hindû manner by smearing the floor with cow-dung moistened with water, and then marking it with broad stripes of white. The Purôhita being now called to celebrate the ceremonies of the purification, makes her sit down on a little stool, holding the child in her arms. Her husband being seated beside her, the Purôhita commences by sacrificing to the god *Puḷḷiyâr* or *Vig'hnêśwara.*[q] He then consecrates some water, and pours a little into the hand of the husband and the wife, who drop a part of it on their hands, and drink the rest. The house is afterwards sprinkled over with the holy water, and what remains is thrown into the well.

By this ceremony all that dwell in the house are deemed to be purified, and may then mix with the world. The newly delivered woman alone is not perfectly clean till the end of a month from the time of her lying-in. During the whole period of her uncleanness she must be kept in a detached place, and must not touch any of the furniture or vessels in the house. The time being expired she may then return to her usual place in the family.

---

[q] The worship of Gaṇêśa, Vig'hnêśwara, or (as in Tamil he is called,) Piḷḷaiyâ is very widely spread in India.

(Gaṇêśa = *Lord of the hosts.* *Gaṇa,* a host + *îśan,* lord. Vig'hnêśwâra = *Lord of obstacles.* *Vig'hna,* obstacle, + *îśwara.* Piḷḷai, *a child* + âr, honorific affix = *the honored child.* Vinâyakan = *he who has to do with hindrances.*)

He is the son of Śiva and Pârvati. Being Lord of the inferior hosts of deities he is called *Gaṇêśa.* He is supposed to remove obstacles and is therefore invoked at the beginning of all undertakings. He has the head of an Elephant, and his familiar trunk and little cunning eye are to be seen in every thoroughfare.

Being a glutton he has a large corporation.

He is the domestic, household god of all the classes. Concerning him multitudes of stories are told. His great festival is called *Vinâyagar Chauṭṭi* or Chatûrthi, and is held on the 4th of Âvaṇi (July-August.)

In some part of the country the kâka tree (cassia fistula) is sacred to him.

Twelve days after the birth, the child receives its name, which is imparted in this manner. The father, and the mother with the infant in her arms, being seated, the Brâhmans who are invited form a circle round them. A plate with rice, raw but free of husks, is brought in, upon the surface of which the father inscribes the day of the month when the child was born, with the name of the ruling star of that day. He adds the name which he wishes to be given to the child, which has been previously chosen out of the calendar of their saints with many long and trifling combinations. Each ceremony is accompanied with several Mantras of the Purôhita, who pronounces them, holding a gold ring in his hand. I ought not to omit that the whole is preceded by the sacrifice of the *Hômam*, which will be afterwards described. In this case it is offered to the nine planets.[r] At last, the whole ceremonies being ended, the father calls the child three times by the name which has been given to it, and the whole is concluded with a sacrifice to the god of the house. Dinner is then served to the Brâhmans, who, after receiving *betel*,[s] and some pieces of money or other presents, take their leave.

When the child has attained the age of six months, they begin to give him solid food; and this gives occasion for a new entertainment to the Brâhmans. The house where it is given, having been first neatly cleaned within and without, in the Hindû fashion, the door is decorated with garlands of mango leaves. In the court, a *pandal* or shed is constructed, under which a little bank of earth is raised, which is used for several purposes. The Brâhmans, who have been previously invited, having placed themselves under the *pandal*, the mother of the child goes thither also, and carrying it in her arms sits down on the little bank of earth. The Purôhita commences this, as well as the former ceremony, by offering the sacrifice of the *Hômam*. When it is over, the married women, but not widows, draw near and, singing all together, perform over the child the ceremony of the *Ârati*.[t]

As this ceremony will be frequently alluded to in the course of this work, it will be proper here to give a short account of it. Upon a plate of copper they place a lamp made of a paste from rice flower. It is supplied with oil and lighted. The married women, but not widows, for their presence would be unlucky, take hold of the plate with both hands, and raising it as high as the head of the person for whom the ceremony is performed, describe in that position a number of circles with the plate and the burning lamp.

---

r These are the Sun, Moon, Mars, Mercury, Jupiter, Venus, Saturn, with Râhu and Kêta (the dragons who swallow the Sun and Moon when eclipses happen).

s The leaves of the *Piper betel* smeared with lime and the nut of the Arîka palm (areka catechu).

t The waving of lighted camphor be re an image, to avert the evil eye. Sometimes it is done as in the text.

Sometimes, in place of the rice lamp, they fill the plate with water, coloured red with a mixture of saffron and other ingredients; and with this describe their circles, raising it as high as the head of the person who is the object of the ceremony.

The intention of this ceremony is to avert fascination by the eye, and to prevent the accidents which arise out of I know not what evil impression occasioned by the jealous looks of certain persons. The credulity of the Hindûs respecting this sort of injury is carried to excess: and it is for that reason that the ceremony of the *ârati*, which is considered to have the virtue of preventing the effect of those glances, is so common and so universal among the Hindûs, and especially among persons of high rank, who, being more observed and having more enemies than private individuals, are more exposed to the evil influence of malevolent or jealous looks. When such persons therefore appear in public, the first thing that is done on their return home, is to perform this ceremony of the ârati over them, as an antidote to the ill designed looks which may have been cast upon them. For the same reason princes have the ceremony repeated several times in a day.

The gods themselves are not considered out of the reach of malicious glances of the eye; and therefore when they are carried in processions in the streets, or in any other way exposed to public veneration, the ceremony of the ârati is always celebrated when they are taken back to their place, to efface the evil they may have sustained by such wicked looks. The dancing girls who daily attend at the temples of the idols to chaunt hymns in their praise, never fail, at the conclusion, to light the lamp of rice paste and to go through the ceremony of the ârati, elevating it to the idols' heads, and whirling in the accustomed circles.

This sort of superstition or idle observance is by no means peculiar to the Hindûs. I have seen cantons in France, (and I suppose it is not different in many other countries,) where the people were scarcely less infatuated. I have known decent villagers who would not have dared to shew their young children to people they did not know, or to persons of bad appearance, lest their invidious or ill-boding look should occasion some mischief to befal them.

The bad consequences arising from the eye or look were not unknown to the ancients. We read in Virgil,

"Nescio quis teneros *oculus* mihi fascinat agnos."

The Hindûs call this evil glance *drishti-dôsham*, or evil which comes from looks; upon which their notions are altogether extravagant. But let us resume our subject.

The ceremony of *ârati* being made upon the child by the married women present, they continue their song and go in a body to seek the god of *the Plate*, who is nothing else than a new vessel of brass given for a present by the maternal uncle of the infant.

This dish has been turned into a god by virtue of the Mantras of the Purôhita. The women, proceeding to the place where it is deposited, cast into it a small quantity of an earth called *Pramâṇam;* after which, each clasping her hands, the whole at once make a devout obeisance to the god of the Dish, and place him beside the child; for whom at the same time they offer up their wishes that he may become great and strong, and enjoy good health and long life. Then they rub his lips with boiled rice, prepared expressly for the occasion, and gird round his middle a little cloth, which is likewise brought out with abundance of ceremonies.

The women having retired, leave room for the men, who put some *akshatâ*[u] upon the infant's head as well as on their own. The *akshatâ*, of which frequent mention will be hereafter made, are nothing but grains of rice tinged with a reddish hue.

This ceremony and the preceding one being accomplished, the whole is finished by a feast given to the persons invited.

When the infant attains its second or third year, they shave its head; and this also is made the subject of a feast. Preparations are made for this important ceremony as on former occasions. On the earthen bank raised under the pandal or shed, in the way before mentioned, they trace a square, in the middle of which they deposit a measure of rice in the husk. In the same square they place the idol *Piḷḷaiyâr* or *Vig'hnêśwara,* to whom they make an offering of cocoanuts, sugar, and betel. The barber then shaves the head of the child, to the sound of musical instruments, leaving only a small tuft of hair, such as the Hindûs always permit to grow on the crown of the head. All who have been invited look on, and are obliged to continue standing until the barber finishes his operation. As soon as it is over, he lays hold of the measure of rice which stands in the little square, takes his payment and retires. The Brâhmans then perform the sacrifice of the Hômam to the nine planets.

The Purôhita presides at all these ceremonies, and accompanies them with the Mantras. As in former cases, they are closed with a repast provided for the Brâhmans that are invited.

About the same time they pierce the ears of the children of either sex; for the Hindû men as well as the women wear pendants at their ears, though of a different shape. They are always of gold, and it is not allowed to wear on the head trinkets of any other metal; only that sometimes the women employ a silver one to bind the hair at the neck.

The ceremony of piercing the ears of the children is not without its entertainments any more than the antecedent ones. It is attended with nearly the same practices, which it would be tedious any more to describe. The jeweller bores them, to the sound of musical instruments, with a very fine gold wire. The hole is gradually widened

[u] *Fried grains of rice*, S.

from time to time by inserting a substance of greater thickness. It is more enlarged in the girls, for the purpose of suspending a greater proportion of ornaments. But in some provinces of the peninsula it is so enormously extended, both in men and women, as to equal at least the size of a Spanish dollar.[c]

I have studiously abridged the account of these ceremonies, as nearly the same will recur in those of the *triple cord*, of marriage, and of burial; where they will be more minutely detailed.

However frivolous and superstitious these ceremonies may be, they possess one advantage at least, that of compelling the Brâhmans to assemble frequently together, and to make their duties reciprocal, which greatly contributes to render the individuals of their society much more refined than those of the other Hindû castes amongst whom these practices do not prevail.

---

c In the extreme South it is much larger.

A

DESCRIPTION

OF

THE PEOPLE OF INDIA, &c.

PART II.

OF THE FOUR STAGES IN LIFE OF THE BRÂHMAN.

CHAPTER I.

STATE OF BRAHMACHÂRI.

THE Brâhmans divide their progress through life into four stages: the first is that of a young man of the caste, when he has been invested with the triple cord, and is then called *Brahmachâri*. The second is when the Brâhman becomes a married man. In this condition, and particularly when he is the father of children, he obtains the appellation of *Grihastha*. He reaches the third stage when, being satiated with the world, he resolves to retire into the desert with his wife; and then he receives the name of *Vanaprastha*, which signifies "an inhabitant of the wilderness." The fourth and last stage is that of *Sannyási*, at which he arrives when he devotes himself to a life of solitude, with no wife; and in a still higher degree of seclusion than the *Vanaprastha*.

It will be proper to consider these several degrees in their turn, with the duties belonging to each. In the first place, then, we shall speak of the *Brâhmachari*, and the manner in which he is instituted into this condition.[w]

All the Brâhmans wear a Cord over the shoulder, consisting of three thick twists of cotton, each of them formed of several smaller threads.[x] It is called *Jandemu* in the *Telugu*, *Pûṇûl* in *Tamil*, and *Janivâram*, or *Yajnôpavîtam* in *Canarese*.[y] The three threads are not twisted together, but separate from one another, and hang from the left shoulder to the right haunch. When a Brâhman marries, he mounts nine threads in place of three.

---

w Compare Manu, Chap. II. 175.

x Manu. chap. II. 44. *Kârpâsam upavîtam syât viprasya urdd'hvavritam trivrit* of cotton the cord should be of the Brâhman, put on from above, three-fold.

y பூணூல். Thread put on. TAM. జందెము. TEL. ಜನಿವಾರ. CAN. The two last are corruptions of S. YAJNÔPVÎTA.

The Brâhmans, and other persons who have a right to wear the cord are as proud of the distinction as an English Nobleman of the badge of the Order of the Garter, a Spanish Grandee of the fleece of Gold, or a French gentleman as of the Order of the Holy Ghost.

The children of Brâhmans are invested with the Cord when they come to the age of seven or nine years. It is not obtained but at a considerable expence; and Brâhmans who are poor are therefore, in order to acquire it, obliged to resort to a contribution; and Hindûs of every caste believe they perform a meritorious act in contributing to the charges of the ceremony. It is called *Upanayanam*, or, *initiation.*

The Cord which is given to the young Brâhmans must be made with much care and with many ceremonies. The cotton of which it is formed ought to be gathered from the plant by the hands of Brâhmans only, in order to avoid the pollution which would pass from the impure hands of men of other castes. For the same reason it should be carded, spun, and twisted, by persons of the tribe, and be always kept exceedingly pure.

I had some difficulty in bringing myself to detail the whole of this ceremony of the Upanayanam, it is so filled with minute and trifling superstition. But I considered that those who would wish to know and to compare together the ceremonies of various ancient nations, would probably be pleased with a regular summary of the true genius of the Hindû superstitions. I have taken that which I here present from the *Directory* (*Nitya-karma*) of the Purôhitas. The father of the Brahmachâri commences by selecting, agreeably to the rules of Hindû astrology, the month of the year, the week, the day of the week, and the minute of the day, most favourable for that ceremony. Part of what is necessary is laid down in the Hindû almanack. The Purôhita is charged with what remains; and it is no trifling affair, so intricate are the calculations and combinations which he has to undertake.

The father of the young Brâhman is in the first instance required to make an ample provision of rice, peas, pumkins, and all other vegetable food, of curdled milk and melted butter, of cocoa and the various kinds of fruit which can be found, to be the ground work of the entertainment to be given to the Brâhmans. It is necessary above all things that he should be provided with betel, and good store of money in silver and copper, together with some pieces of new cloth. All these articles must be distributed to his guests at the close of the ceremony, which continues four days. He must also provide a new dish of copper or brass, and several earthen vessels which have never served for any such purpose before, and must never be used again.

Every thing being in readiness, the ceremony of the first day begins. An invitation is given to all the Brâhmans, their relations, and friends; to those who live in the place, and those who gave invitations on similar occasions of their own. In general, if any one were overlooked of those who have the right or the expectation of being invited, such a neglect would occasion disputes and animosities between the parties concerned, that would rarely terminate but with life.

The Purôhita is called before all the others. He brings on the day that is indicated, the belt itself, mango-leaves, the herb Darb'ha, or *Kuśa*, a sacred plant employed in most of the ceremonies of the Brâhmans. The reader will observe the resemblance which the name of this plant, Darb'ha, the growth of which resembles the common grass or hay, bears to the Latin noun *Herba*.[y] He must also provide an antelope's skin to sit upon; the skin of this animal, as well as that of the tyger, being deemed extremely pure and becoming, as no uncleanness arises from handling or sitting upon them.

When all the guests are assembled, the *Purôhita* begins by invoking the god of the house, which must have been previously well purified and set in order according to the customs of the Hindûs, by rubbing the floors and inside walls with cow-dung diluted with water, while the outside walls are adorned with broad perpendicular stripes in red earth.

The greater part of the ceremonies are performed under a *pandal* or alcove, previously set up for this purpose in the yard, with great care and useless rites. It is supported on twelve pillars of wood, erected by the hands of the Brâhmans themselves. For to them alone, and to the persons connected with the *Right Hand*, belongs the privilege of fixing twelve pillars; those of the Left Hand being limited to ten or to eleven at most.

While the Purôhita is beginning to recite his mantram, they place the Piḷḷaiyâr or Vig'hnêśwara under the pandal. They are often contented, however, with setting up a cone made of mud or cow-dung to represent that deity, which, by the virtue of the Purôhita's mantram, becomes a god. He then offers him a sacrifice of incense, of burning lamps, and akshatâ, or grains of rice tinged with red. This god *Piḷḷaiyâr* is of a disposition much addicted to wrath and contradiction; as his appellation *Vig'hnêśwara* imports, meaning *the God of Obstacles*. For this reason, in all public ceremonies, they begin with invoking him first, that he may not interpose any troublesome obstruction to their happy progress.

The married women (widows being excluded from all scenes of cheerfulness) being purified by bathing; some of them go to prepare the feast, whilst others return to the place of assembly, and having made the young Brahmachâri sit down on a little stool, they rub him well with oil, then wash him, hang a new cloth to his belt, adorn him with several trinkets, and do not fail to put round his neck a string of coral beads, and bracelets of the same material on his arms. They forget not to stain the rim of his eyelids with black. This last is very commonly used by the Hindûs, and is known to have been usual in former times with other nations.

---

y The *darb'ha* is essential in all sacrifices. Rig Vêda Sanhitâ, A. I. Adh. I. Sukta III. 3. "The sacred grass (Poa Cynosuroides) after having had the roots cut off, is spread on the Vêdi or altar and upon it the libation of.......... melted butter is poured out. In other places a tuft of it in a similar position is supposed to form a suitable seat to the deity or deities invoked in the sacrifice." Wilson. See also Stephenson's sâma Vêda, p. viii. Manu, Chap. III. 256.

The father and mother of the young man who is the subject of the ceremonies, make him sit down between them in the midst of the assembly, and the women who are present, perform upon him the ceremony of the *Ârati* which was described in the last chapter. Then they join their voices in chanting praise to the gods, or good wishes for the young man.

This ceremony is followed by an offering which is made to the god of the house for every house has its own deity, male or female according to the fancy of the votary. The sacrifice consists in offering up a little boiled rice with a portion of different kinds of food prepared for the feast, and some betel. This offering is not thrown away, being afterwards eagerly devoured as a sacred morsel yielding happiness.

The principal ceremonies of the first day being thus concluded, all the people are made to sit down in several rows, the women being separated from the men in such a manner that they may not be looked at. The women of the house wait upon the guests, and, with their fingers (spoons and forks being entirely unknown amongst the Hindûs) serve out the rice and other dishes prepared for the occasion. Each receives his portion on leaves of the banana or other trees, sewed together, which can only serve once. The entertainment being over they distribute betel among the guests, who then withdraw for the day.

Next day, early in the morning, the father of the young Brâhman, having purified himself by bathing, waits the proper time, and as soon as it comes, he goes, as he had done the day before, to invite his relations and friends to attend and accompany him to the ceremonies of the second day. He takes with him the *Akshatâs* in a sort of cup, to present them to the persons he has invited. And indeed the offer of such presents to those who assist at these ceremonies is a part of Hindû politeness; and the guests, as a proof of their taking it in good part, pick up a few of the red grains and stick one or two on their foreheads as an ornament.

The assembly being formed, the Brahmachâri, with his father and mother, all ascend the pile of earth thrown up beneath the *pandal*, and seat themselves on three little stools. In the meantime the young man is bathed in the same manner as on the former day; they deck his brows with sandal and akshatâ, and gird his loins with a pure cloth, that is to say a cloth not handled since it was washed. (It is not in this case only that pure cloths must be used by the Brâhmans; for whenever they wash themselves they must employ no other; and it is for this reason that, after bathing, they always wash their towel to remove its impurity, and then wait till it is dry before they put it up.) All these ceremonies are accompanied with the songs of the women, the same as on the preceding day. But on this occasion they do not use the ceremony of the *Ârati*.

These introductory ceremonies being accomplished, the Purôhita enters, carrying fire in an earthen vase, which he places upon the pile; and by means of the mantram, he makes this fire a god. The father of the Brahmachâri then advances and makes the sacrifice of the

Hômam in honour of the fire ; this is succeeded by nine similar sacrifices in honour of the nine planets. The Hindûs reckon them nine, because, in addition to the seven which we admit with them, they had the increasing and waning moon as two distinct planets. These nine are considered as malevolent deities ; and they are generally sent by the magicians on the errand of tormenting the objects of their resentment. On the present occasion, as well as on many others, the design of the sacrifice of the Hômam is to render them propitious.

The sacrifice of the Hômam heretofore repeatedly mentioned, and to which we must again frequently return, is one of the most meritorious. The Brâhmans alone have the privilege of offering it. Their method is to kindle a fire of some kind of consecrated wood, and then to cast on the fire some boiled rice bedaubed with melted butter. This sacrifice, so simple and easy, is nevertheless very famous and in very frequent use.

Those sacrifices made by means of fire, are followed by one made to the Fire itself, to which as a deity they offer incense, with burning lamps and certain viands. The fire thus consecrated is afterwards carried into a particular apartment of the house, and kept up day and night with great care until the ceremony is ended. It would be considered a very inauspicious event, if, for want of attention or by any accident, it should happen to go out. All the sacrifices to fire or made by means of fire, indicate a species of idolatry very striking, but by no means peculiar to the Hindûs.[a]

The following ceremony conducted by the women will not be thought the least ridiculous of the festival. Having procured a large copper vessel, well whitened over with lime, they go with it to draw water, accompanied with instruments of music. Having filled the vessel with water, they place in it perpendicularly some leaves of mango, and fasten a new cloth round the whole, made yellow with saffron water. On the neck of the vessel, which is narrow, they put a cocoa nut stained with the same colour as the cloth. In this trim they carry it into the interior of the house, and set it on the floor upon a little heap of rice. There it is still farther ornamented with women's trinkets; after which the necessary ceremonies are performed to invite the god, and to fix him there. This perhaps is not the same as the god of the house; or rather it is the apotheosis of the vessel itself that is made in this case, for it actually becomes a divinity, receiving offerings of incense, flowers, betel, and other articles used in the sacrifices of the Brâhmans. Upon this occasion only, women act and perform the deification; and it appears that the divinity which is resident in the vessel is female. But, however this may be, the mother of the Brahmachâri, taking up in her hands this new divinity, goes out of the house, accompanied by the other Brâhman women, visits the festival, preceded by musical instruments, and makes the circuit of the village,

[a] *Agni* or fire is the first, as *Vishṇu* is the last among the gods in the Vêdas.

walking under a sort of canopy which is supported over her head. Upon returning home she sets the *vessel God,* which she has in her hands, where it was formerly stationed under the *pandal;* and with the assistance of some of the other women, she fixes, in honour of the god, two new cloths on the pillars of the alcove near which it is placed.

The following ceremony is also, at least in a great measure, performed by women. They go in search of mould from a nest of *karraiyân* which are a species of white ants very common in India and very troublesome. With this they fill five small earthen pots, in which they sow nine sorts of grain, which they moisten with milk and water. When they have finished, the Brâhmans approach, and by the power of their mantras they convert the five earthen pots into as many gods. After offering to these new divinities the accustomed sacrifice of incense, rice, and betel, they are placed upon a little dish and set down under the pandal, near the female god of whom we have just spoken. When they are put by her side, the whole party join in a profound inclination of the body in sign of adoration. They make another to the gods of their ancestors, whom they invoke to be present at the feast. Then turning to the young man who is the object of the whole, they tie a piece of bastard saffron to his arm with yellow cord. The barber once more shaves his head; he is bathed, his brows are decorated with sandal leaves, and his loins are girt with a *pure* cloth.

The ceremony is immediately succeeded by the *feast of the young men,* particularly provided for the young Brâhmans who had been previously invited to partake of it with the new candidate.

This repast is followed by a ceremony more imposing than the preceding. The father of the new Brâhman having made the company retire to some distance, whilst he and his son are concealed behind a curtain, sits down upon the ground, with his face turned towards the west, and making his son sit down beside him with his face towards the east, he whispers a deep secret in his ear out of the mantras, and gives him other instructions analogous to his present situation. The whole is in a style which probably is little comprehended by the listener. Among other precepts I am informed, the father, on one occasion, delivered the following: "Be mindful, my son, that there is one God "only, the master, sovereign, and origin of all things. Him ought "every Brâhman, in secret, to adore. But remember also that this is "one of the truths that must never be revealed to the vulgar herd. "If thou dost reveal it, great evil will befal thee."

In the evening, at the time when the lamps are lighted, the Brahmachâri being made to take his seat in the alcove under the branches, the women, with songs, go in quest of the consecrated fire we have mentioned, which it was a sacred duty to keep alive, and place it close by the youth. The Purôhita, drawing near, recites some mantras over the fire; after which the young Brâhman makes, for the first time, the sacrifice of the *Hômam,* which has been already described; and this he has acquired the right to do by the distinction of the Cord. While he is employed in the sacrifice the women continue their singing, inharmonious as it is, and the instruments make the air resound with sharp and discordant notes. The Hômam is followed by a sacrifice to the holy fire which was recently brought by the women; after which they take it back to its original station. They quickly return, and once more perform the ceremony of the Ârati to the newly initiated disciple. After this they receive betel, as well as the other guests. And thus conclude the ceremonies of the second day.

When all is ended, the father of the Brahmachâri distributes amongst the assistants what remains of the money which he destined for the charges of the feast. He orders the pieces of cloth which were provided to be brought in, and he distributes them also. Those that are wealthy give cloth of higher price, and some add the present of trinkets or a cow. The Brâhmans, always skilful in the art of adulation, extol such liberal donors, idolize their generosity, and assign them a place already with Para-Brahma as the reward of their kindness to the Brâhmans. Those to whom such flatteries are directed listen to them with the utmost complaisance, and think them ample remuneration for the extravagant expences which their folly has occasioned.

Besides the Brâhmans (as we have formerly mentioned) there are some other Hindû castes who wear the triple cord: and in particular the Jains, who will be mentioned afterwards. The *Kshatriya* or Rajas, the *Vaisya* or Merchants, and, amongst the Sûdras, the five castes of artisans in wood, stone, and metals, have also the right to wear this badge; by which means it ceases to be a distinction and occasions ambiguity. The caste of the Râjas receive the cord from the hand of a Purôhita Brâhman; but he makes no other ceremony at its reception than the sacrifice of the *Hômam.* After being invested he must give a great entertainment to all the Brâhmans who have honoured the ceremony with their company, and make them presents. Before he departs, he presents himself before the assembly and makes the prostration of the eight members, whether for the purpose of thanking the Brâhmans, of whom it is composed, for the honour they had conferred upon him in giving him the cord, or whether as a mark of his adoration of those gods of the earth. This ceremony, however, does not bear the name of *Upanayana,* because the Râjas do not acquire through it the right of learning all the sciences. They have not, for example that of perusing the Vedas.[a]

It is thus at the present time, that it is conferred on the five castes of artisans. But it is not by the hands of a Brâhman that they receive it, because, like the Jains, they will not admit them to be superior to themselves. It is the Guru of their own caste that confers it.

---

[a] Manu, Chap. II. 38.

CHAPTER II.

OF THE CONDUCT EXPECTED FROM THE BRAHMACHÂRI, AND THE RIGHTS HE ACQUIRES BY RECEIVING THE CORD.

THE condition of Brahmachâri continues from the *Upanayana* or ceremony of the Cord to the time of Marriage, which is about the age of sixteen. This is not too early a time to marry, because the spouse is a child of four or five years old. This custom of marrying the girls so soon, and indeed as early as possible, though common to all the castes, is most strictly observed by the Brâhmans; to such a degree even, that a marriageable girl would scarcely find a husband among them. In this caste there is often the most disgusting inequality of age between the parties; for it is not at all uncommon to see old widowers of sixty or seventy remarrying with children of six or seven years of age, and giving a preference to them over adult and really marriageable women, whom they will not endure to hear mentioned, although these poor victims of the prejudices of their caste may have uniformly led an irreproachable life. The husband, of course, generally dies long before the wife, and frequently even before she has attained the age of puberty. She finds herself a widow when she has but just grown into a woman; and, according to the customs of her caste, she cannot marry again. Hence disorders arise which tend to the dishonour of all the tribe. The evil is striking, but the idea of curing it, by allowing young widows to remarry, never enters the mind of any Brâhman. In every circumstance that can occur, they are willing to support the utmost inconvenience rather than abolish or even alter the most ridiculous of their absurd prejudices.[b]

The proper business of the young Brâhman, before marriage, is held to be a course of study, of rigorous submission and conformity to the severe discipline of all the rules of the caste. This is the meaning of his appellation of Brahmachâri.[c] It enjoins ready obedience to the orders of his superiors, the utmost deference to his father and mother. But as far as relates to his equals, and to real politeness towards the rest of the world, the sequel of our enquiries will shew what regard is paid to those rules of conduct, when the indolence of parents drops the rein which should keep their children in order.

The young Brâhman is to commence by learning to read and write. He is then taught the Vêdas and the Mantras, which he gets by heart. He then advances to other sciences according to the degree of his docility and quickness of capacity, and if his parents are able to pay teachers, he is above all taught arithmetic in all its branches. The study of the various idioms of India, and especially the *Hindûstânî* or

---

b Of late years the remarriage of widows has been permitted in several places, even among Brâhman families.

c Bramha = *the Vêda* + Châri = *who goes.*

Hindî, at least in the southern provinces, occupies the greater part of his leisure. During this immature period, he is not to use betel, nor put flowers in his hair, nor ornament his body or forehead with sandal. Neither must he look at himself in a mirror. He must bathe daily, and offer the sacrifice of the Hômam twice a day. In short, his whole attention must be occupied in forming himself upon the true model of the institutions of his caste.[d]

It is not easy for children to live under such restraint; and accordingly very few are found who follow all that is prescribed to them. Nothing is more common, for example, than to see them with their foreheads decorated with sandal, and their mouths full of betel. And it is not likely that other rules, which are prescribed on the points of form, should be better observed.

Although a young Brâhman, from being incapable of affording the expences necessary, or from whatever other cause, has not been able to enter into the state of matrimony at the time prescribed, they no longer treat him as a Brahmachâri, after attaining the age of eighteen or twenty; neither does he acquire the name of *Grihast'ha.*[e] But, whatever be his age or condition, as soon as he has obtained the Cord, he is entitled to the six privileges of the caste, of which the Hindû books so often speak. These six privileges are as follows:

To read, and to get read, the Vêdas; to make and to cause to be made, the sacrifice of the Yajna; and, lastly, to receive alms and to give presents to the Brâhmans.[f] The Śûdras have only the last of these privileges, namely, that of giving alms or presents to the Brâhmans, who affect to confer an honour by receiving them at their hands. I shall speak but briefly upon these privileges.

The right to read and learn the Vêdas is so exclusively appropriated to them, that the slightest penalty which a Brâhman would incur by rashly or imprudently lending these sacred books, or communicating their contents to persons of a different caste, would be, as we have elsewhere mentioned, to be ignominiously driven from his caste, without any hope of being admitted again.[g]

It is from these books that the Brâhmans have filched their principal *Mantras,* so famous and so beneficial to them; and it is for that reason, no doubt, that they hold them so precious.

Those who profess the study of science must learn these books by heart. This qualification gains for its possessors the name of *Vaidika.*

---

d Compare Manu Chap. II. The abbé adds in his corrected MS.: "His parents impart to him early that system of imposture, of dissimulation, of trickery and of fraud which characterizes all Brâhmans and forms a principal trait in their character."

This is too strong; but the abbé speaks often from impulse, and his opinions are, in consequence, a little inconsistent, at times.

e *Householder:* Griham = *house* + st'ha = *one who stays.*

f Manu Chap. III. 69—81.

g I have omitted some remarks of the abbé on the Vêdas, as in Prof. Max Müller's Ancient Sanskrit Literature the character of the Vêdas is fully discussed.

But, in devoting themselves to this study, they cannot expect to reap any benefit in point of instruction; because the language in which they are composed is so ancient, and the errors which have crept in by the carelessness of copiers are so multiplied in the manuscripts that still remain, that they are nearly unintelligible to the Brâhmans themselves, who are considered to be the most conversant in that branch.

The greater part of the Brâhmans, who devote themselves to this study, do not understand neither of them, because they have not yet attained a sufficient acquaintance with the *Sanscrit*, the parent language of India, in which the books are written. Their utmost proficiency has been to read it tolerably, by which they are enabled to learn it mechanically and get it by rote, without understanding its meaning. They may be compared to the peasantry in the Roman Catholic countries of Europe, who learn to read Latin that they may be able to chaunt the Psalms cn Sundays at church.

In some parts, however, Brâhmans are to be met with, who are well versed in this mother tongue, although they are in no great number. There are some of them even who are so disinterested as to teach the Vêdas gratuitously to their disciples. But the greater number are too closely attached to their private interests, or too poor to imitate them. It does very well for a wealthy Brâhman to be at such an expence, and to encourage others in the same studies by rewards. Accordingly, some of them act on this plan, and fancy they are performing meritorious works of charity. They have paid the compliment to the caste of Râjas, to associate them with themselves in the right of having the Vêdas read to them ; that is to say, in paying the masters who teach them; and I am well persuaded they would not refuse the same favour to any other person that would contribute to so good a work, even were it a Śûdra.

It is not to be understood, however, that there is any great degree of emulation among them in regard to this sort of study. Poverty prevents the greater number from engaging in it ; and the apathy and indolence so characteristical of all Hindûs keep back the rest from a study sufficiently repulsive in itself.

The third and fourth privilege of the Brâhmans consists in making the sacrifice of the Yajna and in causing it to be made. But, as I propose to detail the principal circumstances in this famous sacrifice when I treat of the Vanaprastha Brâhmans, I will omit them here.

It appears that the Yajna as well as the Hômam, of which we have already spoken, is to be understood as being a sacrifice made to the *fire* already consecrated by the Mantram, and into which the Brâhman to whom alone it belongs to make it, casts the boiled rice bedaubed with melted butter. By the word *Yajna* is understood, in a more extended sense, all the sacrifices accompanied by Mantram.

The fifth privilege of the Brâhmans is that of giving alms and presents ; which it may be supposed they indulge in less willingly than in the sixth, which consists in the right of receiving them. But it must be allowed that there are a great number of people of this caste who practise hospitality and exercise other works of charity. Yet, as in the eyes of all the members of this sect, every other man is an object of indifference and even of contempt, we may be allowed to lay it down as a general remark, that generosity and compassion are virtues not natural to the Brâhmans.

Among the presents which they permit to be made them, there are some which they particularly approve. These are gifts of gold, or in land; gifts of clothing, of grain, and of cows. Milk being their chief article of food, the last sort of gift is one of the most agreeable. Donations of land are extremely common in many places, from the generosity of the princes, who exempt them from the tribute paid by other landholders. These lands descend, with their immunities, from generation to generation. They do not themselves cultivate them, unless poverty compels them, but they keep farmers under them who take the management, for which they receive one-half of the produce for their pains. The villages which are thus exempted from all taxation, and inhabited by Brâhmans are called by the name of *Agrâram* or *Agrahâram;* an expression composed of two words which signify a *portion of ground.* There are many such in the various provinces of the peninsula.

Besides receiving the revenue of these lands, the Brâhmans discharge the various functions of worship in the greater part of the temples. They engross the principal part of the income of the lands assigned to defray their expences, as well as the offerings made by the Hindûs to the idols. These two last sources of wealth are very abundant.

There is also a work of charity which greatly prevails in this country, which consists in giving them great entertainments, which are often followed with presents of money or cloth. But we shall leave this source of their income till we come to treat of the public festivals called *Samarâd'hanam.*[h]

The Brâhmans in asking and receiving alms or donations, seem to proceed upon their right. They have no shame in taking or asking for what they are in want of. When they ask, they do it boldly, but not with insolence, as the Moorish fakirs and the Vishṇuvite mendicants do. Nor do they, like the latter, the *Dâśaru* or *Ândhras,* make a trade of begging by asking alms from door to door.

But if you will not give to the Brâhmans, you must not amuse them with vain promises. This, they say, would be a heinous sin, and would assuredly draw down a severe chastisement upon him who should attempt it. One of their authors proves this by the following illustration.

"Kartâ! Kartâ!" screamed an ape, one day, when he saw a fox feeding on a rotten carcase: "thou must, in a former life, have com-

---

h = General worship.

mitted some dreadful crime, to be doomed to a new state in which thou feedest on such garbage." "Alas!" replied the fox, "I am not punished worse than I deserve. I was once a man, and I then promised something to a Brâhman, which I never gave him. That is the true cause of my being regenerated in this shape. Some good works which I did have obtained for me the indulgence of remembering what I was in my former state, and the cause for which I have been degraded into this." The silly Hindû gives such a story his implicit faith; and the wily Brâhman knows well how to profit by his credulity.

Another privilege which they very generally enjoy is an exemption from the taxes imposed on houses. They are also free from the tolls levied upon goods in the districts which are subject to the princes. And they are rarely subjected to any corporal punishment, however atrocious their offences may be.

The murder of a Brâhman for any cause whatever, is one of the five great crimes acknowledged by the Hindûs, which would without doubt draw down some signal and awful calamity over the whole land where it should be committed.

It is thought quite sufficient to condemn a Brâhman to restitution and heavy fines, when he happens to be guilty of malversation in office and embezzles the public money; which frequently occurs.

However, under the dominion of the Europeans and Mahometans, where their sacred and inviolable character is not so much respected, they must undergo, like other Hindûs, the punishments due to their crimes. The Moors sometimes have them cudgelled to death, unless they redeem themselves at a large price in money, of which their oppressors are still more covetous than of blood. But the Brâhmans are so attached to their wealth, or rather they are so well acquainted with the character and disposition of those who desire to rob them of it, and know so well that if they once were seen to yield to any torture in the smallest degree they would never be free from it, while any property remained to them; that they prefer to suffer patiently whatever can be inflicted rather than submit to the smallest exactions.

I know from good authority that the last Musalman prince who reigned in Mysore, being very desirous to seize upon the wealth which certain Brâhmans of his country possessed, a measure which was very customary with him wherever he suspected a man to be rich; those men set all his cruelty at defiance for the space of eighteen months, in which time he was unable to extract any thing from them. Yet during that whole period he had employed threats, imprisonment, chains, and every kind of bodily punishment which the agents of his cruelty were able to invent. But all was unavailing. They bore all those savage trials with the most heroic firmness. At length, their persecutors were obliged to yield, and to let them go, with the shame of having tortured men for no cause, and without the gain of one farthing, although it was afterwards ascertained that they had considerable wealth.

When the Brâhmans find themselves involved in troubles like these, there is no falsehood or perjury which they will not employ for the purpose of extricating themselves. Nor is this to be wondered at, since they are not ashamed to declare openly that untruth and false swearing are virtuous and meritorious deeds when they tend to their own advantage. When such horrible morality is taught by the theologians of India, is it to be wondered at that falsehood should be so predominant among the people ?

CHAPTER III.

OF THE EXACTNESS WITH WHICH A YOUNG BRÂHMAN MUST SHUN EXTERNAL DEFILEMENT, AND THE DIFFERENT PRACTICES IN THIS RESPECT.

ALL Hindûs, in general, pay the most scrupulous attention and care to avoid whatever can, in their imagination, defile their person or apparel. It is more than probable that the Brâhmans have communicated to them these habits, being themselves more deeply tinctured with them than the Hindûs belonging to other castes. In their conduct and the whole intercourse of life, the Brâhmans have nothing so much at heart as Cleanliness; and as it is this quality, influencing their whole manners, that gives them in a great measure the superiority which they assert over the other tribes, I shall treat of it fully in this chapter; more especially as it is one of the principal objects of a Brahmachâri to cultivate at an early age those habits which in their estimation form a part of good education.

A human dead body inspires horror in every country. It cannot be touched but with the greatest repugnance; and it excites some feeling of uncleanness afterwards. But the Hindûs feel this sensation if they have but assisted at a funeral. When the ceremony is over they instantly immerse themselves in water, and no person can return home from such a duty until he be purified in that manner from the uncleanness which he is thus supposed to have contracted. Even the news of the death of a relation, though at a hundred leagues distance, has the same effect; and a person hearing such tidings would be considered impure by all around him until he had bathed; although it is the near relations only and not strangers that would be so contaminated. This sort of defilment, occasioned by the death of any one, was recognized among the Israelites. Numbers ix. 6, 7, and 10 and xix. 11 and 18. Their manner of purifying themselves from the stain occasioned by a dead body was very nearly the same as among the Hindûs.

Agreeably to the same feeling, a Hindû is no sooner dead than they hasten to inter the body; and until it is carried away, neither those in the house nor any in the neighbourhood can either eat or drink or go on with their occupations. I have seen the ceremonies at a temple where many were assisting, stopped suddenly and suspended until a corpse in the same street should be buried.

It is not thought sufficient to perfume merely the apartment in which a person has died. A Purôhita Brâhman must necessarily purify the house and remove the stain by means of the Mantram and his holy water; and until this is accomplished no person must enter.

Child-birth and periodical changes render a woman unclean. For a month after lying-in she must touch none of the earthen vessels of the house nor the clothes of any one; far less their persons. When the period expires, she washes herself by plunging into the river, if there be one near; or more commonly by having water poured over her body and head.

To efface the periodical stain, they wash themselves in the same manner on the third day, when they return to their home, from which they were excluded for the three days of their uncleanness. Houses of moderate convenience have places separate and distinct, for their reception during that period; but the poor, who have not this advantage, turn their women into the street, to a little corner set apart for that purpose, where they stay the time allotted, without communication with any one.

In the two cases we have mentioned, it would by no means be sufficient to wash in plain water the clothing which the woman then wore; but it is necessary to send it to the bleacher to be scoured. Even when brought home from this last operation, the Brâhmans are not satisfied till they have again passed it through water. This last practice, which they always follow even when they provide themselves with *new* clothes, arises from the consideration that the bleacher and weaver being Śûdras, will necessarily have affected them with a stain which the use of water is necessary to remove.

The wives of the sect of Śiva, under like circumstances, have a practice quite peculiar to themselves, and on that account deserving notice; for they think they sufficiently efface a periodical uncleanness by rubbing their foreheads with ashes; after which easy ceremony they are held to be pure. They call it *B'hasmasnânam* or the bath of ashes. Thus it has happened that, in the one party, frivolous and excessive attentions have degenerated into superstition; and in the other, superstition has occasioned the neglect of a practice perhaps necessary in a hot climate.

It is not, as many authors seem to believe, a prejudice quite confined to the Hindûs, to consider an earthen vessel as much more susceptible of pollution than one of copper or any other metal. The latter may be purified merely by washing it, while the former becomes quite unserviceable and must be broken in pieces. The same rule is prescribed to the Israelites in Leviticus, ii, 32, 33. Among the Hindûs, while the earthen vessels are new, and in the hands of the vender, any person may handle them; but from the moment they have been put in water, they can serve the person only who has employed them or those with whom he can eat according to the rules of his caste. The Brâhmans carry their nicety and delicacy on this point so far as not to permit Śûdras and other strangers to enter their kitchen, or to have any other means of seeing their earthen vessels. A look from them would defile them, and make it necessary to break them. This custom, I imagine, may proceed from the earthen vessels in India being unglazed, which leaves them with open pores, and may lead to the conclusion that they easily attract what is unclean.

It is the same with clothes as with dishes; some being susceptible of being soiled, and others not. Of the latter kind are stuffs made of silk, and clothes of certain vegetable substances. It was on this account that all the ancient Brâhmans of the solitary order, were always clothed with the last mentioned fabrics, and many of the Brâhmans of the present time clothe themselves in the former, in many cases, particularly at their meals. Some physicians of their caste will not feel the pulse of a sick Śûdra but through a shred of silk to prevent immediate contact with his skin. With regard to Cotton, it is unfortunately subject to contract impurity from the touch of persons of an inferior caste, and particularly by that of Pariahs or Europeans. A Brâhman who piques himself on his delicacy, shews, in a case of this kind, a thousand squeamish tricks, and in the intercourse of life is obliged to move under perpetual constraint. Finding it utterly impossible, in towns and other frequented places, to avoid an accidental contact with people of all degrees, the very delicate Brâhmans shun such places and retire into the villages. But those amongst them in whom self-interest predominates over the desire of acquiring the fame of a zealous observance of their rules, relax a little in this observance, and get off by shifting their clothes as soon as they get home. They tumble what they take off into the water, and thus the whole uncleanness is got rid of.

Leather and every kind of skin, except those of the tiger and the antelope, are held to be very impure. They must never touch with their hands the pantoufles and sandals which they wear on their feet. A person who rides on horseback must have some stuff to cover the saddle, the bridle and stirrup leathers, to avoid all contact with skin. The most disagreeable of all European fashions in their eyes is that of boots and gloves; and they hold a man to be extremely unrefined who does not shrink to touch the slough of a carcase.

A Brâhman who is particular in his delicacy must attend also to what he treads upon. It would cost him a washing if he should touch a bone with his foot, or a broken pot, a bit of rag, or a leaf from which one had been eating. He must likewise be careful where he sits down. Some devotees always carrying their seat with them, that is a tiger or antelope's skin, which are always held pure. Some are contented with a mat: the rich take a carpet; but one may even squat on the ground without defilement, provided it be newly rubbed over with cow-dung. This last specific is also used as a daily purification of the Hindû houses from the defilement occasioned by comers and goers. When thus applied, diluted with water, it has the farther advantage of destroying the insects which would otherwise annoy them.

Their mode of eating their meals also requires much circumspection and gravity. However numerous the company may be, it would be unpolite to address conversation to any person during dinner. They eat in silence, and no conversation begins till they have ended the repast and washed their hands and mouths. The left hand, on this occasion, must not be employed, unless to hold the vessel of water from which they drink. This last operation is performed not by applying the vessel to the lips, but by pouring the water from on high into the mouth. This is the Hindû practice universally; and it would be considered a piece of gross impropriety to drink as we do by touching the vessel with our lips. In eating, great care must be taken that nothing drops upon the plate, or on the leaf when one is eating apart. If a single grain of rice should fall, his meal would be at an end; else he must cast away the plate so defiled, and bring another, with a fresh supply of food, in its place.

The reason of this extreme fastidiousness is founded on the Hindû notion that the saliva is the most filthy and impure secretion that proceeds from the body, and consequently held in the utmost horror. It is therefore never permitted to any one to spit within doors. If he has occasion, he must go out.

The fragments of the repast are given neither to the domestics nor to the poor, (unless they be Pariahs, who accommodate themselves to any thing,) but are cast to the crows or dogs. The poor are served with alms of boiled rice in a proper state, untouched by any one. But they who follow the usages of their caste, and who must not eat with those who give them the alms, receive it raw; and it is in this state only that Brâhmans will take it from persons of another caste.

They rarely eat their food from plates; and when they do so, it is only at home. It would be indecorous to use them elsewhere in public. The rice and other articles are served on bits of Banana leaf or some other leaves sewed very neatly together. They serve but once, and when they have done eating they take them to a distant place and throw them away. To offer a Brâhman any thing to eat on a metal or porcelain plate which others had used, however well it may have been washed, would be considered as the grossest affront.

With the same feeling, they will use neither spoon nor fork when they eat; and they are astonished how any one, after having once applied them to their mouths and infected them with saliva, should venture to repeat it a second time. When they eat any thing dry, they throw it into their mouth, so as that the fingers may not approach the lips.

A European once gave a letter of introduction to a Brâhman who had come from a great distance to receive it; and having sealed it with a wafer, which he moistened by putting it on his tongue, the Brâhman who observed this, would not touch the letter, and chose rather to forego any advantage he could derive from the recommendation than to carry a thing so polluted.

The touch of most animals, particularly that of a dog, is a stain to the person of a Brâhman. It is amusing to see the methods they take to shun the touch of one, when they see it approaching. If the dog should actually come in contact with them, they would be obliged instantly to plunge into the water and wash all their clothes in order to get free of such a stain.

The dog, nevertheless, is one of the divinities that the Hindûs pay honour to, under the name of *Bhairava ;* and the image of it may be seen in several of their temples.

There are a thousand other ways by which a Brâhman may receive an outward stain; but what we have already stated is sufficient to shew their feelings in that particular. It is principally for the purpose of purification from all such uncleanness that the bath is so common amongst them. There are certain rivers and ponds which are esteemed to have a particular virtue of this kind, and all the Brâhmans of the neighbourhood repair thither regularly every day to bathe. Those who, by residing too far from such privileged places, are out of the reach of such an advantage, must content themselves with the tank or well of their own village. In many parts, the other castes are not admitted either to bathe or draw water from the places set apart for the ablutions of the Brâhmans. If they should trespass, their audacity would bring down a prosecution upon them. But, in places where they are not absolute masters, they are obliged to be somewhat more forbearing.

A Brâhman rarely passes a day without bathing; and such as desire to attract the particular regard and esteem of the public, by the strict observance of their customs, practice it three times every day.

It is the general practice of the Hindûs to rub their head and body well with oil before they bathe; and they remove the grease by applying the juice of certain plants, and then having warm water poured over all their body. This last ceremony is never omitted with regard to the dead, before they are taken to the grave or the pile; and it belongs to the nearest relations to perform it.

CHAPTER IV

OF THE INTERIOR DEFILEMENT OF THE BODY; OF THE ABSTINENCE OF THE BRÂHMANS, AND THE PARTICULAR HORROR OF THE HINDÛS FOR THE FLESH OF THE COW.

Besides the external pollution which goes no deeper than the skin, the Brâhmans and the greater part of the Hindûs admit another sort which penetrates into the body, and exists there until it is removed by some remedy adequate to that effect. It is difficult to dispute that there is some foundation for their notions on this subject of inward uncleanness. The excessive perspiration of some, and the sort of diseases which many others are affected with, appear distinctly to shew that, from some cause inherent in warm climates, or in the nature of the bodies of those that inhabit them, the blood of most of them is impure. The Brâhmans, setting out upon this principle, have restricted themselves to certain practices by which they pretend that the body is defended from impurities, many of which are caught by infection. The attention to be paid to this consideration is therefore not without foundation, although they have strayed beyond it in an infinite number of silly observances which common sense derides.

Water is the ordinary drink of the Brâhmans. It must be drawn and carried with care, and by none but persons of the caste. To drink what had been drawn or carried by Śûdras would be considered an extraordinary offence, and would cause an internal taint, requiring much time and many ceremonies to purge. Yet in many cases the Brâhmans and Śûdras are obliged to draw their water from the same well. They must be careful, however, that the pitcher of the one does not touch that of the other; for if they should come into contact, the Brâhman would infallibly be obliged to break his, if an earthen one, or if made of metal, to have it well scoured with sand and water. To avoid this inconvenience, the Brâhmans, wherever they are supported, interdict the Śûdras from approaching their wells. This prohibition is still more strongly enforced on the Pariahs, who, when hard pressed for water, are seen bringing their pitchers half way and entreating the Śûdras to give them a supply. Where the Mahometans bear sway, indeed, it is common to see Brâhman, Śûdra, and Pariah all drawing from the same well, regardless of all distinctions. Nor are they much better observed in some European provinces, though I myself can bear witness to an insurrection occasioned by a Pariah woman who irregularly ventured to draw water at the common well.

There is a kind of beverage very prevalent and in great request in India, which is a preparation of curds beat down in water. It is thought to be a wholesome and refreshing drink even although the makers and venders are Śûdras, and that it is often no better than water with a slight dash of white. The Brâhmans drink it greedily, and when reproached for swallowing, without scruple, water brought by Sûdras, they assert in their vindication that the mixture of curd, the product of the cow, purifies the whole. Thus, where their convenience is concerned, they are at no loss to discover a justification.

But they have a great aversion to a liquor called *Kaḷḷu* in Tamul, which is drawn by incision from the cocoa, palm, and some other species of trees. It is sweet and refreshing when newly extracted from the tree, but when drank to excess it inebriates. By distillation, it is converted into a sort of brandy, which is no less prohibited by the Brâhmans and all other good castes than the Caḷḷu itself. All intoxicating liquors occasion internal uncleanness which requires a great number of ceremonies to efface.

Drunkenness is in general very much detested among the Hindûs. A notorious drunkard cannot escape with a gentler punishment than the degrading infamy of being expelled from his caste. There are scarcely any but the vile Pariahs who drink such liquors openly ; and their conduct in this only adds to the universal contempt in which they are held. Some Brâhmans, however, it must be confessed, especially in the European establishments, exceed a little on this score; but they take all possible precautions to keep secret so enormous a breach of their customs.

The air one breathes may also communicate inward uncleanness in certain cases. This would decidedly happen if some whiffs of smoke should reach a Brâhman from a funeral pile where a body is consuming.

In some districts the Pariahs are obliged to make a long circuit when they perceive any Brâhmans in the way, that their breath may not infect them or even their shadow fall upon them as they pass. The Sûdras are obliged to keep at a certain distance when they speak to them, and even then they are bound in good manners to hold their hands, over their mouths to prevent their breath from being offensive.

But the most striking example of the pains taken by the Brâhmans to avoid internal defilement, is the abstinence from Meat, which they all profess. This is to be understood not as relating to all living creatures merely, but to whatever has had the animating principle, such as eggs of all kinds, from which they are as much restricted as from flesh.[i] They have also retrenched from their vegetable food,

[i] In books in all the Vernaculars of India abstinence from the use of animal food is insisted upon, with a vehemence which attests the difficulty which is felt in enforcing it.

In the Tamil *Kural*, chapter xxvi, there are ten couplets in which the poet, deserted I must say by his muse, urges the duty of abstinence from eating any thing that has had life.

The last verse is :

" *Kollân pulâlai marruttânai kaikûppi,*
Ellâ uyirum Torum."

Every living thing will worship with folded hands the man who kills not and eats not flesh !

which is the great fund of their subsistence, all roots which form a head or bulb in the ground, such as onions; and those also which assume the same shape above ground, like mushrooms and some others.[j] Or, are we to suppose, that they had discovered something unwholesome in the one species, and proscribed the other on account of its fetid smell? This I cannot decide, all the information I have ever obtained from those amongst them whom I have consulted on the reasons of their abstinence from them, being, that it is customary to avoid such articles, together with all those that have had the germ of the living principle. This is what is called in India, *to eat becomingly*. Such as use the prohibited articles cannot boast of their bodies being pure, according to the estimate of the Brâhmans. I am aware that, amongst these also, some secret infractions of the rule have occurred; but the secrecy with which it is violated proves that it is generally observed; and it may be fairly assumed that the great body of the Brâhmans rigidly abstain from all sorts of animal food, as well as from whatever has had the principle of vitality.

The history of the world furnishes no example of abstinence so long persisted in as in the case of the Brâhmans, and so religiously and universally observed. This practice, followed by the noblest part of a great nation, by people living in this manner with their wives and children, without ever forming a thought of departing from it in the most grievous diseases, has probably endured amongst them several thousands of years, affording in my judgment a convincing proof of their great antiquity. I conceive it to be the continuation of the life which men led before the flood; in those times when the juices of the earth had not yet suffered any change, and the nourishing herbs and succulent fruits yielded all the nourishment that was required. Men, in that era, even after their corruption, still gave proofs of some remains of their pristine innocence and of the gentleness of their original nature, by the horror which they so long kept up at the shedding of blood. And, in all probability it was the forbearance from every living thing, and the simple use of the vegetable productions, that contributed in part to the long life of the primitive patriarchs. It was not till after the flood, that men, grown more cruel and voracious, or perhaps no longer finding in the fruits of the earth the same nourishing properties they had formerly possessed, fell into the habit of shedding blood, committing murder, and covering their tables with dead carcases.

The Brâhmans, or those rather from whom they derive their origin, separating in good time from the rest of the original descendants of Noah, before the practice of eating flesh had become common, adhered to the first practice of their fathers, and transmitted to their posterity that dread of the effusion of blood[k] which was common to all men before the deluge, and which the Brâhmans alone have kept

---

[j] Manu, Chap. V. 5.

[k] Comp. Manu, Chap. V.

up unaltered even to our times. Is it *their* nature that has degenerated, or is it *ours?*

So far from our having any reason to believe that this rigorous abstinence of the Brâhmans has declined or is falling into disuse, we see that, even amongst the Śûdras, the better classes following the same custom; and the observance of it raises them in the estimation of the public. It is said of persons, when one intends to do them honour, that they are *people who abstain from meat;* and those who aspire, through this practice, to inward purity, are also remarked to become more attentive to their exterior cleanliness by more frequently bathing and wearing more decent attire.

This abstinence, universal among the Brâhmans, and which has for its constituent principle interior purity, is still maintained, as we have already remarked, by those Hindûs who are particularly addicted to the worship of Śiva. No person who wears the Lingam must eat any thing that has had vitality. But as, with all this care about inward purity, the Lingamites are remarked for external slovenliness, they lose on one side what they gain on the other, and their abstinence does not raise them above the other Hindûs who eat meat without scruple. It is a particular reproach to the Lingamites that they do not enforce those proper precautions regarding cleanliness, which in warm climates are no less conducive to health than to purity.

The practice of *eating as is becoming,* as the Hindûs express it, by abstaining from whatever has had life, imparts to those who observe it a sensibility of smell by which they can distinguish the fetid odour of persons who have ate flesh four-and-twenty hours before. This is a fact which I have often witnessed, and which may probably be owing in part to the great perspiration which the heat of the climate produces.

In some castes, they make a curious distinction with regard to abstinence from animal food, by permitting it to the men and denying it to the women.

It is owing in a great measure to the notion of considering as impure those who eat of animal food, that the separation between the *Pariahs* and the other castes has become so extremely wide. They will eat not only animals killed on purpose, but also such as die naturally. Oxen and buffaloes which perish from old age or disease belong to them of right, and they carry home and greedily devour the tainted carrion which they find on the highways and in the fields.

To kill an ox or a cow is considered by the Hindûs as an inexpiable crime, and to eat their flesh as a taint that can never be effaced. The disgust which they all have for such a species of food is so great that the mere proposal of such a thing would excite many to sickness; and there is absolutely no instance of a native of any caste, except the Pariahs, who has ever shewn the desire to taste it.

This rigorous prohibition to kill cows, oxen, and buffaloes, and to feed on their flesh, may proceed in a great degree from superstition, on the idea that all these animals, particularly the cow, are divinities. I believe, however, that its true origin is a motive more powerful in its influence upon the human mind than any that flow from religion itself, I mean interest. The early legislators well knew the extreme value of those animals, in a country where every thing they yielded, even to the dung, serves for the use of man; where there is no other resource for the labours of agriculture, for the carriage of goods and other merchandise from one place to another, and for many other services indispensable to civilized life. But, on the other hand, what would become of the poor inhabitants, who feed only on insipid vegetables, if they were deprived of the rich and wholesome nourishment derived from the teats of the cow? What then might happen if the number of these animals, in other respects so difficult to keep up in the country, should be daily diminished by putting their lives at the discretion of a race which, in all its actions, conducts itself uniformly without reflection, and never thinks of any thing beyond its immediate wants and desires; a people regardless of any evils to which they may be subject to-morrow by the abuse of what they enjoyed to-day?

Another motive not less powerful than those we have mentioned, and which no doubt has also contributed to proscribe this species of food, is the desire of preserving health. It is certain that beef is an aliment too rich and heavy in warm climates, especially for the feeble stomachs of the natives. The custom of eating it would speedily have ruined their health. I know Europeans who, having been accustomed to make it the chief part of their food when in Europe, abstained from it wholly when they came to India, from observing that as often as they fed upon it they were tormented with indigestion.

These observations, and perhaps many more of the same nature, probably occurred to the penetration of those who gave laws to India. On the other hand they knew too well the character of the people to whose discretion they committed the life of the most useful, of the most precious of animals. They knew further that a prohibition would soon be forgotten or violated unless founded on supernatural authority; and so many motives concurring to require their preservation, they made them deities, that a man who slew them might be held as a sacrilegious monster, and he who ate of their flesh should be tainted with pollution not to be effaced.

To kill a cow is a crime which the Hindû laws punish with death. The Pariahs can eat only of the flesh of such of those animals as die naturally. This is not visited upon them as a crime, but they are considered to be wretches as filthy and disgusting as their food is revolting. Indeed the virtuous feeling of indignation is carried to excess against them: but it is the natural disposition of the Hindûs to do nothing of any sort in moderation. There are, however, some epidemic maladies, chiefly cutaneous, which I have often seen effecting the Pariahs exclusively, while their neighbours the Sûdras were exempt from them; which seems to corroborate the opinion that the blood of the former is corrupted by the unwholesome and disgusting food which they use; and this justifies in some degree the treatment which they receive from the other tribes.

What has contributed to render the European name hateful to the Hindûs, and indeed to sink it in their private thoughts beneath the Pariahs themselves, is the use which they undisguisedly make of the flesh of the cow to satiate their gluttony. I am not at all surprised that the first European invaders who penetrated into India should have shewn so little regard for the most sacred and most universally established prejudices of that people, because they were not then aware of their origin and motive. But I am really astonished that the behaviour of the Europeans, when, upon first setting their feet on the boundary of India, they began to slaughter the oxen and the cows, did not excite an universal insurrection, or that one single man of the sacrilegious invaders escaped the indignation which must have burned in the breasts of the Hindûs, on the murder of those sacred creatures, whom they rank in the number of their principal divinities.

So enormous a sacrilege, such positive deicide, would have been ample motive with any other nation to exterminate every individual who was concerned in it, and to render for ever execrable the memory of a people that would thus sport with the lives of creatures who stand amongst the dearest objects of their worship. The forbearance and patience of the Hindûs, who have seen, for upwards of three hundred years, a handful of Europeans established amongst them, sacrificing every day to their voracious appetites the divinities whom they adore, will paint the gentle, the soft, the lenient character of these people more vividly than the pencil of the most eloquent historian.

The Egyptians and many other ancient nations have not been so patient under similar circumstances.

To purify the body from all internal defilement which it can have contracted, no remedy is accounted more efficacious than the *panchakâryam*, or five substances which proceed from the cow, and have been already mentioned. This remedy would be of indispensable necessity for one that had fallen under the last degree of uncleanness; as if, for example, a Brâhman, under any circumstances that could exist, had drank water that had been drawn by a Śûdra.

As to ordinary stains, from which no care can at all times defend the most wary, there are many modes of removing them, which I shall by and by describe; and if they have the virtue to purify the soul, how much more efficacious must they be when applied to the stains of the body?

CHAPTER V.

ON THE DEFILEMENT OF THE SOUL, AND THE REMEDIES USED TO EFFACE IT.

It is a doctrine taught in Hindû books, maintained by the philosophers of that nation, and even sometimes promulgated by the Brâhmans, that the principal, and indeed the only pollution of the soul proceeds from Sin; and that it is the perverseness of the Will that is the cause of it. One of their poets, Vêmana, expresses himself in this manner: "it is the water that brings the mud; and it is the water that washes it away: the will is the cause of sin; and the will alone must remove it."[1] Such a doctrine as this, however badly followed up in practice, proves at least that the Hindûs are not ignorant that the change of the will is an essential condition for obtaining the remission of sins and purifying the soul.

But the lights of nature which reason will never suffer to be wholly extinguished, even in the thickest darkness of gross idolatry, have been much obscured by the passions to which the Brâhmans have become enslaved. These have persuaded them that, without renouncing sin and giving it up from the heart, there is a way of purifying the soul by divers remedies, which, from their extreme facility, are calculated only to diminish the abhorrence of it, and to lull the guilty in fatal security. The *Panchakâryam*, which we have already noticed, serves for the "*remission of all sins committed with a perfect knowledge.*" These are the express words of a Brâhman author. The remedy would appear to us to be of a disgusting nature; but the Hindûs think otherwise, and both recommend and practise the frequent use of it, without shewing any repugnance.

As they consider sin under the notion of an impurity of the soul, it is not wonderful that they should have thought bathing the proper means of purifying it. There are certain places of bathing which have the most complete efficacy. Those who wash their bodies in the Ganges, the Indus, the Câvêry, the Krishna, and some other rivers, whose waters are sanctified by superstition, restore the soul and the body from all sins and corruptions which they may have contracted. Even the distance of those rivers may be obviated, and their benefits obtained without stirring from home; it being quite enough to direct your imagination to their waters, and to think of them while you are performing your purifying ablutions.

---

[1] This is not to be found among the verses of *Vêmana*. But any Telugu verse of which the author is unknown is ascribed to him. In the *Kuraḷ* we find this couplet.

Manattukaṇ mâçilaṇ âdal! anaitt'arran; âgula nîra pirra.

"Be pure in heart! This much is virtue. All else is empty noise."

There are also a great many springs and pools consecrated by superstition, and much renowned for the spiritual effects which they communicate to those who bathe in them. In some of them it is only every twelve years that remission of sin can be found. Such is the case with the lake of *Kumbhakônam* in Tanjore. Some have this virtue every third year. Of this kind is the stream that runs from the mountain of *Tîrtha-malai* in the Carnatic. There are still many other privileged spots which possess a periodical virtue for purifying soul and body from uncleanness.

When the year and the day arrive for bathing in those sacred waters, a crowd of people almost without number, who have been previously apprised of it by messengers sent to all parts by the Brâhmans, who are interested in propagating the superstition, assemble as pilgrims, and arrange themselves all round the water at the happy time. They wait for the favourable hour and moment of the day; and on the instant of the astrologer's announcing it, all—men, women, children, plunge into the water at once, and with an uproar that is not to be imagined. In the midst of the confusion some are drowned, some suffocated, and still more meet with dislocated limbs. But the fate of those who lose their lives is rather envied than deplored. They are considered as martyrs of their zeal; and this happy death lets them pass immediately into the abode of bliss, without being obliged to undergo another life upon earth.

The period of an Eclipse is also a privileged time for washing away the impurity of the soul. Wherever the bathing takes place, it is effectual at that time; but particularly when made in the sea. When performed at the solstices, or the equinox, on the eleventh day of the moon, and some other particular epochs, the virtue is also great. The disemboguement of one river, or the confluence of two are likewise considered very favourable situations. But it would be altogether endless to pursue this subject.

The Mantras, the mere sight of great men, particularly of Gurus, the thinking upon Vishṇu, are not less effectual than bathings for cleansing the soul. Pilgrimage to certain temples or other places, become famous by the superstition of the country, the mere view of the summit of very high mountains, will procure the pardon of sin. One of these privileged mountains exists in the district of Coimbatore in the Carnatic, called *Nîlagiri-malai,* which is supposed to be the loftiest in the province;[m] and, upon that ground alone, the Hindûs, whose principle it is to deify whatever is extraordinary in nature, have converted it into a sacred place. The access to the summit being very difficult, the mere sight of it, which may be had at a great distance, is sufficient to effect the forgiveness of sins in those who visit it with the intention of obtaining this favour. And the visits to it are therefore not unfrequent.

---

m The Nilagiris have become well known since the Abbé wrote. It is now ascertained that the Doḍḍa beṭṭa (great hill) is the highest peak in Southern India. It is 7,850 feet above the level of the Sea.

A Brâhman once, after pursuing a dog four times round a temple of Śiva, killed him with one stroke of his cudgel at the gate of the temple; and for this achievement he obtained the pardon of all his sins, and the distinguished honours of being transported to the *Kâilasa* or Paradise of Śiva. Admission into the *Vaikuṇṭha* or Paradise of Vishṇu, was granted to a great sinner for pronouncing, though in a blasphemous way, the name of *Nârâyaṇa,* one of the appellations of Vishṇu.

All these anecdotes are taken from Indian books. But, even through the thick darkness with which idolatry has overspread the mind of the Hindûs, we may discern a ray distinctly pointing to the fall and corruption of human nature, and the necessity of some remedy for repairing its errors and restoring it to its original state.

Besides the sins committed in his present life, which a Brâhman has to atone for as far as he is able, he must also attend to the expiation of those which he had committed in preceding lives. To be born a Brâhman is no doubt the most blessed of all regenerations, and is bestowed only on the accumulated merit of a long course of good deeds performed in preceding states of existence. But a new birth is itself a proof that some faults remained unexpiated, else the soul would have been transported at once to the residence of bliss, and delivered from the punishment of revolving from one generation to another.

Good works, such as giving alms to the Brâhmans, erecting places of hospitality on the highways, building temples, contributing to the expences of worship, digging tanks, and many other meritorious acts of charity, when united to the various remedies already described, greatly enhance their efficacy, and contribute exceedingly to the cleansing of the soul from recent stains, as well as from those which have adhered to it from its former existence.

I will not say any thing here of the obstacles which the soul continually experiences in its progress towards purification, from its family connection, its caste, perverse disposition, and many other sources of sin which occur in the course of life: but I will return to the subject hereafter.

CHAPTER VI.

CONJECTURES RESPECTING THE ORIGIN OF THE RITES OF THE BRÂHMANS CONCERNING UNCLEANNESS AND PURITY.

THE conduct and the manner of thinking of the Hindûs respecting uncleanness and the means of purification, are so different from any thing to be seen in other nations, that it would be very desirable if we could discover some evidence to enable us to discern with certainty what has given rise to those rules of conduct which they so invariably pursue. Something approaching to their customs is perceivable in several parts of the books of the Old Testament; in the conduct of Jacob, for example, who, in proceeding to offer sacrifice to God, at Bethel, commanded his family to "be clean and change their garments;"* in the aversion of the Egyptians for shepherds,† in their hatred of strangers; and above all in the law prescribed to the children of Israel, through Moses, which directs them in the course to be followed with regard to several real and formal impurities.‡ The rules on this subject, minutely laid down in Leviticus, are in many respects the same with those which are now in full vigour among the Brâhmans.

The learned, I believe, agree almost unanimously that Moses, in prescribing laws on this subject to the people of God, did no more than to regulate and fix the notions of the Jews on many points already established and observed. I suspect, even, that by the rules which he laid down on the subject of different sorts of uncleanness, he sought to moderate the excess which they ran into in such matters in Egypt, as well as in most parts of Asia. In after times the Israelites did not confine themselves to the instructions laid down by their holy legislator; but, as far as appears, exceeded his rules; and probably it is from their extreme eagerness in this respect, acquired in Egypt, that many of the practices of the Jews of the present day have been deduced, for which there is no authority in their own ancient law.

Although, in comparing the rules of the one with those of the other, many of the Jewish rites correspond with those of the Brâhmans; yet, in many others, the difference and even the opposition is so striking, as to make it impossible that the one could have proceeded from the other by any communication. And as I have never seen any thing in the history of the Egyptians and Jews that could induce me to believe that either of these nations or any other on the face of

---

* Gen. xxxv. 2. † Gen. xlvi. 34. ‡ Levit. v. xi. xii. xiii. xiv. xv.

the earth, have been established earlier than the Hindûs and particularly the Brâhmans; so I cannot be induced to believe that the latter have drawn their rites from foreign nations. On the contrary, I infer that they have drawn them from an original source of their own. Whoever knows any thing of the spirit and character of the Brâhmans, their stateliness, their pride and extreme vanity, their distance, and sovereign contempt for every thing that is foreign, and of which they cannot boast to have been the inventors, will agree with me that such a people cannot have consented to draw their customs and rules of conduct from an alien country.

But if it is not by communication with other nations, as old as themselves, that the Hindûs have acquired customs and rules which subsist among them to the present day, and unite them indissolubly in a national mass, from what source do they derive them?

On so obscure a subject we can only offer conjectures; and mine, I hope, will not be wide of probability.

Even before the flood, men distinguished, in the sacrifices which they offered to God, between clean animals and unclean; things that were pure and things that were impure. The Lord approved that distinction, and commanded Noah and his children to observe it when they introduced the various living creatures into the ark. (Gen. chap. vii.) And, although God after the deluge, authorized the human race, who had been, up to that epoch, nourished by the simple productions of the soil, to use thenceforth more solid food, by substituting the flesh of animals, which were then solemnly submitted to the dominion of man (Gen. chap. ix.); it is nevertheless probable that this distinction between clean and unclean animals, and things pure and impure, remained long engraven on the minds of the first men who lived after the flood. Their impressions on this subject were probably deepened by the ordinance of God which allowed them to eat the flesh of the living creatures, but forbade them expressly to taste their blood. (Gen. chap. ix. 4.) At any rate, it appears beyond all doubt that the notions about defilement, founded on the distinction between things clean and unclean, existed before the deluge. It is probable, therefore, that the practices of the Hindûs upon pollution and purity proceed from that original source, and that their tenets on this subject were transmitted to them, at least in part, by their first legislators, who lived soon after the flood.

It is well known that many other ancient nations, in common with the Hindûs, entertain those opinions respecting bodily and spiritual uncleanness, and, like them, have recourse to water or fire, and sometimes to both, for purification. While the people of India were consecrating the memory of the Ganges and the Indus, the waters of the *Phasis* were also regarded as having the virtue to purify the body and the soul from all uncleanness, not only by the inhabitants of Colchis or Mingrelia, but by all who sailed to the mouth of that river; and the Egyptians attributed the same quality to the Nile.

When the Flood was but lately gone by, and mankind still formed but one people, they would naturally turn their attention to the means of preserving health. Cleanliness would at once strike them as serviceable in this respect; and as they could not then procure it by a frequent change of clothing, they would have recourse to the constant use of the bath. In spite of this, diseases would be more common than they had ever been before the deluge, as every thing in nature had degenerated. It would be remarked that many of those diseases were occasioned by the improper food which they took. This would accordingly be proscribed as impure. Many remarks on the subject would occur, some good and others bad, which would spread, and lead to conclusions respecting what was useful and what pernicious, and to distinctions between the clean and the unclean. Nevertheless, in such times, when medicine, like every other science, was in its cradle, it is probable that cleanliness and the bath would long continue to be the universal remedy for all evil, and every species of corporeal impurity.

But, being compelled to separate, and to spread population over the various countries of the earth, they carried with them, under their different leaders, the arts necessary for society, with the customs already established with a view to the preservation of health. The warmth of the climate of India, which probably was one of the first countries inhabited, would incline its original colonists to make strict regulations for the exact observance of the necessary practices. Among the new race, or their immediate successors, men would arise, having authority, but superstitious and extravagant in their notions, who would carry much farther than their ancestors had done, the notions respecting filth and purity. Observing, at the same time, that in the country which had fallen to their lot, every thing tended to carelessness and hurtful indifference, they established severe laws upon the minutest observances. But in their wish to promote the good of the people and prevent a fatal decline, they plunged them into an abyss of error, which has been rendered impassable by the absurd imaginations of their poets.

At the same time, if we have good reason to reproach the Brâhmans with their outrageous strictness in point of purity; are they to be condemned, on the other hand, for manifesting horror at the excessive beastliness of many of the Europeans who come in their way? What ought they to think on seeing the disgusting appearance of those who compose the crews of our ships, or when they observe our soldiers, when not on duty, drunk perhaps, and deprived of reason, rolling in the dirt in presence of the multitude, and scarcely retaining the appearance of men?

CHAPTER VII.

OF MARRIAGE AMONG THE BRÂHMANS.

MARRIAGE is to an Hindû the great, the most essential of all objects; that of which he speaks the most and looks forward to from the remotest distance. A man who is not married is considered to be a person without establishment, and almost as a useless member of society. Until he arrives at this state he is consulted on no great affairs, nor employed on any important trust. In short, he is looked upon as a man out of the pale of nature. A Brâhman who becomes a widower is likewise held to have fallen from his station; and nothing is more urgent upon him than to resume the marriage state.

The case is quite different with respect to Widows. It never enters into their view to procure a new establishment, even when they lose their husbands at the age of six or seven: for it is not rare to see widows no older, particularly among the Brâhmans (as has been already mentioned) where an old man of sixty or upwards takes for his second wife a child of that tender age. Their prejudices, however, on this subject, have taken such firm root in their minds, that the bare mention of remarrying these young widows would be considered by their relations and by themselves as the greatest of insults. Yet they are despised through all India. The very name of widow is a reproach; and the greatest possible calamity that can befal a woman is to survive her husband; although to marry with another would be held a thousand times more to be dreaded. From that moment she would be hunted out of society, and no decent person would venture at any time to have the slightest intercourse with her.

Though Marriage be considered the natural condition of man, yet Celibacy is not unknown in India. It is even a state respected; and those of their Sannyâsis who are known to lead their lives in perfect celibacy, receive, on that account, marks of distinguished honour and respect. But this condition cannot be embraced excepting by those who devote themselves to a life of seclusion from the world, and of perpetual contemplation, such as that class of enthusiasts do; or by such as are bound by their profession to discharge the duties of religion towards their neighbours, such as the Gurus. The Hindûs seem to have felt that the duties of Penitent and Guru were incompatible with those of the master of a family, and that a man ought to be free from the embarrassment and anxiety of one of these stations to be fully able to acquit himself properly of the other. This was perhaps the chief reason for allowing the Sannyâsis and the greater part of the Gurus to live in a single state.

The greater number, however, are bachelors only in name. No virtue is less familiar to them than chastity. It is publicly known that they keep women, and commit breaches of that virtue which they profess, that would disgrace the most profane. But their sacred title of Sannyâsi or Guru raises them above the attacks of the wicked; and such human failings, if not carried to great excess, scarcely diminish the outward reverence and respect which they receive from the silly vulgar.

At the same time, I cannot but believe that the small number of real Sannyâsis or Penitents who are still found living in woods and deserts, wholly retired from the world, and who, through vanity or fanaticism, condemn themselves to all sorts of privations, and inure their bodies to the harshest austerities, actually live in celibacy and altogether unconnected with women. The severe life which they lead scarcely allows the body to war against the spirit. But, as far as concerns the Gurus and Sannyâsis, who scour the country to live on the public credulity, or those who shut themselves up in a sort of monasteries and lead a lazy and voluptuous life, with no other occupation than that of receiving the presents and offerings which their numerous votaries, deceived by their false reputation for sanctity, bring to them from all quarters; such men are to be considered as mere impostors, knaves, who abuse the credulous populace, under the guise of celibacy, while they are revelling in every species of luxury. All that I have heard from various persons who have lived in their service as domestics, and have been admitted to familiar intercourse with them, confirms me in the opinion which I have always entertained, that nothing is more foreign to them than that virtue which they chiefly affect.

Although the state of celibacy be allowed to those who devote themselves to a life of contemplation, it is not so with regard to any class of women. They cannot profess virginity, however much they may be attached to that condition. In ancient times, however, it seems to have been known among the Hindûs; as frequent mention is made in their books of the *five celebrated Virgins*, who are almost as famous as the seven celebrated *Rishi*. The Hindû authors speak in lofty terms of commendation of the care with which they preserved themselves spotless, and of the inflexible firmness with which they resisted the solicitations of some powerful seducers, who used every means to overcome them. Even the most powerful of the gods tried to corrupt them, and were foiled. Many other particulars of these five virgins may be found in the *Bhâgavata* and some other Hindû books.

Now, however, it is not permitted to women to embrace this holy profession. The state of subjection and servitude in which they are held in India cannot admit of their following any employment which would make them independent and place them beyond the power of the men. It is an established national rule that women are designed for no other end than to be subservient to the wants and pleasures of the males. Accordingly, all females without exception, are obliged to marry when husbands can be found for them. They always try to bring it about before they become really marriageable;

and those who arrive at that period without finding a husband, seldom preserve their innocence long. Constant experience proves that Hindû girls have neither sufficient firmness nor discretion to resist, for any length of time, the solicitations of a seducer; which is no doubt a strong reason for disposing of them in marriage so soon.

Those who cannot find a husband fall into the state of concubinage with those who chuse to keep them, or secretly indulge in those enjoyments which, if known, would expose them to shame.

I have taken great pains to learn what is the real spirit of Hindû jurisprudence on the subject of Polygamy, and the indissolubility of marriage; and although I have not arrived at any absolute certainty, all that I have observed appears to demonstrate that the former is prohibited and the latter established. Persons well acquainted with the usages of the country have confirmed me in this conclusion, and have assured me that if there be many instances of polygamy, particularly among the great, who are suffered to have a plurality of wives, yet it is really an abuse and an open violation of the customs of the Hindûs, amongst whom marriage has been always confined to couples; though in all places the powerful will set themselves above the law.

The custom or law in India which limits marriage to one pair has been followed by the principal divinities whom the Hindûs acknowledge. They were married but to one lawful wife. They have given *Saraswati* only, to Brahma; *Lakshmi* to Vishṇu; and *Párvati* to Śiva. *Sîtâ-dêvi*, the wife of *Râma*, was carried off by the giant *Râvaṇa;* but he did not repudiate her on that account, nor marry another wife. He went in pursuit of the ravisher, and commenced a long war against him, in which, after sustaining defeats and gaining victories, he at last subdued his enemy and regained his consort.

All these stories, and many more of the same kind which I could adduce, seem to prove that a plurality of legitimate wives was in ancient times unknown and rejected. It is clear that conjugal fidelity was not one of the attributes of those fabulous gods; but it is no less certain that they never assign to them more than one woman under the appellation of wife. Even in modern times polygamy is not tolerated; although, as we have already remarked, kings and persons of high rank are permitted to take two wives, sometimes three, and in some instances as many as five. Still, this is considered an abuse, although it is not safe to complain against authority.

Where persons in private life are seen to live with several women, they are only concubines; one only being married to him and bearing the title of wife. The children from her alone are considered legitimate. The rest are bastards; whom the law would exclude from any share of their father's property, if he died without a will.

I know of one case only where a man already married may lawfully espouse a second wife; which is, when the first, after a long cohabitation, is pronounced barren. But even in this case, the consent of the first wife is necessary, and she always continues to be considered as the man's principal wife, and as superior to the second. Neither is this second marriage conducted with half the ceremony as the former.

The indissoluble nature of marriage is also, as far as I can judge, equally well established among the Hindûs as that of the marriage of a couple of persons. A man cannot divorce his wife on any ground whatever. If there are any examples of an opposite kind, it is only amongst people of the lowest castes, or of disreputable lives; or because the previous marriage had been attended by such impediments as to render it invalid by the laws of the country. But marriages legally solemnized can never be dissolved amongst persons of a reputable caste, particularly amongst the Brâhmans.

If the husband insists on a separation from his wife on account of adultery, it can only be effected, as with us, *quoad mensam et torum;* and the marriage is not dissolved by it. The woman, after being so discarded, continues to wear the *tâhli* or symbol of marriage, and is not treated otherwise than as the lawful wife of the man from whom she is separated. He also is obliged to support her as long as she lives; and, during that time, he can have no other woman but as a concubine.

After these general remarks upon the marriage state, let us now attend to the ceremonies and pageantry which the Hindûs employ in the celebration of this solemn contract, which elevates both parties into their proper sphere, and, by connecting them with sacred and indissoluble bands, keeps up the renovation of the world. But, of the great variety of ceremonies which precede and accompany the celebration of marriage, the most important and solemn circumstance in life, we shall content ourselves with tracing the most prominent.

The father of a young *Brâhmanâri,* if he be rich and liberal, takes upon himself all the expence of the marriage of his daughter. Some divide the burthen with the father of the intended husband; but in general they take from him a considerable sum of money in return for having given him their daughter, and oblige him besides to bear the whole charge of the marriage.

To marry, or to buy a wife, are synonymous terms in this country. Almost every parent makes his daughter an article of traffic, obstinately refusing to give her up to her lawful husband until he has rigorously paid down the sum of money which he was bound for, according to the custom of the caste. This practice of purchasing the young women whom they are to marry, is the inexhaustible source of disputes and litigation, particularly amongst the poorer people. These, after the marriage is solemnized, not finding it convenient to pay the stipulated sum, the father-in-law commences an action, or more commonly recalls his daughter home, in the expectation that the desire of getting her back may stimulate the son-in-law to procure the money. This sometimes succeeds; but if the young man is incapable of satisfying the avarice of his father-in-law, he is obliged to leave his wife with him in pledge. Now, there is time for reflection; and the father-in-law, finding that the sum cannot be raised, and that his daughter from her youth is exposed to great temptations which might lead to the disgrace of all his family, relaxes a little, and takes what the son-in-law is able to pay. A reconciliation is thus effected, and the young man conducts his wife quietly home.

Men of distinction do not appropriate to their common purposes the money thus acquired by giving their daughters in marriage, but lay it out in jewels, which they present to the lady on the wedding day. These are her private property as long as she lives; and on no account can be disposed of by her husband.

In negociating a marriage, the inclinations of the future spouses are never attended to. Indeed it would be ridiculous to consult girls of that age; and accordingly the choice entirely devolves upon the parents. Those of the husband attend principally to the purity of the caste; while those of the wife are more solicitous about the fortune of the young man, and the disposition of the intended mother-in-law of their daughter.

When a man, with this view, casts his eyes on a young girl, he begins by satisfying himself through some friend, concerning the inclinations of her kindred. When he has ascertained that he is not likely to suffer the affront of a refusal, he selects a fortunate day to visit them, and to solicit her in form, carrying with him a piece of new cloth for women, a cocoa nut, five bananas, some saffron, and other articles of that nature. If he should meet upon his way any object of evil omen; if a cat, for example, or a fox, or a serpent should cross the road before him, so as to intercept his progress, he would instantly return home, and postpone the journey to a more fortunate day.

All the Hindûs have their minds so filled with these silly superstitions, that, however necessary any expedition or journey may be, they will surely defer it, if at the first outset they should be crossed by any of the creatures above mentioned. I have repeatedly seen labourers take back their cattle to their stalls, and spend the whole day in idleness, because, in setting out in the morning, they found that a serpent had crossed their road.

After the young man's father has solicited the girl, and offered the presents he takes with him, her own father defers his answer until one of those little lizards, which creep on the wall, making now and then a small shrill cry, gives a favourable augury by one of its chirps. As soon as the lizard has *spoken* (as the superstitious Hindûs express themselves) and given a favourable prognostic by its assent, the father of the girl declares that he will voluntarily bestow her in marriage on the son of him who asks her; after which a great number of ceremonies are performed, answering to our betrothment, and communicating to the future husband a right to the girl, which prevents her from being given to any other. These ceremonies are followed by an entertainment; after which a fortunate month and day are selected for the marriage, upon due consultation with the astrologer or the Purôhita.

There are, properly, but four months in the year in which marriage can be celebrated: namely, March, April, May, and June. Nuptials for the second time, may indeed be solemnized in the months of November and February; but, in these two months, so much attention must be given to the signs of the zodiac and many other matters, each more trifling than another, that it is not easy to find a day in which all the favorable circumstances combine.

The custom of restricting marriages to those four months, arises, like almost all the other customs of the Hindûs, from superstition. But I conceive that the principal motive which originally induced them to fix on those four months as a fortunate time for marrying was, that the country labours being then all closed or suspended, on account of the excessive heat, and the preceding harvest furnishing the means of supplying what the ceremony requires, they look upon that period as affording more leisure and better resources for this important concern than any other season of the year.

The ceremony of marriage lasts five days. In the course of it, all those rites are exhibited which have been described in speaking of the ceremony of the triple cincture. These we need not repeat; and such as are peculiar to the wedding festival, not being in a better taste, we shall content ourselves with mentioning the most important of them.

The bridegroom and bride are first of all placed under the *Pandal*, or alcove with twelve pillars, as formerly described. This is a common and very useful appendage to the principal houses in India, being erected before the principal door, and covered with boughs of trees, so as to shelter the house from the heat of the sun, and at the same time to afford a convenient recess for strangers who come upon any business with the owner of the house, when perhaps it is not convenient, nor even admissible, for him to enter into the dwelling.

The Pandal, being on this occasion decorated in the most superb manner, the young couple are seated under it upon the little mound of earth, with their faces turned towards the east. The married women then advance, performing before them the rites of the *Ârati*, as they have been already described.

It being desirable to render all the gods, and even the lowest of them, propitious, the whole of them are invited to the wedding, and they are besought to remain there during the whole entertainment of five days. The same prayer is preferred to the *Gods' ancestors;* and the grand fathers, whom they have seen, are entreated to seek and bring with them their more ancient progenitors, whom they themselves could not have known.

A particular sacrifice is then offered to *Brahma;* which is the more remarkable that this god, in consequence of a curse denounced against him by some penitents of former times, has no temple and no regular worship in any part of India.

I ought not to omit that, before any thing is undertaken, they take care to place under the Pandal *Vig'hnêśwara*, the god of obstacles. He is greatly honoured, as has been mentioned, because he is greatly feared. And although the extreme ugliness of his appearance has hitherto kept him without a wife, they never fail to pay him the utmost attention in all public ceremonies, lest his displeasure should cast some impediment in the way of their happy accomplishment; which is the more to be apprehended from his being so prone to take offence.

As it is necessary, in circumstances so important, that the bridegroom should be pure and exempt from all sin, he is called upon to offer a free gift, on the second day, of fourteen flags to one of the Brâhmans, in expiation of the faults he has committed since his investiture with the cord.

This act of charity is followed by a sort of interlude, which appears very absurd after the progress they have made. The bridegroom shams an eager desire to quit the country, upon a pilgrimage to Benares, to wash himself there in the sacred waters of the Ganges. He equips himself as a traveller, and being supplied with some provisions for the journey, he departs with instruments of music sounding before him, and accompanied by several of his relations and friends, in the same manner as when a person is really proceeding on that holy adventure. But no sooner has he got out of the village than, upon turning towards the east, he meets his future father-in-law, who finding the object of his expedition, stops him, and offers him his daughter in marriage, if he will desist from his journey. The pilgrim readily accepts the conditions, and they return together to the house.

After many other ceremonies, the recital of which would be tedious, they fasten on the right wrist of the young man and on the left of the girl, the *Kaṇkaṇam,* which is merely a bit of saffron; and this particular ceremony is conducted with more state and solemnity than any other during the whole course of the festival. It is succeeded by another not less remarkable. The young man being seated, with his face turned towards the east, his future father-in-law approaches, and looking steadily on his countenance, fancies that he beholds in him the great Vishṇu. With this impression, he offers to him a sacrifice; and then, making him put both his feet in a new dish filled with cow-dung, he first washes them with water, then with milk, and again with water; accompanying the whole with suitable Mantras.

This being finished, he must direct his fixed attention and thought to all the gods united; then name each of them separately, one after another, as far as the memory can serve. To this invocation of the gods, he subjoins that of the seven famous penitents, the five virgins, the ancestor gods, the seven mountains, the woods, the seas, the eight cardinal points, the fourteen worlds, the year, the season, the month, the day, the minute, and many other particulars which must likewise be named and invoked.

He then takes the hand of his daughter and puts it into that of his son-in-law, and pours water over them in honour of the great Vishṇu. This is the most solemn of all the ceremonies of the festival, being the symbol of his resigning his daughter to the authority of the young man. She must be accompanied with three gifts; namely, with a present of one or more cows, with some property in land, and finally with a *Sâlagrâma*, which consists of some little amulet stones in high esteem among the Brâhmans, worn by them as talismans and dignified even with the homage of sacrifices.

This ceremony which appears to be the foundation of the marriage, is succeeded by another but little less in importance. All married women in India wear at their necks a small ornament of gold called *Tâhli*, which is the sign of their being actually in the state of marriage. When they become widows, this ornament is removed with great form, as will be afterwards described. There is engraved upon it the figure of *Vig'hnêśwara* or *Lakshmi*, or of some other divinity in estimation with the caste; and it is fastened by a short string dyed yellow with saffron, composed of one hundred and eight threads of great fineness. Before tying it round the neck of the bride, she is made to sit down by the side of her husband; and, after some slight preliminary ceremonies, ten Brâhmans make a partition with a curtain of silk, which they extend, from one to another, between them and the wedded pair, whilst the rest are reciting the Mantras, and invoking *Brahma* with *Saraswati*, *Vishṇu* with *Lakshmi*, *Śiva* with *Parvati;* and several more; always coupling each god with his consort. The ornament is now brought in to be fastened to the neck of the bride. It is presented on a salver neatly decked and garnished with sweet smelling flowers. Incense is offered to it, and it is presented to the assistants, each of whom touches it and invokes blessings upon it. The bride then turning towards the east, the bridegroom takes the *Tâhli*, and, reciting a mantram aloud, binds it round her neck.

Fire is then brought in, upon which the bridegroom offers up the sacrifice of the *Hômam;* and, taking his bride by the hand, they walk thrice round the fire while the incense is blazing.

Last of all, he lays hold of her ankle with his right hand, and brings it into contact with a little stone which he holds in his left, and which is called the stone of *Sandal*, doubtless because it is a kind of paste formed out of that odoriferous wood. In going through this ceremony, the bridegroom must have his thoughts fixed on *the Great Mountain of the North*, the native place of the ancestors of the Brâhmans.

The meaning of the ceremony we have described is not difficult to divine. By the preceding one, we see the surrender of the girl to her intended husband by her father. Here, the acceptance of her is signified by the bridegroom binding the *tâhli* round the neck of the bride. The *Hômam* and the three circuits which the young couple make around the fire, indicate the ratification of a mutual engagement between them, as there is nothing more solemn than what is transacted over this element; which, among the Hindûs, is the most pure of the deities, and therefore the fittest of all others to ratify the solemn oaths of which it is the most faithful memorial.

We have now gone through the principal ceremonials appertaining to marriage, with the omission of not a few of smaller importance. But perhaps we ought to subjoin the following one, which is considered by some to rank as high as the preceding.

Two baskets, made of bamboo, are placed close together; this species of wood being preferred, on account of its being thought more pure and less subject to be defiled by handling. The new married pair go each into one of the baskets, standing upright. Two other baskets are brought, filled with ground rice. The husband takes up one with both hands and pours what it contains over the head of his spouse. She does the like to him in her turn. They repeat this till they are weary, or till they are admonished that it is enough.

In other castes, it is the assistants that sprinkle the heads of the new married couple; and perhaps it signifies only the abundance of temporal blessings which are implored on their behalf. It was practised in other nations with corn; and it still, in some measure, exists among the Jews. In the marriage of great princes, pearls are sometimes used in place of rice or corn.

On the evening of the third day, when the constellations appear, the Purôhita, or astrologer, points out to the new married pair a very small star, close to the middle one in the tail of *Ursa Major*, and directs them both to pay it obeisance; for it is *Arundhati*, he says, the wife of *Vaśistha*, one of the seven famous Ascetics.

Next day, before dinner, the bride rubs the legs of her husband with saffron water; and then he rubs hers in the same manner. I know not the meaning of this ceremony, or indeed whether it has any. Ceremonies of some kind the Brâhmans must have; and they appear to have found nothing more serious than this to fill up the present interval.

While the assembled guests are dining, the bridegroom and bride also partake, and eat together from the same plate. This is a token of the closest union; and two persons the most intimately connected cannot shew a more evident mark of their friendship than this. Well may the woman now continue to eat what her husband leaves, and after he has done; for they will never sit down again to a meal together. That is never permitted but at the wedding feast.

On the last day, a ceremony is practised remarkable for its singularity. When the husband offers the sacrifice of the *Hômam*, and when, in the usual form, he is casting into the fire the boiled rice sprinkled with melted butter, the bride approaches and does the same on her part with rice that has been parched. This is the only instance that I know where a woman may take part in this sacrifice, which is the most sacred and solemn of all, excepting the *Yajna.*

All these ceremonies, with many others which it would be tedious to detail, being concluded, a procession is made through the streets of the village. It commonly takes place in the night, by the light of torches and fire-works. The new married pair are seated in one palanquin, with their faces towards each other. They are both highly dressed out; but the bride in particular is generally covered over with jewels and precious stones, partly the gifts of her father and father-in-law; but the greater part are borrowed for the occasion.

The procession moves slowly; and their relations and friends come out of their houses, as they pass; the women hailing the new married parties with the ceremony of the *Ârati*, and the men with presents of silver, fruits, sugar, and betel. Those who receive such presents are obliged, under the like circumstances, to repay them in their turn. I have sometimes seen these marriage processions truly magnificent, though in a style so extremely remote from ours.

Thus ends the solemnity of marriage among the Hindûs. The pomp which attends their elevation to this state shews the importance which they attach to it, and also the respect which they entertain, or at least once entertained, for the sacred bands which inseparably unite the husband and the wife.

I will say nothing of the entertainments mutually given by the relations of the two parties after their marriage. Those by whom they are given, and the ceremonies which accompany them, differ so little from what I have already described, in speaking of the admission to the *Triple Cord*, that I forbear to repeat them. But there is one thing well deserving of remark; that, amongst the almost infinite variety of ceremonies made use of on the occasion of marriage, there is not one that borders on indecency, or has the slightest allusion to an immodest thought. This is particularly to be noticed amongst a people, who in all other circumstances of life, where feasts and shews occur, make a merit of openly and unreservedly violating the rules of modesty and decorum.

The marriage festival being over, the young spouse is taken back to her father's house, which continues to be her principal abode until she has grown up into a state fit to discharge all the duties of matrimony. This epoch is a new occasion for joy and feasting. The relations attend to celebrate it in the same manner as the marriage, and the greater part of the ceremonies then practised are now repeated. It is notified to the father and mother of the young man that their daughter-in-law has now become a woman, and is qualified to live with her husband. Then, after completing the ceremonies to which this occasion gives rise, she is conducted in triumph to the house of her father-in-law, where she is detained for a while to accustom her to the society of her husband; and after a month or two her own parents return and take her home with them.

The residence of the young woman is thus, for the first and even the second year, divided between the house of her husband and that of her father. This is accounted a mark of good understanding subsisting among them. It is, however, a concord, which most probably, alas! will too soon be dissolved; when this same young wife, beaten by her husband and harassed by her mother-in-law, who treats her as a slave, shall find no remedy for ill usage but in flying to her father's house. She will be recalled by fair promises of kinder treatment. They will break their word; and she will have recourse to the same remedy. But at last, the children which she brings into the world, and other circumstances, will compel her to do her best, by remaining in her husband's house, with the shew of being contented with her lot

In general, concord, the union of minds, and sincere mutual friendship are rarely found in Hindû families. The extreme distance kept up between the two sexes, which makes the women absolutely passive in society, and subject to the will and even the caprices of the men has accustomed these lords of their destiny to regard them as slaves, and to treat them on all occasions with severity and contempt. It is therefore in vain to expect, between husband and wife, that reciprocal confidence and kindness which constitute the happiness of a family. The object for which a Hindû marries is not to gain a companion to aid him in enduring the evils of life, but a slave to bear children and be subservient to his rule.

CHAPTER VIII.

OF THE SECOND DEGREE OF BRÂHMANS; THAT OF GRIHASTHA, AND THE DUTIES WHICH IT IMPOSES.

THE second state of a Brâhman is that of *Grihastha;* a name given to those only who are married and have children. A young Brâhman, upon his marriage, ceases indeed to be a Brâhmachâri; but neither is he considered to be a true *Grihastha,* while his wife, on account of tender age, remains with her parents. The Grihasthas compose the body of the caste, maintain its rights, and settle the disputes which arise. It belongs to them also to watch over the observance of the Brâhmanical rules, and to recommend the practice of them by their precept and example.

A Grihastha Brâhman should rise in the morning an hour and a half before the sun. On getting up, his first thoughts should be directed to Vishṇu. About an hour before sun-rise, he walks out of the village, intent upon a business of great importance to a man of this caste, that of attending to the calls of nature. The place is chosen with great circumspection, and decency requires of him to put off his clothes and slippers.

The demands of nature being discharged, he washes himself with his left hand; which, on account of this impure use of it, is never employed in eating, nor allowed to touch the food. The number of times they must wash, and what particular parts of the body, with the kind of water and earth which they must use in purifying, and many other observances which decency prevents me from enumerating, are detailed in the ritual of the Brâhmans. One of their devotees, called *Vaśishta,* has drawn up a digest of the rules to be followed on the occasion, long enough to fill half a dozen pages. Amongst his admirers, the great King of Lippa is spoken of as one of the most zealous.

I must not omit to notice a particular ceremony, which is never forgotten by a Brâhman, on the occasion alluded to; namely, that of putting the *Cord* over his right ear, which is supposed to have the virtue of purifying from corporeal stains. According to the principles laid down in their writings, the water, the Vêdas, the sun, the moon, and the air, are all contained in the ears of the Brâhmans; and it is upon this notion, that in discharging the function alluded to, they put the cord over the ear, as a means of purification. By the same rule, after sneezing, spitting, blowing the nose; after sleep, or being in tears, and in many similar cases, they seldom fail to touch the right ear in order to purify themselves from the uncleanness which these acts occasion.

We have before observed that exterior cleanness of the body, kept up in the Hindû way, is a higher recommendation than any other quality whatever. Greatness and dignity are supposed to exist wherever it is conspicuous. This feeling has led to the study and invention of a thousand minute and trifling practices, which are more systematically pursued by the Brâhmans than by the other castes: and it is upon this superiority that they chiefly plume themselves, and think themselves entitled to look with contempt on all that neglect it.

After obeying the mandate of nature, the next care of the Grihastha Brâhman is to wash his mouth. This is no trifling matter to him. The care with which he must select the little bit of wood with which he rubs his teeth, the choice of the tree he must cut it from, the prayer he must address to the deities of the woods for permission, and many other ceremonies prescribed for the occasion, make a part of the education of the Brâhmans, and are described at great length in their books of ceremonies.

The scrupulous attention with which they perform this operation every morning, with a piece of wood always fresh cut from the tree, leads them to make a comparison very unfavourable to the Europeans, many of whom altogether neglect the practice; and those who most regularly adopt it, add to the horror of the Hindû, when he sees them rubbing their teeth and gums with brushes made of the hair of animals, and using them again and again, after being soiled with the pollution of the mouth and the saliva.

Happy is he who, after the cleansing of his mouth, can wash himself in a running stream. It is more salutary to the soul and the body than the water he could find at home, or in a standing pool. An affair of so great importance is necessarily accompanied with many rites, as frivolous in our eyes as they are indispensable in theirs. One of the most essential is to think at that moment of the Ganges, the Indus, the Kistna, the Câvêry, or any other of the rivers whose sacred waters possess the virtue to efface sin; and then to implore the gods that the bath they use may be no less available to their souls than one of those nobler streams would be.

While in the water, it is necessary to keep their thoughts fixed stedfastly upon Vishṇu and Brahma; and the bathing ends by three times taking up handfuls of water and, with their faces towards the sun, pouring it out in libations to that luminary.

When he comes out of the water, the Grihastha Brâhman puts on his clothing; which consists of one piece of cloth, uncut, of about a yard in width and three yards in length. It has been already soaked in the water, and thus made pure from all the stains it had contracted. He then completes his dress by rubbing his forehead with a little of the ashes of cow-dung or with the paste made of sandal wood. He then drinks a small quantity of the water which he has taken out of the river; and the remainder he sprinkles around, three times, in honour of all the gods, mentioning several of them by name, with the addition of the earth, the fire, and the deities who preside over the eight cardinal points; and he concludes the whole by a profound reverence to the whole circle of the gods.

It would be tedious to describe the variety of gestures and movements which the Brâhman exhibits in such cases. But we may select one particular, namely the signs of the cross, which he distinctly makes as a salutation to his head, his belly, his right and left shoulders. For, after saluting all external things he commences with the particular salutation of himself in detail. Every member has its particular salutation. Even the fingers are not forgotten, as he touches each of them all round with his thumb. All these actions are accompanied with prayers or the Mantras, of which we shall speak in the following chapter.

It would now seem to be time for the Brâhman to go home, after his leisure has been so long occupied with ceremonies; but he has still a prayer to offer to the tree *Ravi*, consecrated to Vishṇu. He implores the tree to grant him remission of his sins, and then walks round it seven or fourteen or twenty-one times, always increasing by seven.

In going home, he always takes with him a little pitcher of water and some flowers, both of which are necessary for the sacrifice which he is obliged to offer soon after his return to his house. When he enters, he must read some of the *Purâṇas*, or hear them read. He then makes the *Hômam;* after which he may attend to his private affairs.

He orders dinner about mid-day. This is provided by the women; though the ordinary Brâhmans value themselves on their skill in cookery. The great object here is absolute cleanness in the preparation. Many precautions are necessary for this. The clothes of the women employed must be newly washed, their vessels fresh scoured. The place must be neat, and free from dust; and the eyes of strangers must not pervade it.

While dinner is preparing, the Brâhman returns a second time to the river. He bathes again, repeating almost all the ceremonies in the same order as in the morning. But the anxious care is in returning home, lest he should happen to touch any thing on the way that might defile him; such as by treading on a bone, on a bit of a leather, or skin, on an old rag, broken dish, or any other thing of that nature. Upon these points, however, it must be allowed, they are not all equally scrupulous.

This extraordinary purity appears to him necessary, on account of the sacrifice which he is about to offer to the idols which he keeps in his house. Every man has them of his own; and on the present occasion, the offering consists of flowers, some boiled rice, fruit, and a small portion of the dishes provided for dinner. What is thus offered is not lost, but distributed after dinner, and eaten as something sacred.

The Brâhman being seated on the ground, his wife lays before him a banana leaf, or some other leaves sewed together, and sprinkling them with a few drops of water, she serves the rice upon this simple cover; and, close by it and on the same leaf, the different things that have been provided; all of which consist of the simple productions of nature, or of cakes. The rice is seasoned with a little clarified butter, or a kind of sauce, so highly spiced that no European palate could endure its pungency.

The manner of serving up all this would appear very disgusting to us, as it is entirely performed by the hand; unless where the woman, to save her fingers, is obliged to take a wooden spoon. But this rarely happens, as the Hindûs generally have their food cold and their drink hot.

The viands being before him, the Brâhman before he touches them, sprinkles some drops of water round his plate; but, whether to attract the dust that might blow over his rice, or whether as a sacrificial libation to the food, I know not. But, before he puts a morsel into his mouth, he lays upon the ground a little of the rice and the other things set before him; and this is an offering to the *progenitors*, and their portion of the meal.

At length he begins to eat; and he has generally some poor Brâhmans with him as guests, and, more particularly, strangers belonging to the caste, if his means permit him to entertain them. Hospitality is greatly recommended among the Brâhmans; but they are bound to exercise it only towards persons of their own caste.[n]

The repast is quickly finished, as in swallowing they have neither the bones of fish nor of flesh to dread. They rise immediately, and wash both hands, although one only has been soiled; for the left being reserved for other purposes, as we have already mentioned, cannot even be employed in washing the right, and the lawful wife of the Brâhman alone can pour water over it for that purpose.

After washing his hands, he rinses his mouth twelve times. He never uses a toothpick; at least he never uses one twice, thinking that none but such as are inured to filth could use, for another occasion, a thing that had once touched their mouths and been polluted with saliva.

To procure a good digestion, the Brâhman, after his meal, chews some leaves of *basil*, that had been some time before offered in sacrifice. This is a plant consecrated to Vishṇu; and, if he thinks of the famous ascetic Agastya while he is chewing it, or of the giant Kumbhakarna, his digestion will be improved, and will keep him free from every sort of distemper.

Before going out upon his affairs, or to visit his friends, his wife brings him betel; and the interval between dinner and sun-set is quite at his disposal. He commonly employs it in going into company. But, in mixing with the world, he is required, above all things, to attend to the great precept; never to covet the goods or the wife of another man. Such a doctrine, though but ill observed, is nevertheless a proof that the Hindûs have not forgotten the principles of natural morality.

When the man has finished his repast, the wife begins hers,

---

n Manu, Chap. III. 110.

on the same leaf which has served him. As a mark of his attention and kindness, he is expected to leave her some fragments of his food; and she on the other hand, must shew no repugnance to eat his leavings: as an illustration of which I will here quote a story which I have read in one of their books.

"An old Brâhman was so corroded with a leprosy, that one day, "whilst he was at dinner, a joint of one of his fingers fell off and "dropped into his plate. His wife, who sat down, in her turn, to eat "what he had left, contented herself with moving a little to one side "the fragment of her husband's finger, and eat up the rest without "betraying the least disgust. Her husband who was looking on, was "so highly pleased with her conduct, that he bestowed the warmest "praises upon her for such a mark of her attachment, and asked what "recompense she would desire to have for it, in this world. 'Alas!' "cried she, bathed in tears, 'what recompense can I look for? Though "young, I have no children, and have no hope of having any; and I "am likely soon to be placed in the wretched class of widows.' 'No,' "replied the Brâhman, in a firm tone, 'thou shalt not be without a "reward for so meritorious an action. I will provide for thy happi-"ness.' And as he was a man beloved by the gods and full of good "works, notwithstanding his leprosy, he obtained the boon of being "regenerated in this world, with his wife, for as many generations as "they themselves should desire, with the possession of every thing "that was good. They prospered accordingly, in this manner, as "husband and wife, during three generations, with every temporal "enjoyment; and their happiness was crowned with a numerous "progeny. Satiated, at length, with the blessings of life, the good "woman desired that she might not be renewed any more. So she "died, and her husband also; and they were both translated to the "*Satyalôka*, or Paradise of Brahmâ."

But to return to the daily duties of the Grihastha Brâhman. About half an hour before sunset, he returns a third time to the river, and goes through nearly the same ceremonies as on the two preceding occasions of that day. He then goes home, offers the sacrifice of Hômam, and reads the *Bhâgavata*, a book written in honour of Vishṇu, metamorphosed into the person of Krishṇa, and other books of that nature.

The Hindûs divide both day and night into four equal parts, called *Sâmam;* each watch consisting of three hours. The time of going to bed is towards the close of the first watch of the night, or about nine o'clock. The Brâhman visits the temple in the house where he resides, and must carry thither some offering; such as oil, fruit, incense, or even betel, if he is very poor. He walks round the temple four times, if it be dedicated to Vishṇu; thrice if to Śiva; and only once if it be a temple of Vig'hnêśwara or Piḷḷaiyâr. When he bows in adoration of this last divinity, he holds his right ear with his left hand, and his left ear with the right.[o]

o In reference to the subject of this whole chapter compare Manu, Chap. III.

CHAPTER IX.

THE TRIPLE PRAYER OF THE BRÂHMANS.

THE Triple Prayer of the Brâhmans, called *Sand'hyâ,* will be best illustrated by giving extracts from it, which, though they contain nothing but absurdities, will serve to unfold more fully the nature of the Hindûs and the spirit of that idolatry to which they are devoted.

Each *Vêda* has its *Sand'hyâ ;* and every Brâhman employs that which belongs to his Vêda. The following extract is taken from the *Yajurvêda.* The Brâhman thus commences his introduction to the prayer:

"If he that is pure or not pure, in whatever trouble he may be, thinks upon him who has the eyes of the *Nîlôtpalam,* he shall be pure within and without."

The Nîlôtpalam, it will be observed, is the lily of the ponds, and extolled by the Hindûs as the most beautiful of flowers. There are several species of it, having different colours. He who has the eyes of the Nîlôtpalam, is Vishṇu.

The original expressions may be thus translated, word for word, into the language of the learned.

Apavitraḫ	*pavitraḫ*	*sarvâvas'thâm*	*gatôpiva*
Impurus	purus	in quâcumque necessitate	repertus
Yasmarêt	*Pankaruhikâksham*	*Sabahirabhyântaram*	
qui meminerit	oculos lilii aquatici habentem	hic intrâ, intus	

Suchiḫ.
purus (est).

This stanza will probably sound harshly in the ear of a European; but I thought it not unmelodious when I heard it pronounced by a Brâhman, with strong utterance, and without omitting any aspiration.

He then invokes the *seven superior worlds,* the names of which are *Bhûh, Bhuvas, Swarga, Mahtar, Jana, Tapa, Satya.* The first is the earth, and the last the world of Brahmâ, the most elevated of all. They are commonly enunciated by joining to each name the word *Lôka,* which signifies *world,* or more properly *place,* and bears a close resemblance to the Latin word *locus.*

In pronouncing those sacred words *Bhûlôka, Bhuvalôka, Swargalôka,* the Brahman shuts his nostrils and every other opening, sinks apparently into profound meditation, and separating each word by a short pause from the next, he fills up the interval with the sacred and mysterious monosyllable *Ôm;* a word pronounced with as much awe and reverence by him as the holy name *Jehovah* amongst the Jews.

It evidently appears by all the circumstances under which this mysterious monosyllable is used, and the manner in which it is uttered, that it carries with it the idea of a supreme being, one and indivisible, like the sound *Ôm*.

Both in beginning and ending the reading of any Vêda, or when listening to any sacred composition, the Brâhman must always pronounce this monosyllable silently, but distinctly, within himself.

In like manner it is always prefixed in pronouncing the words which represent the seven superior worlds, as if to shew that these seven worlds are manifestations of the power signified by the word Ôm.

In an old Purâṇa, we find the following passage: "All the Rites ordained in the Vêdas, the sacrifices to the fire, and all other solemn purifications shall pass away; but that which shall never pass away is the word *Ôm;* for it is the symbol of the Lord of all things."

Although the interest of the Brâhmans induces them to conceal the true meaning of this mysterious word, of which many of them indeed are ignorant, and all pronounce with the utmost secrecy; I think it can scarcely be doubted that it was invented to represent the idea of the only true God.

The following prayer, which they always recite at their morning bath, has the greatest power of any: "May the Sun, may sovereign Will, may the Gods who preside over our Will, and chiefly thou, O Moon! pardon the sins I have this night committed, by my will, by my memory, by my speech, by my hands, by my feet, by my belly."

To this prayer he adds the following words: "Fire has Brahmâ for its face; Vishṇu for its Head; and Rudra for its Heart. The origin of the Earth is from on high. From smoke is engendered water, into which it is resolved; and from the water is produced the Earth, as a sediment."

At the end of the prayers, the Brâhman salutes the winds lodged in various parts of his body; of which they reckon ten, as follows:

1. *Prâṇa;* a wind which originates at the anus, and pervading the body to the crown of the head, descends from thence to the nostrils, and is the cause of the respiration which issues out of these organs for twelve inches, of which one-third escapes, and the remaining two-thirds are inspired again into the body by breathing.

2. *Apâna.* This wind resides in the region of the navel, and forces out the solid and liquid excretions, as well as the accompanying wind, through their proper channels below.

3. *Vyâna,* or the wind which aids digestion and escapes backwards.

4. *Sâmâna,* a wind which keeps all the rest in regular equipoise.

5. *Nâga,* the wind which occasions hickup and vomiting.

6. *Kûrma,* which causes the tremor of the eyelids.

7. *K'hlêdikam,* which produces phlegm, cough, and sneezing.

8. *Dêvatâ,* which occasions stitches, shootings, and convulsions.

9. *Mukha Malarndu*, which excites to laughter and weeping.

10. *Jananjaya*, which resides in the head. At death, all the other winds dissipate, and this alone remains in the corpse for three days. On the third day it inflates the whole body, bursts the head, and escapes through the cleft.

All these winds are severally saluted by the Brâhman when he prays during bathing; but those that he most frequently addresses himself to are the *Apâna* and *Vyâna*, the winds which depart by the mouth and otherwise.

In the last chapter I mentioned the salutation paid to the fingers, to the two thumbs, the two fore-fingers, and so forth, by the Brâhman, when in the act of prayer. The hands, the heart, the stomach, the belly, and all the other parts of the body are saluted severally in the same manner. He then salutes the four cardinal points of heaven, by turning towards each, and bowing submissively before it.

Heaven, earth, himself, are all objects of his salutation.

He implores the elements, living or not living, to be witnesses of his prayer, and to answer it.

Particular salutation is paid to the famous Mantram *Gâyatri*, and to *Saraswati*, who is the wife of Brahmâ, but here taken only as a personified word.

Lastly, he salutes his prayer itself; and ends his devotions by saluting the whole of the Gods and Penitents in a body.

In the prayer towards the south, they salute "the excellent Brâhmans who have extended their career to the four seas." They reckon but four on this occasion, although they generally admit the existence of seven; namely the Salt Sea, the Juice of the Sugar Cane, Arrack, Liquid Butter, Curds, Milk, and Pure Water.

One of the most striking passages in the *Sand'hyâ* consists of a sort of Litany, comprising the twenty-six names of Vishṇu, under which he is thus saluted: "Hail, *Kêśavâ!* hail, *Nârâyaṇâ!* hail, *Gôvindâ!*" &c. But let it not be imagined that these epithets convey any honourable distinctions in favour of the deity to whom they are addressed. *Kêśavâ* signifies one who has a fine head of hair; *Nârâyaṇâ*, one who makes the waters his abode; *Gôvindâ*, him who keeps the cows; and so on of the rest. All those appellations have a reference to fables related concerning Vishṇu; which fully demonstrates what we have already suggested, that the Vêdas, from which all their prayers are taken, are of a later date than the fables and the idolatry existing among the Hindûs.

The prayer which the Brâhman addresses to the Sun contains less absurdity than the preceding. It runs thus: "Thou art Brahmâ, when thou risest; Rudra (or Śiva), in thy middle course; Vishṇu, at thy setting: Thou art the precious stone of the air; king of day; observer of our deeds; the eye of the world; the measure of time; Lord of the nine planets; he that blotteth out the sins of those who honour him, and expels the darkness on the return of sixty Gaṭikams

(24 minutes); he who, in his chariot, bounds over the mountain of the north, which stretches ninety millions five hundred and ten Yôjanams (about nine miles); thee will I praise with my utmost strength; and do thou, in thy mercy, forgive all mine iniquities." This prayer is closed with twelve, twenty-four, or forty-eight obeisances to the Sun.

The tree *Ravi*[p] (called *Arasa-mara* in Tamul) is thus addressed in prayer: "Thou art the king of the trees. Thy root resembles Brahmâ; thy branches are like Śiva; thou grantest the remission of sins and a blessed world, after death, to those who have honoured thee in their lives by the ceremonies of the Cord and of Marriage; to those who have offered thee sacrifices, have gone round about thee, have saluted and honoured thee. Destroy my sins, and grant me a happy world after I die."

This prayer is followed by several turns round the tree, which is sacred to Vishṇu. Indeed Vishṇu, according to the Hindû fables, is sometimes metamorphosed into this tree: and at the grand ceremonies of the Cincture and Marriage, a branch of it, as we have seen, is always placed under the alcove, and sacrifices are offered to it.

The following prayer is believed to be no less efficacious than the preceding: "As the wearied man leaves the drops of sweat which issue from his body, at the foot of the tree where he reclines; as the bather in a sacred river is cleansed from his impurity; as the holy oblation is sanctified by the blessed herb Dharba: so may this water absolve me from all sin."

When bathing the Brâhman pronounces, with slow utterance, the *Nârâyaṇâ Namah*, or salutation to Vishṇu, and also the Mantras of five letters, *Nama Śivâya*, or salutation to Śiva. These two prayers, though extremely short, possess great virtue to purify both body and soul.

The whole of these, and some other prayers, so dark and unintelligible that I could never comprehend their meaning, are always used by the Brâhman while bathing; and a few after it is over.

On the spot where they recite them, they spread one of the cloths which form their dress, and to one end of it they fasten a brass pitcher filled with water, before which they prostrate themselves. Then they sit down and make several gesticulations. Sometimes they seem to be musing. Some of the prayers are uttered with a loud voice, and others in so low a tone that persons who are moved by curiosity to listen, cannot at all understand them. Their manner of praying resembles that of a school-boy rapidly repeating by rote a lesson which he has learned. In general one cannot suppose, from their outward appearance, that they have any inward feeling of what they are employed in; so much do their prayers, as well as their other ceremonies, appear to be a matter of routine.

---

p The *ficus religiosa*, peepul, or poplar-leaved fig tree.

CHAPTER X.

OF THE FASTS AND FESTIVALS OF THE BRÂHMANS.

THE Brâhmans are bound to keep frequent fasts through the whole year, from the time that they are invested with the Triple Cincture. Age, infirmity, and even disease, unless in extreme cases, affords no exemption from this duty.

The two first days of the new moon, the eleventh, and when it is full; the time of the solstices and equinoxes; the period that precedes and follows their numerous feasts; the time of an eclipse,—are all attended with fasting. It is not so rigidly observed, however, as formerly, or as it is by some other nations. It consists in making, upon those days, the usual ablutions and other practices with more exactness, and with more scrupulous care, than on ordinary occasions, and in abstaining till sunset from all prepared food. But they may eat fruits, or take milk, without prejudice to the fast. This is not called a meal; nor are they supposed to have had dinner unless boiled rice has been served up with its usual seasoning.

After those times of mortification they try to get something more dainty than usual,—but, above all things, liquid butter; of which they are so fond as to drink it like water; and, when dinner time arrives, they replenish their stomachs so heartily as to make up sufficiently for their former privations.

These fasts have for their object two purposes. The first is to obtain the forgiveness of their sins; and the second to avert the malign influence of the stars.

A prudential motive may also have originally tended to the establishment of their frequent fastings, as conducing to their bodily health. The Brâhmans, in general, add to their other numerous vices that of gluttony. When an opportunity occurs of satiating their appetite, they exceed all bounds of temperance. Such occasions are frequent, on account of the perpetual recurrence of their rites and ceremonies, all of which are followed by a repast, at which they load their stomachs with an excess of nourishment. This necessarily brings on frequent ailments, in a climate where all the bodily organs are so relaxed that excess of any kind, particularly intemperance, has the most serious effect. To obviate these consequences, and no doubt also to insinuate themselves into the esteem and good opinion of the public, they have adopted those periods of abstinence which attract the observation of the people, and afford their own stomach the necessary intervals for recovering its tone and natural energy.

Besides the Brâhmans, all the other castes who are entitled to wear the Cord, and also several tribes of Śûdras, who do not wear it, but who wish to make a respectable appearance in public, observe the greater part of the fasts. When the days of abstinence arrive, they lay aside all servile work. The tradesmen shut their shops; the labourers repose, and give rest to their cattle: the mechanics suspend their toil, and the manufacturers quit their looms.

These occasions return so frequently that they amount to a considerable space of time in the course of the year, and are therefore attended with a heavy loss. But, in a country where industry is so little encouraged, this loss of time is not much regarded; and the lazy Hindû finds more leisure than he wants for his simple and uniform round of occupation. Perhaps the love of idleness and the want of rest may have contributed a great deal to the introduction of a custom which affords so good a pretext for relaxation.

The usages and customs which we have hitherto described are so opposite to ours, and the greater part of them appear to us so troublesome and ridiculous, that we find it difficult to conceive how so great a nation, a people so old in civilization should have adhered to them so obstinately as to preserve them to our times without any alteration. The attachment is so powerful that it has never yet entered into the imagination of any one of them to attempt a reform or change. Several of their philosophers, particularly *Vêmana, Agastya, Paṭṭanattu-piḷḷai, Tiruvaḷḷuvan,* and others, have indeed ridiculed them in their writings. But these authors, no doubt considered the danger of innovation, in matters of religion, as well as in government; and while they made the worship and civil usages of their country the subject of their raillery, they recommended a strict compliance with both, and religiously conformed to it themselves.

It is worthy of remark that, amongst the philosophical writings found in this country, where the authors are pleasant and satirical on the subject of religion and ceremonies, there is not one, as far as I know, which has been written by a Brâhman. All that I have seen or heard of are the works of Śûdras. Among these I might again mention *Tiruvaḷḷuvan*, a Pariah, *Agastya*, and *Paṭṭanattu-piḷḷai*, who have composed their poems in the Tamul language, *Saruvigny-Mûrtti*, a Lingamite, who has adopted the Canarese tongue. One of the most celebrated in the whole country is *Vêmana*, whose poems were originally written in Telugu, and now translated into many other dialects. It is affirmed that this philosopher lived within these one hundred and fifty years, and was born in the district of *Kaḍapa*, of the caste of Reddi.[q] His poems are interesting, and written in a philosophical style.

It is also material to observe that all the philosophers who have turned the religion and customs of the country into ridicule, are

---

q Concerning Vêmana little is known. He has not mentioned his own family name. He was by birth a *Câpu* or farmer. It is said that he was of the family of Ana Vêma Reddi, a chief in the Kandanûl (Curnool) country. His dialect seems to show that he was a native of the south western parts of Telingâna, and he lived probably about the beginning of the 17th century of our Æra. See Preface to C. P. Brown's Vêmana.

modern authors, at least as far as I have been able to obtain correct information. There may have been ancient authors who have treated such subjects as philosophers, but their works have perished; and I am led to believe that all the earlier works that tended to expose the absurd worship of the Hindûs have been destroyed by the Brâhmans of late times, in order to arrest the progress of infidelity. They shew themselves equally earnest to discourage the circulation of the modern philosophical writings.

There is so wide a difference between our religion and education and those of the Hindûs, that it is not wonderful that we should at the first glance feel so much dislike to their ridiculous and senseless ceremonies. But, in their judgment, ours are infinitely worse. The European manners, they think, would disgrace a barbarous people; and they cannot at all comprehend how a race, possessed of qualities so eminently above other nations, should retain, in the intercourse of life, manners so low, so coarse, and so remote from theirs.

With respect to the bondage in which we suppose they are kept by these usages, it is not perceived by those who have been trained from their infancy to practise them. They perceive, likewise, that their neglect of them would bring public disgrace upon themselves; as every eye would be upon them, and as respect and esteem are paid only to the zealous observance of the ceremonies; while on the other hand a disregard of them would bring down public and private disgrace. But usages also grow into a habit, and the nature of a people so regularly accustomed to the daily practice of them renders them easy and familiar.

At the same time I have found individuals among the Brâhmans reasonable enough to admit that some of their customs were inconsistent with good sense, and that they practised them merely out of respect to public opinion, and to live like other people. I have also been informed that, in many particulars, there is no rule for their conduct, and that the greater number of the Brâhmans did not so strictly confine themselves to the observance of their customs, but because others practised them, and because they feared their own neglect would be animadverted upon.

The regular observance of all their rites depends very much upon the degree of affluence in which they are placed. The liberality of the princes, as has been observed, endows many of them with villages and considerable territory, for which they make no returns. These villages, called *Agragrâma* are inhabited only by Brâhmans. The labourers who cultivate their lands reside wholly apart from them, in the adjoining villages. Those who live on the *Agragrâma* being thus under the inspection of one another, are compelled, in common decency, to conform to the customs of their caste. Yet I would except such of them as are possessed of so small a piece of ground that they are obliged to cultivate it themselves, in order to procure a livelihood; for their labours in the field occupy them so completely as to afford no leisure for those tedious ceremonies, the rules of which they frequently do not understand. But they are despised on that account by their brethren, who look upon them as degenerate Brâhmans; while they themselves are enabled to be more faithful to their rules by the abundance of leisure which they enjoy and the amusement which the ceremonies supply to divert their lassitude; independently of the credit they derive from their regularity, and the public favour which it conciliates.

The Brâhman Gurus are obliged, and have a right from their station, to watch over the observance of the rules prescribed to the caste. Those who are remiss, and notoriously negligent do not always escape with the severe reprimands or public affronts put upon them by the Guru, when he visits the district, but in most cases have a fine imposed upon them proportioned to their criminality and their means.

The Purôhitas are also compelled, for the sake of giving a good example, and in order to avoid the contempt which their negligence in this respect would draw upon them, to be very rigid with regard to the prescribed observances; and their interest also prompts them to enforce the practice on others, as it is the means by which they live.

Ceremonial precision appears most conspicuously at the *Samarâd'hanâ*, or public feasts, which are often given to the Brâhmans. Those who are at the expence of the entertainment consider it as one of the most meritorious of their deeds. They are given on various grounds; as on the dedication of a new temple, to expiate by so good a work the sins of the dead, or to obtain success in time of war; sometimes to avert an evil constellation; to procure rain in a great drought; to celebrate the birth or marriage of a great prince or other high personage, and for other purposes of the same kind; but chiefly founded on the superstition of the country. It is unnecessary to add that the Brâhmans, feeling the benefits they derive from such institutions, zealously urge their adoption, and assign to them the highest rank in the order of good works.

When a Samarâd'hanâ is announced, a general concourse of men and women assemble at the place from seven or eight leagues around, with appetites well disposed to take every advantage that the generosity of their entertainer can yield them. Sometimes, above a thousand people will attend; and as they must all be Brâhmans, and naturally keeping a strict watch upon each other, all the ceremonies of the caste are observed with the most scrupulous nicety, and every one studies to surpass the rest in the exactness with which he can perform them.

Being now seated on the ground in long rows, the women distinct from the men, they are prepared for dinner. Sometimes one and sometimes another sings a Sanscrit hymn in honour of their gods, or an obscene song; and when it is finished, the whole company, many of whom understand not a word of it, roar out in loud approbation, "Harâ, harâ, Gôvindâ !"

He who gives the entertainment is not permitted to sit down with his guests unless he be a Brâhman himself. If he belongs to any other caste, he does not shew himself in the assembly until the feast is over; and then he prostrates himself before these "gods of the earth," whom he has had the honour to entertain; and they, in their turn give him the *âśîrvâdam* or benediction.

If, in addition to the entertainment, the benefactor makes a present of money or cloth, he is trumpeted forth by ho Brâhmans who share it, and exalted above the gods; and this is a sufficient reward for his profusion.

The Hindûs in general, have the keenest relish for the most barefaced adulation and the most fulsome praises. There is a whole caste of them, consisting entirely of flatterers, called the caste of the *Bhats*, whose only employment is to sneak with base servility into the presence of persons of distinction, reciting or chaunting some verses in their praise, which they have got by heart, filled with the most enthusiastic praise. The great man listens patiently to the sycophant, and has even the vanity to imagine that he is deserving of the lofty compliments which he hears, and rewards them with suitable liberality.

The ceremonies and other practices of the Brâhmans are so numerous and so frequently repeated, that they occupy the whole time of those who sincerely discharge them. But, as we have observed, the greater number content themselves with performing the principal ones, or such as in their opinion cannot be omitted without an open violation of the laws of decorum.

There are but few among them, for example, who bathe oftener than once in the day, and repeat the whole of the long prayers prescribed; and the same is the case with regard to the fasting and abstinence from certain aliments which must never be eaten or touched. They conform to all their customs, while they are seen, but they are not so scrupulous when in their retirement. Hence comes the proverb so general among them: "An entire Brâhman at "the Agragrâma; half a Brâhman when seen at a distance; and "a Sûdra when out of sight."

But the attachment to these customs subsists in its fullest vigour, and they hold in sovereign contempt any one amongst them that would shew himself indifferent in any particular.

CHAPTER XI.

OF CERTAIN PROHIBITED SORTS OF FOOD AMONGST THE BRÂHMANS; AND THEIR SECRET AND NOCTURNAL SACRIFICES.

THERE are three articles of living particularly interdicted to the Brâhmans: the eating of whatever has had the principle of life; the use of inebriating liquors, and the touching of food that has been dressed by persons of a different caste.

The habit they acquire, from their infancy, of never eating flesh, and the aversion instilled into them for this species of food, grows up into such a degree of horror, that the sight of any person using it would induce in many of them the re-action of the stomach. It is not therefore more difficult to such persons to abstain from meat, than to a Jew or Mahommedan to renounce the flesh of the hog.

This abstinence prevails not only among the Brahmans, but, as we have often had occasion to mention, among the various castes who are desirous of conciliating public esteem, and who, being educated in this particular in the same prejudices, keep up an equal aversion to all sorts of animal food. They likewise preserve the same abhorrence of all liquors and drugs that intoxicate, and they would take it as the highest insult if it were proposed to them to taste any thing of that nature.

It is not quite the same with those who reside in secluded places and are less exposed to observation. Not long ago a fire broke out in a village of Tanjore in the house of a Brâhman, the only individual of that caste who lived there. All the neighbours came running, and removed the effects which they found in the house. With other things they discovered a large jar filled with pickled pork, and another half full of arrack. If the accident of the fire afflicted the distressed Brâhman, the discovery made in the house was scarcely less overpowering, although it was long kept up as a diverting joke by the inhabitants of the village as well as of the neighbourhood, through all parts of which the story spread. It may be fairly surmised that this was not the only person of his caste that was guilty of such a breach of its rules.

Transgressions of this kind are still more common in the great towns, where it is more easy to procure the proscribed articles, and to enjoy them without detection. I have been credibly informed that some Brâhmans in small companies, have gone very secretly to the houses of Sûdras whom they could depend on, to partake of meat and strong liquors, which they indulged in without scruple. I also know of instances where these same Sûdras were permitted to sit down with them, and to join in the same secret abomination. The forbidden dishes which they used in common had been dressed by the Sûdras; and to touch any food prepared by persons of another caste is a violation of the rules of the Brâhmans, still more abhorred than that of eating with them in common.

An inconvenience which frequently attends these secret debauches is that the cook-maid is not always to be relied on for keeping the secret. I knew a young Brâhman wench who was inveigled one day by the arts and importunities of a Śûdra woman, whom she frequently visited, to eat of a ragout which the Śûdra woman had dressed. Some time after, they had a quarrel, and this sad indiscretion of the poor Brâhman girl could not be expiated by all the shame and confusion with which the detection overwhelmed her.

The secret use of intoxicating drink is still less uncommon than that of interdicted food, because it is less difficult to conceal. Yet it is a thing unheard of to meet a Brâhman drunk in public. It may be allowed, therefore, that some individuals amongst them occasionally infringe their rules in secret, on this important point; but it would be an injustice to their extreme sobriety if we hesitated to believe that the Brâhmans in general abstain from strong liquors and other inebriating substances, keep up a perpetual fast, and touch nothing that belongs to animals but milk.

The punishment of offences of this class belongs to the Gurus. When they make their circuit, and pass through any place where an offender is detected, he is brought before them, and after hearing the charges against him, he is heavily amerced or corporally punished, or even excluded from the caste when the crime is very flagrant.

But, of the great numbers accused, many are acquitted on the good repute in which they are held, and sometimes to avoid too much publicity. Various other reasons are found to palliate the faults of delinquents, and a Guru allows himself to be easily gained over, by presents, so as to refuse to take cognizance of the charge, or to find some other means of nullifying it. I was an eye witness of the following instance of such connivance.

Being at *Dharmapuri*, a small town in the Carnatic, while a Guru Brâhman was making his visitation of the district, one of the caste was accused before him of having openly violated the rules respecting food, and even of turning them publicly into ridicule. The accusation was as well founded as it was important. The culprit was brought up before the Guru, who had previously taken the evidence against him, and now decreed that he should be divested of the Cord. At this awful moment, the man, apparently unmoved under so grievous a punishment, advanced to the middle of the assembly where the Guru was seated, and, after performing the sâshṭângam in the most respectful way, addressed his judge nearly in the following terms:

" So you, with your council, have decided that I am to be divested " of my Cord. It will be no great loss to me. Two bits of silver will " get me another. But I desire to know what your motive can be for " degrading me in this public manner. Is it because I have eaten " meat? If that is the only reason, why does not the justice of a

"Guru, which ought to be impartial, extend its severity alike over all "offenders? why should I be the only person accused out of so great "a number of delinquents? I look on one side, and there I see two or "three of my accusers, with whom I joined not long ago in devouring "a good leg of mutton. Here, on the other side, I turn my eyes, and "I see some more of them whom I dined with the other day, at the "house of a Śûdra, where we cut up an excellent pullet. Allow me "only to give in their names; and I will also accuse many others "whose consciousness has detained them from appearing at this "assembly. But, if you will allow me, I will instantly bring "testimony of the facts, and justify my accusation."

The Guru was evidently puzzled how to proceed, after a discourse on so delicate a subject, and delivered with so much intrepidity. But, recovering himself, he cried out with much presence of mind: "Who has brought this prattler hither? Don't you see the fellow is "mad? Turn him out, and let us be no longer tormented with his "nonsense." And in this happy way the Guru extricated himself from considerable embarrassment.

But there are instances of more impious infractions of the laws on which we are treating than these, inasmuch as they have been conducted in secret, and consecrated by magical rites and Occult Sacrifices in honour of the gods. It is not very long ago that some magicians, real or pretended, held their nocturnal orgies in secret, in a place which I know. In these they gave themselves up to excesses of every sort. The chief mover was a Brâhman. Some Śûdras were his accomplices, who were previously initiated in the mysteries of darkness which were there solemnized. They eat and drank of all forbidden things; and they closed the ceremonies of each day by some unknown magical sacrifices. The effects of such preparation were so much dreaded by the neighbourhood, that they were about to require the aid of the government to put down such dangerous combinations. But when the gang found they were discovered, they sculked away of their own accord.

But there is one of these Occult Sacrifices in existence, and known to many, secret and abominable as it is. I mean the sacrifice to the *Śaktis;* a word which signifies *force* or *power*. Sometimes it is the wife of Vishṇu, and sometimes the wife of Śiva that the votaries pretend to honour by this sacrifice; but the primary object appears to be the worship of some certain invisible force represented by the emblems of *Power* and *Strength.*[r] It is always celebrated with more or less

---

[r] The worshippers of the Śakti, the power or energy of the divine nature in action, are exceedingly numerous amongst all classes of Hindûs.

It has been computed that of the Hindûs in Bengal, at least three-fourths are of this sect. This active energy is personified, and the form with which it is invested depends upon the bias of the worshipper towards Vishṇu or Śiva.

In the former case the *Śakti* is termed *Lakshmi* (wife of Vishṇu), and in the latter *Pârvati*, *Bhavâni* or *Dûrgâ* (names of the wife of Śiva.) Even *Saraswati* (wife of

secrecy, and is more and more wicked, in proportion as those who assist at it are deeply initiated in its attendant mysteries of darkness.

The least detestable of the sacrifices made to the *Śaktis* are those in which the votaries content themselves with eating and drinking of every thing, without regard to the usage of the country; and where men and women huddled promiscuously together, shamelessly violate the sacred laws of decency and modesty.

These abominable sacrifices are principally conducted by the *Nâmad'hâris*, or those who exclusively profess the worship of Vishṇu. In the meetings which they hold, all castes are invited, without excepting even the Pariahs. All distinctions are abolished, and the Pariah is as welcome as the Brâhman.

They bring before the idol of Vishṇu all sorts of meat that can be procured, without excepting that of the cow. They likewise provide abundance of arrack, the brandy of the country; of toddy; of opium, and several other intoxicating drugs. The whole is presented to Vishṇu. Then he who administers, tastes each species of meat and of liquor; after which he gives permission to the worshippers to consume the rest.

In some varieties of these mysteries of iniquity, still more occult than those we have alluded to, the conspicuous objects of the sacrifice to the *Śaktis*, are a large vase filled with arrack, and a young girl, quite naked, and placed in the most shameful attitude. He who sacrifices calls upon the *Śakti*, who is supposed, by this evocation, to come, and take up her residence in those two objects. After the offering has been made of all that was prepared for the festival, Brâhmans, Śûdras, Pariahs, men, women, swill the arrack which was the offering to the Śaktis, regardless of the same glass being used by them all, which in ordinary cases would excite abhorrence. Here, it is a virtuous act to participate in the same morsel, and to receive from each others mouths the half gnawn flesh. The fanatical impulse drives them to excesses which modesty will not permit to be named.

It cannot well be doubted that these enthusiasts endeavour by their infamous sacrifices, to cover with the veil of religion the two ruling passions, lust and the love of intoxicating liquor. It is also certain that the Brâhmans, and particularly certain women of the caste, are

---

Bramhâ) enjoys some portion of homage, whilst a vast multitude of inferior beings of malevolent character, and formidable aspect receive the worship of the multitude.

In the *Vêdânta* philosophy the active will of the deity is always spoken of as *Mâyâ*, "original illusion."

In the Sânkhya philosophy too nature, termed *Prakriti*, is said to be of eternal existence and independant origin. She is thus regarded as the mother of gods and men, is sometimes identified with *Mâyâ*, as the personified energy or bride of the Supreme.

Connected with this is the worship of Râdhâ, the favorite of the youthful *Krishṇa*.

From *Prakriti* all female nature is secondarily derived. Hence some parts of the Śakti worship, which lead to the introduction of gross impurities. (Wilson's sects.)

the directors of those horrible mysteries of iniquity. Fortunately the great expence of these ceremonies prevents their frequent recurrence.*

The Greeks, the Romans, and other ancient nations likewise had their secret and abominable orgies, as well as the Hindûs. *Vice* was honoured amongst them, and considered essential to the adoration of their gods and the gratification of the worshippers. It still raises our astonishment to perceive how far the wisest and most accomplished of all nations carried its indulgence in tolerating, and even sanctioning, the excesses of every sort that were introduced at the feasts instituted in honour of Bacchus. And we are compelled to blush when we think of Greece, in her highest state of refinement, enduring the abominable mysteries celebrated at the festivals, and in the temple of Venus.

Ancient authors have transmitted some account of the execrable rites practised by the Persians, in honour of their God Mithra; and we also know the infamous ceremonies which the Egyptians adopted in honour of Osiris.

The sacred Scripture also recounts, in part, in different books, the irregularities and crimes committed in honour of Baal. It likewise alludes to the detestable worship of Moloch, as practised by the Moabites and Ammonites; which brought upon these races a dreadful vengeance.

It is thus that the genius and progress of idolatry have been always the same, and that ignorance and fanaticism have in all ages led to similar results.

* The Śakti worship is to a certain extent sanctioned by the Purânas, but it is especially prescribed in a serious of works called *tantras*, and is thence called the *tantra* system. This system seems to have originated in the early ages of Christianity.

The votaries of this sect are divided into the followers of the right hand and left hand ritual.

Among the former *Pârvati* is worshipped under the form and name of *Amman* or mother. The adoration of *Kâli* or *Dûrgâ* (a name of *Pârvati*) is very popular.

In the left hand ritual, called in South India, the Vêda of the eight letters (eṭṭ'eṛuttu vêdam), Śiva is worshipped under the name of *B'hairava*.

Dr. Graul giving an account of the orgies corresponding with the Abbé's adds that there are only two places in the Madras Presidency, as far as he could learn, where these rites are celebrated in their full form, *Puḍukoṭṭei* in Tinnevelly and *Periya Pâḷayam* near Madras.

[Compare Wilson's sect and Graul's Reise nach Ost indien. IV. 135.]

CHAPTER XII.

THE DIFFERENT AVOCATIONS OF THE BRÂHMANS.

If the Brâhmans lived strictly according to the primitive rules of their caste, they would keep themselves retired in the remote villages, occupying themselves with their ceremonies, attending to the management of their families, and particularly to the education of their children; and what leisure remained should be devoted to reading, study and meditation. But a life so philosophical is not compatible with the poverty of some of them and the ambition of the rest.

Their real practice has been to insinuate themselves, by art and address, into the courts of the princes of the country; to conciliate their affection and confidence, and to gain possession of the highest offices. Brâhmans are almost always the chief ministers of those indolent kings who are sunk in pleasure and effeminacy, and have no other employment than the search after new delights and delicacies, for the gratification of their perverted appetites. The happiness of their people, and the good government of their country, are objects foreign to their care. Women, baths and perfumes occupy all their leisure, and they are surrounded by those only who have learned to administer to their round of sensuality, or who can offer any fresh object of pleasure or new mode of voluptuous enjoyment. The cares of government are devolved upon the Brâhmans, to whom they delegate all their authority, and the power of appointing to every office.

It may be easily imagined that, in this exalted sphere, they do not forget their relations and friends, but, on the contrary, attach to their interests such persons of their caste as may aid them, by close union, in maintaining their authority.

It is unnecessary to remark that Brâhmans thus exalted in rank, must be above their proper condition. Engaged in governing a kingdom or a province, they have neither the time nor the inclination to undergo the tedious course of their ceremonies. But having power in their hands, and being the source of punishments and rewards, no person can venture to reproach them with the dereliction of their usages as a crime. Their rank places them out of the reach of the laws.

It is a favourite proverb with them, that *"for the belly one plays many tricks."* And indeed it would be difficult to reckon the number of methods they take to acquire a living. Some practise medicine, and, it is said, not unsuccessfully. Others go into the army; and there are many of these in the Mahrata cavalry.

Some devote themselves to commerce, particularly in the province of Gujrat; and they are considered intelligent merchants. But this a profession in no estimation with the caste; though I conceive the contempt they have fallen into is rather owing to their remissness with regard to ceremonies than to the profession itself.

The collectors of revenue, custom-house officers, writing-masters, village accomptants, and teachers of schools, are generally Brâhmans.

They are very fit to be employed on messages, as they are never stopped by any body. And it is on this account that many merchants, in the countries ruled by native princes, keep them in pay in the quality of *kûlis*, or porters, because the officers of the customs are commanded to search nothing which they carry.

This last sort of employment is the more lucrative to those who follow it, that they can travel any where, almost without expence. For nearly every stage on the highways has a lodge or house of charity, called *Chattram*,[t] erected for Brâhman travellers. They alone can be received, and the keeper of the lodge is not allowed to charge them any thing for their entertainment, being well repaid for all that he lays out by the large endowments and abundant contributions that support these hospitable establishments.

The facility with which they can every where pass renders them excellent spies in war time, when there is any reason to hope that they will not take part with both sides in the contest.

Poverty, or avarice, makes them frequently descend to occupations of a very low sort, and to professions very contemptible in their own eyes. Some of them are dancing-masters to the loose girls that belong to the temples of the idols. Others profess cookery; and, of these, the rich Brâhmans always have one in their kitchens. Neither do they object to perform this office in the service of Śûdras; though this incongruity arises out of it, that the master, being of an inferior caste, must not touch the dishes which his domestic uses for his cookery. Neither, on the other hand, will the prejudices of the domestic permit him to withdraw from the table the plates which he had served up. What he has prepared is pure for his master; but what his master has touched is pollution to him.

In the countries under the government of Europeans, they frequently enter into their service, and become their *Dubâshis*[u] or upper servants; and, when we take their prejudices into account, this last condition of life must appear to a Brâhman the lowest in which he can be placed; because waiting on his master forces him continually to break his own rules, and exposes him to defilement in its utmost degree. Those who are far removed from the neighbourhood of Europeans cannot imagine how people of their caste can be induced, by hire, so completely to divest themselves of all shame, as to become the menial servants of men whom they consider as of the lowest and most

---

t Tam. Çattiram. S. K'shatram. A place where Brâhmans are lodged and fed.

u Hind. Dôb'hâsi. From S. DWI, *two* B'HÂSHÂ, language. An *interpreter*, and general *agent*.

grovelling manners. Those, however, who comply, justify themselves by their old maxim: "for the belly, one will play many tricks."

The superstition, which reigns without controul in India, is a never-failing resource for the Brâhman to supply all his wants. Any malady, dispute, journey, or other undertaking; any bad omen or unpleasant dream, or any of a thousand other things that continually happen in life, makes it necessary to have recourse to them, to learn what evil or good is to follow. In all cases where they are consulted, they resort to the Hindû Almanack, of which each has a copy, where are inscribed the good days and the evil, propitious and unpropitious moments, fortunate and malign constellations. Upon these they pretend to calculate, and give their dupes an answer, more or less favourable, in proportion as they are paid.

Going on in this mountebank way, they have a cure for every disease, and have always an answer ready to suit every occasion. When a matter comes before them that will pay well, they give all possible importance to their response by inventing some fine story that will exactly apply to it. And, in short, wherever imposture and deception can avail, they are never at a loss.

"What is a Brâhman," I was one day asked, in a jocular way, by one of that caste with whom I was intimately acquainted: "he is an ant's nest of lies and impostures." It is not possible to describe them better in so few words. All Hindûs are expert in disguising the truth; but there is nothing in which the caste of Brâhmans so much surpasses them all as in the art of lying. It has taken so deep a root among them, that, so far from blushing when detected in it, many of them make it their boast.

I had once a long conversation on the subject of religion, with two Brâhmans, who came to visit me. They were of that sort who live on the popular credulity. Our conference ended by their frankly confessing the truth of the maxims of the Christian religion, and its excellence when compared with the absurdities of Paganism. "What you say," they repeated to me, over and over again, with the appearance of conviction: "what you say is true." "Well!" I answered, "if what I say is true, that which you teach to your "people must be false; and you are no better than impostors." "That is true also," they replied: "we lie, because we gain our "bread by it; and, if we preached to our people such truths as you "have now inculcated so fully, we should have nothing to put in "our bellies."

Flattery is another of their prime resources. They are by nature of an insinuating turn; and whatever may be their vanity and pride on other occasions, they make no scruple to cringe in the most fawning way before persons from whom they expect any favour. They likewise attach themselves very eagerly to great merchants or other wealthy persons; and all Hindûs being extremely vain, the Brâhmans who thoroughly know them, skilfully take advantage of this disposition in persons who can afford to make it worth their while, and lavish upon them the utmost profusion of praise. They well know how to adapt their flattery to the particular taste of the individual, sometimes by composing verses in his praise, sometimes by publicly relating anecdotes or incidents in his life, true or false, if they are to his advantage. Sometimes they overwhelm him with blessings; tell him his fortune, and give him assurance of the enjoyment of temporal delights for many years. Such flatteries and encomiums, ridiculous as they are, give infinite pleasure to those who receive them, as the blazon of their merits; and the flatterer whose invention has been roused by want or some other cause, receives an ample reward.

CHAPTER XIII.

OF THE TOLERATION OF THE BRÂHMANS IN RELIGION, AND THEIR BIGOTRY IN POLITICAL AFFAIRS.—THEIR CONTEMPT OF STRANGERS.

I HAVE elsewhere observed, that it is a principle among the Brâhmans in general, to honour all the Gods of the country, as there are none of them in direct opposition to the rest; and that the wars and disputes which have occasionally arisen out of that circumstance have not been of long duration, nor hindered them from soon returning to a state of amity. I have also mentioned that, in consequence of this principle, the greater number are displeased with those sectaries who are so closely attached to the worship of any particular deity as to disregard all others, or at least to look on them as inferior and subordinate to him whom they prefer.

But, are those tolerant Brâhmans the less attached, on that account, to the religion of their country and the worship of their idols? What I am going to say on this subject may appear paradoxical; but it is by no means uncommon with them to speak in the most contemptuous style of the objects of their worship. They appear in the temples without the least symptom of attention or respect for the divinities who reside there. Indeed, it is not a rare thing to see them chuse these places in preference, for their quarrels and fights. And, in general, the prostrations they make to their gods of brass and stone do not appear to proceed from any pious impulse.

Their faith and their devotion are sometimes excited by human interests and motives. They exhibit a great reliance on those gods through whom they get their bread; but when they have nothing to gain, or when they are not observed by the profane, they seem to care little about them.

The legends concerning the Pagan gods are universally so trifling and absurd that it is no wonder the people should sicken at the ridicule of addressing them in worship. It is not a dangerous thing to laugh at them; for they will frequently join in the joke and carry it farther. Many of them have songs or scraps of rhymes, abusive of the gods whom they outwardly adore; and these they sing or recite publicly, and with glee, without any apprehension of moving the anger or vengeance of the impotent beings to whom they are applied. The Sûdras, who are more simple and credulous than the Brâhmans, would not be so tolerant; and it would be very unsafe for any one to turn into ridicule the deity whom they profess chiefly to revere.

What mainly contributes to the contempt which the Brâhmans really feel for the gods whom their interest, education, and general custom lead them outwardly to adore, is the clear and distinct knowledge they possess of a God eternal, the author, and first cause of all things; of a Being infinite, all-powerful, extending through all, immaterial, existing of himself, boundless in understanding, who knows all things, who guides all things, infinitely wise, of a purity which excludes all passion, propensity, division, or mixture. This is the idea they entertain, and which their books declare of *Paramparavastu, Para-Brahmâ, Paramâtmâ;* and it is the literal signification of the preceding expressions which the Brâhmans employ to explain the nature and the attributes of the Supreme Being.

These expressions, extracted from their books, and several more which I may likewise produce, signify the perfections of God, to which I have alluded. But the evil is, that the principal part of those high attributes, which only pertain to the Supreme Being, the creator and sovereign master of all things, have been prostituted to the fabulous deities of India, mixed with a number of others, accommodated to the vices and passions of men; and which therefore can have no effect but to degrade and vilify the nature of the true God.

But can it be credited that the Brâhmans, holding opinions so lofty of the deity, should descend to give the appellation of God to that innumerable multitude of living or inanimate creatures which are worshipped by the illiterate crowd? They must, at another æra, have confined their adoration and homage to the supreme and only God, whom they now appear to know but in speculation. Him alone the Hindûs in remote times seem to have adored.

But custom, interest, appearances, and all the other feelings by which human nature is corrupted begin to prevail. They exist no where more powerfully than in the hearts of the Brâhmans; for they have kept the light from their own eyes; they have stifled the cry of their consciences, by substituting for the worship of the only and true God the absurd and irrational adoration of lifeless idols. "Professing themselves to be wise they become fools." God, whose image they have disfigured by their abominations, has justly visited them with that severe judgment which the holy Apostle Paul has informed us fell upon certain philosophers of his time, who shunned the light, as the modern Brâhmans do, and has delivered them up in the same manner, "giving them over to a reprobate mind." These are the words of the Apostle in the first chapter of the Epistle to the Romans; the whole of which, from the eighteenth verse, may be perused as an eloquent description of a community sunk into an abandoned state of manners, to be compared only with the worst part of society in India.

There is this vast difference between the ancient philosophers and the modern sages of India, that the former were too few in number to influence the public mind, and had not sufficient support to combat successfully the errors into which the multitude had fallen; whereas the Brâhmans, from their numbers and the high consideration in which they are held, if they seriously desired it, and if their interest and passions did not run the other way, might throw down by a single effort, the whole edifice of idolatry in India, and substitute without difficulty, in its room, the knowledge and worship of the true God; of whom they themselve still preserve the loftiest conceptions.

But, to return to the religious toleration of the Brâhmans, we add, that they carry it much beyond the universal adoration of all the deities of their own country. It is a principle established and taught in their books, and maintained by themselves in discourse, that, in the world, there must be an endless diversity of laws and of worship (expressed by their word *anantavéda*, which signifies an infinity of religions) not one of which they can condemn.

They would respect Muhammedanism, such as it is professed in India, with all the trappings and superstitious additions of ceremonies with which it has been overloaded: but the weight of the yoke which its propagators have imposed on their necks, with an utter disregard of their laws, has brought both them and their religion into abhorrence.

The Christian religion, in itself, is not disliked by them. They admire its pure morality; but they perceive also that it would not be easy for a plain Hindu to conform to some of its precepts. The Christian religion condemns and abjures the greater part of their usages, on account of the superstition with which they are tainted; and thence, in some districts particularly, it becomes quite insupportable. The Hindus who embrace it appear no longer to be branches of the same national family with themselves, having renounced the usages which the adherents of the ancient faith consider as the only sacred bond which can unite them indissolubly together.

I have often thought, however that interest was a good deal concerned in their hatred of the Christians, as they must perceive that, if that religion gained ground, it must be to their prejudice; and that, if it ultimately triumphed, they would be left destitute of the means of subsistence.

Upon the whole, we must conclude that the tolerant spirit of the Brâhmans, in regard to religion, arises from indifference about it; most of them holding their own worship in contempt.

They have been thought intolerant in their religious practices, because they do not open the gates of their temples to Europeans, but refuse to admit to their ceremonies such of them as are attracted by curiosity to see them. But the reserve which the Hindûs maintain in such cases by no means proceeds from an intolerant feeling with regard to religion, but wholly from a dislike of the unprepared condition and the uncleanness in which, according to their prejudices, the Europeans continually live. If these strangers would cease from taking Pariahs into their domestic service; if they would abstain from eating the flesh of cattle, give up their offensive dress, with their boots, gloves and whatever is made of animal skin, and accommodate themselves, in however small a degree, to the other leading usages of the country, they would experience from the Hindû the most perfect and unbounded toleration.

Having sometimes in my travels come up to a temple where a multitude of the people were assembled for the exercise of their worship, I have stopped for a while to look on; and the Brâhmans, who direct the ceremonies, have come out, and, upon learning who I was, and my manner of living, have invited me to go in and join them in the temple; an honour for which I always thanked them unfeignedly, as became a person of my profession to do.

But if the Brâhmans manifest that it is agreeable to their principles to shew indulgence in whatever immediately concerns their religion, the case is very much altered in regard to their Civil Institutions. In this particular they are the most intolerant of men Nothing appears to them well ordered but their own customs. In the world there are no really civilized men but themselves; and the habits and manners of the strangers, who are now become their masters, and live in the midst of them, they consider to be worthy only of a barbarous people.

This pride and vain prejudice in favour of their customs and practices are so deeply rooted in their nature, that all the mighty revolutions to which they have been exposed have not effected the slightest visible alteration in their manner of living. Several times have they been subdued by conquerors, who have shewn themselves superior to them in courage and bravery; but they have always regarded their vanquishers as infinitely beneath them in civilization, education and accomplishments.

After being subdued by the Muhammadans, in modern times, that fierce people, who could not tolerate any religion but their own among a race whom they had conquered, used every effort to impose their religious as well as civil institutions on the Hindûs, who had all submitted without resistance to the stern invaders. But all endeavours were in vain. The Hindûs, who had surrendered to them all they had valuable on earth, who saw their wives and their children carried away, and made no resistance; who beheld the fierce plunderers ravage their whole land with blood and fire, and yet rested quiet; shewed a spirit never to be subdued, when any attempt was made to change their customs and to substitute those of a foreign people. Even the long residence of their conquerors among them, during which every art of seduction has been employed, without intermission, to entice their new subjects to comply with their modes of life, has produced no visible alteration in the old customs of the country. The lure of wealth and honours held out by the Moslim invader to all who would conform to his religion and rules, and the harsh treatment and contempt reserved for those who persevered in their own worship and forms; were all too feeble to move the Hindûs, particularly the Brâhmans; who have preferred a state of vassalage, with the use of their own rites, to all the dignities and honours which would have been the reward of their compliance. After a long struggle, the haughty conqueror has been obliged to yield, and even, in some measure, to adopt the religious and civil customs of the vanquished people.

It must also be admitted that the harsh and tyrannical system employed by the Muhammadan invaders in the Government of a race of men so gentle, so submissive, so pacific as those they found in India, was but ill adapted to conciliate affection, or to abate the prejudices which, in all times, they have entertained against strangers and their customs.

The period of their emancipation from the iron yoke imposed upon them by those tyrants, and which they have endured for several ages without daring to complain, cannot now be far off. But the poor Hindû, though apparently insensible to the evils of life, cannot easily forget the numberless miseries which he has suffered for several hundreds of years from those cruel oppressors; who, after subjugating an unresisting and obedient race, that never ventured to dispute their dominion, appear to have studied as a science the art of inflicting calamity and woe.

The Muhammadans in India are disliked by the Brâhmans, both on account of the tyranny which they exercise over them, without any respect to the imaginary *lords of the earth*, and also for the small regard they shew to their ceremonies and customs in general. But they also find amongst these strangers, persons who equal or perhaps surpass themselves in haughtiness, in pride, and vain glory, and in most of the vices which are familiar to either race: so that the one is never likely to coalesce with the other.

There is this difference, however, that the Muhammadan on his part maintains but an empty pride, which has no other foundation than the office which he holds, or the dignity with which he is invested; whereas the Brâhman has the consciousness of his own excellence, which never forsakes him, but enables him to support his rank under all circumstances of life. Rich or poor, in prosperous or adverse fortune, he regulates himself continually by the sentiment which tells him, that he is the noblest and the most perfect of all created beings, that all other men are beneath him, and that there is nothing on earth so well ordered and so becoming as his usages and customs.

He is likewise well convinced that there is nothing human in which he does not surpass the strangers who live in his country; particularly in whatever relates to science. For, as to the arts, he considers them as greatly beneath his dignity, and suited only to the degraded castes, who are not permitted to soar into the sublime regions of knowledge, accessible only to the Brâhmans.

The profound ignorance in which the Muhammadans in India live, being incapable even of dipping into the almanack, for which they are compelled to have recourse to the Brâhmans, tends very much to strengthen the good opinion which the latter entertain of themselves; which no beings in the world carry so far. But, if they were impartial, they would descend a good deal from this self-conceit, when they perceive how far the Europeans, with whom they now live in familiarity, leave them behind in all the branches of knowledge which they cultivate in common.

Nevertheless, a Brâhman will always refuse to own that any European can be as wise as he is. He holds in sovereign contempt all the sciences, arts, and new discoveries which such a teacher could communicate, in the injudicious conceit that any thing not invented by himself can be neither good nor useful. And he is persuaded that every thing human that either can or ought to be known, is already contained in his books, while on the other hand, whatever he himself has not found out is suspicious, and ought to be rejected without farther examination.

Such is the education of a Brâhman, and such the principles in which he is universally and invariably trained up; and it would be labour lost to attempt to correct his prejudices or to alter his notions on such affairs.

One frequently sees amongst them some individuals whom interest or other motives have induced to acquire the European tongues, and who understand them very well. But they are rarely seen with a European book of science in their hands; and it would be somewhat difficult to convince them that any such work contained an atom of which they are ignorant, or that is not already to be found in books of their own.

At the same time, although the Brâhmans will not allow that the Europeans equal them in the high departments of knowledge, they confess their superiority in some other respects. In particular, they love to talk of the humanity with which they carry on war, of the moderation and impartiality with which they govern the people under their controul; and, if it were possible for this singular caste to become familiar with any foreigners, it would certainly be with the Europeans; whose good qualities of benevolence and humanity they acknowledge. But among the bright virtues which adorn them, they descry the darkest taints. They see them addicted to habits so gross and abominable according to their notions, so completely opposite to their own education and breeding, as well as to their institutions, that they quickly forget the favourable impressions which their beneficence, moderation and spirit of equity had left, and view them in no other light than as a part of the barbarous nations.

Let us but candidly consider how a Brâhman, or a Hindû of any other caste, can attach himself with affection to an European; an individual who, in his whole conduct, affronts their most sacred and inviolable institutions.

How can a Brâhman repress the horror and the hideous disgust which must arise within him, when he sees Europeans feeding upon the flesh of the cow: he, to whom the murder of one such animal is more appalling than manslaughter, and the use of its flesh more horrible than to gorge on a human carcase?

In what estimation can he hold men who admit Pariahs into their domestic service, or keep women of that vile tribe, as servants, or in a more criminal capacity: he, who feels a stain, and must immediately wash, if even the shadow of such a being passes athwart him?

What respect can he have for men who debauch themselves in public, who appear to consider the detestable act of drunkenness as a gallant feat: he, who has been taught to view it as the most infamous of all vices, and the most debasing to human nature; he, who, if he once offended in that way, would be consigned to the most degrading punishment?

What idea can he form of Europeans, when he sees them bring their females to mix in their intemperance, and beholds women shamelessly laugh, play, and toy with the men, and even join them without blushing, in the dance: he, whose wife dares not sit down in his presence, and who has never known nor imagined that persons of that sex, with the exception of the common girls and prostitutes, could take it in their heads to amble and caper?

Another peculiarity which is nearly as shocking to the Hindûs, is that of the European dress. It is so different from theirs, and in other respects, so cumbersome and incommodious in a warm climate, that it is not surprising they should think it fantastical and ridiculous.

But what disgusts them most of all is the boots and gloves. In their imaginations, leather and all kinds of skins of animals are of so impure a nature that they must wash after touching them; and they do not understand how Europeans can handle, and even put on, without horror, the offals of a beast.

CHAPTER XIV.

OF THE MANNERS OF THE BRÂHMANS.

To complete our knowledge of the character of the Brâhmans, it will be necessary to draw an outline of their manners. Those who are most intimately acquainted with this caste of people, I believe, will generally agree that an exact and faithful portrait of them will not be much to their advantage. I do not intend to enter very minutely into the subject of this chapter; and the greater part of what I have to say will apply, not to the Brâhmans only, but to Hindûs of all other castes.

Amongst the vices peculiar to them, we may place in the first rank their extreme suspicion and duplicity. These feelings appear very prominent wherever their interest is in any degree committed. But, in general, the reserve of the Hindûs, in all the circumstances of their lives, makes it very difficult to discover what is at the bottom of the heart; and the skill which they possess in counterfeiting what best suits their interest takes away all confidence in their most solemn protestations.

I do not suppose, however, that these vices are innate, or that they spring from any natural bias to be rogues and dissemblers. I rather suppose they proceed from the influence of the tyrannical governments under which they have existed for so many ages. Till of late, they have been habituated to live under the rule of a great number of petty and subordinate tyrants, whose sole object appeared to be to emulate each other in the art of trampling on the people whom they governed; which end they could most easily attain by the constant use of shifts and evasions. The feeble and timid Hindû had no other means of warding off so much injustice and vexation, but by opposing trick to trick, and practising in his turn the duplicity and dissimulation which were employed against him. Thus he grows expert in the practice of those arts. They are his defensive armour against despotism, and they are so often called into use that they have become his natural protection.

One of the principal ties that bind human creatures together, the reverence we feel for those from whom we derive our existence, is almost wholly wanting among them. They fear their father, while they are young, out of dread of being beaten; but from their tenderest years they use bad language to the mother, and strike her even, without any apprehension. When the children are grown up, the father himself is no longer respected, and is generally reduced to an absolute submission to the will of his son, who becomes master of him and his house. It is very uncommon, in any caste whatever, to see fathers preserving their authority to the close of their lives, when their children are mature. The young man always assumes the authority, and commands those who are the authors of his being.

At the same time, when these have acquired absolute authority in the house, they are not deficient in attention to their fathers, mothers, and relations; and, when grown old and infirm, they do not suffer them to be in want of any thing.

No where in the world do parents shew more tenderness and attachment towards their offspring than those of India. But this fondness shews itself only in the most absolute indulgence of them, in every thing, whether good or bad. They have not sufficient courage and resolution to correct their faults, nor to repress the growing vices. The experience of how little gratitude a foolish father receives from his spoiled children, has no effect upon them, and makes them neither more severe nor more vigilant.

As no pains are taken to curb the passions of these indocile infants, their minds are left exposed to the first impressions that assail them, which are always of an evil tendency. From their earliest years, they are accustomed to scenes of impropriety, which, at such an age might be supposed incapable of imprinting any image on their fancies: but it is nothing uncommon to see children of five or six years old already become familiar with discourse and actions which would make modesty turn aside. The instinct of nature is prematurely awakened by the state of bare nakedness in which they are kept for their first seven or eight years, and excited by the loose conversation which they frequently hear, the impure songs and rhymes which they are taught as soon as they can speak, and the lewd tales which they constantly listen to, and are encouraged to repeat. Such are the sources from whence their young hearts imbibe their first ailment, and such the earliest lessons which they learn!

It is superfluous to add that, as they grow up, incontinence and its attendant vices increase with them. Indeed the greater part of their institutions, religious and civil, appear to be contrived for the purpose of nourishing and stimulating that passion to which nature of itself is so exceedingly prone. The stories of the dissolute life of their gods; the solemn festivals so often celebrated, from which decency and modesty are wholly excluded; the abominable allusions which many of their daily practices always recal; their public and private monuments, on which nothing is ever represented but the most wanton obscenities; their religious rites, in which prostitutes act the principal parts: all these causes, and others that might be named, necessarily introduce among the Hindûs the utmost dissoluteness of manners.

It is probably with the view of guarding in some measure against this dreadful depravity, that they hasten to marry their children so soon. But marriage itself is but a feeble restraint in many cases on the evil consequences of so profligate an education.

Domestic discord cannot fail to be prevalent in a country where the youths are trained so early to licentiousness, where the number of young widows is so great, and where abortion is so common from most of them knowing the means of procuring it, and from believing it to be a smaller evil to cause the death of an unborn infant than to put to hazard the reputation of a frail matron. But many of this misled women whose minds do not shrink from the crime of infanticide, and who use ingredients to destroy the innocent victim, become the sacrifice to their wickedness; for it frequently happens that the deadly drug extinguishes the life of the mother after that of the child.

When the remedy does not take its intended effect, and when there is no way of concealing the consequences of their frailty, the Brâhman women, to prevent as far as they can the shame which their condition would bring upon the family, give out that they are about to make a pilgrimage to Benâres, a solemn undertaking as common in the Brâhman caste for women as men to engage in. With the assistance of some confidential person whom they have admitted into the secret, they begin their journey, pretending to take the way to *Kâśi*, but go no farther than some neighbouring place, to the house of some relation or friend, where they remain in privacy till they are disencumbered of their load. This being arranged, and the child disposed of in a private way, they quietly return to their families.

Besides the sources of corruption already noticed, which are common to all the Hindûs, there is one of a peculiar kind, known in several districts, though chiefly among the Brâhmans, and some other classes of Hindûs the most distinguished for licentious habits. Many of them possess a detestable book which is known under the name of kokkôga *Sâstra*, in which the grossest lewdness and most infamous obscenities are taught, in regular method, and upon principle. I know not whether this abominable work exists in the various countries of India and whether it be written in their several idioms; but I know it is extant in writing, in the *Tamul*, and that it is met with in the districts where that dialect is used.

Among the Hindûs those men who attach the idea of sin to the violation of the most trifling ceremony, see none in the greatest excesses of profligacy, such as the institution, contrived for their gratification, of the dancing girls, or prostitutes, attached to the idolatrous rites in the different temples. The are often heard repeating a scandalous line, which attributes merit to such vague connections.

It greatly tends to keep up domestic misrule amongst them, that adultery, on the woman's side, although infamous and reprobated, is not so severely punished here as in several of the other tribes. They pay no great attention to it when kept private, and even if it becomes public, as every Brâhman must have a woman, and as he cannot possibly find another in the room of her who has dishonoured his bed, in any other capacity than as a concubine, the shortest way for him is to retain his wife, with all her failings, and to correct them in the best manner he can.

The disgrace, infamy, and shame which are the consequences of an erring wife, and which even extend to all her family, serve as a restraint upon many, and retain them in the path of duty, to put them upon finding the best means of cloaking their frailty, so that it may escape the eyes of the public. Those who are not so fortunate as to escape publicity, must expiate their errors by submitting to be received in public with reproach and insult; and, in a country where no prosecutions take place on account of verbal abuse, when they have any dispute with other women, their slip is most certainly the first thing to be brought up. The confusion into which they are thus publicly thrown is a good lesson to others to be more careful in preserving their honour, or at least in saving appearances.

But it will appear almost incredible that, notwithstanding this state of corruption and the relaxation of manners so widely diffused over all India, external propriety of behaviour is much better maintained amongst them than amongst ourselves. The indecent prattle and fulsome compliments which our fops are so vain of, and study as a science, are here entirely unknown. The women, shameless and dissolute as they are in other respects, would not join in such impertinent gossipping in public. A man who should talk in a familiar way with his wife would be thought an unpolished ridiculous person. One is never asked how his wife does. Such an inquiry would be considered impertinent, and be felt by the husband as an insult. It is still more requisite that when one visits his friends he should never shew any desire to see the wife, or even speak to her if they met, unless they be near relations.

In no country is there a just medium in this respect. Our error is an excess of familiarity. The fault of the Hindûs is too much reserve.

The austere behaviour of the Hindûs towards the fair sex arises from the opinion, in which they have been nurtured, that there can be nothing disinterested or innocent in the intercourse between a man and a woman; and, however Platonic the attachment might be between two persons of different sex, it would be infallibly set down to sensual love. They have not therefore been yet able to familiarize themselves with the European manners in this particular. The politeness, attention, and gallantry which the Europeans practice towards the ladies, although often proceeding entirely from esteem and respect, are invariably ascribed by the Hindûs to a different motive; and they cannot see a European conducting a lady under his arm but they conclude she must be his mistress.

But this habit of reserve which they keep up towards the women of their own nation, together with the other reasons alluded to, and the severity with which they punish those who are guilty or are strongly suspected of such conduct, have the effect to render the violation of honour much more rare, than it would otherwise necessarily be, in a country where the men are, so early in life, accustomed to licentiousness, and where there are so many young widows who have it not in their power to re-marry.

To all these motives for continency, we ought to add that the Hindû women are naturally chaste. In this respect they are undoubtedly of a very different character from what is attributed to them by some authors, who have but imperfectly observed their dispositions, and who have, no doubt, been deceived by the dissoluteness of some females of the nation, who connect themselves with Europeans, or of the still greater number who follow the armies. From these particular instances, they have ventured to brand them in general with the odious imputation of unchastity. I believe their opinion to be erroneous, and I am confident that any person who shall inquire closely, and with impartiality, into their habitual conduct, as I have done, will join with me in revering their virtue.

Having said so much of the methods taken by the Brâhmans to encourage and stimulate that passion which of itself exercises a power sufficiently absolute over the human heart, I will say a few words on their mode of resenting any injury or affront which is offered to them. No creature whatever retains longer than they do the spirit of rancour. When they have nourished a feeling of hatred against any one, it often passes from generation to generation, and becomes hereditary in families. They counterfeit a reconciliation, when their interest requires it; but it is never sincere; and it is nothing uncommon to see a man taking vengeance for an injury offered, many years before, to his father or grandfather.

In their view of obtaining satisfaction, a duel would be sheer folly. Assassinations, and even fisticuffs, beyond a gentle blow or two, are almost unknown among them. Their disposition, naturally timid and cowardly, does not admit of methods of revenge so dangerous and bloody. In cases of deep offence, the Brâhman prefers to avenge himself by the means of some evil-engendering *Mantram*, or by having recourse to some famous magician, who, by his spells and enchantment, may strike his enemies with terror, or effect them with some incurable disease.

Their manner of shewing their wrath is, by scolding stoutly and bandying the grossest and most infamous abuse; in which accomplishment the Brâhmans are not surpassed by any other caste. They will try also to ruin their adversary by calumnies and other secret attacks; in which, sooner or later, they will succeed.

Homicide and suicide, though held in particular horror by the whole of the Hindûs, and though less frequent among them than in many other nations, are however not unknown. It is the women chiefly who resort to self-slaughter, in moments of despair, almost always brought on by the harsh and tyrannical manner in which they are treated. They put an end to their life by hanging themselves, or plunging into a pond or river; and the general cause of this desperate end is, as we have just mentioned, family discord.

Besides that great connecting link of human society, filial reverence, a virtue so little appreciated among the Hindûs, the Brâhmans are likewise destitute of the other high moral sentiments which infuse the spirit of mutual agreement and union into the social body, moulding it into a large community of brothers, aiding one another in every difficulty, and mutually contributing whatever is in their power to each others welfare.

The Brâhman lives but for himself. Bred in the belief that the whole world is his debtor, and that he himself is called upon for no return, he conducts himself in every circumstance of his life with the most absolute selfishness. The feelings of commiseration and pity, as far as respects the sufferings of others, never enter into his heart. He will see an unhappy being perish on the road, or even at his own gate, if belonging to another caste; and will not stir to help him to a drop of water, though it were to save his life.

He has been taught from his infancy to regard all other classes of men to the utmost contempt, as beings created for the purpose of serving him, and supplying all his wants; without any reciprocal duty on his part, to shew his gratitude, or make any other return.

Such are the principals on which the education of the Brâhmans is invariably and universally founded. And, after such a description, shall we be at all surprized at their haughtiness, their pride and self-love, or at their contempt of all other men, of whom they never speak amongst themselves without the addition of some ignominious epithet or expression of scorn?

CHAPTER XV.

OF THE EXTERIOR QUALITIES OF THE BRÂHMANS AND OTHER HINDÛS; THEIR BODILY AND MENTAL WEAKNESS; OF THEIR LANGUAGE, THEIR DRESS, AND THEIR HOUSES.

THAT nothing may be wanting to our description of the Brâhmans, I will add a few words concerning their gait, physiognomy, and other characteristical peculiarities, the greater part of which is applicable in degree to the other castes.

There are among them, as in all other nations in the world, men of every degree of stature and figure. But one hardly ever sees in India certain bodily deformities which are common in Europe. The hump-back, for example, is rarely to be seen. But to balance this deficiency, there is a far greater proportion of blind than in Europe. The extreme heat of the climate, the usual practice of the poor to go with their heads and bodies almost bare, under the strongest influence of the sun, may unquestionably contribute to impair the organs of sight. To guard against this evil the people have a custom of rubbing the head with an ointment composed of several ingredients.

The colour of the Hindûs is tawny, lighter or darker according to the provinces which they inhabit. That of the castes who are constantly employed in the labours of agriculture, in the southern districts of the peninsula, is nearly as dark as that of the Kaffirs. The Brâhmans, and people whose profession admits of their working in the shade, such as painters and many other artisans, are of a lighter hue. A dark-coloured Brâhman and a whitish Pariah are looked upon as odd occurrences; which has given birth to a proverb common in many parts of India, "Never trust to a black Brâhman or a white Pariah." The tint of the Brâhman approaches to the colour of copper, or perhaps more nearly to that of a bright infusion of coffee. I have seen people in the southern parts of France as dusky as the greater number of Brâhmans, and perhaps more so. Their women, who are still more sedentary and less exposed to the rays of the sun, are still lighter in their complexion than the males.

There are some wild hordes on the hills and in the thick forests on the coast of Malabar, who are much less deeply tinged than any of the castes that have been mentioned. In the woods of the Coorg country there is one of these communities, called Malay Kûdiyara who do not yield, in point of complexion, to the Spanish or Portuguese. I can divine no other reason why those savages who inhabit the mountains should be of a whiter hue, but that they are continually under the shelter of trees which protect their complexion.

But, in all castes, without exception, the Hindûs have the sole of the foot and the palm of the hand much whiter than the rest of the body.

It is no uncommon thing to meet with a class of individuals amongst them who are born with a skin much whiter even than that of Europeans. But it is easy to perceive that it is not a natural colour, because their hair is altogether as white as their skin; and, in general, their whole exterior appearance is unnatural. They have this distinguishing peculiarity, that they cannot endure the light of the broad day. While the sun is up, they cannot look steadily at any object; and, during all that time, they contract their eye lids so as apparently to exclude vision. But in return, they are gifted with the faculty of seeing almost every object in the dark.

In India, these beings are looked upon universally with horror. Their parents, even, who have brought them into the world, abandon them. Their colour is supposed to arise from leprosy; and indeed the name they are known by signifies *lepers by birth.* It is reasonable to conclude that so remarkable a deviation from the ordinary course of nature, as the birth of a white infant from black parents, must actually proceed from some disease contracted within the body of the mother; and it may be a kind of leprosy, as that disease, it is said, does not hinder those who are affected with it from arriving at an advanced age.

When they die, their bodies are neither buried nor burnt, but cast upon the dunghill. This custom is founded on a notion arising out of the superstition of the country, which interdicts from the honours of interment all who die under any cutaneous or eruptive disorder. If they did otherwise, the Hindûs firmly believe that a general drought, or some other public calamity would break out that year, over the whole land.

Agreeably to this opinion, these persons, and those who have white spots on their skin, such as are often seen on the soles of the feet and the palms of the hands of some Hindûs, together with those who die of small-pox or other eruptions, or have any ulcer on the body when they die, and pregnant women dying undelivered of the fœtus; in all such cases, the dead bodies are exposed in the open fields to be devoured by wild beasts and birds of prey.

I have, more than once, been in districts afflicted with grievous drought, where the inhabitants, becoming desperate from there being no prospect of rain, and imagining that the defect arose from some corpses, such as we have described, being secretly interred, have gathered in crowds to open the suspected graves. These they dig up, and carefully inspect the bodies which have perhaps lain for months, drag them from their sepulchre, and throw upon the dunghill such as they imagine to have been interred illegally. This horrid custom, of thus rudely violating the ashes of the dead, is very common in those parts where the Lingamites are numerous, as that sect follows the practice of burying their dead, in place of burning them, which is the general custom among the Hindûs.

In general, the Hindûs have the forehead small, the face thinner and more meagre than the Europeans; and they are also very much inferior to them in strength and other physical qualities. They are lean, feeble, and incapable of supporting the labours and fatigues which the other race are habituated to. The Brâhmans, in particular, scarcely ever attempt any laborious effort of the body; and when they do, it is but momentary. This feebleness is, no doubt, occasioned by the nature of the climate, as well as by the quality of the food to which the greater number of Hindûs are restricted. In general, they eat nothing but seeds, or such insipid matters; for, though most of them cultivate rice, which appears to be a production of nature in the highest degree suited to the use of man, and well adapted to sustain his vigour, the mass of the people do not use it for their ordinary fare. They are obliged to sell it, to get what is necessary for paying their taxes, to procure clothes, and supply their other domestic wants. After disposing of their crop of rice, they nourish themselves, for the rest of the year, in the best way they are able, upon the various sorts of small seeds, similar to what are given in Europe to pigs or chickens: and it were to be wished that every Hindû had even this sorry fare at his command.

The same debility and tendency to degenerate, which is so visible in the Hindûs themselves, appear to involve all animal existence in that country, from the plant up to the human species. The grass, vegetables, and fruits, are all sapless; at least, the greater part are devoid of the nourishing qualities inherent in the same productions of nature in other countries.

The domestic and wild animals, with the exception of the elephant and the tiger, are there found in a degraded state, both as to native vigour and nutritive properties. All eatable things, of the most succulent nature elsewhere, are insipid here. Nature seems, in this region, to have fashioned all her productions animate or inanimate, on a scale proportioned to the feebleness of the people. What she has provided for the use or the service of a debilitated being, she has lowered in a corresponding degree.

The imbecility of the mind keeps pace with that of the body. There is no country, I believe, where one meets with so many stupid or silly creatures; and, although in India there are to be found numbers of persons of good sense and moderate talents, and even some who, by means of a good education, have distinguished themselves advantageously amongst their countrymen, yet I think it very doubtful whether, during the three centuries in which the Europeans have been settled in the country, they have ever discovered among them one true genius.

What they are, in point of courage, is well known; their natural cowardice being every where proverbial.

Neither have they sufficient firmness of mind to resist any application that may be made to them on their weak side. Praise and flattery will induce them to part with any thing they possess.

They are not less devoid of that provident spirit, which makes other mortals think of their future wants and well-being, as much as of the present. Provided the Hindû has just enough to support the vanity and extravagance of the day, he never reflects on the state of misery to which he will be reduced on the morrow, by his ostentatious and empty parade. He sees nothing but the present moment, and his thoughts never penetrate into an obscure futurity.

From this want of foresight, chiefly, proceed the frequent and sudden revolutions in the fortunes of the Hindûs, and the rapid transitions from a state of luxury and the highest opulence to the most abject wretchedness.

They support such overpowering shocks of fortune with much resignation and patience. But it would be erroneous to ascribe their tranquillity, under such circumstances, to loftiness of spirit or magnanimity; for it is the want of sensibility alone that prevents their minds from being affected by the blessings or miseries of life.

It was probably with an intention to make some impression on their unfeeling nature, and to stimulate their imagination, that their histories, whether sacred or profane, their worship and laws, are so replenished with extraordinary and extravagant conceits.

We must also ascribe to their phlegmatic temper, more than to any perverseness of disposition, the want of attachment and gratitude with which the Hindûs are justly reproached. No where is a benefit conferred so quickly forgotten as among them. That sentiment which is roused in generous minds by the remembrance of favours received, and which repays in some measure the liberal heart for the sacrifices which its desire to oblige so often requires it to make, is quite a stranger to the natives of India.

But we shall here drop the subject of their mental faculties, in which they do not appear to great advantage, and return to the exterior qualities of the Brâhmans.

It is easy to distinguish a member of this caste, by a certain free and unembarrassed air, something more easy and independent than is in general to be met with in the other tribes. Without betraying any appearance of affectation, their manner and movement sufficiently indicate the consciousness they feel of their superiority in rank and origin. One may recognise them also by their language, which is exempt from the low and vulgar expressions in use among the other castes.[v] Besides its superior purity and elegance, it is more tinctured with the Sanscrit. They have particular phrases also, not employed by the Śûdras. In private conversation their discourse is diversified with proverbial turns and allegorical allusions, briefly expressed. Possessing a great copiousness of phrase, it often happens that, after learning their language tolerably well, one is provoked to find that he

[v] In speaking the vernaculars they make use of many corrupt forms and, in fact, scarcely one speaks correctly.

cannot understand a word that passes between any party of them, when conversing familiarly with each other. In their talk, as well as in their letters, they introduce a thousand graceful flights which they know very well how to apply. Indeed they rather exceed just bounds in this respect, as they have no moderation in the extravagance of their compliments. They make no scruple to elevate above all the gods those to whom they direct their flattery; and truly this is but the first step in their fulsome adulation.

But, to reverse the picture, and turn to their horrid and execrable foulness of language and imprecations; they must be admitted to have a more unbounded supply of these flowers of speech than of the courteous sort. For, although the Brâhmans pride themselves on their politeness and good education, they forget them both when their passion is roused. On these occasions, such a torrent of the most indecent and obscene expressions issues from their impure mouths, that one would be tempted to suppose they had made a particular study of the language of invective and insult.

Nothing can be more simple than their primitive dress. A single piece of cloth, uncut, about three yards long and one in width, was formerly, and in general still continues to be their only apparel. Being wrapped round the loins, one end passes between the thighs, and is fastened behind, while the other end, after being cast into several folds in front, is allowed to hang down in a negligent, though not ungraceful way. This is the habit of those, in particular, who pride themselve the most on propriety and purity. Bathing gives little trouble, with such a garment; and they have generally a spare one for a change, which sometimes they spread over their shoulders.

Many of them provide themselves with a piece of woollen cloth, to wrap themselves in during the night, or in the cool of the morning.

Since the European manufactures have become general in the country, many Brâhmans and other Hindûs, have bought themselves a piece of scarlet, with which they make a great shew.

It appears that they were accustomed to have the head uncovered, or merely with the cloth thrown over it which serves to protect their shoulders. At present, many wear a turban; an ornament which they have borrowed from the Muhmmadans, consisting of a long piece of very fine stuff, sometimes twenty yards in length, by one in breadth; and with this they encircle the head in many folds.

Those who are employed in the service of the Europeans or of the Musalman princes, besides their ordinary dress, wear a long robe of muslin or very fine cloth; which is also an imitation of the Muhammadans, and formerly unknown in the country. The Brâhmans, however, keep up a distinction between themselves and the Musalmans, by fastening it to the left side, in place of the right; and they sometimes wear, above this dress, a cincture of very fine texture passing several times round the body.

The wealthy amongst them do not dress differently from the rest;

but the vesture they wear about their loins, is generally of a finer cloth, and ornamented with a fringe of red silk.

Almost all the Hindûs wear golden ear-rings, of a larger or smaller size, and of different shapes, according to the custom of the various countries. We shall hereafter describe this species of finery.

The plainness of their houses corresponds with that of their dress. They are commonly constructed of earth, and thatched with straw, especially in the country. Those who live in towns are for the most part better accommodated.

The inside of the house is like a small cloister, with a court within it, and a gallery, from which, all round, there are entrances into small chambers, very dark, the use of windows not being known to the Hindûs, and the interior of the house receiving no light but from a narrow passage.

The kitchen is situated in the most retired part of the house, and quite out of the view of strangers, who might happen to come on a visit or any other purpose. In the houses of the Brâhmans, particularly, the kitchen door is always barred; a precaution which they use lest even the gaze of strangers should pollute their earthen vessels for preparing their food, and oblige them to break them in pieces.

The hearth is almost always placed on the south-west quarter, which is denominated the side of the *god of fire,* because they say this deity actually dwells there. Each of the eight points of the compass has its divinity that presides over it.

As men, here, never visit the women, unless they be near relations, and as the females are always occupied with household affairs in the inner apartments which strangers do not generally approach, the fashion is to construct, at the gate of entrance, verandahs or alcoves, both within and without, where the men assemble, and sitting cross-legged, carry on their conversation, talk of business, dispute on religion or science, receive their visitors, or pass their time in empty talk.

Besides private houses, there is generally one or more of public erection in places of any considerable size, known to the Europeans under the name of *choultries,* and which merely consist of a vast empty hall, open on one side the whole length. They serve not only to shelter travellers, but are also used as courts of justice, where the chiefs of the district assemble to discuss the affairs of the village, or to decide differences and accommodate disputes. They likewise serve for temples, in places where there is no other edifice set apart for religious worship.

CHAPTER XVI.

OF THE RULES OF POLITENESS IN USE AMONG THE BRÂHMANS AND OTHER HINDÛS.—OF THEIR VISITS AND PRESENTS.

It would be useless and tiresome to detail the whole rules of politeness which the Hindûs observe with regard to each other. It will be sufficient to mention some of the principal, which will shew their particular turn on this point.

The Hindûs have many modes of *salutation*. In some parts, they manifest it by raising their right hand to the heart: in some, by simply stretching it out towards the person who is passing, if they know him. For they never salute those whom they are not acquainted with. In many parts, there is no shew of salutation whatever. When they meet any of their acquaintance, they content themselves with saying a friendly word or two in passing, and then pursue their way.

They have likewise borrowed the Musalman *salâm;* and they salute both Muhammadans and Europeans with this ceremony, which consists in raising the hand to the forehead. When they address persons of distinction and high rank, they give them the salâm thrice, touching the ground as often with both hands, and then lifting them up to their foreheads. Sometimes they more nearly approach the person whom they wish to distinguish by their attentions, and, instead of touching the ground three times, they touch his feet as often with their hands, which they afterwards raise to their forehead.

The other castes salute the Brâhmans by offering them the *namaskâram.* This salutation consists in joining the hands and elevating them to the forehead, or sometimes over the head. Such a mode of saluting implies great superiority on the part of him to whom it is paid.[w] It is accompanied with these two words *andam arya;* which signify, "Hail! respected Lord!" The Brâhmans, in return, stretching out their hands half open, as if they wished to receive something from the person who pays them homage, answer with this single word, *âsirvâdam,* "benediction!" When people do not intend to carry their reverence to the utmost, they limit it by raising their hands no higher than the breast.

The Brâhmans and Gurus alone have authority to return the âsirvâdam, or to pronounce this sacred word over those who treat them respectfully, or make them presents.

Another very respectful mode of salutation consists in lowering both hands to the feet of the person to be honoured, or even in falling

[w] In regard to the subject of this chapter compare *Manu,* Chap. II, 119 and following couplets.

down and embracing them. This homage is sometimes paid by a son to his father, and sometimes by a young man to his elder brother, when they have met after a long separation: but in general children pass their parents hundreds of times every day without paying them the slightest attention.

Of all forms of salutation, the most striking and the most respectful is the *sâshṭângam,* or prostration of the eight members, elsewhere mentioned, which consists in throwing themselves at their whole length on the ground, and stretching out both arms over their heads. This is practised before the Gurûs or other high personages, and in presence of an assembly, when they appear before it to solicit the pardon of any misdeed.

When relations come in a body from distant parts to pay a visit of ceremony, they make a pause near the place to which they are going, and send a messenger to apprize their friends of their approach. These immediately go in search of them and conduct them home with the sound of music. But it is not customary to embrace on such occasions, or on any other; with the single exception, that in some places, visits of condolence on the death of some very near relation admit of it; but, in the closest embrace, they always avoid touching each others faces. And, in no case whatever, is a man permitted to embrace a woman. It would be considered a monstrous impropriety. A husband, even, cannot in public, use such familiarity with his own wife, nor a brother with his sister, nor a son with his mother.[x]

Relations who have been long separated testify their joy, when they meet, by clinging closely together, chucking each other under the chin, and shedding tears of joy.

The Brâhmans and other Hindûs, in quitting an apartment, follow the same rule of politeness that we do, by letting the visitor walk first. They differ in this from the Spaniards and Portuguese, who shew their civility by doing quite the reverse. The object of this practice is to avoid turning their back on their guest; who, on his part, declines it also, as far as he is able, by going side by side with his entertainer until they are both out of doors.

Agreeably to this usage, when a person retires from the presence of great men, he steps backwards or sidelong to a certain distance; and by the same rule, a servant attending his master on foot or on horseback never goes before him.

To tread in the footstep of any one, even by accident or inadvertency, demands an immediate apology; which is made by stretching both hands towards the feet of the party offended.

---

x Among some tribes, which retain more of primitive usage than the rest, such as the Baḍagars on the Nîlgiris, when any member of the village community returns home after a prolonged absence, he receives a solemn benediction, with the imposition of hands, from those older than himself, while he bestows the same on those junior to him. The younger reverently touch the feet of their elders.

To receive a blow is not considered a great matter, whether inflicted by the fist or the bare foot: but when aimed at the head, so as to make the turban fall off, it becomes a serious insult.

But by far the greatest of all indignities, and the most insupportable, is to be hit with a shoe or slipper. To receive a kick from any foot with a slipper on it is an injury of so unpardonable a nature, that a man would suffer exclusion from his caste who could submit to it without receiving some adequate satisfaction. Even to threaten one with the stroke of a slipper is held to be criminal and to call for animadversion.

One of the reasons which make them dislike to serve the Europeans is the great terror they are under of being kicked by their master with his boots or shoes on; a sort of discipline, it must be owned, not unexampled.

The women, as a mark of their respect, turn their backs to the men whom they hold in estimation. They must at least turn their faces aside, and cover them well with their veils. When they go out of doors, they must keep on their way without noticing goers or comers. If they meet a man, they must hold down their head or avert their countenance. They never are permitted to sit in the presence of men. A married woman is not indulged in this privilege, even in the presence of her husband.

Any person whatever must turn aside when he meets a person of much superior rank. If on foot, he must go off the path, so as to leave it unincumbered; and, if on horseback or in a palanquin, he must light and remain standing till the great personage has passed and got to some distance.

In speaking or saluting a superior, he must cast off his slippers. He must do it also when he goes into his house. One is not permitted to enter into a cow-shed even, with leather shoes on his feet. Wherever he has occasion to go, he must invariably leave his slippers at the door. If he were to pass the threshold of his own house, or of any other, with any integument of leather, it would be considered on all hands as an enormous impropriety.

In addressing any person of note, they must in politeness preserve a certain distance from him, and cover their mouths with their hands while they are speaking, lest their breath or a particle of moisture should escape to annoy him.

It is only among equals that reciprocal salutations are admitted; and superior persons, when they receive this mark of respect from their inferiors, are not required to return it. The Brâhmans, when accosted with the *namaskâram*, content themselves with giving back the *âsirvâdam*. They behave differently indeed to the Europeans and Moors, when their interest engages them to shew their manners. Unless they have some motive of that sort, either of hope or fear, they never salute foreigners in any way; but under those circumstances, they perform their *salâm* in one of the modes described already. But they do not hesitate to make their different salutations, even the *sâshṭângam* itself, to their Gurûs or the Sannyâsis of their caste.

It is the custom in several of the southern provinces of the peninsula for the men to uncover their shoulders and breast, when addressing any person for whom they have respect. It is also observed by the women of certain castes, who always, when under the necessity of speaking to a man, uncover the upper part of the body from the head to the girdle, and wrap round their middle the part of the clothing which usually covers the shoulders and chest. They act in the same way when speaking to their husbands, or other persons at home, whom they are bound to reverence. It would be thought a want of politeness and good breeding to speak to men with that part of the body clothed.

When the Hindûs visit a person of consideration for the first time, civility demands that they should take with them some present, as a mark of deference and respect, or to shew that they come with a friendly intention, especially if their object be to ask some favour in return. But, in any case, to approach respectable people with empty hands would be considered as an act of presumption. When the means of offering presents of value are wanting, they carry with them, on their visits, sugar, bananas, cocoa nuts, betel, milk, and other simple offerings.

Some visits are held to be indispensable, such as those of *condolence* and of *Pongol*, which shall be afterwards explained. They commence on the first day of the return of the sun, when that luminary, according to the Hindû calculation, enters the tropic of Capricorn, and begins his approach, infusing as it were a new life into all nature.

The festival to which this epoch gives rise is celebrated with unusual pomp and solemnity in the Tamul districts. The day itself and the two that follow it are distinguished above all others for the presents which friends and relations mutually offer, consisting of new earthen vessels, on which certain figures are drawn with chalk; of ground rice, slips of bastard saffron, and various fruits. These presents are carried with much solemnity with the sound of musical instruments. A present of this sort is of most indispensable obligation from a mother to a married daughter. If it were neglected the mother-in-law would resent the omission to her dying day.

With regard to the visits in cases of mourning, they never can be represented, as they often are with us, by letters of condolence. Some one of the family must go in person, although at a distance of thirty or forty leagues. Indeed hardly any difficulty can be offered as an excuse for the non-performance of this duty.

CHAPTER XVII.

OF THE DECORATIONS WORN BY THE HINDÛS, AND THE DIFFERENT EMBLEMS WITH WHICH THEY ADORN THEIR PERSONS.

EVERY Hindû, without excepting those even who engage in the profession of penitence and renunciation of the world, wears ear-rings of gold. The penitents, indeed, or Sannyâsis, who were supposed to have overcome the three great lusts of women, honours, and riches, have them made of brass instead of the more precious metal.

These pendants are of different sorts and shapes; but most commonly of an oval form. They are sometimes large enough to admit one's hand to go through them. For the most part they are made of a slender ring of copper, round which gold wire is twisted so as to cover it entirely. People of ordinary condition ornament it with a pearl or precious stone, which is attached to the centre of the pendant and adds to its beauty.

This species of ornament, of a size sometimes so preposterous, will not appear improbable to those who have attended to the practice in the remotest antiquity, as described in the antient writings, sacred and profane. At times they load their ears with four or five pairs, particularly during the ceremony of marriage.

Some likewise wear, at the middle of the ear, a little golden trinket, to which they attach a precious stone; whilst others fix this ornament to the upper part of the cartilage.

The poor people have small pendants of little value dangling at each ear; and, in whatever distress they may be, the universal fashion requires that this organ should not be without its ornament.

Some people of distinction and wealth wear round their necks gold chains, or a species of chaplets of pearls which descend to the bosom.

Many of them are seen with rings of gold and of silver, in which precious stones are set, of very high value. They frequently add to these several ornaments large bracelets of massy gold, of more than a pound weight each. The men, likewise, after they are married, generally wear silver rings upon their toes.

But there is an ornament quite peculiar to the people of India, and which seems to be unknown to other polished nations in modern times, although it appears to have been used in early ages by the nations of antiquity. It consists of various marks or emblems inscribed on the forehead and other parts of the body. The simplest of all, and at the same time the most common, is that to which they give the name of *Pottu*, being nothing more than a small circle of about an inch in diameter, stamped on the middle of the forehead; of a red colour, or sometimes black, or yellow. This last colour is procured by rubbing sandal wood on a flat stone, from whence a liquid odoriferous paste is formed, with which they impress the sign on the middle of the forehead.

Some instead of the *Pottu*, draw between the eye-brows three or four horizontal lines. Others describe a perpendicular line which descends from the top of the forehead to the root of the nose.

Some northern Brâhmans apply this liquid paste of sandal to either jaw, with much effect. Others again use it to colour the neck, the breast, the belly, the arms, with various images and figures; and some have their whole bodies besmeared with it. Many of them mix the paste with vermillion or other ingredients, according to the colour which they prefer.

The Vishṇuvite Brâhmans, as well as the other Hindûs who are particularly devoted to the worship of Vishṇu, adorn their foreheads with the figure called *Nâma*, which has been already described to be a line, generally red, drawn perpendicularly on the middle of the forehead, and two white lines collaterally, which unite at the base with the middle line, and give to the whole the appearance of a trident, producing an extraordinary and at times a ferocious air in those who are so conspicuously marked. Some devotees of the sect have it imprinted, likewise, on the arms, the shoulders, the breast and the belly.

The marks which the disciples of Śiva bear on their foreheads and other parts of the body are always put on with the ashes of cow-dung, or the ashes gathered where dead bodies have been burned. Some devotees of this sect have their whole skin thus speckled from head to foot. Others draw large bars not only across the forehead but on the arms, breast, and belly.

A great number of Hindûs, who are not connected with any sect, likewise rub their foreheads with the ashes. The Brâhmans never lay them on in that manner upon any part of the body, but occasionally, in the morning, draw a small horizontal line over the middle of the forehead, to denote that they have bathed and are pure.

The Hindûs adopt a great variety of other marks, of various shape and colour. Some are peculiar to certain castes; others are in use in some particular countries only, but the most of them denoting the exclusive devotion they entertain for some sect.

It is difficult to explain the origin and meaning of many of these symbols, the greater number of those who use them being ignorant of it themselves. Some may be found who consider it merely as a matter of ornament; though, certainly, the great majority have superstition only for their end and aim.

But, whatever the motive may be, the custom and fashion require that every man should have his forehead adorned with some one of the marks used in the country. To have it bare, is the token of being in mourning, or it signifies that they are yet unbathed and have not broken their fast; and it is as inconsistent with decorum for any one to present himself in that unseemly condition before any company or any individual of respectability, as it would be in Europe to go into polite society with matted hair and disordered apparel.

The women are by no means so attentive to this kindof decoration as the men. They content themselves in general with exhibiting the little circle on the middle of the forehead, of red, black, or yellow, called *Pottu,* which we before described. Sometimes they draw a single red line horizontally or perpendicularly, and rub a little of the ashes on it, according to the custom of their caste. But to make up for their negligence in this species of decoration, they frequently rub the face, legs, and all the parts of the body that are exposed, with a water made yellow by the infusion of bruised saffron.

One finds it difficult to believe that the people of India can imagine such bedaubing and other devices, so ridiculous in our eyes, to be ornamental, and to augment their charms; but, on the other hand, they are disgusted with many of our customs, especially with our wearing wigs, made up of hair, shorn sometimes from a leprous skull, sometimes from that of a prostitute, or perhaps even of a putrid carcase. A bald head, to be sure, is no misfortune in so warm a country; but, at all events, they would think it preferable to the dreadful alternative of covering the crown with such disgusting and abominable offal.

Væ tibi! væ nigræ!
Dicebat cacabus ollæ.[y]

PHÆDR.

[y] "Woe to thee! Woe, ! thou black one! said the kettle to the pot."

CHAPTER XVIII.

OF THE MARRIED BRÂHMAN WOMEN; THEIR DRESS AND ORNAMENTS.

WHAT I have to relate concerning the *Brâhmanâris*, or Brâhman women, will equally apply to other individuals of the sex in different castes. Yet there is but little to be said concerning the Hindû women, from the small consideration in which they are held; always treated as if they were created for the mere enjoyment of the men, or for their service. They are supposed to be incapable of acquiring any degree of the mental capacity which a greater ascendant in society would surely confer upon them, by rendering them of more importance in the affairs of life. But they are so low in estimation that, when a man has done any thing reprehensible, it is quite proverbial to say, that he has acted in the spirit of a woman. She, on the other hand, as an excuse for any fault, lays all the blame on the natural inferiority of her sex.

Agreeably to this mode of judging of the fair sex, the education of the women is utterly neglected. They never cultivate, in any degree, the understanding of the young girls; though many of them are naturally ingenious, and would shine under the advantages of education. It is thought quite sufficient in India that a woman can grind and boil their rice, or attend to the other household concerns, which are neither numerous nor difficult to acquire.

The immodest girls, who are employed in the worship of the idols, and other public prostitutes, are the only women taught to read, to sing, and to dance. It would be thought the mark of an irregular education if a modest woman were found capable of reading. She herself would conceal it out of shame. As to the dance, it is confined entirely to the profligate girls, who never mix in it with the men. In singing, the modest women, in some places, join; but it is only at marriages or other ceremonies among their relations, and never in the company of strangers.

The work of the needle is generally unknown to a Hindû female. Almost all the inhabitants make use of clothing in the piece, uncut; and therefore there is no occasion for employing the art of sewing. For the same reason they are ignorant of knitting; but they are all skilled in spinning cotton. This labour occupies almost all their leisure, and affords to many of the poor the means of living. There are few houses that are not provided with one or more of the little machines used in this domestic art.

We have before observed, that as the Brâhmans marry their daughters extremely young, they make them return to their paternal home as soon as the ceremony is completed, where they continue till they arrive at a marriageable age; and fresh ceremonies take place on this new occasion.

When the event which marks this epoch takes place, it is speedily communicated to the husband, and published with the sound of trumpets; when the relations assemble to festivals, and celebrate the various rites particularly described in the chapter on marriage.

Undoubtedly, the principal motive for this festival is the near prospect which the parents of the young couple have now before them of a new generation about to spring from their immediate descendants. For no people in the world have so ardent a desire, as the Hindûs manifest, to perpetuate their lineage.

This festival has the name of *Marriage complete*. At this time the women make the bride undergo the greatest part of those ceremonies which have been described, particularly such as are designed to counteract the fascination of spells and evil glances. Some days afterwards she is conducted with pomp and state to the house of her father-in-law, where she is trained to live with her husband.

When a woman, particularly of the Brâhman caste, becomes pregnant, the ceremonies which she undergoes have no end. There are some applicable to every one of the months of gestation. It is also absolutely necessary that she should lie-in at her father's house. For this purpose, her mother demands her about the seventh month, and she is not allowed to return until she is perfectly recovered. But on no consideration will she go home, unless her mother-in-law or some other near relation attends to conduct her. This is a general and invariable rule in every caste. Very frequently a discontented wife forsakes her husband; and though it may be for no other reason than a transient fit of ill humour or caprice, and a matter entirely of her own seeking, yet will she never return to her mother-in-law, unless she receives from her the first advances.

These domestic discords, and the consequent flight of the lady to her paternal home, are very common. They generally originate from the extremely harsh and domineering manner in which their mothers-in-law conduct themselves towards them, looking on them as slaves purchased with money. They embroil the husband and wife with false reports, lest they should live too lovingly, and lest the wife, by being too much caressed, should cease to be obedient. Yet this is but an imaginary danger, as the husband looks on his wife merely as his servant, and never as his companion. He thinks her entitled to no attentions, and never pays her any, even in familiar intercourse.

The women, on the other hand, are so accustomed to the austere manners of their husbands, that they would disapprove a contrary behaviour, and despise their husbands if they treated them with easy familiarity. I have seen a wife in a rage with her husband for talking with her in an easy strain. "His behaviour covers me with shame," quoth she, "and I dare no longer shew my face. Such conduct "amongst us was never seen till now. Is he become a *Feringi, "and does he suppose me to be a woman of that caste?"

But, degraded as the Hindû women are in private life, it must be allowed that they receive the highest respect in public. They certainly do not pay them those flat and frivolous compliments which are used amongst us, and which are the disgrace of both sexes; but, on the other hand, they have no insults to dread. A woman may go wheresoever she pleases; she may walk in the most public places (must I except those where the Europeans abound?) and have nothing to fear from libertines, numerous as they are in the country. A man who should stop to gaze on a woman in the street, or elsewhere, would be universally hooted as an insolent and a most low-bred fellow.

We have said enough on the subject of women, in a country where they are considered as scarcely forming a part of the human species. But we shall add something concerning their dress and their manners.

The dress consists of a simple piece of tissue used only by women. It is about nine or ten yards in length, and sometimes more, and its breadth is above a yard. It may be seen, in every variety of quality and price, and of all colours. They are bordered at the ends with a colour different from that of the robe. Each extremity is wrapped round the body two or three times, forming a sort of tight petticoat, falling in front as low as the feet; but not so far behind, because the end of the web, passing between the thighs, is tucked up to the waist, and leaves the legs uncovered behind, as high sometimes as the ham. But this fashion of dress is limited to the Brâhmanâris. The women of other castes fasten the web in a different manner, so as to form a completer and more modest covering than the former. Another part of the cloth passes over the head, shoulders, and breast, in the districts where those parts are habitually covered.

The dress of the women, therefore, is of an entire piece as well as that of the men; and, for that reason, it is extremely convenient for bathing; a practice which the rules of purity require from the females of the tribe as much as from the males; and they are no less addicted to it.

In some parts, they wear a sort of jacket, which does not reach so high as the shoulders; but this is a foreign custom borrowed from the Mahommedans.

I have seen Brâhman women, on the coast of Malabar, who, together with the women of the other castes of that country, always appeared with their bodies half naked; I mean quite uncovered down to the girdle. This appears to have been the ancient mode of dressing all over the peninsula, and is still retained in the mountainous parts, where many other customs are preserved in pristine vigour.

* *Feringi* is a term of reproach by which they designate Europeans. It is derived from the word *Frank*; and was introduced into India by the Muhammadans.

The Hindû women paint on the arms of their young daughters various figures, chiefly of flowers. It is done by slightly pricking the skin with a needle, and inserting into the punctures the juice of certain plants. These marks are never effaced, and continue imperishable on the skin during life. Where the complexion is not very dark, they also decorate the face, by this art, in various places, particularly the chin and the cheeks. These spots resemble the patches sometimes put on by the European ladies to set off their beauty. But, when the skin is very dark, they are considered as useless.

Besides the yellow tincture made with saffron water, already mentioned, which is used chiefly by the Brâhman women, to stain the face and other uncovered parts of the body, they paint with black the border of the eye-lashes, particularly when they are young. It relieves the white of the eyes, and adds to their lustre.

As to their hair, to give it a sleek and glossy appearance, they frequently rub it over with oil; and, separating it into two equal clusters, from the forehead to the crown, one on the right and the other on the left, they unite them together behind, and, rolling them up in a particular way, form a copious bunch which is fixed over the left ear.

The Hindû women, in general, have beautifully black hair, and never of any other colour. But it is wholly different from that of the negroes, being as fine and as smooth as our own. They ornament it with sweet scented flowers, and frequently with trinkets of gold. For, silver embellishments are not permitted to be worn on any part of the body, except a single buckle on the braid behind, which serves to tuck up the hair.

The ornaments of silver are appropriated to the arms, but more commonly to the legs and feet. Those on the legs are truly fetters, weighing sometimes two or three pounds.

Each toe has its particular ring, so broad above as to conceal the whole toe.

The trinkets for the arms are of various kinds. The bracelets are sometimes formed globular and hollow, and more than an inch in diameter: while others have them flat, and perhaps two inches in breadth. Some wear them round the wrist, and others above the elbow. They are either gold or silver, and of various shape, according to the fashion of the country and the caste. The poor have them of brass; and some are seen with more than half the arm covered over with a number of large rings of glass.

Round their necks are hung several chains of gold or silver, and strings of large beads of gold, pearl, coral, or glass, according to the ability of the wearer. Some have collars of gold, an inch broad, set with rubies, topazes, emeralds and other precious stones. With such ornaments all of them are bedecked; each, according to her fancy or means.

There are a great number of other decorations, the names of which it would require long study to acquire. They differ in shape in the various districts. I know eighteen or twenty species of ornaments for the ears alone.

But, as if all these toys were not sufficient, the women, in several districts at least, wear another of a particular form on the right side of the nose, where it is suspended through a little hole purposely bored at the extremity of the nostril. It hangs sometimes as low as the under lip. This last embellishment, the form of which is also varied in the different castes, is scarcely met with in the Tamil country, but is universally seen in Canara and the Telugu countries.

It raises our wonder to see a woman who is invested with all this finery, bearing a pail of water on her head, grinding rice, and performing the other household labours. Thewives of the Brâhmans themselves never scruple to discharge those domestic duties.

It would, however, be too much to suppose that every woman was possessed of all the fine things we have enumerated, their wealth of this kind depending on the riches of their parents and husbands. But it is always a stipulation, in a contract of marriage, how much of this precious commodity is to be contributed by the father-in-law, and how much the bride is to carry with her from home. The jewels, thus obtained, become their inalienable property; which they never fail, when they become widows, to vindicate as their own.

The children of either sex are likewise ornamented with various trinkets of the same form, though smaller than those of grown persons. They have also some that are peculiar. As all children in India go perfectly naked till they are six or seven years old, the parents of course, adapt the ornaments to the natural parts of the body. Thus, the girls have a plate of metal suspended so as to conceal, in some measure, their nakedness. The boys, on the other hand, have little bells hung round them, or some similar device of silver or gold, attached to the little belt with which they are girt.

Amongst the rest, a particular trinket appears in front, bearing a resemblance to the sexual part of the lad.

CHAPTER XIX.

THE STATE OF WIDOWHOOD. SECOND MARRIAGES NOT PERMITTED TO WOMEN.

THE happiest lot that can befal a woman of India, and particularly one of the Brâhman caste, is to die in the married state. Their books pronounce that such an exit is the reward of good deeds done in a preceding existence.

When the husband dies first, just before his parting breath, the wife flies to her toilet; and for the last time in her life, adorns herself with all her jewels and her finest attire. She is no sooner dressed than she returns, with marks of the profoundest grief on her countenance, and throws herself on the body of her dead husband, which she embraces with loud shrieks. She continues to clasp him fast in her arms, until the relations, who are generally quiet spectators of what is going on, thinking she has acquitted herself sufficiently of this first demonstration of grief, attempt to take her away from the body. She will not yield, however, to any thing but force, and appears to make violent efforts to disengage herself from their restraint so as to precipitate herself again upon the corpse. But, finding herself overpowered, she must be contented with rolling upon the ground, as if she were bereft of reason, striking her bosom violently, tearing off her hair in handfuls, and giving several other proofs of the sincerity of her sorrow. She is compelled to act in this manner, were it only in dissimulation, and to save appearances; as it is all in conformity with custom, and appertains to the ceremony of mourning.

After exhibiting these first evidences of despair, she gets up; and assuming a more composed appearance, approaches the body of her husband. Addressing it, in a style rather beyond the limits of real affection she demands—"Why hast thou forsaken me? What evil "have I done that thou hast left me at this untimely age? Had I not "always for thee the fondness of a faithful wife? Was I not attentive "to household affairs? My pretty children, whom I have brought "thee! what will become of them, and who will protect them, now "thou art dead? Did I not neatly serve up thy rice? Did not I "devote myself to provide thee good eating? What did I leave "undone? and who henceforward will take care of me?" Such pathetic appeals as these she utters in a sad and lamentable tone; and, at each demand she pauses, to allow scope to her grief, which then breaks forth in violent screams, and with torrents of blasphemies against the gods, who have deprived her of her protector. The women who are attending wait till she has finished her lamentations, which they re-echo nearly in the same dismal tone.

She continues to apostrophize her husband in this manner, till her wearied lungs can no longer afford her the means of making her afflictions audible, or till her exhausted eloquence has spent all its stores. It is then time for her to withdraw, that she may enjoy some repose, and meditate upon some new harangues to be addressed to the dead body when they are preparing for its obsequies.

The more vehement the expression of the widow's grief on such occasions, and the louder her exclamations, so much the more is she esteemed for her intelligence and sentiment. The young women who are present listen to every word she speaks, and diligently observe all her gestures; and, when they are struck with any thing that appears new or interesting in either, they diligently treasure it up in their memory, to be used at some future time when, in their turn, they are brought into the same predicament.

It would be highly discreditable to a woman, under such circumstances, to forbear these expressions of violent sorrow. I was once appealed to by some relations of a young widow, whose stupidity was so gross, they said, that at her husband's death she had not a word to say; but only wept.

These ceremonies, wailings, and lamentations have been continued from high antiquity.

It is well known that the Romans hired mourners to attend their funerals, who were paid well, in proportion to the apparent vehemence of their sorrow.

In like manner, it is the custom in India to engage women for pay, to assist on such occasions, to add to the solemnity of the mourning by their tears and lamentations. These weeping hirelings when sent for, instantly assemble about the deceased, with hair dishevelled and half their bodies bare, and commence by setting up the loud shout of lamentation in unison; then weep in gentler cadence, and beat time to the measure by thumping their bosoms with both hands. Sometimes, in mild apostrophe, they reproach the dead for his cruelty in departing; and sometimes join in high eulogium on the virtues and good qualities which he exhibited in his life. Each, in her turn, pours out her measure of reproof and commendation. Their assumed grief disappears as soon as the body is carried to its obsequies. They receive their wages, and mourn no longer.

The widows, who, in the learned tongue, are called *Vid'havâ*, which bears a great resemblance to the Latin *Vidua*, are less regarded than any other women, especially if they are without children; in which case they are spurned by all the world. They are then called *Muṇḍai*, a term of derision and even of abuse, as it signifies *shaved head;* which was, indeed, their allotment by the old law, though it be not enforced at present, any more than that which prohibits them the use of betel.

They cannot now wear any ornaments, excepting one of a plain sort, which is fastened round the neck. Coloured clothing is interdicted. In most parts they are allowed *white* only. Neither are they permitted to stain their faces with saffron water; nor even to imprint on their foreheads any of the symbols formerly described. They are excluded from all ceremonies of joy; such as that of marriage, where their appearance would be considered an evil omen.

A woman is constituted *widow*, some days after the death of her husband, by a particular ceremony. The relations and near connexions of her own sex, being assembled in the house of the deceased, after partaking of a repast which has been prepared for them, encircle the widow who is the object of their meeting, and exhort her to be reconciled to her unfortunate destiny. Having joined with her for some time in weeping over it, they make her sit down; and her nearest female relation, after an exordium of some frivolous ceremonies, cuts the thread by which the *Tâhli* is suspended, that little golden ornament which all wives in India wear at their necks as the symbol of their marriage. Then the barber is called, who shaves her head. By these two ceremonies she instantly sinks into the despised class of widows; of which, being conscious, she fails not to make the air resound with her cries while they are going on, and with bitter curses of her unhappy lot.

We have formerly had occasion to remark that, however young or beautiful the widow may be, a new union is altogether impossible, by reason of the invincible customs of the country, which forbid it.

It has also been remarked that, as the progress of libertinism, in our hemisphere, has counteracted the propensity to wedlock, and made Europe the region of single women; so India, from its peculiar habits, has become that of widows. The caste of the Brâhmans is in this respect pre-eminent. The disorders engendered by the prohibition of second nuptials are real, but not so frequently felt as might be supposed; which must in a great measure be attributed to the gravity of the widows, and the naturally chaste temperament of the Hindû women, which is certainly far beyond what is conceded to them by some ill informed writers.

We may enumerate also, among the causes of their reserved behaviour, the constant vigilance and attention which the parents of the young women and widows exert to prevent them from ever being alone; as well as the system of the country, which admits of no familiar intercourse between males and females, but punishes severely the slightest offences against decorum, on the acknowledged ground that they quickly degenerate into greater abuses.

CHAPTER XX.

RULES AND PRECEPTS FOR THE CONDUCT OF MARRIED WOMEN.

I CANNOT better exhibit the manner of thinking adopted by the Hindûs concerning the conduct to be expected from wives, than by copying what is prescribed on that subject in the *Padma purâṇa*, one of the books of highest authority which they possess.

The author introduces, as the speaker, one of the celebrated seven penitents, who was ordained to prescribe the rules which we are about to adduce, and which were compiled for the purpose of attaching every woman to her husband and to the duties of her condition.

I pretend not to approve the whole. Some of them appear to me absurd, or at least useless, and some others injurious to the welfare of society; and the greatest number seem intended to reduce the women to a state of the most abject slavery. But one does not wonder to find here some mixture of the follies of Hindû superstition, which are never wanting in all cases whether grave or unimportant.

I should have been pleased to find a little more of order and connection in the institutes of our author. This portion of his work, although one of the most interesting, is not the best composed. But I shall give it as it is: an authentic model of Hindû diction.

"Hear me attentively, great king of Lippa! I will expound to "thee how a virtuous and affectionate woman ought to conduct "herself towards her husband. So said the great penitent "Vaśishṭa.

"A woman has no other god on earth than her husband. The "most excellent of all the good works she can perform is "to gratify him with the strictest obedience. This should be "her only devotion.

"Her husband may be crooked, aged, infirm; offensive in his "manners. Let him also be choleric and dissipated, irregular, "a drunkard, a gambler, a debauchee. Suppose him reckless "of his domestic affairs, even agitated like a demon. Let him "live in the world destitute of honour. Let him be deaf or "blind. His crimes and his infirmities may weigh him down; "but never shall his wife regard him but as her god. She "shall serve him with all her might; obey him in all things, "spy no defects in his character, nor give him any cause of "disquiet.

"In every stage of her life, a woman is created to obey. At "first, she yields obedience to her father and mother. When "married, she submits to her husband, and her father and

" mother-in-law. In old age, she must be ruled by her children.
" During her life, she can never be under her own controul.

" Diligent she must always be in her domestic labours; watchful
" over her temper; never covetous of what belongs to another.
" She must avoid dispute. She must persist in her task, till
" her husband bids her desist. Her deportment and her mind
" must be always serene.

" She may see things she would be delighted to possess; but let
" her not seek to obtain them, without the consent of her
" husband.

" If a stranger insinuates himself, and woos her with the most
" impetuous passion; if he offers her the richest garments and
" jewels above all price:—by the gods! she will spurn him
" from her presence.

" When a passenger shews a desire to look at her, she must shun
" him with downcast looks, and walk on in utter disregard
" of him, meditating only on her husband. Never will she
" look in the face of any other man. Thus acting, she will
" receive the applause of the world.

" If her husband laugh, she ought to laugh. If he weep, she will
" weep also. If he is disposed to speak, she will join in con-
" versation. Thus is the goodness of her nature displayed.

" She never notices whether any other man be young or well
" made, nor holds conversation with him. So let her act, and
" she shall have the praise of a faithful wife!

" And equally high in reputation shall she stand, who, seeing
" before her the most beautiful of the gods, shall view him with
" disdain, as unworthy of being compared with her husband.

" What woman would eat till her husband had first had his fill?
" If he abstains, she will surely fast also. If he is sad, will she
" not be sorrowful; and, if he is gay, will she not leap for joy?

" In the absence of her husband, her raiment must be mean.

" Holding in low estimation her children, her grand-children
" and her jewels, in comparison with her husband; when he
" dies she will burn herself with him; and she will be
" applauded by the whole world for her attachment.

" Her father-in-law, her mother-in-law and her husband, are all
" entitled to her affection; and if she sees them squandering
" away all the substance of the family, she shall not complain
" of their acts, far less oppose them.

" The labours of the household she must be always ready and
" diligent to discharge.

" Carefully let her perform her daily ablutions, and the colouring
" of her body with the saffron [illegible]. Let her attire be elegant;
" eye-lids be tinged with bl[illegible] on their edges, and her forehead

"coloured with red. Her hair shall also be combed and "beauteously braided. Thus shall she resemble the *Akchimi.*

"Sweetly let her words distil from her mouth; and more and "more to please her husband be her only aim.

"When he goes out for a supply of wood and leaves; for the "purpose of prayer or bathing, or for whatever other cause; "she ought to watch the moment of his return, be ready to "go before him, to introduce him to an apartment, to find him "a seat, and to serve him with the food that he relishes.

"She should remind him of any thing that is wanting at home, "and whatever he supplies she must manage with care.

"Prudent in speech, she must converse with the Gurus, the "Sanniâsi, with strangers, servants, and every one besides, in "a way becoming herself and agreeable to them.

"In using the authority which her husband has committed to her "at home, she will conduct herself with prudence and mildness.

"Whatever money she receives from him, she must faithfully "expend, with no reservation for herself or her friends, not "even for charitable purposes unauthorised by her husband.

"She must meddle in nothing that passes. She must listen to "no tales, whether lively or sad.

"Never let her yield to anger, or bear malice against others.

"She will abstain from whatever food her husband dislikes.

"She shall not anoint her head or her body with oil, when he "forbears to use it.

"When he goes abroad, if he bids her go with him, she shall "follow. If he bids her stay, she shall stir no where during "his absence. There shall be no bathing, nor rubbing with "oil. She shall not clean her teeth or pare her nails, nor eat "oftener than once a day. She shall not recline on a couch, "nor wear her new attire, nor deck her head.

"A woman, when the complaints of her sex occur, shall hide "herself in a place detached from the dwelling, as if she were "a Paria woman, or as if she had slain a Brâhman. During that "time, she must see nobody, not even her children, nor the "light of the sun. On the fourth day she shall go forth to bathe. "Twelve times shall she plunge into the water, and then "twenty-four times; observing all the usages that pertain to "ablution, and which were ordained before the *Kali yuga.*" (Here the Penitent Vaśishṭa describes the whole of those ceremonies with a minuteness and an indecent plainness which we must not imitate.)

"When a woman becomes pregnant, she must conform to all the "rites that are usual on the occasion. She must shun the "company of women of dubious virtue, and of those whose "children have all died. She shall not ruminate on unpleasant "thoughts; nor look at frightful objects. She shall avoid tales "of distress, and abstain from food difficult to digest. By "adhering to these rules, she shall bring forth beauteous "children; but abortion will follow if she disobeys.

"A woman, when her husband is from home, should strictly "conform to his parting counsels. She must forsake all vain "decoration, and must even refrain from rites which would at "other times be grateful to the gods.

"If a man keep two wives, the one shall in no wise intermeddle "with the other, nor speak good or evil respecting her "companion. She must not allude to the beauty or deformity "of her children: but they ought both to live together in good "accord, without a disobliging expression passing between "them.

"When in the presence of her husband, a woman must not look "on one side and the other. She must keep her eyes on her "master to be ready to receive his commands. When he speaks "she must be quiet, and listen to nothing besides. When he "calls her, she must leave every thing else, and attend upon "him alone.

"When her husband sings, she must be in ecstasy. If he dances, "she views him with delight. If he speaks of science, she is "filled with admiration. When in his presence, she must be "always gay. There must be no gloom or discontent.

"She ought above all things to shun domestic quarrels, whether "on account of her relations, or of any other woman that her "husband may keep, or on account of any unpleasant words "that may arise. To leave her house for reasons such as these, "would expose her to public derision, and give occasion for "many evils.

"Her husband may sometimes be in a passion; he may threaten "her; he may use imperious language; nay, he may unjustly "beat her. But, under no circumstances, shall she make "any return but meek and soothing words. Laying hold of "his hands, she should entreat his forgiveness. There shall be "no exclamations; no thoughts of deserting her home.

"But, to retort upon her husband; to say to him, you have in- "sulted me with rude language; you have beaten me; I shall "speak to you no more; I will look upon you as a father; and "you may treat me as an elder sister; I will meddle no more "with your affairs, and do you let mine alone! I will have "nothing more to do with you: such taunting discourse must "never fall from her lips.

"If her relations shall invite her to any festival, on occasion of a "wedding, the ceremony of the Cord, or the like; she shall "not go without leave from her husband, or unaccompanied "by some elderly woman. She will be absent as short a time

" as possible; and, on her return, she shall faithfully recount " to her husband every thing she has seen, and cheerfully " return to her domestic labours.

" When her husband is from home, she must sleep with one of " her relations, but never alone. She must often enquire after " his health. She must urge him to make a speedy return; " and she will intercede for him with the gods.

" Let all her words, her actions and her deportment give open " assurance that she views her husband as her god. Then " shall she be honoured of all men, and be praised as a discreet " and virtuous wife.

" If her husband dies first, and she resolves to die with him; — " glorious and happy shall she be in that world into which " he has passed.

" But, whether she die the first, or survive her husband: a " virtuous woman will surely enter into the enjoyment of " every blessing in the world to come.

" A woman has no true enjoyment but through her husband. " From him she derives children; he provides her with fine " apparel, decorates her with jewels, supplies her with flowers, " with sandal, saffron and every thing her heart can desire.

" It is, moreover, by means of his wife, that a man enjoys all " earthly happiness. This is the perpetual counsel of all our " books of wisdom. It is by the aid of the wife that he performs his good works, that he acquires riches and honour; " and under her auspices all his measures are prosperous. " A man without a wife is an imperfect being."

These dogmas may appear to bear too heavily upon the females; yet are they kept up in full vigour to this day in many particulars. Nay, in some tribes, they are still more severe. I might give an example of this from some districts under the *Vaishṇava* Brâhmans, where the wife is not permitted to speak to her mother-in-law. When any task is prescribed to her, she shews her acquiescence only by signs. But it sometimes happens that, though deprived of the privilege of words, they can make their gestures so expressive and significant as to put the old woman in a rage.

It is said that the same practice of imposing silence on the young women, in presence of a mother-in-law or a step dame, is established in Armenia: a contrivance well adapted for securing domestic tranquillity; dearly purchased, however, by degrading the most useful and interesting portion of the fair sex into the condition of slaves.

CHAPTER XXI.

OF THE CUSTOM OF WOMEN ALLOWING THEMSELVES TO BE BURNED WITH THE CORPSES OF THEIR HUSBANDS.

THE ancient and barbarous custom which imposes it as a duty on women to die voluntarily on the funeral pile of their husbands, although still in force, is by no means so general and frequent as it was in former times. It is also more rare in the peninsula than in the northern parts of India: where it is by no means uncommon, even in the present times, to see women offering themselves up as the willing victims of this horrid superstition, and devoting themselves, out of pride or vanity, to this cruel death. It is confined to the countries under the government of the idolatrous princes; for the Muhammadan rulers do not permit the barbarous practice in the provinces subject to them; and I am persuaded the Europeans will not endure it where their power extends.[a]

As this awful rite was chiefly an appendage to regal and princely state, it has been considered as honourable in itself and as reflecting additional lustre on the caste and family to which the magnanimous victim belonged.[b] In very old times it was considered an affront to the memory of the deceased, and as an evident mark of the want of that ardent devotion which a woman owes to her husband, when she shewed any reluctance to accompany his body to the pile.

A few years ago, I myself was witness to the influence which these false notions retain even in modern times. It was in the case of the wife of the son of a Polygar, or Prince, of Kangendy, in the Carnatic; upon whom neither entreaties nor threats nor reproaches were spared, in order to induce her to allow herself to be burned alive with the body of her deceased husband; and, more especially, as she was of a family celebrated for several generations, for heroic resolution in that splendid devotion. The funeral was long delayed, in hopes that the woman would at length resolve to prefer so glorious and honourable a death to a remnant of life, to be dragged out in contempt and infamy. But threats and entreaties, long continued as they were, had no influence upon her. She stubbornly resisted all the attacks of her relatives; and her husband was obliged to go unaccompanied to the other world.

The wretched condition of widows, on one hand, and vanity on the other, inspiring the hope of renown, are the principal inducements

---

a It need hardly be mentioned that Sati is not permitted by the British authorities; nor can it be necessary to speak of what Lord W. Bentinck effected in connection with this subject.

b The right is called Sati, which means a *good, honorable woman.*

with those who embrace the dreadful proposal. And, certainly, they are canonized after death; vows are paid to them, and recourse is had to them in diseases and other casualties of life, in the faith that a miraculous deliverance will be effected by their intercession. After the fire has consumed her body, they collect the remnants of the bones which have resisted the fire; and erect over the spot little pyramids or monuments, to transmit to posterity the memory of so illustrious a victim of conjugal attachment. This distinction is the more striking that a grave-stone is a thing almost unheard of in India. The ceremony being over, the woman who has submitted to this glorious death is considered in the light of a Deity. Crowds of votaries daily frequent her shrine, imploring her protection, and praying for deliverance from their evils.

To these inducements, which are sufficient in themselves to make a powerful impression on an enthusiastic and fanatical mind, let us add the solicitations of relatives; who if they observe the slightest tendency in the widow to devote herself, never fail to prompt and encourage her to come to a final determination. And to accelerate this object, they sometimes ply her with drugs, which confuse the intellect, and make her easily submit to any thing that is required of her. Her relations are pleased with the result, well knowing that so splendid a death will redound to the everlasting honour of their family.

Some authors who have mentioned this inhuman practice, have taken upon themselves to pronounce that it was introduced from a dread on the part of the husbands, that their discontented wives might seek occasion secretly to procure their death. But I can assure my readers that, after the perusal of the writings of native authors, and the long intercourse I have had with many very enlightened individuals in the country, I can find no ground whatever to justify such an insinuation. Indeed, it must appear evident, from the nature of the thing, that a dying husband can entertain no jealousy of his wife surviving him, inasmuch as she is doomed, after his demise, to perpetual widowhood. The most discontented of wives would have more to gain by submitting to the severest husband than she could expect by becoming a widow, at the expense of such a crime, which could lead to no hope of improving her situation by a new engagement.

Nor, on the other hand, can we ascribe these voluntary deaths to conjugal affection, although it forms the most ostensible pretext, and although the lamentations and demonstrations of despair manifested by the women, at the death of their husbands, might lead one to suppose that it might really be the motive of such a sacrifice. But all their external expressions of grief may be safely ranked under the head of grimace, of which the Hindus under all circumstances of life, are the most absolute masters. During the long period of my observation of them and their habits, I am not sure that I have ever seen two Hindû marriages that closely united the hearts by a true and inviolable attachment.

The Brâhman women no longer continue the practice of burning themselves alive with the bodies of their husbands. This custom is relinquished to other castes, as well as many others which require the endurance of bodily pain. That which we are speaking of is now almost confined to the tribe of Râjas. But though the Brâhmans have found pretences for absolving their women from this dreadful penalty, they still continue to preside exclusively at such tragical proceedings, and to direct the performance.

When a woman of any other caste than their own, declares, gravely and deliberately, that she is desirous of being consumed alive by the side of the dead body of her husband, the matter is conclusive. She cannot afterwards draw back. Her revocation would be disregarded; and if she refused to go to the pile with good will, she would be carried thither by force.

It is a prevailing superstition through all India that if a woman, after taking that resolution voluntarily, shall refuse to fulfil it, the whole country in which she lives shall be visited with some dreadful calamity. To inspire her, therefore, with adequate courage, the Brâhmans, and all her kindred visit her in turn, complimenting her on her heroism, and the immortal glory which she will derive from a mode of dying which must exalt her in dignity to the gods. They excite her fanaticism by every means which cruel superstition can suggest, and keep up the phrenzy of her imagination, until the hour arrives when she is to be led to the funeral pile.

Then is she bedecked with all her jewels, and dressed in her finest apparel. Her brow is adorned with the sacred symbol of her caste. Her body is tinged with the yellow infusion of sandal and saffron. Every thing is prepared. Her spirits are roused and kept up to the highest pitch of exaltation that fanaticism and superstition can impart. The procession begins, and she is led to the pile on which she is soon to expire.

Before describing the rest of the ceremony, I ought to observe that, in cases where a husband has several wives, which often happens in the caste of Râjas, they dispute with each other for the honour of accompanying their common husband to the pile, and to be burnt with him. The Brâhmans who preside at the ceremony determine which of them shall have the preference. An instance of this kind I will here extract from the *Bhârata*, a work of great authority among the Hindûs.

" *Pâṇḍu*, the King, retired, with his two wives, into the forest, " to pursue a course of penitence. He had also entered into a solemn " vow, under the curse of instant death, that he should hold no commerce with either of them. The youngest was extremely beautiful, " and her charms were so powerful as to overcome the terrors of perdition. For a long time she resisted his solicitations, and reasoned " with him on the danger of yielding to them; for she was unwilling " to incur the imputation of being the cause of his death. But all

" was in vain, her refusal only serving to increase the violence of his " passion. He was at length driven to the gratification of it; and " immediately the curse fell upon him with full effect.

"Being now dead, a question arose, which of the two wives " ought to follow him to the funeral pile; and a sharp altercation took " place between them for the preference. An assembly of Brâhmans " was held to decide the dispute; when the elder of the two wives " insisted, that her rank, as his original consort, gave her a precedence " above any posterior one; and farther observed that her competitor " had several young children, whose education absolutely required " the prolongation of her life.

" The second wife then addressed the assembly admitting the " superior rank of her opponent, but insisting that, as she was the im- " mediate instrument of their husband's death, and the fatal cause " which brought down the malediction upon him, that she alone ought " to endure its consequences. 'And, as to the bringing up of the " children,' quoth she, turning tenderly towards her rival, 'are they " not yours as well as mine? Besides, what sort of education could " they expect from a young inexperienced girl like me? Believe me " it will better suit with your gravity and years.'"

In the Bhârata, the debate is carried on to much greater length; but it will be sufficient to relate that, notwithstanding the eloquence of the younger lady, the court gave the preference to the other, and " admitted her," says the author, " to the distinguished honour of " being consumed alive with the body of her husband."

In some other castes of Hindûs, where the custom of burial prevails, instances have occurred of women being interred alive with their dead husbands. The ceremonies are nearly the same in either case; and in the following detail of them I have it in my power to present a more exact and faithful picture than I have yet seen from any other hand.

The first instance that fell under my observation was in the year 1794, in a village of Tanjore, called *Poḍupeṭṭah.* A man of some note there, of the tribe of *Kômaṭi* or *Merchants*, having died, his wife, then about thirty years of age, resolved to accompany him to the pile, to be consumed together. The news having quickly spread around, a large concourse of people collected from all quarters to witness this extraordinary spectacle. When she who had occupied the most conspicuous part had got ready, and was decked out in the manner before described, bearers arrived to bring away the corpse and the living victim. The body of the deceased was placed upon a sort of triumphal car, highly ornamented with costly stuffs, garlands of flowers, and the like. There he was seated, like a living man, elegantly set out with all his jewels, and clothed in rich attire.

The corpse taking precedence, the wife immediately followed, borne on a rich palanquin. She was covered over with ornaments, in the highest style of Indian taste and magnificence. As the procession moved, the surrounding multitude stretched out their hands towards her in token of their admiration. They beheld her as already translated into the paradise of Vishṇu, and seemed to envy her happy lot.

Their progress being very slow, the spectators, particularly the women, went up to her in succession, to wish her joy, and apparently desiring to receive her blessing, or at least that she would pronounce over them some pleasing word, and predict their future fortunes. She tried to satisfy them all; telling one that she would long continue to enjoy her temporal felicity, and another that she would be the mother of many beautiful children. She assured one that she was destined to live many years in happiness with a husband that would doat upon her. The next was informed that she would soon arrive at great honour in the world. These and equally gracious expressions she lavished upon all that approached her, and all departed with complete assurance of enjoying the blessings which she promised them. She likewise distributed amongst them some leaves of betel, which were eagerly accepted, as relics, or something of blessed influence.

During the whole procession, which was very long, she preserved a steady aspect. Her countenance was serene and even cheerful, until they came to the fatal pile, on which she was soon to yield up her life. She then turned her eyes to the spot where she was to undergo the flames, and she became suddenly pensive. She no longer attended to what was passing around her. Her looks were wildly fixed upon the pile. Her features were altered; her face grew pale; she trembled with fear, and seemed ready to faint away.

The Brâhmans, who directed the ceremony, and her relations, perceiving the sudden effect which the near approach of her fate had occasioned, ran to her assistance, and endeavoured to restore her spirits. But her senses were bewildered; she seemed unconscious of what was said to her, and replied not a word to any one.

They made her quit the palanquin; and her nearest relations supported her to a pond that was near the pile, and having there washed her, without taking off her clothes or ornaments, they soon reconducted her to the pyramid on which the body of her husband was already laid. It was surrounded by the Brahmans, each with a lighted torch in one hand and a bowl of melted butter in the other, all ready, as soon as the innocent victim was placed on the pyramid, to envelope her in fire.

The relatives, all armed with muskets, sabres and other weapons, stood closely round, in a double line, and seemed to wait with impatience for the awful signal.

This armed force, I understood, was intended to intimidate the unhappy victim, in case the dreadful preparations should incline her to retract; or to overawe any other persons who, out of false compassion, should endeavour to rescue her.

At length, the auspicious moment for firing the pile being announced by the Purôhita Brâhman, the young widow was instantly divested of all her jewels, and led on, more dead than alive, to the fatal pyramid. She was then commanded, according to the universal practice, to walk round it three times, two of her nearest relations supporting her by the arms. The first round she accomplished with tottering steps; but, in the second, her strength wholly forsook her, and she fainted away in the arms of her conductors; who were obliged to complete the ceremony by dragging her between them for the third round. Then, senseless and unconscious, she was cast upon the carcase of her husband. At that instant the multitude making the air resound with acclamations and shouts of gladness, retired a short space, while the Brâhmans, pouring the butter on the dry wood, applied their torches; and instantly the whole pile was in a blaze.

As soon as the flames had taken effect, the living sacrifice, now in the midst of them, was invoked by name from all sides; but, as insensible as the carcase on which she lay, she made no answer. Suffocated at once, most probably, by the fire, she lost her life without perceiving it.

The other instance which I alluded to is of a more recent date. It was at the death of the late Râja of Tanjore in the year one thousand eight hundred. He left behind him four lawful wives, whom he had espoused, agreeably to the Hindû custom, which tolerates in Princes the abuse of polygamy.

The Brâhmans having decided that two of the wives should be burnt with their husband, and having selected the devoted individuals out of the four; these received the information with much apparent joy. It would no doubt have been a matter of everlasting shame to themselves, and of the deepest ignominy to the manes of the deceased, had they hesitated in their compliance. They had also reason to believe that means would be fallen upon to procure their assent, whether voluntarily or not; and therefore they made a virtue of necessity, and put on the semblance of consenting with a good grace.

The brief account which I here present of this awful ceremony was communicated to me by a person, of veracity to be completely relied on, who was sent on purpose to the place, to take an account of all the circumstances. His detail extends to four and twenty pages of writing, in which are included several particulars exactly resembling those described in the preceding example, which therefore I will not repeat; nor shall I be tedious upon those that were different.

One day only was required to make the necessary preparations for the obsequies; which were conducted in this manner.

In a field, three or four leagues from the royal residence, they made an excavation of no great depth, about twelve or fifteen feet square. Within it they constructed a pyramid of the sweet smelling wood of the sandal, the only species of timber used in this barbarous rite. On the middle of the pyramid, a scaffold was erected to the elevation of a few feet, constructed in such a manner as that the props could be easily withdrawn; by which means the structure would give way at once. On the four corners of the platform large jars were placed, filled with melted butter, to smear the pyramid, that it might be the more easily set on fire.

This was the order of the procession. It was headed by a great number of soldiers under arms. They were followed by a multitude of musicians, chiefly trumpeters, who made the air re-echo to their melancholy sounds. Next came the body of the king, upon a splendid palanquin richly decorated. This was surrounded by the nearest relations and by the Guru of the deceased. They were all on foot, and without their turbans, in token of mourning. A large party of Brâhmans formed round them, as an immediate escort. The two wives, who were to be burned with the corpse of the king, came next, each borne on a palanquin quite open. They preserved, during the journey, a calm appearance and a cheerful air. The escort of troops kept off the immense crowds who were assembled from all quarters, some from motives of interest and others out of curiosity.

The two Queens were attended by some of their favourite women, with whom they occasionally conversed. They were loaded, rather than decorated, with jewels; which were not stripped from them, as commonly happens to women of ordinary rank, when they ascend the pile. They were accompanied by their relatives of both sexes, to many of whom they had made presents before leaving the palace. Thousands of Brâhmans, collected from all parts, made up the rest of their retinue; and an innumerable multitude of persons of all ranks followed in the rear.

When they arrived at the ground where the sacrifice was to take place, the two victims were made to descend from their palanquins, for the purpose of purification and of performing the other preparatory ceremonies. They went through the whole, without hesitation, and without shewing the least embarrassment; but, towards the close, their countenances began to betray them, and the three circuits round the pile were not accomplished without considerable efforts to sustain their equanimity.

During this interval, the body of the King had been deposited on the scaffold over the platform. The two Queens were also laid down beside the corpse, one on the right hand and the other on the left; and they joined hands by stretching them over the body. The astrologer or Purôhita having then declared that the happy instant was come for finishing the ceremony, the Brâhmans recited several Mantras in a loud voice, and consecrated the pile by sprinkling it with their *tîrtham* or holy water. These brief ceremonies were hardly over, when, on a signal given, the pillars, which supported the pyramid and the scaffold, were suddenly withdrawn, and the women were instantly overwhelmed by the falling mass of timber, which tumbled over them with a crash. At the same instant the whole edifice was kindled in all its parts. On one side the nearest of kin to the

King applied his torch, and opposite to him the Guru; while the Brâhmans in every quarter were pouring jars of melted butter on the flames, creating so intense a heat as must have instantly consumed the victims. Then the multitude shouted for joy; and the kindred, approaching the pile, also set up a loud cry, calling upon them by their names. They fancied they heard a voice in answer pronouncing *Enna? What?* But the fall of the platform and the immediate bursting out of the flames must have stifled them at once.

Such was the miserable end of those unhappy victims of a cruel and barbarous superstition; and such are the ceremonies with which it is accompanied, varying in different districts, but fundamentally the same.

Two days after, when the fire was completely extinguished, they dug out from amongst the ashes some portions of the bones which were not wholly consumed, and inclosed them in urns of red copper, which were sealed with the signet of the new King. Soon afterwards, thirty of the Brâhmans, set out with them for *Kâśi* or Benares, to cast them into the holy waters of the Ganges. The reward which was to be paid to them, upon depositing the relics at Kâśi, was previously agreed upon, and was paid them when they returned with certificates from that holy city.

A small portion of these bone-ashes was pounded and swallowed by twelve Brâhmans, who mixed it as an ingredient with some other food. This act, so revolting to our nature, was believed to be expiatory of the sins of the three parties deceased. But, as it is understood that this can be effected only by transferring those sins into the bodies of the Brâhmans, the lucre which they derive from so unnatural an act is not believed to be attended with much ultimate advantage to them.

There were also found among the ashes some small pieces of gold, formed, no doubt, from the trinkets of the Queens, which the violence of the heat had fused.

It then became a question what recompence the Brâhmans should share who had borne a part in the obsequies, or had honoured them with their presence. The King's Guru received a present of an elephant. The three palanquins, which had served to transport the corpse and the two Queens to the pile, were allotted to the three principal Brâhmans. Amongst the rest a distribution was made, in cloth and money, to the amount of about twenty-five thousand rupees, besides several bags of small coin scattered among the crowd, in the course of the procession. Finally, twelve houses were built, which were given to the twelve Brâhmans who had the courage to swallow the pounded bones of the deceased, and by that means to take upon themselves all their sins.

Some days after the funeral, the new King made a pilgrimage to a temple a few leagues distant from his capital. After bathing in a privileged pond in its neighbourhood, and being here thoroughly cleansed from all the impurities contracted during the previous ceremonies of the mourning, he made some further presents to the Brâhmans and to the poor of the other castes.

On the spot where the funeral pile was erected, on which the King and his two unhappy Queens were consumed, a round mausoleum has been built, about twelve feet in diameter, terminating in a dome. Here the present Prince generally stops, when he happens to go out in that direction, and prostrates himself before the tombs of his predecessors.

A great number of votaries of all castes continually repair thither to offer their vows to these new divinities, imploring their help and protection in all the vicissitudes of life. When I was last there, in 1802, a great variety of pretended miracles were current, as having been performed by their intercession.

India is not the only nation in which the abominable practice of sacrificing the wife on the pile of her husband has been adopted. Ancient authors speak of it as not unknown in early times amongst other civilized nations. Herodotus, in particular,[c] speaking of the Crestonæans, asserts that the women dispute with each other for the honour of dying with their husband. She who was esteemed to have been his favourite, had the preference, and was slain on his tomb. The rest, to whom this honour was refused and who were only permitted to be present at the ceremony, returned from it abashed and in confusion. The Indians, however seem to be the only people in the universe who keep up the abominable custom to the present day.[d]

---

[c] Gaisford's Ed. Tom. II. 581.

They were a Thracian race. This custom has prevailed in many countries, among the Teutons. (Val. Max. VI. 1), the Wends, and the Heruli, (Procop. B. Goth. ii. 14), among the Slavonian and Scandinavian races. In reference to the Wends, the words of S. Boniface (Ep. ad Ethelbald, works Giles' Ed. Vol. I. p. 136,) are; "tam magno zelo matrimonii amorem mutuum servant, ut mulier, viro proprio mortuo, vivere recuset; et laudabilis mulier [SATI] inter illas esse judicatur, quæ propriâ manu sibi mortem intulit, *ut in unâ Strue pariter ardeat cum Viro suo.*"

[d] Husband, or man, in Sanskrit is *dhava*. From this the Sanskrit forms the name of the widow by the addition of the preposition *vi*, which means without; therefore VIDHAVA *husbandless, widow.* This word is undoubtedly of the highest antiquity. Now if the custom of widow-burning had existed at that early period there would have been no VIDHAVAS, no husbandless women. Therefore the very name indicates, what can be proved by historical evidence, the late origin of widow-burning in India.

In the passage of the Rig Vêda which has been quoted as the authority for the incremation of Hindû widows a change of two letters has been made. The text is,

Ârohantu janayo yonim agnê ;

They may go the mothers to the altar first.

It has been changed to,

Ârohantu janayo yonim agneh ;

They may go the mothers into the womb of fire.

Few false readings have had consequences so fearful!

Compare Müller's Essay on Comparat. Mythol. Oxford Essays 1856.

CHAPTER XXII.

OF ADOPTION AMONG THE BRÂHMANS AND OTHER HINDÛS.

WHEN a Brâhman finds himself without male issue, whether from the barrenness of his wife or the premature death of the children she may have brought him, he is empowered, nay required, to procure a son by means of adoption, in order to fulfil the obligation which they believe all men to be under, of providing for the succession of society. Besides, as the perfect state of a Brâhman consists in being married, he falls short of that perfection when he is without offspring, particularly males, *to perform his obsequies*. This defect alone is supposed to exclude him from a blessed world after his death.

These notions prevail so strongly among the Hindus, that I have known women not only consenting to their husband taking another wife, but finding him one, when they happened to have daughters only. Yet they could not but foresee the great inconvenience that would result to themselves from the introduction of another wife, who being young and likely to bring male children to her husband, would naturally presume on these claims of superiority over the lawful wife.

We have before remarked, that polygamy was an abuse not publicly tolerated and admitted, excepting in favour of the Princes, to whom the Brâhmans granted the indulgence of marrying as many as five wives in the accustomed way of matrimony. But when persons of ordinary station appear to have other wives besides the legitimate one, it may be inferred that they are merely hired concubines, or wives intended to supply the sterility of the real one. And even, in this last case, the domestic troubles which almost universally spring from it, give a general preference to the practice of adoption.

The Brâhman, who is destitute of male issue, looks out amongst his nearest relations, such as his brothers, or uncles, for a youth whom he may adopt. If he cannot find one in that class of relatives, he goes to his wife's kindred. He may even adopt the children of his own daughter. Those who have several male children very willingly part with one of them to a relation who has none, particularly if he be rich; by which means the property is retained in the family. But if he does not find a proper young man, among his own relations or those of his wife, he has recourse to some poor Brâhman, overloaded with children; and, if he be in tolerable affluence himself, he is not likely to meet with much repugnance in such a quarter. The fundamental rules of adoption are the following:

The adopted son wholly renounces all claim on the property of his natural father, and acquires an unlimited right of succession to all that belongs to his adopted father. From him he is entitled to maintenance and education, as if he were his own son; and to receive, through his means, the advantages of the Triple Cord, and of being settled in marriage. The adopted son is obliged, on his part, to take care of his acquired parents in their old age, and attend to their funeral when they die. Afterwards he enters into possession of their property; enjoys whatever is of value, and is obliged to pay the debts.

He farther enters into the *Gôtra* or lineage of him by whom he is adopted; and is considered as descended from the same ancient stock.

When the ceremonies of adoption commence, the new parents perform one which is held to be the most important and essential of any, by tying round the loins of the youth that little string which every male child in India is ceremoniously invested with at the age of two or three years, and which serves to fix the bit of cloth that is always used to cover those parts of the body. If the ceremony has been previously performed by the natural parents, the adopted ones break the cord, in token of dissolving the Gôtra from which the child descended; and put on a new one, as the sign of his being called to theirs.

On this, as on all other solemn occasions, their first care is to select an auspicious day, and the fortunate moment of the day, by help of the rules of their astrology.

It is unnecessary to enter at large into the remaining ceremonies, as they closely resemble what are used in other solemnities. The Pandal or artificial bower over the door, or in the court before the house, is not omitted. The *Tôraṇam*, of which it is chiefly composed, are easily adapted to that or any other situation, being merely lines stretched in proper directions, thickly strung with mango leaves. When a prince or the governor of a province is expected to pass through a town or village the streets are decorated in this manner, as if with triumphal arches; and, simple as the contrivance is, the effect is exceedingly beautiful.

Within the house, or under this Pandal, the whole relations and friends assemble. The Purôhita commences the ceremonies by offerings or sacrifice to the patron god of the house, and to the *God of obstacles.* He then produces the holy water, of which the adopted son takes a little in the hollow of his hand and drinks it. Some is sprinkled about the house and the Pandal, and over those who are present; and the rest is poured back into the well.

The sacrifice of the *Hômam*, which follows, is made here with some variation, being offered to the *nine planets*, which the Purôhita, by virtue of his evocatory mantras, compels to attend at the ceremony. An offering is also made to them of two measures of rice, in a raw state, which are divided into nine portions. As many Brâhmans, chosen for the purpose, perform the Hômam, with sweet-scented wood; and, after invoking the God of fire, spreading the rice and sprinkling the liquid butter, they make him a profound obeisance with closed hands, and retire.

The sacrifice being over, the adopting father and mother sit down on a little stool placed under the alcove; when the natural mother of the child, after receiving a hundred or perhaps five hundred small pieces of money and a new garment, as her *wages for nursing*, approaches the adopter, who asks her with a loud voice in presence of all the assembly, whether she delivers him her child to be brought up: to which she answers, *I do deliver him to you to bring up.* This phrase is held distinctly to import, that she gives up her son, not as a slave who is sold, but to be reared as a child of the family.

This ceremony applies more particularly to the mother than to the father, as children among the Hindûs until grown up are always considered to belong to her; and if, for any reason, she parts from her husband, she always takes the children away as her own. For this reason the delivering over of the child, in adoption, belongs to its mother; while the reception of it appertains, with equal propriety, to the adopting father.

A dish is then brought in, filled with water, made yellow by the infusion of saffron. It is consecrated with mantras by the Purôhita; and the mother taking the dish, delivers it to the adopter, and at the same time invoking the fire to bear witness, she thrice repeats these words: "I give thee this child; I have a right to him no more." The adopter takes the child, and seating him on his knee, he addresses the relations present, saying: "This child has been given me, and "the fire adjured as a witness of it; and I, having drank of the "saffron-water, promise to rear him as my own son. He enters into "all that belongs to me; my property and my debts."

Then he and his wife, pouring a little saffron-water into the hollow of their hands, and dropping a little into that of the adoptive child, pronounce aloud before the assembly: "We have acquired this "child to our stem, and we incorporate him with it." Upon which they drink the saffron-water, which they hold in their hands, and, rising up, make a profound obeisance to the assembly; to which the officiating Brâhmans reply by the word *Âsirvâdam.*

It is unnecessary to add that the ceremony is terminated by a repast given to the Brâhmans, for which they prepare by bathing; and that the whole concludes with the distribution of betel and pieces of money: for this is the termination of all their festivals.

The circumstance of using saffron-water in this ceremony has given rise to a common appellation for adopted children, who are often called the *water-of-saffron children* of such a one, without meaning it as a term of ridicule or reproach. In this it differs from the nicknames frequently bestowed on individuals there, the most of which are taken from some odd particulars in their lives, and often from some mental or bodily defect.

The Śûdras add one peculiarity to the ceremony, the adopting father and mother pouring on the feet of the child the water from the pitcher, which they hold in one hand; and, catching it with the other hand, and drinking it. In other respects they follow the same customs as the Brâhmans, but they abridge them.

It is not always upon young children that the rite of adoption is performed. Great lads sometimes receive it also, when it suits the interest of their families.

Adoption admits of being effected, in a simpler way, and one better accommodated to the circumstances of people in the humbler situations of life. She who surrenders the child, and he who accepts it, do it in presence of the fire; which they appeal to as being witness to the adoption; and this suffices to render it valid and legal.

Those who inhabit the banks of the Ganges, may perform the act of reddition and acceptance, by taking the river to witness the mutual agreement; and this stands in the place of other ceremonies.

Another species of adoption arises from the wayward circumstances of some of the poorer and meaner Brâhmans; who, finding it difficult to support the cost of the ceremony of the cord and other rites, are reduced to make over the whole or part of their children to richer Brâhmans, who take charge of them; and by this act alone the children are incorporated into the Gôtra and considered as adopted.

The same thing likewise takes place in respect to marriage. A father and mother, unable to support the expence of the ceremonies, give up their son to a man who has girls only. He accepts of him, and gives him one of his daughters for a wife. By this process he is considered as adopted into the family, and enters accordingly into all its privileges and obligations.

But in whatever way adoption is consummated, the adopted child loses all right to the property of his natural parents, and is not at all answerable for the debts they may leave behind them.

The adoption of girls is rare, though not without example.

In the account I have given of the ceremonies used in adoption, as well as in the preceding ones of marriage and the Triple Cord, I have been guided by the Directory or Ritual of the Purôhitas. That book also solves some difficulties respecting the division of the effects; of which we shall now treat.[e]

---

[e] The acknowledgment of this right in the case of Hindû Râjas, by the British Government, is one of the many wise and just measures by which Lord Canning has secured to himself a place in the foremost rank of our Indian Statesmen.

CHAPTER XXIII.

PARTITION OF PROPERTY IN CERTAIN CASES.

In the Ritual above mentioned, the case is put of a man who, after adopting a son, unexpectedly has six children by his wife; four boys and two girls. Two of the boys die, while one of the daughters and the adopted son are severally married. There remain, in a single state, two boys and one girl; and provision must also be made for the subsistence of the mother. The question is, how the effects of the deceased ought to be divided.

The answer given, is to the following effect. First, there must be a sum set apart, sufficient for the expence of the funeral rites of the deceased, to be performed in a decent and creditable way; and also for the marriage of the three children who are not yet established. The sum required for this purpose must be deposited in safe hands.

Secondly. What remains must be divided into six portions and a half. The adopted son takes one portion, with a quarter of the half share. The eldest brother takes as much; after which the remainder shall be divided in equal parts amongst the other brothers and the mother.

If the mother were dead, the division would be into five parts and a half; unless all the brothers should agree to provide their unmarried sister with trinkets out of the share which would have fallen to the mother. If she, at her death, chuses to leave her part of the succession to her daughters, their brothers cannot oppose it. If she does not, the brothers will divide amongst themselves whatever remains of her property, after the charge of her burial.

This decision, laid down by the Brâhmans, appears to vary from the general custom of the Hindûs; by which, in the division of the paternal property, no more is allowed to the elder brothers than to the younger. The mothers, on the other hand, have no share whatever of the property of their husbands, the children being strictly bound to provide for them during their lives.

It may happen that a man who has no children, by reason of the barrenness of his wife, may take another to remedy this defect. If the latter should have a son, the father's estate would descend to him exclusively, and the lawful wife would have nothing whatever at the death of her husband, were the son not obliged to provide for her during her life. If the *great wife*, as the first is called, does not chuse to live with the *little one*, the relations are called in, and a provision is assigned her adequate to her wants.

A rich man, whose wife was unfruitful, being desirous to have progeny, took a second. For the same reason he married a third. The whole proved barren, so that he died without leaving issue. He had an elder brother, and also a younger, as well as several cousins, the sons of his paternal uncles. None of these, however, had been living with him, having long before received their portions, and each maintaining a separate establishment. The question to be determined was, Who is the true heir of the deceased?

The answer given is, that the true heir is the younger brother. As the youngest, the duty of conducting the funeral falls upon him, by the usage of the country; and he who performs the obsequies is held in all cases to be the successor of him to whom he renders those honours. In becoming the principal at the interment, he also becomes the head and master of the house. He will therefore take on himself the maintenance of the three wives left by his deceased brother; and if any of them should wish to return to her relations, she will be free to do so, and to take with her the jewels which she had received from her husband. Besides this, an assembly of the relations will determine upon the allowance which her brother-in-law, the heir to her husband, shall be bound to afford her. If she incline to remain in the house that was her husband's, and to have an establishment there, apart, she will be indulged in her wish; and in that case her brother-in-law would not be under the necessity of assigning to her any considerable income. She would make it up by begging alms; a profession not disgraceful in such a case, being one of the six privileges of her caste.

The brother-in-law is also obliged to bear the expence of the funerals of the three widows, if they die before him.

If there were no junior brother, it would be the elder alone who would have every right centred in him, whether regarding the obsequies or the succession; and in default of both, they will pass to the nearest relation on the father's side.

The book from which I have quoted does not enter more deeply into the division of property in difficult cases. The relatives assembled decide any dispute, according to the rules of the country or the caste, and more frequently still according to the wealth and generosity of him who best rewards them for a favourable decision. This, of course, leads in such popular courts, to innumerable intrigues, and perversions of justice.

From what has been remarked, it will be seen that the right of succession and that of performing the obsequies are inseparable. When a rich man dies, without issue, or other direct descendants, a crowd of remote relations appear, who dispute with each other the privilege of conducting the obsequies. The contest is often prolonged till the corpse becomes putrid in the house. But the case is very different when a poor man dies under the like circumstances. Nobody contends for the right of disposing of his body. On the contrary, all his relations keep aloof; knowing that he who took charge of his funeral would also have the burden of his debts.

There is still another rule respecting succession among the Hindûs that differs wholly from ours, and which would appear to us somewhat irreconcileable with the principles of public justice, which ought to be observed in all civilized nations.

A father dies, leaving several male children, who, from negligence or perhaps unwillingness to separate, or from his having left nothing, have none of his property to divide. Some of them, by industry, application and economy, acquire considerable wealth, while the rest becoming vagabonds, thoughtless and dissolute, sink into difficulties and debt. After scouring the country for many years, these probably discover that some of their brothers, by industry and good conduct, have acquired some degree of opulence; and from them they confidently claim an equal share of what has been acquired by the sweat of their brows, and devolve upon them a proportion of the debts which they themselves have contracted by debauchery and misconduct. If this be refused, the creditors come forward, and, by the process of law, compel the industrious part of the family to make good the waste of the prodigals.

If brothers, for the reasons we have alluded to, or any other, neglect to make a partition of property; when they die, the community of effects and debts attaches to their children: and, if these are equally negligent it descends to their posterity.

Accordingly, it is by no means rare to see cousins of the fourth or fifth degree, engaged in law-suits concerning the division of goods, founded on the right thus transmitted from their great-grandfathers. It is not difficult to imagine, that, under such circumstances, the thriving part of a family are frequently molested by their poorer relations; or that, in a country where there is no public system of law, and where custom, as various as the tribes, regulates every thing, there should be abundance of litigation and chicanery.

There is one advantage however, arising from this singular custom, which in some measure compensates for its bad effects; namely, that it gives brothers and other relations who are liable to be affected by the law of partition, the right to watch over the conduct of each other, and to restrain the debauchery and extravagance of those whose misconduct might involve them all in distress.

In no case, have daughters a title to share in their fathers' property. When a man dies, leaving girls only, they are entirely excluded from the inheritance; and all the effects of the deceased pass to his nearest male relations. They are obliged, no doubt, to rear and maintain the young women, and to dispose of them in marriage when grown up. But this last is no burden, as they receive money on such occasions, instead of paying any. A contract of marriage in India can be only considered as a bargain and sale, by which a father or any other owner of a girl disposes of her at a certain price, to any person who is willing to buy a wife.

CHAPTER XXIV.

OF THE LITERATURE OF THE BRÂHMANS AND PARTICULARLY THEIR POETRY.

It is not to be doubted that from the earliest times the sciences have been cultivated by the Hindûs, or rather by the Brâhmans, who have been in all ages, as it were, the depositaries of them. They have always considered them as a property exclusively their own; and perceiving the ascendant which their learning gave them over the other castes, and the reputation which it acquired them, they have always made a mystery of it to the vulgar, and taken the greatest pains to prevent its spreading among other classes of men.

But, have they themselves cultivated the sciences with success, or have they made any advancement in them? This we must answer in the negative, if we judge from the scientific remains of their ancient authors, compared with their present literary men. I do not believe that the modern Brâhmans have made the smallest progress in any branch of learning which they cultivate, beyond their ancestors of the era of Pythagoras and Lycurgus. That long space of time, between epochs so remote, during which so many barbarous races have emerged from the darkness of ignorance to the brightest splendour of civilization, and have extended their intellectual researches beyond the natural sphere of the human mind, has been employed to no purpose by the Hindûs. They have continued on the very spot where they stood more than two thousand years ago. During that period half the world has become enlightened; but, amongst the Hindûs, one can trace no improvement in the sciences or arts; and the most partial observer must admit that they are now far behind many communities who were not so soon inscribed in the roll of cultivated nations.

The sciences which rendered them most famous amongst external nations, in times of superstition and ignorance, and which conciliated at the same time the awe and reverence of their own countrymen, were Astronomy, Astrology, and Magic. The first shall be considered hereafter. The other two have been discussed in a treatise by the late P. Pons, missionary in the Carnatic, published in the memoirs of the Academy of Sciences, and copied by the Abbé Lambert into his *General History of All People.*

No comparison can be drawn between the schools of science in that country and those established in Europe. All that can be pretended is that in some large towns, or in the precincts of some large temples of their idols, certain Brâhmans, learned or affecting to be so, teach gratuitously what they themselves know to such as are willing to take lessons from them; while some others do so with more attention to their own interests. But the whole is carried on without method, without any place for study, without discipline. He may learn who has a mind, and as long as ever he chuses; but there is nothing in their institutions which can excite the student to emulation, or encourage the teacher; no examinations to undergo, no places to gain, no premiums to contend for, no privilege held out to those that excel. The reputation of wisdom, to be sure, draws reverence from all the world; but this is not a motive sufficiently powerful to stimulate the Brâhmans. It would be necessary that they should taste more frequently than they do of the liberality of their Princes. But these great men are too much lulled by pleasures, and too deeply immersed in ignorance to be able to appreciate the value of science, or to feel the least impulse of generosity towards those who cultivate it.

So much, then, for the course of study, the universities and the literati of India.

In reference to the literature of the Hindûs, I shall here confine myself to the Hindû poetry.

I suppose there is no country on earth where Poetry was more in vogue than it was in former times in India. It seemed impossible for them to write but in verse. They have not a single ancient book that is written in prose; not even the books on medicine, which are said to be numerous in the Sanskrit tongue. All Hindû books that are not in verse are modern. The translators of the eighteen Purâṇas from the original Sanskrit into the other idioms of India, have all written in verse. At least I know it is so in the Tamil tongue, the Telugu and Kanarese; and I have no doubt it is the same in the other dialects of the country.

The *Tamil* Poetry has been chiefly cultivated by the Śûdras, who, by labouring to preserve the turn of the Sanskrit Poetry, have so multiplied the rules of their rhyme that it is very difficult to make correct verses in their language.

The Poetry in the Telugu and Kanarese has been principally cultivated by the Brâhmans; and it has such a resemblance to the Sanskrit, even in prosody, that I do not believe the Śûdras had meddled in these two dialects. Of the Sanskrit poetry itself I shall endeavour to give some idea, such as may apply generally to the various sorts, as they exist in the several idioms of India.

I shall consider, 1. The various Species of their Poesy. 2. The long and short *Letters*. 3. The *small Feet* of the measure. 4. The *large Feet*. 5. The Rhyme. 6. The Versification. 7. The style or taste of Hindû Poetry. But, having no intention to compile a Hindû Prosody, which would be little amusing to my readers, I shall say but a few words on each of those heads, and merely what may be necessary to give a general view of the subject.

1. *The different Species of Poesy.*

There are several sorts, such as, *Padam* (Ode) *Padyam*, (Stanza) *Dwipada*, (Couplet) *Daṇḍaka*, (blank verse.) Another kind has been specified under the name of *Padya,* but as it is not composed of feet, we do not include it with the others.

Under the head of *Padam,* they comprehend the odes in honour of their Princes and other great men; songs of gallantry and lewdness; libertine addresses to the gods and goddesses; lines composed by adulators in honour of those whom they wish to flatter, or upon more ordinary occasions. This species of Poetry is likewise called *Sringâram* or *ornamented,* because it is often the vehicle of eulogiums on women, and the ornaments they wear on various parts of their dress.

Amorous songs are likewise denominated *Sittimbam* or the *Joy of Pleasure;* a name no doubt derived from the licentious. Of this sort there is an infinite variety. They are chanted by beggars when they carol from door to door for alms. The more indecent and gross the allusions, the dissolute audience are the better pleased.

The hymns in honour of the gods are also called *Kírtanâ* or *Praise,* being intended to glorify the divinities of the land.

The word *Padam* is likewise used for the *strophe* of a poem.

The second species of Poesy, called *Padyam* comprises the great poems, composed in honour of the gods, the kings, and other mighty personages. This kind is formed of several stanzas, like the *Jerusalem Delivered* of Tasso; but they are not uniformly constructed. There are at least thirty sorts, which may be successively used or intermixed at pleasure in the course of the poem.

These *Stanzas,* are also employed on subjects of morality and satire. The Poet Vêmana, who wrote in Telugu, and Tiruvaḷḷuvan who wrote in Tamil, have distinguished themselves in this measure, to which we shall afterwards return.

The species called *Dwipada* or *two-footed,* is much less rigorous than the other kinds, and is indeed merely a measured prose, written in poetic fashion. It has been employed by the authors of little histories, or local exploits, whether true or imaginary.

From these three examples, the other sorts belonging to this class may be imagined, without farther illustration.

2. *The long and short Letters.*

The Hindû verses, like the Latin and Greek, are composed of short and long syllables. From these simple feet, are formed hemistichs; by combining which, the full verses are evolved.

I have mentioned that the *short feet* were composed of *Letters,* because in the Indian languages Letters are actually Syllables. Every consonant carrying its vowel along with it, they pronounce Ba, Be, Bi, &c. Da, De, Di, &c. but never B, D, mute, or separate from a vowel. Even a double syllable such as Bra, Dla, Ksha, Rma, &c., in many dialects, is considered as making but one letter.

Of the Letters some are short and called *Laghu.*[f] The others are

---

[f] Light.

long, and called *Guru.*[g] Even in familiar writing, they seldom fail to distinguish the long and short letters with their particular marks. It is still more regularly attended to in pronunciation; and, in verse, it is quite indispensable.

In Hindû Poetry, as well as in Latin, a long letter is equivalent to two short, and two long to four short. Thus the word *Māttā* is equal in quantity to *Kălăgădŭ*, composed of four shorts. But there are letters which, though short in writing and in ordinary discourse, become long in verse, by position. Thus the *a* which begins the word *Akcharam* though short in general, becomes long in versification, as being placed before two consonants *K* and *Cha*. In the same manner the letter *Ka*, though naturally short, is long, in verse, in such a word as *Karman*, on account of the two consonants which follow it. Two examples of this occurring to me from Virgil, in the lines, "*Brontesque,* "*Steropesque et nudus membra Pyracmon,*" and—"*date tela, scandite* "*muros;*" I expressed my doubt one day to a Brâhman, who was explaining to me the rules of Poetry. His vanity and self-conceit had been already a little humbled by finding that a foreigner could so easily comprehend matters which he thought quite sublime; but when I started my difficulty, he stood fixed for a while in astonishment, and stared me in the face without speaking. At length he answered, "You are right; but I am astonished how such a thought could have "entered into your mind, knowing so little as yet of our Poetry." I told him that the Poetry of my own country bore some resemblance to that of his, and that my acquaintance with the former led me to the observation I had made. These words served to increase his astonishment, as he had always supposed, till then, that no creatures on earth knew any thing of Poetry but the Brâhmans. This prejudice made me easily pass with him for a man of wonderful penetration. This at least I gained by it, that he became more diffident in our future intercourse.

The last letter of a verse may be of any quantity, at pleasure; but the distinction must always be marked in pronunciation. The Latins took the same licence; and it is likely that Horace, when he said "*Sic* "*te Diva potens Cypri,*" pronounced the last syllable short, and in the verse "*Amice propugnacula,*" long; because in the one the last foot is a dactyl, and in the other an iambus.

As, in an idolatrous nation, every thing tends to superstition, the poets of India hold some letters to be *amritam*, or *ambrosial*, and others to be *Visham*, or *poisonous*. The one are of good omen, and the other mischievous. This distinction is not regarded in poetry relating to the gods, who are supposed incapable of being affected by the good or evil qualities of letters; but, in verses which concern human beings, the case is very different, and particular care must be taken never to begin any thing, addressed to them, with a visham, or unlucky letter. The letter which has the sound of *Ke*, and that which sounds *Ki* are of that quality in some idioms, because their form in

[g] Heavy.

writing is such that the point turns down towards the ground. The *Ko*, on the contrary, is fortunate, because the point of that letter turns up on high.

3. *The small Feet in Verse.*

There are two kinds of feet in verse, the small and the large; the latter being composed of the former. The feet have the name of *Gaṇam*, of which there are two kinds, the simple *Gaṇam* and the *Upagaṇam*. The chief of this are:

1.	The Iambus:	Sanskrit.	Lagam: ∪ — .
2.	The Trochee:	„	Galam: — ∪ .
3.	The Spondee:	„	Gangâ: — — .
4.	The Tribrach:	„	Nanuhi: ∪ ∪ ∪ .
5.	The Dactyl:	„	Bhactapa: — ∪ ∪ .
6.	The Amphibrach:	„	Jajâpa: ∪ — ∪ .
7.	The Artibacchic:	„	Tampaśya: — — ∪.
8.	The Anapœst:	„	Sarasâm: ∪ ∪ — .
9.	The Cretic:	„	Rakshâya: — ∪ —.
10.	The Bacchic:	„	Yatistê: ∪ — — .
[h] 11.	The Molossus:	„	Mantrâṇâm: — — —.

The Hindû poets discover a certain relation between the *Gaṇam* and the Upagaṇam; one or the other causing good or evil, according to the god who presides over it. Those that fall under the rule of the Moon, which is, in India, the emblem of cold, are deemed favourable; while those, on the contrary, which are governed by the Sun, are injurious. Agreeably to this superstition, a copy of verses must not begin with a malign *Gaṇam*. The Hindû prosodies are very diffuse on this subject.

4. *The long Feet.*

The Gaṇams, then, are the true materials from which the *Feet* of the verse are made, which are called *Padam* or *Charanam*; both which words signify *Feet*. They may be compared to the hemistichs of pentameter lines, or the pause which we make in the middle of the verses of ten and twelve syllables, in French and English. They enumerate a variety of these *Padams*, according to the number of *Gaṇams* they contain; some having three, five, seven, or more.

As in pentameter verse, two dactyls or two spondees may be put in the first hemistich; so also, in certain Padams, they may use one Gaṇam or another at pleasure, provided the number of shorts and longs is preserved. This mixture, however, must be managed without affectation, to avoid the appearance of pedantry.

But every species of Gaṇam is not equally admitted into all sorts of poetry; some of which require certain fixed Gaṇams. On this point the Hindû prosody enters into a great variety of particulars not

[h] See Brown's Telugu Grammar.

very important. The case is nearly the same in the Latin Ode, where a rigorous restriction to certain feet is required, and where others, though on the whole equal in quantity, cannot be admitted.

The *Long Feet*, in Hindû verse, have each their particular name; as the Elephant, the great Tiger, the Serpent Capella, and so forth.

5. *The Rhyme.*

The Hindûs have a two-fold Rhyme in their verses. The one sort falls on the first letter or syllable of the line, and is called *Yati*. Thus, in two verses, where one begins with the word *Kîrti* and the other with *Kîrtana*, *Kî* is the Yati or Rhyme. The other sort falls on the second letter or syllable from the beginning of the line, and is called *Prâsam*. In two lines, one beginning with the word *Capagny* and the other with that of *Dipantram*, *pa* is the *Prâsam*.

Although they are unacquainted with blank verse, yet they are not very rigid in point of metre. For the *Yati*, they make Ka, Ksha, Kta, all rhyme together; or Pe, Pte, and so forth. There is still more licence in the Rhyme of the *Prâsam*, in which nothing is positively required but to attend strictly to the consonant, without any regard to the vowel. Thus, for example, Da, De, Di, Do, Du, all rhyme together. But these metres are avoided as far as possible; and the lines that have the *Yati* and the *Prâsam* exactly to correspond, are most admired. The nearer this resemblance is attained so much the more palatable to the Hindû; though, to us, such sort of chimes would appear ridiculous play, like the comical line of Ennius so often in the mouths of schoolboys as very ludicrous—"*Tu tibi, Tite Tati, mala tanta, tyranne, tulisti.*"

The only thing remarkable in Hindû prosody, with regard to rhyme, is this complete opposition between our custom of putting the rhymes at the ends of the lines and theirs of placing them at the beginning; which also adds to the difficulty of their composition of verses.

6. *Of the Verse.*

Padams, or feet, arranged artfully with regard to quantity and rhyme from the *Padyams*, which are sometimes called *Slôkams*.

The Hindû poets have several species of *Padyams*, each of which has its particular name. In the simple *Cawdapadyam*, certain feet, and no other, can be introduced; in the same way as in the hexameter verse, dactyls and spondees only can be used. But a single *Gaṇam* may sometimes compose a whole verse, such as *Devaki, desuki, Camsudu*. There are a great many minute instructions to be attended to on this subject, which are too minute to detail.

It will appear from what has been said, that the Hindû versification is by no means easy; and accordingly, though great numbers in every caste dabble in verses, there are but few who make them correct or conformable to the strict rules that are laid down. Their poets, however, possess an advantage which does not attend most of the European tongues, and particularly the French, in the numerous synonymes with which the Indian languages abound.

7. *Of the Taste and Style of Hindû Poetry.*

The poetical expression of the Hindûs perhaps offends by too great loftiness and emphasis. One may understand their books and conversation in prose; but it is impossible to comprehend those in verse, until diligent study has rendered them familiar. Quaint phrases, perpetual allegories, the poetical terminations of the words, contracted expressions, and the like, render the poetical style obscure and difficult to be understood, excepting to those who are inured to it.

One of the principal defects of the Hindû poets, at least when compared with our taste or our prejudices, is that their descriptions are commonly too long and minute. For example, if they are describing a beautiful woman, they are never contented with drawing her likeness with a single stroke, as a European would generally do in similar cases; saying, perhaps, that she possessed all the charms that nature could confer. Such an expression would not be strong enough for the gross comprehension of a Hindû. The poet must be more exact; he must particularise the beauty of her eyes, her forehead, her nose, her cheeks, and must expatiate on the colour of her skin, and the manner in which she adorns every part of her body. He will describe the turn and proportion of her arms, legs, thighs, shoulders, chest, and in a word, of all parts, visible or invisible; with an accurate recital of the shape and form which best indicate their beauty and symmetry. He will never desist from his colouring till he has represented in detail every feature and part in the most laboured and tedious style, but at the same time with the closest resemblance.[i]

The epithets, in their poetical style, are frequent, and almost always figurative; which makes them approach very nearly to the Latin poetry.

---

[i] Mr. Brown's remarks concerning Telugu poetry will apply mutatis mutandis, to Tamil, Kanarese and Malayâlim poetry also, and in fact to the poetry of all the vernacular languages of India.

"Telugu poetry has now lasted for more than six centuries: and the earliest compositions manifest a high state of literary refinement. Their taste is often such as we must condemn, but we have no means of framing a *fair* judgment until we are able to read the original. Were Horace to be judged of from our English translations, who could imagine him to be a poet? The French translation of Paradise lost is a similar failure.

Much however that is admired in Telugu is in the worst taste of literary frippery. At the conclusion of poems, in particular, we find verses framed in fantastic shapes, such as that of a sword, a square, a wheel, a serpent or any other laboured conceit. Another refinement relates to the language: wherein the same verse is made to bear two entirely different imports, every word involving a poem.

The Telugus evince a remarkably vivid attachment to the literature of their language, and it greatly endears a foreigner to them to know that he has studied the poems which among them hold a reputation as permanent as that of Paradise lost among ourselves."

The brevity and conciseness of many modes of expression in the Hindû idioms, does not hinder their style, upon the whole, from being extremely diffuse.

Their verses, in many of their dialects at least, would appear harsh and inharmonious to a European ear, on account of the frequent aspirations to which many of the letters or syllables are subject, which in many cases seem incapable of being joined together. Yet this mode of pronunciation has a certain firm and masculine tone, which makes up for its uncouthness. The observation, however, does not apply to the poetry in the Tamil language, in which many of the poets write; because that dialect has no aspirations.

To give an exact idea of the different species of Hindû poesy would not be much relished by the greater number of readers, so different is their manner from ours. All their little pieces that I have seen are in general very flat.

I know not whether they have any regular dramatic pieces, all that I have seen of this nature being mixed with songs and dialects of which I can give no distinct idea, never having taken the trouble to study any of them.

As to epic poems, they have several. The two most celebrated are the *Râmâyaṇa*, which contains a rapid sketch of the history of *Râma*, or of *Vishṇu* metamorphosed into the shape of that hero, and the *Bhâgavata*, which relates chiefly to the adventures of *Vishṇu*, under the name of *Krishṇa*. These two poems are of an unconscionable length. Their authors have introduced into them all the fables on which the religion of the Hindûs is founded. Their narratives of the same story are often at variance; and they do not at all adhere to the rule of Aristotle, who confines the duration of the epic poem to the period of one year; for the Bhâgavata takes up its hero before his birth, and does not leave him till after he is dead.

The extraordinary and marvellous adventures which are related in the Eneid of Virgil and the Iliad of Homer do not in any degree approach to the incredible prowess and the wonderful achievements of the Indian heroes, whose exploits are celebrated in these books. All that ancient story hands down of Enceladus and his terrific companions, cannot bear a comparison with what is here related of the giants, who sometimes fought against Râma, and sometimes on his side. Tasso himself is feeble in the description of mighty feats, when compared with these transcendent fabulists.[j]

---

[j] As the Tamil metrical system differs considerably from the Sanskrit, adopted by the Telugu, Kanarese and Malayâlim poets, I add a few words regarding this subject.

For further information see *Babington's Beschi's Shen Tamil Grammar*, and Pope's IIIrd Grammar, 2nd part, where also the Native authorities are given.

It will be necessary to consider

FIRST, Tamil meterical feet.

These are

I. Single feet.

1. Nêr : —.
2. Nirai : pyrrhic : ◡ ◡ (or iambus ◡ —.)

II. Double feet.

3. Nêr + ner : spondee. — —.
4. Nêr + nirai : dactyl : — ◡ ◡.
5. Nirai + nêr : anapæst : ◡ ◡ —.
6. Nirai + nirai : proceleusmatic : ◡ ◡ ◡ ◡.

☞ Each successive foot is formed from one of the preceding by the resolution of a long into two short.

III. Triple feet.

7. Nêr + nêr × nêr : Molossus. — — —.

The remainder are formed by adding successively a *nêr* and a *nirai* to each of the double feet giving, 8. *Ionicus a majori*, 9. *Choriambus*, 10. *dactyl + pyrrhic*, 11. *Ionicus a minori*, 12. *anapæst* + pyrrhic, 13, 14—two nondescript feet.

IV. Quadruple feet are formed in the same way, but they are not now used.

SECOND, the connection of feet in lines.

There are various methods in which feet may follow one another in lines. Of these the most used are the methods called the *Veṇ* or pure, and the *Viruttam*, or expanded.

I. The pure metre. [Veṇ.]

Using only double feet, those triple feet that end in a nêr, and occasionally a single foot, its law is this : *the arsis of a double foot must follow the thesis of a preceding foot, and vice versâ ; but the arsis of the triple foot is followed by an arsis.*

II. The Expanded. [Viruttam.]

This is used in free and lengthened compositions, and the feet of one line may be connected in any way, provided those of the next line have precisely a parallel connection. This consonance of lines is maintained for forty or fifty quatrains. These lines often resemble in Rythm the various Choriambic measures of Horace.

THIRD : Verses.

Of these the kuraḷ couplet of the veṇ metre, and the quatrain of either metre, are most used.

The kuraḷ of Tiruvaḷḷuvan is in the first, most of the ethical works of the Minor poets in the veṇ quatrain, and the Ethics, (Râmâyaṇam, Chintâmaṇi &c.) in the Viruttam quatrain.

The following are peculiarities of South Indian metres.

1. The Rhyme is in the beginning of the line.
2. Each line must have an alliterative consonance between its first syllable and the initial syllable of some one of the succeeding feet.
3. Every foot MUST have *incision*, but there is no Cæsura.
4. The last syllable of any foot, long or short, with a preceding short, forms a nirai.
5. A redundant syllable at the end of a word, is considered a nêr, whether it be long or short.

CHAPTER XXV.

THE EPISTOLARY STYLE OF THE BRÂHMANS.

The epistolary style of the Brâhmans and of the other Hindûs in general is in many respects different from ours. I cannot better explain it than by adducing examples taken from their own letters.

I have selected the three following specimens, to shew, by the first, how a Brâhman addresses a person who is his inferior; by the second, one who is his equal; and, by the third, a person who is above him.

Letter to an Inferior.

"They, the Brâhman Śubâya, to him Lakshmaṇa, who has all "good qualities, who is true to his word, who by the services he "renders to his relations and friends, resembles the Chintâmaṇi;[k] Asirvâdam.

"Year of Kilaka, the fourth day of the month Phalguna, I am "at Banavara, in good health. Send me news of thine. As soon as "this letter shall have reached thee, thou shalt go to the most excel-"lent Brâhman Ânautâya, and prostrating thyself at all thy length "at his feet, thou wilt offer him my most humble respect, and then, "without delay, thou shalt present thyself before the Cheṭṭi" (that is, the merchant) "Rangapa, and declare to him that if he shall now "put into thy hands the three thousand rupees which he owes me, "with interest at twenty-five per centum, I will forget all that is "passed, and the matter shall then be at an end. But if, on the con-"trary he makes shifts and continues to defer the payment of the "money, tell him that I am acquainted with a method of teaching "him that no person shall safely break his word with a Brâhman, "such as I am. This is all I have to say to thee. Asirvâdam."

Letter to an Equal.

"To them the Lord, to the Lord Râmâya, who possesses all the "good qualities which can render a man esteemed; who is worthy "to obtain all the favours which the Gods can bestow; who is the "beloved of beautiful women, who is the particular favourite of "Lakshmi; who is great as the Mount Mêru, and who has a perfect "knowledge of the Yajur vêda: the Brâhman Śubâya; Namaskâram" (respectful greeting).

---

[k] S. *Chintâ*, thought; mani, jewel: the jewel which imparted all gifts which its possessor could think of. The word *Asirvâdam* = a blessing

"The year Durmati,[l] the fifteenth of the month Phalguna,[m] I "am at Bailore, where I and all the members of my family enjoy "good health. I shall learn, with great gladness, that it is the same "with you; and I trust you will inform me particularly of all the "subjects of satisfaction and contentment which you experience.

"On the twenty-second of the month above mentioned, being a "day in which all good omens unite, we have chosen that the mar- "riage of my daughter Vijaya Lakshmi shall be celebrated. I beg you "will honour the ceremony with your presence, and be here before "that day with all the persons of your household, without excepting "any. I expect you will put yourself at the head of the solemnity, "and that you will be pleased to conduct it.[n] And if there is any "thing in which I can be of service to you, have the goodness to let "me know it. This is all I have to apprise you of. Namaskâram."

Letter to a Superior.

"To them the Lord,[o] to the Lord Brâhman, to the great Brâh- "man Ânantâya, who are endowed with every virtue and all good "qualities; who are great as Mount Mêru; who possess a perfect know- "ledge of the four Vêdas; who, by the splendour of their good works, "shine like the Sun; whose renown pervades the fourteen worlds: I, "Kishṇâya, their humble servant and slave, keeping my distance, "with both hands joined, my mouth closed, mine eyes cast down; "wait, in this humble posture, until they shall vouchsafe to cast their "eyes on him who is nothing in their presence. After obtaining "their leave, approaching them with fear and trembling, and "prostrating myself at my whole length before the lotūs flowers "on the ground where they stand; and, thus submissive, with respect- "ful kisses, will I address their feet with this humble supplication:

"The year Vikari,[p] the twentieth of the month Paushya,[q] I, your "humble servant and slave, whom your Excellence has deigned to "regard as something, having received with both hands the letter "which you humbled yourself by writing me; after kissing it and "putting it on my head, I afterwards read with the profoundest "attention, and I will execute the orders it contains, without departing "from them the breadth of a grain of millet. The affair on which "your Excellence has vouchsafed to command me is in good progress, "and I hope that, by the efficacy of your benediction, it will soon "terminate to your entire satisfaction. As soon as that happens, I, "your humble servant and slave, shall not fail to present myself

---

l The 55th of the Hindû Cycle.

m The Month of March—April.

n This is an expression used out of politeness to every one who is invited under similar circumstances.

o A superior is always addressed in the plural, both in speaking and writing.

p The 39th of the Cycle.

q December—January.

"(agreeably to the orders of your Excellence) at the lotūs flowers "of your holy feet. I now entreat your Excellence to impart to "me the commands and instructions necessary to enable me so to "demean myself as to be agreeable to their will, and that you will "clearly point out to me in what manner I may render myself "most acceptable to your blessed feet. For this, it will suffice, if I "receive from your bounty a leaf of betel[r] indented with your nail, "in care of some confidential person, who can verbally explain the "orders of your Excellency. Such is my humble prayer."

The style of these letters strikes us at first as extraordinary, and very remote from what we use in similar circumstances. But, if we attentively consider the epistolary forms that still prevail in Europe, and analyze the letters which Europeans often write to their equals, generally concluding with soliciting as an honour to be favoured with admission into the number of their *most humble and most obedient servants*, it will not appear so easy to determine which style of the two is the more ridiculous and servile. The principal difference, perhaps, is that, in their letters, the fulsome compliments are inserted at the beginning, and in ours at the end.

It is not to be denied that the fawning, tumid and bombastic phrases which the Hindûs use, appear to be arrayed with too much affectation; and we ought to admit still more readily that, in our translations, we come far short of the expressive vigour of the Indian terms. The simple structure of the European tongues does not succeed in translating them literally.

The compliments with which all letters between man and man in India commence are often much longer and more extravagant than those we have adduced. I have seen epistles in which the complimentary effusion covered a whole sheet. But it is chiefly, when writing to persons of great dignity of rank, or when some object is expected to be gained, that the full plenitude of complimentary blandishment is drawn out. The real source of all is to be found in the eager and passionate desire for praise and adulation, which all Hindûs feel.

In letters, written by one Hindû to another, one never sees respects or compliments offered to their wives. Such an attention would be misplaced, and would be considered not only ridiculous but as a gross breach of politeness. They can only be mentioned under particular circumstances, such as condoling with a man on the death of his wife. Then the woman might be praised for her excellent qualities, and wishes might be expressed that the husband might soon find another wife of equal merits. For it is not singular to see a Hindû widower marrying fifteen days or a month after the death of his wife.

When there is occasion to communicate to any one the decease of a relation, the custom is to singe a little the point of the palm leaf on

---

[r] A person dispatched on a verbal message, is frequently supplied with no better credentials than a betel leaf with the print of the nail.

which the afflicting news is written. This has alike import as the black seal used by us in such cases. The same practice takes place when one serves another in writing with a severe rebuke. The application of fire to the palm leaf shews that he who sends it entertains a feeling of resentment.

When a superior writes to his inferior, he puts his own name before that of the person to whom he writes; and quite the reverse when he writes to his superior. Indeed it would be considered as the grossest rudeness if he happened to set his own name first.

Having treated of the language of Poetry and of the Epistolary style among the Hindûs, I will now offer some remarks that I have made on their writing.

CHAPTER XXVI.

ON THE HINDÛ HAND-WRITING.

THE Hindû books attribute the invention to the great Brahmâ, the creator of man and author of his destiny. Each individual carries his doom inscribed on his forehead by the hand of God himself.[s] The sutures of the head, seen on a skull, are the hand-writing of Brahmâ; and the letters there impressed contain the future lot of the individual. This is a fable, no doubt; but it must be also admitted that it is one of very great antiquity, and sufficiently proves, at least, that when it was invented, they had already the knowledge of writing in India; otherwise how could they imagine traces of writing in those marks?

That this knowledge existed amongst the Hindûs, in the most ancient times, is proved by another authority of as old a date as the former. The four Vêdas are attributed to Brahmâ, who wrote them on leaves of gold. These books, which contain the detail of the idolatrous ceremonies which this people practises, are the most sacred of all, and at the same time the most ancient which they acknowledge. Their other books, of which many are, without contradiction, very old, speak of these as of a far earlier date. The language also in which they are written has become unintelligible, in many places, from desuetude by age.

Here, therefore, we find books, and consequently the use of writing, among the Hindûs, in times extremely remote.

One of the principal articles of the Hindû faith is that which relates to the ten incarnations of Vishṇu. The first and earliest of the whole is the change of this God into a Fish. And what was the cause of it? It was the loss of the four books which contained the four Vêdas. Brahmâ, under whose care they were left, fell asleep; and a giant, his enemy, took that opportunity of stealing the sacred volumes. Having escaped unperceived, he flew to the sea, with his precious booty, which he swallowed and deposited in his bowels, the better to secrete it. Vishṇu, metamorphosed into a fish, went in pursuit of his enemy; and, after a long search, discovered him at length, in the deepest abyss of the ocean. Having attacked him there, fought him and vanquished him; he tore him in pieces, plucked the concealed books from his lowest entrails, and restored them to him who was their author and guardian.

Books, therefore, are the subject of one of the oldest fables of India.

---

s Hence "the writing on the skull" is used for *fate*.

The Fourth Vêda of the Hindûs teaches *Magic*; and thence probably all ancient nations derived their Occult Arts. There are practices in India very much resembling those that the soothsayer Balaam employed against the camp of the Israelites, as detailed in the twenty-second and two following chapters of the book of Numbers. This wicked science, having been cultivated, from very early times, by the Egyptians (who might have acquired it from the Brahmâns of India), may have spread, in the same manner, to the nations bordering on Egypt. And it was, no doubt, from that country that the false prophets, or magicians, who so frequently made their appearance among the Jewish tribes, drew their instruction. But, however this may be, Idolatry and Magic are twin sisters, who are seldom found separate. The Hindû idolatry has so much the higher claim to antiquity, that it does not appear, like that of the Greeks and Romans, to have been borrowed from any foreign source, and that some of the writings which contain its details are perhaps among the most ancient that exist in the world.

Some of the native authors ascribe the invention to a famous penitent called *Agastya;* so short, that he was not a hand's breadth in stature.[1] He is one of the oldest authorities to which they refer, having been contemporary with the Seven Penitents who were saved from the flood in the vessel of which Vishṇu was the steersman: the whole being probably nothing else, as we have already observed, than the story of Noah and his family, disfigured by the fables of idolatry.

All these proofs on which I found the antiquity of writing among the Hindûs, I shall be told, are nothing more than a tissue of fables, so absurd that no reasonable conclusion can be drawn from them. Let it be so: but, at least, the whole world must confess that these same fables, however absurd, are of high antiquity; and that their existence, in such ages, necessarily implies the existence of writing also in those very early times.

But it is clear it can be no fable, that in the times of Lycurgus, nearly a thousand years before the Christian æra, there were philosophers in India who were more eagerly sought after than those of Egypt, and who would have been unheard of by the Grecian literati, if they had been recent, or of ordinary repute. Such philosophers therefore, who were also astronomers, must have been long accustomed to the art of writing, which such sciences as these essentially pre-suppose.

Having premised so much on the origin of writing in India, let us now consider its present state. Our observations here will be directed to the characters which the Hindûs use in writing; the material on which they inscribe them; their mode of writing; and, finally, the form of their books, and of the letters which they address to each other.

---

[1] Hence in Tamil called குறுமுனி : *Kuru-muni* — little ascetic.

1. *The written Characters.*

It is said there are eighteen living languages used in India; and though some of them bear a resemblance to others, yet the characters of the greater number are quite dissimilar. What resemblance, for example, between the letter அ (*a*, short) and ஆ (long *a*) of the Tamil tongue, and the corresponding letters of the Telinga, అ, ఆ. The difference is not less striking in every other letter of the alphabet; and the same diversity, as between these two, exists in almost all the rest. Different, however, as they are in the signs which they employ in writing, there is a wonderful similarity in the idioms, in the turn of their phrases, and the arrangement of the words, which scarcely admit of any inversion. In these last particulars, they differ widely from the European languages; which, with a general resemblance in the idiom and the character, are altogether unlike in the particular turn, cast and arrangement of the style.[*]

Notwithstanding the diversity of the written characters in the several dialects, there is an affinity between the languages themselves; so that a person who has learned one, may easily understand those of the contiguous districts: and it is very common to meet with Hindûs who speak fluently seven or eight languages, or more.

But, what is most remarkable here, and makes it almost impossible to describe the difference of character among the various dialects, is first, that all the languages of the country that I am acquainted with have the same arrangement of letters in the alphabet; 2, that all the letters are double, each having a long and a short; 3, that the short and long vowels are always placed at the beginning of the alphabet, and before the consonants, as â *ā*, ĭ *ī*, û *ū*, &c. 4, that these vowels are letters purely initial, which are never so written but at the commencement of a word, and vary their form when used in the middle or after a consonant; 5, that each consonant has a vowel combined, and forms a syllable; thus, one never pronounces *b* or *d* mute, but *ba*, *da*. A slight change in the character will make the *a* vanish, and substitute another vowel according to its new shape. Thus, in the Canarese language, the consonants ಬ (*ba*) and ದ (*da*) undergo the following change of sound by the slight alteration of the shape of the letter:

ಬ	ಬೆ	ಬಿ	ದ	ದೆ	ದಿ
ba	be	bi	da	de	di

How is it that there is so great a resemblance in the idioms of these languages, as well as in the structure of the composition, and so wide a discrepance in the signs and characters? The mother language of all that are spoken in India, from which each derives a common

[*] The student who would fully understand this subject should consult Dr. Caldwell's Drâvidian Comparative Grammar, in which the origin and affinities of the South Indian language are discussed in such a manner as to leave nothing to be desired.

idiom and method, having an alphabet so arranged as we have seen; how comes it that the daughters should have adopted a character so different from that of their common parent?

The like difference is observable in the form of their ciphers, or arithmetical figures, as in their alphabet; and indeed in this case the abberration is greater. For though they all follow the decimal scale, they have different modes of expressing it. In the Tamil language, they do it by a single sign; thus:

௧	௰	௱	௲
1	10	100	1000

In the Telugu language and the Canarese, they follow exactly the same process which we have adopted from the Arabians, expressing the units by a single sign, the tens by two signs, the hundreds by three, and so on. Their arithmetical scale approaches still nearer to ours, by their employing our cipher, and even giving it the same form of a circle, as will be seen in the following example:

1	2	10	11	20	22	100	104
౧	౨	౧౦	౧౧	౨౦	౨౨	౧౦౦	౧౦౪

120	1000	1001	1020
౧౨౦	౧౦౦౦	౧౦౦౧	౧౦౨౦

Such is the *Telugu* arithmetical notation, corresponding very nearly with what was communicated to Europe by the Arabs, at the end of the tenth century. Such a coincidence can hardly have arisen from chance, and it is therefore extremely probable that the one must have been taken from the other.

The *Tamil* notation seems to have greater resemblance to the Roman mode than to the Arabian; for they express the Arithmetical signs by letters of their alphabet, and use but a single letter to denote unity, ten, a hundred, and so forth.

But different as the Hindûs are, in this particular in their several divisions; they are still farther removed from the characters used by other ancient nations, which have come down to us; such as the Phœnician, the Syriac, the Arabic, the Greek. The notation differs no less than the mode of arrangement, seeing that two of the last mentioned nations wrote from right to left, while the Hindûs write as we do.

2. *The Material on which they write.*

Paper is not unknown to the Hindûs. They manufacture it, not from cotton, as is generally believed, but of old bags made of the rind of a plant, having first separated the coarser filaments which supply the place of hemp. I believe, however, that the use of this coarse paper is modern in India, and posterior to the invasion of the Moguls, who are acquainted with no substitute for paper, and still follow the Persian mode of writing. Some Hindûs, particularly such as live in the provinces where it is difficult to find palm leaves, also use paper; but more generally black tablets, on which they write with a white crayon. The ordinary practice, however, is to use the palm leaves, both in common writing and for books. The palm tree is a generic name, which is extended by Europeans to the cocoa tree and the date tree, though the leaves of neither of these be at all adapted for writing on. What they actually employ are those of the Palmyra. They are cut in breadths of about three fingers, and two feet long. Each of them will admit of seven or eight lines; and they are thicker, stiffer, and stouter than double paper, so that after writing, or rather engraving on one side, they turn to the other, without at all injuring what is on the reverse.

Quintus Curtius relates, that the Indians, when they were invaded by Alexander the Great, wrote with an iron point on the smooth and tender bark of trees. I cannot help thinking, however, that the Palm leaves, which are soft and polished, must have been taken by that author for the rind of a tree; more especially as one can see no trace in India of any writing being done upon bark.

The Cumæan Sybil in the Eneid is conjured not to write her oracles on the leaves of trees, which the wind would speedily disperse:

> "——— Tantum foliis ne carmina manda,
> Ne dispersa volent rapidis ludibria ventis."—[ÆNEIDOS VI, 74.]

Whence could the idea have arisen of the prophecies of the Sybil being inscribed on leaves?

3. *The Hindû method of writing.*

They execute it with an iron spike, sometimes six inches long, the upper end of which is commonly formed into a cutting edge to trim the sides of the leaves, so as to make them all straight. In writing with the spike, neither chair nor table is wanted. The leaf is supported on the middle finger of the left hand, and is kept steady by being held between the thumb and the forefinger. The right hand, in writing, does not slide upon the leaf, according to our practice in writing on paper; but, after finishing a word or two, the writer fixes the point of the spike in the last letter, and pushes the leaf from the right hand towards the left, so as to enable him to finish his line. This becomes so habitual and easy, that one often sees a Hindû writing as he walks along.

As this species of penmanship is in fact only a sort of faint engraving, the strokes of which are indistinct and not easily read, especially by weak eyes, sometimes they besmear the leaf with fresh cow-dung, rubbing the surface well, so as to leave nothing behind but the finer parts that adhere to the engraved lines. This they afterwards tinge with black, and thus the writing becomes more visible, and easier to read.

This mode of writing is undoubtedly more simple and easy than ours, for small occasions. Neither does it require, like ours, the apparatus of table, chair, inkstand, and so forth. But I own that ours has the advantage when we have to do with large affairs, or the keeping of journals and ledgers.

The Hindû writing is not exempt from the great inconvenience which attends our old manuscripts, by the absence of points and marks, as well as of the separation between the words and sentences. Besides, their orthography is so extraordinary and complicated, in some dialects, that the best reader cannot decypher what he has before him without hesitation, and without close attention to the subject, especially when it is not set down according to the rigorous grammatical principles, which the greater number are ignorant of or neglect. This difficulty is most severely experienced in the Tamil tongue.

When the Hindûs write on paper, they do not use a pen; the fowls which furnish the quill, such as geese and swans, being unknown in most districts of their country. They use for the purpose, a *Calam* or reed, somewhat thicker than our pens, and cut in the same manner: this word *Calam* is remarkable on account of its resemblance to the Latin *Calamus;* from which the Hindû word must be derived, as I conceive the use of paper in that country is not old.[v]

4. *The manner in which their Books and Letters are made up.*

In making up a book of several leaves of palm tree, there is no occasion for a bookbinder. A small hole is bored at each extremity of the leaves, through which they are strung together by a small cord. Two thin boards are then applied, the one above and the other below, of the same length and breadth as the leaves, so as to form a cover to the book. These are likewise pierced at the extremities, and small pieces of wood or iron are passed through the holes in the boards and the leaves, so as to connect the whole together. A long string is fastened to each end of the bits of wood or iron; and by wrapping it several times round the book the whole is kept shut. If this mode be simple, it certainly is not commodious; for, as often as one consults the book, he must unlace the string, take out the pegs and throw the whole volume into disorder.

The Hindû manner of writing, as well as the binding of their books, approach nearly to the customs of the Romans on the same occasions; for we are informed by Seneca that the ancient Latins wrote on plates of wood, which they strung together and formed into a *Caudex;* from whence, as he observes, is derived the Latin word *Codex.*[w]

I have spoken already of the epistolary style of the Hindus. With regard to the form of their letters, they content themselves with rolling up the leaves of palm on which they are written, and enveloping the whole in an outer leaf, upon which they write the

---

[v] It is the Arab KELEM.

[w] Tom. I. 314 [Elzevir.]

address. Care must be taken about the due length and breadth of the leaves, as well as the manner of putting them up in the outer case, in proportion to the rank of the party addressed.

We are not to judge of the antiquity of writing in India by the dates which we find inscribed on some pagodas or temples of idols; because it has been a trick of the Brâhmans to put up such dates, as, though evidently recently written, would make the origin of the building ascend to the commencement of the *Kaḷi-yuga.* I have seen temples which have been erected within these few years, bearing inscriptions that would carry them as far back as the flood; and that too in the presence of those who had helped to build them, some of whom are still living. Such is the Hindû abhorrence of falsehood!

The gradual change in writing, which takes place in some countries in the lapse of time, is not a safe ground of conjecture as to the age of Hindû manuscripts. I have seen an act of donation written on a plate of gold, in Canarese characters, more than two hundred years ago; the letters of which are perfectly legible, and exactly like those at present in use. No alteration has therefore taken place in that great interval of time.

In some inscriptions, however, of very high antiquity, characters are found not now in use, although they resemble letters employed in writing in other idioms of the country. Some are also found in various places, where the characters are evidently foreign and wholly unknown. It is probable that such inscriptions have been cut by artists brought from distant parts to embellish the edifices on which they appear, and who, being jealous of their architectural fame, would not leave it at the mercy of those who had employed them, or who had assisted them in the labour. By these they might have been robbed of all the praise, if the writing had been made in the ordinary characters.

The remarks I have made concerning the dissimilarity of the letters, and the resemblance of style, in the writing of different districts in India, may be equally applied to the *Siamese* dialect. The alphabet, and particularly the vowels, are there arranged, in the same manner as in the Hindû idioms: *a, i, u, e, ai, o, au, am, ah.* In some languages of India, the point or mark which denotes the vowel that always accompanies the consonant, is placed before it; as in the Tamil syllables தெ, *te,* பெ *pe,* the sign ெ prefixed to the consonant represents the *e*, pronounced after it though placed before it. The same practice is followed in the Siamese writings in several letters; which can scarcely have been fortuitous, and rather indicates that these two different dialects spring from the same source.

The *Páli* language, or learned tongue of Siam is a corrupted Sanskrit. It is not to be doubted that the people of that country anciently spoke this primitive language of the Hindûs. It would even appear to have extended much farther, as I have had several Sanskrit words pointed out to me in the Malay tongue.

The shape of the characters of the Siamese writing, at least as far as I have seen, is indeed altogether different from that of the Hindû. But the same dissimilarity is remarked among the different idioms of India; and it may be farther observed that the Siamese follow the Hindû mode of writing from left to right, and not from right to left, as the Arabs do, nor from top to bottom, like the Chinese. Though they appear therefore, to have a strong affinity to the latter race in the features of the face, as well as in their religious and civil ceremonies, their language and manner of writing seem to approximate them more closely to the people of India, and to assign them the same origin.[x]

---

x The date of the introduction of writing into India is discussed by Dr. Max Müller, history of antient sanskrit literature, pp. 497—524. He announces the following results:

1. No single allusion to writing, reading, paper or pen is to be found in the Vêdic hymns.

2. Before the time of Pâṇini, and before the spreading of Buddhism in India, writing was for literary purposes unknown.

3. The Indian alphabet cannot be traced back much beyond Alexander's invasion.

4. The first actual writing, the first well authenticated inscription in India, is of Buddhist origin.

5. Writing was first used in India probably towards the latter half of the Sûtra period (between 600 B. C. and 200 B. C.)

The alphabets of all the vernacular languages of India have doubtless had a common origin, the original alphabet used by the Brâhmans and probably derived from Aramæan sources, and introduced about 400 B. C. This was brought into South India by Agastya, the traditional father of South Indian Civilization.

CHAPTER XXVII.

DEATH AND OBSEQUIES OF THE BRÂHMANS.

THE decease of a Brâhman is attended and followed by such a number of foolish and ridiculous ceremonies, as clearly prove the determination of that sect to outdo the rest of their countrymen in this as well as in all other things. And indeed they are not at all rivalled, in regard to rites performed for the dying and the dead. We shall first briefly mention such as accompany the agony, and then such as follow the death.

When it is evident that a Brâhman is in extremity and has but a little time to live, a space is prepared with earth, well spread with cow-dung, and strewed with the holy herb of Dharba; over which a cloth that is pure is stretched. By this is understood on the present occasion, a cloth which has neither been worn nor washed in suds. The dying man is placed upon it at his full length, and another pure cloth is wrapped round his loins. This being done, they ask his permission to perform upon him the ceremony of expiation; which is to be made by the Purôhita, assisted by the *chief of the funeral.* This appellation is given to the person who, by proximity of kindred, or by the customs of the country, has the charge of conducting it. The dying man having given his consent, the chief of the funeral brings on one plate, some small pieces of silver or copper coin, and on another, the Akshatâ, the Sandal, and the Panchakâryam. The Purôhita pours a little of this last into the mouth of the sick man; and by the virtue of that nauseous draught the body is perfectly purified. But this does not supersede the general cleansing called *Prâyaschita.* This is accomplished by the Purôhita and the chief of the funeral going up to the dying man and making him recite within himself, if he cannot articulate, the proper Mantras; by the efficacy of which he is delivered from all his sins. For this reason, the ceremony is called *Prâyaschita,* or *general expiation.*[y] But how shall we gravely describe the next ceremony? A cow is introduced with her calf. Her horns are decorated with rings of gold or brass, and her neck with garlands of flowers. A pure cloth is laid over her body; and thus bedecked, she is led up to the sick man, who takes hold of her tail. Mantras in the meantime are sung, the prayer of which is that the cow would conduct him, by a blessed path, to the next world. He then makes a gift of the cow to a Brâhman, in whose hand a little water is poured while he accepts the present; which is the ordinary ratification of a gift.

The donation of a cow, which is termed *Godânam,* is, in this crisis, of indispensable aid in helping the soul to arrive, without accidents, at the *Yama Lôkam,* or the world of hell, which has Yama for its king and lord. In this progress they come to a river of fire, which all must pass after death. Those who have made the Godânam, or the

---

[y] Vishṇu Purâṇ, p. 42.

gift of the cow, to a Brâhman before they die, are met by one of these favoured creatures from the dwelling of Yama, the moment they arrive at the bank of the stream; and by her help, they are enabled to cross, without injury from the flames.

The Godânam being ended, a distribution of the pieces of coin is made amongst the Brâhmans present; and their value united should amount to that of the cow.

On this occasion also, are prepared the *Daśa-dânam*, or *Ten Gifts*, (reminding us of the Latin *Decem Dona*) to be distributed on the day of the funeral, which is conjectured not to be far off. These ten presents consist of the following articles: cows, lands, millet-seed, gold, butter, clothes, grain of various kinds, sugar, silver, and salt. Such costly gifts offered to the Brâhmans, being very acceptable to the gods, will accordingly secure to the dying man a blessed world after his death.

It is fitting that a Brâhman should die upon the ground, not on a bed, nor even on a mat; and the reason is this: his soul being disengaged from his body must enter into another, which will carry it to the world that is destined for it. And if he should die in his bed or on a mat, he must carry with him these moveables wherever he goes; which would be very tormenting. If, on the other hand, he should happen to die, by any accident, in a different way from what has been here supposed, a much more liberal distribution of presents, and a longer tract of ceremonies would be required to get him extricated from the burdens attached to him. This absurd and ridiculous idea, in which the Brâhmans are educated, has given rise to a curse very common among them, when they quarrel; namely: "mayest thou "never have a friend to lay thee on the ground, when thou diest."

As soon as the breath has departed, all who are present must weep for a reasonable time, and join in lamentations, in unison, and with a melancholy air adapted to the circumstances.

The chief of the funeral then goes to the bath, and after ablution, closely shaves his beard and mustaches; makes a second ablution, to cleanse him from the pollution contracted from the touch of the barber who shaved his head; and indeed on all occasions, ablution must follow the contact of the barber. The conductor, on his return, brings several things to the dead body; and amongst others a piece of pure cloth to serve as a handkerchief for the decease, and fire for the sacrifice of the Hômam, which he himself offers up without delay.

After these introductory ceremonies, the corpse is well washed, and the barber is called to shave all hair from the body. He is invested with his finest clothes, and decorated with all his jewels. He is rubbed with sandal where he is uncovered; and the accustomed mark is affixed to his forehead. Thus dressed, he is placed on a species of state bed, where he remains exposed until the preparations are ready for carrying him to the pile.

Every thing being in order, the chief of the funeral approaches the body; and with the assistance of some relation or friend, strips it of its clothing and jewels, and covers it with the handkerchief provided for the occasion; one corner of which he tears off, and wraps in it a small bit of iron and a few seeds of sesamus. I never discovered the reason of this practice.

The litter on which the body is placed to be carried to the pile, is constructed in this manner. To two long poles, placed parallel, they fasten seven pieces of wood across, with ropes of straw. Upon this frame the body is laid at all its length. Then they bind the two thumbs together, and also the two great toes. The handkerchief, which was before negligently thrown over the body, is now carefully wrapped all round it, and firmly bound by straw-ropes. They leave the faces uncovered of those only who have died in the state of marriage. The litter, adorned with garlands of flowers and foliage, and sometimes decked with valuable stuffs, is borne by four Brâhmans chosen for that purpose. The procession is thus arranged.

The chief of the funeral marches foremost, carrying fire in a vessel. The body immediately follows, surrounded and attended by the relations and friends, all unturbaned, and with nothing on their heads but a plain bit of cloth, in token of mourning. The women never attend at the funeral, but remain behind in the house; where they set up hideous cries as it is setting out. While advancing on the road, the custom is to stop three several times on the way, and at each pause, to put into the mouth of the dead a morsel of unboiled rice moistened. But the object of the stoppage is very important. It is not without example, they say, that persons, supposed dead, have not been actually so; or, even when lifeless, have been reanimated and restored; and sometimes also, it has happened that the gods of the infernal regions have mistaken their aim, and seized one person instead of another. In any view, it is but right to afford time and the opportunity for rectifying such mistakes, so as not to expose to the flames a person who may be still alive. Hence the propriety of the three pauses; each of which continues half the quarter of an hour.

Having at length arrived at the place set apart in each district for burning the dead, they commence by digging a trench of inconsiderable depth, and about six or seven feet in length. The small space which it occupies is consecrated by the mantras of the Purôhita. It is slightly sprinkled with water to lay the dust; and a few pieces of money in gold are scattered upon it. Here the pile is erected, of dry wood; on which the body is laid out at full length. The chief of the funeral kindles a piece of dried cow dung,[1] and puts it on the breast of the corpse, over which he makes the sacrifice of the *Hômam*, which is immediately succeeded by the most extravagant of all ceremonies. The conductor places himself close to the deceased, and addresses certain mantras to each aperture in the body; at the same time, applying his mouth to every one of them in its turn. There are nine in all, accord-

[1] It is well known that in India the scarcity of fire-wood is so great as to oblige the inhabitants to burn the dung of the cow or buffalo, which has been previously flattened and made thin like a cake.

ing to the Hindû account, which includes the two eyes, the ears, the nostrils, the mouth, the navel, &c. When he has concluded the appropriate mantram to each orifice, he pours into it a little liquid butter, which operates a perfect cleansing of the body. The disgusting and indecorous spectacle is closed by his putting a bit of gold coin into the mouth of the corpse; which each of the assistants follows up with a little crude rice that has been steeped in water.

They at last strip it of the few ornaments which were left, and even of the handkerchief with which it was enveloped, and the little belt to which the bit of cloth is appended which all Hindûs wear before them. Over the body a quantity of twigs are laid, which are slightly sprinkled with Panchakâryam; and the chief of the funeral, taking on his shoulders a pitcher of water, goes three times around the pile, letting the water run aslant over it through a hole made in the vessel; which he then breaks in pieces, near the head of the corpse. This act and the more important one that follows constitute him the universal heir to the deceased.

At last, the torch is brought for setting fire to the fatal pile, and is presented to the chief of the funeral. But, before receiving it, he is obliged to make some grimaces to prove his sorrow. He rolls about a little on the ground, beats his breast, and makes the air resound with his cries. The assistants also cry, or appear to cry, and embrace each other, in testimony of their true or counterfeited grief. Fire being then applied to the four corners of the pile, the whole crowd retire, excepting the four Brâhmans who carried the body; and they remain until the whole is consumed.

The chief of the funeral flies immediately to the bath, and plunges in, without taking off his clothes. All dripping, and in the open air, he boils some rice and pease, and exposes them to the crows, which, it is well known, are numerous in India; but on such an occasion, the crows are not crows, but devils or malevolent beings, under that shape, whom they wish to appease and render propitious by this offering. If they should refuse to eat, which the Hindûs say has sometimes happened, it is taken for an evil presage of the future state of the deceased; and people would thence have a right to conclude that, so far from having been admitted into a region of bliss, he had been kept fast, notwithstanding all the mantras and purifications of his brethren, in the *Yama Lôkam*, or place of torment.

The body being consumed, the four individuals who alone continued about the pile, repair to the place of assembly of the other Brahmans who have assisted at the funeral. After three times walking round the assembly, they request permission to go to purify themselves in the Ganges. This boon being obtained, they formally wash themselves from the sin, as they term it, of carrying the carcase of a Brâhman.

All present are then invited to join in the bath of death, with a particular application to him who has just been consumed. After the dreadful heat he must have undergone, the bath, they suppose, must be refreshing to him. When it is finished, some presents of money and of betel are distributed among the assistants, after presenting them with the Daśa Dânam or Ten Gifts, which had been previously got ready. The assembly then shew themselves before the gate of the house of the deceased, into which no person can enter in its present polluted state; and, after washing their feet, they return home.

The chief of the funeral, however, has still something more to perform. He must fill with earth a small vessel, in which he sows nine sorts of grain: Rice, Wheat, Sesamum, Millet, and several sorts of pease. They are well watered, to make them shoot soon, and be ready for the ceremonies to which they are applied.

But there is an intermediate one to be performed, not less curious. It consists in placing in the house of the deceased a small vessel filled with water, supported by a thread, fixed to the ceiling or to a beam. This thread serves as a ladder for one of the Prâṇas, or winds of the body of the deceased, to descend every day to drink. It remains ten days; on each of which a handful of boiled rice is put into the dish to serve as food for the Prâṇa.

After the completion of all these ceremonies, and not till then, the people of the house may eat. But, for that and several following days, the food must be simple and unseasoned, so as to accord with the idea of sorrow.

All the rites we have mentioned, and many others we have omitted, are observed with the most scrupulous exactness, either from superstition or respect to appearances. The omission of the most frivolous or ridiculous of all would probably excite the greatest murmuring and offence. Poverty, indeed, necessarily excuses the performance of those that are attended with great expence, such as the ceremony of the Daśa Dânam, or Ten Gifts.

Though the customs of the other Hindûs are in the same taste as those of the Brâhmans, yet they differ from them in some striking particulars. Such are the dull and deafening sounds of their drums, trumpets, and other instruments of music which accompany the funerals of the Śûdras, and which are not in use among the Brâhmans. Among the instruments alluded to for aiding the expression of grief, the most remarkable of all is a kind of trumpet called *Túri* in Tamil, five or six feet in length, whose awful and dismal roaring spreads consternation all round. Two of these instruments at least must be employed, and they are sounded with a most piercing, though monotonous, tone. The one thunders out a sort of *Si Bemol*, on which it dwells near half a minute; and, after a moment's pause, the other groans in a *Sol Diez*, which he prolongs in the same manner. Their obstreperous alternations, which are continued through the whole ceremony and are heard afar off, are intended to inspire dread, and are indeed well adapted to increase the solemnity of funeral rites, by spreading consternation through the whole neighbourhood. But it is still more remarkable that these same lugubrious instruments accompany the wedding festivals, among some castes, with their tremendous braying.

The greater part of the ceremonies which we have attempted to describe, afford complete evidence of the distinct knowledge which the people of India have preserved, in the midst of the darkness of their gross idolatry, of the immortality of the soul, and above all of the necessity of a remedy to obtain the remission of sin; though the emblem of pollution, under which they represent this condition of the soul, no doubt has often led them to confound the voluntary corruption of the mind with the stains which affect the body alone.

In the different Prâṇams, where this subject is frequently in view, and by which sometimes the soul itself is signified, and sometimes the principle of life, under the notion of *Wind*, can one avoid recurring to the *Breath of Life* of the Holy Scripture, by which the Creator animated the clay which he had formed, and man "became a living soul." But, in all ages, it has been the particular tendency of superstition and idolatry to darken and corrupt the purest ideas of natural religion.[a]

---

[a] In illustration of this chapter, I append an account written at the time of the funeral ceremonies of the late Râja, Sivajee, of Tanjore.

"It was certainly one of the most solemnly thrilling spectacles I have ever seen when the poor remains of the last Râja of Tanjore, dressed with the utmost magnificence, and loaded with jewels of rare value, were borne out, in a state palanquin, inlaid with ivory, through the long streets of his royal city, the last remnant of the inheritance of his ancestors.

A fortnight before I had attended Lord Harris, when he visited the Râja in full durbar. Then he was loaded with jewels and gold, and presented a spectacle of almost unparalleled gorgeousness.

And even now, as the light of the torches fell on the nodding head, one could almost imagine he still lived and was gravely acknowledging the salutations of the crowds around him.

The death change seemed to ennoble him. A majesty, an air of quiet power, seemed to pervade his features. Something eagle-like in the face called up the remembrance of the portraits of the first Mahratta chief, so mighty and so daring, who shook the throne of the Mogul into dust. Before the funeral procession, as chief mourner, walked the representative of the now ruling power, and, after him, the European inhabitants of Tanjore. Vast multitudes lined the streets, and crowded the fronts and tops of the houses, over which the light of many torches cast an unearthly glare. In the crowd there was a strange mingling of races, the Mahratta, with brooding sorrow on his brow, the Tamilian with his accustomed apathy, jostled by Englishmen, Muhammadans, Afghans, and other tribes whom the court had attracted to Tanjore. Wild discordant music sounded, and ever and anon, as the sad procession moved slowly forward, the wail, such as is never heard in other lands, the loud wail of a nation mourning for the last of its royal race filled the air. Whatever may have been their estimate in some respects, of the poor Râja while he lived, tens of thousands of sincere mourners attended him to the funeral pyre that night.

And then when on a plain, by the river's side, the royal garments were taken off one by one, and at last the body wrapped in a simple muslin robe, was lifted on to the pile of sandal wood, a long, loud, mournful cry was raised and the vast multitude swayed to and fro as though with agony unutterable.

Quickly the fuel was heaped up till the face too was hidden. Then the nearest male relative, a boy of twelve years of age, was borne around the pile three times, and at the end of the last circuit a pot of water being dashed to the ground, a sign that as water poured on the ground such is the life of man, the pile was lit by the youth, and the flames rushed up, throwing a livid glare over the whole scene. Again the wailing sound, but louder, was heard, and as we thoughtfully wended our way home, it was long ere its distant echoes died away on our ears. The next morning a little shed of exquisite workmanship covered the heap of white ashes which was all that was left of Sivajee, Maha Râja of Tanjore!"

CHAPTER XXVIII.

THE CEREMONIES PRACTISED BY THE BRÂHMANS FOR THE DEAD, AFTER THE OBSEQUIES.

THE rites which the Brâhmans celebrate for a whole year for their dead will perhaps appear more tedious than those we have already described. To avoid this as much as possible, we shall be contented with giving a brief outline of the principal ones, leaving it to the reader to imagine the constant recurrence, upon every occasion, of the bathing, the Mantras, and the eleemosynary presents to the officiating Brâhmans.[b]

The day after the obsequies, besides the ordinary alms to the Brâhmans in general, a special mark of attention is shewn to one in particular, by giving him a piece of cloth, and money sufficient to provide him with a good repast. Both are given with a view to the deceased, who, as they observe, can be hungry no more nor stand in need of clothing.

The third day, the relations and friends re-assemble, and proceed to the place where the body was burnt. The chief of the funeral collects the remains of the bones which have withstood the flames, and after moistening the ashes with water and milk, he puts them into a little new basket, and throws them into the water, if there be any at hand, or if not, into some desart and solitary place. A part, however, is reserved, which, after being properly wet and made into a kind of paste, is fashioned into something of a human shape; and this is understood as the representative of the deceased, and has sacrifices offered up to it with the usual ceremonies. Some reserve a part of the ashes, to be cast, at some future time, into one of the famous rivers which possess the sacred virtue of purifying, and even sanctifying whatsoever they touch.

After this first ceremony, a small bank of earth is thrown up, on which three little stones are set; one called by the name of the deceased; another by that of *Yama*, or the god of hell, and the last denominated *Rudra*, or he that is the cause of tears. It is likewise one of the titles of Śiva, the god of destruction; and the place where the dead are burned is called *the land of Rudra*.

After decorating the three stones with flowers and small slips of

---

[b] Consult Wilson's Vishṇu Purâṇ, p. 315, &c., especially the notes.

new cloth, a sacrifice is offered up to them with great solemnity; and then the assembled Brâhmans set up a cry of lamentation, all in one tone, and embrace the chief of the funeral. He, in his turn, makes them the usual presents, and after exposing to the crows, or rather the demons in the shape of those birds, some rice and boiled pease, he takes up the three stones, and carries them home with him, to be used in the rites of the ten following days. For the present all is finished, and every one betakes himself to his home.

On the fourth day, the chief of the funeral after bathing, performs the *sankalpana*, or *application of thought.* His meditation must be wholly fixed upon Vishṇu, of whom he is to think as master of the world. To this consideration, he must add that of the metamorphosis of this divinity into a hog. He must also think of Brâhma, of the earth, the sun, the moon, and several other gods. He must call to mind the year, the month, the time of the month, the day of the week, on which the deceased yielded his breath. Many other considerations must be present to his mind, which we cannot stop to enumerate.

In general, the *application of thought* is recommended in all the ceremonies, which are made by Purôhitas; and it would be a very commendable practice if it were employed on rational objects.

In most of the ceremonies practised during the twelve days of mourning for the death of a Brâhman, they make great use of the sacred herb *dharba.* Mention is made of this plant so regularly, in almost every rite of the Brâhmans, that a short account may not be here misplaced of the origin of that veneration which the Hindûs entertain for it.

It is found every where, but chiefly in wet and marshy places, where it grows spontaneously. In some parts, it is so plentiful that the natives thatch their houses with it. It reaches to about three feet in length. The blade resembles that of the common grass. In the Hindû books, there is no end to the praises bestowed on this herb, and the good it occasions. It is this great estimation in which it is held that recommends it to the Brâhmans to be used in all their ceremonies. The cause of its virtue is that when the gods and the giants joined together to churn the sea of milk, by means of Mount *Mandara Parvata* or (probably the Caucasus,) which served them for a churn, and when from this operation emerged the vase which contained the *Amrita,* it was first set down upon this herb; which acquired from the sacred contact, the most excellent qualities.[c]

But, to return to the ceremonies of the mourning. Those which are carried on up to the tenth day, being nearly in the same style as those which have been already described, require no farther notice.

See Vishṇu Purâṇ, p. 74—80.

On the tenth day, they vary in several particulars. The chief of the funeral then provides some dishes of savory food in the manner of the Brâhmans, but in no great abundance. He adds to them flowers and fruits; and the whole being covered with cloths stained yellow with saffron water, is placed on a sort of tray, and carried to the widow of the deceased. She then adorns her forehead with some scarlet emblem, the edges of her eyelids with black, her hair with red flowers, her neck and bosom with sandal, and stains her face, arms, and legs with the ordinary dye of the country, which consists of water made yellow by a mixture of powdered tumeric. She then puts on her jewels and her finest robes.

All who are present then proceed to the brink of the nearest tank or well. The chief of the funeral marches at their head, bearing the several articles necessary for the ensuing ceremony. He is followed by the widow, by several other married women who accompany her, and a great number of the relations and friends. They repeat the ceremony of the three little stones, and receive the offering of rice and other articles, brought for that purpose from the house. The women have then permission to weep; which they employ with loud shrieks, beating their bosoms till their grief real or pretended is exhausted. The chief then introduces a ceremony which is worthy of notice. He takes the three little stones, and the vessels in which is commonly prepared the ricc offered either to the stones or to the crows. Then, going into the water up to the neck, he turns towards the sun, whom he addresses in these words: "Up to this day, these stones have "represented the deceased. Henceforth let him cease to be a corpse. "Now let him be received into the *Swarga.* There let him enjoy "all blessings, as long as the waters of the Ganges shall continue "to flow." In pronouncing these words, he casts behind him the stones and the vessels he held in his hands, and returns to the bank of the pond.

It deserves to be remarked; as a thing perhaps now peculiar to the idolatry of the Hindûs, though admitted in some degree into the ancient religion of other nations, that they rank the carcases of the dead among the subordinate and malevolent deities. It appears also that it is only those that suffer a violent death, or that have been deprived of the ordinary funeral rites, who remain in this abhorred condition of carcases, and who prowl through the vast regions of the universe to inflict evil upon men. Such as perish by an ordinary death, and who receive the accustomed funeral rites, retain but for a few days this hideous form.

In this aspect of Hindû Paganism, a considerable resemblance appears to the *Manes* of the Greeks and Romans, or to the shades of their dead, fluttering on the banks of the river Styx; and, perhaps, still more to the walking spirits which are to this day believed in by many persons in Europe.

The women have likewise their own particular ceremonies; the most important of which is that performed in constituting the wife of the deceased a widow. We have elsewhere described this ceremony, as applied to women in general; but a difference takes place in regard to the wives of Brâhmans.

On the bank of the pool where they are assembled, a shed is constructed, on which they place a ball of earth, to which they give the name of the deceased; and his wife, stripping off her jewels, lays them on the ball, pronouncing these words: "I divest myself of these as the evidence of my love." She then, with her own hands, cuts the *Tâli* from her neck; the emblem of matrimony, which is worn by all wives.

These ceremonies are accompanied with the tears and loud cries of her who is the object of them; and the other women, embracing her by turns, join in the cries and lamentation.

The custom is, in such cases, not to untie the string by which the Tâli is suspended, but to cut it; and hence arises the curse so often imprecated by women, when they quarrel: "may your Tâli "be cut;" meaning, may you become a widow. For it is by this sign, above all others, that the state of widowhood is published and declared.

After the lamentation is ended, they bathe, in order to purify themselves for the following ceremony. The chief of the funeral extends on the ground, in a suitable place, a long piece of new and pure cloth, on which he places a vessel filled with water, and whitened on the outside with chalk. Close to the vessel is placed a small heap of saffron powder, which represents the god *Vig'hnêśwara,* to whom they sacrifice, as well as to the vessel itself; by which means the water it contains becomes the holy element of the Ganges. All the assistants must drink a little of this water, to cleanse them from all the impurities they have contracted during the celebration of the funeral. Every one then receives an areca nut and a leaf of betel, and the widow a new dress.

The ceremonies of the eleventh day are not more interesting, and therefore we shall lightly pass them over. On this day the chief of the funeral repairs to the tank, attended by the Purôhita and nine Brâhmans. There he digs a little trench, which he fills with cow-dung. This he kindles; and on the fire he performs the sacrifice of the Hômam. He then rolls up two little balls of boiled rice, and casts one after the other into the fire. Prostrating himself before that element, he prays for a blessed world to the deceased; and immediately he returns to the house for the *Deliverance of the Bull.*

To celebrate this rite, one of those animals is selected, which must be all of one colour, and that either white, red, or black. Having decorated him well with garlands of flowers, they brand on his right flank, with a hot iron, the figure of a sort of weapon called *Śûla, (a trident)* which is appropriated to Śiva. In honour of him the bull is set at liberty, and has a right to pasture at large. This emancipation of the bull is considered as one of the most meritorious acts that can be performed for the welfare of the deceased.

The celebration of the twelfth day is of a piece with the preceding. From amongst the eight Brâhmans who are invited by the chief, he selects one, whom he constitutes, in his thoughts, a dead carcase. He puts in his hand the herb Dharba, and washes his feet; upon which he then puts some grains of Sesamum. Seating him then in a particular place, he puts Dharba on his head, pendants of gold at his ears, and a ring on his finger, and, after making him some presents of cloth, he ends by putting a string of *Rudrâksha* about his neck. These are a kind of beads, of which necklaces are often made, and are nearly of the size and shape of a nut.

Afterwards they proceed to one of the funeral rites which the Brâhmans deem the most important of all. In a place prepared for the purpose the chief deposits four little balls made of rice and other vegetables, kneaded together. The first is for the deceased; the second for his father; the third for his grandfather; and the fourth for his great-grandfather. He pours a little water on each, and adds a few grains of Sesamum. Then addressing himself to the Brâhman, who represents the corpse; "thou hast been till now," says he, "a "dead carcase; henceforth thou shalt be a progenitor; thou shalt "dwell where they reside, and enjoy all happiness." He has no sooner spoken than he takes up the ball which was dedicated to the father of the deceased, divides it into three parts, and kneading each portion with one of the three other balls which have remained entire, he offers to them a sacrifice in common.

Although the Brâhmans, in the invocation of their ancestors, on this and similar occasions, confine themselves to the three latest generations, yet they by no means exclude those that are more remote. On the contrary, they particularly enjoin upon those whom they invoke, to bring with them their forefathers.

After having accomplished all the ceremonies of which we have given this brief detail, the chief of the funeral goes to the tank and bathes, and then returns home, well wrapped up in a sort of cloak. On reaching the house, he embraces all his relations there assembled, and addresses them in words of consolation. An entertainment succeeds for all those who have assisted at the ceremonies of mourning; after which he resumes his turban: a matter so important as to require an ostentatious display of ceremonies peculiarly adapted to the occasion.

The rites which we have described are not the only ceremonies practised on the death of a Brâhman. The same, or similar ones, are repeated at least fifteen times in the course of the year in which he dies; and the day of the anniversary of his death, called *Tit'hi* must be kept for a succession of years. The same ceremonies, or nearly so, are repeated, of which we have furnished so tiresome a detail.

The ceremonies practised at the death of married women, are not much unlike those performed for the men. To die in the state of matrimony, is so happy an event for a woman, that it can be nothing less than the reward of the fervent worship she has paid to Lakshmi, or some other distinguished goddess, during her life.

But I will close this long and tedious detail concerning Mourning, after recounting one remarkable ceremony which is practised by all the castes.

The Hindû Astronomy attributes to the Moon a sort of zodiac consisting of twenty-seven constellations, having a relation to her periodical course of the same number of days. The four last are more or less unlucky; and miserable is he who happens to die when the Moon is in that part of her orbit. Or, unhappy rather are his relations. The body of a person who dies under so inauspicious a planet, can in no wise be carried over the threshold. In taking it to the funeral, an aperture is made, by demolishing a part of the wall, through which it is brought, to escape the perilous consequences which would otherwise ensue upon so ill-starred a demise. It is necessary to abandon the house for six or at least three months, according to the degree of malignity of the lunar influence, at the time of dying. While this is going on, the door is barricadoed with bundles of thorns. The time being elapsed, the briars are removed, the door opened, and all the apartments carefully garnished. The Purôhita attends to accomplish the purification by his rites. It is then in a condition to admit of a feast and donation to the Brâhmans; after which its owner may dwell in it as before.

The same superstitious observance takes place with respect to *Births.* When they occur on days when the Moon is passing through a malign constellation, the relations are so much alarmed at the evils which cannot fail to ensue, both to themselves and to the children born in so evil an hour, that they secretly get rid of them either by delivering them over to people who are less credulous on that score, or, when they cannot find such an opportunity, by exposing them on the highways or streets.

In admitting the absurdity of the Hindû superstition in general, and that of the funeral rites in particular, we are not compelled, thank God! to insult over the blindness of those who have so erred. I view their conduct only with eyes of compassion. Such, and lower still, perhaps, were our own ancestors; and such would we ourselves have been, but for the undeserved gift of Revelation, which the Father of Light has condescended to impart unto us, in his infinite mercy, for the purpose of rescuing us from the thick darkness in which our forefathers were so long immersed, and of exalting us to the glorious light of truth. Thanks without end be to Him for those His inestimable blessings ! [d]

---

[d] The following verses will illustrate this subject. They are natural, unaffected, earnest : rare qualities in oriental poetry.

Extracts from the song of Paṭṭaṇaṭṭu Piḷḷai as he performed the funeral rites for his mother.

1. In which future birth shall I see HER, who for ten moons, burdened, bore me, and when she heard the word Son, lovingly took me up in her rosy hands and fed me from her golden breast ?

2. Shall I kindle the flame to consume HER, who for three hundred days of weariness and longing, morn and evening imploring Śiva's grace, was borne down by me a burden ?

3. Shall I place HER on the pile and kindle it,—HER who in the cradle, on her bosom, on her shoulder, caressed me, fanned me, singing soothing lullabies ?

4. Shall I put the rice into that mouth, my mother's, with which she was wont to call me her honey, nectar, her only wealth, her boy ?

5. Shall I heap up rice on the head of HER, and place the firebrand, with unflinching hand and steady eye : who softly raised me, pressed her face to mine, and called me oft her son ?

6. Formerly the fire was kindled, in the three towns, (1) then was kindled in Lanká's isle ? (2) Sorrow for my mother kindles the fire, deep within, and I too have kindled the fire ! See it burns ! it burns !

7. It burns ! It burns to ashes—Alas !—the hand which soothed me, and reared me, and led me so tenderly that its touch would not have frightened away the timid bird !

8. Is she ashes now ? Hath she come already to thy feet, O wondrous Lord of Sôṇa's hill ? Hath she, evermore gazing on thee, rejoicing, forgotten me, her son ?

9. She was erewhile ! She walked in the way ! She was here but yesterday ! To-day burned, become ashes ! Come all, unlamenting, sprinkle milk, ALL IS IN ŚIVA'S POWER !

(1.) Alluding to the burning of the three towns of the Aśur by Mahâdêva.

(2.) By Râma, in his war with Râvaṇa, to recover Śîtâ.

CHAPTER XXIX.

OF THE THIRD CONDITION OF THE BRÂHMANS, THAT OF VÂNAPRASTHA OR INHABITANTS OF THE DESART.

THE third order of Brâhmans is that of *Vânaprastha*, or Inhabitants of the Desart.[e] I know not whether any of this order still remain in the territory washed by the Indus, or in the north of India; where it is certain they once abounded and flourished. This sect of philosophers is now to be found no where in the peninsula, and I believe it to be there absolutely extinct.

The ambition of acquiring a name, and also that of attaining the utmost degree of perfection by purification in solitude, impelled many of the Brâhmans, in ancient times, to forsake the towns and all intercourse with men, and to retire into the woods, with their obsequious wives. They who assumed this distinction, were kindly received by those who had embraced it before them, and were initiated by them into the rules of a solitary life.

From this class of philosophers, the Brâhmans of pristine times acquired all their original lustre; nay, it appears that they were the true founders of the caste. To them, undoubtedly, it was that Alexander the Great, after invading their territory, applied for instruction; and to them allusion is made by the ancient Greek and Latin authors, when they speak of the Brâhmans of India. At the time, therefore, when the conqueror of Greece penetrated into their country, they were still famous, and were esteemed the only real Brâhmans. There were, no doubt, a great many who lived in intercourse with the world; but they were not held in equal reputation with the Vânaprastha.

The most celebrated amongst them, and the most ancient, were the Seven great *Rishis* or Penitents, whom we have already mentioned. Their successors enjoyed nearly the same degree of respect. Even their Kings did not disdain to shew them honour, and to pay them marks of reverence which almost approached to adoration. They looked for no success but through their benediction, which they preferred to all the honours they could elsewhere obtain. On the other hand, they stood in extreme awe of their curse, which was believed never to fall innoxiously.

The reception accorded to some of those solitary Brâhmans by a great monarch, is thus described by the author of the *Padma Purâṇa:*

"Penetrated with joy and respect beyond expression, he pros-"trated himself at full length before them. When he rose, he made

---

[e] Compare Vishṇu Purâṇ, p. 294—296, Manu. vi. 3.

"them sit down, and washed their feet. He then poured the water "that had been so used, upon his own head. This was succeeded by "a sacrifice of flowers, which he offered to their feet. Then, with "both hands clasped and raised over his head, he made them a "profound obeisance and addressed them in these words: 'The "happiness which I enjoy this day in seeing your holy feet, is a suffi-"cient reward for all the good works I have yet performed. I possess "all happiness in beholding those blessed feet, which are the true "lotus flower. Now is my body become wholly pure. Ye are the "gods whom I serve, and besides you I acknowledge no others on "the earth. Nothing is purer than I shall henceforth be.'"

Such is the degree of honour in which the Penitents are held, and such the style of Hindû compliment. It indicates a sentiment of the lowest flattery in those who use it, and no great degree of reverence for their gods. The same taste subsists, in its full vigour, to the present day, and particularly among the Brâhmans: for, when they have any thing to hope or to fear, even if it were from a Pariah, there is no strain of compliment too high for the occasion.

It is not surprizing that Kings should pay such honours to the penitent philosophers, seeing that the gods themselves respect them, and feel honoured by their visits. There is no sort of approbation or distinction which the deities do not manifest for them; while they, in return, treat them with haughtiness, and sometimes even insolently. Witness him, who paid a visit to each of the three principal divinities of India, and began his interview by giving each of them a kick! His object was to know how they would demean themselves, and to find out their temper, by the conduct which they would adopt upon such a salutation.

The penitents always maintained a kind of superiority over the gods, and punished them severely when they found them in fault. It has cost Brahmâ, Śiva, Dêvendra,[f] and some other deities, pretty dear to have incurred their maledictions, on account of their infamous obscenities. These stories, silly as they are, prove the high opinion that has been entertained of the penitents, and the antiquity of the institution; on which I shall hazard some conjectures.

The Hindû fable of the seven penitents that were saved from the waters of the deluge in a vessel of which Vishṇu was the pilot, seems to shew that sons of Noah, or at least of Japhet, to the number of seven, having been dispersed by the famous event which confounded their language at Babel; some of them might have reached India by the way of Tartary, and so have become the first founders, not only of the Brâhmans, but also of the other people who gradually settled in the country in which they had instituted laws. It happened to the people who inhabited India, as it has done to all other ancient nations, that the laws prescribed to them for their worship, their morals and

---

[f] Brahmâ was cursed by Śiva, for falsehood.
Indra was cursed by Durvâsas. Vishṇu, Purâṇ, p. 70, and by Gautama. Râmayaṇam. I. XLVIII. Schlegel's. Vol. I. p. 180.

good order in society, as well as the dogmas for preserving health, suffered in a length of time great alterations, occasioned by prejudice, interest, and a thousand other causes. At length, they degenerated into a philosophy ill understood in many respects, to which certain Brâhmans attached themselves; forming at once a sect of philosophers and a community separate from the rest of the nation. Their retreating to the woods, the austerity of their lives, and their contempt for temporal wealth; the purity of their morals, and their high cultivation of science, were qualities which could not fail to establish their reputation and to gain the public esteem.

It can scarcely be doubted that these sages of India are of higher antiquity than those of Greece. For, what was the philosophy of Greece before Pythagoras, and what its legislation before Lycurgus? It was because legislation had been established in India on fixed rules, and because the philosophy of that country had spread its renown as far as Europe, that those two celebrated philosophers undertook, at different periods, so long a journey, in order to see the Hindû Vânaprasthas, and to study their precepts and their example. Nor, were they, as far as appears, the only persons that visited India with similar views.

It is true that the philosophy of the Greeks, though later in its origin, soon surpassed that of the Hindû Brâhmans, by the clearness of its conceptions on all the points which it discusses, by the beauty of its morality, by the success with which it cultivated every science, by its researches into the nature of the Divinity, and by the abhorrence which it inspired for the ridiculous gods of paganism. Yet it would be unjust to deny that the Brâhman Vânaprasthas also would have made great proficiency in the knowledge of morals and of divinity, had they not suffered their minds to be pre-occupied by the idle dogmas respecting the means of purifying the soul; which they thought indispensable in practice, although with the certainty of spoiling their whole philosophy. In this way, the wisest of the Hindûs became the most besotted.

This illusion concerning uncleanness and the corresponding purification from it, which they pursued, as one may say, till they lost sight of it, made them stumble from one error upon another, from precipice to precipice; and the current which hurried them away carried with them the whole nation, of whom they had been the oracles. This was the more unavoidable that the people of the north had just subdued India, bringing with them the Brâhmans, who were hardly known till then, and who established their religion upon the ruins of that of Buddha; the one altogether as absurd as the other.

It may be asked, whether there was any communication between Zoroaster, or his disciples, and the Vânaprasthas of India: a question to which I do not consider myself capable of giving an answer. A great affinity has been demonstrated to exist between these two different races of people by a modern author,* whose profound and

* Sir William Jones.

interesting researches into Oriental literature have challenged the attention and admiration of the learned of Europe. This author, in comparing the *Zend*, or sacred idiom of the ancient Persians with the Sanscrit of India, has found so great a resemblance between these two ancient tongues as to lead him to pronounce that they were in ancient times the same dialect. Nevertheless, the worship of Zoroaster and that of the Brâhmans are so different, and in many particulars so opposite to each other, that it would be very difficult, on comparison, to persuade one's self that they both sprang from the same fountain. And if at the present time, some slight resemblance is observed between the *Pârsis*, and the Hindûs, in the worship of fire, which is common to both; their religion and customs are wholly different in every thing besides. But that which constitutes the fundamental basis of the Hindû philosophers is so exclusively peculiar to them, that I believe no traces of it can be observed in any other nation; nor can it be shewn that there is any thing in their practices, religious or civil, in which other nations have been their instructors.

I pretend not but that, in some particular points, there is a resemblance between them and philosophers of other countries. Their morality has a great affinity to that of Zeno and the Stoics. Their manner also of teaching, by imposing a great deal on the memory, bears a likeness to that of the Druids. The spirit of seclusion which characterises the Vânaprasthas, is also found among the Rehabites, the children of the prophets, and the Essenians of Egypt. But no certain knowledge can be thence derived concerning the philosophy of India, the antiquity of which seems to go beyond that of those other nations.

CHAPTER XXX.

RULES OF THE VÂNAPRASTHAS.

THE life of the Brâhman Recluse was regulated by the observance of certain rules of conduct to which those who embraced it were restricted. They are thus described in the *Padma Purâṇa*, to my quotation from which I will add a few remarks to make it more intelligible.

1. The Vânaprastha must renounce the society of other men, even the Brâhmans, and take up his abode in the desert, far from towns and inhabited places.

The renunciation, however, was not so complete but that they might be permitted occasionally to revisit the world, for several purposes; instances of which are seen in the Hindû writings.

2. They shall carry with them their wives, who must be subject to the same course of life as themselves.

It is here that the Vânaprastha is chiefly distinguished from the Sannyâsi Brâhman, who is bound to live single, or to put his wife away, if he has one. But though the Vânaprastha be not condemned to absolute continence, it is yet required of him to use his conjugal rights with moderation.

3. They must inhabit no house that is covered otherwise than with leaves, as any other dwelling would ill become those who profess to have renounced the world.

Houses thatched with palm leaves are very common in India.

4. They must not wear garments of cotton cloth, but must always have their dress of a fabric made from grass.

This last species of cloth is still common in the north of India. It is as soft to the touch as silk, and has the advantage of not being subject to be soiled like the cloth of cotton.

5. They ought to practise, with the greatest exactness, all the rules prescribed to the Brâhmans in general, particularly that of bathing three times every day; with the accompanying prayers.

6. They must be particularly attentive in the choice of whatever is used for food. They should always confine themselves to such herbs as are found within the forests they inhabit. They ought scrupulously to abstain from all roots that form a bulb in the ground, and particularly from onions.

The Brâhmans of the present time as well as the other castes of Hindûs who live on vegetables, still keep up this regulation. Onions, garlic, mushrooms, and some other productions of the same kind are prohibited to them, although their women, who are not so scrupulous, sometimes introduce, very secretly, both garlic and onions for a relish to their ragouts. In the practice itself, a similarity will be found to the Egyptian superstition, in which onions are considered sacred, and even as the objects of worship.

7. They must be continually meditating and pondering on Para-Brahmâ; by which means they may attain that spiritual temperament which shall re-unite them with the divinity.

We shall speak, in the sequel, of the various modes in which this re-union may be effected.

8. The sacrifices, and above all that of the *Yajna*, ought to be their principal occupation.

In the next chapter will be found the description of this sacrifice, the most famous of all that are offered up by the Brâhmans.

I am surprized that the author of the work had not inserted among the occupations of the Recluse Brâhmans the study of the Sciences; for it is certain that at least a very great number of them cultivated learning with assiduity, particularly those branches that relate to Theology, Morals, Astronomy, and Magic. To them we are indebted for the Hindû books, which still exist on those subjects of science.

These ascetic philosophers, as far as we can judge, observed their rules in all their force at the time of the invasion of Alexander the Great; and there is reason to believe that they persisted in them long after the era of that famous conqueror. Their conduct was far superior to the general rules we have quoted, as may be inferred from the following account of their principles.

Men, according to these philosophers, are born with three leading impulses; the Love of Land; the Love of Gold; and the Love of Women. By the Love of Land, they mean not only the various property which one may acquire during his life, without even excepting a throne, but also employments and posts of honour.

So far were they from grasping at wealth or aspiring to dignities of this kind, that their exhortations and example sometimes prevailed upon Kings themselves to make a sacrifice of their worldly possessions, and to renounce their state and dignity, to lead with them a philosophical and penitential life in their forests. The Hindû books make frequent reference to those penitent and secluded Princes. They sometimes went beyond the Brâhmans, their masters, in the fervour and austerity of their penitence. And, so far from being jealous of their illustrious rivals, these have frequently, in admiration of their extraordinary devotion and zeal, conferred upon them the signal distinction of becoming Penitent Brâhmans like themselves, and have incorporated them accordingly with their caste.

By the passion for gold, these philosophers meant not only the desire of possessing that metal, but also whatever else it could acquire as money; such as precious stones, fine houses, rich dress, sumptuous feasts, and whatever appertains to the table. The Vânaprasthas had the same indifference for all these good things as they professed to have for worldly honours and possessions in land. The simple furniture of their cabins consisted of some vessels of copper and earthen ware. They accounted themselves sufficiently rich if they had some cows to supply them with the milk which was the chief ingredient of their food. For this reason the present of a cow was gladly accepted by them from any of their votaries.

Many very extravagant fables are still extant regarding these cows of the Penitents. I have found in the Bhâgavata the history of one which could supply, not milk only, but every species of food, for a large army. A neighbouring Prince being desirous to possess so valuable a treasure, went to seize her by force; but the Vânaprastha to whom she belonged had received her from the gods, as a recompence for the favour of his devotion, and the merit of his sacrifices; and the cow, being endowed with as much courage as exuberance, rushed into the midst of the enemy's force, which had come to carry her away, and put the whole army to the rout.

As these solitary devotees lived in great simplicity, their expences were but small; and they found, in the offerings which were brought them by their numerous votaries, not only enough for their own wants, but also for the alms which they gave to the necessitous among their visitants. They confined themselves to one meal daily. Inebriating liquors were not in their thoughts; nor was the want of them felt as any privation by men accustomed, from their infancy, to consider the use of such an indulgence as impure and debasing. They had contracted in good time a salutary detestation of it, and no crime appeared in their eyes so degrading to human nature as drunkenness.

By the passion for women they understood all the sensual pleasures connected with the sex, excepting what the legitimate union of a man with his wife permits; and, even in that case, their moderation in the use of authorized enjoyment was extreme.

On this subject we may perceive, in the conduct of those philosophers, vestiges of the primitive races of men, who held sacred the command of their Creator to our first parents: "Increase and multiply "and replenish the earth." They held it as an indisputable obligation imposed by nature on all living creatures, to transmit, by a new generation, the existence which they received from their predecessors. But they were so strongly impressed with true sentiments concerning marriage, and with the purpose of Him who ordained it, when He created the first man and woman, that they abstained from all intercourse but as it promised to be fruitful: so different in this respect from the *Manicheans*, who, as St. Augustin relates, from their dislike of progeny, never acted the husband but under circumstances where conception was not likely to ensue.

They were convinced, in short, that a spiritual life was unattainable, excepting by subduing all the passions, and that passion in particular which chiefly predominates over our nature. It was not lawful for them even to look in the face of a woman; and they were impressed with the belief that a single act of incontinence would erase all the merits of a life of devotion for a number of years. The Hindû books are filled with instances of this kind. But as it is the fatality of their authors to corrupt all narration by an intermixture of the wildest and most contradictory fables, we shall find, tacked to a true story of a penitent who was punished for not effectually controlling his desires, some wonderful and highly embellished tale of his excesses, in voluptuousness of every kind, committed by some devotee, and continued for thousands of years; and unaccountably supported, during that long period, in full vigour, by the fervency of his devotion.

I shall not go into any long detail of the virtues of the Vânaprastha Brâhman. If, on the one hand, they cannot be considered as real and genuine, upon the ground that they are not founded on the natural feelings of humanity, but rather practised for ostentation and shew; on the other hand, we must allow that, whatever was the motive, they are at least on a level with the virtues of the vaunted philosophers of Greece. For they practised hospitality, and enjoined it so strongly upon others, that the Brâhmans, on going to their meals, were bound to look into the street, to observe if any wretched wanderer stood in need of a morsel. And it is still more remarkable that, in such a case, no distinction was made between a friend and an enemy. I will not indeed avouch that their practice always kept pace with morality so pure.

Their highest boast is their moderation in resenting the injuries which they suffer; and they strongly inculcate upon others the duty of restraining the feeling of wrath. The ebullitions of this passion in themselves, which some times break out against the gods, they ascribe rather to zeal than to anger, as they are never excited but by the contemplation of the disorderly conduct and lascivious practices of those celestial personages.

Yet, notwithstanding the purity of their principles on this topic, it is certain that a small vexation serves to irritate them, and that they do not well exemplify their own precepts. Their maledictions have become formidable, because they may be incurred by a trifling fault; and because, though unjustly fulminated, they never fail to take effect.[g]

---

[g] The Purâṇas and Epics are full of instances of this. Compare Kuraḷ. Chap. II.

CHAPTER XXXI.

OF THE SACRIFICES OF THE ANCHORET BRÂHMANS; PARTICULARLY THE YAJNA.

THE sacrifice most in use amongst the Vânaprasthas was that of the *Hômam*, so often mentioned; and which was commonly performed by producing new fire from the flint, and casting upon it some boiled rice and liquid butter, and pronouncing over it the appropriate Mantras. This easy and simple sacrifice appears to have had the Fire for its object, and to have been generally offered up to the Sun, as being the most obvious symbol of that element; and occasionally to the whole Heavenly bodies.

The penitents likewise offered to the gods several other sorts of sacrifices, all of them consisting of the simple productions of nature; such as flowers, rice, pulse, and various sorts of fruit. These sacrifices were repeated every day, and occupied all the leisure they had after their ablutions, their hours of meditation, and their contemplation of Para-Brahmâ.

Although it appears certain, from the perusal of the Hindû books, that bloody sacrifices of animals were habitual to them in very remote times; and although it be affirmed that they are required by the *Atharvana Vêda;* yet it does not appear that the Brâhmans in person lent their assistance to such sacrifices, by slaying the victims with their own hands. These functions have always been devolved upon persons of another caste. That of the Râjas, the next in rank to the Brâhmans, has not considered it beneath its dignity to exercise the office of sacrifices. But, in more recent times, the Brâhmans have always kept aloof from sacrifices where blood was spilled; and they assume no employment in temples where victims are slaughtered.

The only case in which the Vânaprastha Brâhmans, as well as those of the present day, could possibly offer up a living victim, is at the sacrifice of the Yajna, at which a ram is immolated. But even here, to testify their horror of blood, the animal offered up in sacrifice is not slaughtered in the ordinary way, but crushed and smothered.

This sacrifice is the most exalted and the most meritorious of all that human beings can devise. It is the most grateful to the gods. It calls down all sorts of temporal blessings, and blots out all the sins that can have been accumulated for four generations. Nothing but the unbounded benefits which it imparts could have surmounted the horror which the Bráhman feels at murder; unless he be, in some degree, supported by the arrogant feeling of having the exclusive right of offering this sacrifice, at which no man of any other caste can be present. They extend the privilege of contributing to the expence, it must be allowed, very widely. But, with every aid, this is so enormous, on account of the numbers of Brâhmans who assemble from all quarters, not so much to grace the solemnity, as to share in the presents which he who presides is obliged to lavish amongst them, that such sacrifices are but rarely attempted.

He who presides at them must select a ram, entirely white, and without blemish ; of about three years old, well shaped, and fat. He must also proclaim the day of the sacrifice through the whole district, and invite the attendance of the Brâhmans of the four Vêdas. If any one of the four should fail to be represented, the ceremony must necessarily be put off. The Śûdras, of whatever rank, are not permitted to attend; and Brâhmans themselves are excluded, when affected by disease or infirmity, or when blind, lame, or labouring under any other bodily defect ; as well as widowers not remarried.

Every thing being prepared, the Purôhita, after announcing the favourable moment of the day for commencing, goes to the place of assembly, attended by the concourse of Brâhmans, sometimes amounting to two thousand. As usual, they begin by digging a shallow trench, three or four feet square. The ground is then consecrated with Mantras, and the sacrifice of the Hômam ; the trench being half filled with dried wood of the following species : the wood of the tree *Ravi* or *Arasu*. of the *Âla-marû*, the *Icha-maram* and the *parsu-maran*. These are all trees consecrated by the superstition of the country. Dharba, the sacred grass, is also used in abundance ; and the whole is sprinkled with liquid butter, that they may the more easily be set on fire. Every stage of the ceremonies is accompanied by the appropriate Mantras, which the Purôhita pronounces with a loud voice, while the attendants are responsive, irregularly, and with tumultuous exclamation.

When the fire is properly kindled, the ram is conducted into the midst of the assembly, after being duly washed, and consecrated by the service of Mantram. He is decorated with flowers and akshata, the grains of rice dyed red. He is bound with cords made of Dharba, the sacred grass, and Mantras are offered up, which are of a nature to kill the ram, although their efficacy is somewhat aided by stopping the ears, nostrils, and mouth of the animal. During this process, several of the Brâhmans assail him with heavy blows with their fists, and one of them, by violent pressure of the knee on his neck, chokes him outright. If the animal, during these cruel torments, find an interval to bleat, it would be held an evil omen. The Purôhita, all the while, recites his Mantras to accelerate the death of the victim.

When the ram is dead, the chief of the Yajna opens the paunch, and taking out the caul, holds it over the fire until the grease dissolves and drops into the flame. Melted butter is likewise added, as an appropriate libation to that element, serving to render it more intense.

The carcase being scorched, is cut into small pieces, some of which are soaked in butter and cast into the fire one after another.

A part, however, is preserved for him who presides at the sacrifice, and part for him who is at the expence of it. These share their portions with the Brâhmans who are present; amongst whom a scuffle ensues, each striving for a small bit of the flesh. Such morsels as they can catch they tear with their hands, and devour as a sacred viand. This practice is the more remarkable, as being the only occasion in their lives when they can venture to touch animal food.

The fire is then supplied with boiled rice and also with raw, but cleaned and washed as if intended for being dressed. All being now ended, each assistant receives his portion of betel, which had been laid out in readiness around the fire of the Yajna, and is now chewed like some hallowed dainty. Then he who is at the expence gives a splendid entertainment to all the Brâhmans present, and concludes the whole by distributing money and apparel among all the Brâhmans; which, on account of their great number, is a matter of large expence.

The president of this solemnity, who is by no means to be confounded with the Purôhita, who is merely the director of the ceremony, is ever afterwards considered a person of consequence. He acquires by it the right of keeping up a perpetual fire; and when it is extinguished by any accident, he rekindles it, not with sparks from a flint, but with heat generated by the friction of one piece of wood against another. When he dies, his funeral pile is lighted from that same fire; which is extinguished only with his ashes.

I have not learned whether this famous sacrifice which at first view seems to be offered solely to the fire, may not have a reference to some particular divinity. But it appears probable that he who conducts it is entitled to address it to any god he pleases, provided it be one of the superior order. But, on the other hand, the fire of the Yajna bears the appellation of *Yajnêswara*, or the god fire; and the word Yajna is derived from *Agni*, fire; as if it were to this god that the sacrifice were really offered. I need not point out the resemblance between the word *Agni* and the Latin *Ignis*.

This most renowned sacrifice, the most meritorious and efficacious of all others, is one of the six privileges of the Brâhmans; who alone have the right to assist in it, while other castes are only admitted to participate in the expence. It was more common amongst the Anchoret Brâhmans of old, than it is at present; but at the same time, in those ancient days, it was carried on in a way more simple, and exempt from the extravagant expence which interested motives on one side, and vanity on the other, have loaded it with in the present times.

The *Great* Sacrifice of the Yajna, which was still more famous, is no longer in use. But I have been assured by persons of credit that, towards the beginning of the last century, the King of Ambhir in Hindustan, had it celebrated with all the pomp and expence which pertain to it. His present to the Guru alone was a lac of rupees;

and the Brâhmans who attended, to the number, it is said, of twelve thousand, all received gifts according to their rank and dignity.

The fabulous history of the Hindûs commemorates, in numerous passages, this sacrifice of the Grand Yajna and its powerful effects. It was practised in its utmost splendour, by the Gods and the Giants, when they warred against each other.

The effect of so high a sacrifice was to insure the certainty of victory to those who practised it, over all their enemies; and in this it never failed, if the preparations and ceremonies were not imperfect.

The Brâhmans flocked to it from all quarters; and the Prince, or God, or Giant, to whom it belonged, could not reject the claim of any one of them. They who know the nature of a Brâhman may well judge of the rate of the expence. I remember to have read somewhere in a Hindû book, of an ancient King, who, on such an occasion, gave away a bushel of pearls to each of the Brâhmans present, who amounted to thirty thousand!

At this sacrifice, every species of victim was immolated; and it is beyond doubt that human beings even were offered up. But the horse and the elephant were the most common. Before the great ceremony began, it was held necessary to make a long excursion, and to go over a great tract of country, attended by a numerous army. The Kings, Giants, or Gods, against whom the sacrifice was designed, came in array against them with all their forces, and endeavoured to carry off the victim by violence or stratagem. If they succeeded, the sacrifice was at an end. The Prince, Giant, or God, who was preparing it, lost all the advantages that he promised himself from it; and those against whom it was directed were delivered from the evils which would have arisen from its success. For, this terrible rite produced no less advantage to those who succeeded in making it, than to render them always victorious in battle, and to throw an enchantment upon their arms by which one man was enabled to overthrow a whole army.[h]

I shall pass over the long ceremonies of the Grand Yajna, having been unable to procure an accurate account of them. But I will extract from one of the Hindû books, a specimen of the innumerable fables which they contain with respect to the virtue of this sacrifice; the more particularly as it is the history of one of the metamorphoses of Vishṇu.

"The Emperor Bâli, the Giant, was performing this sacrifice; and, "if it had been accomplished, the whole of the Princes of India would "have perished, and he would have been absolute lord of the country. "But, before it took effect, Vishṇu, the Preserver, descended from his "throne, and presenting himself before the tyrant, in the shape of a "Brâhman dwarf, entreated of him the humble boon of a bit of ground

[h] See Râmâyaṇa, Schlegel's Ed. I. p. 103.

"of the bigness of three prints of the sole of his foot, merely that he "might sacrifice upon it. The Giant smiled at the request, and very "readily granted it; and immediately Vishṇu, resuming his own mighty "form, covered with one foot-step the whole earth; with the second, "all the space that lies between the earth and the firmament. 'And "where,' he demanded, 'shall I place the third?' 'On my head,' "replied the Giant Bâli; who saw, too late, with whom he had to treat, "yet believed he might preserve his life by submitting to the discretion "of Vishṇu. But the unrelenting god made his third step on the head "of Bâli, and crushed it flat; then hurled down to hell the monster "who had been the oppressor of the earth."[i]

---

[i] This story is beautifully told in Kamba Râmâyaṇam. I. (IX.) 18—39.
See also Vishṇu Purâṇ, p. 265.
Bhâgavata, VIII. 15—23.

CHAPTER XXXII.

OF THE GIANTS, THE ADVERSARIES OF THE ANCHORETS.

THE Vânaprastha Brâhmans were exposed to great difficulties in the accomplishment of their sacrifices, by the opposition of their declared enemies, the Giants. They were likewise frequently thwarted by the Gods. Such opponents could render themselves invisible, by ascending into the skies, from whence they rained down lumps of flesh upon the offerings of the unhappy Penitents; by which they were altogether profaned. In this manner they avenged themselves, in part, of the impediments thrown in their way by the maledictions of those pious men.[j]

The Giants of India are represented to be of a size so enormous, that, in order to wake one who had fallen asleep, they were obliged to make several elephants walk over him at once; and, even then, it was a long time before he was sensible of their weight. The hairs of his body were like the trunks of the largest trees. At one time, in a skirmish with some Gods with whom he was at war, he fixed a rock upon each hair, and advancing into the midst of his enemies, with a sudden twirl of his body, he made the huge stones project around him, with such fury, as to overwhelm them all.

The Giant Râvaṇa, the same who stole away the wife of Râma, that is to say of Vishṇu personating that Prince, had ten heads. The palace which he possessed in the island of Ceylon, of which he was King, was so prodigiously lofty, that the Sun passed every day at noon under one of the arches.[k]

All the Giants were extremely debauched, and of a very malevolent disposition; particularly those that were Brâhmans: for some there were of that caste, and they were the most wicked of all. They had been transmuted into Giants, on account of their evil deeds when in the condition of men. They were very numerous; whole armies of them being sometimes seen, who occasionally made war on each other, but more frequently joined together in attacking the Gods; who, in many instances, have been subdued by those formidable opponents.

Sometimes they devoted themselves to an ascetic life, but with no view of reformation. The Giant *Bhasmêswara* supported a life of penitence so long as to compel Śiva to grant him at last the power he had long and earnestly solicited, of reducing to cinders all persons on whose heads he might lay his hands. The ruffian was willing to make

---

[j] Compare Southey's curse of Kehâma.

[k] Vishṇu Purâṇ, p. 385.

the first experiment of this miraculous power upon Śiva himself. The hapless god knew not whither to fly from the pursuit of the giant. But Vishṇu, the Preserver, seeing his distress, came up to his relief, and saved him, by artfully engaging the giant inadvertently to raise his hand to his own head; by which means he was consumed to ashes. With stories like this the Hindû Mythology is filled.

With respect to the giants who were in hostility to the Brâhmans, I am led to believe that they were merely the chiefs of the people in the neighbourhood of their hermitages, who would sometimes take offence, and annoy them in the performance of their magical rites; the effects of which they were taught to dread. This is a feeling not without example amongst ourselves; if we consider that, though not perhaps the first of our philosophers, yet many of their successors, have been held in dread, as being conversant in Occult science and dangerous necromancy. Some feeling like this, no doubt, it was that attended those ancient Hermits of India, which rendered their malediction so terrible, their wrath so awful; and it would naturally follow, that the fear of falling under such a perilous influence would excite those around them, both Kings and people, to league against them. And thus may have been effectually extirpated those renowned Vânaprastha Brâhmans; of whom no vestige now remains.

It was a fit theme for some poet, in his frenzy, to describe their contests with the neighbouring Kings and people, as a war with gigantic enemies. And, whatever the imagination of the poet could invent, there was credulity enough amongst the Hindûs to devour.

CHAPTER XXXIII.

OPINIONS OF THE HINDÛ PHILOSOPHERS ON THE NATURE OF GOD, OF THE DIFFERENT BEINGS IN THE UNIVERSE, AND PARTICULARLY THE SOUL.

THE Vânaprastha Brâhmans, or Ascetics, being bound, by their rules, to devote a large portion of their leisure every day to the contemplation of Para-Brahmâ; it is not surprizing that they should have acquired some tolerably pure notions of the Divinity.[1]

"God," to use the words of the philosophers of India, "is an "Immaterial Being, pure and unmixed, without qualities, form, or "division; the Lord and Master of all things. He extends over all, "sees all, knows all, directs all; without beginning, and without end. "Power, strength, and gladness dwell with Him."

This is but a slight sketch of the lofty terms in which the Hindû writings, after their philosophers, describe the Para-Brahmâ or Supreme Being. But it is painful to see these sublime attributes unworthily profaned, by prostituting them to the false gods of the country, and blending them with innumerable other attributes, as ridiculous and absurd as the fables to which they are attached.

The earliest of these philosophers, maintaining ideas of the Godhead so pure, in all probability never strayed into the absurdities of polytheism and idolatry. Their successors, however, adopted them by degrees, and insensibly conducted the nation, whose oracles they were, into all the extravagances in which we see them now involved. Hence we may conclude, that the speculations of those spurious teachers have prevailed no farther than to corrupt the purity of the inherent notions, and of regular tradition, respecting the nature and unity of God, as well as the worship which was paid to Him by those who flourished immediately after the Deluge.

These philosophers soon separated into two parties, upon the nature of God, and that of the universe. Up to the present times, each has its numerous partisans. The first is called *Dwaitam*, the *Sect of Two;* that is to say those who hold the existence of *two* beings or substances, namely, God, and the World, which He created, and to which He is united.

The other sect is called *Adwaitam; not Two;* meaning, those who acknowledge but one being, one substance, one God.

---

1 "There is a monotheism that precedes the polytheism of the Vêda, and even in the invocations of their innumerable gods the remembrance of a God, One and Infinite, breaks through the mist of an idolatrous phraseology, like the blue sky that is hidden by passing clouds."—MÜLLER.

The professors of the last doctrine designate the foundation of their system by the two technical expressions *Abhavanê Bhavanâsti: From nothing nothing comes.* They maintain that *Creation* is an impossibility, and that, on the other hand, a pre-existing and eternal substance is absolutely chimerical. From these premises they infer, that, whatever we imagine to be the universe, and the various objects which appear to compose it, is nothing but a pure illusion, or *Mâyâ.*

From the various tales which they have invented for illustrating their system, I have selected the following:

"A man, in a dream, imagined that he was crowned King "of a certain country, with great pomp and many ceremonies. On "waking, he met a man who had just come from that country, and "who related to him the whole circumstances of a King being chosen "and crowned there. His narrative agreed in all points with what "the other had seen in vision. There was, therefore, no more reality "in what the one person believed that he had seen, than in what the "other certainly had dreamed. The illusion was equal with regard "to both: for that which we take to be a reality is nothing more "than a deception from the Deity, the only being that exists: and "the various things we behold are but appearances, or rather modi-"fications of the Divinity."[m]

I know not whether these philosophers deduce from their pernicious system, all the consequences which naturally follow from it. Some of them I know have done so. I have read, in a Hindû book, an extract from the celebrated poem of the *Bhârata,* the author of which introduces on the scene the god Ṡiva, instructing his wife *Pârvati,* in familiar discourse. He tells her plainly, amongst other things, that the most abominable crimes, such as adultery, fraud, and violence are mere sports in the eye of the Divinity.[n]

In the system of *Dwaitam,* which admits of two essences, *God* and *Matter,* our souls are nothing but a portion of the Divinity; which is enveloped, as it were, by real objects, and shaded by the various passions which affect those several substances, and are inherent in them. The supporters of this last opinion try to explain it by the image of the sun, which appears in many vessels of water, all distinct from each other; or by an ingot of gold, from which various trinkets and vessels are formed: while there is but one sun and one ingot.

The ordinary Brâhmans, less learned, but more intelligent than those of the caste who attach themselves to the controversies of Dwaitam and Adwaitam, acknowledge one Supreme Being, the author and creator of the universe and of our souls. But they do not confound these created things with God, by whom men are governed, punished, and rewarded, according to the goodness or evil of their doings.

---

[m] The *Gnâna Vaṡishtam* is full of stories of this kind. It is in Tamil, and is well worth the careful study of all who wish to understand the system which has the most powerful influence of any over the minds of the people of South India.

[n] This has often been urged upon me by Hindûs in defence of their system.

There is still another scheme of philosophy, which is utterly rejected by the Brâhmans, and is said to be followed and taught by the Jainas and the votaries of Buddha. This system is nothing else than the pure *Materialism,* which Spinosa and his disciples have endeavoured to pass for a new discovery of their own. The materialists of India appear to have long preceded them in this doctrine, and have drawn from it the same practical deductions which their European brethren have done, and which have been propagated in modern times with such pernicious success.

Agreeably to this system, there is no god but matter; which, separating into various masses, forms as many gods, according to some; and the whole forming but one god, according to others.

Thence they conclude that there can be neither sin nor virtue, no migration nor transmigration of souls; that after death, there is no *Swarga,* or place of delight; no *Naraka,* or abode of torment. The truly wise man, according to them, is he who seeks after all the pleasures of sense, and who believes in nothing that he does not see. All beyond this is a chimera.

God, says a philosopher of this abominable school, possesses four *Śakti* or *Faculties;* which are like so many wives. These are knowledge, desire, energy, and deception or illusion.

The body, in applying the first Śakti, which is *Knowledge,* to its whole senses at once, enjoys perfect pleasure. It is but imperfect, if the diffusion is limited to a part of them. From this partial extension of knowledge proceed pain and sleep. Death is a total suspension of the knowledge of the body regarding its senses. It thus becomes insensible and perishes.

It is to amuse and divert Himself with the pleasures of infancy, that God creates his own substance into children, while at the same time He is enjoying the varying gratifications of maturity and age. Such, in a few words, is the whole secret of the causes of the commencement of life, and of its close.

The second Śakti of the Divinity is *Desire,* which changes with the various impressions it receives. God is man, horse, dog, insect, or in short whatever He wishes to be. His desire extends to each living creature, and varies with the instinct of each individual. He is delighted by enjoying what is adapted to the particular gratification of each.

But the Śakti of *Desire* unfortunately obscures that of knowledge, and hinders it from perceiving that there is no other deity but the material body, propagation, life, and death. From this ignorant deviation, occasioned by *Desire,* the inclinations of men are derived; such as the affection of a mother for her children, and the pains she takes in rearing them. The truly wise man, who would acquire the enlightened knowledge of truth and nature, must therefore renounce desire.

The third Śakti is *Energy*, upon which these pretended philosophers speak still more mysteriously.

All the universe, according to them, lay in confusion. Men lived without subordination, without laws or castes. To remedy this mighty disorder, a general consultation of bodies was held. *Energy* proposed to them the following scheme: "let us collect," quoth she, "from all bodies, whatsoever is found most excellent in each. From "such materials I will form a complete man, who, by the union of "beauty, wisdom, and strength, shall make himself master of the "whole earth, and become its only King. I shall be his spouse; and "from our marriage shall spring bodies innumerable, each more "perfect than another." The project was approved, and carried into effect. It fully succeeded; and from the body of the wife of a Brâhman, called Sutadâna, was born the god *Buddha;* a being, incomparable in all perfections; who has promulgated laws, the transgression of which is the most heinous sin. No iniquity can be more enormous than to deny Buddha to be what he is. He who acknowledges him, is the true Buddhist, a Brâhman indeed; the Guru among Brâhmans. His own body is his only god. To his body alone he offers up sacrifice. He procures for himself all possible enjoyments; he has no dread of any thing; he eats indiscriminately of all food. He scruples not to lie, in order to attain the objects of his wish. He acknowledges neither Vishṇu nor Śiva, nor any other god but himself.

"But, as all individuals are so many deities, or rather modifica-"tions of the same god, why are they not all endowed with the same "talents and equal penetration? Why are the greater part devoid of "sublime intelligence?" Such was the objection started by a new proselyte to one of the sages of the sect. His answer was, that "the "evil entirely proceeded from the fourth Śakti called *Mâyâ* or *Illusion.* "It is the cause of all deception, and makes men take what is false "for what is true. It has misled men into a belief that there are "gods; that there are such vicissitudes as living and dying, pollution "and purification. The only means of shunning the errors of *Mâyâ* "is to cling to the doctrines of Buddhism."

The author of the *Tantra Śastra,* from whom I have borrowed this exposition of the system, proceeds next to explain creation, and to make us comprehend how God, united to Mâyâ, should have produced men differing so greatly in their inclinations. But what he advances could only have proceeded from an extravagant imagination, and is no more worthy of attention than the talk of a sick man who is deprived of his reason by delirium.

He then returns to the principles and doctrine as above described. He sneers at the Brâhmans for their ablutions, fasts, penitence, sacrifices, mantras, vêdas. The true vêda, he exclaims, is for a man to please himself, to procure all sensual enjoyments, to take vengeance upon an enemy, and pursue him to death; to disclaim all sentiment of humanity, and to think only of his own advantage.

It is not wonderful that persons, who promulgate doctrines like these, should have created enemies to themselves; or that the Brâhmans, in particular, should be at open war with a sect that sets their principles so completely at defiance.

But the most odious part of this detestable doctrine is the gravity with which it inculcates the renunciation of all natural feelings, such as filial piety, compassion for the distressed, and similar propensities; which they sometimes denounce as sinful.

In tracing the course of this system, we encounter the history of a certain King, who scarcely ever left the apartments of his wives; but notwithstanding condemned to death a man whose crime was the practice of humanity and of charity towards his fellow-creatures.

Nevertheless, I doubt whether the genuine Buddhists would avow such horrid doctrines; and I rather believe the calumny must have been invented by some envious Brâhman, for the purpose of casting odium on a sect for which his caste entertains the most implacable hatred.

While employed in writing these pages, I am in the midst of a district, where there are great numbers of *Jainas* or followers of Buddha; and, after much enquiry into their character and conduct, I can assert that, in the practice of the moral virtues, they are not beneath the level of other Hindûs; and that, in good faith, in probity, and disinterestedness, they far surpass their antagonists the Brâhmans.

I can also recognise in the present description of the system in question, the bias of some Hindû philosophers, which always prompts them to extremes, in their theories as well as in their actions.

One prominent custom amongst them is, never to yield to their taste or appetite in eating or drinking; but to habituate themselves to the most nauseous aliments.

They must elevate themselves above the prejudices of the vulgar, and always pursue, in their conduct and mode of thinking, a course opposite to that of others.

They hold it improper to give themselves up to sensual pleasures in this present world, in which the desires of the body must be suppressed by mortifying penance.

At any rate, it must be admitted, that, if the Buddhists actually hold the odious and detestable tenets which are ascribed to them, in the reports which we have here abridged; these have no visible influence on their behaviour, or the slightest effect in relaxing the social ties which bind them, equally with other castes, to the great stock of society. Whatever is peculiar to their order they abstain from making public, by writing or in act; and this reserve, which is still continued, is probably occasioned by the memory of ancient persecution, which has at length softened down a rugged and pernicious system into a harmless theme of speculation.[o]

[o] On the subject of this chapter compare the Calcutta Review No. XLVII, for March 1855. Art. 2. "On the Shaktas."

CHAPTER XXXIV.

ON THE INFLUENCE OF PENITENCE IN PURIFYING THE SOUL; AND ON PURIFICATION BY FIRE.

THE doctrine of the Ascetic philosophers was, that Retirement should dissipate the clouds of Illusion which lead us astray, and break the chains which unite us too closely with the created beings that surround us; as well as with our own evil passions, which entangle, depress and pollute the soul. Being thus set free, it rejoins the Divinity, even Para-Brahmâ; and the penitent now cleansed from the stains of guilt which defile other men, can boldly exclaim "Behold a Brâhman! I "am wholly divine: I am Brahmâ!"

Men, whom a vain philosophy has beguiled into this ecstatical pride, cannot fail to look upon all other mortals with contempt; as wretches whose accumulated pollution and sins require the revolution of generation after generation to expiate.

This pride was farther inflamed by the marks of attention, or rather of adoration, which the greatest Princes lavished upon them; and which they accepted with absolute coolness, or in a manner which shewed that they considered the honour as not more than their due.

After this, one ceases to wonder at the behaviour of one of these philosophers called Maṇdanis; who, according to Strabo, refused to visit Alexander the Great, when he sent for him, and even wrote a haughty epistle to that sovereign. He was no doubt a *Vânaprastha* Brâhman, and doubtless he shewed great condescension in taking the trouble to write to any one. But, if the letter of this Hindû philosopher, as preserved by Strabo, be not a forgery, at least it is certain that, by paraphrasing and tricking it out in fine Greek, it is so disguised that, I venture to say, it never came out of the hands of a Hindû Muni or Rishi in that shape.[p]

But, how did this penitence or purification operate upon the Anchoret, in his solitary state? It operated in three ways; by subduing the passions, by the habit of contemplation, and by the mortification of the body. By the first, they pretended not only to eradicate the three great propensities before-mentioned, as relating to land, money, and women; but also to extirpate all ordinary prejudices, concerning castes, distinctions and honours. Their wish was to extinguish the most natural feelings, and even the instincts implanted in us by nature for our preservation. They required of their disciples to be insensible to heat and cold, to wind and rain; and to eat, without reluctance, not only the most offensive and disgusting scraps,

---

[p] Strabo, Geo. xv. He is called Dandamis by Arrian and Plutarch.

but even things of which nature herself shews her utmost abhorrence. They called this discipline by the name of *Môksha Sâdhakam*, or *Exercise of Deliverance*. In many respects, then, they were more Stoical than Zeno, and more Cynical than Diogenes himself.

It is probable, at the same time, that the great number of the solitary Brâhmans did not enter into these extremes, but left them to be practised by some enthusiastical penitents of an inferior order; although it cannot be disputed that their rules led implicitly to all the excesses that have been mentioned.

Even at the present time there are pretended penitents, who teach and practise the detestable *Môksha Sâdhakam*. Some of them go entirely naked, and affect, by that evidence, to shew that they are insensible to the passion that has the most powerful influence over men, and that the objects most capable of exciting it have no influence whatever upon them.

Many of these naked Sannyâsis are still met with about the country, to whom the Greek authors gave the name of *Gymnosophists*. They all exercise the profession of mendicity; and under the appellation of Sannyâsis are mere vagabonds, without house or habitation. Though completely naked, no appearance of any throb or involuntary motion is ever seen in parts of the body, over which the will has often but little control. Sights the most apt to produce excitement, appear to make no impression on this race of knaves. The multitude who are unacquainted with the means by which this control has been acquired, and who believe them to be out of the reach of passion, hold them in great admiration. And the European authors, who are not much better informed, have ascribed this power of restraint to cooling medicines; of which, according to them, they make constant use for the purpose of deadening their feelings. But the utmost austerity of living is not likely, of itself, to make them so callous to the impressions which affect the senses, and irresistibly influence that animal affection which these penitents boast that they have subdued. But, so far from their leading an austere and regulated life, I can testify that they are, of all Hindûs, the most intemperate; eating publicly, and without shame, all sorts of meat, and immoderately using strong liquors and intoxicating drugs. These transgressions are imputed to them as nothing. They are Sannyâsis; and the use of the Môksha Sâdhakam, which they are supposed to practise under those circumstances, exempts them from all blame.

The real means employed for producing the quiescence alluded to are quite mechanical. Before venturing to exhibit themselves, they attach a heavy weight, so as to swing between their feet towards the ground. This is augmented from time to time, and they drag it about with so great an effort, that the muscles are deracinated, or so weakened as no longer to be capable of their functions. Such I have been positively assured, is the sole cause of the famous inertia in the Gymnosophists or naked Sannyâsis of India.

Others amongst them boast of having conquered natural feelings of another kind; and they give horrible proofs of it, by eating human excrements, without shewing the slightest symptom of disgust. The stupid Hindû, who is never tickled but by extremes of some sort or other, looks at the fanatic with admiration, and feels nothing but respect and reverence.

Contemplation fills up the outline sketched by the mortification of the passions, by replenishing the soul with thoughts of the Divinity, and re-uniting it to that first being from whom it emanated, and of whom it is a part. This re-union is not effected all at once, but by several degrees, as will be explained under the head of the Sannyâsis. It is to bring about, by little and little this happy union, that the Vânaprastha is obliged, by his rules, to devote a considerable portion of his time every day to contemplation.[q]

The third degree of perfection consisted in the *mortification of the body*; by which was understood, not only that hard and austere mode of living, which every one must lead who aspires to perfection; but also frequent bathing, according to the usages. These philosophers confounded the pollution of the body with that of the soul, and were persuaded that they reciprocally passed into one another; and therefore they believed that the bath, by cleansing the body, had also the virtue to purify the soul. This was more particularly the case when it was performed in the Ganges, or any of the other rivers which superstition had rendered famous.

The little that now remained to complete the work of purification was accomplished by *fire*. It was for this reason that all the devotees were burned after death. Their obsequies were attended only by the solitary Brâhmans, their companions; and were in the same taste as those we have formerly described; though much less protracted than those of the ordinary Brâhmans. It could not indeed be supposed that they should stand so much in need of purificatory ceremonies, after renunciation of the world, the gloomy life they had led in the deserts, and their continued labour of purification during the whole course of their existence.

But, the uttermost perfection of purity was only to be attained by terminating their earthly course by *fire*, and offering themselves alive on the burning pile. Strabo relates the history of the Brâhman *Calanus*,[r] in which there is nothing improbable; who exhibited this spectacle before the whole army of Alexander. At the same time, I do not believe that examples of this kind were frequent among the Vânaprasthas. I remember but one instance in all the Hindû books I have perused or heard read; which was of an ascetic and his wife. Both were advanced in years; and they joined together in erecting the funeral pile; seated themselves very quietly upon it, set fire to it themselves, and were consumed together. After the highest degree

---

[q] Manu. Chap. VI. 8.

[r] Kalânas or Kalyâna.

of purification which human beings can reach, their souls were speedily reunited to the Divinity, without the slightest danger of being called upon to revisit the earth.

Such were the melancholy and deplorable effects of the Hindû superstition, and of the chimerical notions of their most enlightened philosophers.

Calanus was undoubtedly one of the *Vânaprasthas.* Certainly he could not have had the education and the manners of the Greeks; and that was a sufficient reason with that vain nation to treat him as a barbarian. Cicero, who has copied this story from the Greek historians, treats him in the same manner.[s] But it may be reasonably doubted that he was not so ignorant a man as the great Roman imagines; although at the same time, I do not pretend that our Vânaprastha had any knowledge of Grecian mythology, as Cicero seems to suppose, or that he chose the manner of his death in imitation of that of Hercules;[t] a name which probably he had never heard of.

What Cicero mentions of Calanus being born at the foot of the Caucasus, confirms what I have already said concerning the origin of the Brâhmans; and tends to shew, that the discoveries made at the time of the invasion by Alexander, at a period so near the establishment of these philosophers in India, are evidence of their deriving their descent from the environs of that famous mountain.

---

[s] Calanus Indus, indoctus ac barbarus, in radicibus Caucasi natus, suâ voluntate vivus combustus est. Tusc. ii. 22.

[t] Est profecto quiddam etiam in barbaris gentibus præsentiens atque divinans: siquidem ad mortem proficiscens Calanus Indus, cum adscenderet in rogum ardentem, O præclarum discessum, inquit, é vitâ, cum, ut Herculi contigit, mortali corpore cremato, in lucem animus excesserit! Cumque Alexander eum rogaret, si quid vellet, ut diceret: Optime inquit; propediem te videbo. Quod ita contigit. Nam, Babylone, paucis post diebus, Alexander est mortuus. Divin. i. 23.

CHAPTER XXXV.

OF THE LEARNING OF THE SOLITARY BRÂHHMANS AND OF THE EPOCH OF THE FLOOD.

HAVING already treated on the devotion, and the moral and philosophical system of the Vânaprasthas, it would be now proper to consider the *learning* or science to which they were addicted. But what has been elsewhere said on the sciences of the Brâhmans in general, applies so nearly to those of the devotees, that it is unnecessary to repeat it. There are two sciences, however, the one useful and the other pernicious, to which they in a particular manner apply themselves; namely, astronomy and magic. I have already given my reasons for not entering minutely into the former; but it is so connected with the epoch of the universal deluge, an event famous through all the world, and the point from which they date their astronomical calculations, as well as their commercial and ordinary eras; that I shall detail a few of the principal notices which the ancient Vânaprastha Brâhmans have transmitted to us on this subject. They have been treated very superficially by such authors as have come in my way.[u]

They recognize four ages of the world; to which they give the name of *Yuga.* They attribute to each of these, a duration, which would extend that of the world to several millions of years.

The first is called *Satya-yuga*, or *the age of innocence*, which they prolong to 1,728,000 years. The second, which they call *Treta-yuga*, lasted about a fourth part less than the preceding, or 1,296,000 years. The third, called *Dwapara-yuga*, continued for one-third less than the second, or 864,000 years. And the last, in which we now live, and which is called *Kali-yuga*, or *the age of misery*, will endure one-half less than the third, and will consequently amount only to 432,000 years.

This last age commences with the epoch of the Hindû deluge; and the year of the Christian era, 1805, in which I am now writing these pages, corresponds to the year 4906 of the Kali-yuga.[v]

---

u There are portions of the Vêdic writings which are only to be studied by the Vânaprasthas, or those who, having fulfilled all the duties of a student and householder, as detailed in the preceding chapter, retire from the world to the forest to end their days in the contemplation of the Supreme. Of these the Upanishads are a part; and they contain the most elevated portions of the whole Vêdic writings.—Müller, p. 313, &c.

v Vishnu Purâṇ, p. 24. From which this calculation is taken.

Each *yuga* or age has its Sand'hyâ consisting of as many hundreds as the yuga has thousands, and its Sand'hânsa of an equal duration.

Thus the computation stands :

At the close of each of the yugas which they admit, a revolution in nature took place, so universal, that not a vestige of it subsisted in that which followed. The gods themselves have had their share in the general change. Vishṇu, who was white in the last revolution, is become black in the present.

It is therefore clear that the commencement of the true era of the Hindus, that is to say the Kali-yuga, in which we now live, must ascend very nearly to the epoch of the universal flood; an event most distinctly marked by the Hindû authors, who give it the name of *Jala-praḷayam*, or water deluge.

The author of the Bhâgavata gives a very clear and detailed account of this deluge, which covered the whole surface of the earth. It is said in this book, one of the most ancient and famous of any which the Hindûs acknowledge that the Jala-praḷayam, or universal inundation of water, swept off all mankind, with the exception of the seven famous Rishis or Penitents; who, with their wives, were saved from the total ruin of the human race, by means of a ship, into which Vishṇu made them embark, and of which he himself became the pilot.

Besides this narrative in the Bhâgavata, frequent allusions to the Jala-praḷayam are found in several authors; some of whom add, that, besides the seven penitents, who embarked in the ship provided by Vishṇu, there was also preserved in it *Manu*, who appears to be the great Noah himself.

I believe that the universal flood is not more clearly announced in any ancient writings whatever, that have alluded to it, nor described in a manner more close to the recital of Moses, than in the Hindû book to which we have referred.

KRITÂ YUGA	4,000	years.
Sand'hyâ	400	
Sand'hânsa	400	
		4,800
TRETÂ YUGA	3,000	
Sand'hyâ	300	
Sand'hânsa	300	
		3,600
DWÂPARA YUGA	2,000	
Sand'hyâ	200	
Sand'hânsa	200	
		2,400
KALI YUGA	1,000	
Sand'hyâ	100	
Sand'hânsa	100	
		1,200
		12,000

These are years of the gods, 365 of which make one year of mortals.

Hence 4,800 × 365 = 11,728,000 — Kritâ yuga.
3,600 × 365 = 1,296,000 — Tretâ yuga.
2,400 × 365 = 864,000 — Dwâpara yuga.
1,200 × 365 = 432,000 — Kali yuga.

The ages deteriorate in a series 4, 3, 2, 1, units are counted into thousands and they are multiplied by 365, according to a mythological Fiction.

Thus a concurrent testimony of this remarkable epoch is afforded us, whose antiquity cannot be called in question; by the only people, perhaps, on earth, which has never been humbled into a state of barbarism, and whose territory, from its situation, climate, and fertility, must have been settled amongst the earliest of all; a nation which, perhaps, above all others, has been rigidly attached to its rites; and in whose customs no considerable change has been ever known. That nation, in its civil institutions, dates always from the epoch of the abatement of the flood. It appears, in its civil and popular intercourse, to have entirely rejected its other fabled ages, and to cling solely to this; since, as we have shewn above, all the eras promulgated in public, take their source from the commencement of the Kali-yuga, that is, the precise period of the flood. Every public and private act bears that it is done on such a year of its cycle of sixty years; and it expresses exactly, how many such cycles have elapsed from the deluge downwards. How many facts connected with historical truth are considered to be immutably fixed, which have not nearly so solid a foundation as this?

Besides their civil Cycle of sixty years, they have also adopted one of ninety; which is used only in astronomical calculations. They both commence from the same epoch, that of the cessation of the flood, or beginning of the Kali-yugam. It may be questioned, however, whether the astronomical Cycle be of the same antiquity as the civil; and it may be well supposed that the astronomers, having arisen after the establishment of the nation, made it to accord with that which they found already established, and that they could not, or durst not, change it. They likewise saw that the two modes of calculating could never occasion the least confusion; because, in every third succession of the Cycles, they started together afresh.

The Hindû astronomers admit into their calculations another epoch, still more modern; as it commences only about the middle of the first century of the Christian era. It is called the *Sâlivâhana* epoch, because it takes its date from the death of a famous King of India of that name, who reigned in a province called Sagam.[w]

The Chinese likewise have a civil Cycle, of sixty years, in common with the Hindûs; but there is this difference between the two races, that the Chinese are ignorant of any relation which their era bears to that of the flood. It is hardly to be imagined that the two nations could have communicated with each other, seeing that they do not agree in the computation. For, according to some authors who have written on the affairs of China, the birth of our Saviour falls on the fifty-eighth year of the Chinese Cycle, while it coincides with the forty-second of the Cycle of the Hindûs. This at least confirms the

---

[w] This æra synchronizes with A. D. 77. He was a king of the Mahrattas and his capital was Paitûn on the Godâvery.

The æra current north of the Nerbudda is that of the Râjpût king of Ujein, Vicranâditya, = 56 B.C.

antiquity of the Cycle of sixty years still in use with the two most ancient races of people on the face of the earth.

It would be useless perhaps to inquire whether this Cycle was instituted before the flood, and whether it be from Noah or his immediate descendants that the Hindûs have derived it. All that we know for certain is, that the *weekly* Cycle was instituted and acted upon before that famous epoch, and that the Hindû week agrees exactly with that of the Hebrews and with ours. The days of their week correspond precisely with those of ours, and are numbered just in the same way.

But what is peculiar to them is that, in the same manner as every day of the week and every month of the year has its particular name, so has each of the sixty years of the Cycle. Thus, they do not say that a certain event happened on the twentieth or thirtieth year of the Cycle; but they give the year its name, and say that it happened in the year *Krôdhi*, the year *Viswâsu*, the year *Pingala*, and so forth.

CHAPTER XXXVI.

OF THE MAGIC PRACTISED BY THE VÂNAPRASTHA BRÂHMANS, AND STILL IN USE AMONG THE HINDÛS.

THE secrets of Magic are taught in several Hindû books, and particularly in that of the four Vêdas, which bears the name of *Atharvaṇa Vêdu.* The Brâhmans assert, and wish to have it believed, that this *Vêda* is not in existence; being desirous to avoid the suspicion of being initiated in the pernicious science which it teaches. But this assertion is the less to be believed, because books of this sort are sure to be preserved, in preference to all others, in an idolatrous country.[x]

The Brâhman Devotees were accustomed to study these Vêdas, and particularly that of the Atharvaṇa. We have had occasion to remark elsewhere, that their sacrifices frequently bore a great resemblance to magical operations; and the power which such sacrifices were supposed to possess over the Gods themselves, makes it extremely probable that those who practised them were conversant in the mysteries of that pernicious art.

We have also mentioned that the Solitary Brâhmans, at first cherished and respected by the kings and their people, became at last detestable to all their neighbours, on account of the terror which their malediction and their magical sacrifices inspired; and that this was probably the real cause which united against them the Princes in the vicinity of their retreats, who at last extirpated that sect of philosophers; so that no vestige of them now remains.

There is no reason, therefore, to doubt that the Brâhmans in the remotest times, have been conversant in all the mysteries of the art of magic. They still give it a place in the table of their sciences; and indeed it holds a high rank among the sixty-four divisions which they arrogate to belong exclusively to themselves. It is no less certain that many of them dabble in magic to the present times, and are publicly known to be initiated in all the secrets of the Occult art.

---

x The Atharvaṇa Vêda is undoubtedly very rarely found. It contains the magic formulas by which the priests sought to avert any malicious and hostile influences which might destroy the efficacy of the sacrifice.

It thus served as a shield to the other three Vêdas, since only by its verses could the rites and sacrifices ordained in them be performed and offered with success.

The Atharvana is thus full of mystic formulas, of expressions possessing a hidden meaning and a miraculous power.

Its incantations are designed to remove sicknesses, to bring wealth and success and to effect any end great or small desired by the sorcerer.

Compare Max Müller's Sanskrit Lit. p. 454.

W. Vishṇu Purâṇa, p. 276—283.

There still exist, in all the castes, numbers of persons, who pretend to be skilled only in some one of the many branches of magic, such as that of divination, augury, and other branches of the science which imply nothing of a pernicious tendency. It is not to be wondered at that in a country like India, plunged in the thick darkness of gross idolatry, and of every sort of superstition, impostors should abound, who find their interest in promoting such abuses. In every quarter, tellers of good fortune are to be found, who will distribute good luck to those who are willing to pay for it. Brâhmans, and even Pariahs, called *Vâḷḷuvar*, announce the good and the evil days, favourable and inauspicious omens, tell fortunes, by observing the features of the face or the lines on the palm of the hand: and those who exercise this profession are consulted by incredible numbers.

But these common soothsayers are by no means dreaded, or held in fear; while those who are understood to be initiated in the profound mysteries of magic, or such as possess the art to detect robberies, and the most secret crimes, to cure diseases, or to bring them on, to infuse a devil into the body of any one, or to expel him, and to produce other similar effects of supernatural influence, are looked upon with horror and awe.

Those pretenders to real magic are often consulted by persons who wish to avenge themselves of some enemy by way of malediction; and also by sick persons, who are persuaded that their disease has been caused by some magical operation directed against them, and who would gladly recover their health by a counteracting art, able to repel the malady and return it upon those from whom it proceeded.

There is no sort of good or evil which these magicians will not undertake to produce; although they are more inclined to the evil. There is no species of malady which they do not pretend to be able to cure: fever, dropsy, retention of urine, pain in the whole members, fatuity, madness, and all other disorders. But all this is nothing compared to the energy with which they denounce the destruction of an enemy's army besieging a place, the death of the commander of the besieged fortress, and the inhabitants it contains.

The Muhammadans in India, being equally superstitious as the natives of the country, are no less infatuated with the notion of magic. I knew, from the best authority, that the last Musalmân Prince who reigned in the Mysore, the fanatical and superstitious Tippu, in his last war, in which he lost his kingdom and his life, resorted to the most celebrated magicians he could find in his own country and elsewhere, trusting that, by the operation of their art, the English army, which was then marching to besiege his capital, and which he could not expect to repel by ordinary means, might be destroyed. The magicians whom he consulted on this occasion, acknowledged their impotence, and were obliged to confess that their operations, so potent amongst other races of men, were utterly inefficient against the Europeans.

But if magic teaches the means of drawing down evil, it also affords, by counter-spells, not only a defence against imminent peril, but the power of causing the pernicious effects of sorcery to recoil on the heads of those by whom it is meditated.

The magicians are likewise provided with many Antidotes against witchcraft, which they distribute among those who consult them. There are certain enchanted beads; some sorts of roots; very thin plates of copper, on which extraordinary figures are engraved, with inexplicable words and unknown characters; amulets, also, of various kinds; all which are worn by the Hindûs, to serve as talismans, and to preserve them from every species of incantation.

Secret methods of inspiring love are likewise understood by the professors of the magical art; and this is not the least lucrative part of their trade. A wife or a mistress resorts to them eagerly, in quest of a spell to restrain the husband or lover from deviating into other amours. Debauched gallants and lewd women consult them on the means of seducing the object of their passion.

The Hindûs believe in *Incubus* Demons. Those of India are not quite the same in their practices as the beings of that nature in Europe, which some country people still believe in. In India they exceed so much in the fierceness and frequency of their attacks on women, whom they haunt in the shape of a dog, or some other brute, that the harrassed female dies in consequence. A superstitious people take dreams for realities; and it would be in vain to attempt to convince a Hindû that these are not operations of the devil.

But the great subject of the work is the means of communicating enchantment to the arms used in war. Enchanted armour is celebrated in all Hindû writings. The gods in their wars, constantly made use of it. One weapon was called the arrow of Brahmâ, and that was never shot without effect. Another was named after the serpent Capella, which, when launched against an army, lulled to sleep the whole troops that composed it. To the present day, those who have weapons charmed by magical sacrifices, bid defiance to wounds in battle. Cannon balls and musket shot levelled against them become harmless, and tumble at their feet. Cutting instruments cannot penetrate their skin, but bend or break when directed against them.

There are also secrets for obtaining all sorts of temporal blessings, and wealth unbounded, and charms which have the virtue to make barren women conceive. Generals and soldiers may be provided with certain bits of bone, which will not only render them invulnerable, but make them appear terrible in battle. There are also enchanted drugs, which, when rubbed on the face and eyes, will enable them to discover concealed treasure. But I find no secret to insure immortality; which I rather wonder at, as the Hindû Charlatanry does not generally stick at trifles.

The next question relates to the means used by the magician to insure success to his incantations.

In Europe, as long as the belief in magical arts subsisted, it was understood that their virtue depended on a compact entered into with the evil spirits. But, in India, it is sufficient for the practitioners to receive a few lessons in the art from their masters; whom they thenceforth style their Gurus. If, upon experiment, the disciples give any orders to a demon, spirit, or god, and these are disregarded; they have only then to command obedience, in the name of their masters, and instantly their orders are executed.

In using the word *Gods* on this occasion, the very highest even are to be understood, Brahmâ, Vishṇu, Śiva, being as much under the control of the magicians as the inferior deities. Some indeed are called upon, in preference to others, when something evil is to be invoked upon any one. The Planets are of this class. Their name *Grahana*, which signifies the *act of seizing*, points out their office of laying hold of those against whom the magician employs them. The *Bhûta*, likewise, or *Elements* pass for extremely malevolent beings, fit to be employed for such purposes; as well as the *Pisâchi* other wicked spirits, under which appellation the Hindû Christians denote the devil. The Śakti, female divinities and wives of Śiva, the God of Destruction, are also much employed in evil purposes. *Maraṇa Dêvi*, or *Goddess of Death, Mâri, Kâli*, and some other gods of the same sanguinary and malevolent kind, also perform a great part in this game.

In order to put all those gods and spirits in action, the magician offers up sacrifices of the Mantram, with many ceremonies peculiar to the occasion. The sacrifices are much in the same taste as those before described, although they are sometimes accompanied with particular ceremonies. The magician, for example, while he offers up his sacrifice to Lakshmi, the wife of Vishṇu, must be entirely naked; and on the contrary, he must be decorously dressed when he sacrifices to Râma. The flowers, which are presented to the god invoked must be red; and, when the object is to procure the death of any one, the boiled rice offered up must be sprinkled with blood. And, upon the same principle, when the utmost effect is required from magical operation, a human victim is sacrificed; and particularly a young girl.

We have already spoken of the virtue of the Mantras; but it is in the work of magic that they are most efficacious. They imperiously dictate to the great gods; and compel them to act in the heavens, in the air, or on earth, whatsoever the magician requires.

It is in incantation, chiefly, that certain Mantras, called *fundamental*, are employed. They are composed of some barbarous syllables, of harsh utterance and difficult pronunciation. Some of them, though almost impossible to be expressed in European characters may be imitated by the sounds *Hrom, Shrim, Shram.* Sometimes the magician employs his Mantras in a humble and supplicatory style, conciliating the god whom he invokes; but he soon assumes an imperious tone, and exclaims in a vehement and impassioned key: "Seize, grasp! If thou dost, it is well: if not, I command thee, in "the name of God, and in the name and for the feet of my Guru!" Such awful invocations enforce the ready compliance of the god.

The ingredients employed by the magician, in his magical operations, are without number. A specimen of them will here suffice.

In some direful acts of fascination, it is necessary to use the bones of various animals; those, for example, of the elephant, of a black dog, of a scorpion, a tyger, a black cat, a bear; of a man born on a Sunday when it falls on the new moon, of a woman born on a Friday; the footbones of an European, of a Mahometan, and of a Pariah, and several others; to the amount in all of sixty-four species of bones of different sorts.

This osseous compound, after due charms and incantation by Mantras and sacrifices, has the potency to slay whomsoever it is directed against. This effect will surely follow, if, when a certain star is in the ascendant, a portion is buried in the house of one's enemy.

Equipped with these relics, the magician has only to advance to a hostile army, in the silence and darkness of the night, and to bury the bones at the four cardinal points of the camp. He then retires to some distance, and one hundred times denounces the Mantram of destruction against the army; and, within seven days, it will either disband itself, or perish to the last man.

Thirty-two weapons, consecrated by the sacrifice of a human victim, will scatter such dismay amongst a besieging army, that a hundred of their opponents will appear, in their sight, as a thousand.

A quantity of mud is collected from sixty-four of the filthiest and nastiest places, and moulded into small figures; on the breasts of which they write the names of the persons whom they mean to annoy. When incantation is made over them, and sacrifice performed, the Planets or the Elements environ the parties so represented, and inflict upon them a thousand pangs. Sometimes they pierce the images with thorns, or mutilate them, so as to communicate a corresponding injury to the person represented.

Sixty-four roots of different plants, have a similar efficacy in producing evil, when duly prepared with Mantras and sacrifice.

This variety of sorcery and spells calls to our recollection the similar apparatus of the Canidia and Sagana of Horace; when the explosion of Priapus terrified the hags into a hobbling retreat, leaving behind them their enchanted relics and clothes.

> "———— At illæ currere in urbem.
> "Canidiæ dentes, altum Saganæ caliendrum
> "Excidere, atque herbas, atque incantata lacertis
> "Vincula, cum magno risuque jocoque videres." [Hor. Serm. I. viii 47—50.]

Thus ends the small specimen we have selected out of the great depositary of Indian jugglery.

The next thing to be considered is the risk of danger which the magician himself incurs in the exercise of his profession. This is great and imminent, on account of the reluctance of the gods to be so controled by his Mantras. Often do they take vengeance upon him for this compulsory obedience. He cannot err in the slightest ceremony, nor make the smallest mistake, without exposing himself to their fury. The rites he is obliged to perform are without number; and the omission of any one of them, however minute, through inadvertency or any other cause, would instantly make the whole mischief he was preparing for others revert upon his own head.

But it is from rivals, who exercise the same trade, that the conjuror has most to dread. These do what they can to counteract his projects and to make the effects of his own wicked contrivances fall upon himself, by employing spells of still greater efficacy. This being the case, they bear a mortal hatred towards each other, or at least pretend to do so. When they meet, their mutual dislike breaks out into loud defiance, calling on those within their reach to decide as judges between them and pronounce which of the two is the most skilful. The contest begins. The problem perhaps is, to lift a straw from the ground, or a piece of money, without touching it. Both advance; but they stop one another's progress by flinging enchanted cinders, or by reciting Mantras. They both feel, at the same instant, an invisible but irresistible force which repulses and drives them back. They again approach, redoubling their efforts. The sweat exudes in drops: blood is discharged from their mouths. One of them, in the scramble, gets hold of the piece of money or the straw, and he is clamorously proclaimed the victor.

Sometimes one of the combatants is violently precipitated upon the ground by the force of the Mantras of his antagonist. In this state he remains for a long while stretched at his whole length, breathless and (as he makes it appear) deprived of sensation. At length he gets up, covered with shame and confusion, hangs his head, retires to bed, and affects to be very ill for several days.

It will readily be supposed that I attribute such disputes and their consequences to a premeditated understanding between the quacks; but, through all India, the people are firmly persuaded that these processes result from magical secrets known only to the initiated few, who, by their means, produce such wonderful effects. And it must be owned that effects are occasionally produced by them, of which it would not be easy to divine the cause.

CHAPTER XXXVII.

OF THE SANNYÂSI, THE FOURTH STATE OF THE BRÂHMANS: THE MANNER OF INAUGURATION AND THE RULES.

THE fourth degree to which a Brâhman can attain, is that of Sannyâsi; a state so sublime, as the Hindû books declare, that it imparts, in a single generation, a larger stock of merits than ten thousand could produce in any other sphere of life. They add, that, as soon as a Sannyâsi dies, he passes straightway to the world of Brahmâ, or to that of Vishṇu; exempt, for ever, from the penalty of being re-born upon earth, and of revolving from generation to generation.

The Sannyâsi Brâhman takes precedence of the Vânaprastha, inasmuch as the latter does not absolutely renounce the world, being in some degree connected with it by his wife and children;[y] whilst the true Sannyâsi is obliged to sacrifice all those connections, and at the same time to assume the most rigid of the rites of the Vânaprasthas. He takes the profession also of mendicity; and, from the moment of his installation into that lofty order, he must live solely upon alms.[z]

But, before embracing this holy profession, they must devote several years to the state of Grihastha, or a married life; in which they may have children, and so acquit the debt they owe to their forefathers; which consists, as the Brâhmans hold, in perpetuating the succession of their race.

There are, however, examples in the Hindû books, of Sannyâsis, who embraced that state from their infancy, and before being married. Something of that sort is still to be met with.[a] But such varieties are not to be found in the class of the Brâhmans.

It must not be from humour nor any temporary fit of zeal that a Brâhman resolves to assume this rank. His resolution must be the fruit of mature reflection, and must be founded on a true and sincere separation from the spurious enjoyments and all the pleasures of this world; which he must heartily renounce, in order to aspire after a more perfect existence. In this renunciation of the world, he must so thoroughly detach himself from whatsoever pertains to fortune, pleasure, and honours, as no longer to have any hankering after such distinctions. If he wilfully encouraged, in his heart, the slightest longing after any thing that other men most ardently pursue, such a swerving towards earthly vanities would alone suffice to deprive him of all the fruits of his penitence.

---

[y] Manu VI. 3. [z] Manu chap. VI. 33. [a] Manu VI. 38.

When a Brâhman, therefore, has well considered the bent of his own disposition, and has finally made up his mind to that high calling, he convenes the principal Brâhmans of his district; and, having communicated to them the resolution he has formed, he intreats them to instal him in the situation which he feels himself destined to fill. A matter of such importance, however, cannot be transacted without abundance of ceremonies.

The first care is to select a proper day; one, in short, to which there can be no objection. This having arrived, the aspirant, in his way to the place of the ceremonies, undergoes the purification of bathing. He takes with him ten pieces of cloth, such as are frequently worn in India, somewhat like our bed-quilts, and envelopes his whole body in them. Four of these cloths must be dyed of *câvi* colour, which is a deep yellow approaching to red. It is the established colour worn by the penitents, and, in imitation of them by the Musalman Fakîrs. These four are for his own use; and the other six are to be given as presents to individuals of the caste.

He must also provide himself with a long bamboo cane with seven knots, a gourd scooped and dried, an antelope's skin, some small pieces of silver and copper money, Flowers, Akshatâ, Sandal wood; but above all, a quantity of Panchakâryam. To this liquor he sacrifices, and divides it into five earthen pots, afterwards pouring it all back into one vessel. He then mixes it well, and quaffs a portion of the disgusting preparation. Taking up what is left of it, together with the other articles that form his stock of materials, he proceeds to the place appointed for the ceremonies.

The Guru who presides and directs, whispers in his ear some Mantras accompanied with a few instructions relative to the new state which he has embraced; after which, he orders him to dress himself in one of the cloths of a yellow colour which he has brought with him, to cut the Triple Cord, as a token of his renunciation of the caste itself, and to shave off the lock of hair which the Brâhmans and other Hindûs allow to grow on the crown of the head.

All this being accomplished, he takes the seven-knotted cane in one hand, the gourd filled with water in the other, and an antelope's skin under his arm. The whole equipage of a Sannyâsi consists in these three articles.

Lastly, he drinks thrice of the water in the pitcher which he carries in his hand, he recites the Mantras which had been taught him by the Guru; and thus he is constituted a Sannyâsi. There are no other ceremonies required at his installation; which is completed by the distribution of the cloth, the pieces of money, and the other materials among the persons present.

The new Sannyâsi must conform strictly to the instructions given him by his Guru, and must follow the rules prescribed to those who assume this profession. I here subjoin such of them as have come to my knowledge, with necessary remarks.

1. A Sannyâsi, every morning, after bathing, must rub his whole body with ashes.

The difference here between the Sannyâsi and other Hindûs, all of whom make this use of ashes, is, that they apply them only to the forehead. The reason for his spreading them over the whole body is to conceal his lineaments and beauty from those who come to visit him, and to shew that he has renounced the pleasures of life and the decoration of his person.

2. He must restrict himself to a single meal every day.[b]

The Hindûs, as we have elsewhere observed, are not supposed to be making a meal unless when they sit down regularly to their boiled rice, with its ordinary accompaniments. At other times, they may sip milk, and eat fruit or other raw substances, without any breach of their fast. The Sannyâsi may likewise avail himself of the same indulgence.

3. He must give up the use of Betel.

It is generally known that this is the leaf of a creeping plant, of a poignant taste, which the Hindûs incessantly chew. It is even a greater mortification to them to abstain from this luxury than it would be for an European to renounce his tobacco when most habituated to it.

4. Not only must he shun the company of women, but he must even avoid looking at them.

5. Once every month he must shave his beard, his mustaches, and his whole head.

6. He must wear on his feet only wooden clogs.

This species of shoe is extremely convenient, being no otherwise fastened to the foot than by a peg, the extremity of which passes between the great toe and the second. It is on account of cleanness that the Sannyâsis adopt this custom; for they would be defiled either by going barefooted, or in leather shoes.

7. When a Sannyâsi travels, he must carry in one hand his seven knotted staff, in the other his gourd, and the antelope skin under his arm.[c]

The use of the gourd is to carry water for his drink, and the skin makes a convenient seat when he has occasion to sit down.

8. He must live only upon alms, and he can demand them of right.[d]

In this way, some Sannyâsis become extremely rich. But, on the other hand they are bound to bestow the wealth so acquired in alms or other charitable acts. Some lay them out in the construction of public works, such as houses for travellers, temples, tanks and

---

[b] Manu vi. 55.

[c] Manu vi. 41.

[d] Manu vi. 56.

other reservoirs for containing water. They are likewise hospitable to passengers and persons who come to visit them.

8. He must erect a Hermitage on the bank of a river or lake.

This regulation has in view the greater facility of bathing; a practice strongly recommended to the Sannyâsi. The habitation itself must be very plain: a mere shed, open on all sides.

There are, no doubt, many other rules appertaining to this class of individuals; but I have confined myself to such as have fallen under my own knowledge.

CHAPTER XXXVIII.

THE VARIOUS DUTIES OF THE SANNYÂSI, PARTICULARLY CONTEMPLATION.

THE primary and chief care of a Sannyâsi ought to be to divest himself entirely of any lingering attachment to the world that may adhere to him. It is a feeling that will always be shooting out afresh, if it be not completely eradicated.

A wife, children, relations and friends, a caste, a bias to sensual pleasure, indulgence of the palate; and, in short, all the passions invelope the soul in the same manner as the integuments in which some insects involve themselves, composed of threads of straws, from which they can never extricate themselves any more. Or they may be compared to the wind, which agitates the surface of the water, and prevents it from reflecting the true image of the sun.

Comparisons such as these abound in the Hindû writings, by which they endeavour to impress on the mind the interruptions which the passions and other stimulants of sense occasion to the perfect re-union of the soul to the Divinity: a consummation which ought to be the sole object of solicitude with a Vânaprastha Brâhman, and still more with a Sannyâsi.[e]

He has shaken off the chains which bind other men to the earth by a voluntary renunciation of the world, and the abandonment of all he there held dear. Any slight hankering after terrestrial things, that might still insensibly adhere, is washed away by continual ablutions by the Panchakâryam, of which he often drinks, by his daily sacrifices and the various ceremonies which accompany them; by the devout life which he leads; and, above all, by the habitual exercise of contemplation.

This operation of the mind is so striking a quality amongst an idolatrous people that it merits particular attention, if we are desirous to know how far the spirit of fanaticism and superstition can mislead men; especially when it is nourished by vanity and self-love, or the wish to be distinguished and to acquire a name.

Contemplation, in this sense, is termed *Yôgam*[f] by the Hindûs; from which is derived the name of *Yôgi* which is given to some

---

e Manu vi. 61—96.

f Mythologically *Yôga* or devotion is daughter of *D'harma* or virtue. Technically yôga signifies all those exercises by which reunion with the supreme spirit, the union of the discriminated with the universal soul is obtained. These exercises are taught by Patanjali, the founder of the yôga system.

Vishnu Purân. p. 155—157—652. Bhagavat Gitâ, passim.

amongst the Devotees, who are supposed, though perhaps wrongfully, to be more addicted to this virtue than others of the same profession. According to the Hindû doctrine, the exercise of the Yôgam spiritualizes the Sannyâsi, and renders him absolutely faultless, by conducting him through four stages, each more perfect than another.

The first of these degrees, and lowest of all, is called *Sâ-lôkyam*, or *Unity of place.* In this state, the soul perceives itself in some measure to be in the same place with God, and as it were in his presence. Thence it passes to the second stage, called *Sâmîpyam*, *proximity*; meaning, as I understand it, that by the exercise of contemplation and the advance beyond sublunary things, the notion and conception of God become more familiar, and the contemplative Sannyâsi is brought more nearly into his presence. The third degree is called *Sâ-rûpyam, resemblance*; because, in this state, the soul attains a likeness to the Divinity, and acquires in degree some of his principal attributes. This leads to the fourth and highest state called *Sâ-yûgyam,* in which a perfect transformation into the divine nature is effected, and an intimate re-union with it.[g]

I am disposed to think that, upon a candid consideration of what we have now before us, our mystical teachers, and such of us as devote ourselves to a contemplative life, ought not to be scandalized with such doctrine. At any rate, it shews that the ancient devotees of India reflected more profoundly than is commonly understood on spiritual concerns.

More pure, undoubtedly, and more rational, before the introduction of foul idolatry, this spirituality was afterwards contaminated, and existed no farther than to inflame the pride of the devotees. They pretended that they had at length arrived at that intimate re-union with Para-Brahmâ, by which they became one essence; while the rest of mankind, whom they looked down upon with sovereign contempt, were crawling in the mire of materiality and passion.

But whence did those pretended penitents derive this habitual contemplation so much boasted of?

Before the prevalence of idolatry in India, and while the traditions transmitted from the patriarchs who were near the period of the flood, inculcating religious purity, external and internal, and such worship as the primitive generations paid to the Supreme Being, were not yet forgotten; perhaps the spirit of contemplation might have still possessed energy sufficient to keep up the feelings of piety and

---

Baron Von Humboldt's definition of *Yôga* is "the steady direction of the mind towards the Godhead, which abstracts from all other objects, even from its own thoughts, puts a stop, as far as possible, to every motion and function of the body, meditates exclusively on the essence of the Godhead, and strives to unite itself to it."

The object of this *Yôga* is "the transmutation of the human into the divine nature."

[g] There is some confusion here.

These are Vaishṇava terms and do not belong to the yôga system.

devotion towards God. But this must have been confined to ancient times. At present, a vain phantom only remains.

I cannot better represent the sórt of contemplation that exists among the present spurious devotees of India, than by giving a brief account of a conversation I once had with two Hindûs who were aspiring to the contemplative life, and had for a long time studied under eminent Sannyâsis, in whose houses they had been placed.

"I was a novice," said the first, "under a celebrated Sannyâsi, "who had fixed his hermitage in a remote situation near Bellaburam. "As he prescribed, I devoted great part of the night to watchfulness, "and to endeavours to expel from my mind every thought whatever. "Agreeably to other instructions, daily repeated to me by my master, "I exerted all my might to restrain my breathing as long as it could "be possibly endured. I persisted in thus containing myself, con-"tinually, till I was ready to faint away. Such violent efforts brought "on the most profuse perspiration from all parts of my body. At "length, one day, while I was practising as usual, I imagined I saw "before me the full moon, very bright, but tremulous. At another "time, I was led to fancy, in broad day, that I was plunged into thick "darkness. My spiritual guide, who had often predicted to me that "the practice of penitence and contemplation would disclose to me "very wonderful appearances, was quite delighted with my spiritual "progress, when I related to him what I had experienced. He then "set me some new tasks, equally difficult, to join to those I had "been employed in; and told me that the time was not far distant "when I should find still more surprizing effects from my penitence.

"Wearied out at last with these tiresome follies, I gave them up, "fearing they would altogether discompose my brain; and I again "betook myself to my old employment of a labourer."

The second, who, though rather advanced in years, was of a shrewd intellect, gave me the following account of his studies.

"My master," quoth he, "who was a Sannyâsi of more than "ordinary reputation, and with whom I served as a novice five or six "months, had fixed his residence in a desert place, at some distance "from *Nâma Kallu.* After making me go through some preparatory "exercises of no great difficulty, he prescribed me others, according "to the progress I was making, rather more severe. He ordered me, "amongst other things, to look steadily at the sky, with my head "elevated, and without winking. I was obliged to repeat this exercise "several times every day; and my organs of sight soon became "inflamed in an extraordinary degree, which occasioned me violent "head-achs. Sometimes I fancied I saw sparks, and sometimes globes "of fire in the air. The Sannyâsi, whose disciple I was, appeared "highly satisfied with my proficiency in my studies. He was blind "of one eye, and I learned that he had lost it by the same experiment "which he imposed upon me, as quite indispensable to conduct the "mind to spirituality. Being afraid at length that his schemes would "end in the total loss of my sight, I resolved to leave him and his "contemplation also.

"I had likewise made trial of another sort of exercise not less "painful than the former. The great hinge on which spirituality turns, "as my master told me, is to keep all the orifices of the body so closely "shut that none of the winds from within should escape. For this "purpose, it was necessary to stop the ears with the two thumbs. "The little finger and the ring finger were brought together, and "held the lips close. Each fore-finger blocked up an eye, and each "middle finger pressed upon a nostril. In order to secure the lower "aperture, the penitent sat accurately upon the end of his heel. In "this position," continued he, "I shut one of my nostrils with one of "my middle-fingers, and drew in as long a breath as I could through "the other; which I then closed, and allowed the breath to escape "gradually through the first. This I managed for a long time, only "taking care never to inhale and respire by the same nostril."

As I had some difficulty in comprehending the trick which the novice had described to me; I desired him to place himself before me in the attitude he alluded to. This he most readily did; and never, surely, was there seen any thing more laughable than the posture he put himself into for a few moments; but which he was soon obliged to quit, in order to give way to the bursts of laughter which the remembrance of his past follies still provoked.

There are several other postures, still more irksome and ludicrous than this, in which these pretended contemplatists put themselves, to help their meditations. One of them is to stand upright on one foot, till the leg swells, suppurates, and breaks out in ulcers. Some will reverse the position, and continue, great part of a day, with their head on the ground and their feet in the air. Some hold their arms cross-wise over their heads, until the muscles, by continued tension, assume the new direction given to them, as if it were natural, and can never recover their original position.

It would be useless to describe the other various modes of doing penance, every one of which seems more painful than another. They reckon eighteen different kinds: but the specimen we have given will be sufficient to shew the nature of their usages, and the extravagant follies to which superstition, fanaticism, and delusion will lead, when supported by a feeling of vanity and pride.

The Hindû authors, however, speak in high terms of this contemplation, and of the admirable effects it produces. They mention one horrible instance of it, to which forsooth they attach the highest degree of merit. It consists in subduing all sensation, and retaining the breath with such determined perseverance, that the soul, abandoning the body, bursts through the crown of the head, and flies to re-unite itself with the great Being, with Para-Brahmâ.

In the present times, the great body of contemplatists do not go such lengths, though some are still met with who practise these extravagancies. Most of them content themselves with holding their heads immoveable, their arms across, and their eyes closed; excluding from their minds by this posture, all manner of thought. Others, again, keep their nostrils constantly shut, by squeezing the nose between the fore-finger and thumb, bending the head forward, and keeping the eyes stedfastly fixed to the ground, without raising them to notice any of the objects around, or even the persons who may be addressing them.

I know that the practice of one of those modern Contemplators, who was for some time a neighbour of mine, consisted in representing vividly to his own imagination an image or idol of Vishṇu, to which he mentally offered garments, jewels, flowers, and different kinds of viands. He then fancied that he was addressing various petitions to the gods; all of which were granted. He passed an hour and a half, daily, in this exercise; though I did not find that he became richer by it.

The first true Contemplators in India, dedicated a portion of each day to tranquil reflection, in the presence of him whose perfections and benefits they meditated upon; a race has now succeeded of foolish and extravagant bigots, who, retaining nothing of their predecessors but part of the external shew, gave the reins to their enthusiasm, and seek no middle course in their observances. But we have often had occasion to remark that it is the natural disposition of the Hindûs neither to embrace nor to follow up any thing that does not border upon the wonderful.[h]

---

[h] Compare Wilson's Hindû Sects, p. 132.

The perfect fulfilment of the duties prescribed by the yôga system is impossible in the Kali age.

Hence the proverbial expression, frequent in the mouths of Hindûs :—

"Na sid'hyati kalou yôgâ.
Na sid'hyati kalou tapaḥ."
Yôga is not attainable in the kali yuga;
Penance is not attainable in the kali yuga.

CHAPTER XXXIX.

OF THE FUNERALS OF THE SANNYÂSI BRÂHMANS.

THE ceremonies at the Obsequies of Sannyâsi Brâhmans differ in several particulars from what are used in the case of ordinary Brâhmans, and even from the Vânaprasthas. The bodies of all these are burned after death. The Sannyâsis, on the other hand, are all interred, even such of them as have attached themselves during their life to the sect of Vishṇu. The bodies of the devotees of the last sect when they die, we have seen, are burned on a funeral pile, in the same manner as those who are attached to no particular sect; whereas, by the custom of the country, all who have in their lifetime professed the worship of Śiva, and wear the Lingam, are buried when they die. The number of the last is exceedingly great in the western provinces of the peninsula.

In the interment of a Sannyâsi, his son, if he had one before he assumed his profession, takes the lead. If there be none, it is conceded to some Brâhman, who voluntarily takes it on himself, at his own expence. There are never wanting persons who offer themselves for this generous service. It is considered to stand in the highest class of good works.

After washing the body, it is again invested with two pieces of cloth stained with the *Câvi* yellow. The whole corpse is rubbed over with ashes of cow-dung, so as to give it a thick coating. The necklace is then put on which they call *Rudrâksha,* meaning the *eyes of Rudra* or Śiva, from whose tears the beads are supposed to have been crystallized. All the while, some of the Brâhmans are rattling a sort of castanets of brass, common in that country, which make a piercing sound.

After these preparatory ceremonies are over, the body is placed in a sitting posture, cross-legged, in a large basket; which is suspended with straw ropes upon a strong pole of bamboo, and carried by four Brâhmans. They proceed, without noise or tumult, to the trench which has been prepared on the bank of the river, if there be one in the neighbourhood. It is dug so as to resemble a well, about six feet in depth, and is filled about one-half with salt, on which the body is placed, in the posture that has been described. It is then covered up to the neck with the salt, which they press closely all round, so as to keep the head immoveable. This is succeeded by the strange ceremony of breaking cocoanuts upon the head of the deceased, which is continued till the skull be quite shattered; after which, more salt is thrown into the pit, and the head covered out of sight.

Earth is then accumulated over the trench, to the height of several feet; and upon the heap so raised a *Lingam* is erected, about three hands breadth high, which is immediately consecrated by the Brâhmans with mantras; and an offering is made of lamps lighted, of fruits, flowers, incense, and, above all, of the *Paramânnam*.[i] This is a dish which the Brâhmans use often, and are very fond of; consisting of boiled rice, cocoa, and sugar. All the offerings are accompanied with hymns, or rather obscene songs, which they all join in chanting to the honour of Vishṇu.

As soon as they have ended the uproar, for their singing deserves no other name, every one bawling in a note of his own; the president of the ceremonies paces round the Lingam three times; after which, he makes a profound obeisance, with his hands clasped, and offers at the same time prayers for the deceased: that, "through the sacri-" fice made to the Lingam he may be completely blessed; and may "it please Śiva and Brahmâ to receive him into their world, that he "may not have to live any more in this."

After finishing his prayer, he pours out upon the ground a little water and rice, and then collects all the bits of the cocoa nuts which were broken on the head of the deceased, and distributes them among those present; who eat them as a sacred and well-boding morsel.

The *Paramânnam* is distributed among such as are without children, as this sacred food is supposed to be efficacious in rendering barren women fruitful. The ceremonies of the day end with the bath: not that this is necessary for the purpose of purification on the present occasion; for no impurity can be contracted when assisting at the funeral of a Sannyâsi; but merely as one of the three regular ablutions which a Brâhman makes every day.

For ten days after the funeral, the person who presided appears every morning at the tomb, accompanied by several other Brâhmans, and offers sacrifices as before to the Lingam, which still remains over the grave. These are repeated also on the anniversary of the funeral; but with this variation, that after entertaining those who assist at the ceremony with a suitable repast, he walks round, saluting each, and takes leave of them all without offering any presents. The company, as they retire, compliment him on the good work which he has performed.

Some tombs of Sannyâsis have become famous, and are visited by crowds of pilgrims, who come from afar with offerings and sacrifice. They seem to be considered as a part of the divinities whom the people adore.

---

[i] PARAMA, *best* + ANNAM, good.

The ceremony of battering the head of the corpse, strange as it appears, is intended merely as a species of sacrifice, instead of an injury. Where stones are set up to represent Lingas, they generally assail them in the same manner, as they pass them on the highway.

The prayers and vows offered up for the Sannyâsis, after their death, with the ceremonies which accompany and follow their obsequies, seem to indicate that all their faults are not considered to have been expiated or their state of felicity to be beyond all doubt. But this is not the only point on which Paganism is at variance with itself.

Some aged or infirm Brâhmans, when conscious that they have not long to live, become Sannyâsis towards the end of their days. This conversion, though tardy, and probably not very sincere, never fails to obtain for them after death the same distinction they would have received if they had passed the best part of their lives in all the austerities of the profession. I may also remark, in passing, that what I have had occasion to mention respecting the clothing of the real Sannyâsi and Vânaprastha Brâhmans, shews that ancient authors were under a mistake when they gave them the name of *Gymnosophists* or *naked* philosophers.

Some modern authors are no less mistaken in giving the appellation of Sannyâsi Brâhmans to some pretended penitents, who live secluded in hermitages, or sometimes even in a kind of convent, spacious and convenient. The last sort is the most common, and extends to all the castes. They do not in general adhere to the rule of the Sannyâsi Brâhmans, which requires that, before embracing the profession, they should have entered into wedlock, and propagated children. Many of those here alluded to have never been married, although I would not warrant their having lived in a state of exact continency, as they have generally a licence to keep several women in the quality of servants, some of whom have the superintendence over a set of runners whom they send abroad in every direction to collect alms and offerings, which are in some way shared amongst them.

The appellation of Sannyâsi is still more improperly applied to a vast number of vagabonds who scour, the country, with no settled place of abode, and usurp that venerable title, to impose on the people. Many cheats of this kind are to be met with; but the most common are the pretended penitents called *Vairâgis*, who sometimes make excursions in great bodies, and live on alms; which they always demand with great importunity and insolence, as a thing absolutely due to them. The Vairâgis belong entirely to the sect of Śiva: yet they do not wear the Lingam, the ordinary badge of the devotees of that god. But, in token of their special devotion to his worship, they are continually blackened over with ashes, and they profess a life of celibacy; although those who are acquainted with their habits best know how scrupulous they are on the point of chastity.

The *Vairâgis*, in the sect of Śiva, resemble very closely the

Dâśaru in that of Vishṇu, as far as regards their wickedness. In that, neither yields to the other. There is visible between them the same aversion and hatred towards each other, and the same intolerance towards others, which are observable in all sects who permit themselves to be swayed by the impulse of superstition and fanaticism; and, upon that ground, it is impossible but that even in modern times, religious wars must have prevailed in India, and that the Vairâgi and Dâśaru must have been mutually engaged in sanguinary contests.[j]

---

[j] Compare Wilson's Hindû Sects; p. 115.

The words Sannyâsi, Vairâgi and Fakîr have the same meaning—a wandering beggar of any religious order. The words are sometimes limited and when they are so a *Fakîr* is a Muhammedan, a Sannyâsi is a Śaiva, and a Vairâgi a Vaishṇava mendicant.

The affrays mentioned in the text chiefly take place between the Nâgas of the two sects, who are an extremely worthless set of Vagabonds.

These contests have by no means ceased, though the strong hand of authority represses them, so that they do not lead to the same sanguinary results as in former times.

A

DESCRIPTION

OF

THE PEOPLE OF INDIA.

PART III.

RELIGION.

CHAPTER I.

THE ORIGIN OF THE TRIMÛRTTI, AND THE PRIMITIVE IDOLATRY OF THE HINDÛS.

THE Hindûs understand by the word *Trimûrtti*, the three principal divinities whom they acknowledge; namely, Brahmâ, Vishṇu, and Śiva. It signifies *three powers*, because the three essential energies of *Creation*, *Preservation*, and *Destruction*, severally pertain to these three gods. The first is the leading attribute of Brahmâ, by whom all things were created. The second belongs to Vishṇu, the preserver of all that exists: the last to Śiva, the destroyer of what Brahmâ creates, and Vishṇu preserves.

These three deities are sometimes represented singly, with their peculiar attributes; and sometimes as blended into one body with three heads. It is in this last state that they obtain the name of Trimûrtti, or three powers. It appears also that this union of persons may have been intended to denote, that existence cannot be produced and reproduced, without the combination of the three-fold power of creation, conservation and destruction.

The Trimûrtti is acknowledged and adored by all Hindûs, excepting the tribe of *Jainas* or *Bauddhists*. And in general it may be remarked that although some castes attach themselves, in a special manner, and almost exclusively, to the sect of Vishṇu, or that of Śiva; yet when these gods are united with Brahmâ, and form but one body, they pay undivided worship to all three, without regard to the particular doctrines which distinguish the special followers of the different deities.

The difficulty of tracing the origin of the Trimûrtti is increased by the disagreement of the Hindû authorities with each other on this subject. In some Purâṇas, it is declared to have sprung from a woman called *Âdi-sakti*, or *Original Power*, who brought forth the three gods; and the fable adds that, after having brought them into the world, she became desperately in love with them, and took her three sons for husbands.[a]

In other Purâṇas, the origin of the Trimûrtti is differently accounted for. In the Bhagavata, in particular, it is mentioned that a flower of *Tâmarai*, or lily of the lakes, grew out of the navel of Vishṇu, and that Brahmâ sprung from the flower.[b]

In some, the Trimûrtti is stated to have originated from *Âdi-sakti*, the *first power*; who produced a seed from which Śiva sprung, who was the father of Vishṇu.

But it must be allowed that the fable of the Trimûrtti, or of the three principal deities being united in one body, is less consistently supported than any other doctrines in the Hindû books. All that they contain on the subject is a mass of absurdities, which do not even agree with each other. The point which the whole of them discuss the most diffusely, is what relates to the debaucheries and abominable amours of the three deities in their combined form.

But, great as the power of the Trimûrtti is, it is frequently compelled to endure the superiority of some virtuous personages, with the dreadful effects of their malediction and wrath. Shocked at the sight of the infamous proceedings of the three deities, those purer minds attain the power of punishing and of fully subduing them by the irresistible potency of their Mantras. In this high rank, the virgin *Anasûyâ* was conspicuous, a woman as much renowned for inviolable chastity and piety towards the gods, as for tender compassion towards the unfortunate.

The Trimûrtti having heard the praises of this virtuous woman, became enamoured of her and disguised as mendicants, went to ask her for alms. She readily complied, and made a liberal distribution amongst them. The pretended beggars, having thus partaken of her bounty, proceeded to urge their suit.

Anasûyâ, amazed and terrified at language to which she had been so little accustomed, took vengeance, by pronouncing certain Mantras over her suitors, and sprinkling them with a holy water of such efficacy as to convert the Trimûrtti into a calf. The transformation of the gods being complete, she yielded to the tenderness of her nature, and nourished the fatling with her own milk.

The Trimûrtti remained in this humiliating state of servitude, till the female deities, apprehending some unpleasant accidents from the absence of their three principal gods, consulted with each other, and

---

a This is the idea of the Mâdhwas, or followers of Mâdhwâchârya.

b This is substantially the account given in all the Vaishṇava Purâṇas.

determined upon employing all the means in their power to relieve themselves from the degraded condition into which they had fallen. They went therefore in a body, in quest of Anasûyâ, whom they humbly besought to give up the Trimûrtti, and restore the three gods to their accustomed splendour. This petition of the goddesses was granted, with great difficulty, and only upon the hardest of all conditions. But they chose rather to lose their honour than their gods. They discharged the penalty (to whom or by what means the story says not), and the virgin restored the Trimûrtti to their original state, and allowed them to return to their ancient residence.

The Hindû books abound in abominable stories of this kind respecting the Trimûrtti. What we have related is one of the least indecent amongst them.

But the obscure, and, in many respects, contradictory, manner in which they describe the origin of the Trimûrtti, and the extreme confusion which pervades all the fables relating to it, have convinced me that the three chief divinities who compose it are something wholly different from what they are there represented to be.

At the commencement of their idolatry, the Hindûs, confining their worship to sensible objects, such as the sun, the moon, stars and elements, never resorted to images of stone or other materials; because the objects of their adoration were always present and continually in their view. But, when the spirit of idolatry had made progress, and the people of India had deified their heroes or other mortals, they began then, and not before, to have recourse to statues and images to preserve the memory of such illustrious beings, and transmit it to posterity. By degrees they assigned a bodily form to all the objects of their worship, believing it to be the only means of fixing durable impressions of them in the minds of a people nearly insensible to every thing that did not directly affect the senses.

It is from this period, I presume, that the true origin of the Trimûrtti is to be taken, being long posterior to the establishment of idolatry in India. The *three powers* contained in the etymology of the word, appear to shew that, under the representation of three divine persons in one body, the ancient Hindûs intended the three great powers of nature; namely the earth, the water, and the fire. In course of time this original notion would gradually vanish; and an ignorant race, directed solely by the impressions of the senses, gradually converted what at first was a simple allegory, into three distinct godheads.[c]

Before pushing our inquiries farther, it will be proper to make some remarks on the origin which the learned of Europe, in modern times, have assigned to this triple god of the Hindûs. They resolve

---

[c] There is not the slightest hint in the Vêdas of this important feature of later Hindûism, the Trimûrtti, or, Tri-une combination of Brahmâ, Vishnu and Śiva, as typified by the mysterious syllable ÔM.

Wilson's Rig Vêda Sanhitâ. xxvii.

it into the three principal deities of the Greeks and Romans under different names, and according to them, Brahmâ is no other than Jupiter, Vishṇu is the same as Neptune; and Śiva is Pluto.

Jupiter, in Greek Mythology, is the author and creator of all things; the father, master, king of men and gods. But all these attributes pertain no less to the Hindû Brahmâ. All men were created by him and issued from various parts of his body. The universe is his work and belongs to him. It is called the *Egg of Brahmâ;* and when it was laid, according to the Hindû expression, he *hatched* it.

He also more particularly resembles Jupiter in his scandalous amours. Jove had his own sister Juno for his wife. Brahmâ is both the father and the husband of Saraswati. Many other points of resemblance might be pointed out between these two divinities, sufficient to induce the belief that the one was derived from the other.

I find the resemblance equally striking between Neptune and Vishṇu. The former makes the waters his abode. The sea is his empire. There he holds sovereign sway, armed with his formidable trident. The cheerful tritons accompany him, sounding their conch shells all around.

Vishṇu is distinguished by attributes nearly the same. The name by which he is principally invoked is that of *Nârayâṇa,* which signifies *one that sojourns in the waters.* He is represented as quietly asleep on the bosom of the wide ocean, if no accident occur to awake him; with no trident in his hand, indeed, nor tritons around him. But the symbol of the trident is borne by his devotees on their foreheads, represented by the mark called *Nâmâ;* and some remembrance of the tritons may be suggested by their blowing of the sea-horn, the figure of which they likewise represent with hot iron on the shoulders.

But as to Pluto, the grim monarch of hell, king of the dead, ruler over the regions of desolation; is he not the exact model on which Śiva is formed? To Śiva belongs the power of destruction. He reduces all things to dust. Where carcases are burnt, there he delights to dwell; there he raises his howlings and his cries. *Rudra* is his name, *the cause of lamentation.*

Pluto, finding no female willing to accompany him to his dismal abode, carried off Proserpine by force, and concealed her so well that she escaped for a long time the search of her mother Ceres. It was by roaming in unfrequented places, and with infinite difficulty, that Śiva also found a wife. Having long failed in his search, he obtained one at last by applying to the mountain *Pârvata,* who gave him his daughter *Pârvati,* in consideration of his long and rigid penitence in the deserts. And to prevent her escape, he constantly carries her on his head enveloped in the enormous folds of his bushy hair.

But when a resemblance is found between the fabulous deities of different nations, is that sufficient to justify the conclusion that they are in reality the same, though under different names? If it were so, I could exhibit Jupiter in Vishṇu and in Śiva, as well as in Brahmâ;

for those two gods, have a coincidence of character, as much as Brahmâ himself, with the chief deity of the Greeks and Romans.

It was Vishṇu, in fact, who purged the earth from a race of giants by whom it was over-run, and who far exceeded in stature, as well as in strength and power, the Enceladuses and Briareuses that were subdued by Jupiter.

The Roman deity rode upon an eagle. Vishṇu was also mounted on a fine bird of prey, of the species of eagles. It was called *Garuḍa*, and though originally of little size, it became enormously large, and fit to bear the *Master of the World:* for by this high title was Vishṇu, as well as Jupiter recognized.

Other points of resemblance, not less striking, exist between the other gods of India and of Greece. Juno, the wife of Jupiter, is the goddess of wealth. And so is Lakshmi, the wife of Vishṇu, whose name denotes *Riches.* But there is a greater similitude between these illustrious females in their jealousy, for which they are equally conspicuous, arising in both from the perpetual infidelities of their husbands, and producing the same dissension and domestic quarrels.

The Romans, in their public spectacles, exhibited in honour of their gods, chiefly introduced Jupiter and Juno on the stage. The Hindûs have the same practice in respect to Vishṇu and Lakshmi.

There is still another high deity in India who bears no small resemblance to Jupiter in several particulars: I mean *Indra* or *Dêvêndra.* The word signifies *King of the Gods;* and he who bears this name is *monarch of the sky.* The world which he inhabits is called *Swarga* or *the place of sensual delight.* Dêvêndra reigns here over a great number of inferior deities, who enjoy, in his paradise, all the pleasures of carnal voluptuousness. He distributes amongst them the *Amrita,* a liquid which may be well compared to the *Ambrosia* of the Greeks.[d] Thunder is the armour of Dêvêndra; and he, as well as the son of Saturn, launches it against the giants. But, amongst the points of resemblance between them, there is this essential difference, that Dêvêndra, with all his high titles, is but of an inferior class in the order of the gods, and that his authority is but of a subordinate kind.

The same parallel which I have drawn, between Jupiter on one side, and Brahmâ, Vishṇu, and Dêvêndra on the other, I could equally apply to several others of the Grecian and Hindû gods; and by that means shew that the one class has not been copied from the other, as from a model. Indeed whatever resemblance may be traced between the objects of idolatry in different countries, it will scarcely afford sufficient grounds to infer that the whole was originally the same, or the one borrowed from the other.

But if it was not from abroad that the Hindûs received their three principal divinities, whence can they have originated? This will require explication. But let us first attend to an essential article in

[d] Amrita = immortal = (ambrotos): hence *Ambrosia.*

which the Hindû idolatry differed widely from the European paganism, as it anciently flourished at Athens and in Rome. It was not the *Sea* they worshipped there, but its monarch, the god Neptune who presided over it. His attendants, the Nereids and Tritons, had a share in his worship. It was not to fountains and forests that sacrifices were offered, but to the Naiads and Fauns who ruled and had their dwellings there.

The idolatry of India is of a grosser kind, at least in many circumstances. It is the water itself which they worship; it is the fire, men, or animals; it is the plant, or other inanimate object. In short they are led to the adoration of things, from the consideration of their being useful or deleterious to them. A woman adores the basket, which serves to bring or to hold her necessaries, and offers sacrifices to it; as well as to the rice-mill, and other implements that assist her in household labours. A carpenter does the like homage to his hatchet, his adze, and other tools; and likewise offers sacrifices to them. A Brâhman does so to the style with which he is going to write; a soldier to the arms he is to use in the field; a mason to his trowel, and a labourer to his plough.

It is true, there is another species of idolatry much less rude than this, which relates to idols of distinction. These are withheld from public adoration until the divinity they represent has been invoked and inserted by the Mantras of the Brâhmans; and in this instance, therefore, we must allow that it is the god who resides in the idol that is the object of worship, rather than the image itself. But this last species of idolatry, though of later origin than the preceding, I conceive, is by no means opposed to it. Both kinds are followed and approved, although the first be undoubtedly the most common; and indeed it is founded on a maxim universally admitted amongst them, that honour is due to whatsoever may be the cause of good or of evil, whether it be living or inanimate.

"My God!" exclaimed one day to me a person of some consideration amongst them, "what vast evil or good the man has it in his "power to do me, who is at the head of the husbandmen, who cultivate my grounds under his orders!"

I have somewhere read a conversation between the wives of the seven famous penitents of India, in which they all agreed in the principle that a woman's chief god is her husband, by reason of the good or evil which he can bring upon her.[e]

It was upon the same principle that the Hindûs in ancient times, rendered divine honours to certain grand penitents, from the strong conviction they felt of the mischief that might result from their maledictions, or the good that would flow from their blessing.

---

[e] In the Kuraḷ this verse is found: "deyvam toṛâaḷ koṛunan toṛud 'eṛuvâḷ pey ena peyyum maṛai.

"*If the woman who worships no god, but rises up adoring her husband, bids it rain, it will rain.*"

Nor is it from a dissimilar feeling, that at the present day, they so readily prostitute the name of God by applying it to any mere mortal whom they have reason to view with fear or hope.

But the poor Hindûs are not the only people that have degraded themselves by such humiliation and sacrilegious flattery. The Romans scrupled not to follow the same course ; and Virgil was not the only adulator who dishonoured religion, in venturing to burn incense upon altars dedicated to his benefactor Augustus, then living, and to bedew them with the blood of the best lambs of his flock.

The principle amongst the Hindûs of deifying whatsoever is useful, has extended to the mountains and the forests. In such sequestered places, castes of persons are found who lead a vagabond and savage life, acknowledging none of the gods of the country; but they have one of their own institution, a thick and long Root, which these wild men are fond of, and make the principal part of their food. They adore it, and in its presence they celebrate their marriages and take their oaths and vows. They know of nothing that can be more useful to them ; and therefore they have assumed it for their god.

The same idea gave birth to the apotheosis of the three principal deities of India; for I am persuaded that they were originally, in the Hindû idolatry, nothing else than the three most obvious elements of the Earth, the Water, and the Fire. These were the real gods whom they originally worshipped; and we shall soon find that the same worship, though not so visible, still subsists at the present day.*f*

Earth is the element from which all the productions most necessary to man proceed. From her bosom are collected the grain and the plants which serve for his nourishment. She is the universal mother of all living creatures. She is therefore the first of the Gods: she is *Brahmâ.*

But, without the seasonable visitation of the Rain and the Dew, in a land hot and without water, the labours of the husbandman would be fruitless, and the soil, now so exuberant in its increase, would become barren and deserted. *Water* is the great preserver of whatever the earth engenders, or makes to germinate with life. Water, with all its blessings, has therefore become the second God of the Hindûs, and holds the honours of *Vishṇu.*

But what could the sluggish earth, even with the aid of the water, so ungenial and cold in its own nature, have effected, in their sterile union, but for the *Fire,* the principle of warmth, which came to vivify and quicken the mass? Without this enlivening element, the chilled plants would have refused to shew their gay attire, or to acquire the maturity necessary to constitute a fit aliment for man. But fire not

---

f "The stories of Śiva, Vishṇu, Mahâdêva, Pârvati, Kâli, Krishṇa, &c., are of late growth, indigenous to India, and full of wild and fanciful conceptions. There is no system of religion or Mythology in the Vêda. If we want to tell the Hindûs what they are worshiping—mere names of natural phenomena, gradually obscured, personified and deified,—we must make them read the Vêda." Max Müller, Oxford Essays 1856.

only invigorates all animated nature, and developes every thing to its utmost perfection; but it also accelerates dissolution and decay; a process not less necessary, because, from corruption, nature is restored, and germinates afresh. Fire, therefore, has contributed as much as the other elements, and equally deserves the general adoration and worship, which have bestowed on it the title and the honours of *Śiva.*

What I have here proposed is not a system gratuitously invented, for the purpose of explaining the original idolatry of the Hindûs. It is their own doctrine, reduced into daily practice; and the direct worship of the *Elements*, though less observable now than it was in former times, is still maintained in vigour. "Hail! Earth, mother most mighty!" are the words of the *Yajur-vêda;* or, as they are afterwards explained, "Health to her, from whom we derive the "blessing of nourishment." In the same Vêda the following words are also found: "Health to thee, O Fire! God that thou art."[g] And, in other respects, nothing more strongly indicates the divinity that was ascribed to this element, than the sacrifice of the Hômam, so much used by the Brâhmans, and that of the *Yajna* formerly described; both of which seem evidently an offering to *Fire.* In presence of that element, the Hindûs take their most solemn oaths. It is also adjured as the witness of whatever they assert and affirm; and a perjury committed, under such circumstances, could not fail to draw down the dreadful vengeance of the God.

The divinity of *Water* is recognized by all the people of India. It is the object of the prayers and of the adorations of the Brâhmans, while they perform their ablutions. On that holy occasion, they particularly invoke the sacred rivers; and above all the Ganges, whose venerable waters they adore.

On many occasions the Brâhmans and other Hindûs offer to the Water oblations of money, by casting into the rivers and tanks, in the places chiefly where they bathe, small pieces of gold, silver, and copper, and sometimes pearls and ornaments of value.

Sailors, fishermen, and others who frequent the sea and the rivers, never fail, upon stated occasions, or as circumstances require, to hold a solemnity on the bank, where they sacrifice a ram, or other suitable offering. But, to whom do they offer this worship? "To *that* God," they will answer, pointing to the water of the sea, or of the river or pond near which they stand.

If, after a long drought, a plenteous shower descends to renovate the hopes of the despairing husbandman, filling the great tanks or reservoirs that contain the water collected for the irrigation of the fields of rice; instantly the population of Brâhmans and Śûdras assemble on the brink, with loud exclamations of the "*Lady*" being arrived. Every one joins in congratulation. Every one clasps his

---

[g] Weber's Yajur Vêda Part I. p. 444.
Rig Vêda. I Ashṭaka. 7.

hands, and makes a deep obeisance, in sign of gratitude to the *Water*, which replenishes their cisterns. The sacrifice of a Ram is also made, from time to time, at the brink of the water.

At the season of the great inundations of the Kâvêri, which generally take place in the middle of July, the inhabitants of that part of the peninsula make a solemn pilgrimage to its banks, many of them coming from a great distance, so that, in some places, the concourse is altogether innumerable. Their object is to congratulate *the Lady* or *the Flood* on her arrival, and to offer sacrifices of rejoicing.

When I had occasion to speak of the *Triple Prayer* of the Brâhmans, I mentioned that they place a copper vessel filled with water on the ground, and make several prostrations and other signs of reverence before it. From this, one might be led to conclude, that the vessel, and the water it contains, are placed in honour of Vishṇu, and that the signs of adoration are addressed to that God. But my reason for thinking that the worship is directed exclusively to the *Water* in the vessel, is, that the same practice exists among the Brâhmans, whether belonging to the sect of Vishṇu or not.

The homage and worship which the Brâhmans offer *directly* to the Elements, may be remarked in several of their daily rites. When, for example, they commence reading in the Vêdas; on coming to the *Yajur-vêda* and *Atharvêna-vêda*, they must offer a prayer to Water; but if it be the *Rik-vêda* and *Sâma-vêda*, the supplication must be addressed to Fire.

The worship of the *Elements* among the Hindûs was, no doubt, in ancient times, consecrated by temples erected to their service. I have never been able to discover that any vestiges of such buildings remain; but if we give credit to Abraham Rogers, and the Brâhman who was his authority, there was a temple standing, in his time, in a district bordering on the coast of Coromandel, which was built in honour of the *Five Elements*.

It may be said, perhaps, that the Hindûs are not the only people that have paid adoration directly to the object, without regard to the Gods who were ultimately considered as the inherent Kings and Rulers; and that, in almost all countries, the Elements have been worshipped. The Persians, in particular, as we learn from Herodotus, offered them sacrifices. This serves to confirm what I have advanced concerning the Hindû worship of them; nor is it wonderful that they should have fallen into a practice, so gross and absurd, in imitation of all other ancient nations.

From those three elements were formed the three gods, Brahmâ, Vishṇu, and Śiva, or the Trimûrtti; which bears the double meaning of *three bodies* and *three powers*. The Hindû writers affect allegory above all things; and the simple readers, being easily misled, take the whole in a literal sense, and worship the image instead of what it signifies.

The mode of explanation by allegory, is so familiar to the Hindû poets, that they usually refer to their three chief gods under the symbolical attribute of each. In regard to the human race, they find three distinct characters or dispositions, which they call *Guṇa;* namely, the *Tama Guṇa*, or *serious and grave;* the *Satwa Guṇa*, or the *gentle and insinuating;* and the *Raja Guṇa*, or the *choleric and ardent.*[h] These qualities they have transferred to the three gods; making the first apply to Brahmâ, the second to Vishṇu, and the third to Śiva. The agreement is no less exact when applied to the three elements combined in the Trimûrtti; the Earth, represented by Brahmâ, having solidity for its characteristic; the Water, under the appellation of Vishṇu, with its insinuating qualities; and the Fire, with the semblance of Śiva, containing the power of destruction.

The *Tama*, or *grave* character attributed to Brahmâ, is so suitable to the nature of the earth, which is distinguished by ponderosity and density, that the Hindû authors confound it frequently with the earth itself. Thus, in a lunar eclipse, when the opacity of the earth intercepts the rays of the sun in their way to illuminate the moon, they use the word *Tama*, and say that the *Tama Bimbam*, or disk of the earth, obscures that of the moon with its shadow.

The *Raja Guṇa*, or *ardent* disposition, is no less indicative of Śiva. The appellation is therefore frequently given him by the poets. And though his usual name of Śiva signifies Joy, yet he often passes under others which denote *Fire* only. Such is that of *Jwâla*, under which he is known, signifying *a flame.*

I may here allude to a custom, which supports my opinion respecting the Trimûrtti. The Hindûs, sometimes imagining that the god Śiva has waxed extremely wroth, and fearing, during periods of excessive heat, that everything will be set on fire by the burning ardour that inflames him, place over the head of his idol a vessel filled with water, in which a little hole has been pierced, to let drop after drop fall down, to refresh him and check the vehemence of the fire which consumes him.

The *Satwa Guṇa*, or *gentle and insinuating temper*, is no doubt expressive of the *water*, which filters and insinuates itself into the earth, and renders it fertile. The word *Vishṇu* means, that which *thoroughly penetrates;* which perfectly agrees with the quality of water, which is emblematical of him. Indeed the name by which he is chiefly known by many of his devotees is that of *Ap* or *Water*.

What I have here attempted to prove respecting the three principal deities of India as being nothing else than the three principal elements of earth, water, and fire, is an article of doctrine well understood by many Brâhmans belonging to the sect of Vishṇu. I have conversed with several of them, who have informed me that their opinion on the subject was not different from mine, and have even furnished me with

---

h The three qualities are SATYA, goodness, or purity, knowledge, quiescence: RAJAS, foulness, passion, activity; and TAMAS, darkness, ignorance, inertia. Vishṇu Purâṇ. p. 2.

some of the arguments I have made use of. They told me farther, that they themselves treated all that is commonly taught concerning the mystery of the Trimûrtti as fabulous or allegorical. But as their mode of thinking visibly tended to the overthrow of the established religion of the country, and at the same time, not only to dry up the principal source of their emoluments, but actually expose them to public detestation; they preferred to keep their opinions private, or at least to communicate them only to one another, or in company where they were confident they should be safe.

Taking for granted the reality of the metamorphosis of the three elements into the three principal deities of India, it will be easy to give a very simple and natural explication of certain expressions to be found in the Hindû writings, which might lead many persons to believe that the people of that region possessed, from the earliest times, some knowledge of the mystery of the Trinity. "These three gods," it is there said, "make but one only. It is a lamp with three lights;" with many other expressions seeming to import one God in three persons.[i]

If it were true that the primitive Hindûs had it in their contemplation to transmit an idea of the Trinity under the form and attributes of the Trimûrtti, it must be owned that they have most wofully disfigured that august mystery. But it does not appear to me that we are authorised to draw such consequences from the expressions we have alluded to, and others of the same kind ; for the reunion of their three elements into one body, relates only to that natural admixture of three substances, no two of which, without the third, could possibly produce what is necessary for the wants of man, but must remain barren and unfruitful.

The fathers of the first ages of the church, such as Justin Martyr, St. Clement, Theodoret, St. Augustin, established the truth of the Trinity by the authority of the ancient Greek philosophers, and particularly by that of Plato, or of his principal scholars Plotinus and Porphyry; and they successfully availed themselves of these authorities, in those times, against the Pagans, amongst whom they preached the Christian religion. The fathers found, in the works of the authors alluded to, the words of *Father, Son,* and *Spiritual Word:* the Father comprehending what was perfect in goodness; the Son altogether resembling the Father ; and the Word, by whom all things were created ; and these three hypostases made but one God.

---

[i] "In the epic poems the Vêda is but imperfectly known ; the ceremonial is no longer developing, it is complete. The Vêdic legends have been plucked from their native soil, and the religion of Agni, Indra, Mitra and Varuṇa has been replaced by an altogether different worship. There is a contradiction running through the religious life of India, from the time of the Râmâyaṇa to the present day. The outer form of the worship is Vêdic, and exclusively so ; but the eye of the religious adoration is turned on quite different regions. The secondary formation, the religion of Vishṇu and Brahmâ began with the epic poetry, and remained afterwards as the only living one, but without the power to break through the walls of the Vêdic ceremonial, and take the place of the old ritual."—*Prof.* Roth quoted by Müller.

These were not idle words, casually escaping from those philosophers. They were the foundation of the system of Plato, who could not venture to make them public amongst a people attached to polytheism, lest he should be treated with the same cruelty as befel the virtuous Socrates. But I strongly suspect that those venerable fathers of the church would not have chosen to resort to the authority of those philosophers, had they not found in their works expressions more decided, more consistent, and more spiritual, than what can be found in Hindû writings.

I might subjoin to what I have said respecting the change of the three principal elements into the divine nature, a similar transformation of the other two, the *air* and the *wind.* The latter, which the Hindûs have created their fifth element, appears to be the god Indra or Dêvêndra, the greatest of the subordinate deities, and king of the *Air*, in which he dwells. His name signifies *Air;* and it is in that region that the winds have the strongest power.

In the *Indra Purâṇa*, these words are found: "Indra is nothing "else than the Wind, and the Wind is nothing but Indra. The wind, "by condensing the clouds occasions the thunder; which has been "given to Dêvêndra as his weapon." He is frequently represented as having warred against the Giants, sometimes victorious and sometimes overcome. The clouds, which often resemble giants in their shape, sometimes arrest the progress of the wind; while the wind, more frequently, purges the air of the clouds.

It has happened to the poets of India, as well as those of other nations, in early times, that their fables and fictions were originally mere allegories, which were afterwards taken as real by a rude people. Succeeding poets preserved some part of the allegories of their predecessors; but they more frequently gave reins to the mad enthusiasm of a wild imagination, and fabricated new fables, often incongruous with the others, and still more remote from credibility. Thus in searching after the origin of the gods of the Pagans, recourse must be had to something behind the chaos of ill digested and absurd fables, which obscure the view.

CHAPTER II.

THE PRINCIPAL FESTIVALS OF THE HINDÛS, PARTICULARLY THAT OF THE PÔNGOL OR SANKRÂNTI.

BESIDES the Feasts peculiar to each district and temple, which return several times in the course of a year, and are celebrated by the inhabitants of the neighbourhood, the Hindûs have a great many more, which are held but once a year, and are commonly observed through the whole country. It would be a useless labour to enter into a particular detail of these numerous festivals, with the object and ceremonies of each. But we may remark that all of them are occasions of joy and diversion. On such days, the people quit their servile employments. Friends and relations unite in family parties, in their best apparel; decorate their houses as finely as they are able, and give entertainments more or less splendid, according to their means. Innocent pastimes are intermixed, and every other method of testifying their happiness.

They reckon eighteen principal Festivals in the course of the year; and no month passes without one or more of general observance. Some, however, are of so much more celebrity than the rest, as to demand particular notice.

In this number we must place the first day of their year, which falls on the new moon in March. At that period, the Hindûs make rejoicings for three days; exhibiting fire-works, letting off chambers or guns, and shewing their joy in every other way.[j]

The festival of *Gauri*, which is held in the beginning of September, and which last several days, is also to be commemorated, as one of the most solemn. The name of *Gauri* is one of the appellations of Pârvati, the wife of Siva, and it appears to be principally in honour of this goddess. It is likewise held to be in honour of the gods of the household, who are not the same in this instance as the *Penates* formerly mentioned.[k]

At this time, every artisan, every labourer, all the world, in short, offer sacrifices and supplications to the Tools and Implements which they use in the exercise of their various professions. The labourer brings his plough, hoe, and other instruments which he uses in his work. He piles them together and offers to them a sacrifice consisting of incense, flowers, fruits, rice, and other similar articles; after which he prostrates himself before them at all his length, and then returns them to their places.

---

j Special worship is paid to the Almanack on this day.

k GAURÎ— *a young damsel.*

The mason offers the same adoration and sacrifice to his trowel, his rule, and other instruments. The carpenter is no less pious with regard to his hatchet, his adze, and his plane. The barber, too, collects his razors in a heap, and adores them with similar rites.

The writing-master sacrifices to the iron pencil or style with which he writes; the tailor to his needles; the weaver to his loom; the butcher to his cleaver.

The women, on this day, heap together their baskets, the rice-mill, the wooden cylinder with which they bruise the rice, and the other household implements; and fall down before them, after having offered the sacrifices we have described. Every person, in short, in this solemnity, sanctifies and adores the instrument or tool which he principally uses in gaining his livelihood. The tools are now considered as so many deities; to whom they present their supplications, that they would continue propitious, and furnish them still with the means of living. So universal is the feeling among the Hindûs to deify and honour whatever can be useful or pernicious, whether animate or inanimate!

The festival of Gauri is concluded by erecting a shapeless statue in each village, composed of paste from grain. It is intended to represent the Goddess Gauri or Pârvati; and, being placed under a sort of canopy, it is carried about through the streets with great pomp, and receives the homage of the inhabitants, who flock to render it their adorations.

Another festival, of equal celebrity, is called by the Hindûs *Mahâ-Navami*, which is destined principally to the honour of deceased ancestors. It is celebrated in the month of October, during a period of three days; and is so religiously kept that it has become a proverbial saying, that those who have not the means of celebrating it should sell one of their children to procure them.

When the day of the festival arrives, all Hindûs, each for himself, make offerings of boiled rice and other food to their departed ancestors, that they may be well regaled on that day. They afterwards offer sacrifices of burning lamps, of fruits and flowers; and to these they add new articles of dress for men and women, that their ancestors of both sexes may be fresh clothed.

This festival, which lasts several days, is selected by the Princes and those who follow the profession of arms, to offer up sacrifices to the accoutrements used in the field, in order to obtain success in war. On the appointed day, all the arms, offensive and defensive, are collected together. A Brâhman Purôhita is called, who sprinkles them with his holy water, and pronounces mantras over them; by virtue of which the whole are deified. The ceremony, which is conducted with great solemnity, finishes, by sacrificing a Ram to the armour. It is called the ceremony of *Âyudha Pújâ*, or *Sacrifice to the Arms*, and is celebrated in all parts by the military with the utmost animation.

On the same day, the Princes give public shews, with a distribution of prizes. The spectacle consists chiefly in fights of wild beasts with each other, or with men; and also in combats of pugilists, some of whom come from a great distance to contend for the prize which it is customary to assign to the victor. This species of contest, which much resembles the shew of gladiators among the Romans and other ancient nations, is entirely committed to a particular caste of Hindûs, called Jeṭṭi. The members consist of youths selected from their infancy, and trained to this kind of sport: and their principal employment is to mangle each other with blows in the presence of those who chuse to pay for the enjoyment of so barbarous a spectacle; which is nevertheless one of the principal amusements of the Hindû Princes.

Before entering the lists, the pugilists, as if the blows with fists which they discharge upon each other were not sufficient to satisfy the barbarous appetite of the multitude, arm their fingers with a sort of iron cases or ferrules. Thus equipped, they commence by words of defiance and threatening gestures; and then setting on with signs of fury, they assail each other with terrible blows from their armed hands. Then, struggling, they throw each other down; and when they get upon their legs again, with their heads and bodies streaming with blood, they recover their breath, and engage in the combat anew, till one is declared the victor; unless indeed when the strength of both is equally exhausted, and the humane umpire of the sport separates them, to make room for another pair. The dismissed combatants retire, bathed in blood, and often with broken bones; and yield the arena to the new set, who repeat the horrid spectacle. When it is over, the Prince grants prizes and other rewards, both to the victors and the vanquished, in proportion to the savage ferocity with which they have belaboured each other.

When the shew is ended, the bruised combatants are attended by persons of their caste, who come provided with plasters for their wounds, or with skill to set their dislocated bones. In operations of this sort the *Jaṭṭis* have the reputation of being expert.

In the month of October—November, (Kârtika) another feast is celebrated, which is called *Dîpâli,* and which does not yield in solemnity to the preceding. It is instituted in memory of the two celebrated giants, one of whom bore the name of *Bala-chakravartti,* and the other that of *Narakrâsura.* The latter had become the scourge of the human race, and infested the earth with his crimes. Vishṇu at length delivered both gods and men from the terror of this monster, whom he slew after a dreadful combat. The contest ended but with the day.[l] Thus Vishṇu, not having it in his power to make his diurnal ablutions before the setting of the sun, was under the necessity of performing them, contrary to all rules, in the night. The Brâhmans, in commemoration of this great event, when that day returns, put off their ablutions to the night; and this is the only occasion, in the course of the year, in which they can transgress the ordinance of never bathing

[l] Vishṇu Purâṇ, 582.

after sunset. But this exception, of the nocturnal bathing, possesses the highest degree of merit; and it is therefore conducted with particular solemnity.

But the word *Dîpâli* signifies *a row of Lamps;* and I therefore suppose it must have been instituted in honour of fire; and, at this season, the Hindûs actually light a great number of lamps round the doors of their houses. They make paper lanterns, also, which they hang in the streets with a burning lamp in each; which in many places gives this festival the name of the *Feast of Lanterns.*

The husbandmen celebrate this festival of Dîpâli in a different way. Being then the harvest time for grain, they assemble with much pomp at the corn fields, and offer their supplications and sacrifices.

In many places they also offer sacrifice, on this day, to the *Dunghill,* which is afterwards to enrich the ground. In the villages, every one has his particular heap, to which he makes his own offering, consisting of burning lamps, fruits, flowers and other matters, which are deposited on the mass of ordure.

There is another festival, of great celebrity amongst the Lingamites called *Śiva-râtri,* or *Night of Śiva.* It is celebrated towards the end of February or beginning of March, when the votaries of that god purify their Lingas, and cover themselves with a new garment. After various sacrifices, they must pass the night in watchfulness, employing the time in reading some purâṇas relating to Śiva, or in visits to their Jangama, but without defiling themselves with any servile work.

The feast called *Nâga Panchami* is also one of the eighteen annual festivals, and one of the most solemn. It takes place in the month of December, and is instituted in honour of the *Serpents.*[m]

All these festivals are celebrated as family rites, and are not to be confounded with those that are carried on in the pagodas or temples, to which multitudes of people resort, and where all the rules of decency and modesty are violated without shame or remorse.

But, of all festivals, the most famous, at least in most countries, is that which is called *Pôngol,*[n] celebrated in the end of December or the winter solstice. It lasts three days; during which time the Hindûs employ themselves in mutual visits and compliments, something in the same manner as the Europeans do on the first day of the year.

This portion of Hindû Paganism is too remarkable to be passed over without a short description of the principle circumstances which attend it. The feast of the Pôngol is a season of rejoicing, for two special reasons. The first is, that the month of *Magha* or December, every day in which is unlucky, is about to expire; and the other, that it is to be succeeded by a month, each day of which is fortunate.

For the purpose of averting the evil effects of this baleful month

---

m Or Pythons, Krishna slew the serpent Kâli this month.

n Or "boiling."

of Magha, about four o'clock in the morning, a sort of Sannyâsis go from door to door of every house, beating on a plate of iron or copper, which produces a piercing sound. All who sleep, being thus roused, are counselled to take wise precautions, and to guard against the evil presages of the month, by expiatory offerings, and sacrifices to Śiva, who presides over it. With this view, every morning, the women scour a space of about two feet square before the door of the house, upon which they draw several white lines with flour. Upon these they place several little balls of cow-dung, sticking in each a citron blossom.

I have no doubt that the little balls are designed to represent the idol of Piḷḷaiyâr or Vighnêśwara, *the god of obstacles*, whom they desire to appease with the flower; but I know not why the blossoms of the citron are chosen above all others. Each day these little lumps of cow-dung, with their flowers, are picked up and preserved in a private place, till the last day of the month Magha; and when that comes, the women, who are alone charged with this ceremony, put the whole in a basket, and march from the house, with musical instruments before them, clapping their hands, till they reach the tank or other waste place where they dispose of the relics.

The first day of this festival is called *Bhôgi Pôngol*, or the *Pôngol of Rejoicing*,[o] and it is kept by inviting the near relations to an entertainment, which passes off with hilarity and mirth.

The second day is called *Sûrya Pôngol*, or *Pôngol of the Sun*,[p] and is set apart of the honour of that luminary. Married women after purifying themselves by bathing, which they perform by plunging into the water, without taking off their clothes, and coming out all dripping with wet, set about boiling rice in the open air, and not under any cover. They use milk in the operation; and when it begins to simmer, they make a loud cry, all at once, repeating the words, *Pôngol, O Pôngol!* The vessel is then lifted off the fire, and set before the idol of Vighnêśwara, which is placed close by. Part of the mess of rice is offered to the image; and, after standing there for some time, it is given to the cow; and the remainder of the rice is then distributed among the people.

This is the great day of Visits among the Hindûs. The salutation begins by the question, "Has the milk boiled?" to which the answer is "It has boiled." From this the festival takes its name of Pôngol; which is derived from the verb *Ponghêdi* in Telugu, and *Pongu* in Tamul, both of which signify "to boil."

The third day, not less solemn than the preceding, is consecrated with ceremonies still more absurd, and is called the *Pôngol of Cows.*

In a great vessel, filled with water, they put some saffron, the seeds of the tree *Paratti*[q] and leaves of the tree *Vêpu.*[r] After being well mixed, they go round all the cows and oxen belonging to the

---

[o] Or rather Indra's pôngol, he being Lord of Swarga.

[p] Or Perum pôngol, *great pôngol*

[q] Cotton.

[r] Margosa.

house, several times, sprinkling them with the water, as they turn to the four cardinal points. The Sâshṭângam, or prostration of the eight members, is made before them four times. Men only perform this ceremony, the women staying away.

The cows are then all dressed out, their horns being painted with various colours, and garlands of flowers and foliage put round their necks and over their backs. They likewise add strings of cocoa-nuts and other fruits, which are soon shaken off by the brisk motion of the animal which these trappings occasion, and are picked up by children and others, who follow the cattle on purpose, and greedily eat what they gather, as something sacred. They are then driven, in herd, through the villages, and made to scamper about from side to side by the jarring noise of many sounding instruments. The remainder of the day, they are allowed to feed at large without a keeper; and whatever trespasses they commit are suffered to pass without notice or restraint.

At last the festival concludes by taking the idols from the temples, and carrying them in pomp to the place where the cattle have been again collected. The girls of pleasure, or dancers, who are found at all ceremonies, are not wanting here. They march at the head of a great concourse of people; now and then making a pause to exhibit their wanton movements and charm the audience with their lascivious songs.

The whole terminates with a piece of diversion, which appears to be waggishness rather than any part of the ceremony. The numerous rabble who are present form themselves into a ring, and a live hare is let go in the midst of it. Poor puss, finding no outlet by which it can escape, flies to one side and the other, sometimes making a spring over the heads of the throng, which produces incredible mirth in the crowd, till the creature is at length worn out and caught. The idols are then reconducted to the temples, with the same pomp as when they were brought away. And thus closes the festival of the *Pôngol;* the most celebrated, undoubtedly, of all the rites which are performed during the course of the year.

Thus have we given an abridgement of the extravagant absurdities to which the Hindûs give themselves up, in the celebration of their festivals; and such is the excess of folly to which the human mind can surrender itself, in matters of religion, when it has no other light to guide its steps than its own, or when it takes the dreary road of superstition.

The grossness of the idolatry which universally prevails in India is such, that persons, educated in a way altogether dissimilar, find it difficult to comprehend how an intelligent people should be attached to so absurd a worship, and should never have attempted to emerge from the gloom of darkness into which they have been plunged: just as if it were possible to reason wisely on the subject of religion, and to form a rational system, when the human understanding has God no longer for its ruler, nor revelation for its guide.

Besides, humanly speaking, we feel less surprize in this respect, when, upon attentive examination, we clearly perceive that the laws and customs, both civil and religious, of this people, are so closely combined together, that any infringement of the one is sure to break down the other. Education, prejudice, and national bias have, in all times, led them to consider the two principal pillars of civilization, religion and civil rule, to be indissolubly connected.

The very extravagance, also, of the Hindû idolatry, the whole ritual of which is nothing less than the subversion of common sense, serves to give it a deeper root in the hearts of a people, sensual, enthusiastic, and fond of the marvellous. They cannot see, in all the world, a religion preferable to their own; and, infatuated with their idols, they shut their ears to the voice of nature, which cries so loudly against it.

But the Hindûs are still more irresistibly attached to the species of idolatry which they have embraced, by their pride, sensuality, and licentiousness. Whatever their religion sets before them tends to encourage these vices; and, consequently, all their senses, passions, and interests are leagued in its favour. It is made up of diversion and amusement. Dances, shews, and lewdness, accompany it, and form a part of the divine worship. Their festivals are nothing but sports; and, on no occasion of life, are modesty and decorum more carefully excluded than during the celebration of their religious mysteries. How can a people, ignorant of all enjoyment but that of sensual gratification, fail to be attached to a religion so indulgent to its peculiar passions?

Interest, also, that powerful engine, which puts in motion all human things, is a principal support of the edifice of Hindû idolatry. Those who are at the head of this extravagant worship, most of them quite conscious of its absurdity, are the most zealous in promoting its diffusion, because it affords them the means of living. Such impostors will suffer no opportunity to escape by which they may more deeply infatuate the people with the idolatry and superstition in which they have been bred. Well acquainted with the sway which their senses maintain over them, they take care to accompany the public rites and ceremonies with all the pomp and splendour which can impose upon their fancy.

These artifices are employed, above all, in some celebrated Pagodas. The persons who preside there, who live the year round, in voluptuous indolence, upon the abundant offerings brought to them on the anniversary of their festival, spare no pains to gratify the superstition which animates their votaries. Triumphal cars, superbly decorated in the Hindû fashion, on which the idols are placed in all their splendid finery, are exposed to public veneration. Songs, dancing, shews, fire-works, and an unceasing round of diversions; the sight of an immense assembly, where numbers of the wealthy contend with each other for the palm of luxurious extravagance and shew; and above all, the extreme licence which prevails through all classes, and the facility with which every individual can humour the bent of his desires: all these things are infinitely delightful to a people who have no relish for any pleasure but that of the senses. They fly to these festivals, therefore, from all quarters. Even the poor husbandman, to whom, with a numerous family, the scanty crop scarcely affords subsistence through the course of the year, forgetful of his future wants, sells a part of his stock for a contribution to this ridiculous worship, and for offerings to the impostors who thus entertain them at the expence of the public credulity.

The places where these festivals are held are famous all around, and are considered as holy and consecrated spots; in order to keep up the delusion and increase the confidence of the people. The Brâhmans, who have the charge of the temples, besides the pomp and splendour with which they dazzle the multitude, have recourse to another species of imposture, not less powerful, amongst a race credulous in the extreme, and lovers of the marvellous. They preserve a long list of miracles, which they pretend to have been wrought by the God of stone who resides in their temple, in behalf of those who have brought him rich offerings and trusted in him. Sometimes it is a barren woman whom he has blessed with fertility; sometimes one blind whom he has restored to sight; sometimes lepers who have been cured, or cripples who have recovered the use of their limbs. The silly Hindû swallows the bait, and never dreams of the designs of the impostors.

This digression has insensibly led me too far out of my course; my intention having been merely to shew, by the way, that the very extravagance of the ceremonies I have been describing, so far from rendering them ridiculous or contemptible, is the strongest aid to the progress of superstition and idolatry among the Hindûs.

If one adds to this the prodigious antiquity from which they draw their fabulous religion; the wonderful and astonishing incidents in the lives of their Gods, Giants, and early Kings; the enchantments, true or imaginary, effected by their philosophers; the austere seclusion of their ascetics; the rigid abstinence from animal food of all the nobler part of the nation; their daily and scrupulous purification; and, finally, their prayers and vain contemplation: all this may at least serve to excuse the excess of their superstition; and, at the same time, by shewing us the monstrous aberrations to which the human mind is subject in regard to religion, may lead those amongst ourselves, who are conscious of clearer views and sounder information on that important subject, to be thankful to the Father of Mercies; who, by the blessing of the shining light of revelation, has relieved us from the thick darkness of idolatry, in which, for some secret purpose known only to Himself, and which it is not lawful for us to scrutinize, He has permitted so many nations to grope; some of which, perhaps, might have turned to a better account than we have done, that inestimable blessing, which, being a free and unmerited gift, is the more to be prized.

CHAPTER III.

OF THE TEMPLES OF THE HINDÛS AND THE CEREMONIES THERE PRACTISED.

THERE is not, perhaps, in the whole world, a land in which the Buildings destined for religious uses are so numerous as in India; and there are few in which the popular credulity and superstition have better answered the purposes of the founders of the false religions which have been there established.

One hardly sees a village, however small, in which there is not a Pagoda, or building set apart to the worship of the divinities whom they adore. It has become proverbial amongst them, that a man should not live where there is no temple; and they are satisfied that, sooner or later, some mischief must befal those who disregard this maxim.

Of the good works recommended to the rich, one of the most honourable and most meritorious is to lay out a part of their fortune in erecting buildings for religious worship, and endowing them with a suitable revenue. Such works of merit never fail to draw down upon those who practise them the protection of the gods, the remission of sin, and a happy world after death.

Yet it happens that the greater number of those who ruin themselves by these works of merit, generally undertake them from motives of vanity and ostentation rather than of devotion. These are the predominant vices amongst the Hindûs; and in this case, above all others, the desire of renown and of obtaining the praises of men has, assuredly, more influence on their conduct than any expectation of meriting the protection of the gods, in honour of whom they incur those foolish expences.

Besides the Temples of Idols that are seen in all the villages, we meet with many in places insulated, and remote from all habitation; in woods, on the banks and in the middle of rivers, near great lakes and other places; but, above all, on mountains and even the steepest rocks.

This propensity for erecting temples and other religious houses, on mountains and other elevated situations, is observable throughout India, in such a degree, that scarcely a summit is to be seen that is not surmounted with some building of this nature.

This propensity I have thought worthy of remark; and I cannot attribute it solely to the desire of exhibiting their temples to greater advantage, or of rendering the glory of the founders more conspicuous in the eyes of posterity, but to other motives. Indeed, the conduct of the Hindûs, in this instance, is by no means peculiar. The Holy Scripture informs us that the same feeling existed, not only among the ancient idolatrous nations, but also extended to the chosen people of

God. The Israelites were accustomed to chuse a mountain, when they offered their supplications and sacrifices to the Lord. Solomon himself, before the building of the Temple of Jerusalem, religiously conformed to this practice, by selecting Mount Gibeon, the highest eminence in his neighbourhood, on which to sacrifice his burnt-offerings. And when the ten tribes separated themselves, in the reign of Jeroboam, they erected their sacrilegious altars on the mountain of Samaria.

When God prescribed to the Israelites the conduct they were to pursue, in taking possession of the land of Canaan; he commanded them, above all things, to demolish the temples of idols, which the nations who inhabited that country had erected on the mountains, and other "high places;" to break the images in pieces, and to destroy the "Groves" which they had planted, and under the cover of which they probably hid (as the Hindûs do at the present day) the objects of their idolatrous worship.

Besides the temples of the idols, there are to be seen in all parts of India, objects of the popular worship, represented by statues of stone or of baked earth, but most commonly sculptured in blocks of granite. Many of these are met with near the high roads; at the entrance into villages; on the banks of the lakes; but, above all, under bushy trees of that kind, chiefly, which are held sacred by the superstition of the country. Such are the *Aruli-maram, Âla-maram, Bevina-maram,* and other trees; and under the shadow of their branches the Hindûs delight to deposit the gods whom they adore. Of the infinite number of images of stone, that are scattered all over the country, some are placed under niches, but the greater number are exposed in the open air.

The most of the Hindû temples have a most miserable appearance, and resemble ovens rather than places designed for the residence of gods. Some of them likewise answer the purpose of a court of justice, a town hall, or a choultry for the reception of travellers, as well as a temple for religious worship. But there are some also, which, from a distant view, have a majestic appearance, and which, by the taste of their architecture, sometimes excite the admiration of the traveller, and recal those times of antiquity when artists laboured for posterity as well as for contemporary fame, by erecting solid and durable works, which outlast the flimsy, though more elegant erections of others.

The form of the larger temples, both ancient and modern, is always the same. The Hindûs are attached in all things to the ancient customs of their ancestors; and they have not departed from them in the style of their public edifices. For this reason, their architecture most probably exhibits a more faithful model of the manner of building used by the first civilized nations than that of the Egyptians or the Greeks can do.

The gate of entrance of their great pagodas is cut through a huge pyramid, which gradually becomes narrower, and almost always finishes at the top in a crescent. This pyramid fronts the east, towards which the gate of every temple small or great is turned.

In pagodas of the first order, beyond the pyramid, there is commonly a large court; at the end of which another gate appears, cut like the former, through a second pyramid, massy, but not so lofty as the first. This being passed through, there is another court; at the end of which the temple for the residence of the idol is built.

Opposite to the gate of the temple, and in the middle of the second court, there is placed, upon a large pedestal, or in a kind of niche, supported by four pillars, and open on all sides, a grotesque figure, representing a cow or bull, lying flat on its belly. Sometimes it represents the Lingam, sometimes the god Vighnêśwara, Hanumân, the serpent Capella, or some other of the principal objects of their idolatry. The divinity, situated in this niche, is the first object to which the votaries present their homage. They adore it by making the Sâshṭângam before it; at the same time, touching the pavement with both corners of their forehead. Some, less ardent, instead of the Sâshṭângam, content themselves with the Namaskâram, by joining their hands together, and raising them to their forehead, thumping their cheeks with the right hand. After this homage to the exterior object of worship, they are allowed to enter into the interior of the temple.

The door is generally narrow and low, although it be the only aperture through which air and the light of day can enter, the use of windows being wholly unknown to the Hindûs. The building is divided into two, and sometimes into three parts; all on a level. One of these divisions is very large, to accommodate all persons of good caste who chuse to enter. This may be called the Nave; and the smaller one, which we may call the Sanctuary, is separated from the other, communicating only by a door, which can be opened by nobody but him who holds the office of sacrificer and chief functionary of the temple. He only, and a few of his attendants by his leave, can enter into this sacred place to dress the idol, to wash it, to offer it flowers, incense, lighted lamps, fruits, betel, butter, milk, rich apparel, ornaments of gold and silver, and a thousand other articles of which their sacrifice and offering consist.

The nave of the temple is sometimes arched with brick, but generally with a ceiling constructed of large and massy blocks, supported by pillars of hewn stone rising from the floor, the capitals of which are composed of two other solid stones, which cross each other and support rafters of the same material, which also extend crosswise through the whole length and breadth of the ceiling. Upon these rafters are placed other hewn stones, flatter and broader, with which the temple is roofed. The chinks are stopped with good cement to keep out the water.

The scarcity of timber in India may probably account for its being never used in the construction of their temples. Perhaps also the ambition of having solid and durable edifices has determined them to use only brick and stone. But, it is certain that wood is no where employed in a Hindû temple but for the doors.

The sanctuary or receptacle of the idols is generally constructed with a dome. The whole building is low, no doubt from the difficulty of finding stones adapted to the length of column necessary for the support of the roof. The proper proportion of height is therefore deficient in the Hindû temples; which, being added to the want of circulation of air, by the narrowness of the doors, often occasions unpleasant consequences to those who frequent them.

If we combine with these horrors, the infectious effluvia arising from the smell of decayed flowers, burning lamps, libations of oil and melted butter, added to the rank perspiration of a multitude squeezed together in such a place, we may form some idea of the stench which exhales from the shrines of the deities of India.

The horrid filth, too, in which these divinities are kept, cannot fail to be disgusting to unpractised eyes. It would be difficult to imagine any thing more hideous than their appearance. They are generally represented in frightful or ridiculous attitudes; but no distinguishing feature can be perceived, on account of the dark hue they contract by being perpetually daubed with oil and melted butter, mixed with other ingredients. They have the same custom of blackening the triumphal cars, which are every where seen transporting the idols through the streets, in their processions; but this dingy and filthy appearance is admired, as proceeding from the frequent oblations of butter and oil, to which they give the name of NIVÊDYAM or consecration. Without this, objects of worship could not be consecrated; for no statue or image can be exhibited to public adoration until the Purôhita Brâhman has invoked into it the Divinity, by virtue of his mantras, and has consecrated it by drenching it with oil and liquid butter.

Something analogous to this practice may be observed in the Holy Scripture. Thus Jacob, after his dream, "rose up early in the "morning, and took the stone that he had put for his pillows, and set "it up for a pillar, and poured oil upon the top of it." (Gen. xxviii. 18.) And afterwards, in alluding to it, the angel says to him: "I am "the God of Bethel, where thou anointedst the pillar, and where "thou vowedst a vow unto me." (Gen. xxxi. 13.) Libations of oil were employed in the same manner, by many ancient nations, in the consecration of living and inanimate objects.

But to return to the Hindû temples. Besides the idols in the interior or sanctuary, other objects of worship are set up in different parts, sculptured on the pillars which support the building; and on the walls.

In the outer court, the niches, in which the images of men or animals are set, have the front filled with figures bearing allusion to their fables, or in some cases with the most monstrous obscenities. The principal walls without, which are of strength proportioned to the rest of the building, are likewise covered with them, in some instances, all round.

Some of these idols, and in particular the principal one which resides in the sanctuary, are clothed with valuable garments, and adorned with jewels of great price. A golden or silver crown is never wanting, or rays of glory of the same metal, for their heads. In the great temples these ornaments are enriched with precious stones, encreasing their value to many thousand pagoda coins. But all this finery, lavished on such hideous forms, tends only to make them more horrid; and, what still increases their deformity, is the eyes, mouth, nose and ears of gold and silver, which are frequently stuck upon their sooty heads.

On the outside of the temple, opposite to the door of entrance and at a small distance, there is commonly a pillar of granite erected, of an octagonal shape, cut from a single block, sometimes forty or fifty feet in height. It is inserted in a huge pedestal, formed of one or more pieces of freestone. Its base is square, and has several figures sculptured on it. The capital of the column terminates in a square, from the corners of which small bells are commonly hung. On the middle of this square, at the summit of the column, there is a sort of grate on which incense is sometimes burned; but they, more commonly, have lighted lamps.

High columns of this kind are frequently met with on the highways; and where they stand, in desert places, the devotees in the neighbourhood keep the lamps occasionally burning on the tops.

I am led to believe that these lofty pillars, which are always placed towards the east, are erected in honour of fire, or rather of the sun, the brightest emblem of that element. In the festival of Dîpâli formerly described, which appears to be instituted in honour of the fire, many lamps are lighted on the tops of the pillars, as long as the festival continues. Sometimes they are wholly in a blaze, by wrapping many pieces of new cloth round the column, and setting them on fire.

There are some celebrated temples, whose income is sufficient to maintain several thousand persons, employed in the various functions of idolatrous worship. These are of various castes, though the greater number are Brâhmans.

Of these various ministers of the temples, the sacrificers occupy the first rank. They may be either Brâhmans, or of any other caste; for, in some temples, under certain circumstances, even Pariahs assume the office of sacrificers. This I know to be the case in a celebrated temple in the Mysore, called *Mêlcôtta*, at a solemn festival celebrated there every year.[8] The Pariahs, on that occasion, are the first to

[8] For a full account of this place see Buchanan, Vol. ii. p. 69, &c.

enter into the sanctuary of the temple, with offerings to the idol; and the Brâhmans do not begin till they have ended.

The oblations or sacrifices offered in most of the Hindû temples consist of the simple productions of nature, such as boiled rice, flowers, fruits, and the like, but above all of lamps, of which many thousands are sometimes seen burning in the temple. They feed them with butter, in preference to oil.

The Hindû priests regularly offer up sacrifice twice every day, evening and morning. They always begin the ceremony by washing the idol that is the object of it. The water used is brought from the river or tank, with processional pomp and state. In some great pagodas, it is brought on the backs of elephants, escorted by many of the Brâhmans and other ministers of the temple, preceded by the musicians and dancers belonging to it.

In smaller temples, the Brâhmans themselves bring it morning and evening, on their heads, in copper pitchers, attended by the music, the dancing girls and other assistants. The water, so set apart for washing the idols, is called *Tîrtham*, or holy water.

When the sacrificer has washed the images, he offers up the sacrifice; the material of which is generally brought by the votaries.

Two things are indispensably necessary to the sacrificer in performing the ceremony: several lighted lamps, and a bell, which he holds in his left hand during the whole time, while, with his right hand, he offers his oblation to the gods, and adorns them with flowers; imprinting on their foreheads, and various parts of their bodies, some of the marks which the Hindus are accustomed to apply to themselves, with sandal wood and cow-dung ashes. The followers of Vishṇu in this case, impress on their idols the figure of the *Nâma*. All the sacrifices are accompanied with mantras suited to the circumstances, and with innumerable bows and gesticulations, the most of which would appear exceedingly ridiculous to an European.

During the actual performance of the sacrifice, the priest is quite alone in the sanctuary, the door of which he closes. The unholy multitude remain in the nave, silently waiting till he has done. What he does they cannot know, only hearing the sound of his bell. The whole ceremony is performed with the utmost rapidity, and with no signs of reverence or awe.

When it is over, he comes out, and distributes part of the articles which had been offered to the idols. This is received as something holy, and is eaten immediately, if it be fruit, rice, or any article of food. If flowers, they stick them in their turbans; and the girls entwine them in their hair. Last of all, the priest takes some of the Tîrtham or holy water in the hollow of his hand, which is drank by those who can reach it; after which the assembly breaks up.

Next to the sacrificers, the most important persons about the temples are the dancing girls, who call themselves *Dêva-dâsi*, *ser-*

vants or slaves of the gods. Their profession, requires of them to be open to the embraces of persons of all castes.

Every temple, according to its size, entertains a band of these, to the number of eight, twelve, or more. The service they perform consists of dancing and singing. The first they execute with grace, though with lascivious attitudes and motions. Their chanting is generally confined to the obscene songs which relate to some circumstance or other of the licentious lives of their gods.

They perform their religious duties at the temple to which they belong twice a-day, morning and evening. They are also obliged to assist at all the public ceremonies, which they enliven with their dance and merry song. As soon as their public business is over, they open their cells of infamy, and frequently convert the temple itself into a stew.

They are bred to this profligate life from their infancy. They are taken from any caste, and are frequently of respectable birth. It is nothing uncommon to hear of pregnant women, in the belief that it will tend to their happy delivery, making a vow, with the consent of their husbands, to devote the child then in the womb, if it should turn out a girl, to the service of the Pagoda. And, in doing so, they imagine they are performing a meritorious duty. The infamous life to which the daughter is destined brings no disgrace on the family.

These prostitutes are the only females in India who may learn to read, to sing, and to dance. Such accomplishments belong to them exclusively, and are, for that reason, held by the rest of the sex in such abhorrence, that every virtuous woman would consider the mention of them as an affront.

These performers are supported out of the revenues of the temple, of which they receive a considerable share. But their dissolute profession is still more productive. In order to stimulate more briskly the passion which their lewd employment is intended to gratify, they have recourse to the same artifices as are used by persons of their sex and calling in other countries. Perfumes, elegant and attractive attire, particularly of the head, sweet-scented flowers intertwined with exquisite art about their beautiful hair, multitudes of ornamental trinkets adapted with infinite taste to the different parts of the body, a graceful carriage and measured step, indicating luxurious delight; such are the allurements and the charms which these enchanting syrens display to accomplish their seductive designs.

From infancy they are instructed in the various modes of kindling the fire of voluptuousness in the coldest hearts; and they well know how to vary their arts and adapt them to the particular disposition of those whom they wish to seduce.

At the same time, notwithstanding their alluring demeanor, they cannot be accused of those gross indecencies which are often publicly exhibited by women of their stamp in Europe; particularly the exposure of the person and the lascivious airs which one would think capable of inspiring the most determined libertine with disgust: on the contrary, of all the women in India, the common girls, and particularly the dancers at the temples, are the most decently clothed. They are so nice in covering every part of the body, as to have the appearance of being affectedly precise, or as if they intended, by the contrast with the more open attire of other dames, to excite more strongly the passion which they wished to inspire, by carefully veiling a part of the charms which it covets.

Neither can they be reproached with that impudent assurance exhibited in public by the Messalinas of Europe. Shameless as the dancing girls of India appear to be, they will not venture, upon any occasion, to stop a man in the streets, or to take any indecent liberty in public. And, on the other hand, a man who would take such liberties, even with a prostitute, so far from being applauded, or joked with, by the spectators, as happens in some other countries, would be obliged to hide his head for shame, and would be treated with marks of indignation.

Relaxed as the manners of the Hindûs are, they know how to observe, in public, that decorum which every class of people owes to another, in the intercourse of life; and which are never violated, with impunity, but in nations arrived at the last degree of corruption.

After the Dancing Women, the next order of persons employed in the service of the temples is that of the Players on Musical Instruments. Every Pagoda, of any note, has a band of Musicians; who, as well as the dancers, are obliged to attend at the temple twice every day, to make it ring with their discordant sounds and inharmonious airs. They are also obliged to assist at all public ceremonies and festivals, to enliven them with their music; and they, likewise, are paid from the revenue of the temple.

Their band generally consists of wind instruments, resembling clarionets and hautboys; to which they add cymbals and several kinds of drums. They produce, out of these instruments, a confusion of sharp and piercing sounds, little suited to please an European ear. They are acquainted, however, with music in two parts. Intermixed with the instruments, they have always a bass and a high counter; the first of which is produced by blowing into a kind of tube, widened below, and yielding an uninterrupted and uniform stream of sound resembling the braying of a wide horn.

Part of the musicians execute the vocal part, and sing hymns in honour of the gods. The Brâhmans, and other devotees, sometimes join in the chorus, and sometimes sing, separately, airs or other sacred pieces of their own composition.

The Dancing Women, the Singers, and the Instrumental Performers relieve one another, by taking up their several parts, in rotation, to the close of the ceremony; which is often terminated by a procession around the temple; whilst, night and morning, the jovial girls fail not to perform the Arati over the idols of the temple, for the purpose of averting the fatal influence of the looks and glances of envious or evil-minded persons; the gods themselves not being exempt from that species of incantation.

In the band of musicians belonging to each temple, the most conspicuous performer of all is the Sâṭṭuva, who beats time. He does it by tapping with his fingers on each side of a sort of drum tightly braced. As he beats, his head, shoulders, arms, and every muscle of his frame, are in motion. He rouses the musicians with his voice, and animates them with his gestures; and, at times, he appears agitated with violent convulsions.

To a European ear, as we have already remarked, the vocal and instrumental music of the Hindûs would appear equally contemptible. Yet they have a Gamut like ours, composed of seven notes; and they are taught music methodically. They are likewise expert in keeping time, and they have also our variety of keys.

In their Vocal Music, a monotonous dulness prevails; and, in the Instrumental, they produce nothing but harsh, sharp, and piercing sounds, which would shock the least delicate ear.

But, although the Hindû music, when compared with the European, does not deserve the name, I conceive that we have degraded it beneath its humble deserts. European ears and musicians are by no means impartial judges. To appreciate their music rightly, we ought to go back two or three thousand years, and place ourselves in those remote ages when the Druids and other leaders of the popular belief in the greater part of Europe, used, in their rites, nothing but dismal and horrid shrieks, and had no instrumental music but what was produced by clashing one plate of metal against another, by beating on a stretched skin, or raising a dull and droning sound from a horn or a rude instrument of twisted bark.

We ought to recollect that the Hindûs have never had the thought of bringing any thing to perfection; and that, in science, arts, and manufactures, they have remained stationary at the point where they were two or three thousand years ago. Their musicians, in those remote ages, were as skilful as those of the present time. But if we compare the Hindû music, as we now hear it, with that of Europe, as it was two or three thousand years ago, I have no doubt that the former would take high precedence over all others in a similar stage of society.

The gamut of the Hindûs is exactly the same as ours, being composed of the same number of notes, and arranged in the same way. It is expressed by the signs or syllables following:

Sa, Ri, Ga, Ma, Pa, Da, Ni, Sa; or
ut, re, mi, fa, sol, la, si, ut.
and also *Sa, Ni, Da, Pa, Ma, Ga, Ri, Sa*; or
ut, si, la, sol, fa, mi, re, ut.

The musicians of India have no more than three and thirty tunes; each of which has its particular name. Yet, though their whole musical knowledge is limited to these thirty-three airs, there are few that know them all; and the greater number are not capable of playing one-half of them.

All the musicians belonging to the temples are taken from the caste of *Barbers*, one of the lowest among the Sûdras. The department of wind-instruments belongs, almost exclusively, to this caste, or to others of a rank equally low; and, so degraded has the employment become in the eyes of the Hindû people, that no individual of a respectable caste would condescend to put a wind-instrument to his mouth. But the Brâhmans themselves disdain not to practise upon *stringed* instruments: a preference which will be afterwards accounted for.

The expence of the idolatrous worship of the Hindûs being very considerable, the several Pagodas have, necessarily, resources for defraying it. In several districts they draw a sort of tithe out of the produce of the harvest. In other parts, they have the absolute property of extensive lands, exempted from all taxation; the produce of which is exclusively assigned to those who perform the rites of the temple. Besides, the humblest Pagoda is not without great numbers of votaries and devotees; who bring in considerable offerings, in money, trinkets, cattle, provisions, and other articles; all which are divided amongst the functionaries of the temple, according to their dignity and rank.

Sometimes the revenues of a temple, arising from such offerings, have been large enough to tempt the cupidity of some of the Princes, particularly of the Mahommedan race. These considerate rulers have sometimes found it convenient to lay hold of more than one-half of the income proceeding from the offerings made to the temple by the devotees; which they represented to be but a fair indemnification for their trouble in protecting the religion of the country.

In the several Pagodas, the Brâhmans, who are the principal ministers, omit no sort of imposture to keep up the popular credulity, and to allure votaries to the worship of that deity by which they live. For this purpose, they resort to various means; amongst which may be enumerated the Oracles, which they ascribe to their deities, and the Miracles which they perform. The oracles are managed by some expert Brâhmans, who understand this sort of roguery, and contrive to introduce some person within the images, which are generally hollow, or conceal themselves hard by so as not to be observed, and, from that concealment, harangue the multitude; all of whom firmly believe that it is the image itself that speaks, and therefore listen to the oracular admonition with awful silence. The impostors who carry on this deception, sometimes take upon themselves to predict future events, but in so obscure and ambiguous a way, that, however the issue may turn out, they may always have it in their power to make it accord with their predictions.

But the most successful artifice is generally in causing complaints to be made to the idol, that the number of his votaries and the value of their offerings are decreasing. They represent him as saying, in reply, that if the zeal of the people does not wax warmer, and the offerings increase, instead of falling off, he will quit the temple, abandon a people so ungrateful for his protection, and retire into some other country where he will be better received.

At other times the priests put the idols in irons, chaining their hands and feet. They exhibit them to the people in this humiliating state, into which they tell them they have been brought by rigorous creditors, from whom their gods had been obliged, in times of trouble, to borrow money to supply their wants. They declare that the inexorable creditors refuse to set the god at liberty until the whole sum, with interest, shall have been paid. The people come forward, alarmed at the sight of their divinity in irons; and, thinking it the most meritorious of all good works to contribute to his deliverance, they raise the sum required by the Brâhmans for that purpose; and this being settled, the chains are soon dissolved and the idol restored to liberty.

In some famous temples, such as that of *Tirupati,* they make use of silver chains, instead of iron, when it is necessary to put the idol under restraint.

Another sort of imposture is often practised by the Brâhmans in many parts; which consists in announcing to the people, and making them believe, that the idol is afflicted with a dreadful malady, brought on by the vexation of perceiving the devotion of the people and their former confidence abating from day to day. In such cases, the idol is sometimes taken down from the pedestal, and placed at the door of the pagoda, where they rub his forehead and temples with various drugs. They set before him all sorts of potions and medicines, shewing the most earnest endeavours to cure him by these ordinary means: but all the resources of art proving useless, while the disorder continues to increase, the Brâhmans send out their emissaries to all parts to spread the afflicting news. An ignorant and stupid people implicitly believes in the ridiculous imposture, and hastens with gifts and offerings. The deity beholding such proofs of reviving piety and confidence, feels himself instantly relieved from his melancholy, and resumes his station.

The Brâhmans who direct the public worship, frequently resort to another species of trick, equally gross as the former, for the purpose of inspiring a salutary fear of the idol, and of attracting ample donations to his temple. This is effected by representing their god as enraged against certain individuals who have offended him, into whose bodies he has sent a *Pisâcha* or demon, to avenge his insulted honour upon them by every species of torment.

Persons accordingly appear, wandering about in all parts of the country, exhibiting, by dreadful convulsions and contortions, every symptom of being possessed by the evil spirit. Well instructed in their art they tell a marvellous story, wherever they go, of some god or other, to whom they are obnoxious, having sent a fiend to dwell within them and to torment them. To prove that it is really a wicked demon that haunts them, they babble in various languages, of which they have had a previous smattering, but which now appears to be the immediate inspiration of the demon who resides within them. They publicly devour all sorts of meat, drink inebriating liquors, and openly violate the most sacred rules of their caste. All these transgressions are laid to the charge of the devil that possesses them; and no blame attaches to the unwilling instrument. The people, before whom these impostures are exhibited, unsuspicious of the fraud, are filled with dismay; and prostrate themselves before the evil spirit, with sacrifice and oblations, to render him innoxious. Whatever he asks they bring. They give him to eat and to drink abundantly; and, when he leaves them, they accompany him with pomp and with the sound of instruments, till he arrives at some other place, where he plays the same game, and finds as silly dupes. In the lucid moments, which he can easily command, he exhorts the crowds of spectators to profit by the awful example before them, to have more regular confidence in that god by whom he himself has been so grievously punished, to conciliate his friendship by offerings and gifts, that they may not be subject to the same severe punishments which have befallen him for his defects in piety and faith.

Another contrivance of the Brâhmans, employed with no less success, consists in the public testimony they give to a vast number of pretended Miracles wrought by the god of their temple, in favour of numerous votaries, who have shewn their faith, in him, and brought him abundant offerings. These miracles comprehend the cure of all sorts of disease; of the blind who have regained their sight; the lame who have recovered their limbs; and the dead who have been raised.

But the miracle which takes precedence of all others, and is always listened to with the highest delight and admiration, is the fecundity conferred on numbers of women, who remained in a barren state, till their prayers and their offerings obtained from their divinity the gift of children. We have seen that sterility in India is accounted a curse, and that a childless woman is always despised.

The Hindûs consider a man to be rich only in proportion to the number of his children. However numerous a man's family may be, he ceases not to offer prayers for its increase. A fruitful wife is the highest blessing, in the eyes of a Hindû; and no misery can be compared with that of a barren bed.

The children become useful at an early age. At five or six years old they tend the smaller animals. Those that are stouter, or a little more advanced, take care of the cows and oxen; whilst the adult assist their fathers in agricultural labour, or in any other way in which they can afford comfort to the authors of their being.

Superstition has a powerful influence in keeping up this vehement desire of having children, which prevails among the Hindûs; for, according to their maxims, the greatest misery that can betide any man is to be destitute of a son, or a grandson, to take charge of his obsequies. In such a state he cannot look for a happy world hereafter.

In pursuance of this system, we see their barren women continually running from temple to temple, ruining themselves frequently by the extravagance of their donations to obtain from the ruling divinities the object of their ardent desires. The Brâhmans have turned the popular credulity on this point to good account; and there is no considerable temple, whose residing deity does not, amongst many other miracles, excel in that of curing barrenness in women.

There are some temples, however, of greater celebrity than others in this way, to which women in that state resort in preference. Such is that famous one of *Tirupati* in the Carnatic. Sterile women frequent it, in crowds, to obtain children from the God *Vencaṭa Râma* who presides there. On their arrival, they apply, first of all, to the Brâhmans, to whom they disclose the nature of their pilgrimage and the object of their vows. The Brâhmans prescribe to the credulous women to pass the night in the temple, in expectation that, by their faith and piety, the resident god may visit them and render them prolific. In the silence and darkness of the night, the Brâhmans, as the vicegerents of the god, visit the women, and in proper time disappear. In the morning, after due inquiries, they congratulate them on the benignant reception they have met with from the god; and, upon receiving the gifts which they have brought, take leave of them, with many assurances that the object of their vows will speedily be accomplished.

The women, having no suspicion of the roguery of the Brâhmans, go home in the full persuasion that they have had intercourse with the divinity of the temple, and that the god who has deigned to visit them must have removed all impediments to their breeding.

There are many other excesses, still more extravagant, to which the credulity and superstitious bias of the Hindûs have led them, in this particular. Among many examples of this kind which I could mention, I shall take notice of one only; which some of my readers will find as much difficulty in believing as I do in relating it: so repugnant it is to all decency and modesty; though I know it to be true.

At about ten leagues to the southward of Seringapatam, there is a village called *Nanjanagud*, where there is a temple, famous over all the Mysore. Amongst the numbers of votaries, of every caste, who resort to it, a great proportion consists of barren women, who bring offerings to the god of the place, and pray for the gift of fruitfulness in return. But the object is not to be accomplished by the offerings and prayers alone, the disgusting part of the ceremony being still to follow. On retiring from the temple, the woman and her husband repair to the common sewer, to which all the pilgrims resort in obedience to the calls of nature. There, the husband and wife collect, with their hands, a quantity of the ordure; which they set apart, with a mark upon it, that it may not be touched by any one else; and with their fingers in this condition, they take of the water of the sewer in the hollow of their hands, and drink it. Then they perform ablution, and retire.

In two or three days, they return to the place of filth, to visit the mass of ordure which they left. They turn it over with their hands, break it, and examine it in every possible way; and, if they find that any insects or vermin are engendered in it, they consider it a favourable prognostic for the woman. But, if no symptoms of animation are observed in the mass, they depart, disappointed and sorrowful, being convinced that the cause of barrenness has not been removed.

But these abominable practices, detestable as they appear, are not the worst that the inordinate desire of having posterity gives rise to in India. There are some, so enormously wicked, that every thing recorded in history of the debauchery and obscenities that were practised among the Greeks in the temple of Venus, by the courtesans consecrated to that goddess, sinks to nothing in the comparison.

There are temples, in some solitary places, where the divinity requires to be honoured with the most unbounded licentiousness. He promises children to the barren women who will lay aside the most inviolable rules of decency and shame, and, in honour of him, submit to indiscriminate embraces.

An annual festival is held, in the month of January, at those infamous sinks of debauchery; where, I need not say, great numbers of the libertines of both sexes assemble, from all quarters. Besides barren wives, who come in quest of issue, by exposing their persons, some of them having bound themselves by a vow to grant their favours to numbers, many other dissolute women also attend, to do honour to the infamous deity, by prostituting themselves, openly and without shame, before the gates of his temple.

There is an abominable rendezvous of debauchery of this sort at the distance of four or five leagues from the place where I am now writing these pages. It is on the banks of the Kâveri, in a desert place called *Junjinagati*. There is a mean-looking Pagoda there, in which one of those detestable idols resides who require to be honoured by the grossest abominations. The January festival is regularly celebrated there by great crowds of both sexes, with all their ceremonies and vows.

In the district of Coimbatore, near a village called *Kara-madai*, I have seen a temple of this description; and it was pointed out to me that such places of debauchery were always situated in desert places, far removed from all habitations.[t]

I shall, next, take notice of another sort of Vows, very common amongst the Hindûs; which are absolved by suffering mutilation in various ways, or by enduring bodily torments. They are generally undertaken on occasions of disease, or any other danger, from which they suppose they can be delivered by their efficacy. One of the most common consists in stamping, upon the shoulders, chest, and other parts of the body, with a red-hot iron, certain marks, to represent the armour of their gods; the impressions of which are never effaced, but

---

[t] The celebrated Mahârâja—trial in Bombay throws light upon the statements in the text.

are accounted sacred, and are ostentatiously displayed as marks of distinction.

A practice very common among the devotees consists in laying themselves at their whole length on the ground, and rolling in that posture all round the temples, or before the cars on which the idols are placed in solemn processions. On such occasions, it is curious to see the numbers of enthusiasts who roll in that manner before the car, over the roads and streets, during the whole of the procession, regardless of the stones, thorns, and other impediments which they encounter in their progress, and by which they are mangled all over. It is in this class of enthusiasts that some individuals are found so completely inspired by the demon of a barbarous fanaticism, or seduced by the first incitements of a delirious glow, that they roll themselves under the car on which the idols are drawn, and are voluntarily crushed under the wheels. The surrounding crowd of enthusiasts, so far from trying to prevent this act of devotion, loudly applaud the zeal of the victims, and exalt them amongst the Gods.

One of the severest tests to which the devotees of India are accustomed to expose themselves, is that which they call in many places *Chidi Mari*. The name arises from this species of self-infliction being generally practised in honour of the goddess *Mari-ammâ* (or *Marima*) one of the most wicked and sanguinary of all that are adored in India. At many temples, consecrated to this cruel divinity, a sort of gibbet is erected, with a pulley at the arm, through which a line passes with a sharp hook at the end. Those who have vowed to undergo the rough trial of Chidi Mari, place themselves under the gibbet, from which the rope and iron hook are let down. Then, after benumbing the flesh of the middle of the back of the votary by rubbing it very roughly, they fix the hook into it; and, giving play to the other end of the string, they hoist up to the top of the gibbet, the wretch, thus suspended by the muscles of the back. After swinging in the air for two or three minutes, he is let down again; and the hook being unfixed, he is dressed with proper medicines for his wound, and is dismissed in triumph.[u]

Another well known proof of devotion, to which many oblige themselves, by vow, in cases of illness or other troubles, consists in walking or rather running over burning coals. When this is to be performed, they begin by kindling a blazing fire, and when the flames expire and all the fuel is reduced to cinders, the votaries commence their race, from the midst of a puddle of earth and water, which has been previously prepared for the purpose; running quickly, over the glowing embers, till they reach another puddle of the same kind on the other side of the fire. But notwithstanding this precaution, those who have a tender skin cannot fail to be grievously burnt.

Others, who are unfit for the race, in place of going through the fire, take a cloth well moistened with water which they put over their

---

[u] This is the famous Charak Pûjâ, now interdicted by the British Government.

head and shoulders, and lift up a chafing-dish filled with live embers, which they discharge over their heads. This is called the Fire Bath.

Another species of torture submitted to, in the fulfilment of vows, is to pierce the cheeks, through and through, with a wire of silver or other metal, fixed in such a manner that the mouth cannot be opened without extreme pain. This operation is called locking the mouth, and is often protracted through the whole day. While under this discipline, the votary repairs to the temple which he has come to visit, and pays homage to the god; or walks about, with ostentation, amongst the admiring throng. There are several temples frequented by this species of votaries, in preference to the Pagoda of Nanjanagud before mentioned; and numbers of devotees of both sexes are there seen, with their jaws thus perforated through the teeth, and their mouths completely locked.

I once met a fanatic of this sort, in the streets, who had both lips pierced through and through with two long nails, which crossed each other, so that the point of the one reached to the right eye and that of the other to the left. He had just undergone this cruel operation at the gate of a temple consecrated to the goddess Mari-ammâ; and, when I saw him, the blood was still trickling from the wounds. He walked in that state for a long time in the streets, surrounded by a crowd of admirers, many of whom brought him alms, in money or goods, which were received by the persons who attended him.

There are a great many other sorts of tortures and bodily pains thus voluntarily inflicted by the Hindûs, with the view of rendering their gods propitious. Each devotee chuses the sort which is suggested by an imagination heated with barbarous fanaticism; and, still more frequently, by the desire of acquiring a name, and becoming conspicuous amongst the people.

Some make a vow to cut out their tongues, and acquit themselves of their vow by coolly executing it with their own hands. The custom is, when they have separated the half or any other portion of that organ, at the door of the temple, to put it on a cocoa shell, and offer it, on their knees, at the shrine of the deity.[v]

---

[v] The following extract from a Madras Newspaper, dated Oct. 30, 1861, will illustrate the Abbé's statements.

CORONER'S INQUEST.—The inquest on the body of Soobroy Chetty, who died under the extraordinary circumstances reported in a late issue, has been brought to a close, the jury finding a verdict of "deceased died from a wound in the tongue inflicted by himself in the performance of a vow." Three witnesses were examined at the adjourned hearing. The first was a Policeman who deposed that he saw the deceased lying at the door of the temple after a portion of his tongue was cut off, and offered to take him to the hospital, for which purpose he brought a cart to the place, but the friends of the man interfered and took charge of him.—Anantha Charry, the pagoda conicopillay, swore that he knew that the deceased cut his tongue in the same way three years ago. It was quite a common practice and many had followed it and recovered from sickness. When people were ill, they came to the pagoda and cut off their tongues and when they recovered they fed brâhmans. Witness had been in the pagoda 15 years, and since that time seven or eight men had performed the vow and recovered. There was nothing to prevent food being given them if they liked; the priests did not interfere. It was always the man who made the vow who performed the operation. Witness had never heard any authority for believ-

This disposition of the Hindûs to bind themselves by vows to painful or costly works, in honour of their gods, is visible in all unpleasant circumstances that befal them; but particularly in disease. There is hardly a Hindû who, in that case, does not take a vow to perform something or other when he recovers. The rich make vows to celebrate festivals at certain temples. Those less opulent offer, at the Pagoda, a cow, a buffalo, pieces of cloth, or trinkets of gold and silver. Those who are affected with any disorder of the eyes, mouth, ears, or any other outward organ, vow to their idols a corresponding resemblance of it in silver or gold.

Amongst the innumerable sorts of vows practised by either sex, the following, which is very common in all parts of the peninsula, appears to me so curious as to deserve notice. It consists in the offering of their hair and their nails to the idol.

It is well known that the men in India have the custom of frequently shaving the head, and allowing only a single tuft to grow on the crown. Those who have taken the vow suffer their hair and nails to grow for a long space of time; and, when the day of fulfilment arrives, they go to the Pagoda, have their head shaved and their nails pared, which they offer up to the divinity whom they worship. This practice is nearly peculiar to men, and is held to be one of the most acceptable of all others to the gods.

Before concluding our remarks on the vows of the Hindûs, it may be proper to observe, that all such as relate to painful operations of the nature above described, with many others that are attended with bodily suffering, are always declined by the Brâhmans, who lead the merit of them to the Ŝûdras; and those of the latter class who practice them are for the most part fanatical sectaries of Vishṇu or Ŝiva, particularly of Vishṇu, who aspire by that method to the public admiration, rather than to do honour to the gods, by such barbarous and ridiculous works.

Besides the practices already mentioned, which are carried on in almost every temple of any note, there are many others, not less revolting, which are confined to some particular pagodas of great renown, where the concourse of pilgrims and other devotees is not to be numbered.

The most celebrated of the Hindû temples, in the south of the peninsula, is that of *Tirupati* in the north of the Carnatic. It is

---

ing that good would result from such a proceeding, nor did he hear priests advise it. It was a practice.—Soobroya Charry, a carpenter, deposed that six years ago he cut his tongue taking off an inch from it because he suffered from pain in the belly. It was at the Cundaswamy pagoda. The next day the goddess came upon one of the hermits at the temple and the hermit came and told witness that he was permitted by the goddess to drink milk. He took milk for a week and then his tongue grew; and in a month he began to speak and then took rice. The hermit was not present when he cut his tongue. The operation of cutting off his tongue cured his belly ache immediately. The thought occurred to him by chance that being a creature of the deity, if he cut his tongue and put his trust in the deity he should get better. No one told him to cut his tongue. He had heard of many having done so before he tried it himself.

dedicated to the god *Venkaṭa Râma*. Crowds of pilgrims resort to it, from all parts of India, chiefly from amongst the followers of Vishṇu. Those who are indifferent about castes also attend in great numbers; but the disciples of Śiva never appear. The infinite number of enthusiasts, who are continually journeying to this holy station, pour into it such abundance of offerings of all sorts, in goods, grain, gold, silver, jewels, precious stuffs, horses, cows and other cattle, and in all other articles of value; that its revenue serves to maintain several thousands of persons, who are employed in the various functions of the idolatrous worship, which is there conducted with extraordinary pomp.

Amongst the great number of ceremonies practised at this celebrated place, that of the Ravishment of Women is too remarkable to be passed over. It generally takes place at the time of the grand procession of the image of the god drawn through the streets, in a triumphal car, when curiosity to see the august spectacle attracts an inconceivable throng.

While the procession is going forward the Brâhmans who preside over the ceremony disperse themselves among the crowd, selecting the most beautiful women they can find, and begging them of their friends, for the use of the god Venkaṭa Râma, for whose service the choice is declared to be made. Some persons, more intelligent, or at least less stupid than the rest, and who are so well acquainted with the knavery of the Brâhmans as to know that it is not for a god of marble that their wives are solicited; resist them, with violent reproaches, and publicly expose their impostures. Their own wives they will not deliver up; but they look on, while other more credulous husbands give up theirs; not only without repugnance, but glorying in the honour, that a person of their family should have been chosen by their deity for a wife.

When a woman, thus obtained, and kept in the temples, by the Brâhmans, in the name of the god, is declared too old for his purposes, or when he has taken any dislike to her, they make a mark on her breast, representing the arms of the Venkaṭa Râma, and give her a patent, which certifies that she has served a certain number of years as one of the wives of the god of Tripati, who is now tired of her, and therefore recommending her to the charity of the public. Thus they are all dismissed in their turn; and under the appellation of Kali-yugam Lakshmi, or the Lakshmi of the Kali-yugam, they go about respected; and, wherever they appear, they are suffered to want for nothing.

This constupration of women, on the pretence of devoting them to the idols which are venerated by the Hindûs, is not wholly confined to the temple of Tripati, but extends to other famous pagodas, such as that of the Jaganâth and some others.

The temple of Jaganâth[w] is scarcely less famous than that of

[w] JAGAT + NÂTAN—*Lord of the Earth.*

Tripati. The religious ceremonies are conducted there with the greatest magnificence. It is situated on the north of the coast of Orissa. Its principal divinity is represented under a monstrous shape, without arms or legs.

One thing peculiar to this pagoda is, that it appears to be the Temple of Peace, and the centre of union among the Hindûs. The distinction of sects and castes is here unknown. Every individual whatever is admitted, and allowed to pay his homage, in person, to the divinity. Accordingly, a great number of pilgrims frequent it from all quarters of India. The disciples of Vishṇu and those of Śiva attend, with equal zeal. The Vairâgis, the Dâśaru, the Jangama, and every variety of religious fanatics, when they approach this temple, lay down their animosity; and it is perhaps the only spot in India where they suspend their hatred and contention. Whilst sojourning here, they seem to compose but one community of brothers.

Several thousands of functionaries, chiefly Brâhmans, are engaged in the performance of the ceremonies of religious worship in this Temple of Concord. The crowd of votaries never abates. Those of the south, who undertake the holy pilgrimage to Kâśi or Benares, never omit the Temple of Jagaṇâth in their way; and those from the north, in their holy journey to Cape Comorin, always visit it, as they pass, to offer their adorations to its presiding deity.

There are also many temples in the various provinces of the peninsula, as well as other sacred places, which are famed for some particular advantage or other, or for some singularity in their worship.

At *Combaconam,* (Kumbhacôṇam) in Tanjore, there is a consecrated pond, which possesses the virtue, at intervals of twelve years, to cleanse all who bathe in it from spiritual and corporal impurities, though accumulated for many generations. When that moment of plenary indulgence arrives, one beholds innumerable swarms of both sexes, many of whom have come from the remotest provinces of the north of the peninsula.

Near Madura, there is a very famous temple, in a place called *Paṛani,* to whom the devotees bring offerings of a singular kind. They consist of large leathern shoes, of the shape of those which the Hindûs wear on their feet, but much bigger and more ornamented. This god being addicted to hunting, these shoes are intended for his use when he traverses the deserts in the chase.

It is unnecessary to carry much farther the detail of the ceremonies and rites, general and particular, which are exercised in the temples of India. What I have already stated, I hope, will give insight into the religious worship of the people. I will conclude, therefore, with a few words concerning their Processions, and the Cars of triumph on which they exhibit their gods, in procession, through the streets.

There are no temples from which Processions of great magnificence and splendour do not take place, once in the year, or oftener

On those occasions the idols are taken out of their sanctuaries, and raised on high triumphal carriages constructed for the purpose. They are upon four wheels of great strength; not composed, like ours, with spokes within a rim, but of three or four thick pieces of wood, rounded and fitted into each other. The whole being compacted of solid timber, supports an erection of sometimes not less than fifty feet in height. The boards of which it is composed are carved with images of men and women; frequently representing the grossest obscenities. Over this first elevation, composed of solid timbers, they raise several stories of slighter materials; the whole contracting and narrowing into a pyramidal form; resembling the shape of the temples, as we have described them.

On the days of procession the cars are adorned with precious stuffs, painted cloth, garlands of flowers, and green foliage. Under a niche in the centre the idol is placed, in glittering attire, to attract the admiration of the people.

Having fastened ropes to the enormous vehicle, they set thousands of people to work, who draw it slowly along, accompanied with the awful roaring of their voices. At certain periods they make a pause; at which the immense crowd, collected from all parts to witness the ceremony, set up one universal shout, or rather yell, in proof of their exultation and joy. This, joined to the piercing and dissonant sounds of their instruments, and of the numerous drums which rattle amongst the disorderly throng, produces a confusion and uproar surpassing all imagination. Sometimes, as may be easily supposed, the cumbrous car gets into embarrassment, and sometimes to a total stand, in the crowded and narrow streets, by unforeseen accidents; and then the tumult and the clamorous roar redouble.

It may be easily imagined, that, in such a chaos of confusion, where men and women are indiscriminately blended in the crowd, and their conduct wholly unobserved, many irregularities must take place. And, in fact, these consequences do arise from the processions; because every individual may, without constraint, follow the immediate impulse of desire. For this reason, it is generally the rendezvous of debauchees, and also of young persons of both sexes, who, having conceived a mutual attachment for each other in secret, and being afraid, or unable, to gratify it in any other way, without exposure, chuse the day of procession to accomplish their desires without restraint.

Such is the outline of the religious ceremonies of the Hindûs, and such the spirit of idolatry which prevails among them. A religion more shameful or indecent has never existed amongst a civilized people. At the same time, I am far from believing that the present worship of the Hindûs corresponds with that of their first legislators; but, rather, that it is a corruption by the Brâhmans, who invented, in after-times, the monstrous worship which now prevails; for the greater number of the shocking fables, mentioned in this chapter and the preceding one, appear to be modern inventions.

Absurd as the worship of the Hindûs is, their attachment to the species of idolatry which they have embraced is so powerful, that none of the great revolutions that have taken place in their country, in modern times, have inspired them with the slightest idea of renouncing the foolish rites of Paganism, and assuming the more rational religion of their conquerors. The Christians and Mohammodans have, equally, laboured to introduce their respective religions amongst them; and the latter, no doubt, have made many proselytes, but only in the way which they have pursued every where else, of violence and compulsion. But, after all, their doctrines have never taken root, nor become predominant, in any of the provinces of India. Yet, in many of them, persecutions of every sort have been exercised against the Pagan inhabitants; and the Moslem Princes have also tried every other method of persuasion, by putting wealth and honours within the reach of those who should renounce the worship of idols for the faith of their Prophet.

The religion of. Christ, which offers itself only in the way of gentleness and persuasion, that holy and benevolent faith, which would seem so well adapted to sweeten and cheer the life of a people subdued to misery and oppression; that religion from God, whose penetrating truths have softened the rugged hearts of so many barbarous nations, has been announced to the Hindûs for more than three hundred years; but with no remarkable success. It even sensibly loses the little ground it had gained against a thousand obstacles, through the zeal and persevering efforts of the ministers who first preached it there. The prejudice against it unhappily increases every day. The conduct of those who, though born in countries where Christianity alone is professed, are now spread over all India, is often so unworthy of their faith, as to increase the prejudices and dislike which the natives entertain for every foreign religion, and for that above all others.

It is unnecessary to remind the reader that the manners of a people who have adopted religious customs so indecorous as the Hindûs have done, must necessarily be very dissolute. Accordingly, licentiousness prevails almost universally, without shame or remorse. Every excess of debauchery or libertinism is countenanced by the irregular lives of their gods, and by the rites which their worship prescribes. This connexion illustrates the truth of the remark of Montesquieu, that, "in a country which has the misfortune to possess "a religion that does not proceed from God, it necessarily falls in "with the morals which prevail, because even a false religion is the "best guarantee that men can have for the honesty of men."

CHAPTER IV.

OF THE PRINCIPAL DIVINITIES OF INDIA.

It would be a work of volumes to enter into a detail of the fables that relate to the different deities which the commonalty adores; for there is scarcely an object in nature, living or inanimate, to which the Hindûs do not offer worship. But they acknowledge three principal gods whom they specially venerate, under the names of *Brahmâ*, *Vishṇu*, and *Śiva.*[x] When worshipped, in union, they form, as we have already seen, the Trimûrtti; and they are also separately adored with peculiar rites. These three have given birth to an infinite number besides; and the Hindûs, in all things extravagant, have shewn this disposition no where more conspicuously than in the number of the divinities they have formed. They have gone far beyond all other idolatrous nations in this particular; as they reckon no less than thirty-three *kôṭi* of gods, each kôṭi being equal to ten millions, so that the whole number amounts to three hundred and thirty millions.

I shall confine myself to a short description of the principal ones that are universally acknowledged through the whole country. The full detail would be quite insupportable. We have already spoken of the Trimûrtti, or three principal gods united in one person, and we shall now proceed to a short view of the leading attributes of each.

Brahmâ.

Brahmâ occupies the highest place among the Hindû divinities. He is fabled to have been born with five heads; but he is represented with four only, because he lost one in a violent contest with Śiva, whose wife Pârvati he had ravished; and the indignant husband could not be appeased till he had cut off one of the heads of the adulterer.[y]

His wife, it is said, was his own daughter, *Saraswati*, whom he keeps always in his mouth. Having conceived for her an incestuous passion, he durst not gratify it in the human shape which he bore; and therefore he converted himself into a stag, and changed his daughter into a bitch. Under this form, he gratified his unnatural desires; and it is because he violated the most sacred laws of nature, as many believe, that he is without worship, without temples or sacri-

---

x "The one only god, Janarddana, (= the object of adoration to mankind) takes the designation of Brahmâ, Vishṇu, and Śiva, according as he creates, preserves, or destroys." Vishṇu Purâṇ.

y The account in the Kâsi k'hâṇdam of the Skanda Purâna, is that Śiva in the form of Kâla Bhairava, tore off Brahmâ's fifth head for presuming to say that he was Brahme, the Eternal and Omnipotent cause of the world, and even the Creator of Śiva.

See Wilson's Sects. p. 3.

fices; that no one, in short, performs any exterior ceremony of religion in honour of Brahmâ.

Others affirm that the sort of neglect into which this god has fallen, so as to be unworshipped, proceeds from a curse launched against him by a certain penitent, to whom Brahmâ was deficient in respect when the holy man entered the regions of bliss.

Three important energies, in the nature of attributes, are ascribed to this deity. The first is that of being author and creator of all things. The second makes him the giver of all gifts and of all blessings; and the third assigns to him the control over the destinies of all men. Every individual bears his mark, impressed on the forehead, by the finger of the deity himself. He also possesses the power of granting the gift of immortality to whomsoever he pleases; and it is to him that many fabulous personages are indebted for it; such as the Giants *Râvaṇa*, *Hiraṇya*, and several others.

Being the author of all things, he is consequently the creator of men. The four great castes, of which the world consists, namely, the Brâhmans, the Râjas, the merchants, and the agriculturists, were formed and instituted by him. The first and noblest sprung from his head; the second from his shoulders, the third from his belly, and the last from his feet.

This is the story of the creation of man most generally adopted, although some give it a different turn. They say that Brahmâ, in his first essay to create a human being, made him with only one foot; which not answering, he destroyed the work, and formed the next with three; but the third foot being more an incumbrance than a help, he destroyed this model also, and finally resolved upon the two legs.

Vishṇu.

Next after Brahmâ, comes *Vishṇu,* also called *Perumâl.*[1] His worship extends far and wide; and of all the gods he seems to have the greatest number of followers. They are divided into several classes or sects, known by the general appellation of *Matam.* Each Matam has its secrets, its sacrifices, its mantras, and particular signs. The most numerous of all is that whose members bear the mark of the Nâma, or three perpendicular lines, imprinted on their foreheads, as a particular symbol of their extreme devotion for that divinity.

The particular titles and attributes of Vishṇu are those of Redeemer and Preserver of all things. The other gods, without excepting Brahmâ himself, have often stood in need of his assistance; and, but for his powerful help, must, on many arduous occasions, have fallen into perdition.

His title of *Preserver of all things,* has made it necessary for him, on various occasions, to assume different forms, which the Hindûs call *Avatâras,* a word which may be rendered into *Metamorphoses.* Ten of these are enumerated, namely:

[1] —*Mighty being.*

1. *Mat'ya-avatâra*, or transformation into a *Fish*.
2. *Kûrmma-avatâra*, that into a *Tortoise*.
3. *Varâha-avatâra*, or *Boar*.
4. *Narasingha-avatâra*, change into *half man and half lion*.
5. *Vâmaṇa-avatâra*, that into a *dwarf Brâhman*.
6. *Paraśurâma-avatâra*, the change into the god of that name.
7. *Râma-avatâra*, or Vishṇu representing that hero. [Râma Chandra.]
8. *Balâ-râma-avatâra*, change into the Indian Hercules.[a]
9. *Bhadra-avatâra*, or metamorphosis into the tree *Ravi* or *Aruli*; and
10. *Kalki-avatâra*, or change into a *Horse*.

A few words will suffice on each Avatâra, the detailed account of which would occupy a large volume.

The first Avatâra, or metamorphosis into a *Fish*, takes its rise from the following accident, reported, at great length in the Bhâgavata. Brahmâ, one day being overpowered with fatigue, fell asleep. The four books called Vêdas, which had been assigned to his particular care, seeing their guardian completely sunk in somnolency, took advantage of it, and made their escape. All unprotected, they were met on the road, in their flight, by a Giant called *Hâyagriva*, who laid hold of them; and, in order to secure so precious a treasure, swallowed them, and put them next his heart. But, to avoid all danger of detection, he concealed himself in the midst of the waters of the great ocean. Vishṇu, when he heard of the loss that Brahmâ had sustained, and that the Giant was the robber, departed from his abode and followed his enemy into the waters, under the form of a fish. After a long search, he found him at last in the deepest abyss of the sea, and there, attacking him with fury, he overcame him, and, penetrating into his bowels, there found the Vêdas, and restored them to Brahmâ their keeper.

The second Avatâra was into a *Tortoise*, and was brought about in this manner. Whilst the Gods and the Giants were at open war, the Giants, with the mighty Bali at their head, were victorious over the Celestials, whom they treated with the greatest severity. In this disastrous state the gods were satisfied to obtain peace on any terms that their enemies might propose. Having thus concluded a treaty, they lived in apparent amity; but the Gods were, all the while secretly invoking Vishṇu to protect them from the power of their dangerous enemies. He granted their prayers, and at the same time ordered them to pull up the mountain *Mandara Parvata*, and cast it into the sea. In executing this task, some of them were so much fatigued as to be incapable of proceeding, which Vishṇu perceiving, flew to their aid, on the wings of the bird Garuḍa, his ordinary vehicle, and fixed the mountain in the sea of curdled milk. Afterwards, the gods being

[a] There is some difference in the enumeration in various books: some omit the Bâla-râma, and insert Buddha.

See Vishṇu Purâṇa, ii., li., xliii, 29, 75, 145, 384, 492.

desirous to navigate the sea, made a ship of Mount Mandara; and, having taken a serpent for a rope; they fastened one end of it to the head of one of the stoutest of their number, and the other end to the right arm of a second. While they were thus towing Mount Mandara as a ship, the gods, who were in it began to perceive that it was sinking; upon which they put up their fervent supplications to Vishṇu, the preserver, to rescue them from the imminent danger to which they were exposed. Vishṇu flew again to their relief, and seeing them all about to perish, he metamorphosed himself into a tortoise; plunged into the sea, and supported the sinking mountain on his solid back.

The third Avatâra was his transformation into a *Hog*. Vishṇu, being in pursuit of the Giant *Hiranyâksha*, a monster of whom he wished to rid the world, discovered that he was concealed in Patâla, which is the lowest of the seven inferior worlds; and, being determined, at all hazards, to reach him, he converted himself into a large Hog, and dug a passage through the earth with his snout, continuing his pursuit till he caught and slew this enemy of the human race.

The fourth Avatâra is called *Narasingha*. The three preceding were changes into the forms of animals. This was a mixture of Man and Lion. It took its rise from the following adventure. The younger brother of the Giant Hiranyâksha, hearing that his brother had been slain by Vishṇu, resolved to be avenged; and, with that design, he attacked the god in his abode of felicity, the Vaikuṇṭha. Vishṇu, apprehensive of a contest with so powerful an enemy, avoided him, and hid himself. The Giant being unable to find him, sought to avenge himself on the other gods who lived in the same residence with his enemy, and treated them with cruelty. The son of the Giant, who was one of those gods, interceded for them with his father, and endeavoured to appease his wrath. But, so far from listening to these entreaties, on finding that his son was a supporter of Vishṇu, he determined to put him to death. That god, seeing the danger that his votary was in, burst from beneath a cauldron, in the double shape of man and lion. He had still a long and bitter contest to sustain with the Giant; but, at last, having proved victorious, he seized his enemy, laid him across his thigh, tore his belly open with his lion's claws, sucked his blood, and extracted his bowels, which he afterwards twisted round his neck as a trophy of his victory.

The fifth Avatâra, was the change into a Brâhman Dwarf. The Giant Bali, always terrible in his wars with the gods, had already subdued three worlds, and reduced the gods he found there into the hardest subjection. Vishṇu, being desirous of delivering so many gods and mortals from their savage enemy, metamorphosed himself into a dwarfish Brâhman, and visited Bali under that disguise, soliciting a bit of ground no bigger than three prints of his little feet, which he required to offer sacrifices upon. The request appeared ludicrous to the Giant, and he granted it without scruple. Vishṇu immediately resumed his godlike form, and with one footstep covered the whole earth. With another, elevated in air, he overshadowed the whole space between the earth and firmament, and nothing being left to receive the third impression of his foot, he trod upon the Giant's head, and hurled him down to the infernal Patâla.

The sixth Avatâra, was the transformation into the person of *Paraśu-Râma*, by which Vishṇu became the son of *Jamadagni* and *Rênuki*. The Giant *Kîrtavîryanârjana*, having conquered and reduced under his dominion the father and mother of Paraśu-Râma; he, or Vishṇu in his shape, resolved to revenge the insult offered to the family. He attacked the Giant, slew him, and brought the carcase to his father Jamadagni. The sons of the Giant, desirous of vengeance, in their turn, went in search of Jamadagni; found him, and cut off his head. Paraśu-Râma, incensed at the cruelty; and being resolved to inflict adequate punishment on the murderer of his father, attacked not only those who committed the crime, but many other Kings who had leagued with them. Twenty-one assaults were sustained; but, in the last he gained the possession of their persons, and put them all to death.

The seventh Avatâra is the metamorphosis of Vishṇu into the hero called *Râma*. It is described, in a very prolix and tedious way, in the Râmâyaṇa, a book well known and read by all Hindûs. It has raked together, in the history of Râma, a collection of all the fables of the country. It commences with the moment of the conception of its hero. The principal adventures in his life, which would require a folio volume to describe, were, in the first place, his journey into the desert for the purpose of soliciting Swamitra to give him his only daughter Śîta in marriage; next, his pilgrimage to the city of Ayôdhya, and the war which it led him into with Paraśu-Râma, the same person with himself, in reality, being only different forms of Vishṇu, which for a long time unfortunately they did not discover; then the abduction of Śîta by the Giant Râvaṇa; the grief and despair of Râma on this event; the consolation and advice given him under such circumstances by his brother Lakshman, and the mode he points out for the recovery of his wife Śîta; an army of Apes, commanded by the great Ape *Hanuman*, who met him while searching for Śîta, and informed him where she dwelt, with her ravisher Râvaṇa, and the manner of life which she led; how Râma, at the news, inrolled the army of Apes in his service, to help him to fight Râvaṇa; and, being ignorant of war, received instruction from the Apes, who taught him to build bridges, to draw up an army in array, and to surprize the enemy; how he conquered the Isle Lanka, or Ceylon, where his enemies had rendezvoused, and which he assaulted with his Ape auxiliaries, by means of a bridge from the main land; and how, lastly, after a long and cruel war, in which the hero gained victories, and suffered defeats, he was joined by Vishṇu, the brother and enemy of the Giant Râvaṇa, who taught Râma the certain means of subduing his enemy; how his advice is pursued; and how Râma, having gained a decisive victory over Râvaṇa and the united Giants, at length regains his beloved Śîta.

The eighth Avatâra, in which he is transformed into the person of *Bâla-Râma*, exhibits Vishṇu so disguised for the purpose of making war against an Army of Giants, who were desolating the earth. He took for his weapon a Serpent of enormous size, and, by its means, soon succeeded in destroying all the Giants against whom he had taken arms.

The ninth Avatâra is the transformation into the tree *Ravi* or *Áruli*.[b] Vishṇu having entertained impure desires towards the daughter of a Giant, a beauty renowned for her virtues, employed all manner of artifices to gain her. This modest female having resolutely rejected his illicit solicitations, he at last made a desperate effort for the gratification of his wicked design; and finding it impracticable, under an animal form, he assumed that of the tree Ravi; in which semblance he succeeded in satisfying his passion. This metamorphosis is, no doubt, the cause why this tree is so famous and so much venerated by the Hindûs.[c]

The tenth Avatâra is the transformation into a *Horse*.[d] This last Avatâra has not yet taken effect; but the Hindûs trust that it will be realized. They expect it with the same ardour as the Jews look forward to their Messiah. This tenth Avatâra is to be the most beneficial and the most wonderful of all. The books which announce it do not assign the period when it will arrive, nor how it will be brought to pass, but the Hindûs confide that it will restore the *Satya-yuga* or Age of Happiness.

Krishṇa.

Besides the Ten Avatâras of Vishṇu, the Hindûs recognize another, which is that of his change into the person of Krishṇa. This metamorphosis, and all the fables that accompany it, are contained in the book called *Bhâgavata*, which is scarcely less famous than the *Râmáyaṇa*.

Krishṇa, at his birth, was obliged to be concealed, in order to avoid the attack of a Giant who sought his life. He escaped his enemy under the disguise of a beggar. He was reared by persons of that caste, and soon exhibited marks of the most unbridled libertinism. Plunder and rape were familiar to him from his tender years. It was his chief pleasure to go every morning to the place where the women bathe, and, in concealment, to take advantage of their unguarded exposure. Then he rushed amongst them, took possession of their clothes, and gave a loose to the indecencies of language and of gesture. He maintained sixteen wives, who had the title of queens, and sixteen thousand concubines. All these women bore children almost without

---

[b] The ninth *Avatâra* is generally said to be Budd'ha. Vishṇu appeared in this shape to spread infidelity and so counteract the power which many had acquired by their austerities.

[c] The Basil (Ocymum Sanctum) is also sacred to Vishṇu, and is cultivated very largely by Brâhmans.

[d] Kalki.

number; but Krishṇa, fearing they would league against him and deprive him of his power, murdered them all. He had long and cruel wars with the Giants, with various success.

In obscenity, there is nothing that can be compared with the Bhâgavata. It is nevertheless the delight of the Hindûs, and the first book they put into the hands of their children, when learning to read; as if they deliberately intended to lay the basis of a dissolute education.[e]

Śiva.

This God has likewise the names of *Îśwara, Rudra, Sadâśiva,* and *Paraméśwara.*[f] He is generally represented under a terrible shape, to shew, by a menacing exterior, the power which he possesses of destroying all things. To aggravate the horrors of his appearance, he is represented with his body all covered with ashes. His long hair is plaited and curled in the most whimsical way. His eyes, unnaturally large, give him the appearance of being in a perpetual rage. Instead of jewels, they adorn his ears with great serpents. He holds in his hand a weapon called *Śûla.* I have sometimes seen idols of Śiva, of gigantic proportions, admirably contrived to inspire terror.

The principal attribute of this God, as we have mentioned, is the power of Universal Destruction; although some authors also give him that of Creation, in common with Brahmâ.

His fabulous history, like that of all the other Hindû Gods, is nothing but a tissue of absurd and extravagant adventures, invented, as it would seem, for the mere purpose of exhibiting the extremes of the two most powerful passions which tyrannize over man, Luxury and Ambition. They relate to the wars which he maintained against the Giants; to his enmity and jealousy in opposition to the other Gods; and, above all, to his infamous amours.

It is related that, in one of his wars, being desirous of completing the destruction of the Giants, and of obtaining possession of Tripura, the country which they inhabited, he cleft the world in twain, and took one-half of it for his armour. He made Brahmâ the general of his army. The four Vêdas were his horses. Vishṇu was his arrow. The mountain Mandara Parvata was used for his bow, and a mighty serpent supplied the place of the string. Thus accoutred, the terrible Śiva led his army to the abode of the tyrants of the earth, took the three fortresses they had constructed, and demolished them in a moment. This, and other stories of Śiva, are given at great length in the Hindû sacred books.

---

e The Śâlagrâm or Ammonite found in the Gundick and *other* rivers flowing through Nepâl is said to be a form of Vishṇu. The account of its origin given in the Skânda Purâṇa, and of the birth of Hari-hara Putra or Aiyenâr, Son of Vishṇu and Śiva is most monstrously and incredibly abominable.

f He has a thousand names: such as, Mahâ dêva — *mighty God;* Trilôchana — *three eyed one;* Tripurâri, *destroyer of the three towns;* Nîlakanṭa — blue throated one; Sômanât'ha — *Lord of the moon;* Sambhu — *The self existing one.* &c. &c.

Śiva had great difficulty in obtaining a wife; but having made a long and austere penitence at the Mountain Parvata, that lofty eminence was so affected by it as to consent at last to give him his daughter in marriage.

The Lingam.

The abomination of the *Lingam* takes its origin from Śiva. This idol which is spread all over India, is generally inclosed in a little box of silver, which all the votaries of that god wear suspended at their necks. It represents the sexual organs of man, sometimes alone, and sometimes accompanied. The long account given of the origin of this mystery in the Linga-Purâṇa may be thus abbreviated.

Śiva having one day, in presence of the seven famous penitents, exhibited himself in a state of nature, began to play several indecent vagaries before them. He persisted till the penitents, being no longer able to tolerate his indecency, imprecated their curse upon it. The denunciation took immediate effect, and from that moment Śiva was emasculated. Pârvati, having heard of the misfortune of her husband, came to comfort him;—but I have not the courage to return to the pages which contain the topics of consolation which she used, or the methods she employed to repair his loss.

In the meantime, the penitents having more coolly considered the disproportion of the punishment to the offence, and wishing to make all the reparation in their power to the unhappy Śiva, decreed that all his worshippers should thenceforth address their prayers, adoration and sacrifices to what the imprecation had deprived him of.

Such is the infamous origin of the Lingam, which is not only openly represented in the temples, on the highways, and in other public situations, but is worn by the votaries of Śiva as the most precious relic, hung at their necks, or fastened to their arms and hair, and receiving from them sacrifices and adoration.

The Lingam is the ordinary symbol of all the followers of Śiva.[g] That sect spreads over the whole of India, but particularly in the west of the peninsula, where the Lingamites compose, in many districts, the chief part of the population. The particular customs of the sect have been before noticed; the most remarkable of which are their abstinence from whatever has had the principle of life, and the practice of interring their dead in place of burning them, as most other Hindûs do.

We know to what excess the spirit of idolatry may lead the ignorant; but it is incredible, it even seems impossible, that the Lingam could have originated in the direct and literal worship of what it represents; but rather that it was an allegorical allusion of a striking

---

[g] The Linga is in fact the only form in which Śiva is worshipped. In many temples there are 108 lingas; in some 216. They are not much frequented.

In South India numberless legends relating to devout worshippers of Śiva are current. Some of them are curious, and they are exclusively of Southern origin.

kind, to typify the procreative and regenerating powers of nature, by which all kinds of being are reproduced and maintained in the wide universe. It was, no doubt, to this fecundating and reproductive energy of nature, that the early idolators of India paid their adoration; while their successors, from the propensity to embody every thing abstract into sensible images, transferred it to the gross emblem; and, forgetting by little and little the ideas of their ancestors, came at length to adore the abomination itself, and to rank it amongst their principal divinities. From the same principle, as far as we can perceive, arose the worship of the Phallus among the Greeks, that of Priapus among the Romans, and probably that of Baal-peor mentioned in Scripture: objects of worship amongst other ancient idolatrous nations, which differed but little from that of the Lingam, and were equally abominable.

Vig'hnêśwara.

The god Vig'hnêśwara is likewise known by the names of *Piḷḷaiyâr*, *Gaṇêśa*, and *Vinâyaka*. He is one of the most universally adored deities.[h] His image is every where to be seen; in the temples, in the choultries, in places of public resort, in the streets, in forts, by the side of streams and tanks, on the highways, and generally in all frequented places. He is taken into the houses; and in all public ceremonies, he is worshipped the first of all. We have already spoken of him as the God of Obstacles, and mentioned that the honours he received proceed from the apprehension that he would otherwise cast difficulties and impediments before them, in the ordinary occurrences of life.

He derived his birth from the excrement of Pârvati. His mother made him her guard and door-keeper. In this situation, the god Kumâra, who had long entertained a grudge against him, finding him alone one day, cut off his head. Śiva was much grieved when he heard of the misfortune; and, being desirous to repair it, he made a vow that he would cut off the head of the first living creature he should find lying down with its crown towards the north, and unite it to the trunk of Vig'hnêśwara. In setting out on this design, the first animal he met with, lying in that position, was an elephant; the head of which he cut off, and set it on the neck of Vig'hnêśwara, and thus restored him to life. Pârvati was terrified when she first saw her son in this condition; but, by degrees, she became reconciled to the frightful change, and gaily asked him one day what sort of a wife he would wish to marry. The son, who had for a long time looked with an incestuous eye on his mother, replied that he would like one altogether the same as she was. Alarmed at his answer, she exclaimed, in her wrath: "a wife like me! go then and seek for her, and never mayest "thou marry until thou findest exactly such an one." From that time, though Vig'hnêśwara has diligently visited all places frequented by women, he has never found one to suit the condition in the curse; or rather, no woman will unite with so unseemly a husband.

---

h Comp. p. 65.

Indra or Dêvêndra.

This God, as we have before stated, is King of the Inferior Deities, who sojourn with him in his paradise called *Swarga,* or seat of Sensual Pleasures; for in this voluptuous abode, no other are known.

The god Dêvêndra rides an elephant, and has a cutting instrument called the *Vajra* for his weapon of offence. The colour of his garment is red.

Those who seek to establish a connection or resemblance between the false gods of the different idolatrous nations of antiquity, will find several points of approximation, in comparing the divinities of India with those of Greece and Rome. The short account we have given of the history of some of the principal ones would serve to establish this congruity. At the same time I do not consider it sufficient to justify, in its full extent, the conclusions drawn from those marks of similitude, by some modern writers, who are desirous of tracing the Indian and Grecian gods from a common origin.

The metamorphosis of Jupiter; at one time into a satyr, in the rape of Antiope; at another into a bull, when he carried Europa away; then into a swan, for the purpose of abusing Leda, or into a shower of gold for the corruption of Danaë; and many other changes, for facilitating his amours, have a great resemblance to the adventures of Brahmâ and of Vishṇu. Nor does the Lingam of the Hindûs, as we have shewn, differ widely from the Phallus of the Greeks and the Priapus of the Latins.

But there is another particular in which the gods of these different nations seem to bear a more striking analogy to each other than in any other yet mentioned; and that is the arms or weapons which they respectively bore. The gods of Greece were always represented armed; as the Hindû gods are also.

The Greeks armed Saturn with a scythe, Jupiter with the thunder, Neptune with the trident, and Pluto with his two pronged fork. They assigned a club to Hercules, a thyrsis to Bacchus; to Minerva a shield or Egis, and to Diana the bow and arrows.

The Hindûs, in like manner, have put arms in the hands of each of their principal deities, with the exception of Brahmâ; who, as we have seen, neither wears arms, nor rides; who has no temple, nor sacrifice, nor any other worship whatever.

The various weapons which the Hindûs assign to their several gods, and which appear to be such as were anciently used by that people in war, are thirty-two in number. Of these, some are missile, such as the arrow; the *vâṇa,* composed of combustible materials, and the *chakram,* which will be afterwards mentioned. Some are defensive, as the shield; but the chief part are offensive. It is not easy to describe, in an European tongue, the form of the different sorts of arms that were anciently used by the Hindûs in battle, and which are still to be seen in the hands of their idols. No just idea of them can be communicated without a drawing. Of the weapons, not missile, some are used to stab, some to hack, and some to fell. Others seem intended for grappling, and some for warding off.

Five weapons are given to Vishṇu, called in the aggregate *Panchâyudha*, and which he severally used, according to the various characters which he assumed. Their names are *Sankha, Chakram, Khaḍga, Gaḍa, Sâranga.* The two principal, with which he is most commonly equipped, are the sankha, which he wields in his left hand, and the chakram, which he bears in the right.

Śiva has two weapons, the *triśûla* and the *damru;* and every other principal deity has his peculiar instrument, with which he is always represented.

Another point of resemblance between the Hindû gods and those of ancient Greece consists in the manner in which they were mounted. The Greeks and Romans represented Jupiter as seated on an eagle, Neptune in a chariot drawn by two sea-horses, Pluto in one drawn by four black horses, Mars mounted on a cock, Bacchus with a team of tigers, Juno with her peacocks, and Pallas with the solemn owl.

The Hindûs have, in like manner, assigned to each of their chief gods their peculiar vehicle, Brahmâ alone being excepted. Vishṇu generally rode on the bird Garuḍa, and Śiva on the bull.

The following is a table of the Ashṭa-dik-pâla-kar, or gods who preside over the eight principal divisions of the world.

Names.	Quarters over which they preside.	How mounted.	Weapons.	Colour of Clothing.
1. INDRA	- East	- The Elephant	- Vajra	Red.
2. AGNI	- South-east	- The Ram	- Sikhi	Violet.
3. YAMA	- South	- The Buffalo	- Daṇḍa	Bright-yellow.
4. NIRUT	- South-west	Man	- Cûkâ	Deep-yellow.
5. VARUṆA	- West	- The Crocodile	- Paśa	White.
6. VÂYU	- North-west	The Antelope	- Dwaja	Blue or Indigo.
7. KUVÊRA	- North	- The Horse	- Khadga	Rose colour.
8. IŚÂNA	- North-east	The Bull	- Triśûla	Gray.

CHAPTER V.

OF THE WORSHIP OF ANIMALS, AND THAT OF THE BÛTAM OR MALEVOLENT BEINGS.

OF all kinds of superstition by which the human intellect has been clogged, degraded, and debased, the worship of Brute Animals seems to be the most humiliating to our species. If we did not attend to the origin and the predisposing causes, we could hardly credit that rational beings should descend so far beneath the dignity of their nature as to stoop to the adoration of brutes. But it may be suggested, as some apology for this monstrous aberration of human reason, that, in all ages, the superstitious bias has received an impulse, through the channel of Religion, from motives of fear or interest; and that it has been a natural impression amongst all idolatrous nations to pay adoration to whatever can be detrimental or useful.

It is sufficiently known that animal worship was established and universally observed amongst the Egyptians. The noxious kinds, and the useful, shared alike in their adoration. They erected altars and offered incense to the Bull Apis, the Bird Ibis, to the Kite, the Crocodile, and a vast variety of other animals.[i]

The Egyptians, however, limited their religious adoration of animals to a small number of sorts, the most beneficial or the most dangerous; while the Hindûs, in all things extravagant, pay honour and worship, less or more solemn, to almost every living creature, whether quadruped, bird, or reptile. The Ape, the Tiger, the Elephant, the Horse, the Ox, the Stag, the Sheep, the Hog, the Dog, the Cat, the Rat, the Peacock, the Eagle, the Cock, the Hawk, the Serpent, the Chameleon, the Lizard, the Tortoise, all kinds of amphibious creatures, Fishes, and even Insects, have been consecrated by Hindû folly. Every living creature that can be supposed capable of effecting good or evil in the smallest degree, has become a sort of divinity and is entitled to adoration and sacrifice.

But, amidst the variety of animals, some have been more interesting than others, and have consequently received higher honours; either on account of their superior utility, or the greater dread they inspire. Here we may rank the Cow, the Ox, the Ape, the bird of prey known there under the name of *Garuḍa*, and the serpent Capella. We shall add a few words concerning each of these four species, whose images are represented in every quarter.

---

[i] See Plutarch's "Isis and Osiris."

The Ape, known by the name of Hanumân.

The motive which induced the early idolaters of India to make the Ape one of their principal divinities was, in all probability, founded on the striking resemblance which they remarked between that animal and man, in exterior appearance and physical relations. They considered it as holding the first rank in the order of brutes, and consequently as the king of the animals; and, after deifying it, they chose to perpetuate its honours by inventing the infinite collection of fables with which their books are filled.

It was with an army of Apes that their great hero Râma conquered Lanka, or Ceylon; and the achievements of this host of satyrs, under the command of the great Ape Ḥanumân, occupies the greater part of the Râmâyaṇa, the most celebrated of their historical works. The worship of this leader extends over all the territory of India, and especially amongst the followers of Vishṇu, but the sect of Śiva does not admit of his claim.[j]

His idol is every where seen in the temples, choultries, and other places frequented by the people; and it is also frequently found in the woods, and under thick trees in desert places. But particularly where the Vishṇuvites abound, one meets almost every where with the favourite idol of Hanumân. The sacrifices offered to it consist of the simplest productions of nature.

In parts frequented by apes, devotees are often seen to make it their duty to give them part of their food; and they consider it as a very meritorious act.

Baśwa or The Bull.

The Bull is the favourite God of the worshippers of Śiva. They constantly represent the God as its rider, and as performing all his journies on its back.[k]

The image of it is seen in almost every temple, and in most other places frequented by the people.

But among all the worshippers of this animal, the sect of Śiva pay it the most particular devotion; and, in the districts where they predominate, nothing is to be seen but the representation of their favourite idol Baśwa, or the Bull, on a pedestal, lying flat on his belly.

Monday in every week, as before hinted, is set apart to the honour of Baśwa. On that day, the Śivites give repose to their cattle, and release them from labour.

---

[j] He is Son of Pavana, the *wind*, and Anjarâ, a female monkey, an incarnation of Śiva! The Hindûs worship him on their birth day to obtain long life.

On this account Natives do not like to kill monkeys.

[k] He is a manifestation of *Nandi* doorkeeper and confidential servant of Śiva in his abode of *Kailâs-am*, the silver mountain.

The Bird Garuḍa.

The Garuḍa is of the nature of a bird of prey, and is held in the highest veneration by the Hindûs, and particularly by the tribe of Vishṇu. It is the ordinary vehicle on which that God performs his journies. The Vishṇuvite Brâhmans, every morning after ablution, wait for the appearance of one of those birds, in order to pay it adoration.

It is every where to be seen about the villages. It is bigger than our falcon, but much smaller than the least of our eagles. Its plumage is handsome. The feathers of the head, neck, and breast, are of a very bright and glossy white; and those of the back, wings, and tail, form a sort of mantle of a beautiful brown. But when it approaches near, it becomes offensive, from its unpleasant odour. Its ordinary cry is a kind of *kree, kree!* uttered with a hoarse and croaking scream, prolonging the sound at the end in a very disagreeable way.

Although it appears a vigorous bird; and it actually possesses great advantages in its strong hooked bill and powerful talons; yet it never attacks other birds that can oppose the least resistance. It by no means has the courage of the hawk. Its timid and indolent nature would rather rank it with the buzzard or raven; though it does not, like them, pounce upon carrion. Its ordinary food is the lizards, mice, and, above all, the snakes, which it carries up alive in its claws to a great height, and there lets them fall upon the ground. It descends after them, and, if it does not find them dead after one fall, it gives them a second, and then quietly retires to some neighbouring tree to devour them.

It is probably the service which it does to society, in destroying noxious reptiles and other disgusting animals, that has been the means of protecting it, and raising it to the rank of a principal divinity. It was the same motive that prompted the Egyptians to consecrate the Ibis, and pay it homage.

The Garuḍa also devours frogs and little fishes, which it catches with its claws in shallow waters. It is also a dangerous enemy to the poultry yard; but it is so cowardly that an angry hen can put it to flight; and it can only venture on some unguarded chicken.

I have entered into these details, because the bird seems but little known to our European orinithologists. Being under the protection of superstition, it approaches a man without fear, and is seen every where about the villages, from which it seldom strays. It is of heavy flight, and never mounts high in the air.

Sunday is the day particularly set apart for the worship of this sacred fowl. Troops of people are then seen uniting in their adoration and sacrifice; after which, they call the birds, and throw bits of meat in the air, which they nimbly catch with their talons.

It would be held as heinous an offence, particularly among the followers of Vishṇu, to kill one of these fowls as to commit manslaughter; and when they find one dead, they bury it ceremoniously, and crowds of people attend, with instruments of music, and with every demonstration of deep affliction.

They observe the same practice on the death of an ape or of a Capella serpent, and use many ceremonies for the purpose of expiating the destruction of those sacred creatures.

The Serpent.

Of all noxious animals found in India, there are none that occasion more frequent or more fatal evils than the serpents. Those inflicted by the tiger, though very frightful also, more seldom occur and are less universally felt than what proceed from the venom of these dangerous reptiles. During my whole residence in India, hardly a month has passed without some person in my neighbourhood suffering sudden death by the bite of a serpent.

One of the commonest, and at the same time the most venomous, as its bite sometimes occasions instant death, is what in Europe is generally called the *Capella*. It is met with, unfortunately, every where; and it is for that reason that the Hindûs offer sacrifice and adoration to it, above all others. It is more venerated than the rest of the pernicious creatures, beeause it is the most dreaded of any. Fear of the dreadful and frequent evils which it occasions, has indeed made it the most sacred of animals, upon the same principle that the Egyptians pay divine honours to the crocodile.

In order to impress more strongly on the mind, the danger of this baleful agent, and the necessity for worshipping it, so as to render it propitious, the Hindûs have filled their books with tales concerning so active an enemy of the human race; and, on the other hand, figures of them are represented in most of the temples and on the other public monuments and buildings. They seek out their holes, which are generally excavated in the hillocks of earth thrown up by the kariah or white ants; and when they find one, they go from time to time, and offer to it oblations of milk, bananas and other articles for nourishment.

When one of these dangerous guests intrudes himself into their houses, so far from turning him out, many of them will rather make sacrifices to him, and give him food every day. Some instances are known where Capella serpents have been entertained in houses, in this manner, for several years; but in no case are they ever injured, and it would be a heinous crime to kill them.

One of the eighteen annual festivals of the Hindûs is especially consecrated to the worship of the serpent Capella, which is celebrated on the fifth day of the moon in December, called for that reason *Nâga Panchami; nâga* being the Hindû name for this serpent.

Temples are also erected to them in many places, of which there is one of great celebrity in the west of the Mysore, at a place called

Subrahmaṇya; a name derived from the great serpent Subraya, which is renowned in Hindû fable, and the principal deity honoured at this pagoda.

When the festival comes round, a vast crowd of people assembles to offer sacrifices to the creeping gods, in their sacred dome. Many serpents, both of the Capella and other species, have taken up their residence within it, in holes made for the purpose. They are kept and well fed by the presiding Brâhmans with milk, butter, and bananas. By the protection they here enjoy they multiply exceedingly, and may be seen swarming from every cranny in the temple: and a terrible sacrilege it would be to injure or molest them.

But the Hindû superstition is so inexhaustible that other kinds of animals, besides those we have enumerated, come in for a share of their adoration. Even fishes are not excluded. Devout Brâhmans are often seen casting rice into the waters to feed them; and, in many places, all fishing is prohibited. In times before the Pagan Princes ceased to rule in the Mysore, they made it their constant practice to throw a quantity of boiled rice into the Kâveri for the sustenance of the fishes.

The Bhûta or Malevolent Fiends.

All nations of the earth, civilized or barbarous, have acknowledged the existence of certain evil spirits, whose nature and constant employment it is to injure men in various ways. Revealed religion alone gives just and rational views of the subject. Superstition, on the other hand, engendered by fear and nourished by ignorance, has conjured up a thousand absurd and ridiculous fables, on a subject so well suited to them. People, who have not surmounted their crude notions concerning the general dispensation of Providence, when they find themselves unable to discover the causes of the cross accidents, however common, which befal them in the ordinary course of nature, cannot help ascribing them to the agency of invisible and wicked beings, who delight in bringing upon men the various ills and miseries to which they are exposed. The next step is to seek to propitiate the fiend by prayers, adoration, and sacrifice.

We have seen, in the course of this work, to what pitch the Hindûs carry their credulity in this particular. The worship of demons is universally established and practised amongst them. They call them *Bhûta* which also signifies *Element;* as if the elements were in fact nothing else but wicked spirits personified, from whose wrath and fury all the disturbances of nature arise. Malign spirits are also called by the generic names of *Piśácha* and *Daitya.*

In many parts we meet with temples specially devoted to the worship of wicked spirits. There are districts also in which it almost exclusively predominates. Such is that long chain of mountains which extend on the west of the Mysore, where the greater part of the inhabitants practise no other worship but that of the devil. Every house and each family has its own particular Bhûta, who stands for its tutelary god; and to whom daily prayers and propitiatory sacrifices are offered, not only to incline him to withhold his own machinations, but to defend them from the evils which the Bhûtas of their neighbours or enemies might inflict. In those parts, the image of the demon is every where seen, represented in a hideous form, and often by a shapeless stone. Each of these fiends has his particular name; and some, who are more powerful and atrocious than others, are preferred in the same proportion.

All evil demons love bloody offerings; and therefore their ardent worshippers sacrifice living victims, such as buffaloes, hogs, rams, cocks, and the like. When rice is offered, it must be tinged with blood; and they are also soothed with inebriating drinks. In offerings of flowers the red only are presented to them.

The worship of the Bhûtas and the manner of conducting it are explained in the fourth veda of the Hindûs called Atharvana-vêda; and it is on that account very carefully concealed by the Brâhmans.

I have very generally found that the direct worship of demons is most prevalent in deserts, solitary places, and mountainous tracts; the reason of which is that in such parts the people are less civilized than those of the plains, more ignorant and timid, and therefore more prone to superstition. They are therefore more easily led to attribute all their misadventures and afflictions to the displeasure of their demon.

Many hordes of savages, who are scattered amongst the forests on the coast of Malabar, and in the woods and mountains of the Carnatic, who are known by the names of Maly-arasar, Kurumber, and Irular, acknowledge no other deity but the Bhûtas.[l]

The nature of the Hindûs is so much disposed to idolatry, that all visible objects are adored whether animated or inanimate. Of the latter class, the vegetable race affords them several subjects of particular adoration.

The feast of Dîpâli formerly described, is the occasion generally taken to pay special reverence to plants, by offering them sacrifices. The farmers repeat them many times in the course of the year.

Among the trees, there are some which the Hindû superstition has distinguished with particular honours, on account of the good or evil they are capable of producing. Of the mischievous kind, there is a prickly shrub, the points of which are venomous; to avert the effect of which they offer a sacrifice of a particular nature. It consists in sticking rags on its branches, with which it is sometimes wholly

[l] The system of Demon worship seems to have been that of the tribes whom the Hindûs supplanted, and drove into the mountains or into the extreme South. The Brâhmans have given a place to those demons in their system, and represent them as attendants of Śiva (Bhûtêśa = *Lord of demons.*) The method of worship, the ceremonies and observances of this ancient system are foreign to the genius of Hinduism. Compare app. iv. to Dr. Caldwell's Draviḍian Grammar.

covered. Those who have travelled in the southern provinces must have observed many examples of this.

Amongst the useful trees which are worshipped with particular reverence, less regard is shewn to those which excel in fruit than to such as afford the coolest shade by the thickness of their foliage. The principal of these are the *Âruli* or *Arasa Maram*, *Vêpam* or *Bêvina Maram*; *Âlimaram*, and some others which yield a grateful shelter from the burning climate.

But the most celebrated of all is that which goes by the name of *Âlimaram*. The branches of this tree extend sometimes to the distance of more than a quarter of a league. It darts roots from its branches, which hang like a tissue of fibres, till they reach the ground, into which they gradually make their way; each creating, in a short time, a new trunk, which invigorates the branch it descended from, and shoots out new ones; which, after a while, eject young fibres, in their turn, to produce fresh trunks to the tree; which thus continues to expand, as long as it finds an appropriate soil, or meets with no insuperable obstruction.

CHAPTER VI.

OF THE PARIAHS AND OTHER INFERIOR CASTES OF HINDÛS.

AFTER having so long dwelt upon the Brâhmans, in particular, and the other castes of Hindûs, in general; I am called upon to say something concerning certain tribes, who from their inferiority of rank, and the contempt in which they are held, are considered as a separate race, cut off from the great family of society. The best known and the most numerous of these is the tribe of the *Pareiyar*, as they are called in the Tamil tongue, from which is corrupted the European term *Pariah.*[m] The caste is found every where, and I compute that it must include at least a fifth of the whole population of the peninsula. It is divided, like the other subordinate tribes, into several classes, each of which disputes with the rest for superiority; but they are all held in equal contempt by the generality of the other classes.

What I have to report concerning this caste will form a decided contrast with what I have remarked relative to the Brâhmans, and will afford an additional proof of what I have so often repeated, that the Hindûs are unable, under any circumstances, to preserve a middle course. It will be now shewn that they are not less vehement in the contempt and distance with which they treat the persons here alluded to, than in the honours which they accumulate on such of them as are elevated above the rest, by having acquired a sacred character.

In all districts of the peninsula, the Pariahs are entirely subjected to the other castes, and rigorously treated by them all. In general, they even have not permission to cultivate the ground for their own use, but are compelled to hire themselves to other castes; for whom, for a small allowance, they are obliged to undergo the most severe labours, and to submit to be beaten at pleasure; and, in truth, the Pariahs of India are not to be considered in any other light than as the born slaves of the other tribes. At least there is as great a distance between them and the other castes as subsists in our colonies between the planters and their slaves. These lead not a harder life than the Pariahs, and the usage of both is equally severe.

The distance and aversion which the other castes, and the Brâhmans in particular, manifest for the Pariahs are carried so far that, in many places, their very approach is sufficient to pollute the whole neighbourhood. They are not permitted to enter the street

---

[m] *Parrai* is a drum. Their office is to beat the drum on festival occasions. In Telugu they are called *mâlars* (out-castes,) in Canarese *Poleyaru* (polluted ones) and *Puliar* (polluted persons) in Malayâlam.

Compare app. I. in Dr. Caldwell's Dravidian Grammar.

where the Brâhmans live. If they venture to transgress, those superior beings would have the right, not to assault them themselves, because it would be pollution to touch them even with the end of a long pole, but they would be entitled to give them a sound beating by the hands of others; or even to make an end of them, which has often happened, by the orders of the native Princes, without dispute or inquiry.

He who is touched, even without being conscious of it, by a Pariah, is defiled, and cannot be purified from the stain, or communicate with any individual, without undergoing a variety of ceremonies, more or less difficult according to the rank of the individual and the custom of the caste to which he belongs.

Any person who, from whatever accident, has eaten with Pariahs, or of food provided by them; or even drank of the water which they have drawn, or which was contained in earthen vessels which they had handled; any one who has set his foot in their houses or permitted them to enter his own, would be proscribed, without pity, from his caste, and would never be restored without a number of troublesome ceremonies and great expence.

This extreme detestation of the Pariahs by other castes, is not carried to the same extent in all districts. It prevails chiefly in the southern parts of the peninsula, and becomes less apparent in the north. In that quarter of the Mysore, where I am now writing these pages, the higher castes endure the approach of the Pariahs; for they suffer them to enter that part of the house which shelters the cows; and in some cases they have been permitted to shew their head, and one foot, in the apartment of the master of the house. I have been informed that this wide distinction between these castes becomes less apparent as you go northward, till at last it almost totally disappears.

But the distinction itself appears to be of very old standing, being particularly referred to in several of the ancient Purâṇas. The distance, however, which exists between the Pariahs and the other tribes does not appear to have been so great, at the first, as it is at present. Although the lowest of the castes, it is ranked, nevertheless, with that of the Ŝûdras; and they are considered to have derived their origin from the same source. Even at the present time, they pass for the descendants of the first caste among the Cultivators; who do not disdain to call them their children. But we must also observe, that if the better class of the Ŝûdras considers the Pariahs to be sprung from the same stock with themselves, and represents them, in speculation, as their children, they are very far from reducing their theory to practice. In no instance, indeed, can the Hindûs have shewn a wider difference between their professions and practice.[a]

[a] "The class with which Europeans have generally had most to do is that of the *Pariahs*. While the *Ŝûdras* have in a great degree taken to themselves the position and duties of the *Vaiŝyas* (p. 1), the *Pariahs* in turn have come to occupy the place assigned by Manu to the Ŝûdras. In one respect indeed their status is higher, inasmuch as they are not now slaves to any class. Although belonging to the lowest *class*, they have their own civil rights and honours. Their title of honour is 'Peṭṭa pillai' (Child of the house.) This title indicates indeed a tenderer relation between them and the higher castes than

The European inhabitants are under the necessity of employing Pariahs for servants, because a great part of their work could not be done by persons of any other caste. There is, for example, no member of a Sûdra tribe that would submit to brush the shoes of his master, or to draw off his boots to clean them; but far less could any such person be induced, by any reward, to be his cook; because the Europeans make no secret of violating the prejudices of the people amongst whom they live, by commanding beef to be prepared for their tables. They have no other choice, therefore, but to make use of the unscrupulous Pariah in that department of their household. And it may well be imagined, that if Europeans are detested by the superstitious Hindûs, on account of the nature of their food, this sentiment will not be weakened by considering what degraded beings are necessarily employed in preparing it. For the prejudices of the country will not permit that any one but a Pariah shall eat what has been dressed by a Pariah.

It cannot be questioned that the admitting Pariahs into their menial service, gives offence to the Hindûs, and prevents persons of other castes, from serving them in that capacity.

Another consideration, which creates a dislike to serve Europeans, is the great distance at which they keep their domestics, and the indignities and bad treatment which they frequently make them submit to, but above all the kick of a foot covered with the pollution of a leathern shoe or a boot.

The Pariahs, who are accustomed to servile treatment from their infancy, patiently endure all these indignities; but it is far otherwise with the other castes, who are by nature high-spirited and proud. Besides, the condition of a servant in India is by no means degrading. The footman eats with his master, the maid-servant with her mistress,

---

really exists. Eighteen marks of honour are claimed by the Pariahs, which they can claim and make a parade of on festal occasions, when their means permit and inclination prompts. These are, a white umbrella, a white fan, garlands of flowers suspended across the roads, garments spread in the way, a white horse, or elephant, a palanquin, &c., &c.

The Pariahs are divided into thirteen principal classes, of which the *Vaḷḷuvar* are the most respected. They are the *Gurus* and priests of the class, and are the more respected because tradition assigns to this subdivision of the class, the foster-father of the monarchs of the realm of song, who 'as an eagle outsoars all in his flight,' TIRUVAḶḶUVAR.

They are often Physicians, and some of them enjoy such a reputation that Sûdras often resort to them and allow them to feel their pulse, but always through a thin silken covering.

Among the lowest of these subdivisions is the *Vettyân*. To him belongs the occupation of burning the bodies of the dead, performing the duties of watchman and conveying the intelligence of deaths. The whole community permits him for these general Services to occupy a piece of land without payment of rent, besides allowing him a certain share of the annual produce of the village lands.

Alas ! there are also many pariahs, frequently in consequence of slighter offences, in a state resembling slavery and altogether dependant on a master.

From this springs much trouble and distress to all, but those who become christians.

Yet almost more mournful is the condition, in many respects, of those who must support themselves by kûli work of various kinds. The former obtain a certain, though meagre subsistence, and the most inhuman master is compelled by a sense of his own interest to care for them as for a costly kind of cattle.

and they all go on side by side, in the intercourse of life. The conduct of the European settlers being so opposite in this respect, it is no wonder that their service should be held in dislike by all persons of decent sentiments and habits, and be left entirely to the refuse of all castes.

But, if the caste of the Pariahs be held in low and vile repute, it must be admitted that it deserves to be so, by the conduct of the individuals, and the sort of life which they lead. The most of them sell themselves, with their wives and children, for slaves to the farmers; who make them undergo the hardest labours of agriculture, and treat them with the utmost severity. They are likewise the scavengers of the villages, their business being to keep the thoroughfares clean, and to remove all the filth as it collects in the houses. Yet these, notwithstanding the meanness of their employment, are generally better treated than the others; because there is superadded to the disgusting employment we have mentioned the cleanlier duty of distributing the waters of the tanks and canals for irrigating the rice plantations of the inhabitants of the village; who, for that reason, cannot avoid feeling some kindness in their behalf.

Some of them, who do not live in this state of servitude, are employed to take care of the horses of individuals, or of the army, or of elephants and oxen. They are also the porters, and run upon errands and messages. In some parts they are permitted to cultivate the lands, for their own benefit; and in others they can exercise the profession of weavers. Of late, they have occasionally been admitted into the European armies, and those of the native Princes, in which they have sometimes attained considerable distinction. In point of courage, they are not inferior to any other Hindû caste.

The vices of the Pariahs lean to sensuality, as those of the Brâh-

---

These latter must often endure the sharp pangs of hunger or appease them with the flesh of crows or squirrels, or even carrion.

And when they earn some small sum so great is the weariness that their hard labours and the uncertainty of their subsistence induces that they hasten to avail themselves of the earliest opportunity to drink away their little earnings and their understanding at the same time.

A third class contrives to push its way along in service to Europeans performing the offices of cook, horse-keeper, gardener and so on. These get on for the most part very well, since they are not hindered by any caste rules from eating the food left by their masters or even making use of his stores. It is true that the Pariahs who come thus into contact with Europeans, seem cleaner, more polite, more cultivated and more awake than the others of their tribe, but this is, with few exceptions, all. The desire of drink is encouraged by their intercourse with Europeans and their skill in deception is rendered more refined. They learn to detect and to conceal European wants, weaknesses and vices, and since their wages will not permit them to indulge in similar pleasures honestly, all this acts as a spur to make them go on in dishonest practices.

Some of them even begin to assume the European dress. When in Madras I received an invitation from one of them, requesting the presence of the "honoured Sir," at a wedding and musical entertainment. Some ill-judging Europeans, confounding European manners with European Christianity rejoice in this. It is, however, to be deeply lamented."

From Dr. Graul's Reise. Theil IV. 190, 191.

mans do to knavery. There is a coarseness about them which excites abhorrence. They are exceedingly addicted to drunkenness. The liquor which they most enjoy is the juice of the palm, which they commonly drink when in a state of fermentation; and, though it then stinks abominably, they seem to take it for nectar.

Besides the caste of Pariahs, which is spread over all the provinces of the peninsula, there are some others, peculiar to certain districts, which equal, or even surpass it, in brutality of sentiment, irregularity of life, and also in the abhorrence in which they are held. Such is the caste of the *Paḷḷar*, which is little known but in the kingdom of Madura and other parts bordering on Cape Comorin. They boast a superiority over the Pariahs, because they do not eat the flesh of the cow or ox; but the Pariahs hold them to be far beneath themselves, as belonging to the *left-hand*, of which they are the dregs; whilst they themselves pertain to the *right-hand*, of which they account themselves the firmest support. The history of the *two hands* we have already given; and we failed not to commemorate the effectual aid which the Pariahs are accustomed to lend in turning the tide of battle against the heresy of the *left-hand*.[o]

In the mountainous tract of the Malabar Coast there is to be seen a caste still more low and depressed than any we have yet mentioned. They are called *Puliars;* who are considered to be far beneath the beasts who traverse their forests, and equally share the dominion in them. It is not permitted to them to erect a house, but only a sort of shed, supported on four bamboos, and open on all sides. It shelters them from the rain, but not from the injuries of the weather. They dare not walk on the common road, as their steps would defile it. When they see any person coming at a distance, they must give him notice, by a loud cry, and make a great circuit to let him pass. The least distance they are permitted to keep from persons of a different caste, is about a hundred paces.[p]

In all the provinces of the peninsula, the caste of the (Chakkili) *Shoemakers* is held to be very infamous, and as below the Pariahs. They are inferior to them, from the baseness of their sentiments, and the total want of honour and of all feeling of shame. Their manners are also more gross, and they are more addicted to gluttony and intemperance. They get merry towards the evenings; and it is not long before the villages resound with the cries and quarrels occasioned by their cups. They are all wretchedly poor. These, though rarely, enjoy a temporary abundance, but the wretched *Chakili*, or coblers, exist in absolute indigence. But they can the less complain, as their misery arises chiefly out of their ebriety; a privilege which is nearly peculiar to themselves. They will never work while they have any thing to drink, and they never return to their work till their purse is exhausted; passing in this manner, alternately from labour to drunk-

o They derive their name from *Paḷ* = hollow, because their occupation is digging. They are in a certain way slaves to the cultivators, though many of them are weavers.

p These are the *pariahs* of the western coast. *Pulei* = defilement.

enness, and from drunkenness to labour. Their women do not allow themselves to be surpassed by their husbands in any vicious habit, and particularly in that of intemperance. And nothing more need be said of their morals or behaviour.

Among the Pariahs, there is one sort greatly elevated above the rest; with whom they form no alliance, but consider themselves as their Gurus or *Valluvers*, as they are called. They are likewise named in derision, the *Brâhmans of the Pariahs;* in allusion, no doubt, to their conducting the marriage-rites and other ceremonies of that people. They likewise publish a part of the lies contained in the almanac; such as the good and evil days, the favourable and unfavourable moments for commencing an enterprize; and other follies. But they are not allowed to be editors of the astronomical part of the publication, relating to the eclipses, new and full moon, and such important matters; which entirely belong to the Brâhmans.

Besides those low and despised sects, there are many others, which though greatly above them, are still regarded with contempt by the generality of Hindûs, and held to occupy the lowest rank of all the kinds of Sûdras. These tribes have sunk in the public opinion by living in a sort of vassalage beneath the other castes, or by exercising trades which frequently expose them to pollution; or, in many instances, because they lead a wandering and roving life, which involves them in frequent breaches of the most revered and established customs.

Of the vulgar castes, two of the lowest are the *Barbers* and the *Washermen.* One or more families belonging to each of these castes, exercise their respective trades in every village; from which they must not pass into a neighbouring village to work, without leave. These two trades descend from father to son, from one generation to another; and those who exercise them form two distinct tribes. The Barber is obliged to shave and to cut the hair and nails of all the inhabitants of the village. In many districts, the custom is to be shaved in every part of the body where hair grows; and this custom is very generally observed, particularly by the Brâhmans, on their marriage day and other solemn occasions.[q]

As to the Washerman, he is bound to wash not only all the clothing which men and women wear, but also the filthiest rags that have been used in keeping the children in decent order, or even for more disgusting purposes. These two professions reduce those that practise them to a state of dependence, which does not admit of their declining to do any thing at all connected with their trade. They are paid by the inhabitants, in kind, once a year, after the grain is got in. Their

---

[q] The barbers or Ambattar (Corr. of S. *ambasht'ha*) practice their art, while their women are generally midwives. Their daughters are often temple-girls and their sons musicans to the temple, and thus the whole caste occupies a somewhat lower position in the social scale than it otherwise would. Graul.

The barber of the East is the barber-surgeon of the olden times in the west; and the same chatty, news-loving, gossipping disposition characterizes the brethren of the craft in Asia as in Europe.

servile condition, and the filthy nature of their employment, naturally produce the general contempt in which they are held by all the castes, who look upon them almost as their slaves.[r]

The caste of *Ottar*,[s] whose principal employment consists in building walls of earth, digging tanks, and keeping their banks in repair, are likewise considered as low tribes, by the Śûdras. The education of these people corresponds to the meanness of their origin. Their mind is as uncultivated as their manners; and every thing seems to justify the small esteem in which they are held.

The tribe of *Mochiyar*,[t] or workers in the skins of animals, used in dress, though not so much despised as the preceding, yet possess no degree of consideration. They are not admitted, by the other castes, into any familiarity, or to eat or drink out of the same vessels with them. This is accounted for by the filth they are exposed to in handling the skins.

The other working castes, such as carpenters, blacksmiths, goldsmiths, founders, and in general all who exercise handicraft trades enjoy no great degree of consideration among the other castes of the Śûdras.

The ornamental arts, such as painting, instrumental music, and the like, are extremely low in estimation. Hardly any but the low tribe of the Mochis exercise the first of these; and music is nearly confined to the Barbers and Pariahs: instrumental music wholly so. The small encouragement these two arts receive is, no doubt, owing to the little progress they have made. In painting, nothing can be seen but mere daubing, set off with bright colours and extravagant glare. And, although all Hindûs are great lovers of music, introducing it into all their civil and religious ceremonies, yet I can vouch that it is still in its infancy; and probably they have made no progress in it for three thousand years. In their festivals, and on other occasions; it is not the concord of sweet sounds that they require from their musicians. Confusion and obstreperous noise is more agreeable to their untutored senses, with sounds so harsh and piercing as would almost rend the drum of an European ear. And it must be owned that their taste in this respect is fully gratified by their performers.

But, harsh and discordant as their music is, it pleases them infinitely more than ours. This I have often experienced. Of our instruments they love only the drum. The sound of our sweetest

---

r Among the Vaṇṇar, or washermen, there are found many who have embraced Christianity. Eash caste has its own washermen, and any who should venture to wash for a lower caste, would of necessity lose all employment in his own caste. Graul.

Vaṇṇar is from Veḷ, veṇ, or Vaṇ = white. The Hind. is *Dhobi*.

s The Ottar (from S. OD'HRA = Orissa, because they come from that district) speak a mixed dialect, work very hard. and take their meals together with their wives. They leave a conical pile of earth in the centre of their excavations to measure the depth to which they have dug.

t From the Hind. *Mochi* = a worker in leather. This name is given now to those who repair saddlery, to painters, gilders and ornamental workers. In courts the *Mochi* is the man who makes pens and ink, provides paper, seals letters, &c.

instruments, producing a melody which soothes and delights our perceptions, and excites the most pleasant emotions, has no effect whatever on ears so perpetually stunned with loud and jarring dissonance.

Their vocal music is almost as little adapted to delight an European ear. An insipid monotony pervades their singing; and, although they have a gamut, composed of seven notes, like ours, they have never applied it to create the diversity, proportion, and combination which have so many charms for us.

The contempt in which players on wind instruments are held, I believe, arises chiefly from the defilement which is supposed to be contracted by applying the mouth to apertures so often polluted with spittle. Stringed instruments being free from this objection, the highest castes, even the Brâhmans themselves, do not disdain to make an accompaniment to their own voices, by touching a small harp called *Vîṇâ*, which is used all over India. Its notes are so far from lacerating the ear, like those of their wind instruments, that, on the contrary, they may be listened to with pleasure by an European; though they would give greater pleasure if they were more diversified. The Brâhmans almost exclusively practise on this instrument.

The use of the Vîṇâ is very ancient among the Hindûs. Its name is mentioned in almost all their early writings, as an instrument in favour with the great. Brâhmans, Kings, Princes, and the Gods themselves, learn to strike it; and many of them are extolled for their proficiency.

It appears to me very probable that the Vîṇâ of the Brâhmans is the same as the Kithara, or the Hebrew Harp, so often mentioned in the sacred writings; on which the holy King David so much excelled, and from which he drew sounds that could tame the fury of his unfortunate master Saul, when forsaken of God and agitated by all the passions.

The Harp appears to have been the instrument of the upper ranks amongst the Hebrews, as the Vîṇâ is amongst the Hindûs. We have observed that the Brâhmans alone are proficients on this instrument; but truly they pay dear for the distinction, and their time of probation is very tedious. It is a great deal if the scholar is able to play the two and thirty Hindû airs after four or five years of practice.

Besides the Vîṇâ, they have a stringed instrument called Kinnara a sort of guitar, which is also in great esteem.

The strings of their instruments are never made, as ours often are, of the guts of animals, but always of metal wires. The purity of the Brâhman could not possibly finger the catgut.

A second description of men of degraded rank, in the eyes of the Hindûs, consists of those who are addicted to a vagrant and wandering life, which leads them into a continual violation of the received practices, and makes them suspected characters. There are several castes of this sort, who have no permanent abode, but are in continual migration. Such are the *Kuravers*, the *Lambady*, and many others; some of whom we shall briefly point out.

The vagrants called Kuravers are divided into three branches.

One of these is chiefly engaged in the traffic of Salt, which they go, in bands, to the coasts to procure, and carry it to the interior of the country on the backs of asses, which they have in great droves; and when they have disposed of their cargoes, they reload the beasts with the sort of grain in greatest request on the coast; to which they return without loss of time. Thus their whole lives are passed in transit, without a place of settlement in any part of the land.

The trade of another branch of the Kuravers is the manufacture of osier panniers, wicker baskets and other household utensils of that sort, or bamboo mats. This class, like the preceding, are compelled to traverse the whole country, from place to place, in quest of employment. All of them live under little tents, constructed of woven bamboos, three feet high, four or five broad, and five or six in length; in which they squat, man, wife, and children, and shelter themselves from the weather. When they find no more work in the district, they fold up their tents and remove to the next population.[u]

---

[u] The name *Kuraver* belongs originally to all the hill tribes.

It is from the tamil *Kunru* — a hill. The 3rd part of the Tamil grammar allots to them three occupations :

(1.) The preparation of intoxicating liquors ; (2) the sale of Hinnah ; (3) the watching the young plants of millet ; (4) the collecting red honey ; (5) the digging up roots ; (6) the bathing in water-falls and springs. The present race of Kuraver, who wander over every part of the country, are employed as follows :—

They make baskets of bambû or from the pliant twigs of the icchu (Phœnix farinifera ;) they manufacture small boxes of palmyra leaves, mats and sieves of split bambûs ; they catch birds and hunt for tortoises ; they breed pigs and asses ; teach snakes to dance ; pierce the ears of little girls for the insertion of jewels and tatoo marks on the body. Their women practise fortune-telling and the men conjuring. These latter moreover manufacture thread of steel, copper and iron : some of them beg.

To wander over the country is their universal occupation. They build themselves huts wherever they find a convenient spot, and by any employment reputable or disreputable, by begging or stealing they obtain food to eat. When this fails they pull down their huts and wander onward.

They bury their dead by night, no one knows where. Thence originates the common saying, in regard to anything which has vanished, leaving no trace behind : "It has gone to the burial place of the Kuraver, and to the dancing room of the wandering actors." Another Proverb is : Kurangu piṉamum kurravan çuḍu kâdum kaṇḍadillai : *no one has seen a monkey's dead body, or the Kuravan's burning ground.*

It is no wonder that, such being their mode of life from their childhood, the Kuraver should be a rough and uncouth race.

In some divisions of this people, (who have moreover the bye-rule that no one shall engage in the same employment as his neighbour) they do not scruple to pawn their wives for debt. If the wife who is in pledge dies a natural death the debt is discharged. If she should die from hard usage the creditor must not only cancel the debt but must defray the expenses of a second marriage for his debtor. If the woman lives till the debt is discharged and if she has children by the creditor, the boys remain with him, the girls go back with her to the husband.

When family quarrels arise the relatives form a court of arbitration. Plaintiff and defendant deposit 5 fanams (about 2 shillings) each, and a quantity of intoxicating drink, for "with dry mouth nothing can be uttered," and while the liquor is consumed the process goes on. This protracts their disputes, and "a Kuraver's quarrel," is something equivalent to "a Chancery suit" among ourselves. See Graul. IV, p. 186.

There is a proverb in Tamil: "Kurra vaṟakkum, Iḍai vaṟakkum, Konjattil tîrâdu," *a Kuravan's quarrel and a Idaiyan's quarrel are not easily decided.*

Their name indicates a connection with the Kholes, or hill tribes of Hindûstân.

These vagabonds never think of saving any thing for future wants, but spend every day all they earn, and sometimes more. They must therefore live in grievous poverty; and, when their work fails them, they have no resource but in begging alms.

The third species of Kuravers is generally known under the name of *Kaḷḷa-Bantru*, or Robbers; and indeed those who compose this caste are generally thieves or sharpers, by profession and right of birth. The distinction of expertness in filching belongs to this tribe; the individuals of which it consists having been trained to knavery from their infancy. They are instructed in no other learning, and the only art they communicate to their children is that of stealing adroitly; unless we except that of being prepared with a round lie, and with a determined resolution to endure every sort of torture rather than to confess the robberies which are laid to their charge.

Far from being ashamed of their infamous profession, they openly glory in it; and when they have nothing to fear, they publicly boast, with the greatest self-complacency, of the dextrous robberies they have committed, at various times, during their career. Some who have been caught and wounded in the act, or have had their nose and ears, or perhaps their hand, cut off for the offence, exhibit their loss with ostentation, as a mark of their intrepidity; and these are the men who are generally chosen to be the chiefs of the caste.

It is commonly in the dead of the night that they commit their depredations. Then they enter the villages silently, leaving sentinels at the avenues, while others seek out the houses that may be attacked with the least danger of detection, and so make good their entry and pillage them. This they effect, without attempting to force open the door, which would be a noisy operation; but by quietly cutting through the mud wall with a sharp instrument, so as to make an opening sufficiently large to pass through. The Kaḷḷabantru are so expert in this species of robbery, that, in less than half an hour, they will carry off a rich lading of plunder, without being heard or suspected till day-light discloses the villainy.

The Muhammedan Princes have always in their service a great number of Kaḷḷabantru, whom they employ in their calling; which is that of plundering for their master's profit. The last Musalman Prince who reigned in the Mysore had a regular battalion of them on service, in time of war; not for the purpose of fighting in the field, but to prowl and infest the enemy's camp in the night, stealing away the horses and other necessaries of the officers, spiking the cannon, and acting as spies. They were rewarded in proportion to the dexterity they displayed in these achievements; and in time of peace they were dispatched into the various states of neighbouring Princes, to rob, for the benefit of their master; besides discharging their ordinary duty of spies.

The Polygars,* who are chiefs of particular districts, have in their

* Pâḷayam—kârar — *camp-men.*

pay several of these rascals, who are sent from place to place to steal, or to do any other similar service, in the manner of the Kaḷḷabantru.

In the provinces where they are tolerated by the Government, the poor inhabitants, having no other means of escaping from pillage, pay them a yearly subsidy of a quarter of a rupee and a fowl for each house; the chief of the gang agreeing to take them under his protection, and to be answerable for every robbery that shall be committed.

The caste of Kaḷḷabantru is spread over all the Mysore; where they are also infested with another sort, under the name of *Kanôji*, who are equally formidable.

But, of all the vagrant castes, the best known, and also the most detested, is that of the *Lambâḍis*. Their origin is not well understood, as they are different in manners, customs, and language, from all the other castes of Hindûs. They appear to have more affinity with the Mahrattas than any other nation; and, I believe, it is from that marauding race that we must trace their descent. It is certain that it is in their armies that they are trained to that course of pillage and rapine which has obliterated all notions of property, when they feel themselves the strongest, or when they are out of the reach of jûstice. At the same time, the exemplary punishments which the police has inflicted on them in several places, of late, has made them somewhat more circumspect, and they no longer dare to plunder openly. But, woe to the traveller whom they meet alone in a solitary place, especially if they think him a prize.

Their rendezvous, in times of war, is with some army; and generally with the most undisciplined one, about which they swarm in great crowds, to take advantage of the disorder and confusion which they expect to find, and which serve as a cloak to their depredations. They make themselves useful by supplying the markets with provisions, which they have foraged in all quarters. And they also make a trade of lending out to the side that will best pay them their numerous herds of bullocks to carry necessaries for the supply of the armies. It was thus that, in the last war with the Sultan of the Mysore, the English took into their pay many thousands of them for transporting their provisions. However, they had soon reason to repent their connection with such faithless wretches, devoid of all honour and discipline, when they saw them laying waste the country over which they passed, and causing more damage than the whole army of the enemy would have done. The frequent punishments inflicted on their chiefs had no effect on that horde of robbers, whom the scent of plunder allured more powerfully than even their extravagant perquisites and hire.

In times of peace, these banditti return to their trade in corn, which they carry from one place to another. Their rude and uncultivated manners, with their coarse and deformed features, both in the men and the women, at once betray the character and disposition of their minds. In all parts of India they have justly become the objects of the watchfulness and suspicion of the police; for, in no circumstances, can any reliance be placed on them.

Their women are every where held to be most dissolute.

The Lambâḍis form a caste entirely distinct from the rest of the Hindûs, with whom they have but very little intercourse; being wholly different from them in religion, language, manners, and customs. All other castes treat them with distant and thorough contempt.[w]

There is yet another tribe of vagrants, who are also a separate sect, and live universally despised. They are the class of mountebanks, buffoons, posture-makers, tumblers, dancers, and the like; who form various parties, to exhibit their several arts and tricks, in all places where admirers and dupes are to be found. The most dissolute body is that of the *Dombar*. It is not surprizing that, in a country where the love of all that approaches to the marvellous reigns with unbounded sway, such sorts of jugglers should prevail. Nevertheless, the castes who follow these professions are vilified, and universally looked down upon, though the practitioners are, at the same time, considered as expert magicians, initiated in all occult and necromantic arts, who are to be feared as well as distrusted. They may be compared, indeed, to the mountebank order in Europe; but they are more universally and cordially despised. Yet I have seen them perform tricks and feats which put them at least on a level with their brethren in Europe.[x]

The most usual exhibition is that of the keepers of serpents, who have them taught to dance to the sound of a kind of flute. They perform various tricks with them; which, though apparently terrible, are not very dangerous, as they always take the precaution to deprive them of their fangs, and to extract the vesicle in which the venom is contained. They are believed to have the power of charming those dangerous reptiles, and of commanding them to approach and surrender themselves, at the sound of their flute. The same art appears to have been laid claim to in other ancient nations, as appears from the allegory of the prophet, where he compares the obstinacy of an obdurate sinner to a serpent that shuts its ear against the voice of the charmer. (Jer. viii. 17.) Without dwelling on the literal accuracy of this striking passage of Holy Writ, I may confidently assert, that the skill which the pretenders to enchantment, in India, claim in this particular, is rank imposture. The trick is to put a snake, which they had tamed and accustomed to their music, into some remote place, and they manage it so, that, in appearing to go casually in that direction, and beginning to play, the snake comes forward at the accustomed sound. When they enter into an agreement with any simpleton, who fancies that his house is infested with serpents, a notion which they sometimes

---

w The word is found in all the dialects of India. They are also called Banjâris [= traders.] They are a very mixed and anomalous race.

x They are an aboriginal race called sometimes Doms.

contrive to infuse into his brain, they artfully introduce into some crevice of the house one of their tame snakes, which comes up to its master, as soon as it hears his flute. The potent enchanter instantly whips it up into his pannier, takes his fee, and gravely presents himself at the next house, to renew his offers of assistance to similar dupes.

Another race of vagrants live at the public expence, by exhibiting a kind of comedies, or rather farces, of the indecent kind both in the characters and the dialogue. They likewise exhibit puppet shews, mixed with gross obscenity and absurdity, but well adapted to the stupid multitude that gaze and admire. They know they could not gain the attention, far less the laugh of such people, without sacrificing decency, modesty, and common sense.

In the Mysore and the Telugu country, there is another distinct caste of wanderers, more peaceable and innocent than any of the former. They are called *Pakanaty*,[y] and speak the Telugu. They were originally natives of that country, and were employed in agriculture. They belonged to the tribe of Gôlaru or shepherds. It is now a hundred and fifty years since they first took up their present vagrant and wandering life; to which they are grown so much accustomed, that it would be impossible to reclaim them to any fixed or sedentary habits. The cause of their detaching themselves originally from society arose from some severe treatment which the governor of the province where they lived was going to inflict upon some of their favourite chiefs. To avert this insult, and to be revenged against their rulers, they took the resolution of quitting their villages and abandoning their agricultural labours; and they have never since entertained a thought of resuming their ancient course of life. They sojourn in the open fields, under small tents of bamboo, and wander from place to place, as humour dictates.

Some of their chiefs, with whom I have conversed, have informed me, that they amount in all to seven or eight thousand individuals. Part wander in the Telugu country and part in Kanara. They are divided into different tribes, the heads of which assemble, from time to time, to decide any disputes that may have arisen, and to watch over the general good order of the caste. They are under an exceedingly good police; and, though always roving in bands through the country, they maintain a great respect for property, and no instance of pillage is ever heard of among them.

They all live in the most wretched condition. The wealthiest among them have nothing beyond a few buffaloes or cows, whose milk they sell. They are mostly all herbarists; and wherever they roam, they are careful to collect the various plants and roots which serve for medical purposes, or which are used in dying, or as physic for horses and cows. They sell these simples to the dealers in spices; and by this traffic they partly maintain themselves, and make up for what is wanting by hunting, fishing, or begging.

---

[y] *Pakkaṇa* = an abode of fowlers and outcastes. *Pakka* is a corruption of *Pakshi*, a bird.

Among the vices which are the reproach of the various wandering tribes, intemperance, and the want of delicacy in the choice of food, are chiefly complained of; and these are, at the same time, the most odious and degrading of any, in the eyes of the other castes. Drunkenness pervades them all; the material of which is the Toddy, or juice of the palm; to which men and women are equally addicted.

As to food, every thing is alike to them; and, with the exception of the flesh of the cow, they put up with any other sort of victuals, however offensive. Tiger's flesh, that of the fox, the cat, the crocodile, the serpent, lizard, crow, and of many other creatures, equally revolting to the generality of Hindûs, constitute the principal nourishment of all the different wandering hordes we have described.

Each caste of vagrants forms a little republic in itself, governed by its own laws and usages. They have but little to do with social duties, or even with authority. Wandering continually from place to place, they pay no tribute; and, being scarcely possessed of any thing, they have no occasion for the protection of the Prince to enable them to live unmolested: neither do they importune the magistrate for justice or favour. Each little community has chiefs of its own, elected or deposed by a majority of voices; and who, as long as their authority continues, are invested with power to enforce their rules, to inflict punishment and fines on those who violate them, and to terminate all disputes that arise.

The whole of these wanderers, in going from place to place, take with them not only their wicker tents and all their goods, which indeed are no great matter, but also the provisions necessary for their subsistence during several days, and the utensils requisite for preparing and cooking their food. When they have beasts of burden, they load them with part of their furniture; but, when without that accommodation, they are sometimes in great straits. I have frequently seen poor creatures, of this kind, carrying on their heads and shoulders every thing they possessed in the world, with what was necessary for their present subsistence. The husband took the burden of the tent, the provisions, and some earthen vessels for boiling them; while the wife, with half of her body left bare, in order to spare a part of her garment to wrap the child that dangled at her back, carried on her head the little millstone which they use for grinding the corn that makes a part of their food, and held, under one arm, the pestle for pounding the rice, and the mortar under the other. Such is the touching spectacle I have often seen, with feelings of tender sympathy and compassion; and such is the kind of existence that thousands of Hindûs are doomed to abide; and which they endure without a murmur, and without envying those who enjoy the real blessings of life. And never does it come into their thoughts to improve their condition, by entering into the bosom of society, and engaging in some employment more reputable and easy.

There are still a great many other detached castes in the southern parts of India besides those we have mentioned; all living in a state of degradation and contempt. Amongst others, there is that of the *Kurumbars.* The baseness of their nature and their total want of instruction seem to justify the detestation in which they are held by the superior castes of Ŝûdras. Their occupation is that of Shepherds; but they are not to be confounded with the caste of Herdsmen called *Iḍaiyar* and Gôlam,[z] who are one of the highest castes among the Ŝûdras, and have the cows and goats under their care, while the others are confined entirely to sheep, of which they have considerable flocks. The meanness of their employment seems to spread its influence over their manners. Being confined to the society of their woolly charge, they seem to have contracted the stupid nature of the animal; and, from the rudeness of their nature, they are as much beneath the other castes of Hindûs, as the sheep, by their simplicity and imperfect instinct, are beneath the other quadrupeds. The stupidity of the Kurumbar is become proverbial; and when a person of another caste does any thing thoughtless and foolish, he is said to be as stupid as a Kurumban. This sect prevails in the Telugu, Kanarese, and Tamil countries, but chiefly in the first, from which it appears to have originated, and where they are still found in great numbers in every district.[a]

---

z The *Iḍaiyar* are so called from *Idai*, the middle, being a kind of intermediate link between the farmers and the merchants.

They are divided into eight principal divisions, and each of these is subdivided into eighteen branches. Among these eighteen there is one only which associates familiarly with the seventeen above it, the so called, "Branch of charitable works."

When a bride of the Idaiyar caste enters the room decorated for the ceremonies of marriage, her followers must pay to the sister of the bridegroom the money called the "Bride's room gold," and the relations of both parties must see that this praiseworthy custom is adhered to. When the bridegroom betakes himself to the house of the Mother-in-law, his young companions arrest him by the way, and do not release him till he has paid them a piece of gold. On the third day when the favorite amusement of sprinkling saffron water on the guests in sport is over, the whole party betake themselves to the village tank. The friend of the bridegroom brings a hoe and a basket and the young husband fills three baskets with earth from the bottom of the tank, while the wife takes them away and throws the earth behind. They then say "we have dug a ditch for charity." This singular practice probably may be explained by remembering that in the arid districts where these Idaiyar often tend their cattle, the tank is of the greatest importance. So it is, indeed, with many customs which obtain in India which Europeans think so senseless and which good men oppose with perhaps unnecessary earnestness. Many of these customs are by no means the immediate fruit of Heathenism; very many of them have had a natural origin, and the key to them is now and then to be found.

In their funeral ceremonies too there are many interesting and peculiar observances. Among other things, a man of the *Marraver* caste, a slave, who styles himself "the father of the Grandfather," comes into the assembly and addresses them in enigmatical and mysterious language: "the slave, who intrudes himself of his own accord, spreads his foot over the way, and will thrust a spear into the breast of the strong." These Marraver are with few exceptions plunderers by profession and are employed, therefore, as watchers and policemen. This ceremony seems to indicate an agreement between the Idaiyar and Marraver, for the protection of their flocks. See Graul's reise nach Ostindien IV, 175.

a *Kurrumban* is probably a word allied to Kurravan and means mountaineer. But it is generally derived from *Kurru* small, they being very diminutive in stature.

They are found on the middle slopes of the Nîlagiris, between the *Baḍagar* above on the table land, and the *Iruḷar*, below at the foot of the hills. They speak a purer dialect of Canarese than the Baḍagar. They are regarded with intense fear and dislike by the other hill tribes, and are supposed to be malignant sorcerers.

I have already mentioned the castes of *Savages* met with in the forests and on the mountains of the southern parts of the peninsula. They are divided into various tribes, each of which is subdivided into separate hordes. They seldom quit their haunts, and are not often visited there, on account of the dread they are held in as reputed sorcerers or magicians, whose malice would occasion disease or misfortune. And, indeed, when any of the neighbouring castes are affected with any calamity which they suspect to have proceeded from their machinations, they fall upon them with severity, and sometimes revenge themselves by their death.

Many of these savages spare themselves the trouble of building houses; although, by living in the midst of a wood, they might have abundant materials. In the rainy season, they shelter themselves in caverns, hollow trees, and clefts of the rocks; and, in fine weather, they keep the open fields. In the night, every horde collects in a body; and each lights large fires, all around, to keep them warm and to scare the wild beasts, while they sleep in the centre, in a promiscuous heap. They are almost entirely naked. The women wear nothing to conceal their nakedness but some leaves of trees stitched together, and bound round their waists.

They think it too great a hardship to perform agricultural labour; and therefore they never engage in it but when urged by extreme necessity. Knowing nothing beyond the absolute demands of hunger, they find enough in their forests to assuage it. Roots and other spontaneous productions of nature; reptiles, and animals which they entrap in snares or kill in the chace; and honey, which they find in abundance within the chinks of the rocks, or on the trees, among the branches of which they skip with the agility of monkeys, afford all that is necessary to appease the cravings of nature.

More stupid than the African savage, he of India is ignorant even of the use of the bow.

The inhabitants of the plains apply to them, when they have occasion for timber for building their houses, or for any other works of magnitude; and, for a matter of small value, such as some copper rings, a few glass beads, or a little corn, the savages will cut them as much wood as they want.

They are always considered, by the other inhabitants, to have the power, through the means of incantation and magic, to charm the

In former times when any calamity befell a Toda or Badagan, his first impulse was to slay the first Kurrumban he met, in revenge for the evil, which he supposed to be caused by the incantations of some member of that hateful tribe. These diminutive beings, with their uncouth manners, thickly matted locks and supple limbs, are industrious and not unskilful. They make baskets, cultivate the ground, and cut down trees; but conjuring is their main business. Their knowledge of healing herbs, roots, &c. is very great. Curiously enough they seem to be the high-priests of the Badagas, their deadly enemies. At the commencement of the season, a Kurrumban ploughs the first furrow and gives his benediction to the field, without which there would be no harvest!

tigers, the elephants, and the venomous reptiles which share with them in their forests, so that they have nothing to fear from their attacks.

They train up their children from their earliest infancy, to the hard life that nature seems to have intended for them. The day after lying-in, the woman is obliged to scour the woods for food. Before setting out, she suckles the new-born infant, digs a little trench in the ground for a cradle, where she deposits the naked babe, upon the bare earth; and, trusting to the care of Providence, goes with her husband and the rest of the family, in quest of wherewithal to supply their wants for the day. This is not quickly obtained; and it is evening before they return. From three days old they accustom the child to solid food; and, in order to inure it betimes to the rigour of the seasons, they wash it every day in dew collected from the plants; and until the infant is able to accompany or follow the mother, it remains in this manner, from morning to night, in the recesses of the wood, exposed to the rain, the sun, and all the inclemency of the weather, stretched out uncovered in the little tomb, which is its only cradle.

It appears that the only religion of these savages consists in the worship of the Bhûta or Demons, which they exclusively adore, paying no acknowledgment to the divinities of the nation.

These are, in the greatest number, in the forests of Malabar; but there is also a different species of savages in various parts of the Carnatic, roaming in the woods of that province, and known under the name of *Irular.*[b] Like the Kurumbar, they lead a savage life, and have scarcely any communication with the more polished people of the plain. Their principal means of living are roots and honey, which they find in the woods. They barter the last, and its wax, with the inhabitants of the neighbourhood, for such articles as they have to spare. In other particulars they scarcely differ in any thing from the preceding class, and are equally dreaded for enchantments and sorcery by their jealous neighbours of the plains.

The savage caste of *Malai Kudiar*[c] has been already noticed. Though living in the woods, they have made some approach to the social state. Their occupation is to extract the juice or *Kallu* from the palm trees, selling a part and drinking the remainder. It is the women that ascend the trees; and they do it with great agility. The husbands go to market with the liquor.

This tribe is hardly found beyond the district of Koorg. Here there is also another tribe, known by the appellation of *Yeruvaru.* It consists of several hordes dispersed through the woods. Being without the resources for subsistence which the others possess, they are compelled to provide for their wants by making themselves useful in society. For this purpose they quit their cabins, and repair to the habitations of their more polished neighbours; who, for a small allowance of grain, obtain the services of the savages in the most toilsome

---

b Sons of Darkness.

c — Mountaineers.

labours of husbandry. But, such is their improvidence and indolence, that as long as a single morsel of rice remains in their huts, they obstinately refuse to renew their labour. Their employers, however, are obliged to put up with their humour, because they cannot otherwise exempt themselves from drudgery; and, if they should offend a single individual amongst them, by ill treatment, or in any other way, the whole horde would resent the affront, and, in a body, desert their accustomed abodes for the hidden recesses of the forests. There they would sulkily remain, till their superiors, being at a loss for their assistance, were reduced to the necessity of making the first advances, by an apology for the injury, or such indemnification as the savages might require.

All the various savage tribes, having much difficulty in procuring the absolute necessaries of life, have no means whatever of attaining to the petty luxuries which are within the reach of the lowest orders of the other castes. Betel, tobacco, oil for rubbing the head and body, and some other indulgences which habit has rendered necessary to the ordinary Hindûs, are quite unknown to the savage tribes, and do not even seem to be coveted by them. They think it quite sufficient to be favoured by strangers with a little salt and pepper to season the roots and insipid vegetables which form their principal nourishment.

All these savages are of an inoffensive and quiet disposition. The sight even of a stranger is enough to put a whole horde of them to flight. Their indolent and lazy habits result from the climate. Far different from the Cannibals of America, or those which people an extensive region of Africa, they know not the meaning of war; and they seem to be ignorant of the practice of repaying evil with evil. Buried in the thick forests where they were born, or in the deep grottoes of the rocks which they inhabit, there is nothing they are more afraid of than the approach or appearance of a civilized man; and so far from envying him the boasted happiness of social life, they shun all intercourse with him, out of fear that he designs to strip them of their independence and liberty, and reduce them to the bondage of society.

They preserve, however, some of the leading prejudices of their countrymen. They never eat cows flesh. They have the same notions concerning cleanness and inpurity, and they observe, in the principal occurrences of life, several other rules which are in common use in the country.[d]

[d] The Veddar, and malai-arasar, (hill-kings) belong to this class. They are becoming gradually accustomed in some districts, to associate with other tribes and to engage in regular employments.

ADDITIONAL NOTE TO
CHAP. VI.

I. By far the most interesting of those tribes, whom the immigrant Brâhmanical races have driven to the hills and furthest recesses of the land, are the *Tuḍas*, [*Toṛuvar* = herdsmen] who are found on the plateau of the Nîlagiris.

Of these there are now, probably, between 4 and 500, including children. They are scattered abroad in the four districts into which they divide the hills, in about 100 hamlets, called *Mands.* [Tam. *Mandai,* a fold or flock.]

Their occupation (or rather that of the men; for the women do absolutely nothing but dress their hair) is tending buffaloes, of which they have large herds. These are splendid creatures, almost wild, but obedient to the least sound of the herdsman's voice. Real work of every kind they absolutely disdain.

They are a very fine race in appearance, tall, straight, and manly; with, in many cases, aquiline noses, and always with a full, bright eye, that never shrinks from encountering your steadiest look. They wear a single cloth of thick material, which thrown toga-like over the shoulders gives an air of antique dignity to their figures, which has helped to produce the impression that they were, in some way or other, of Roman origin.

Of course this fancied resemblance soon vanishes, and a closer examination of their language, habits, and features reveals the fact that they are of the same race, though perhaps one of its earliest and most unsophisticated offshoots, as that from which the Tamilians, Telugus and Kanarese have sprung.

Their traditions point to a Northern origin, and it would seem that they have never lived in a plain country.

Their huts resemble the tops of large stage waggons, set on the ground. They are generally found three or four together, with the milk-house at a short distance. Near this latter no woman must come, and the whole management of the dairy assumes a semi-religious character. They have certain sacred spots in the forest called *tiriari* (= *holy room ?*) where a priest, the *Pâl-âl,* (*milkman*) resides. He is elected, must be young, an ascetic, and devote himself wholly to the task of keeping a bowl of milk in the hut, which is his dwelling as well as temple, and of ringing a bell at certain times. This bell, with the relics of certain deceased *Todas,* are the only objects of veneration that I have detected among them.

At a death their custom (stopped by the British Government,) was to beat to death with clubs a number of buffaloes proportioned to the rank of the deceased. The other ceremonies connected with this sacrifice to the Manes, resemble those of the demon worship of the *Shânârs* in the south.

Their language resembles very nearly old or high Tamil, spoken very roughly.

The *Badagas* and others who have come up from the plains pay them tribute as lords of the soil; but they are themselves in deadly fear of the *Kurumbar.* This fear however is simply superstitious. They are, in their turn, regarded as sorcerers by the Badagas.

Their custom of polyandry, and their utter want of regard to chastity, are reducing their numbers rapidly. A married woman among them belongs to all the brothers, and her children are apportioned to the brothers in order of seniority.

They are divided into four classes and seem to have a somewhat strict idea of Caste. They have evidently resided on the hills for many centuries.

II. The KÔTAS (? *Gô-hatas* = cow killers) seem to have come from the same district as the Tudas. Their language differs little from the Tuda dialect, though their way of speaking makes it sound very different. In habits they are disgustingly brutal, living on carrion. They are artificers and cultivators at the same time. They have seven villages on the Nîlagiri plateau, inhabited by about 1,000 persons. They are ethnologically a link between the Tudas and the other South Indian tribes.

III. The BADAGAS (= people of the North) are the most numerous of the hill tribes in South India, and are scarcely in fact to be called hill men, since they have taken up their abode there within a comparatively short period. Their relatives are still to be found in the low country, more especially between the foot of the hills and the city of Mysore.

Many fled with the Râjah of Oomatoor in 1613, when he was driven from his city by Râj Wadaiyâr. [See Wilks I, 45.]

They are divided into 18 classes. The highest caste, and at the same time the least numerous, is that of the Woodairu. [Tam. *Udaiyar* = *possessors,* lords of the soil.] This is a title of honour among the Kanarese. Most of the Baḍagas are nominally worshippers of the Linga, as their Mysore ancestors were. But local traditions and intercourse with the other hill tribes have introduced a number of objects of worship, relics of first settlers, remarkable stones, &c. They have Brâhmans too, whom they have themselves, it seems, selected and constituted to bear the name. They themselves say that there are 338 idols worshipped on the hills. I have examined the few inscriptions to be found on the various stones on the hills, and feel assured that they relate to various expeditions of Poligâr chiefs from the Coimbatûr side of the hills, and that they throw no light on the history of the *Baḍagars.*

Their language is Kanarese with many corruptions. These corruptions evidently tend (though they have not gone so far) to place the Baḍagar dialect of Kanarese in the same relation to modern Kanarese, as the Malayaḷam dialect of Tamil occupies to the Tamil now in use.

IV. The caste of the SHÂNÂR in Tinnevelly has attracted much attention from the fact that upwards of 50,000 of them have embraced Christianity, and afford to the traveller the pleasing spectacle of a humble and unintellectual, but orderly and earnest minded Christian population dwelling in villages in the centre of which the most conspicuous object is a Christian Church or Prayer house. A work entitled the "Tinnevelly Shânârs" by Dr. Caldwell gives the fullest information in regard to this caste.

They are probably immigrants from North Ceylon, as are the Iḷavar or Tîrs of Travancore, a kindred race. They seem to have brought with them the seeds of the Palmyra and the majority of them are engaged in climbing these trees to take the juice, from which their wives prepare a coarse sugar.

They are divided into two classes, the Nalla (good) Shânâr and the Kalla (spurious) Shânâr. The former for the most part own the trees, and assume the position of masters; while the latter who probably immigrated at a later period, are in some parts of Tinnevelly almost slaves.

Their religion is a kind of Demon worship, the principal demons being Bhadra-Kâli, Çudalaiâḍum-Perumâḷ (the great one who dances in the burning ground.) Any person who was distinguished during life, or who has died a violent death, becomes a local demon, and is supposed to haunt the place where he or she flourished or died. The same practise obtains among the lower castes throughout India.

CHAPTER VII.

OF THE METEMPSYCHOSIS. THE HINDÛS THE INVENTORS OF THE DOCTRINE. CAUSES AND NUMBER OF THE TRANSMIGRATIONS. OF THE PAINS OF HELL AND THEIR DURATION. ABODES OF BLISS.

SEVERAL writers, both ancient and modern, have been of opinion that Pythagoras was the author of the system of the Metempsychosis, called by the Hindûs *Pûrva Janma*, or regeneration, and that it was communicated by that philosopher to the sages of India, when he visited their country. But all who are acquainted with the spirit and education of the Brâhmans, both ancient and modern, will be easily satisfied of the contrary, and will be convinced that, so far from receiving lessons from Pythagoras, they were his masters in this respect. The desire of learning something new, and of attaining perfection in the sciences, induced that philosopher to penetrate into every country where they had begun to flourish in those remote ages; and, having heard of the renown of the philosophers of India, which long afterwards spread into Europe, he undertook a long voyage to see them, and to profit by their doctrines.[e]

What makes it more probable that it was from them that he derived his system of the transmigration of the soul of one body into another, is that he did not publish it till after his return from India; and no circumstance of his life shews that he had any notion of it before his journey.

Is it at all to be imagined that the Brâhmans would consent to borrow a system so abstracted and extraordinary from a stranger? Those who know their pride and arrogant presumption, will find great difficulty in believing it. Never can a Brâhman be persuaded that sciences, which he is ignorant of, can be lodged in the mind of a man of any other caste, far less of a foreigner; and never would he lend an ear to any individual who should pretend to be acquainted with any new science or useful discovery, of which he himself would not assume to be the inventor.

We have before had occasion to remark, that this caste of persons has been regarded, in all times, as the universal and exclusive heir of every art and science. They are all educated in the belief that no man can possibly know what they are ignorant of. Such is the fundamental principal in which they have been nurtured, in ancient

---

e On the other hand compare Ritter's history of Philosophy I. 155.

and modern times: a principle which their long intercourse with nations far beyond them in every branch of science has never been able to shake.

Their books, which appear to be more ancient than Pythagoras, are filled with the doctrine of the Pûrva Janma or Metempsychosis, and treat of it as a system coeval with their most ancient institutions, civil and religious, and established beyond all controversy.[f]

But, whoever he was that was the original inventor of that absurd system, which some modern authors have called sublime, Greece and the other countries into which it was introduced by Pythagoras and his disciples, do not appear to have derived much benefit from the discovery. It appears wonderful that Empedocles, Socrates, and Plato, philosophers otherwise so enlightened, should have adopted it, without examination. Aristotle and the whole Peripatetic school justly rejected it. But it continues to this day to be the universal belief of every Hindû.

Pythagoras drew from it a very natural inference, when he asserted that they ought to abstain from eating the flesh of any living creature, lest the son might possibly feed on the body of his father, whose soul had, peradventure, passed into the substance of a fowl or sheep; so that the horrid feast of Thyestes might be often repeated. Several of the disciples of that philosopher, to act consistently with his doctrines, confined themselves to live entirely upon liquids. They even rejected the bean from their meals, as the Brâhmans have rejected the onion and some other simple productions of the same nature. But these rigorous precepts of the strict disciples of the Greek philosopher were less followed than their doctrines, and the people never relinquished the use of flesh.

The Hindû philosophers, in all probability, gave birth to this notion of Pythagoras, when he adopted their system of the Pûrva Janma. He saw their abhorrence of the murder of animals. He likewise saw that the Brâhmans and all the cultivated people of India most religiously abstained from eating whatsoever had been alive; and his conclusion would naturally be that their extreme abstinence in that respect must have arisen from the apprehension they were in of slaying an ancestor, perhaps, in the creature which was served up for their food.

If this was the inference which that philosopher drew from the custom of the Hindûs, and their mode of living, I have no difficulty in saying it was a false one. The abstinence from meat amongst the Hindûs, is founded upon two principles, very different from those which were assumed by the Pythagoreans; and the practice appears to be foreign to the doctrine of Metempsychosis. The first principal is the dread of being defiled by the use of animal nutriment; and the second is the abhorrence of the murder which must have been committed before they could enjoy such a feast. In consequence of the former

[f] Compare Manu xii. Vishṇu Purâṇ, p. 210.

principle, of shunning all defilement, the nobler part of the nation is restricted to the use of liquids only, and of the simple productions of nature, for their aliment. The Brâhmans could use nothing that proceeded from an animal, with the exception of milk, which constituted the most substantial and delicious portion of their food. The horror which a dead body generally inspires; the fetid stench which it exhales, from the moment almost of dissolution, are widely different from the decay of vegetables, which rot without putridity. The revolting idea of being obliged to gratify the appetite by loading the table with carcasses of slaughtered animals, and a thousand other considerations not less reasonable, concerning the nature of what is pure and what is impure, have determined the opinions of the Hindûs on this subject. They have been instilled by education, and so deeply rooted in the mind, that those who have once imbibed the prejudice have not even a thought of ever departing from it, under any circumstances that can befal them through life.

The second motive which influenced their conduct, in this particular, was the dread and horror of murder, which it was necessary to commit as often as they might have recourse to this diet; a dread, which by many is carried so far, as even to induce them to spare the most vile and troublesome insects; such as never fail to disturb the repose of men and brutes. This is more congruous and consistent than the conduct of the disciples of Pythagoras. The Hindûs believe that no difference exists between the souls of men and of animals; and that the sins of human beings in one generation are the cause of their being degraded to the condition of a beast in another. Hence they conclude, that it is equally wicked to slay a beast or an insect as to murder one of their own species.

But, with the exception of the Brâhmans, the Kshatriya and the Vaisya, the greater number of the Śûdras kill animals and eat their flesh. They have amongst them butchers and hunters by profession. The caste of the Vêṭṭar, who generally live in the mountains and forests, have scarcely any other occupation than the chace. I have read somewhere, in an Indian book, that one of the ancient penitents, who were almost entirely Brâhmans, and who never tasted of any creature that had lived, amused his leisure with the diversion of hunting serpents, which were common in the woods where he exercised his penitence, and killed all he could find; although this reptile is particularly reverenced by the Hindûs, and placed in the number of such as the vulgar adores. But this is not the only particular in which the Hindû paganism is found to be inconsistent with itself.

The Pythagoreans were neither so steady nor so consistent as the Hindûs, in their opinions on the same subject; for they reproach them for rendering the transmigration of souls common and promiscuous amongst all living creatures; for thus, they say, the soul of a King might pass into the body of an ape, and of a Queen into that of a grasshopper. In order to escape the ridicule to which such a system was exposed, certain philosophers of that sect, such as Plotinus and

Porphyry, endeavoured, though too late, to limit the transmigration of the souls of men to human bodies, and those of brutes to their own species; and they would fain have passed these inventions for the doctrine of the original founders of their sect. But the testimony of all the ancient writers is too direct and conclusive, on this topic, to admit of any faith being paid to the tardy retractation of their disciples.

The Hindûs recognize two principal causes of the transmigration of souls; and their system of Pûrva Janma seems to have been invented to justify, under a gross allegory, the administration of Providence in dispensing rewards and punishments. The first cause which they assign is common to them with the Pythagoreans. Transgression must be punished, and virtue rewarded. This does not take place in the present life; for we often see vice triumphant, and virtue beaten down. As a remedy for this great irregularity, the Gods, who hold in their hands the destinies of men, have decreed that he who, during his life, was a wicked man, a robber or homicide, shall, in requital of his crimes, be regenerated after his present life, and become a Pariah, some voracious animal, or a creeping insect, or be born blind or crooked; so that, according to this doctrine, lowness of birth or bodily defects, are an incontestable proof of the perverseness that reigned in a preceding existence. On the contrary, to have been born beautiful, handsome, rich, powerful, a Brâhman, or even a cow; every circumstance of that nature, is a clear proof of the pure and virtuous life which had distinguished the fortunate object in a preceding generation. Such is the feeling of all the people of India, and, as it appears, of all the Asiatics; and such was very nearly that of the early Pythagoreans.

But, independently of this first cause of transmigrations, the Hindûs assign another, which is peculiar to them. As their notions concerning defilement and purity must be combined with every thing else, they pretend that a soul after death, must retain something of the dispositions and stains which it had contracted in a preceding generation, just as an earthen vessel retains for a long time the odour of some strong liquor which was put into it when new. They strengthen this comparison by the instance of a woman, who had been a fish in her preceding generation; and who, though, in the present, a real woman, still retained the fishy odour. It is necessary, therefore, that a long succession of generations shall cleanse the impurities of the past; which must be followed by a vast number more, if, in place of purifying themselves from ancient stains, they contract new ones, by a dissolute life.

When the Hindûs are interrogated on the number of these transmigrations which must take effect, and from what epoch they commence; they answer, that they take their beginning from the period when the earth began to be populous, and vice had begun to reign in it. As to their duration, it has been, and will continue to be, commensurate with the various Yugas or ages of the world. As to the number of transmigrations, the poets have exceedingly exaggerated or extenuated them, according as their extravagant imagination impelled. But the most rational of their philosophers agree that the number cannot be fixed, as it must be proportioned to the measure of virtue or vice predominant in each individual, which must require a greater or less succession of new births before arriving at that sublime state of purity which at last puts a period to this transition of the soul from body to body, and inseparably reunites it to the great Being, to Para-Brâhma.

On this point, the philosophers of India appear to me to be wiser and less empirical than the divine Plato himself; since that great philosopher scruples not to determine the period for which a soul shall continue to pass from one body to another. He fixes it at three thousand years for some, and at ten thousand for others. He likewise ventures to pronounce upon the sort of transmigration which some famous individuals have sustained. Thus the soul of Agamemnon he holds to have passed into an eagle, and that of Thersites into the body of an ape; just as if, by the multiplication of lies, he could render his system of the Metempsychosis more probable or less absurd.

One point in which the Hindû system may probably appear defective and inferior to that of the Greeks, is that of consciousness. How can it happen, it is asked, that one should have no remembrance of what passed in the preceding generation? The Grecian poets had fabled the river Lethe, whose waters had the power of creating an oblivion of all that had been done or learned before death. Some chosen souls, however, were exempted from the general rule, and preserved distinctly the memory of the sort of life which they formerly passed. Of this number was Pythagoras himself, who in order to enhance the credit of his new system, had the hardiness to declare that he was originally Æthalides, the reputed son of Mercury; afterwards Euphorbus, who was wounded by Menelaus at the siege of Troy; then Hermotymus; and then a fisherman of Delos, called Pyrrhus; and last of all Pythagoras.

The Hindûs confer that privilege upon but a very small number of virtuous souls; but, as to the bulk of mankind, they affirm that the mere circumstance of regeneration is sufficient to obliterate all memory of what they formerly saw, and all knowledge of former events. A child under two years of age, they observe, cannot remember to-day what he did yesterday; and much less likely is it that he should recollect what took place before his new birth. Is this explanation less satisfactory than that of the river Lethe?

Of Hell.

The *Pûrva Janma* or Metempsychosis, being designed perhaps, as a vindication of the system of Providence, by establishing a balance between virtue and vice, in rewarding the one and punishing the other, did not require the addition of places of torment and felicity after death. As far as punishment was concerned, it was sufficient to renew for several times an evil regeneration to the wicked, while the righteous were, with less delay, reunited to the Divinity, that universal soul of the world from which they were originally detached. But no civilized nation has ever held these abstract and general notions in religion; the offspring of some exalted and enthusiastic spirits. But there are fundamental truths, so deeply engraven on the heart of man by the Author of his being, that neither the vain sophistry of a false philosophy, nor the madness of an overbearing idolatry, shall ever succeed in wholly obliterating their impression.[g]

The Hindûs, above all nations, strictly preserved, in the midst of the thick darkness of a gross idolatry, the remembrance of the principal truths of natural religion, as they existed amongst the earliest men; and of those, in particular, which relate to the rewards and punishments reserved for mankind in another life.

These precious doctrines, with many others not less important, were unfortunately corrupted and disfigured by innumerable fables such as this of the metempsychosis. The Hindûs also invented a king of the infernal regions, who had under his orders judges of the dead, and messengers to execute their awards.

In this infernal kingdom, which they call *Naraka* and sometimes *Pâtâla*, they acknowledge a God or sovereign Judge, to whom they give the name of *Yama*. This chief of the council of hell consults his records formed by the agency of scribes and others under his authority, who keep an exact account of all the good and all the evil which take place on the earth. They lay their report before their master, who decides on each case; and the punishment, proportioned to the sins of the dead, immediately follows. Executioners, cruel and inexorable, are appointed to torment the guilty, without respite, by means of steel, of fire, and a thousand other ways, which their cruelty suggests. In the detail which the Hindû books give of these varied punishments of hell, I have been struck with one as somewhat remarkable, and not less disgusting. It is related that some very guilty souls are plunged several times a day into a lake of mucus. I should not have so much marvelled if they had chosen to drench the culprits in a lake of spittle; for that is the fluid on which the Hindû looks more aghast than on any other excrement or secretion of the body.

But Yama is not the only god that is continually on the watch to seize upon the souls of mortals when they die. Other deities, and above all Śiva and Vishṇu, have likewise their invisible emissaries on earth, who know the votaries of their respective masters; and the death of such persons is often the subject of a sharp contest between the imps of those divinities and the servants of Yama; each of them striving to bear away the departed soul to his own master. But the attachment to Vishṇu or Śiva, however moderate it may have been,

---

[g] Vishṇu Purâṇ, p. 207.
Manu, iv, 88-90.
Ritter's antient Philosophy I, 125.

is so full of merit, that their emissaries generally have the advantage in the disputes for dominion over the souls of the dead, while those of the god of Naraka are compelled to a disorderly retreat.

The duration of the punishment of the sinners condemned by Yama, is in proportion to the heinousness and number of their crimes. The Hindûs admit that the retribution is severe and long, but by no means eternal. They hold that, at the end of every age, a universal revolution of all nature takes place, and a new order of things commences. Unconnected with past times, we now live in the last age or *Kaliyuga;* and we have elsewhere related how much of it has elapsed, and how long it has yet to run. When it ends, all souls shall be reunited to the divine essence from which they were originally taken; and the world being dissolved, the pains of the damned shall terminate also.

The Greeks, less presumptuous than the Hindûs, did not venture to fix the period when their iron age was to expire. Neither did they attempt to assign limits to the thirst of Tantalus, or to predict the moment when Ixion's wheel should stop. Probably they believed that these torments were everlasting. Plato admitted the eternity of punishment for some enormous crimes, for which the guilty were hurled to Erebus.

The Abodes of Happiness.

The Hindûs have invented several places of enjoyment for those who have expiated their faults by repeated transmigrations and the torments they have suffered from Yama in Naraka; but there are four of particular celebrity. One is called *Vaikuṇṭha*, the residence of Vishṇu, into which, besides his own devotees, are admitted those of Brahmâ and Śiva, and all others, without distinction of caste or person. The same report is given of the *Kailâsa*, or world of Śiva, into which his votaries are received after death. These seats of happiness are represented by some Hindû writers to be vast mountains on the north of India; the Kailâsa being a mountain of silver.[a]

The Swarga, another blissful residence, is situated in the air, and has Dêvêndra for its king, although a god of lower rank than Śiva and Vishṇu. His paradise, notwithstanding, is more celebrated than theirs. Music, dancing, sensual enjoyment and carnal voluptuousness are amongst the delights which it affords. There is no reason, however, to suppose that the other places of bliss are destitute of such enjoyments; for the presiding deities of them all, according to the Hindû fables, were equally celebrated for all excesses of sensual indulgence, while they sojourned on this earth.

The paradise of Brahmâ is called *Satyalôka*, or the *World of Truth.* It is elevated far higher than the rest, and is more pure than any. It is watered by the Ganges; a stream which never flowed out of that

[a] Vishṇu Purâṇ, p. 48.

sacred land, until the fervent and rigorous devotion of an illustrious penitent prevailed to draw down its hallowed current upon earth. With such an origin, we cannot wonder at the high virtues ascribed by all true Hindûs to this mighty river.

Brâhmans, almost exclusively, are admitted into the Satyalôka, when they have concluded a life truly virtuous upon earth. But they are not irrevocably stationed there; for neither they, nor those who have been admitted into the other seats of beatitude, are exempt from the necessity of being again born upon earth, and with repeated transmigrations. This shews how limited and imperfect their scheme of celestial happiness must be. This renewed and protracted purification seems contradictory to their system; and paradise, with them, forms no security for its possessor.

But, at last, when these repeated new births, joined to the practice of virtue and repentance, have completely purified the soul, and have corrected its slightest bias towards terrestrial objects; then, and not till then, does it re-unite with the divine Para-Brahmâ, to that unbounded spirit, as drops of water return to the ocean, from whence they were exhaled. This is the complete and glorious beatitude of the Hindûs; to which they give the appellation of *Môksham*, which signifies *deliverance*.

Idolatry, the natural tendency of which is to corrupt all things, by absurd and ridiculous fables, has nevertheless respected certain fundamental truths which are engraven on the hearts of all men; the knowledge of which appears indispensably necessary to the stability of all civilized society. The people of India, though immersed in the thick darkness of the grossest idolatry, have yet preserved the knowledge of a Supreme Being, his providence, bounty, and justice; and of the immortality and spiritual nature of the soul. They have admitted the necessary existence of a future life, accompanied with rewards and punishments. What are we to conclude, then, from their persuasion respecting these fundamental articles of the popular faith? This, surely; that the sacred truths, which are born, as it were, with man, and remain imprinted on his heart, during the whole course of his existence, can never be effaced from the memory of our species. The Atheist and Materialist may resort to the sophisms of a false philosophy, to obliterate the memory of truths which press them hard; they may exhaust the faculties of a mind perverted by the passions, and endeavour to interpose a cloud to prevent their light, which shines like the sun, from reaching the hearts of other men. All their efforts shall be ineffectual. The vivid brightness of those eternal and unchangeable truths shall continue to penetrate athwart the thin vapour, which the unbeliever endeavours to raise, for the purpose of intercepting their splendour. The testimony of conscience shall triumph over the vain sophisms of a false philosophy; and be relied on, while reasonable men exist upon earth.[i]

---

[i] Manu xii. 85--91.

Of Human Sacrifices offered by the Hindûs.

The history of the world teaches us that the different nations by which it is peopled, have, in ancient times, made the sacrifice of human victims a part of the worship which they rendered to their divinities. Man, environed on all hands with evils, and in all cases conscious of his own guilt, imagined, after the spirit of idolatry had biassed his understanding, that the best means of appeasing the gods, and of rendering them propitious, was to offer to them the noblest and most valuable victims which the earth could afford; thinking it lawful, for their gratification, to pour human blood, as well as that of beasts, upon their altars.

I believe there are few nations, civilized or barbarous, in the world, who may not be justly reproached with that horrid kind of sacrifice; and, though some modern authors have questioned the fact of the Hindûs having, in common with other ancient nations, spilt the blood of their fellows, in the sanctuaries of the deities whom they adore, and have sought to acquit that people of so abominable a crime; yet it has never appeared a matter of doubt to me. On the contrary, I believe it is quite certain that the various nations of India have immolated human victims to their gods, both in ancient and modern times.

Incontestable evidence of the fact has been given in several parts of this work. On the subject of magic, we related that, when any very extraordinary effect was intended, the magician could not depend upon a certain result without offering the sacrifice of a young girl to the demons of mischief; and also that when people in authority come to a magician for information on any great event, this barbarous sacrifice is generally the prelude to the ceremonies. It appears, therefore, that the *Atharvana-vêda*, or that book of the four sacred volumes which teaches the magical art, recognises this horrible ceremony.

In the sacrifice also of the Yajna, where the noblest victim is required to be offered, although it was more usual to take an elephant or horse, as the most valuable of animals, for the purpose; yet it is not without example that a man has been chosen, as a creature still more noble.

Indeed, we may easily convince ourselves that no nation can have less repugnance to human sacrifices than the Hindûs, if we examine the conduct which they exhibit at the present time. In many provinces, the natives still can trace, and actually point out to the curious traveller, the ground and situation where their Rajas sacrificed to their idols the prisoners whom they had taken in war. The object of the awful rite was to render their divinities more placable, and to obtain their favourable aid in battle. I have visited some of those abominable places, which are commonly in the mountains or other unfrequented parts; as if those awful beings who delighted to see their altars moistened with human gore, and their sanctuaries strewed with the carcasses, were themselves conscious of the enormity of the crime, and therefore desired to veil the horrid spectacle from the eyes of men. In the secret places where these detestable sacrifices were performed of old, a little temple of mean appearance is generally found, and sometimes but a simple niche, in which the idol is preserved, to obtain whose favour so horrid a price is paid. The victim was immolated by decapitation, and the head was left exposed for a time in the presence of the idol.

I have been conducted to see several of those sad charnel dens, in various districts. One of them is not far from Seringapatam, on the hill near which the fort of Mysore is built. On the top of that mountain, the pagoda may still be observed, where the Rajas were accustomed to sacrifice their prisoners of war, or state delinquents.

Sometimes they were satisfied with mutilating their victims, by cutting off their hands, nose, and ears; which they offered up, fresh and bloody, at the shrine of the idol, or hung them up, exposed on the gate of the temple.

But I have also conversed with several old men, who have entered familiarly into the object and circumstances of these sacrifices, and spoke of them to me as events of their own days, and as publicly known.

It appears, indeed, that this practice of sacrificing prisoners taken in war, amongst the pagan Princes, was not in opposition to our notions of the law of nations, being reciprocal, and acknowledged as the legitimate reprisals of one sovereign upon another. The people look on, without horror, or even surprize. They still speak of it, without emotion, as a thing just and regular, and as being fitly appropriate to the state of war.

Of late, the intercourse of the Hindûs with the Europeans and Musalmans, and the just horror which these invaders have expressed of such atrocious crimes, have nearly effected their total abolition: nearly, I say, because I cannot answer with confidence for what may have taken place, under some petty native Princes, who have preserved a precarious independence up to the present day. Neither would I like to risk the falling into their hands, as an enemy or prisoner of war. What I have heard of some of the petty Mahratta Princes, confirms my suspicions that human sacrifices are not yet wholly renounced.

It cannot therefore be reasonably doubted that in India men have been offered up as holocausts, both in ancient and in modern times, upon the altars of the idols, who are supposed to be gratified by seeing their shrines inundated with human blood. Still, in many places, they keep up the remembrance of these horrible sacrifices; and, although they are no longer permitted to shed the blood of their fellow-creatures, in honour of the gods, they have thought it necessary to supply the deficiency, and in some degree, at least, to satisfy the taste of several of their deities for this horrid sacrifice, by forming a human figure of flourpaste, or clay, which they carry into the temples, and there cut off its head or mutilate it, in various ways, in presence of the idols.

This species of unbloody sacrifice, plainly representing the human victims anciently offered up to the same gods of the country, is seen in many places. In the kingdom of Tanjore there is a village called Tiruśhankaṭam Kuḍi, where a solemn festival is celebrated every year, at which great multitudes of people assemble; each votary bringing with him one of those little images of dough, into the temple, dedicated to Vishṇu, and there cutting off the head in honour of that god.

This ceremony, which is annually performed with great solemnity, was instituted in commemoration of a famous event which happened in that village. Two virtuous persons lived there, *Sirutaṇḍan* and his wife *Vanagata-ananga*, whose faith and piety Vishṇu was desirous to prove. He appeared to them, accordingly, in a human form, and demanded no other service of them but that of sacrificing, with their own hands, their only and much-beloved son Sirâḷan, and serving up his flesh for a repast. The parents, with heroic courage, surmounting the sentiments and chidings of nature, obeyed without hesitation, and submitted to the pleasure of the god. So illustrious an act of devotion is held worthy of this annual commemoration, at which the sacrifice is emblematically renewed. The same barbarous custom is preserved in many parts of India; and the ardour with which the people engage in it leaves room to suspect that they still regret the times when they would have been at liberty to offer up to their sanguinary gods, the reality, instead of the symbol.

If farther evidence were wanting that such sacrifices were actually in existence among the Hindûs, and that they were thought acceptable to the divinities whom the people adore, we should find it in the *Kâlikâ-Purâṇa*, a work written under the direction of Śiva. In this book, one of the most esteemed of any, we find the most minute detail of the mode, the ceremonies, and the advantage of sacrificing human and other living victims. The nicest distinction is also laid down concerning the species of animals, amongst the quadrupeds, birds, and fishes, which might serve for an offering, and to which of the gods those sacrifices were pleasing. Of these, the chief were *Bahira, Yama, Dharmarâja, Kâli, Mariammâ*, and several other of the infernal and malignant demons; most of whom are the progeny or near relations of Śiva the god of destruction.

All these are delighted with human sacrifice, but, above all, *Kâli*, a female divinity, and the most wicked of all. Such an offering gives her a gleam of pleasure that endures a thousand years; and the sacrifice of three men together, would prolong her ecstacy for a thousand centuries.

In the abominable book from which I am quoting, human sacrifices are held to be a right inherent in the Princes; to whom they are the source of wealth, the cause of victory, and other temporal blessings; none of which can be enjoyed by any other man without their consent.

The work describes, at great length, the qualities which the victim, whether human or bestial must possess.

A woman cannot be offered, nor a she animal: neither Brâhman nor Prince.

If it be a human victim that is offered, he must be free from corporal defect, and unstained with great crimes. If it be an animal, it must have exceeded its third year, and be without blemish or disease.

In the same Purâṇa, we find a description of the various instruments, such as the kind of knife and axe, with which the several victims are to be slain. It also contains a minute account of the favourable and unlucky omens to be drawn from the sacrifice, according to the side on which it falls, the manner in which the blood gushes, or the convulsions and cries which attend its last moments.

The same volume assures us that the gods who take delight in bloody sacrifices, are not less pleased with offerings of strong liquors and inebriating drugs, such as arrack, toddy, and opium.

But though such bloody and murderous sacrifices are permitted, and even recommended, to Princes and others of high rank, as the means of acquiring the protection of the gods, and success in their enterprises; they are nevertheless expressly prohibited to the Brâhmans, who are not allowed even to assist at them.

CHAPTER VIII.

OF THE HINDÛ FABLES.

THE particular taste of the Hindûs for poetry and fiction has given rise to an incredible number of Fabulous Stories which are current among them. In their books we often meet with apologues of an instructive nature and well adapted to the subject in hand; and they are much accustomed to relate similar stories in conversation. Some of these popular tales are well imagined and contain a good moral.[j] Out of a great number of this sort I have selected the following, which is very generally known and which I have seen inserted in many of their books; and I have likewise heard it related in familiar conversation by persons of good understanding among them.

The Tale.

" A Traveller, having missed his way, was overtaken by darkness " in the midst of a thick forest. Being apprehensive that such a wood " must naturally be the receptacle of wild beasts, he determined to " keep out of their way by mounting into a tree. He therefore chose " the thickest he could find, and having climbed up, he fell fast asleep, " and so continued until the light of the morning awoke him, and " admonished him that it was time to continue his journey. In pre- " paring to descend, he cast his eyes downwards, and beheld, at the " foot of the tree, a huge tiger sitting, and eagerly on the watch, as if " impatient for the appearance of some prey, which he was ready to " tear in pieces and devour. Struck with terror at the sight of the " monster, the traveller continued for a long while immoveably fixed " to the spot where he sat. At length, recovering himself a little, " and looking all round him, he observed that the tree on which he " was had many others contiguous to it, with their branches so inter- " mixed, that he could gradually pass from one to another, until at " last he might get out of the reach of danger. He was on the point " of putting his design in execution, when, raising his eyes, he saw a " monstrous serpent, suspended by the tail to the branch immediately " over him, and its head nearly reaching his own. The monster " appeared, indeed, to be asleep in that posture; but the slightest " motion might wake it and expose him to its fury. At the sight of " the extreme danger which environed him on all sides; a frightful " serpent above, and a devouring tiger beneath, the traveller lost all " courage: and being unable, from fear, to support himself longer on his

j In the Tamil Reading book published by the Editor, and to be obtained from the publisher of this work a collection of these stories is given, in which only those have been inserted the moral of which is good and the language unobjectionable.

" legs, he was on the point of falling into the jaws of the tiger, who " stood ready gaping to receive him. In awful consternation, he " remained motionless; having nothing before him but the image of " death, and believing every moment to be his last. He had yielded " to despair; when, once more raising his head, he saw a honey- " comb upon the top of the highest branches of the tree. The comb " distilled its sweets, drop by drop, close by the side of the traveller. " He stretched forward his head, and put out his tongue, to catch " the honey as it fell; and, in the delicious enjoyment, thought no " more of the awful dangers which environed him."

Besides detached fables, which are quoted in books, and often brought forward in conversation, the Hindûs have a regular systematical collection of them called *Pancha-tantra,* which is circulated in every district, and translated into all languages. They are very old, and worthy of deep attention. They have been translated into several European languages; and therefore it would be superfluous to enter into a more minute account of them here.

The author was a Brâhman Gymnosophist or Philosopher, called *Pilpay* or *Bidpay.* The following is a summary of the introduction to the Pancha-tantra.

In the city of *Pâtaliputra,* King *Sudarśana* reigned. He had three adult sons, who seemed to vie with each other in coarseness of disposition and manners. The good Prince, in great affliction, at length communicated the subject of his grief to his Council. The Brâhman Sômajanma, one of the number, offered his services to the King, being willing to undertake the reformation of the three Princes, by correcting the errors of their former education. The King accepted his offer with joy, and put his sons under his care. The Brâhman, with great patience and toil, succeeded at length in his enterprize, and subdued the dispositions, habits, and morals of his disciples, by frequently inculcating five principal fables, each embracing a great number of subordinate ones.

These fables compose the Pancha-tantra, or five points of industry. They are five little romances, which are entitled " instructive," although their morality be not very sound, sometimes conducting to what is evil, rather than teaching the means of avoiding it.

The first story explains how dextrous knaves contrive to sow divisions between the best friends. The second teaches the advantage of true friends, and how they should be selected. The third explains how one is to destroy his adversary by artifice when he cannot succeed by force. The fourth shews how a man loses his property by misconduct; and the last exhibits the bad effects of thoughtlessness and precipitate decision.

The first fable appears to teach false morality, in shewing how a breach of the most intimate friendship may be effected, and how a faithful minister may be ruined in the good opinion of his Prince; unless the intention of the Brâhman, in instructing his pupils how the fox undermined the faithful bull in the favour of the lion, was not rather to caution them against the sycophants that haunt the palaces of Kings, and by false insinuations carry poison to the royal ear, and ruin the credit of the most meritorious servants. The following is a short abstract of this fable, which I think superior to the rest.

A Bull, who had been left by his owner in the midst of a forest, became at first the friend, and afterwards the confidant, of the Lion, who ruled there. A Fox, who had till then enjoyed the entire confidence of the king of the woods, had introduced the Bull, and recommended him to the Lion, very much against the opinion and advice of another aged Fox, his friend, who endeavoured, by many apologues, to dissuade him from so dangerous a step. These were answered, by relating other fables; and the advice was rejected. It turned out, however, that the old Fox was right. The upstart Bull conducted himself with so much gentleness, candour, and good faith, that he soon acquired the unbounded confidence of the Lion, became his first minister, and, without artifice, supplanted the Fox that introduced him. Thus degraded, and neglected by his sovereign, after having so long directed his councils, the Fox now strove to undo his own work, and to pull down the minister whom he had elevated to that dignity. For this purpose, he employed every art and all sorts of duplicity, and managed so well, by innumerable fables which he invented and recited to the Lion, every day, that a deep distrust of the faithful animal was engendered in his royal mind; and being led to suspect, at last, that the Bull was about to dethrone him and usurp the dominion of the forest, he fell upon him and tore him in pieces.

The author of the Pancha-tantra has taken occasion to introduce into his work a great number of fables, in which animals are the speakers. They are very much the same with those of Æsop, though far more prolix. They are so constructed, that one fable, before it is finished, gives rise to another, from one of the attending beasts, and so on to a third. There is some ingenuity in this method; but by thus involving one tale within another, we are in danger of losing sight of that which was first commenced. The author returns to it, no doubt; but a reader of fable does not willingly submit to the fatigue and trouble of so intricate an arrangement.

In the last of the four fables which follow, the dialogue is not confined to beasts. The principal subject of this fable is a tame Stork, which a Brâhman had carefully reared in his house. Seeing it one day coming out all bloody from the apartment where his infant child slept, he imagined it to be the blood of the child who had been devoured by the stork. Struck with horror at the thought, in a moment of rage, he slew the fowl. But what was his regret and despair, when he saw the infant in tranquil slumber, and an enormous serpent stretched out dead by the side of the cradle, and immersed in its own blood? At once he perceived that the faithful stork had saved the life of the babe, by flying upon the serpent when in the act of stifling it.

It is impossible to determine the age of these fables, no authentic document of their era being now extant. The Hindûs rank them with their oldest productions; and the estimation in which they are held through all India, is a proof of their antiquity. They are at least as old as those of Æsop; who probably derived his taste from this source, as in many passages of his writings there is a strong resemblance to the Pancha-tantra.

But to take the question in another light: could the Brâhman Sômajanma have had any knowledge of the stories of the Grecian fabulists, so as to have drawn his ideas from them? This will appear rather improbable, when we consider the contempt which the Brâhmans have, in all ages, entertained for literary productions of which they were not themselves the inventors; and the impossibility of their adopting them. We also know that ancient sages sometimes travelled from Europe into India, to receive lessons of wisdom from its philosophers and Brâhmans. Some Greek philosophers undertook this journey, long before the birth of Æsop; and at a time when their country passed for the most cultivated, wisest, and best regulated country in the universe.

It is uncertain whether these fables were originally composed in verse or prose. They were most probably in verse, as that was the most ancient mode of composition in India. It is certain at least that they have them in Sanskrit verse. Thence they may have been translated into prose, for the convenience of those to whom the poetic language was not familiar. They have passed, in this way, into the Tamil, Kanarese, and Telugu languages. The style, in prose, is extremely ornamented, and of a poetic strain; which would naturally be derived from the original poetry.

The five principal fables, together, form a considerable volume, on account of the great number of interlocutory tales that are interwoven with them. If closely translated, they would compose two duodecimo volumes, of three or four hundred pages each.

It is not surprising, that such a work should have an extensive circulation among a people like the Hindûs, prone to fiction and the marvellous. This natural disposition lays them open to the craft of innumerable adventurers, who make it their profession to ramble over the whole land, with fables and stories utterly devoid of reason or sense.[k]

---

[k] In our intercourse with Hindûs of all classes, both as individuals and as a Government, we do not fully recognize this marvellous credulity, which makes the people around us receive the most ridiculous stories regarding our plans and intentions. No rumour is too absurd to find acceptance in every nook and corner of the land.

CHAPTER IX.

HINDU TALES.

The subject of this chapter will perhaps appear to some readers unworthy of any attention. But there are also many to whom nothing is without interest that belongs to the manners and dispositions of an ancient people; and for their sake I will transgress a little on this subject.

Among the tales which are current in the country, some are written and known to many; while others are local, and can be considered only as old women's stories, or the traditions of the district. Both are equally devoid of sense, and fit only to amuse children.

Of the written tales which I have seen, the three following may be taken as a specimen, fit to amuse an idle reader, and at the same time, as characteristical of the general taste that pervades them all.

Tale of the Four Deaf Men.

A deaf shepherd was, one day, tending his flock, near his own village; and though it was almost noon, his wife had not yet brought him his breakfast. He was afraid to leave his sheep, to go in quest of it, lest some accident should befal them. But his hunger could not be appeased; and upon looking round, he spied a *Talaiyári*, or village hind, who had come to cut grass for his cow near a neighbouring spring. He went to call him, though very reluctantly, because he knew that, though those servants of the village are set as watchmen to prevent theft, yet they are great thieves themselves. He hailed him, however, and requested him just to give an eye to his flock for the short time he should be absent and that he would not forget him when he returned from breakfast.

But the man was as deaf as himself; and, mistaking his intentions, he angrily asked the shepherd: "What right have you to take this "grass, which I have had the trouble to cut? Is my cow to starve, "that your sheep may fatten? Go about thy business and let me "alone!" The deaf shepherd observed the repulsive gesture of the hind, which he took for a signal of acquiescence in his request, and therefore briskly ran towards the village, fully determined to give his wife a good lesson for her neglect. But, when he approached his house, he saw her before the door, rolling in the pains of a violent colic, brought on by eating over night too great a quantity of raw green peas. Her sad condition, and the necessity he was under to provide breakfast for himself, detained the shepherd longer than he wished; while the small confidence he had in the person with whom he left his sheep, accelerated his return to the utmost.

Overjoyed to see his flock peaceably feeding near the spot where he left them, he counted them over; and, finding that there was not a single sheep missing: "he is an honest fellow," quoth he, "this "*Talaiyâri;* the very jewel of his race! I promised him a reward, "and he shall have it." There was a lame beast in the flock, well enough in other respects, which he hoisted on his shoulders, and carried to the place where the hind was, and courteously offered him the mutton, saying, "you have taken great care of my sheep during "my absence. Take this one for your trouble."

"I!" says the deaf hind, "I break your sheep's leg! I'll be "hanged if I went near your flock since you have been gone, or "stirred from the place where I now am." "Yes," says the shepherd, "it is good and fat mutton, and will be a treat to you and your family "or friends." "Have I not told thee," replied the Talaiyâri in a rage, "that I never went near thy sheep; and yet thou wilt accuse me of "breaking that one's leg. Get about thy business, or I will give thee "a good beating!" And, by his gestures, he seemed determined to put his threats in execution. The astonished shepherd got into a passion also, and assumed a posture of defiance. They were just proceeding to blows, when a man on horseback came up. To him they both appealed, to decide the dispute between them; and the shepherd, laying hold of the bridle, requested the horseman to light, just for a moment, and to settle the difference between him and the beggarly Talaiyâri. "I have offered him a present of a sheep," says he, "because I thought he had done me a service; and, in requital, "he will knock me down." The villager was at the same time preferring his complaint, that the shepherd would accuse him of breaking the leg of his sheep, when he had never been near his flock.

The horseman, to whom they both appealed, happened to be as deaf as they; and did not understand a word that either of them said. But, seeing them both addressing him with vehemence, he made a sign to them to listen to him, and then frankly told them that he confessed the horse he rode was not his own. "It was a "stray that I found on the road," quoth he, "and being at a loss, I "mounted him for the sake of expedition. If he be your's, take him. "If not, pray let me proceed, as I am really in great haste."

The shepherd and the village hind, each imagining that the horseman had decided in favour of the other, became more violent than ever; both cursing him, whom they had taken for their judge, and accusing him of partiality.

At this crisis, there happened to come up an aged Brâhman. Instantly they all crowded round him; shepherd, Talaiyâri, and horseman; each claiming his interposition, and a decision in his favour. All spoke together; every one telling his own tale. But the Brâhman had lost his hearing also. "I know," said he, "you want to compel "me to return home to her" (meaning his wife); "but do you know "her character? In all the legions of the devils, I defy you to find "one that is her equal in wickedness. Since the time I first bought "her, she has made me commit more sin than it will be in my power "to expiate in thirty generations. I am going on a pilgrimage to "Kaśi (Benares), where I will wash myself from the innumerable "crimes I have been led into from the hour in which I had the mis-"fortune to make her my wife. Then will I wear out the rest of "my days, on alms in a strange land."

While they were all four venting their exclamations, without hearing a word; the horse-stealer perceived some people advancing towards them with great speed. Fearing they might be the owners of the beast, he dismounted and took to his heels. The shepherd, seeing it was growing late, went to look after his flock; pouring out curses, as he trudged, against all arbitrators, and bitterly complaining that all justice had departed from the earth. Then he bethought himself of a snake that crossed his path in the morning, as he came out of the sheepfold, and which might account for the troubles he had that day experienced. The Talaiyâri returned to his load of grass; and finding the lame sheep there, he took it on his shoulder, to punish the shepherd for the vexation he had given him; and the aged Brâhman pursued his course to a choultry that was not far off. A quiet night and sound sleep soothed his anger in part; and, early in the morning, several Brâhmans, his neighbours and relations, who had traced him out, persuaded him to return home, promising to engage his wife to be more obedient and less quarrelsome in future.

Tale of the Four simple Brâhmans.

In a certain district, proclamation had been made of a Samaradanam being about to be held. This is one of the public festivals given by pious people, and sometimes by those in power, to the Brâhmans; who, on such occasions, assemble in great numbers from all quarters. Four individuals of the caste, from different villages, all going thither, fell in upon the road; and, finding that they were all upon the same errand, they agreed to walk in company. A soldier happening to meet them, saluted them in the usual way by touching hands and pronouncing the words, always applied on such occasions to Brâhmans, of *daṇḍam-ârya*, or *health to my lord.* The four travellers made the usual return, each of them pronouncing the customary benediction of *âśirvâdam*; and, going on, they came to a well, where they quenched their thirst, and reposed themselves in the shade of some trees. Sitting there, and finding no better subject of conversation, one of them asked the rest, whether they did not remark how particularly the soldier had distinguished him, by his polite salutation. "You!" says another, "it was not you that he saluted, but me." "You are both mistaken," says a third, "for you may remember that, when the soldier said "*daṇḍam-ârya*, he cast his eyes upon me." "Not at all," replied the "fourth, "it was me only he saluted; otherwise should I have answered "him as I did, by saying âśirvâdam?"

Each maintained his argument obstinately; and, as none of them would yield, the dispute had nearly come to blows, when the least stupid of the four, seeing what was likely to happen, put an end to the brawl by the following advice: "How foolish it is in us," says he, "thus to put ourselves in a passion! After we have said all the "ill of one another that we can invent, nay after going stoutly to "fisticuffs, like Śûdra rabble, should we be at all nearer to the deci- "sion of our difference? The fittest person to determine the contro- "versy, I think, would be the man who occasioned it. The soldier, "who choose to salute one or other of us, cannot be yet far off. Let "us therefore run after him as quickly as we can, and we shall soon "know for which of us he intended his salutation."

The advice appeared wise to them all, and was immediately adopted. The whole of them set off in pursuit of the soldier; and at last overtook him, after running a league, and all out of breath. As soon as they came in sight of him, they cried out to him to stop; and, before they had well approached him, they had put him in full possession of the nature of their dispute, and prayed him to terminate it by saying, to which of them he had directed his salutation. The soldier instantly perceiving the nature of the people he had to do with, and being willing to amuse himself a little at their expence, coolly replied, that he intended his salutation for the greatest fool of all the four; and then, turning on his heel, he continued his journey.

The Brâhmans, confounded with this answer, turned back in silence. But all of them had deeply at heart the distinction of the salutation of the soldier, and the dispute was gradually renewed. Even the awkward decision of the warrior could not prevent each of them from arrogating to himself the pre-eminence of being noticed by him, to the exclusion of the others. The contention therefore now became, which of the four was the stupidest; and, strange as it was, it grew as warm as ever, and must have come to blows, had not the person who gave the former advice, to follow the soldier, interposed again with his wisdom, and spoken as follows.

"I think myself the greatest fool of you all. Each of you thinks "the same thing of himself. And, after a fight, shall we be a bit "nearer the decision of the question? Let us therefore have a little "patience. We are within a short distance of Dharmapuri, where "there is a choultry, at which all little causes are tried by the heads "of the village; and let ours be judged among the rest."

All agreed in the soundness of the advice; and having arrived at the village, they eagerly entered the choultry, to have their business settled by the arbitrators.

They could not have come to a better season. The chiefs of the district, Brâhmans and others, had already met in the choultry; and no other cause offering itself, they proceeded immediately to that of the Brâhmans. All the four advanced into the middle of the court, and stated, that a sharp contest having arisen among them, they were come to have it decided with fairness and impartiality. The court desired them to proceed and explain the grounds of their controversy.

Upon this, one of them stood forward, and related to the assembly all that had happened, from their meeting with the soldier to the present state of the quarrel; which rested on the superior degree of stupidity of some one of them over the others.

The detail created an universal shout of laughter. The president, who was of a gay disposition, was delighted beyond measure to have fallen in with so diverting an incident. But he put on a grave face, and laid it down, as the peculiarity of the cause, that it could not be determined on the testimony of witnesses, and that in fact there was no other way of satisfying the minds of the judges, than by each, in his turn, relating some particular occurrence of his life, on which he could best establish his claim to superior folly. He clearly shewed that there could be no other means of determining to which of them the salutation of the soldier could with justice be awarded. The Brâhmans assented, and upon a sign being made to one of them to begin, and to the rest to keep silence, the first thus commenced his oration.

" I am poorly provided with clothing as you see; and it is not " to-day only that I have been covered with rags. A rich and very cha- " ritable Brâhman merchant once made me a present of two pieces of " cloth to attire me; the finest that had ever been seen in our *Agrâ-* " *grama.* I showed them to the other Brâhmans of the village, who all " congratulated me on so fortunate an acquisition. They told me it " must be the fruit of some good deeds that I had done in a preceding " generation. Before I put them on, I washed them, according to the " custom, in order to purify them from the soil of the weaver's touch; " and hung them up to dry, with the ends fastened to two branches of " a tree. A dog then happening to come that way, run under them, " and I could not discern whether he was high enough to touch the " clothes or not. I asked my children, who were present; but they " said they were not quite certain. How then was I to discover the " fact? I put myself upon all fours, so as to be of the height of the " dog; and, in that posture, I crawled under the clothing. Did I " touch it? said I to the children who were observing me. They " answered 'No:' and I was filled with joy at the news. But after " reflecting awhile, I recollected that the dog had a turned up tail; " and that, by elevating it above the rest of his body, it might well " have reached my cloth. To ascertain that, I fixed a leaf to my " rump, turning upwards; and then, creeping again on all fours, I " passed a second time under the clothing. The children immediately " cried out that the point of the leaf on my back had touched the " cloth. This proved to me that the point of the dog's tail must have " done so too, and that my garment was therefore polluted. In my " rage, I pulled down the beautiful raiment, and tore it in a thousand " pieces, loading with curses both the dog and his master.

" When this foolish act was known, I became the laughing stock " of all the world; and I was universally treated as a madman. " 'Even if the dog,' they all said: 'had touched the cloth, and so "brought defilement upon it, might not you have washed it a second "time, and so have removed the stain? Or might you not have "given it to some poor Sûdra rather than tear it in pieces? After "such egregious folly, who will give you clothes another time?' "This was all true; for ever since, when I have begged clothing of "any one, the constant answer has been, that no doubt I wanted "a piece of cloth to pull to pieces."

He was going on, when a bystander interrupted him by remarking that he seemed to understand going on all fours. "Exceedingly well," says he, "as you shall see;" and off he shuffled in that posture, amidst the unbounded laughter of the spectators.

"Enough, enough!" said the president. "What we have both "heard and seen goes a great way in his favour. But let us now hear "what the next of you has to say for himself, in proof of his stupidity." The second accordingly began, by expressing his confidence, that, if what they had just heard appeared to them to be deserving of the salutation of the soldier, what he had to say would change that opinion.

"Having got my hair and beard shaven one day," he continued, "in order to appear decent at a public festival of the Brâhmans (the "Samârâdanam), which had been proclaimed through all the district, "I desired my wife to give the barber a penny for his trouble. She "heedlessly gave him a couple. I asked of him to give me one of "them back; but he refused. Upon that we quarrelled, and began "to abuse each other; but the barber at length pacified me, by offer-"ing, in consideration of the double fee, to shave my wife also. I "thought this a fair way of settling the difference between us. But "my wife, hearing the proposal, and seeing the barber in earnest, "tried to make her escape by flight. I took hold of her and forced "her to sit down, while he shaved her poll in the same manner as "they serve widows. During the operation, she cried out bitterly; "but I was inexorable, thinking it less hard that my wife should be "close shaven than that my penny should be given away for nothing. "When the barber had finished, I let her go, and she retired immedi-"ately to a place of concealment, pouring down curses on me and the "barber. He took his departure; and meeting my mother in his "way, told her what he had done; which made her hasten to the "house, to inquire into the outrage; and when she saw with her own "eyes that it was all true, she also loaded me with invectives.

"The barber published every where what had happened at our "house; and the villain added to the story, that I had caught her "with another man, which was the cause of my having her shaved; "and people were no doubt expecting, according to our custom in "such a case, to see her mounted on the ass, with her face turned "towards the tail. They came running to my dwelling from all "quarters, and actually brought an ass to make the usual exhibition "in the streets. The report soon reached my father-in-law, who "lived at a distance of ten or twelve leagues, and he, with his wife, "came also to inquire into the affair. Seeing their poor daughter in

" that degraded state, and being apprised of the only reason; they " reproached me most bitterly; which I patiently endured, being " conscious that I was in the wrong. They persisted, however, to " take her with them, and kept her carefully concealed from every " eye for four whole years; when at length they restored her to me.

" This little accident made me lose the Samârâdanam, for which " I had been preparing by a fast of three days; and it was a great " mortification to me to be excluded from it, as I understood that it " was a most splendid entertainment. Another Samârâdanam was " announced to be held ten days afterwards, at which I expected to " make up for my loss. But I was received with the hisses of six " hundred Brâhmans, who seized my person, and insisted on my " giving up the accomplice of my wife, that he might be prosecuted " and punished, according to the severe rules of the caste.

" I solemnly attested her innocence, and told the real cause of " the shaving of her hair; when an universal burst of surprise took " place; every one exclaiming, how monstrous it was that a married " woman should be so degraded, without having committed the crime " of adultery! Either this man, they said, must be a liar, or he is " the greatest fool on the face of the earth! Such I dare say, " gentlemen, you will think me; and I am sure you will consider my " folly," (looking here with great disdain on the first speaker) " as " being far superior to that of the render of body clothing."

The court agreed that the speaker had put in a very strong case; but justice required that the other two should also be heard. The third claimant was indeed burning with impatience for his turn; and, as soon as he had permission, he thus began.

" My name was originally Anantya. Now, all the world call " me Betel Anantya; and I will tell you how this nickname arose.

" My wife, having been long detained at her father's house, on " account of her youth, had cohabited with me but about a month; " when, going to bed one evening, I happened to say, carelessly I " believe, that all women were prattlers. She retorted, that she " knew men who were not less prattlers than women. I perceived " at once that she alluded to myself; and being somewhat piqued at " the sharpness of her retort, I said, Now let us see which of us " shall speak first. 'Agreed,' quoth she; 'but what shall the loser " forfeit?' A leaf of betel, said I; and our wager being thus agreed, " we both addressed ourselves to sleep without speaking another word.

" Next morning as we did not appear at our usual hour, after " some interval, they called us, but got no answer. They again " called, and then roared stoutly at the door; but with no success. " The alarm began to spread in the house. They began to fear that " we had died suddenly. The carpenter was called with his tools. " The door of our room was forced open; and, when they got " in, they were not a little surprised to find both of us broad awake, " in good health, and at our ease, though without the faculty of "speech. My mother was greatly alarmed, and gave loud vent to "her grief. All the Brâhmans in the village, of both sexes, assembled, "to the number of one hundred; and, after close examination, every "one drew his own conclusion on the accident which was supposed to "have befallen us. The greater number were of opinion, that it could "have arisen only from the malevolence of some enemy, who had "availed himself of magical incantations to injure us. For this reason "a famous magician was called, to counteract the effects of the witch-"craft, and to remove it. As soon as he came, after stedfastly con-"templating us for some time, he began to try our pulses, by putting "his finger on our wrists, on our temples, on the heart, and on vari-"ous other parts of the body; and, after a great variety of grimaces, "the remembrance of which excites my laughter, as often as I think "of him, he decided that our malady arose wholly from the effect of "malevolence. He even gave the name of the particular devil that "possessed my wife and me, and rendered us dumb. He added that "this devil was very stubborn and difficult to lay; and that it would "cost three or four pagodas, for the expence of the offerings necessary "for compelling him to fly.

"My relations, who were not very opulent, were astonished at "the grievous imposition which the magician had laid on. Yet, "rather than we should continue dumb, they consented to give him "whatsoever should be necessary for the expence of his sacrifice; and "they farther promised, that they would reward him for his trouble, as "soon as the demon by whom we were possessed should be expelled.

"He was on the point of commencing his magical operations, "when a Brâhman, one of our friends who was present, maintained, "in opposition to the opinion of the magician and his assistants, that "our malady was not at all the effect of witchcraft, but arose from "some simple and ordinary cause; of which he had seen several "instances; and he undertook to cure us without any expence.

"He took a chafing dish filled with burning charcoal, and heated "a small bar of gold very hot. This he took up with pincers, and applied "to the soles of my feet, then to my elbows, and the crown of my head. "I endured these cruel operations, without shewing the least symptom "of pain, or making any complaint; being determined to bear any "thing, and to die, if necessary, rather than lose the wager I had laid.

"'Let us try the effect on the woman,' said the doctor, astonished "at my resolution and apparent insensibility. And immediately, taking "the bit of gold, well heated, he applied it to the sole of her foot. She "was not able to endure the pain for a moment, but instantly screamed "out: 'Appâ, enough!' and, turning to me, 'I have lost my wager,' "she said; 'there is your leaf of betel.' Did I not tell you, said I, "taking the leaf, that you would be the first to speak out, and that "you would prove by your own conduct that I was right in saying "yesterday, when we went to bed, that women are babblers?

"Every one was surprized at the whole proceeding; nor could "any of them comprehend the meaning of what was passing between "my wife and me; until I explained the kind of wager we had made "overnight, before going to sleep. 'What!' they exclaimed, 'was "it for a leaf of betel that you have spread this alarm through your "own house, and the whole village? for a leaf of betel, that you "shewed such constancy, and suffered burning from the feet to the "head upwards? Never in the world was there seen such folly!' "And from that time I have been constantly known by the name of "Betel Anantya."

The narrative being finished, the court were of opinion that so transcendant a piece of folly gave him high pretensions in the depending suit; but it was necessary, first, to hear the fourth and last of the suitors; who thus addressed them:

"The maiden to whom I was betrothed, having remained six or "seven years at her father's house, on account of her youth, we were "at last apprized that she was become marriageable; and her parents "informed mine that she was in a situation to fulfil all the duties of a "wife, and might therefore join her husband. My mother, being at "that time sick, and the house of my father-in-law being at the distance of five or six leagues from ours, she was not able to undertake "the journey. She therefore committed to myself the duty of bringing home my wife, and counselled me so to conduct myself, in words "and actions, that they might not see that I was only a brute. "'Knowing thee as I do,' said my mother as I took leave of her, 'I "am very distrustful of thee.' But I promised to be on my good "behaviour; and so I departed.

"I was well received by my father-in-law, who gave a great "feast to all the Brâhmans of the village on the occasion. He made "me stay three days, during which there was nothing but festivity. "At length, the time of our departure having arrived, he suffered my "wife and myself to leave him, after pouring out blessings on us "both, and wishing us a long and happy life, enriched with a numerous posterity. When we took leave of him, he shed abundance of "tears, as if he had foreseen the misery that awaited us.

"It was then the summer solstice, and the day was excessively "hot. We had to cross a sandy plain of more than two leagues; and "the sand, being heated by the burning sun, scorched the feet of my "young wife, who being brought up too tenderly in her father's "house, was not accustomed to such severe trials. She fell a crying, "and being unable to go on, she lay down on the ground, saying she "wished to die there.

"I was in dreadful trouble, and knew not what step to take; "when a merchant came up, travelling the contrary way. He had a "train of fifty bullocks, loaded with various merchandize. I ran to "meet him, and told him the cause of my anxiety with tears in my "eyes; and entreated him to aid me with his good advice, in the "distressing circumstances in which I was placed. He immediately "answered, that a young and delicate woman, such as my wife was, "could neither remain where she lay, nor proceed in her journey, "under so hot a sun, without being exposed to certain death. Rather "than that I should see her perish, and run the hazard of being "suspected of having killed her myself, and be held guilty of one of "the five crimes which the Brâhmans esteem the most heinous, he "advised me to give her to him, and then he would mount her on "one of his cattle, and take her along with him. That I should be a "loser, he admitted; but all things considered, it was better to lose her, "with the merit of having saved her life, than equally to lose her, under "the suspicion of being her murderer. 'Her trinkets,' he said, 'may "be worth fifteen pagodas. Take these twenty, and give me your wife.'

"The merchant's arguments appeared unanswerable: so I yielded "to them, and delivered to him my wife, whom he placed on one of "his best oxen, and continued his journey without delay. I con- "tinued mine, also, and got home in the evening, exhausted with hunger "and fatigue, and with my feet almost roasted with the burning sand, "over which I had walked the greater part of the day.

"Frightened to see me alone, 'Where is your wife?' cried my "mother. I gave her a full account of every thing that had happened "from the time I left her. I spoke of the agreeable and courteous "manner in which my father-in-law had received me, and how, by "some delay, we had been overtaken by the scorching heat of the sun "at noon, so as that my wife must have been suffocated, and myself "suspected of her murder, had we proceeded; and that I had pre- "ferred to sell her to a merchant who met us, for twenty pagodas. "And I shewed my mother the money.

"When I had done, my mother fell into an ecstacy of fury. She "lifted up her voice against me with cries of rage, and overwhelmed "me with imprecations and awful curses. Having given way to "these first emotions of despair, she sunk into a more moderate tone. "'What hast thou done, wretch!' said she 'what hast thou done! "sold thy wife, hast thou! delivered her to another man! A Brâhma- "nâri is become the concubine of a vile merchant! Ah! What will "her kindred and ours say when they hear the tale of this brutish "stupidity, of folly so unexampled and degrading!'

"The relations of my wife were soon informed of the sad adven- "ture that had befallen their unhappy girl. They came over to attack "me, and would certainly have murdered me, and my innocent "mother, if we had not both made a sudden escape. Having no direct "object to wreak their vengeance upon, they brought the matter "before the chiefs of the caste, who unanimously fined me in two "hundred pagodas, as a reparation to my father-in-law, and issued "a prohibition against so great a fool being ever allowed to take "another wife; denouncing the penalty of expulsion from the caste, "against any one who should assist me in such an attempt. I was "therefore condemned to remain a widower all my life, and to pay dear "for my folly. Indeed, I should have been excluded for ever from my "caste, but for the high consideration in which the memory of my "late father is still held, he having lived respected by all the world

"Now that you have heard one specimen of the many follies of "my life, I hope you will not consider me as beneath those who have "spoken before me; nor my pretensions altogether undeserving of "the salutation of the soldier."

The heads of the assembly, several of whom were convulsed with laughter while the Brâhmans were telling their histories, decided, after hearing them all, that each had given such absolute proofs of folly as to be entitled, in justice, to a superiority in his own way; that each of them therefore should be at liberty to call himself the greatest fool of all, and to attribute to himself the salutation of the soldier. Each of them having thus gained his suit, it was recommended to them all to continue their journey, if it were possible, in amity. The delighted Brâhmans rushed out of court, each exclaiming that he had gained his cause.

Tale of Apaji, Prime Minister of King Krishnarâya.

Although the composition I am now about to describe be placed in the list of tales, yet it is believed to be founded on historical truth; the memory of the good King Krishnarâya, and his faithful minister Apaji, being still held in reverence among the Hindûs. They flourished a short time anterior to the first invasion of the country by the Muhammadans; and their sole ambition was to make their subjects happy. But, whether history or tale, the narrative affords a good illustration of the customs and usages of the people.

In the happy times, when the race of Hindûs was governed by native Princes, one of their monarchs, called Krishnarâya, bore rule over one of the most extensive and richest provinces of that vast country. His only study was to gain the respect and love of his people, by rendering them happy; and, with that view, he was particularly solicitous to admit none into his service or counsels but men whose experience and prudence would insure a wise administration of the state. His prime minister Apaji, stood highest in his confidence, because, with many other excellent qualities, he possessed the happy talent of displaying truth in entertaining and striking allegories.

One day, when at the court of his master, nothing of greater importance being under consideration, the King proposed to him the following question.

"I have often heard it said, Apaji, that men in their civil and "religious usages, only follow a beaten track; and that the form of "worship, or of other customs, being once established, continues to "be blindly acted upon by the undiscerning multitude, however "absurd and ridiculous it may be. I desire that you will prove to "me the truth of that opinion, and shew me the justice of the trite "adage so constantly employed through the whole country, '*Jana* "*Marulô? Jâtrâ Marulô?*'[1] the meaning of which I take to be: Is "it the men or their customs that are ridiculous?"

[1] This is still a common proverb. Kannada Gâdegalu, p. 28, No. 888. Bibliotheca Karṇaṭaca.

Apaji, with his usual modesty, promised the King to apply himself to the solution of that proverbial question, and to give his answer in a few days.

After the King had dismissed his council, Apaji wholly occupied with the question which his master had given him to resolve, went home, taking with him the shepherd who had the care of the King's flock; a man of a gross and rough nature, as those of his profession generally are. He thus addressed him: "Hear me, Kurubâ; you "must instantly lay aside your shepherd's clothing, and put on that " of a Sannyâsi or Penitent, whom you are to represent for a certain " time. You will begin, by rubbing your whole body with ashes. " You will then take in one hand, a bamboo rod with seven knots, " and, in the other, the pitcher, in which a penitent always carries " his water. Under your arm, you will take the antelope skin, on " which persons of that profession must always sit. This being done, " go without delay to the mountain nearest to this town, and enter the " cavern in the middle of the hill, which every one knows. Going to " the farther end of it, you will spread the antelope skin on the ground, " and sit down upon it, in the manner of a penitent. Your eyes must " be fixed on the ground, while one hand keeps your nostrils shut, and " the other is resting on the crown of your head. But be careful to " perform your part well, and see that you do not betray me. It may " happen that the King himself, with all his retinue, and vast multi- " tudes of people, may go to see you; but, whether I, or even the " King himself, shall be there, you must remain immoveable in the " posture which I have described. And, whatever pain you may " suffer, even if they shall pluck up all your hairs one by one, you " must appear to feel as little as if you were dead; complaining of " nothing, attending to nothing; looking at nobody, speaking to " nobody. There, shepherd! That is what I demand of thee. And if " thou transgress my orders, in the slightest degree, thy life shall " answer for it; but if on the contrary thou shalt execute them as I " expect, thou shalt be most liberally rewarded."

The poor shepherd, having been all his life accustomed only to feed his sheep, had no ambition to change his employment for that of a Sannyâsi; but his master's commands were uttered in so determined a tone, that he saw any attempt of his to alter them to be altogether useless, and therefore prepared to play the part of the Penitent. Every thing being in order, he betook himself to the cave appointed, with the resolution of executing the orders of his master.

Apaji, in the meantime, went to the palace, where he found the King already surrounded by his courtiers. Having approached him, he addressed him to this effect:

" Great King! While you are occupied in the midst of your wise " counsellors with the means of making your subjects happy, I am " under the necessity of interrupting you, by announcing to you the " most happy news, and that the day is arrived when the gods, " delighted with your virtues, have chosen to give you a signal proof of

" their protection and favour. At the time I am now speaking, a " great wonder is exhibited in your kingdom, and very near your own " palace. In the middle of the mountain, which is but at a short " distance from your capital, there is a cave, in which a holy penitent, " descended without doubt from the dwelling place of the great " Vishṇu, has taken up his abode. In profound meditation on the " perfections of Para-Brâhma, he is wholly insensible to all terrestrial " objects. He has no other nourishment than the air which he breathes, " and none of the objects that affect the five senses make the slightest " impression on him. In a word, it may be truly said, that the body " alone of this great personage resides in this lower world, whilst his " soul, his thoughts, and all his affections, are closely united to the " divinity. I have no doubt that the gods, in sending him to visit " your kingdom, have deigned to give you an unequivocal proof of " their favour and kindness to you and your people."

The King and all his court listened, with earnest attention, and remained for some time looking at each other in deep amazement. At last the King, with their unanimous concurrence, determined to visit the illustrious stranger, and implore his blessing. He went accordingly, in magnificent procession, with his court and troops attending. The royal trumpets sounded in all parts, to announce the object of the visit, and invite all persons whatever to attend. As they came near the mountain, the numbers encreased; and, never before, had such an assembly been seen. Every face was cheerful, and every heart rejoiced to have lived to see so distinguished a personage upon earth.

The King and the splendid throng had ascended the mountain, and approached the cave where the pretended Sannyâsi lived, in deep seclusion from the world, and in intimate union with the deity. The King, already penetrated with religious awe, entered the holy retreat, with marks of submission and reverence in his demeanour. There he saw the object of his respect, in a remote corner. He paused awhile, and gazed at him in silence. It was a human form he saw, sitting on the skin of an antelope, with a pitcher of water on one side, and a seven knotted bamboo rod on the other. Its head hung down, and its eyes were fixed on the ground. One hand kept the nostrils shut, and the other rested on its head. Its body seemed as motionless as the rock on which it lay.

The King was struck with reverential dread. He drew near to the penitent; and thrice he prostrated himself at his feet, and then addressed him in these terms:

" Mighty Penitent! Blessed be my destiny which has prolonged " my existence to this day, when I have the inexpressible felicity of " seeing your holy feet. What I now behold, with mine own eyes, " infinitely exceeds the public renown which emblazons your virtues. " The happiness of this hour, I know not whence it comes. The few " good deeds I have performed, in the present generation, are surely " inadequate to so distinguished a favour; and I can attribute it only " to the merits of my ancestors, or to some signal work which I may " have been enabled to perform in a preceding generation, the memory

" of which I no longer retain. But, however that may be, the hour, " in which I now first see your hallowed feet is far the happiest of my " life. Henceforth, I can have nothing to wish for in this world. It " is enough for any mortal to have seen those sacred feet; for, so " beatific a vision will blot out all the sins I have committed in this " and all preceding generations. Now am I as pure as the sacred " stream of the Ganges, and I have nothing more to wish for on earth."

The counterfeit penitent received the flattering speech of the monarch without emotion, and inflexibly maintained his posture. The numerous spectators were amazed, and could only whisper to each other, what a great being that must be, who could hear the submissive addresses of such a King, without deigning to cast a glance of approbation towards him. Well might it be said, they thought, that the body only of the holy penitent remained upon the earth, while his thoughts, his sentiments and his soul had been reunited to Para-Brahma.

King Krishnarâya continued to gaze with admiration, and tried by farther flattering and compliment, to gain but a single look of the Sannyâsi; but the penitent continued absorbed in thought.

The King was then about to take his leave; but the minister Apaji interposed. " Great Monarch," he said, having come so far to " visit this holy personage, who will henceforth be the object of " public veneration, and not having yet received his benediction, it " would be desirable at least, to have some memorial of him, to " preserve as a precious relic; if it were no more than one of the " hairs, which grow so profusely on his body."

The King approved the advice of his minister, and immediately advanced, and neatly plucked a hair from the shaggy breast of the Sannyâsi. He put it to his lips and kissed it. " I shall enshrine it," said he, " in a box of gold, which I shall always wear suspended to " my neck, as the most precious of my ornaments. It shall be my " talisman against all accidents, and the source of perpetual good."

The ministers and other courtiers, who were about the King, followed his example; and each plucked a hair from the breast of the penitent, to be preserved as a holy relic. The innumerable multitude, who were spread over the mountain, gradually learned what was going on in the cave. Every one burned with desire to be possessed of so precious a memorial. Each plucked his relic, till the tortured shepherd had not a hair left on his body. But he endured his sufferings with heroic fortitude; and never winced, nor altered his stedfast look.

On his return to the palace, the King informed his wives of all that had passed, and showed them the relic he had brought from the breast of the Sannyâsi. They heard and looked with curiosity and wonder, and sorely lamented that the rigorous rules prescribed to the sex had not permitted them to accompany their husband to the cave, and to share in the general happiness and joy, by visiting the holy man. But the King might, as the greatest of favours, graciously permit the famous penitent to be brought to the palace, that they also might have the happiness of seeing him, and of selecting a hair from his body with their own hands.

The King made many difficulties, but at last consented to indulge the wishes of his wives; and, being desirous, at the same time, to do honour to the Sannyâsi, he ordered out his whole court, with his troops of horse and foot, to serve for an escort. On arriving at the cave, which was still surrounded by a part of the multitude, who had not yet got their hairs, the four chiefs of the cavalcade went up to him, and having unfolded the nature of their mission, they took up the motionless penitent in their arms, and placed him in a superb new palanquin, in the same posture in which they found him in the cave.

The shepherd sat immoveable in the palanquin, still keeping up the appearance of a Sannyâsi in contemplation, and was conducted in state through the streets of the city, in the midst of an immense concourse of people, who made the air resound with their rejoicings. The poor shepherd, in the meantime, who had eaten nothing for two days, during which his whole skin had been lacerated and torn by the perpetual plucking of the hairs, felt but little enjoyment from the triumph, and would have betrayed the plot, but for the dread of his master's anger. "Why should I," he would say to himself, "carry on a trick like this in the midst of torment and pain? I "would be in the company of my sheep, and hear tigers roaring in "the woods, rather than be deafened with the noise of their accla-"mations. Had I been with my flock, I should have had three good "meals before now; whereas after two days of fasting, I know not "when I may be relieved."

While such thoughts were passing in his mind, they arrived at the palace, and he was immediately introduced into a superb apartment, where he received a visit from the Princesses. They prostrated themselves, one by one at his feet; and after a pause of silent admiration, each of them would have a hair also, to be enshrined, like their husband's, in a box of gold, and to be worn continually, as the most precious ornament. It may be supposed that, after so much pincing and plucking, it would be no easy matter to find any thing remaining on the hide of the poor shepherd; and in fact it was not without carefully exploring various creases and folds, that each lady could be accommodated with a relic. At last, they concluded their devout visit, and retired; leaving the shepherd still maintaining his inflexible attitude of contemplation; from which he was at length relieved by the King giving orders, that the Sannyâsi should be left alone all night, in order to enjoy repose, after so much fatigue and suffering.

But Apaji found a secret entrance by which he introduced himself in the night to the hungry and smarting shepherd; and thus he addressed him in soothing accents: "Kurubû! the period of your "probation is accomplished. You have well performed the part I set "down for you, and you have fulfilled my expectations. I promised "you a recompence and you shall not be disappointed. In the "meantime, put off that dress, and resume your coarse woollen "*cambali.* Get something to eat, and go to bed, as you have need; "and, in the morning, go out as usual with your sheep."

The shepherd did not wait a second bidding, but quickly got into the fields, resolved not to act the Sannyâsi any more.

Early next morning, the King went with his retinue to renew his humble salutations to the holy penitent. They found him not, and they remained astonished for a while. But, on reflection, their veneration was augmented, for they could not doubt that it was some divinity, under a human form, who had come amongst them, on a temporary visit, to convince them of his being their protector; and had returned, in the night, to his heavenly abode. The advent and departure of this wonder were the only subject of conversation in court, town and country for several days. Then it gradually grew stale, and at last was but occasionally remembered, like any other antiquated miracle.

A good while afterwards, when Apaji was one day at court, the King put him in mind of the old proverb of *Jana Marulô, Jâtrâ Marulô,* and asked him whether he still thought that a people followed a particular track, merely because it happened to be laid down for them, and that, however ridiculous the ceremony and usages of a nation might be, those who practised them were still more ridiculous.

Apaji, who waited only for an opportunity like this, to enter on his favourite speculation; and having obtained permission to express himself without reserve, thus addressed the King:

"Great King! your own conduct some days ago decided this "question, when you condescended to visit the cave in the mountain, "and the pretended Sannyâsi who was there. You have allowed me "to speak without constraint, and I will therefore confess that the "venerable penitent was no other than the shepherd, who has been "all his life employed in keeping my sheep: a being so rough and "uncultivated as to approach nearly to utter stupidity. Such is the "personage whom you and your court, upon my sole testimony, have "treated with honours, almost divine, and have elevated to the rank of "a deity. The multitude, without examination, have blindly followed "your example, and, without any knowledge of the object of its adora-"tion, run with you into the excess of fanatical zeal, in favour of a keeper "of sheep, a low-born man, uneducated and almost a fool. From this "striking instance, you must be satisfied, that public institutions are "matters of example and habit, and that we ought to direct our "ridicule of the absurd usages of a country, not so much against the "usages themselves, as against those who practise them."

The king, like a wise sovereign, took in good part the strenuous efforts which his minister had boldly adopted to enlighten him on matters so important and abstruse, and continued to repose upon him as his most faithful subject and friend.

CHAPTER X.

OF THE MILITARY SYSTEM OF INDIA.

I OUGHT perhaps, in prudence, to close my description of the Hindû people and their customs, with the last chapter. My profession will justly appear to disqualify me from giving a full or satisfactory account of what relates to the subject of war. At the same time, as almost the whole of their public monuments, religious and profane, represent the image of war, and all their histories are filled with military details, a few remarks on that subject will not be deemed inconsistent with the nature of my work.

The caste of *Kshatriya*, or Kings, and that of *Râjaputras*, or descendants of Kings, were at one time the exclusive possessors of authority and government in the various countries of India; and to them the trade of war exclusively belonged. No others had a right to enrol themselves in the profession of arms.

The Hindû customs have undergone a great change in this particular. The ambition of conquerors has overstepped and subverted those primitive rules of their institution. At present, there are few Kings to be seen of that caste, from which, in right of birth, they ought all to spring. In India, as well as every where else, territory becomes the inheritance of the strongest, and in most of the provinces Princes of base extraction have, by boldness or cunning, raised themselves to the throne.

The right of bearing arms, which, in early times, belonged only to the Râjaputras, is now universal; and all castes, from the Brâhmans down to the Pariahs, may now become soldiers. Sometimes, Brâhmans are found commanding armies, and sometimes, particularly in the Mahratta service, standing in the ranks.

Although the rules and practices followed by the Hindûs seem to have been intended to enervate the natural courage, and to oppose insurmountable obstacles to the other qualities of a good soldier, yet the art of war amongst them appears as old as any other of their institutions; and, as a profession, it originally had, with them, the preference which it merited. In the scale of society, it had the second rank, and stood immediately after the priesthood, who had the pre-eminence due to those functions which place them between god and the human race.

Next to the Brâhmans, the soldiers enjoyed the highest privileges of any other citizens. Some of those privileges were common to them with the Brâhmans; such as the high distinction of being permitted to read the Vêdas, the right of being invested with the triple cord, and some others which the Brâhmans conceded to them, in consideration, no doubt, of the great benefits which they, as well as the society at large, derived from their services.

But although the profession of rms was known and honoured among the Hindûs of ancient times, and although the history of no country furnishes so many examples of wars, conquests, sieges, battles, victories, and defeats, as that of India, in old though fabulous periods; yet it must be admitted that there is probably no nation on earth where, though less honoured, the art was not cultivated with greater advantage and success.

Until the era of the modern invasions, by those fierce and sanguinary conquerors, who, at the head of their warlike and barbarous hordes, passed the mountains of the north to lay waste the fertile and peaceful provinces of India, inundating them with the innocent blood of a harmless race, whose undefended territories they usurped as lawful spoil; until then, the art of war was but in its infancy in India, and the same as it had been for three thousand years. The feeble resistance they made to those ferocious conquerors who so unworthily used the right of the sword, and who, (a thousand times worse than the swarms of locusts which frequently spread dismay over the land by devouring the sources of existence,) carried desolation and death wherever they directed their course, sufficiently proves the inferiority of the Hindû in discipline and courage.

Their wars are of three sorts: those of fabulous times, those of the ancient Kings, and those of modern date. In speaking of the last, I must premise, that I profess to treat only of such as were carried on by the Princes of the country with each other, before the experience of European tactics and skill had induced them to admit foreigners into their armies, for the purpose of being trained and disciplined by their superior abilities. This arose from their ambition, or rather from their narrow comprehension and dim perception of their own true interests, which hindered them from seeing the dangers which, sooner or later, must result from admitting such dangerous auxiliaries into their service. What I shall observe upon is antecedent to that epoch; which, I believe, does not go back more than sixty or seventy years.

I do not at all touch upon the fabled wars of their gods, with each other, or against the giants, which are so tediously given in their books; because they are entitled to no more attention than a sick person in a fit of delirium. They would introduce us to armies of giants, whose heads reached the stars, riding on elephants of a size adequate to their high stature. One of them will appear putting his shoulders under the firmament and lifting it up. Then, with awful concussion, he overturns the gods who dwell there, and shews what he is capable of doing, and what they have to fear. In the same style, a god goes forth to combat a giant, makes the earth his chariot, the rainbow his bow, and Vishnu his arrow. He discharges this tremendous shaft, and, at one stroke, utterly overwhelms an immense city, in which the giants, his enemies, were intrenched, and are now all buried in the ruins.

It would be easy for me to bring forward a thousand fooleries of this sort; which I have read in Hindû books; but they could answer no other purpose than to disgust the reader, and to prove that their poets are the most senseless of mortals.

The history of the wars of the ancient Kings of India is scarcely less extravagant than the other, and deserves no greater attention. It is not composed, in sober prose by historians, but by wild poets in enthusiastic verse; who, in this and in every thing besides, follow the bias of their disordered imagination. What truth can be described through the thick veil of their fable? The million of soldiers whom Xerxes conducted for the overthrow of Greece, are but a handful, when compared with the almost innumerable hosts of warriors that composed the armies of the ancient Princes of India. But there is nothing wonderful in such impostures, when we advert to the incurable tendency of the Hindûs to every kind of extravagance, whether in their narration, in conversation, in civil affairs, in religious opinions, or in any other circumstance of life.

But there is one thing connected with this subject, that is not fabulous; which is, that their armies were made up of four arms, which the Hindûs express by the word *Chatur-angam*. These four were elephants, chariots, cavalry, and infantry. United, they composed a complete army.

This mode of constructing an Indian army subsisted at the time of the invasion of Alexander the Great. It was followed in the army of Porus, who was subdued and taken prisoner by that great conqueror. Quintus Curtius remarks that, in the line of battle, there were arranged eighty-five elephants, three hundred chariots, and thirty thousand infantry. He does not enumerate the cavalry of the Indian King, but he afterwards alludes to it in his narrative.

What we have said of the four divisions of the ancient Indian armies, may serve to fix the origin of the game of chess, which has been the subject of so many disputes and researches, as well as to reform the mode of playing it in Europe; at least, as far as regards the chess-men. I believe it is generally admitted to be a military game. Castles, knights, pawns, and other terms justify that idea. But is it not ridiculous, in the European way of playing it, to see castles marching about; a queen in every part of the battle, and stoutly fighting; bishops, at the side of the King, maintaining a conspicuous share in the combat; and the like?

The Hindûs, who play this game as we do, with some slight variations, call it Chatur-angam, an army of four arms. At the two opposite sides of the chess board they plant the elephants, which were formerly surmounted with small towers. We have substituted in their place, thick solid castles with regular battlements all round, and we make those great masses fly nimbly about in all directions.

Instead of the bishops we employ, the Hindûs make use of cars, representing the vehicle anciently used in their armies. In place of our queen, whom we make very active in the battle, rather unsuitably to her sex, they bring forward what they call *Mantri*, or minister of state, a leader who changes from place to place during the fight, and sometimes strikes a blow, as he passes. All this we think sufficiently demonstrates that the Hindûs were the original inventors of chess.

The field of battle is called *Pura-Sthalam*, or place of combat. From this word is probably derived the name of Porus, which the ancient Greeks give to the King whom Alexander conquered on the banks of the Indus. They probably confounded the name of the place of the battle with that of the Prince who fought. This, probably, is not the only error into which the authors would fall who give such erroneous accounts of India and its inhabitants. But it is time to return from this digression to the constituent parts of the armies of the ancient Kings of India, beginning with the elephants.

All the ancient authors speak of towers, supported by these animals, filled with combatants, in the armies of the Asiatic Princes. But I believe we shall not form correct ideas on the subject, without making great allowances for the imagination of those writers. If these turrets were at all high, the motion of the animal, which from its manner of walking, is more jolting than that of any other, would necessarily make it lose its balance and tumble down. For the elephant does not move like other quadrupeds, advancing the legs alternately, but brings forward the two legs of one side together. If they were constructed with much solidity, they would be too heavy for the animal, which, though the strongest of any, does not support a weight proportioned to his size. For, powerful as he is, they can scarcely venture a heavier load on his back than twelve hundred weight; and they must take some pains to reconcile him even to that.

Of all that has been written, therefore, of castles filled with armed men, on the backs of elephants, a great deal must have been borrowed from indistinct observers, unacquainted with the nature of the animal, who, being astonished at its enormous bulk, fancied its strength to be equally great. Towers such as have been described are therefore plainly absurd. At the same time, I do not assert that the elephant has not been used, to great advantage, in war. The soldiers on his back were furnished with numbers of arrows, or other missile weapons, which they could employ with great effect against an enemy's army. The elephant himself, when accoutred for the combat, was still more terrible than his riders, and wonderfully contributed to spread terror and confusion amongst enemies unaccustomed to that species of warfare.

These extraordinary creatures, even at this day, are of great use in the armies of the Indian Princes. But they serve more for parade than for war. It belongs to the dignity of generals, and other chiefs, to be mounted on elephants, superbly harnessed; and, when they take the field, they are armed with the bow, with fire-arms, and often with a long spear; which they change in battle according to circumstances.

The elephant, by nature, has a great dread of fire; and they are obliged to train him by practice to endure it, and even habituate him to actual burnings, that he may not in battle be terrified and rendered unmanageable by the fire-works which are thrown amongst them. In sieges they are of great use, in forcing the gates of fortified places. And, to increase their efficiency, they are sometimes equipped with strong points of iron of great strength.

In the Mogul armies, an elephant always led the way in a march, having a long pole fixed on his head, with a great flag hoisted on its top. Another elephant generally followed, who carried on his back a small casket set in a niche, inclosing some relics, precious to the Muhammadans; sometimes, even, a true or pretended hair of the beard of the prophet.

The only unequivocal service which the elephant renders is in the transport of artillery. When the bullocks which draw the cannon are stopped by a slough or a ditch, or any similar impediment, one elephant or more are brought, who raise up the carriages with their trunks, and greatly assist in carrying them through bad roads. In passing rivers and canals, where there are no fords, the people and heavy baggage are transported on their backs. But these advantages, and others which might be mentioned, are greatly overbalanced by the expence of their keeping.

The chariots are the next department of the ancient armies of India. They appear to have been very numerous and of vast size. All the principal officers rode in them, and that of the King was particularly splendid. When two Princes were at war with each other, they still kept up the forms of politeness, and never commenced a battle without saluting each other from their chariots; concluding with mutual defiance. We read in one of their books that one of those Kings, when he rode up to give battle to his enemy, first shot an arrow of compliment, which dropped at the foot of his chariot. The other returned the civility in the same way, and then the combat began.

I have never seen a minute description of those vehicles; but the books in which they are mentioned describe them as being large, and drawn by five horses. In one book, I remember to have read of some Prince who, in preparing for war, got a troop of devils for a team; so that he could not fail to drive at a good pace. It was a regular appendage to all chariots, to be hung round with large bells, which would create a fine clangor in the field of battle, and serve to spread terror and dismay through the enemy's ranks.

Perhaps, it is in imitation of those ancient chariots of war, that the Hindûs of the present day decorate their carriages with many bells, the tinkling of which announces their approach from afar. But the cars, in which the Hindûs now sometimes travel, are of modern taste, and bear no analogy to the ancient war chariots.

Cavalry formed the third division of the Hindû army. Their strength, however, did not consist in that arm, their whole dependence being on the foot. This is now wholly changed in modern times, when the infantry are almost entirely laid aside, with the exception of a few undisciplined bands of freebooters, whose principal and indeed only business, is, not to fight, but to spread themselves about in the defenceless villages; to pillage, ravage, burn, and destroy whatever comes in their way; and to scatter havoc and desolation through the whole territory of the enemy.

The Moguls and Mahrattas, who, till lately, were the two principal powers who disputed the mastery, in many long, obstinate, and bloody wars, sometimes brought, on each side, upwards of a hundred thousand horse into the field. The Mahratta Princes, if united, could make a muster of three hundred thousand.

But they have never been able to bring forward any thing like this immense number of combatants; because they knew scarcely any thing of the military art. The severe lessons which the Europeans have continually afforded them, for more than three hundred years, since they have had a footing there, have scarcely yet opened their eyes to the defects of their ancient system of tactics, and the great superiority of those of their opponents. They have never yet known what the severity of discipline in an army may effect, or the advantage of the arrangement of the troops, the order of marching, and encampment. They are wholly devoid of the skill by which large masses of men are moved, without confusion or trouble; and they think they have done every thing when they have got together an immense and indiscriminate multitude, without order, and acting in the field from individual impulse and at random.

The General has under him a great number of chiefs, who command such horse troops as they can raise upon pay. Each man brings his own horse, and receives certain wages for himself and beast, which he keeps at his own expence; and when it dies or is lost, he also is dismissed from the service.

This method of recruiting their armies is extremely prejudicial to the enterprize of the soldier; because the great object of his care being to preserve the horse, upon the safety of which his own bread depends, he is always ready to make his escape, when any real danger appears.

In these armies, desertion is very frequent; nor are the deserters either strictly sought after or severely punished. What they chiefly depend upon as a preventive, is to keep up a good arrear of pay; which compels the soldier to remain at his colours, or to relinquish what he has earned. Sometimes, indeed, they mutiny in such cases, and arrest their General, or threaten him with the sabre: all which he is obliged to put up with, without blaming, far less punishing, the agitators. He reconciles them, in the best way he is able, by giving them acknowledgments at least of the debt; and the same slippery service is renewed.

Troops so undisciplined and mercenary cannot be expected to be very courageous; but marks of valour are often seen in their leaders, particularly among the Moors. They never fly in battle, though overmatched, while any of their people support them; and the point of honour is more concerned amongst them, in submitting to a retreat, than amongst us.

The privates in the Moorish and Mahratta cavalry are in general very poorly mounted. Parties of them sometimes make excursions, and burst into a district where they were not at all expected. It is not that good horses are not to be found in India, particularly in the northern states; but they are sold so high that private individuals cannot afford to buy them. The chiefs, however, take none but the best; and they are at great pains to find them. They decorate them in various ways, and often paint them over with different colours. They dress them also with infinite neatness, and mount them with perfect grace.

The Mahrattas accustom their steeds to stop when a certain cry is given. The horseman dismounts, and the horse stands still as if he were tied. I knew a late instance of a robber who, seeing a horse thus standing still, got upon his back to fly beyond the reach of his pursuers, and had got the animal into a gallop, when the owner perceived him, and instantly gave the accustomed cry to halt. The docile creature obeyed its master's call, perceived its error, and suddenly stopped. The robber tried all means to spur him on, but they were ineffectual; and he was fain to dismount and make his escape on his own legs.

The Moorish and Mahratta cavalry are armed with lances and arrows; to which some of them add the musquet. Many have a wretched sabre, and a great number carry cataris or daggers. Several have no other armour than the whip or rod, with which they push on their steed. Each individual provides his own horse and arms; and there is nothing like uniformity in their weapons or accoutrements.

They scarcely understand marching in a line, nor are they exercised in the evolutions of cavalry: which is indeed less necessary, as a general engagement is a thing almost unheard of amongst them. In their first wars there was nothing beyond skirmishes, or sudden surprizes by one party upon another, which generally ended with little bloodshed. The operations of an undisciplined army must always have consisted, as they do to this day in India, in burning and laying waste the enemy's country, in pillaging the poor defenceless inhabitants and putting them to the torture, to force them to disclose their concealed treasures. It is not therefore to be wondered at that small detachments of European cavalry or infantry should have been recently found to rout ten times their number of such a miserable host.

The infantry force was still more wretched before the present practice began, of permitting their troops to enter into the service of the Europeans, for the purpose of giving them discipline. Till then, foot soldiers were little known in the Mogul and Mahratta armies.

Infantry, however, were more esteemed among the Kings of antiquity; then forming the fourth order of their military establishment. It was then the most numerous part, and what was most relied on in their battles. And still it constitutes to this day the only strength of the little Princes of the country known commonly under the name of Poligars.

These Poligars, who may be compared, in several respects, with the Barons of France and England during the thirteenth century, who from their lofty castles and towers could brave and insult the royal authority, which they often found means to bridle and subdue, are very numerous in various provinces of India; and were still more so, before the great European power, which of late has extended its rule or influence over the country, had diminished the number of those privileged robbers. Their defences are thick forests, or steep mountains, where they can set at defiance those who rule over the countries which inclose them. The higher power, finding it impossible to reduce them without much labour; and fearing at the same time, by unnecessary violence, to rouse them to acts of pillage and devastation, is contented to live with them in the best manner it may.

The confined and barren territory, possessed by the Poligars, not being adequate to their maintenance and that of their horde, they keep a great number of robbers and plunderers in their employment, whom they send out, from time to time, in the night, to the neighbouring country; from which they return with their booty, and share it with their masters.

The English, however, after experiencing some loss, have, by perseverance, almost wholly eradicated this evil; and have shewn the robbers, to their cost, what military discipline and vigour can accomplish, in the most difficult enterprises.

The arms of these chiefs, and of those they have in their service, are bows and arrows, spears, and match-lock guns. They are utterly ignorant of regular battle or of maintaining a contest in the open field; but, when pursued, they betake themselves to their thick woods or steep rocks, where they endeavour to decoy the enemy into some narrow defile, suited to their active and desultory attacks. It was not without penetrating into the heart of their forests, and after great labour and loss, that the English succeeded in laying hold of their leaders, and establishing in their territory a state of order and tranquillity, which they had never known before.

Castrametation is as little understood by the Hindû Generals as the order of fighting. In their march, and encampment, there is the utmost confusion. When it is necessary for the army to halt, the great object attended to is the facility of obtaining water. A large supply is not every where to be found, particularly at certain times of the year: and whole armies have been seen reduced to the utmost extremity of distress by being deprived, even for a short time, of an article of such indispensable necessity in a burning climate.

A great flag, which goes first, and is raised very high, marks the place where the army is to halt. Every division takes up its ground beyond the standard, without regularity or order. The chief pitches his tent in the midst of his party, and hoists his flag upon it; every leader having one appropriate for himself, which may be distinguished by his own party. Thus every thing is in confusion, with the exception of a small space about the tent of the General, where some degree of order is observed; and likewise in the market place, where a very good police is kept up. Here all sorts of goods are to be seen, and various kinds of merchandise, in abundance, which are chiefly supplied from the plunder of the country through which the army has marched. For no Hindû army has any respect for property. Wherever they spread, rape, conflagration, pillage, devastation and every sort of excess accompany their progress.

The wasteful Hindûs scarcely know what it is to form a magazine, or to have convoys of provisions; trusting wholly to their foraging parties to supply their wants. And, so effectually is this done, that numbers of purveyors follow the armies, buying at a cheap rate, from the soldiers, the goods and property pillaged in the march, which they bring regularly to the market. On the other hand, when their march lies through a country already laid waste, these dealers follow with their oxen laden with provisions.

The most abominable profligacy exists in all their armies, but particularly among the Moors. The persons, who so devote themselves, have separate quarters which are perfectly well known, and not less frequented. The General makes them an object of revenue.

Among the followers of the camp there are numbers of mountebanks, all sorts of magicians, soothsayers and fortune-tellers, rope-dancers, slight of hand men, sharpers, thieves, faquirs, blind beggars, and in short so many useless mouths that they out-number the effective soldiers. Besides, every soldier is accompanied by his whole family; so that an army of twenty or five and twenty thousand soldiers, is attended by a train of two or three hundred thousand other individuals, whose chief employment it is to take advantage of the confusion which reigns in a camp, and to addict themselves to plunder and every other sort of licence. The Mahrattas are not so subject to this evil, because it is not so easy to keep up with them in the forced marches they are accustomed to make.

The tents of the chiefs, particularly amongst the Moors, are large and commodious, suited to the taste for luxury and voluptuousness which characterises the Asiatic Princes. They are filled with superb and useless finery, and divided into several apartments, of which some are for their wives or concubines, by whom they are always attended. In the midst of the tumult of camps, a Hindû Prince never forgets any thing that can administer to his appetites or enervate his courage.

To take an army of this sort by surprise, is no difficult operation;

for they keep no outposts. Their spies in the enemy's camp, in some measure, make up for the defect, by apprizing their friends, when they perceive any extraordinary movement of the enemy, and so putting them on their guard.

Assaults by night are but rare, the parties being more disposed to enjoy their own slumber than to disturb that of their enemies, at unseasonable hours.

The art of besieging towns was also, till of late, but little understood. Famine or capitulation were, in general, the only means resorted to for gaining possession of any place of strength. To attempt to take a town by storm, would have been considered an undertaking of desperation and madness: and it has often happened that places, surrounded only with old earthen walls, and defended by a few hundred of the neighbouring peasantry, with no arms but a few matchlock musquets, have been defended for a long time, against considerable armies; who, being fatigued and worn out by the continued repulses of the besieged, have been obliged to retire from the place, with the disgrace of having made no impression upon it whatever.

The state of safety in which the governor of a town, so besieged, considers himself to be, against all the efforts of a beleaguering army, is carried to a degree of confidence so unconquerable, that, even in these days, when they have had experience of what European courage and conduct can do, and have seen the awful consequences of a successful siege, followed up by an assault, they still retain their obstinacy. Instances have lately occurred of the commanders of these paltry earthen forts refusing to surrender, at the summons of an European army, defying it with insolence, and demeaning themselves, at the moment of the assault, as if they were only attacked by some undisciplined hordes.

In general, it is held a point of honour in the commander of a town, never to surrender at the first summons, however inconsiderable and defenceless the place may be, and however powerful the army that attacks it; let the terms proposed for capitulation be ever so reasonable. To surrender under such circumstances, would bring public disgrace upon the sovereign; and all the world would consider it an act of treason on the part of the governor.

The use of trenches has been long known to the Hindûs, and they have been accustomed to make their approaches by that means to the places they besiege. When the two parties thus get near to each other, they fall to mutual defiance and reproaches. "If you "cannot take this place," say the besieged Pagans to the Muhammadan aggressors, "you will look as queer as if you had been eating pork." "Very true," reply the Musalmans, "but if we do take it, "it will be as pleasant to you, as if you had eaten up a cow." Bravery is a virtue laid claim to by all nations, even by the most indolent and timid: and when people of that stamp, amongst whom we cannot refuse the Hindûs the very highest rank, feel themselves out of the reach of danger, they are the most apt to give a loose to vain glory and gasconade.

One method of taking a fortress, very much practised, is that of incantation. The besiegers employ magicians and sorcerers, who exert all the power of their wicked arts to paralyze the exertions of the besieged, and to make their leader fall. He, again, puts contrary spells in operation, fit to counteract these machinations, or even, of so potent a nature, as to aim at the total destruction of the besieging army. I know that, since I have been in India, all this has been practiced: with what advantage to either party, I leave to the reader to imagine.

The fortifications of places of the first order formerly consisted, and, in many parts, still consist, in one or two thick walls, flanked with round or triangular towers; upon which some pieces of cannon, but poorly supplied, are commonly mounted. A wide and deep ditch is on the outside; but, as the Hindûs are unskilful in the construction of bridges, they always leave a causeway from the gate of the town over the ditch, which is generally masked by a wall, that conceals it from without.

But, since the Europeans have introduced themselves among the Hindûs, as their masters in homicide; since they have made them the fatal present of their destructive tactics, and have taught them to cut each others throats with more method and effect, according to the refinements of military art; since, in furnishing them with engines more murderous than their own, they have had the abhorred distinction of teaching them by rule, the dreadful uses to which those instruments can be turned, for the destruction of the species: since that epoch, which they have for ever to deplore, the Hindûs have changed their modes of warfare, in the camp and field, as well as in the fortress.

The most considerable of their ancient places of strength are the castles, built on mountains of steep rock; many of which appear impregnable. They are called *Dûrgas,* and are seen in great numbers in that part of India which is most hilly. We find in Quintus Curtius* a description of one of these Dûrgas called *Aornus,* on the banks of the Indus, which stood out against Alexander, and which he was unable to take until abandoned by the garrison.

The Dûrgas that have a great elevation, have the inconvenience of a cold and humid atmosphere; while, in the valley, or at the foot of the rock, the air is mild, and sometimes hot. For this reason, those who are stationed in these high forts are unhealthy, and are subject to fevers, which are very difficult to cure.

I shall conclude this branch of my subject with a few words on the Arms of the country. The Hindûs have thirty-two different kinds of weapons, each of which has a particular name and description in

* Lib. viii. c. xi.

their books. Models of them are also to be seen in the hands of the images of their principal gods. Each of the thirty-two gods has his own peculiar weapon. It would be difficult to give in writing, any tolerable description of them, as hardly one of them bears the smallest resemblance to such as are known in Europe. All that can be said in general, is, that some are edged for hacking, some pointed for the thrust, and others obtuse and weighty for the purpose of contusion. Among the defensive, are the helmet and the shield, the latter is the more common, and is made of leather, studded with nails, with large round heads; and is generally about two feet in diameter.

Some Hindû soldiers, instead of a cuirass, wear a kind of thick and quilted jackets; a sort of armour greatly in use amongst the Hebrews of old, and other ancient people. They were made with great art, and could ward off the blows of cutting instruments; and the same advantage is attributed to those of the Hindûs: but they certainly are not impenetrable to musket-shot; and I cannot imagine that any advantage they afford can be at all equivalent to the inconvenience they occasion in sultry climates.

The most common weapon of offence, in ancient times, was the bow and arrow. It is still practised with skill and effect. Their arrows are small, not being more than two or two and a half feet long. The bows do not exceed that length, although their fables make those of their gods to be of a prodigious sweep. It is stated that the bow of Rama was carried with difficulty by fifty thousand men.

The favourite weapon of Vishṇu is the *Chakram;* which is a round or circular machine, of which many devotees of the god bear the emblem, imprinted on their shoulders with hot iron. It is still used in some places, and is nothing more than a large circular plate of iron, the outer edge of which is made very sharp. Through the centre a shaft passes, by means of which a rotatory motion is given to the plate, which whirls with great rapidity, and cuts whatever it approaches. I am inclined to believe, that neither this, nor several other weapons that I have seen represented in the hands of the idols, are at all used in any other nation.

Another species, very much in use among all the Hindû Princes, is a sort of large rocket, hooped with iron, and eight or ten inches long. They fire it in a horizontal position, and employ it chiefly in spreading confusion and disorder amongst the cavalry. They wound whatever they approach; and some emit a crescent of fire, which makes them exceedingly dangerous. In general they do not make so loud a report as our hand-grenades, but they have a more extensive range.

From the Hindû books, it appears that the use of these fire-works, which are called *Vâṇa* or *Bâṇa,* is very ancient. Mention is made in the Râmâyaṇa of the Váṇa or Rocket of Rama, as one of his principal missiles. The Váṇa is also one of the thirty-two species of arms enumerated by the ancient Hindûs; which is a proof that the use of gunpowder was not unknown to them, at an early period; for, without that material, it would be impossible to charge the rockets, which, from the oldest times to the present day, have been employed by this people.

Besides, the knowledge and practice of the various sorts of fire-works known in Europe, must have been of ancient date amongst the Hindûs; since there are some castes, whose ordinary, and sometimes only occupation, has always been the making of such preparations of gunpowder. It is probable that the Europeans have borrowed the art from them. But it is certain that they possessed it before the period of the modern invasions of the Christian and Muhammadan powers; which evidently establishes the invention of gunpowder, among them, to have preceded its discovery in Europe by many centuries.

At the same time it appears that the Hindûs were not formerly acquainted with the destructive effects of this powerful agent, when strongly compressed in metallic tubes. It was reserved to the Europeans to instruct them in this deplorable and pernicious science. For, till the invasions from Europe, the people of India made no use of gunpowder, but for pleasure and amusement. Their invaders taught them its murderous qualities.

Besides several of the ancient instruments peculiar to the nation, the Hindûs have lately adopted the lance, the dagger, and the sabre. The last is now their favourite weapon. They have masters of defence who teach the art; and they practise it very gracefully. But these arms are not often stained with the blood of an enemy.

The musket has also become a favourite amongst them, although, in their hands, it is not very fatal. Till lately, they had only match-locks, and their powder has been always very bad.

The Hindû armies are never exercised in firing. Their Princes think it a useless expence to waste powder in any other way than in the field of battle.

Of late, the Europeans have provided them with pieces of cannon, of brass and cast iron. They had iron ones before, but they were composed of separate bars, fastened together, and of an enormous calibre; and, with this miserable artillery, they shot stone balls of more than a foot in diameter. They did not understand any way of pointing them but horizontally. Their ignorance of the European mode of serving the artillery was often the cause of many of them losing their lives. I have read, in a manuscript written here about sixty years ago, that, about that time, the Râjah of Tanjore, for some grudge, having declared war against the Dutch, sent a considerable body of troops to take the fort of Negapatam. Some cannon shots were fired upon them from thence without taking effect. The King's troops, remarking that the bullets went high over their heads, advanced to the glacis, thinking they had nothing to fear from the artillery of their enemies. But the Dutch, taking the opportunity of their near approach, loaded their guns with grape-shot, and, taking a good aim, threw the whole army into disorder, and taught them, to their cost, how easy it was to change the direction of a cannon.

The author, from whom I quote, adds, that, on the same occasion, a Brâhman, in the service of the Râjah, having gone too near the fort, his palanquin was struck with a cannon-shot, and shivered in pieces. He himself was unhurt, having cautiously quitted it a little before; but his fear was so excessive that he fled, with the utmost precipitation; swearing, from time to time, by the three hundred and thirty millions of gods, that he would never again, while he lived, go within ten leagues of any colony inhabited by European dogs.

CHAPTER XI.

ON THE SECT OF THE JAINS AND THE PRINCIPAL DIFFERENCES BETWEEN THEM AND THE BRÂHMANS.

THE details which I propose to give on the sect of the *Jains*, their doctrines and particular customs, have been communicated to me by several learned persons, belonging to that sect, in various districts, and at different times. But, as my instructors did not agree in all points, I have thought it most prudent to avoid all uncertainty, by omitting every thing on which there was a diversity of opinion, and to admit that only on which they were all agreed. I have likewise taken pains to ascertain the authenticity of great part of what follows, by consulting several Jain books, which were for some time in my possession, and from which many of the particulars here given are abridged. So that I can venture to vouch for the accuracy of what I report.

The name *Jaina* is composed of two words *Ji* and *Na*, signifying a person that has renounced the ordinary modes of thinking and living among mankind.[m] For a true Jaina is bound to this separation from society, by his religion, which prescribes it, and also that he may avoid the scorn and sneers which the due performance of his sacred duties would there bring upon him; and by that firm belief in holy things which he must hold inviolable to his dying hour. Yea, his religion is the only true one upon earth; the primitive faith of all mankind.

In the progress of time, the true religion was gradually abused in different essential points; and abominations, corruptions, and superstitions of every kind have usurped its place. The Brâhmans who gained the ascendant, swerved from all the old religious maxims of their Hindû ancestors, laying aside the venerable traditions of their masters, and substituting in their place a monstrous combination in which there cannot be seen a trace of the primitive doctrines.

The Brâhmans are undoubtedly the inventors of the Vêdas, the eighteen Purâṇas, the Trimûrtti, and the extravagant fables of the Avatâras of Vishṇu, the infamy of the Lingam, the worship of the Cow and other animals, and of sensible objects, the sacrifice of the Yajna, and many other absurdities not less reprehensible. The whole of these are rejected by the *Jains*, who hold them to be a mass of abominations, innovations, and corruptions of the true and primitive religion.

---

[m] This is not the true Etymology: JINA is *one who has overcome human infirmities and passions;* and JAINA = appertaining to a JINA.

These depravations of the Brâhmans were not indeed introduced suddenly and at once, but insensibly and little by little. The Jains who then formed, with the Brâhmans, a part of the same general body of Hindûs, all possessing the same common religion, were unwilling to come to an open rupture, but never ceased, from the outset, to oppose with all their might the dangerous innovations and changes which that proud body were introducing into the pure system which every class of Indians had professed from the remotest times.

But the sound believers at that period, perceiving that all their endeavours to preserve the true religion pure and unspotted, were unavailing, and that the Brâhmans were continually advancing in apostacy with rapid strides, and seemed determined to bring matters to a crisis by drawing over the thoughtless multitude into the torrent on which they themselves had embarked, were forced into the unpleasant necessity of an open rupture. This became absolutely unavoidable when, after so many other innovations, the Brâhmans introduced the dangerous novelty of the sacrifice of Yajna, in which a living offering, generally a ram, is sacrificed, in contradiction to the most sacred and inviolable principles of the Hindûs, that uniformly and rigorously interdicted every species of slaughter, which, in its most innocent form, no necessity could justify.

After that detestable innovation, matters came to an extremity. The *Jains* assumed that appellation, which sufficiently denoted the course they were to pursue. They kept no longer any terms, but declared themselves in a state of open insurrection against the corrupters of the true primitive religion. They withdrew from the Brâhmans and all their adherents, and formed the body of Jains such as it now exists, and composed of some faithful Brâhmans, of Kshatriya or Soldiers, of Vaisya or Merchants, and of Sûdras or cultivators. These four divisions now compose the posterity of the Hindûs of every caste who united together, in early times, to oppose the innovations of the Brâhmans, and who have preserved in purity the pristine religion of the country.

After this rupture, the Jains, or true believers, never desisted, during a long course of time, to oppose the progress of the Brâhmans, and to reproach them with their apostacy and impious conduct. The points on which they differed had been till then the subjects merely of learned controversy, but now afforded grounds for a long and bloody war, in which the Jains held up for a long time against their adversaries. But the wicked innovations of the Brâhmans having gradually been adopted by most of the Kshatriya or Râjas, and the great majority of the other tribes, they became the more powerful party, and succeeded at last in beating down the Jains and reducing them to a state of abject submission; every where demolishing the places and objects of their worship, depriving them of their religious and civil liberty, excluding them from all places and employments, and reducing them to such absolute distress that in many provinces of India there does not remain the slightest vestige of the Jains or their worship.

This persecution and religious war, the commencement of which cannot be exactly ascertained, as, according to all appearances, it must have begun at a very remote period, seems to have continued to modern times; as we are assured that Kings and other Jain Princes exercised their government in many countries of the peninsula within these four or five hundred years; and it is asserted that it was under their protection, and by their assistance, that several of the temples and other public monuments were erected, which are at present held by that sect and are to be found in the different provinces.

The Brâhmans are now universally predominant. The Jains no where possess the land nor even confidential employment; but conform themselves in all places to the ordinary life of other Hindûs, addicting themselves, like the rest, to agriculture and trade. The tribe of Vaisya, the most numerous of any, is almost exclusively engaged in traffic, and chiefly in that of vessels of copper and other metals used by the Hindûs in their kitchens.

The Brâhmans intermixed with the Jains are not numerous. I have been informed, however, that in the south of the Mysore, at the distance of three or four days journey from the place where I am now writing, there are fifty or sixty families of Brâhman-Jains who have a temple for their own special use, with a Brâhman Guru of their sect, who officiates in it, at a village called Malaiyûr.[n]

In the principal temples pertaining to the sect, those for example of Belligolu, Madhu-giri and others, the Gurus or priests who perform the sacred functions, are taken from the tribe of Vaisya or Merchants, and not from that of Brâhmans. This usurpation on the part of the Vaisya, added to the reproach they lie under of having corrupted or altered the true religion of the Jains, by mixing it with several superstitious practices of their opponents, has excited against them the jealousy and distrust of the Brâhmans of the sect, who treat them as heretics. But the differences between them have never broken out into an open rupture.

The body of Jains is divided into two principal sects, one of which bears the name of *Jaina-Basru*, and the other *Kâshta-Sanghi-Swetambara.*[o]

Religious System of the Jains.

They acknowledge but one Supreme Being, one God only, to whom they give the appellations of *Jainéswara, Paramâtmâ, Parâparavastu*, and several others, all expressive of his infinite nature.

To this Being alone men ought to offer up their adoration and sacrifices.

The adoration and other marks of respect which the Jains frequently offer to their Tîrthakâras, their Chakravartis and to several

n Many interesting details regarding the JAINS are to be found interspersed through Dr. Buchanan's three Volumes.

o Meaning *White robed.*

other objects of worship held sacred among them, and represented under a human shape, naturally refer to the Supreme Being alone: for those holy personages, in taking possession after death of the Moksha or Mukti, the supreme felicity, have become intimately united and inseparably incorporated with the Divinity.

The Supreme Being is one and indivisible, spiritual and without parts or extension. His four principal attributes are as follows:

1. *Ananta Gnânam*:—Wisdom infinite.
2. *Ananta Darśanam*:—Intuition infinite; or knowing all things, and being every where present.
3. *Ananta Vîryam*:—Infinite power.
4. *Ananta Sukham*:—Infinite happiness.

This great Omnipotent is wholly absorbed in the contemplation of his own infinite perfections and in the enjoyment of his own blessedness.

He concerns not himself at all with earthly things, and intermeddles not with the order and government of this great universe.

The virtue and vice, the good and evil which prevail in the world are equally indifferent to him.

Virtue, being just and good in its own nature; those who practise it in this world, shall find an unbounded reward in another life, in a happy regeneration, or in immediate introduction to the *Swarga.*

Vice, being unjust and wicked in its nature, the vicious shall find a suitable punishment in an evil resurrection, or in descending straight into the infernal *Naraka,* there to expiate their crimes. But, in neither case, does the divinity interfere. He takes no concern in their actions here, nor in their rewards or punishments in a future state.

Matter is eternal, and independent of the Divinity. Whatever exists now, has always existed, and will continue for ever.

Not only is matter eternal, but the order also that prevails in the universe, such as the fixed and uniform motion of the stars, the separation of light from darkness, the succession and renovation of the seasons, the production, and reproduction of animal and vegetable life. In short, whatsoever is visible is also everlasting; and whatsoever is shall endure without considerable alteration.

Metempsychosis.

The most prominent dogma of the religion of the Jains is that of the transmigration of the soul of one body into another after death. The transition is from the body of one man into that of another man, or into that of a brute: and a soul is either elevated or degraded in this way, according to the previous virtue or vice of the possessor.

The Jains attempt to explain their system of future retribution in the following way.

Although a man may not have to reproach himself with great crimes, yet still the slightest tinge of vice discolours the genuine hue of virtue, and the offender must suffer transmigration into the body of an insect, a reptile, a bird, or a quadruped, and is degraded in this respect, less or more, according to the degree of his offences.

When the balance of virtue and vice stands nearly equal, and still more when the good outweighs the evil, the soul removes into the body of a rational creature, and regains a new existence, more or less happy in proportion to the degree of virtue which it preserved in the other world. The noblest transmigration of all is into a Brâhman or into a cow.

When an individual has led a life eminently virtuous, he passes directly after his decease to Swarga.

When a wicked man dies, he goes headlong into Naraka.

In these several particulars, the system of the Jains differs very little from that of their enemies the Brâhmans; but they differ more widely in their opinions concerning the *Lôkas* or *worlds*. For the Jains entirely reject the fourteen Lôkas of the Brâhmans and also their three principal abodes of happiness, the *Satya-lôka*, *Vaikuntha* and *Kailaśa*, the paradises of Brâhma, Vishṇu and Śiva.

The Jains admit but of three worlds, which they express by the generic name of *Jagat-triya*. It comprises the *Urddhwa-lôka*, the paradise, which is the highest of all; the *Adha-lôka*, hell, the lowest of all; and the *Madhya-lôka*, or middle world, the earth, the abode of mortals.

1. *The Urddhwa-lôka or Swarga.*

That world, the first of the Jagat-triya, has Dêvêndra for its king, and has for inhabitants only the virtuous few. There are sixteen mansions in the Swarga, in which a higher and a higher degree of happiness is enjoyed in proportion to the degree of virtue. The first and best of the sixteen, in which the highest felicity is found, is called *Sadhu-dharma*, and is attainable only by the eminently holy, who will here enjoy uninterrupted bliss for a period of thirty-three thousand years. The last and the lowest of the sixteen abodes is called *Achuda Karpa*, where the moderately virtuous are admitted and enjoy happiness for a thousand years. In the intermediate places a degree of enjoyment greater or less is inherited; and every virtuous soul has its mansion assigned according to its rank in merit.

The chief happiness enjoyed in these abodes arises from the company of many women of exquisite beauty, from whose society the blessed draw the purest delight, by indulging the senses of sight and hearing alone, and without animal gratification. They are ravished to ecstacy by the continual view of those enchanting creatures, whose melodious voices fill them with transports of delight infinitely beyond what carnal pleasures can bestow.

But this life does not continue for ever. After enjoying it for a fixed number of years, in a state of less or greater intensity of happiness according to the elevation of their respective merits, they are all doomed, each at his own prescribed period, to revisit the earth, where their souls renew the transmigration from body to body.

Adha-lôka or Naraka: Hell.

The Second World of the Jagat-triya is called *Adha-lôka* or *Naraka.* This is the lowest world of all, where those who had led the most wicked lives on earth, whose sins were too numerous and flagrant to be expiated by the vilest possible state of transformation, are doomed to linger in some one of the seven dungeons, each more hideous than another.

Sinners of all classes have their assigned periods, places, and degrees of punishment; and even in this ultimate place of horrors, the retribution is suited to the relative excess of wickedness and crime. One of the punishments, to which great criminals are there exposed, is to place them between two mountains, the sides of which are made to approach, and, by collapsing, flatten the bodies of the culprits, braying their bones to powder and spreading their substance over the whole face of the mountains like a thin leaf of a tree. The mountains re-open and recede, and again unite with a shock, disclosing the unhappy wretch and crushing him again by turns. Nor does time bring relief, by ending his existence or deadening his sensibility to pain, until the long period revolves and returns him again to the earth, to animate in rotation a new series of bodies.

In no region of the *Naraka* is the punishment perpetual; never exceeding three and thirty thousand years, nor falling short of a thousand.

The Madhya-lôka.

The Third World of the Jagat-triya, is the *Madhya-lôka,* the intermediate state, or world which men inhabit; the abode of virtue and vice.

This *Lôka* is a *Reju* in extent, or the space which is traversed by the sun in half his yearly course. But *Jambu-dwîpa,* the earth in which we live, is but a small part of the Madhya-lôka, and is no more than a vast continent, environed on all sides by a wide ocean. It contains a lake, extending a lak of Yôjana in length, or about four hundred thousand leagues; in the midst of which the famous mountain of *Mahâ-mêru* raises its summit.

The Jambu-dwîpa is divided into four parts; *Purva-videha, Apara-videha, Bharata-kshetra,* (in which India is situated,) and *Ahi-vratta.* These are situated on the east, west, south, and north of the Mahâ-mêru, respectively. They are likewise divided from each other by boundaries consisting of six enormous mountains, called *Himavat, Mahâ-himavat, Nishâdha, Nîla, Ahrumani, Śikâris:* the three first situated to the north of the lake, and the others to the south.

All these mountains stretch in one direction from east to west, and cross the whole Jambu-dwîpa from sea to sea.

In the space which intervenes between one mountain and another, immense plains are situated, where the trees, the shrubs, and the fruits are of a crimson hue. Children of either sex, born in those regions, are fit for propagation forty-eight hours after their birth. Men there are exempt from pain and disease. Ever happy and contented, they feast on the succulent plants and delicious fruits which the unsolicited earth yields them spontaneously: and placid even is their death, which translates them into the elysium of *Swarga*.

On the summit of Mount *Mahâ-himavat*, a mighty fountain springs, from which the Ganges and Indus, with twelve other great rivers, take their origin. These fourteen streams preserve a regular and unintermitting flow. Unlike the spurious Indus and Ganges of the Brâhmans, they are always unfordable, and subject neither to flooding nor desiccation, to ebbing or flowing; but keep their even course through the boundless plain, till they mingle their waves with the ocean.

The sea which encircles the Jambu-dwîpa is two laks of yôjana in breadth, or eight hundred thousand leagues. Beyond this great expanse of waters there is another *Jambu-dwîpa* or continent called *Mahâ-lavani*. It has also a race of inhabitants, with its own *Mahâ-mêru*, and sacred rivers intersecting its ample plains. This Jambu-dwîpa is two laks of yôjana in extent, and is surrounded with a sea four laks of yôjana across.

Beyond this sea there is another *Jambu-dwîpa*, called *Dahata-kishendah*, which is double the extent of the preceding, and has two Mahâ-mêru mountains. It is inhabited by human beings also, and has its holy fountains and rivers. The sea is here eight laks of yôjana across.

On the other side of this ocean a fourth Jambu-dwîpa is situated, with the imposing appellation of *Puskara-vratta-dwîpa*, which again doubles the preceding in all its proportions; has its two Mount Mahâ-mêrus, its streams, and its surrounding ocean.

On the farther shores of this utmost sea, at a distance of sixteen laks of yôjana, a mountain rears its head, with the name of Manush'-otra-parvata, forming the Thermopylæ of the human race, beyond which no earthly being has ever passed. The islands in that extreme ocean have never been visited by man.

In each of the four Jambu-dwîpas, there are several *Tirthan, Kâras, Chakravarti, Vasudevata*, and other holy persons. The numbers of each class vary, but there are not less than twenty of any one, nor more than eighty.

Succession and Division of Time.

The duration of Time is divided into six periods, which have been succeeding each other without interruption from all eternity. At the close of each, a general and total revolution takes place through all nature; and the world is renewed.

The first and longest of these periods is called *Pratama-kâla,* and endures four koti of koti, or forty millions of millions of years.

The second, *Dwitîya-kâla,* last thirty millions of millions.

Tretîya-kâla, the third, diminishes to twenty millions of millions.

Chatûrta-kâla, the fourth, comes down to ten millions of millions, bating forty-two thousand years.

The fifth period, called *Panchama-kâla,* or time of inconstancy and change, is the very age in which we now live, and will last twenty-one thousand years. This present year of the Christian æra, 1807, is the two thousand four hundred and fiftieth year of the *Panchama-kâla* of the Jains.

The recency of the commencement of this period, going back only 2450 years, strikes me as something remarkable, and inclines me to believe that it takes its origin from the epoch of their open rupture with the Brâhmans, and their separation from the other Hindûs. So famous an event might well give rise to a new era. If this point could be well ascertained, it would enable us to fix with more probability than we can do now, the origin and antiquity of the greater number of Hindû tales; because it was the invention, as it is thought, and the introduction of these fables into the religious system of the Hindûs, that created the schism which still subsists between the Brâhmans and Jains.

The sixth and last of the periods is called *Shashta-kâla,* and will continue a thousand years. When it arrives, the element of fire shall disappear from the earth, and those who are then alive shall feed on unwholesome reptiles and such roots and herbs as they can find in their precarious search.

In that last age there will be in the earth neither division nor abolition of castes, no public nor private property, no form of government, no kings nor laws. Men shall then have passed into a savage state.

The period will close with a *Pralayam,* a flood which shall inundate all the earth except the mountain *Vidyârtha,* which is of silver, and will alone remain unburied by the waters.

The flood will be occasioned by unceasing rain of forty-seven days, attended with a mixture and confusion of the elements.

Some persons living near the mountain of silver will take refuge in the caves that are about it, and shall be saved from the universal ruin. When the flood retires, they will come forth from the mountain and replenish the earth. The six periods will commence again in their regular order and succeed one another as before.

Knowledge and Learning of the Jains.

The learning and science of the Jains is wholly deposited in four *Vêdas,*[p] twenty-four *Purâṇas,* and sixty-four *Sâstras.*

[p] They have no *Vêdas,* but *Âgamas* which are of corresponding authority.

The names of the Purâṇas are the same with those of the twenty-four Tirthurus formerly mentioned, there being a Purana devoted to each Tirthuru and containing his history.

The names of the four Vêdas are *Pratamani yôga, Charanani-yôga, Karanani-yôga, Dravyani-yôga.* They were written by the most ancient and famous personage known among the Jains. He flourished before the twenty-four Tirthurus, and burst upon this world from the Swarga. Assuming our nature, he underwent the life of a Brâhman, a penitent, and a Nirvâṇi. He lived a whole *Purva Koti* or a hundred million of millions of years. He is not only the author of the sacred books which he wrote with his own hands; but he also divided men into different castes, laid down the rules by which they were to be directed, their form of government, and all the ordinances which still unite the Jains to one another.

Besides Adhíśwará, who is considered as the most perfect of beings who ever appeared on our earth in human shape, the Jains acknowledge various other famous personages of Shalaka Purusha; whose history is found recorded in the Pratamaṇi-yôga, and also in the twenty-four Purâṇas. Of these holy personages, twenty-four are Tirthankârar, twelve Chakravartis, nine Vaśu-dêvatâs, nine Bâla-vaśu-dêvatâs, and nine Bâla-râmas.

The twenty-four Tirthankârars are the most celebrated of these holy personages. Their condition was the most elevated that any human being can attain. They all lived in the most absolute state of *Nirvâṇi* or naked penitents. They were subject to no human infirmity, weakness, or want, not even to mortality. After sojourning long upon earth in purity and holiness, they chose at last to depart, and by slow degrees their physical frame dissolved, yielding up to the five elements the particles belonging to each, which were gradually attracted to the *Môksha*, the abode of the divinity, and united to his nature for ever.

During their lives they gave an example of all the virtues, exhorting men to conform to the precepts and rules enjoined by former Jains, and devoted themselves to the practice of penitence and contemplation. Several of them lived very long. The first existed some millions of years. The lives of the rest gradually diminished, and the last of all lived no more than eighty years. They flourished in the age called *Chartûrta Kâla,* which immediately preceded that of our own times, and lasted a kôṭi of kôṭis, or ten millions of millions of years.

There are no Tirthankârars at present in this division of the Jambu-dwîpa, which those holy persons have disappeared from, several thousand years ago; although they will return in future ages.

Rank of Sannyâsi Nirvâṇi, among the Jains.

The highest station to which a human being can attain is that of *Sannyâsi Nirvâṇi* or naked penitent. A person in this situation is no longer a man but becomes a part of the divinity, to whom he is in some measure assimilated by his devotions. When he has arrived at the highest possible degree in this profession, he voluntarily lays it down, and, without dying, his earthly frame is attenuated, and he obtains the *Môksha* by absorption into the godhead.

No true Nirvâṇi penitent now exists in this division of Jagat-triya; and consequently no mortal is now capable of obtaining the Môksha or supreme felicity; because, to be qualified for that distinction, a man must have been a Brâhman born, and must also pass through the state of a Nirvâṇi penitent.

Women never having aspired at any time to this rank, it follows that in no age, can persons of that sex have been qualified to receive the Môksha.

After many millions of years and several millions of transmigrations from body to body, all men ultimately attain to the state of Nirvâṇi penitent, and terminate their course by reunion with the divinity through the blessing of Môksha.

But, before arriving at the sublime condition, it is requisite to pass through eleven inferior degrees of contemplation, forming a noviciate or course of preparation for the degree of Nirvâṇi, during which the penitent is gradually acquiring advancement in purity until he arrives at ultimate perfection.

When he has reached this lofty summit, the penitent is no longer of this world, but becomes wholly insensible to earthly concerns. He sees, with equal indifference, the good and the evil, the virtue and the vice which prevail amongst men. He is entirely exempted from human passions and their effects, and neither loves nor hates. He is beyond the wants of nature, and can bear all sorts of privations without pain. Hunger and thirst are no longer felt, and he can pass weeks or months without sustenance. When he submits to food, he takes indiscriminately whatever nourishment, either animal or vegetable, comes in his way. An excrement, if it comes the readiest, is not rejected. He knows not the shelter of a roof, the bare plain or shady forest being his only alternative. Having no wants, he lives in absolute independence and in total estrangement from other men. Though quite naked, he is utterly regardless of wind or rain, of heat or cold. He is exempt from disease and infirmity. He has a lofty contempt for all men, let their rank or condition in life be ever so high. Whether they do right or wrong he cares not. He casts not a look away on any man, nor receives any visit. He suffers no thought, nor affection, nor inclination, to wander from the Deity; of whose essence he already considers himself to be a part. Absorbed in the contemplation of the divine perfections, what consideration has he to bestow on the world and all its vanities?

But a life of abstinence, hardship, and contemplation, during the eleven stages which have been enumerated, must gradually impair the bodily frame of the devotee. It wastes away like *Karpûra,* the Indian camphor, in the furnace. The five principles of which it consists are imperceptibly dissipated; the earth, the water, the fire, the wind, and the air, rejoining their kindred and native elements; till nothing but a shadow or phantom of the Nirvâṇi remains.

Arrived at this incomparable state of perfection, he quits this sublunary world, and goes to unite himself inseparably with the deity, and to enjoy in his bosom spiritual happiness, complete and everlasting.

Civil rules of conduct among the Jains.

Their civil ordinances are in many respects the same as those of other castes of Hindûs, and particularly those of the Brâhmans. Their scrupulosity respecting purity and impurity is nearly as great, and they follow nearly the same modes of purification from external and internal pollution. For this purpose, the ablutions of the Jains are not less frequent than those of any other tribe, and they are accompanied also with Mantras and other ceremonies. The customs of the Brâhmans respecting the Triple Cord, Marriage, Mourning, Funerals and the other affairs of life, are also observed in substance by the Jains.

But they have some usages peculiar to themselves, such as the following.

All castes and ranks amongst them wear the Triple Cord, which they are invested with when very young by the Gurus with much pomp and ceremony.

They are not permitted to take any solid food before sunrise or after sunset. All meals are therefore served up while the great luminary is above the horizon; and no circumstance of life can occur in which this rule may be dispensed with.

They have no *Tithi,* or days appointed for celebrating the memory of the dead; which is one of the most prominent institutions among the Brâhmans. With the Jains, the dead are forgotten almost as soon as they are buried; and, in three days after the funeral, there is no farther mention of them.

They do not, like most other Hindûs, rub their foreheads with the ashes of cow-dung. But as, in India, it would appear rude to shew the bare skin of the whole forehead, they take the decoction of sandal wood and imprint upon it the little circular mark called Pota, or merely a straight line. Some of them exhibit the Pota, in form of a cross, on the head, neck, stomach, and each shoulder, in honour of their five principal Tirthankâras.

They are still more rigid than the Brâhmans with regard to food. They scrupulously abstain not only from all inebriating drink and from all animal matter, but they also reject for nourishment some of the simple vegetable productions, such as the onion and garlic, with other simples on which the Brâhmans subsist.

Their motive for this extreme reserve is the dread of committing murder by destroying the insects which abound in such plants. So that the principal and almost the sole article of food which remains to the Jains, besides rice and milk, are the different species of peas and beans that grow in the country.

They have a particular abhorrence of assa fœtida, which the Brâhmans, on the contrary, are so excessively fond of that it has become an indispensable article in their kitchens.

The Jains eat no honey, not even as a medicine in sickness.

Their dread of committing murder is so excessive, that the women, in cleaning their houses, when they come to scour the floors with cow-dung, according to the general Hindû custom, commence with lightly sweeping the surface, to remove the insects which are hopping about, lest any of them should fall a victim to the scrubbing brush.

For the like reason, when they are preparing to cook, they carefully examine every article and ingredient they are to use, and tenderly shake off all the creeping creatures they find. Indeed, being of opinion that it is as great a crime to kill an insect as a man, the Jains will not maltreat even those that seem formed by nature for the sole purpose of tormenting human repose. When a bug is very teasing, they will remove him softly and put him on the ground without injury.

Being afraid, for the same reason, of swallowing animated beings in the water which they drink, when they go to the tank or well to draw it, they carefully cover the mouth of the pitcher with a bit of gauze to exclude the insects from entering with the water. A thirsty traveller, in the same manner, when he wants to drink on his way, stoops down to the stream, and puts a cloth over his mouth, through which he sucks the water, and so avoids the danger of committing murder.

Notwithstanding these peculiarities of customs and opinions, the Jains enjoy a very extensive toleration in most parts of the peninsula. They have many elegant temples in various districts, where they perform their ceremonies, without interruption, and with abundance of pomp and splendour.

There is a celebrated temple of this sect, in the Mysore, in a village called Srâvaṇa-Balagola, at some distance from the fort of Seringapatam. Vast numbers of pilgrims of this sect, from various provinces of the peninsula, are daily flocking to this sacred place to perform their vows. Of late years, however, it has lost much of its celebrity, on account of the frequent visits of Europeans from curiosity; which, in the eyes of the devout natives, injure the sanctity of the place. I have been informed that the Guru or pontiff of the sect, who formerly resided at this temple, felt himself so greatly insulted by these frequent and inquisitive intrusions of European strangers, which he had no means of preventing, and so deeply affected with the grievous pollution which the very presence of this sort of people, followed by their Pariah servants and dogs, brought upon the temple, that he quitted it in despair four years ago, and sought a refuge on the Malabar Coast, where he might avoid such importunate guests.

The village of Srâvaṇa-Balagola is surrounded with three little hills, and it is in the bason which they form that this celebrated Jain temple is erected.

At the top of one of those hills there is hewn out of the rock a gigantic image sixty or seventy feet high; which may be seen at a distance of several leagues. It must have been a work of great labour to cut out so enormous a figure to such a depth in the rock. It may be taken as a sample of the Hindû style of sculpture; and it has appeared to many European travellers who have visited it not to be devoid of proportion. It represents a celebrated ancient Nirvâṇi penitent, called Gautama, a younger son of their great Adiswara. It is in a standing posture and altogether naked.[g]

The same figure is represented in the interior of the temple at the foot of the mountain, also naked, but sitting cross-legged. On the outside of the walls there are niches containing images of the twenty-four Jinas and several other objects of Jain worship.

It appears deserving of notice that the principal objects of veneration to be met with in the greater part of the large temples of the Jains are represented of a gigantic size, and all naked; which proves that they have generally been intended to commemorate some of their Nirvâṇi penitents.

The Jains meddle not at all with the ceremonies of the Brâhmans; nor will they on any account suffer their own to be touched by them; shewing upon all occasions the utmost jealousy of any attempts at superiority on the part of that sect, to whom they never yield the smallest mark of attention or deference.

So strongly does this sentiment prevail on both sides, that the two sects cannot possibly live together or agree in any one point. A perpetual distrust keeps them asunder; and if self-interest leads them at any time to a good understanding and familiar intercourse with each other, it is altogether insincere and hollow, their secret hatred and abhorrence being generally the greatest when they appear to be the most in union. It is said that some castes of Brâhmans introduce into their daily prayers a malediction against the Jains; who, by way of reprisal, every morning, as soon as they are awake, pronounce these words: "*Brahma Kshayam,*" Let the Brâhmans perish!

---

g Compare Buchanan's Mysore, Vol. III. p. 410, where the image is figured.

The decided hatred that subsists between the two sects is outwardly manifested in their conduct to each other under all circumstances of life. In the countries where the Brâhmans have the ascendant, they exclude the Jains from all employments, and where the latter are the strongest they lose no occasion of mortifying the Brâhmans, of humbling their pride, and making them feel that they have not yet forgotten the injuries and persecutions of every kind which their ancestors had to endure from the Brâhmans of former times.[r]

---

[r] This sketch of the Jains is very imperfect. For fuller information the reader is referred to Wilson's Hindû sects, to Buchanan's Mysore, in which numerous interesting details of the Jains are interspersed, to Wilks' Mysore, vol. I. p. 507, and the Asiatic Researches, vol. IX. The following is a summary of the most important particulars regarding them.

1. They deny the divine authority of the *Vêdas.*

2. They pay peculiar homage to certain deified mortals, who by austerities have acquired a station superior to that of the gods.

3. They manifest an extreme aversion to the destruction of animal life.

4. The 24 *tîrthankâras* [TÎRYATE = it—the world—is crossed over] are especially reverenced, and their colossal images are to be found in their temples.

5. They do not exclude the Hindû gods from worship, though their own saints are the chief objects of adoration.

6. Their ministrant priests are Brâhmans, by whom all ordinary rites of ceremonial worship are performed.

7. The Jain system seems to be the most recent of the *great systems* which have obtained followers in India.

8. The system probably originated about 12 Centuries ago.

9. The Jain system is probably founded upon, and an extension of, some parts of the Buddhist religion. It is a Buddhist sect, and the Jains have superseded and persecuted those from whom they sprung.

10. The Jains succeeded the Buddhists on the Coromandel Coast in or about the ninth Century, and in the 10th Century were in power under Guṇa Pâṇḍya.

11. Between those periods the Jains were the chief writers in Tamil. To them we owe the *Nannûl, Chintâmaṇi, Nâlaḍi* and perhaps the *Kuṛal.*

12. *Guṇa Pâṇḍya* became a Śiva. Vishṇu Verddhana, the Jain Râja of Mysore, became a Vaishṇava in the 12th Century. From that time they have declined in the South, though still found in great numbers.

APPENDIX I.

Note to page 1.

The legend of Paraśurâma, in the Mahâbhârata, shews that there were fierce struggles between the Brâhmanical and Kshatriya races, which ended in the extirpation of the latter.

See Wilson's Vishṇu Purâṇa. Book II. Chap. VII. Müller's ant. Sanskrit lit. p. 17.

The same Paraśu-Râma (Râma of the axe) is said to have introduced Brâhmans into Kerala or Malabar, previously to which he caused the ocean to retire. Wilks' Mysore I. 157, and the *Kérala Urpatti.*

APPENDIX II.

Note to page 3.

The following note from Wilks' Mysore, vol. I. p. 442, 443 confirms the statement of the *Abbé.*

"In passing from the town of Silgut to Deonhully in the month of August last, I became accidentally informed of a sect, peculiar, as I since understand, to the north-eastern parts of Mysoor, the women of which universally undergo the amputation of the first joints of the third and fourth fingers of their right hands. On my arrival at Deonhully, after ascertaining that the request would not give offence, I desired to see some of these women, and the same afternoon seven of them attended at my tent.

"The sect is a sub-division of the *Murresoo wokul,* and belongs to the fourth great class of *Hindoos,* viz. the Souder. Every woman of the sect, previously to piercing the ears of her eldest daughter, preparatory to her being betrothed in marriage, must necessarily undergo this mutilation, which is performed by the blacksmith of the village for a regulated fee, by a surgical process sufficiently rude. The finger to be amputated is placed on a block: the blacksmith places a chisel over the articulation of the joint, and chops it off at a single blow. If the girl to be betrothed is motherless, and the mother of the boy have not before been subjected to the operation, it is incumbent on her to perform the sacrifice.

"After satisfying myself with regard to the facts of the case, I inquired into the origin of so strange a practice, and one of the women related with great fluency the following traditionary tale, which has since been repeated to me with no material deviation by several others of the sect.

"A Rachas (or giant,) named *Vrica*, and in after times *Busmaasoor*, or the giant of the ashes, had, by a course of austere devotion to *Mahadeo* obtained from him the promise of whatever boon he should ask. The Rachas accordingly demanded, that every person on whose head he should place his right hand might instantly be reduced to ashes; and Mahadeo conferred the boon, without suspicion of the purpose for which it was designed.

"The Rachas no sooner found himself possessed of this formidable power, than he attempted to use it for the destruction of his benefactor. Mahadeo fled; the Rachas pursued, and followed the fugitive so closely as to chase him into a thick grove, where Mahadeo, changing his form and bulk, concealed himself in the centre of a fruit then called "TUNDA PUNDOO," but since named *linga tunda*, from the resemblance which its kernel thenceforward assumed to the *ling*, the appropriate emblem of Mahadeo.

"The Rachas having lost sight of Mahadeo, enquired of a husbandman who was working in the adjoining field, whether he had seen the fugitive, and what direction he had taken. The husbandman who had attentively observed the whole transaction, fearful of the future resentment of Mahadeo, and equally alarmed for the present vengeance of the giant, answered aloud that he had seen no fugitive, but pointed at the same time with the little finger of his right hand to the place of Mahadeo's concealment.

"In this extremity Vishnu (Dignus vindice nodus) descended in the form of a beautiful damsel to the rescue of Mahadeo. The Rachas became instantly enamoured: the damsel was a *pure* bramin, and might not be approached by the *unclean* Rachas. By degrees she appeared to relent; and as a previous condition to farther advances, enjoined the performance of his ablutions in a neighbouring pool. After these were finished, she prescribed as a farther purification the performance of the *Sundia*, a ceremony in which the right hand is successively applied to the breast, to the crown of the head, and to other parts of the body, The Rachas thinking only of love, and forgetful of the powers of his right hand, performed the *Sundia*, and was himself reduced to ashes.

"Mahadeo now issued from the *linga tunda*, and after the proper acknowledgments for his deliverance, proceeded to discuss the guilt of the treacherous husbandman, and determined on the loss of the finger with which he had offended, as the proper punishment of his crime.

"The wife of the husbandman, who had just arrived at the field with food for her husband, hearing the dreadful sentence, threw herself at the feet of Mahadeo. She represented the certain ruin of her family if her husband should be disabled for some months from performing the labours of the farm, and besought the deity to accept two of her fingers, instead of one from her husband. Mahadeo, pleased with so sincere a proof of conjugal affection, accepted the exchange, and ordained that her female posterity in all future generations should sacrifice two fingers at his temple as a memorial of the transaction, and of their exclusive devotion to the god of the ling.

"The practice is accordingly confined to the supposed posterity of this single woman, and is not common to the whole sect of Murresoo wokul. I ascertained the actual number of families who observed this practice in three successive districts through which I afterwards passed, and I conjecture that within the limits of Mysoor they may amount to about two thousand houses."

Note to page 195.

THE MAHÂBHÂRATA.

"The Mahâbhârata is the second great Sanskrit epic, and is a work containing so many episodes, referable to various periods, that it has with some reason, been designated a Cycle of Poems. The wars of the two rival families, known as the Pâṇḍus and the Kurus, constitute the main subject, and this portion Akbar the Great thought worthy of translation into Persian; but the appearance of the Gods upon earth, their consultations in heaven, and the episodes are all omitted in the Persian copy.

The Pâṇḍus and Kurus were descendants of a king named Bharata, much respected but apparently quite distinct from him whom we left to reign at Ayodhya. In the Mahâbhârata the scene of Government is Hactinapura to the North of Delhi; and for this ancestral inheritance we find the rival families contending."

"The Râmâyana is the more ancient, and also the more connected of these poems, and commences with the History of a king of Ayodhya, an ancient city on the river Gogra, then called the Srâyu (tributary to the Ganges). King of Ayodhya is his title, although Ayodhya was merely the capital of the province of Kosala corresponding nearly with the modern province of Oude, where remains of old buildings are still visible."

[Mrs. Spiers.]

INDEX.